RICHARD WRIGHT READER

RICHARD WRIGHT READER

Edited by
Ellen Wright and Michel Fabre
Notes by Michel Fabre

Da Capo Press • New York

Library of Congress Cataloging in Publication Data

Wright, Richard, 1908–1960.
  Richard Wright reader / edited by Ellen Wright and Michel Fabre; notes
by Michel Fabre.—1st Da Capo Press ed.
    p.   cm.
  Originally published: New York: Harper & Row, 1978.
  Includes bibliographical references.
  ISBN 0-306-80774-2 (alk. paper)
    1. Afro-Americans—Literary collections. I. Wright, Ellen. II. Fabre, Michel.
III. Title.
PS3545.R815A6   1997
813′.52–dc21   96-45124
                                                                              CIP

First Da Capo Press edition 1997

This Da Capo Press paperback edition of the *Richard Wright Reader*
is an unabridged republication of the edition first published in New York
in 1978. It is reprinted by arrangement with the Estate of Richard Wright.

Published by Da Capo Press, Inc.
A Subsidiary of Plenum Publishing Corporation
233 Spring Street, New York, N.Y. 10013

Contents

Introduction   vii

NONFICTION

Black Boy (excerpt)   3

Joe Louis Uncovers Dynamite   31

Blueprint for Negro Writing   36

Letters: Richard Wright/Burton Rascoe   51
   Richard Wright/David L. Cohn   57
   Richard Wright/Antonio Frasconi   67

Review: *Wars I Have Seen* (Gertrude Stein)   74

There's Always Another Café   79

Black Power (excerpt)   86

Pagan Spain (excerpt)   110

12 Million Black Voices   144

Poetry: I Have Seen Black Hands   243
   Between the World and Me   246
   Red Clay Blues   248
   The FB Eye Blues   249
   Haikus   251

FICTION

Long Black Song   257

Fire and Cloud   287

Lawd Today (excerpt)   346

Native Son (excerpt)   416

The Man Who Lived Underground   517

The Outsider (excerpt)   577

Savage Holiday (excerpt)   706

Big Black Good Man   720

The Long Dream (excerpt)   737

Chronology   872

Bibliography   877

Introduction

The literary reputation of Richard Wright has been secure since the 1940s, when he became famous with the publication of *Native Son* and *Black Boy*. Most Americans know these books by title, yet few people under forty have actually read them, and students are often inclined to consider Wright as a forefather, whose outspokenness was indispensable to the blossoming of Ralph Ellison and James Baldwin, but whose aesthetic achievement has been somewhat overshadowed and superseded by these writers. To some degree, the revival of interest in black literature that began in the sixties has led the public to reconsider its view of this special body of American writing and to reassess its central figures. Among other things, the uniqueness of the Afro-American perspective and its relationship to Western culture have been gauged anew, and Wright's historical importance is more widely recognized. The complexity and scope of his works, however, remain largely unsuspected for a number of reasons. First, Wright's style is widely regarded as visceral and inspired, but at the same time too simple and too naturalistic to be truly literary. It has been held that such writing cannot rival the supposedly more sophisticated and universal achievement of, say, Ellison's *Invisible Man*. Second, it has been alleged that Wright's exile in France, where he lived from 1946 to his death in 1960, dealt a death blow to his creative imagination by estranging him from the situation of the blacks at home. A third line of criticism, mostly espoused by black nationalist critics, contends that Wright's vision of black life in the United States was too white-oriented and too generally bleak to allow him to relate to the more vital aspects of Afro-American culture.

This *Reader* was not conceived to illustrate any argument in the literary or ideological debates about Wright, but grew, simply, out of the need for a more comprehensive view of Wright's total production, a need to let readers judge for themselves its rich, if apparently contradictory diversity.

As in the compilation of any such reader, the decisions of what to include and what to omit have not been easy. Those who believe that Wright's best and most enduring books are *Native Son* and *Black Boy* may be surprised at finding here only the first section of the novel and relatively short extracts of the autobiography: those outstanding works deserve to be read *in toto* and they are easily available. As for short stories, the aesthetic quality of all those in the 1938 collection *Uncle Tom's Children* is so high that other choices surely could have been made. For example, one can easily consider "Big Boy Leaves Home" and "Down by the Riverside" as fitting alternatives to our selection of "Long Black Song" and "Fire and Cloud," illustrating as they do individual rebellion in a pastoral setting or collective resistance couched in the metaphors of black religion. Conversely, the inclusion of *Twelve Million Black Voices: a Folk History of the Negro in the United States* in its entirety together with important sections of *The Outsider* and *The Long Dream* does indeed reflect an attempt at helping reevaluate neglected or little available pieces. All of Wright's book-length works are represented here, with the exception of *The Color Curtain,* a report on the 1955 Bandung Conference, because it duplicates the essential conclusions reached in *Black Power.* As a complement to Wright's best in fiction and in poetry, either revolutionary or intimate, Wright's interests and talents as a reporter, reviewer, literary and social critic are illustrated in selections which testify to the commitment and coherence of his vision as an artist.

Numerous, and often excellent, appreciations of Wright's

importance for Afro-American literature and American culture have been published, and the meaning and implications
of individual works, *Native Son* and *Black Boy* especially,
have been analyzed at length. Less has been said, however,
of the unity of Wright's perspective, of its expanding range,
of the way his ideological vision found its roots in early emotional reactions and existential choices. Although the present
Reader was not organized with the aim of illustrating such
unity and growth, it seems relevant to consider each individual piece, meaningful as it may be separately, within the
context of Wright's whole career.

The depiction of the black struggle under adverse social
and racial conditions often explicitly constitutes the subject
of Wright's writing, but because of his sometimes conflicting
attitudes towards black life in the United States the coherence of his purpose is not always apparent. It does not appear, either, that his major purpose was to demonstrate the
universality of the black struggle as a reflection and example
of the condition of modern man (although certainly much
can be made, as will be seen, of Wright's contention that "the
Negro is America's metaphor"). Wright's enduring concern
was, in fact, more personal and more basic: it amounted to
nothing less than the interchange and conflict between the
individual and society.

Rooted as it is in an existential sense of freedom, Wright's
blossoming into print should be construed as an act of defiance, an assertion of the equation between literature and
rebellion, an avatar of the myth of Prometheus who stole fire
and knowledge from the Gods for the benefit of all men. In
Wright's case, the gap between life and literature is so narrow that the awakening and development of his avocation
closely follow the expanding circles of his self-awareness and
his intellectual growth.

It is largely through—books even more than through experience—that Wright progressively emerged from the desti-
tution of his lower-class Southern childhood, from the restric-

tive definition imposed upon blacks by racism, from the anti-intellectual climate of post-war America, and finally from a self-complacent definition of Western humanism. By the time he put together, in *White Man, Listen,* the lectures that constitute his ideological testament, he saw himself as one of those men "who carry on their frail but indefatigable shoulders the best of two worlds—and who, amidst confusion and stagnation, seek desperately for a home which, if found, could be a home for the hearts of all men." His individual growth thus went along with his affirmation of human solidarity and of the writer's special duty.

Such an affirmation was already foreshadowed in the opening chapters of *Black Boy* and Wright's later, humanistic commitment can appear as a rationalization and acceptance of what was originally a compulsive need for self-assertion in the face of a crushing environment. To put it another way, Wright always wanted to recreate himself, and others, against the definition imposed by society.

From whatever source his sense of freedom may have sprung, if we consider him as the product of the sharecropping South, his conviction of his innate worth and dignity constitutes the cornerstone of his personality. Conversely, such childhood traumas as his father's desertion of the family, his mother's strict enforcement of obedience, finally the necessity for him to depend on the support of relatives, all these rooted Wright's outlook in precariousness, thus increasing his tendency to self-protective rebellion. In *Black Boy,* he describes himself as emotionally deprived, and he projects upon the community in which he lived an unexpected lack of warmth. Before Wright could confront white racism, he had to assert himself against a black familial environment where Seventh Day Adventism seemed oppressive because it served to justify frugality and the banning of secular entertainments.

From his feelings of deprivation Wright sought refuge in fantasy. Books became for him a vicarious means of establish-

ing meaningful relationships with others. But his use of literature as a means of self-fulfillment also alienated him further
from his community which perceived it as a deviant practice.
Wright's originality was considered, in fact, a possible source
of trouble since it challenged the whites' desire to have
Negroes conform to the stereotype. Wright therefore seldom
saw his black environment as a sustaining community, but
rather as a network of constraints aimed at securing subservient behavior.

Wright's conception of individual freedom was thus forged
in opposition to the discipline imposed by the family and
religion. His attempt to reconcile freedom and a definition of
himself not only made him flee the repressive racial order of
the Deep South but it partly alienated him from the restrictive (black) way of life he had known; it increased his emotional kinship with the sort of liberal or social writing to
which he had access, starting with H. L. Mencken and the
American naturalists.

Reaching Chicago at the outset of the Depression enabled
Wright to further conceptualize his problem of relating to
society. Daily experiences at the relief stations convinced
him that his plight was by no means exceptional. Also, racism,
which had loomed so large in the South, now appeared as
only one aspect of capitalist oppression. Although Wright had
to bear the special onus of being black in America, there
were, in fact, millions of people in the country who were
alienated by displacement, urbanization and the societal
changes inherent in industrialization.

Wright joined the Communist Party in 1932 largely in
order to reconcile his desire for a sustaining society and his
need for freedom. In this broader circle, his rebellion was not
directed only against the subservience inculcated by racial
oppression but against the American capitalist system. In
moving terms, which come out lyrically in his revolutionary
poetry, he dreamed of building a world of brotherhood. More
important still, he joined the Party in order to continue his

association with the Chicago John Reed Club, a left-wing artists' and writers' group in which he had found for the first time an acceptable and rewarding peer-group.

It was unavoidable that, when confronted with Party demands tending to limit the freedom of the intellectual or with conciliatory tactics disregarding black protest in the era of the United Front, Wright should have reasserted his emotional, moral and racial individualism. One may even wonder why he continued Party activities until as late as 1942. His novellas of black militancy, like "Fire and Cloud" or "Bright and Morning Star" definitely sprang out of his revolutionary convictions but, in order better to understand what has been called Bigger Thomas' political confusion, one must reflect that *Native Son,* far from being a one-sided propaganda novel, also reflected Wright's belief that Communism did not represent a totally satisfactory approach to the racial question.

Ever and again in his public utterances at that time, like the letter to Antonio Frasconi included in this *Reader,* Wright asserted the writer's duty to proclaim his personal vision against the pressures of political expediency. When he ended his relationship with Communist intellectuals, Wright lost, however, an emotionally satisfying community and, at the apex of success, he found loneliness again, although he was not without sustenance. "The best American Negro novelist," he wielded some power, although the title conferred upon him by critics and audiences tended to impose subtle limits to the recognition thus granted him. His sense of being a "representative Negro," a spokesman denouncing the outrages suffered by his race, accordingly prompted him further to assert his solidarity with them. *Twelve Million Black Voices* and *Black Boy* partly came out of this sense of racial responsibility. At the time, Wright also launched several projects in order to fight segregation and discrimination. His choice probably amounted more to intellectual adhesion than to instinctive, emotional kinship. This did not detract from its validity and sincerity but it helps explain why Wright kept looking for answers to social problems beyond the scope of racial, and even political, commitment.

An agnostic, opposing the repression of institutionalized religion, Wright was still by no means indifferent to the manifestations of the spiritual. His sense of waging a somewhat solitary fight and his growing alienation from American society, now that he had measured what it could offer him, drove him again to explore, this time in philosophical terms, the conflict that he was experiencing between the self and society. Out of his quest grew "The Man Who Lived Underground," completed as early as 1942, and *The Outsider* which was published in 1953 at the close of a seven-year period of self-examination and doubts.

Far from being initiated by the French existentialists, whom Wright befriended only after he went to Paris in 1946, this philosophical interest stemmed from his early existential experiences as well as from the sense of being both inside and outside American culture, which he considered typical of the Afro-American and which he had already explored in "The Man Who Lived Underground." Indeed, anguish, dread and alienation were to be found in *Native Son* as forceful, emotional components before appearing as governing concepts in *The Outsider,* in which the influence of Heidegger and Kierkegaard is more perceptible than that of Camus and Sartre.

Despite its structural and stylistic flaws, *The Outsider* is a novel whose ideological importance rivals that of *Native Son. Native Son* mostly attempted to explore the psychological effects of racism and the ambiguous potentialities, be they fascistic or revolutionary, underlying Bigger Thomas' deviant act of self assertion. *The Outsider* analyzed and repudiated both Fascism and Communism as models for society, and it probed the source of alienation lying at the heart of modern man, not as an effect of oppression but as a manifestation of his destiny. It carried individual freedom to its ultimate limit only to conclude on the necessity of the social bond: "Alone, man is nothing."

It may be argued that Bigger Thomas has potentially more in him of the black nationalist than of the left-wing revolutionary but it is difficult to claim him for a metaphysical rebel. In "The Man Who Lived Underground," Fred Daniels went beyond Bigger in terms of transcending everyday conditions of socialized behavior: in his territory under and beyond, on the reverse side of reality, he experienced the alienation that plagues the human condition. Cross Damon, the protagonist in *The Outsider,* provides even more speculative rationalization for his acts. Only accidentally due to his race, his alienation is that of a present-day intellectual whose philosophical beliefs remove him from the rules of society. Liberated by chance from the snare of economic and familial dependence, he undertakes to remold his destiny according to individual choice and shuns conventional morality. Like Wright, Damon is a product of secularization and he is driven, emotionally and intellectually, to extol the subjective in himself and thereby affirm the value of his individual personality against the collective discipline that reduces people to fragments in the social whole. It should be emphasized that Damon is not defeated because of the intransigence or single-handedness of his attempt but because of the violent methods he is compelled to use. Violence contaminates him and breaks his bond with others. The woman he loves commits suicide out of horror at what he has become: a murderer playing God to other men. Wright thus clearly stresses the necessity for emotional attachment, compassion and solidarity.

Completed at the end of a long transitional period, *The Outsider* constitutes Wright's spiritual autobiography for those years, a dramatization of his dilemma in his quest for balance between individual freedom and the necessity for social order.

Wright's attraction towards existentialism was, however,

more than a search for philosophical illumination. The end of World War II had brought about a new surge of consumerism and materialism in the United States, which Henry Miller was describing as "the air-conditioned nightmare," and it was possible to believe, at the time, that humanism could only be restored through an infusion of the traditional European values of the Enlightenment and the Age of Revolution. Western Europe was then struggling to recover an identity independent of both Soviet Russia and the United States. Among others, the French existentialists embodied a type of humanism which appeared as a bulwark against the dislocations attending urbanization and industrialization. Like Wright, they were dissatisfied with American materialism and with Stalinist totalitarianism, although, like him, they strove for action along Marxist lines. What has sometimes been described as "Wright's roll in the hay with existentialism" should therefore be seen as more than a fad or an experiment on his part. It was a sincere attempt at recreating the sustaining and purposeful community he had once known in the John Reed Club. And, this time, he started from ideological premises which were more sophisticated and more likely than Communism to guarantee individual freedom. Also, whereas in the 1930s he had embraced Communism as he would a religion, Wright now explored the ontological implications of existentialism with a critical eye.

To the degree that Wright projected in *Black Boy* his development as representative of black Southern youth, one is tempted to read the insecurity and alienation of Cross Damon as a projection of existential conditions or personality features construed in order to make the American Negro a representative of modern man. However, although he linked Damon's psychological make-up with his lack of social values and to the utter desacralization of his universe, Wright did not project Negro alienation as typical of modern (or Western) man. Contrary to what existentialism might have led him to do, he stopped short of using the Negro as a choice

metaphor for the alienation of modern man because he gradually came to see existentialism as a philosophy born of "the
decline of the West" and to believe that Afro-American
history was more than a part of Western history, because it
not only reflected the disruptions brought about by the passing of the Third World from feudalism to the modern age but
also foreshadowed the renewal of civilization to come.

Wright thus found himself grappling with problems not
only of racial definition or struggle against oppression but of
the shape modern society was to take if the humanity in man
were to be preserved. In the thirties and forties he had considered that his role as a black writer forced him first to
destroy the stereotypes of the "noble savage" and Uncle Tom
and then to expose the definition of "the Negro" given by
America. Already in *Twelve Million Black Voices* he had
viewed the history of Africans in America as a parable for the
transition from agrarianism to industrialism, but by 1946 he
claimed that American Negroes were the symbol of modern
man's transition to an industrial way of life now starting *on
a global scale.* In a July 1946 letter published in the French
magazine *Les Nouvelles Epitres,* he clearly defined the scope
of his metaphoric reference:

By social definition, I am an American Negro and what I'll have to
say deals with Negro life in the U.S., not because I think that life or
its problems are of supreme importance, but because Negro life in
the U.S. dramatically symbolizes the struggle of a people whose
forefathers lived in a warm, simple culture and who are now trying
to live the new way of life that dominates our time: machine-civili-
zation and all the consequences flowing from it.

It must be understood that when I talk of the American Negroes,
I am talking about everybody . . .

In the next paragraph, Wright describes the plight of Afro-
Americans as that of an "internal colony" (a concept often
used by Black Power theoreticians in the 1960s) and he sets
up two conflicting cultural choices:

The Negro is intrinsically a colonial subject, but one who lives not in China, India, or Africa but next door to his conquerors, attending their schools, fighting their wars, and laboring in their factories. The American Negro problem, therefore, is but a facet of the global problem that splits the world in two: Handicraft vs. Mass production; Family vs. the Individual; Tradition vs. Progress; Personality vs. Collectivity; the East (the colonial peoples) vs. the West (exploiters of the world).

Nowhere on earth have these extremes met and clashed with such prolonged violence as in America between Negro and white, and this fact alone endows the American Negro problem with a vital importance, for what happens between whites and blacks in America foreshadows what will happen between the colored billions of Asia and Africa and the industrial whites of the West. Indeed, the world's fate is symbolically prefigured today in race relations in America.

One may remark that neither paradigm corresponded to Wright's personal preferences: although he might sentimentally cling to "handicraft" and "the East" and he definitely preferred "personality" to "collectivity," he undoubtedly chose "the individual" rather than "family" and "tradition," as can be seen in his strategies for the modernization of Africa.

In 1946, however, Wright was more interested in the plight of the *individual* subjected to the jump from tradition to modernization than in political systems. He stated in the same letter that he was "merely a man who is curious about the tissue and texture of human experience," and he exclaimed:

Imagine people stolen from the warm nest of their ancient living, stripped of their culture, defined in economic terms, worked for 300 years and suddenly freed! . . . How did these people fare? What happened inside of them? What personality traits did they acquire as a result of such an experience? What kinds of cultural manifestations did they express?

In this perspective, the Afro-American's psychological pattern appears clearly to be the result of social change and industrialization rather than a primarily racial component setup. Speaking for all comparable peoples and groups, Wright thus took the Afro-American experience as a unique instance of the most advanced step taken from traditional society to modern society, not as an instance of metaphysical alienation.

Partly due to the influence of his friend George Padmore, one of the major proponents of Pan-Africanism, Wright's ideological preoccupations shifted from his metaphysical concerns. His opposition to Americanism and Stalinism in the name of European humanism soon became opposition to Western colonialism for the sake of Third World liberation. He turned away from a community of Western intellectuals bent upon preserving the freedom of man in Europe and toward the "lonely outsiders," the colored elites attempting to restore freedom in Africa and Asia.

Most of his later work, including his fiction, should be evaluated in that light. To many critics, *The Long Dream* seemed at the time to be merely a return to the roots of Wright's inspiration, that is, the closed Mississippi society he had known as a child, yet the novel was conceived as only the first step in a trilogy. In the initial volume, Wright examined the psychological survival and forced alienation of Fishbelly in a racist (colonial) context. He then, in a second novel, the still unpublished "Island of Hallucinations," proceeded to analyze the sequels of this conditioning in the freer (post-colonialization) atmosphere of Paris. The third volume, which was sketched but never written, would have taken the protagonist to Africa, where he would have discovered new allegiances and overcome his lingering intellectual oppression before returning to the American soil.

Of course, there is a good deal of wishful thinking in such an ending. But Wright's interest lay in that direction. In a different, often more humorous vein found in later short stories like "Big Black Good Man" and "Man, God Ain't Like That," he explored white fears of black power and the psychological havoc inflicted by missionaries trying to impose Christianity upon paganism. Practically all of Wright's nonfiction in the fifties was concerned, directly or indirectly, with the Third World.

Often opposed to Leopold Sengor's *"négritude,"* the strategies that Wright considered fit for the liberation of Africa would deserve separate treatment. In "Tradition and Industrialization," a paper given at the First Conference of Black Artists and Writers in September 1956, Wright, who had often regretted the lack of traditions in the United States, advocated the destruction of stifling African beliefs in unambiguous terms:

> The white Western world, until relatively recently the most secular and free part of the earth . . . labored unconsciously and tenaciously for five hundred years to make Asia and Africa (that is, the elite in those areas) more secular-minded than the West! . . . I do say "Bravo!" to the consequences of Western plundering, a plundering that created the conditions for the possible rise of rational societies for the greater majority of mankind. . . . That part of the heritage of the West which I value—man stripped of the past and free for the future—has now been established as lonely bridgeheads in Asia and Africa. . . . It means that the spirit of the Enlightenment, of the Reformation, which made Europe great now has a chance to be extended to all mankind!
>
> *White Man Listen,* pp. 62–63

Wright clearly fell back on his own childhood experience to advocate the moves that had liberated him: breaking the shackles of religion and any world-view making for human stagnation. He distrusted the mystical tenets of *"négritude,"* like the concept of "the sensitive African" opposed to "the rational European," not because he was unable to perceive the mystical components of African life, but because such conceptions defeated colonial independence by fettering the individual in communal cultures ill-equipped to confront the technological and cultural domination of the West. Wright's attitude towards institutionalized religion was the same as his unrelenting opposition to the oppressive, self-denying beliefs once prevalent in his grandmother's house. Especially after he witnessed the role played by race and religion at the Bandung Conference, he held the religious world-view of Asia and Africa largely responsible for the deprivation and immobility of millions whose emotional satisfaction he could only construe as a dream. He had personally experienced the stresses inflicted by desacralization and industrialization in America, yet he claimed that the Third World should go the way of the West in order not only to confront the West but to establish a freer sort of society:

My decalogue of beliefs does not imply that I've turned my back in scorn upon the past of mankind. . . . Men who can slough off the beautiful mythologies, the enthralling configurations of external ceremonies, manners, and codes of the past, are not necessarily unacquainted with, or unappreciative of, them; they have interiorized them, have reduced them to mental traits, psychological problems. . . . It is my profound conviction that emotional independence is a clear and distinct human advance, a gain for all mankind.

White Man Listen, pp. 52–53

It has been said that Wright had finally settled into the role of a detached observer of Third World nations, a black man of the West, an outsider on the margins of two cultures. Such a view does not, however, take into account his continuing conflict and spiritual questioning. The more he appeared to trust rationality as a means towards political freedom and social development, the more concerned he seemed with the emotional and irrational dimensions of spirituality. As an artist, it had always been his inclination to "revere the fanciful and the imaginative," which, in his eyes, made for the powerful creativity of folk life. His visceral reactions to the impact of African beliefs during his visit to the Gold Coast show that he had grown ever more aware of the spiritual dimension of life, to the point of reconsidering some of his assumptions, or at least of wondering about the dangers of modernization:

The pathos of Africa would be doubled if, out of her dark past, her people were plunged into a dark future, a future that smacked of Chicago or Detroit . . . What would be the gain if these benighted fetish-worshippers were snatched from their mud-huts and their ancestor idolatry, and catapulted into the vast steel and stone jungles of cities, tied to monotonous jobs, condemned to cheap movies, made dependent upon alcohol? Would an African, a hundred years from now, after he had been trapped into the labyrinths of industrialization, be able to say when he is dying, when he is on the verge of going to meet his long-dead ancestors, those traditional mysterious words:

> I'm dying
> I'm dying
> Something big is happening to me . . . ?
> *Black Power*, p. 227

Considered as a mode of living rather than as an institution, religion was not condemned by Wright. On the contrary, closer contact with African beliefs prompted him further to explore the religious foundations of the human personality. He did so in Freudian terms in *Savage Holiday*, his nonracial psychoanalytical novel. He did so, again, in the broader sociological context of *Pagan Spain*, in which he described the heathen substratum of the most Christian, and the least European, country in the West. At the end of his life, his delight in recreating the spiritual moods of Japanese haiku poetry denoted a similar falling back on intuition, on feeling, very possibly because the models of rational societies thus far propounded to man threatened to turn into well-organized nightmares.

In evaluating Wright's conception of individual freedom and fulfillment in relation to organized society, one must make allowances for the changes that occurred between the 1930s and the 1960s, as even quasi-feudal Mississippi grew into an industrial society, with some attending racial liberation. Also, Wright's major theme and lifelong concern, the issue that, in his eyes, made the plight of the Afro-American symbolic of the modern world, was a question no single man could answer. In a review of Michel Del Castillo's novel, *The Disinherited,* which he wrote shortly before his death, Wright expressed his doubts that the rational society he envisioned might be able to answer man's deepest needs:

May it not develop that man's sense of being disinherited is not mainly political at all, that politics serve it as a temporary vessel, that Marxist ideology in particular is but a transitory makeshift pending a more accurate diagnosis, that Communism may be a painful compromise containing a definition of man by sheer default?

As a result of this unreconciled striving for a balance between rational organization and imaginative creativity, Wright's works reflect more than a critical commitment to his race and his country, far more than a passionate fight for social justice. His intellect craved progress and modernity, his feelings could not be content with such. The poet in him always hankered after wholeness of vision, after an organic view of existence which the thinker could not achieve. Speaking of pre-colonial Africa, he remarked in *Black Power* that social change might destroy the organic vision that made "people want to live on this earth and derive from that living a sweet even if sad meaning."

The nostalgic note evoked by that phrase is indeed present in Wright's own writings, in his early fiction and haiku poetry alike, as an essential though subdued counterpart to his more naturalistic approach. Only through the exclusion of such imaginative, organic moods and quasi-pastoral metaphors can Wright's style be restrictively defined as stark realism, lacking in symbolic quality.

This quality is most obvious in the almost surrealistic pattern of imagery and situations that helps make "The Man Who Lived Underground" a masterpiece. It is also evident in a number of novellas where it serves the function of balancing Wright's often bleak picture of black life couched in naturalistic terms. It must be borne in mind that, while evoking the deprivation inherent in the poverty and oppression characteristic of *Native Son* and *Black Boy*, Wright also suggested, in *Uncle Tom's Children* and *Twelve Million Black Voices*, the communal and sustaining qualities black life could take in the South. In the early novellas of *Uncle Tom's Children* the organic world-view of the black peasant is often evoked in lyrical terms even though white violence is ever present. This nearly pastoral approach stands in dramatic contrast to the social realism prevalent in *Native Son*. Without taking it into account one cannot do justice to Wright's non-naturalistic style of writing or to his portrayal of the positive qualities of black life. He does indeed set up believable figures of proud, militant blacks like Preacher Taylor in "Fire and Cloud." Far from being content with terse "realistic" prose, he turns to Biblical imagery, patterns of color, and poetic indirection, all of which make "Down by the Riverside" a success in symbolism through the metaphorical value of the flood as immediate source of, and image for, the trials and confusion of Brother Mann.

Even if one discounts the positive, at times heroic, quality of characters ranging from Tyree Tucker in *The Long Dream* to Aunt Sue in "Black and Morning Star," the most cursory appreciation of *Lawd Today*, not to mention later humorous stories like "Man of All Works" and "Big Black Good Man," reveals that Wright's preference for realism did not prevent him from creating funny and congenial figures and situations. Nor indeed from incorporating into his writing many elements characteristic of black folk culture. Although in *Lawd Today* Wright does not turn to Southern pastoralism but to what rural folkways have become after a generation in Northern ghettos, he recreates in passing the whole context of verbal creativity which explodes in songs, jokes, the dozens, toasts and bombast. When contrasted with the uptight utterances of the whites, this makes for a warm image of black life even if it is also pathetic in the light of the facts of economic oppression. As he expressed it at the time, Wright's interest lay in exposing the system which imposed a "cheap" quality of life upon lower-class blacks, but his desire for authenticity made him emphasize those cultural rituals and interchanges that ensured cohesion and solidarity in the day-to-day struggle of ghetto existence.

Wright's style appears at times as visceral, inspired and naturalistic as it is supposed to be, yet he is by no means the innocent and interesting neo-Dreiserian primitive some critics have contrasted with Ralph Ellison's virtuosity and technical flexibility. The unequalled emotional power Wright attains in his best stories stems just as much from an extremely skilled *poetic* realism, in which intense suffering is achieved through symbolic connotation, as from the climaxing of comparatively short and self-contained dramatic episodes. This poetic, even prophetic, dimension should not be overlooked. In many ways, Wright's art was vision just as his writing was force, meaning and direction. His quest was largely and ultimately an attempt to establish a political and cultural context for the birth of the (black) man in world-wide terms. His vision rested both upon his confidence in the individual self and upon his belief in the power of writing. Was this not the message he expressed when he wrote in *White Man, Listen:*

I am convinced that the humble, fragile dignity of man, buttressed by a tough-souled pragmatism, implemented by methods of trial and error, can sufficiently sustain and nourish human life, can endow it with ample and durable meaning . . . I believe that art has its own autonomy, a self-sufficiency that extends beyond, and independent of, the spheres of political or priestly power or sanction.

Was it not Wright's way of saying that the real struggle is humanism against totalitarianism, imagination against fear? A way of saying that art is soul?

MICHEL FABRE

NONFICTION

Black Boy

It was in 1942, following a lecture at Fisk university, that Wright considered the idea of writing his autobiography.

I gave a clumsy, conversational kind of speech to the folks, black and white, reciting what I felt and thought about the world, what I remembered about my life, about being a Negro. . . . It was not until half-way through my speech that it crashed upon me that I was saying things that whites had forbidden Negroes to say. . . . Later, I learned that I had accidentally blundered into the secret, black, hidden core of race relations in the United States. That core is this: nobody is ever expected to speak honestly about this problem.

The success encountered by Black Boy *was a testimony to America's readiness to confront the truth about Southern racism and the Negro's determination to succeed in spite of it. The world success that makes Wright's autobiography a classic is proof that the story has struck deep chords in the hearts of all men, beyond the circumstances of time and place.*

Wright retraces his childhood memories as the son of a farmhand and a country schoolmistress in the Mississippi delta, the disruption of his home after his father's desertion

Black Boy was originally published by Harper & Brothers in 1945.

and his mother's protracted sickness, his forced dependence upon a Seventh Day Adventist grandmother whose repressive religious code deepened his childhood traumas and curbed his attempts at finding compensation in reading and in the writing of fiction. He emphasizes the losses he sustained through physical and emotional deprivation, as well as through his stubborn attempts at overcoming adversity and the restrictive definition of himself imposed by white racism. Occasional lyrical outbursts and dramatic episodes, however, give evidence of his enjoyment of folk culture and the power of imagination, even though he tended to view black life in the South in terms of cultural deprivation.

After brilliantly graduating from the Smith-Robinson secondary school in Jackson, where he wrote his first stories, Wright moved to Memphis, working there in an optical company. It was during this time that he discovered not only the rigors of Jim Crow but also the more welcome intellectual nourishment in the writings of H. L. Mencken and the American naturalists.

Black Boy *describes the first steps of Wright's coming of age. A later part of his autobiography, originally titled* American Hunger, *was published as a whole for the first time in 1977. It takes Wright from Chicago to New York, from his struggles at the height of the Depression to his position in the Federal Writers' Project, from his enthusiasm for the possibilities of Communism to his disenchantment with its methods, from the revolutionary poetry to the embattled prose of* Uncle Tom's Children. *Just as* Black Boy *is an indictment of the racist South,* American Hunger *is a powerful indictment of the shallow, oppressive materialism in American culture.*

TO HELP SUPPORT the household my grandmother boarded a colored schoolteacher, Ella, a young woman with so remote and dreamy and silent a manner that I was as much afraid of her as I was attracted to her. I had long wanted to ask her to tell me about the books that she was always reading, but I could never quite summon enough courage to do so. One afternoon I found her sitting alone upon the front porch, reading.

"Ella," I begged, "please tell me what you are reading."

"It's just a book," she said evasively, looking about with apprehension.

"But what's it about?" I asked.

"Your grandmother wouldn't like it if I talked to you about novels," she told me.

I detected a note of sympathy in her voice.

"I don't care," I said loudly and bravely.

"Shhh— You mustn't say things like that," she said.

"But I want to know."

"When you grow up, you'll read books and know what's in them," she explained.

"But I want to know now."

She thought a while, then closed the book.

"Come here," she said.

I sat at her feet and lifted my face to hers.

"Once upon a time there was an old, old man named Bluebeard," she began in a low voice.

She whispered to me the story of *Bluebeard and His Seven Wives* and I ceased to see the porch, the sunshine, her face, everything. As her words fell upon my new ears, I endowed them with a reality that welled up from somewhere within me. She told how Bluebeard had duped and married his seven wives, how he had loved and slain them, how he had hanged them up by their hair in a dark closet. The tale made the world around me be, throb, live. As she spoke, reality changed, the look of things altered, and the world became peopled with magical presences. My sense of life deepened and the feel of things was different, somehow. Enchanted and enthralled, I stopped her constantly to ask for details. My imagination blazed. The sensations the story aroused in me were never to leave me. When she was about to finish, when my interest was keenest, when I was lost to the world around me, Granny stepped briskly onto the porch.

"You stop that, you evil gal!" she shouted. "I want none of that Devil stuff in my house!"

Her voice jarred me so that I gasped. For a moment I did not know what was happening.

"I'm sorry, Mrs. Wilson," Ella stammered, rising. "But he asked me—"

"He's just a foolish child and you know it!" Granny blazed.

Ella bowed her head and went into the house.

"But, Granny, she didn't finish," I protested, knowing that I should have kept quiet.

She bared her teeth and slapped me across my mouth with the back of her hand.

"You shut your mouth," she hissed. "You don't know what you're talking about!"

"But I want to hear what happened!" I wailed, dodging another blow that I thought was coming.

"That's the Devil's work!" she shouted.

My grandmother was as nearly white as a Negro can get without being white, which means that she was white. The sagging flesh of her face quivered; her eyes, large, dark, deep-set, wide apart, glared at me. Her lips narrowed to a line. Her high forehead wrinkled. When she was angry her eyelids drooped halfway down over her pupils, giving her a baleful aspect.

"But I liked the story," I told her.

"You're going to burn in hell," she said with such furious conviction that for a moment I believed her.

Not to know the end of the tale filled me with a sense of emptiness, loss. I hungered for the sharp, frightening, breath-taking, almost painful excitement that the story had given me, and I vowed that as soon as I was old enough I would buy all the novels there were and read them to feed that thirst for violence that was in me, for intrigue, for plotting, for secrecy, for bloody murders. So profoundly responsive a chord had the tale struck in me that the threats of my mother and grandmother had no effect whatsoever. They read my insistence as mere obstinacy, as foolishness, something that would quickly pass; and they had no notion how desperately serious the tale had made me. They could not have known that Ella's whispered story of deception and murder had been the first experience in my life that had elicited from me a total emotional response. No words or punishment could have possibly made me doubt. I had tasted what to me was life, and I would have more of it, somehow, someway. I realized that they could not understand what I was feeling and I kept quiet. But when no one was looking I would slip into Ella's room and steal a book and take it back of the barn and try to read it. Usually I could not decipher enough words to make the story have meaning. I burned to learn to read novels and I tortured my mother into telling me the meaning of every strange word I saw, not because the word itself had any value, but because it was the gateway to a forbidden and enchanting land.

. . . The eighth grade days flowed in their hungry path and I grew more conscious of myself; I sat in classes, bored, wondering, dreaming. One long dry afternoon I took out my composition book and told myself that I would write a story; it was sheer idleness that led me to it. What would the story be about? It resolved itself into a plot about a villain who wanted a widow's home and I called it *The Voodoo of Hell's Half-Acre*. It was crudely atmospheric, emotional, intuitively psychological, and stemmed from pure feeling. I finished it in three days and then wondered what to do with it.

The local Negro newspaper! That's it . . . I sailed into the office and shoved my ragged composition book under the nose of the man who called himself the editor.

"What is that?" he asked.

"A story," I said.

"A news story?"

"No, fiction."

"All right. I'll read it," he said.

He pushed my composition book back on his desk and looked at me curiously, sucking at his pipe.

"But I want you to read it *now*," I said.

He blinked. I had no idea how newspapers were run. I thought that one took a story to an editor and he sat down then and there and read it and said yes or no.

"I'll read this and let you know about it tomorrow," he said.

I was disappointed; I had taken time to write it and he seemed distant and uninterested.

"Give me the story," I said, reaching for it.

He turned from me, took up the book and read ten pages or more.

"Won't you come in tomorrow?" he asked. "I'll have it finished then."

I honestly relented.

"All right," I said. "I'll stop in tomorrow."

I left with the conviction that he would not read it. Now, where else could I take it after he had turned it down? The next afternoon, en route to my job, I stepped into the newspaper office.

"Where's my story?" I asked.

"It's in galleys," he said.

"What's that?" I asked; I did not know what galleys were.

"It's set up in type," he said. "We're publishing it."

"How much money will I get?" I asked, excited.

"We can't pay for manuscript," he said.

"But you sell your papers for money," I said with logic.

"Yes, but we're young in business," he explained.

"But you're asking me to *give* you my story, but you don't *give* your papers away," I said.

He laughed.

"Look, you're just starting. This story will put your name before our readers. Now, that's something," he said.

"But if the story is good enough to sell to your readers, then you ought to give me some of the money you get from it," I insisted.

He laughed again and I sensed that I was amusing him.

"I'm going to offer you something more valuable than money," he said. "I'll give you a chance to learn to write."

I was pleased, but I still thought he was taking advantage of me.

"When will you publish my story?"

"I'm dividing it into three installments," he said. "The first installment appears this week. But the main thing is this: Will you get news for me on a space rate basis?"

"I work mornings and evenings for three dollars a week," I said.

"Oh," he said. "Then you better keep that. But what are you doing this summer?"

"Nothing."

"Then come to see me before you take another job," he said. "And write some more stories."

A few days later my classmates came to me with baffled eyes, holding copies of the *Southern Register* in their hands.

"Did you really write that story?" they asked me.

"Yes."

"Why?"

"Because I wanted to."

"Where did you get it from?"

"I made it up."

"You didn't. You copied it out of a book."

"If I had, no one would publish it."

"But what are they publishing it for?"

"So people can read it."

"Who told you to do that?"

"Nobody."

"Then why did you do it?"

"Because I wanted to," I said again.

They were convinced that I had not told them the truth. We had never had any instruction in literary matters at school; the literature of the nation or the Negro had never been mentioned. My schoolmates could not understand why anyone would want to write a story; and, above all, they could not understand why I had called it *The Voodoo of Hell's Half-Acre*. The mood out of which a story was written was the most alien thing conceivable to them. They looked at me with new eyes, and a distance, a suspiciousness came between us. If I had thought anything in writing the story, I had thought that perhaps it would make me more acceptable to them, and now it was cutting me off from them more completely than ever.

At home the effects were no less disturbing. Granny came into my room early one morning and sat on the edge of my bed.

"Richard, what is this you're putting in the papers?" she asked.

"A story," I said.

"About what?"

"It's just a story, granny."

"But they tell me it's been in three times."

"It's the same story. It's in three parts."

"But what is it about?" she insisted.

I hedged, fearful of getting into a religious argument.

"It's just a story I made up," I said.

"Then it's a lie," she said.

"Oh, Christ," I said.

"You must get out of this house if you take the name of the Lord in vain," she said.

"Granny, please . . . I'm sorry," I pleaded. "But it's hard to tell you about the story. You see, granny, everybody knows that the story isn't true, but . . ."

"Then why write it?" she asked.

"Because people might want to read it."

"That's the Devil's work," she said and left.

My mother also was worried.

"Son, you ought to be more serious," she said. "You're growing up now and you won't be able to get jobs if you let people think that you're weak-minded. Suppose the superintendent of schools would ask you to teach here in Jackson, and he found out that you had been writing stories?"

I could not answer her.

"I'll be all right, mama," I said.

Uncle Tom, though surprised, was highly critical and contemptuous. The story had no point, he said. And whoever heard of a story by the title of *The Voodoo of Hell's Half-Acre?* Aunt Addie said that it was a sin for anyone to use the word "hell" and that what was wrong with me was that I had nobody to guide me. She blamed the whole thing upon my upbringing.

In the end I was so angry that I refused to talk about the story. From no quarter, with the exception of the Negro newspaper editor, had there come a single encouraging word. It was rumored that the principal wanted to know why I had used the word "hell." I felt that I had committed a crime. Had I been conscious of the full extent to which I was pushing against the current of my environment, I would have been frightened altogether out of my attempts at writing. But my reactions were limited to the attitude of the people about me, and I did not speculate or generalize.

I dreamed of going north and writing books, novels. The North symbolized to me all that I had not felt and seen; it had no relation whatever to what actually existed. Yet, by imagining a place where everything was possible, I kept hope alive in me. But where had I got this notion of doing something in the future, of going away from home and accomplishing something that would be recognized by others? I had, of course, read my Horatio Alger stories, my pulp stories, and I knew my Get-Rich-Quick Wallingford series from cover to cover, though I had sense enough not to hope to get rich; even to my naïve imagination that possibility was too remote. I knew that I lived in a country in which the aspirations of black people were limited, marked-off. Yet I felt that I had to go somewhere and do something to redeem my being alive.

I was building up in me a dream which the entire educational system of the South had been rigged to stifle. I was feeling the very thing that the state of Mississippi had spent millions of dollars to make sure that I would never feel; I was becoming aware of the thing that the Jim Crow laws had been drafted and passed to keep out of my consciousness; I was acting on impulses that southern senators in the nation's capital had striven to keep out of Negro life; I was beginning to dream the dreams that the state had said were wrong, that the schools had said were taboo.

Had I been articulate about my ultimate aspirations, no doubt someone would have told me what I was bargaining for; but nobody seemed to know, and least of all did I. My classmates felt that I was doing something that was vaguely wrong, but they did not know how to express it. As the outside world grew more meaningful, I became more concerned, tense; and my classmates and my teachers would say: "Why do you ask so many questions?" Or: "Keep quiet."

I was in my fifteenth year; in terms of schooling I was far behind the average youth of the nation, but I did not know that. In me was shaping a yearning for a kind of consciousness, a mode of being that the way of life about me had said could not be, must not be, and upon which the penalty of death had been placed. Somewhere in the dead of the southern night my life had switched onto the wrong track and, without my knowing it, the locomotive of my heart was rushing down a dangerously steep slope, heading for a collision, heedless of the warning red lights that blinked all about me, the sirens and the bells and the screams that filled the air.

ONE MORNING I arrived early at work and went into the bank lobby where the Negro porter was mopping. I stood at a counter and picked up the Memphis *Commercial Appeal* and began my free reading of the press. I came finally to the editorial page and saw an article dealing with one H. L. Mencken. I knew by hear-say that he was the editor of the *American Mercury,* but aside from that I knew nothing about him. The article was a furious denunciation of Mencken, concluding with one, hot, short sentence: Mencken is a fool.

I wondered what on earth this Mencken had done to call down upon him the scorn of the South. The only people I had ever heard denounced in the South were Negroes, and this man was not a Negro. Then what ideas did Mencken hold that made a newspaper like the *Commercial Appeal* castigate him publicly? Undoubtedly he must be advocating ideas that the South did not like. Were there, then, people other than Negroes who criticized the South? I knew that during the Civil War the South had hated northern whites, but I had not encountered such hate during my life. Knowing no more of Mencken than I did at that moment, I felt a vague sympathy for him. Had not the South, which had assigned me the role of a non-man, cast at him its hardest words?

Now, how could I find out about this Mencken? There was a huge library near the riverfront, but I knew that Negroes were not allowed to patronize its shelves any more than they were the parks and playgrounds of the city. I had gone into the library several times to get books for the white men on the job. Which of them would now help me to get books? And how could I read them without causing concern to the white men with whom I worked? I had so far been successful in hiding my thoughts and feelings from them, but I knew that I would create hostility if I went about this business of reading in a clumsy way.

I weighed the personalities of the men on the job. There was Don, a Jew; but I distrusted him. His position was not much better than mine and I knew that he was uneasy and insecure; he had always treated me in an offhand, bantering way that barely concealed his contempt. I was afraid to ask him to help me to get books; his frantic desire to demonstrate a racial solidarity with the whites against Negroes might make him betray me.

Then how about the boss? No, he was a Baptist and I had the suspicion that he would not be quite able to comprehend why a black boy would want to read Mencken. There were other white men on the job whose attitudes showed clearly that they were Kluxers or sympathizers, and they were out of the question.

There remained only one man whose attitude did not fit into an anti-Negro category, for I had heard the white men refer to him as a "Pope lover." He was an Irish Catholic and was hated by the white Southerners. I knew that he read books, because I had got him volumes from the library several times. Since he, too, was an object of hatred, I felt that he might refuse me but would hardly betray me. I hesitated, weighing and balancing the imponderable realities.

One morning I paused before the Catholic fellow's desk.

"I want to ask you a favor," I whispered to him.

"What is it?"

"I want to read. I can't get books from the library. I wonder if you'd let me use your card?"

He looked at me suspiciously.

"My card is full most of the time," he said.

"I see," I said and waited, posing my question silently.

"You're not trying to get me into trouble, are you, boy?" he asked, staring at me.

"Oh, no, sir."

"What book do you want?"

"A book by H. L. Mencken."

"Which one?"

"I don't know. Has he written more than one?"

"He has written several."

"I didn't know that."

"What makes you want to read Mencken?"

"Oh, I just saw his name in the newspaper," I said.

"It's good of you to want to read," he said. "But you ought to read the right things."

I said nothing. Would he want to supervise my reading?

"Let me think," he said. "I'll figure out something."

I turned from him and he called me back. He stared at me quizzically.

"Richard, don't mention this to the other white men," he said.

"I understand," I said. "I won't say a word."

A few days later he called me to him.

"I've got a card in my wife's name," he said. "Here's mine."

"Thank you, sir."

"Do you think you can manage it?"

"I'll manage fine," I said.

"If they suspect you, you'll get in trouble," he said.

"I'll write the same kind of notes to the library that you wrote when you sent me for books," I told him. "I'll sign your name."

He laughed.

"Go ahead. Let me see what you get," he said.

That afternoon I addressed myself to forging a note. Now, what were the names of books written by H. L. Mencken? I did not know any of them. I finally wrote what I thought would be a foolproof note: *Dear Madam: Will you please let this nigger boy*—I used the word "nigger" to make the librarian feel that I could not possibly be the author of the note —*have some books by H. L. Mencken?* I forged the white man's name.

I entered the library as I had always done when on errands for whites, but I felt that I would somehow slip up and betray myself. I doffed my hat, stood a respectful distance from the desk, looked as unbookish as possible, and waited for the white patrons to be taken care of. When the desk was clear of people, I still waited. The white librarian looked at me.

"What do you want, boy?"

As though I did not possess the power of speech, I stepped forward and simply handed her the forged note, not parting my lips.

"What books by Mencken does he want?" she asked.

"I don't know, ma'am," I said, avoiding her eyes.

"Who gave you this card?"

"Mr. Falk," I said.

"Where is he?"

"He's at work, at the M—— Optical Company," I said. "I've been in here for him before."

"I remember," the woman said. "But he never wrote notes like this."

Oh, God, she's suspicious. Perhaps she would not let me have the books? If she had turned her back at that moment, I would have ducked out the door and never gone back. Then I thought of a bold idea.

"You can call him up, ma'am," I said, my heart pounding.

"You're not using these books, are you?" she asked pointedly.

"Oh, no, ma'am. I can't read."

"I don't know what he wants by Mencken," she said under her breath.

I knew now that I had won; she was thinking of other things and the race question had gone out of her mind. She went to the shelves. Once or twice she looked over her shoulder at me, as though she was still doubtful. Finally she came forward with two books in her hand.

"I'm sending him two books," she said. "But tell Mr. Falk to come in next time, or send me the names of the books he wants. I don't know what he wants to read."

I said nothing. She stamped the card and handed me the books. Not daring to glance at them, I went out of the library, fearing that the woman would call me back for further questioning. A block away from the library I opened one of the books and read a title: *A Book of Prefaces*. I was nearing my nineteenth birthday and I did not know how to pronounce the word "preface." I thumbed the pages and saw strange words and strange names. I shook my head, disappointed. I looked at the other book; it was called *Prejudices*. I knew what that word meant; I had heard it all my life. And right off I was on guard against Mencken's books. Why would a man want to call a book *Prejudices?* The word was so stained with all my memories of racial hate that I could not conceive of anybody using it for a title. Perhaps I had made a mistake about Mencken? A man who had prejudices must be wrong.

When I showed the books to Mr. Falk, he looked at me and frowned.

"That librarian might telephone you," I warned him.

"That's all right," he said. "But when you're through reading those books, I want you to tell me what you get out of them."

That night in my rented room, while letting the hot water run over my can of pork and beans in the sink, I opened *A Book of Prefaces* and began to read. I was jarred and shocked by the style, the clear, clean, sweeping sentences. Why did he write like that? And how did one write like that? I pictured the man as a raging demon, slashing with his pen, consumed with hate, denouncing everything American, extolling everything European or German, laughing at the weaknesses of people, mocking God, authority. What was this? I stood up, trying to realize what reality lay behind the meaning of the words . . . Yes, this man was fighting, fighting with words. He was using words as a weapon, using them as one would use a club. Could words be weapons? Well, yes, for here they were. Then, maybe, perhaps, I could use them as a weapon? No. It frightened me. I read on and what amazed me was not what he said, but how on earth anybody had the courage to say it.

Occasionally I glanced up to reassure myself that I was

alone in the room. Who were these men about whom Mencken was talking so passionately? Who was Anatole France? Joseph Conrad? Sinclair Lewis, Sherwood Anderson, Dostoevski, George Moore, Gustave Flaubert, Maupassant, Tolstoy, Frank Harris, Mark Twain, Thomas Hardy, Arnold Bennett, Stephen Crane, Zola, Norris, Gorky, Bergson, Ibsen, Balzac, Bernard Shaw, Dumas, Poe, Thomas Mann, O. Henry, Dreiser, H. G. Wells, Gogol, T. S. Eliot, Gide, Baudelaire, Edgar Lee Masters, Stendhal, Turgenev, Huneker, Nietzsche, and scores of others? Were these men real? Did they exist or had they existed? And how did one pronounce their names?

I ran across many words whose meanings I did not know, and I either looked them up in a dictionary or, before I had a chance to do that, encountered the word in a context that made its meaning clear. But what strange world was this? I concluded the book with the conviction that I had somehow overlooked something terribly important in life. I had once tried to write, had once reveled in feeling, had let my crude imagination roam, but the impulse to dream had been slowly beaten out of me by experience. Now it surged up again and I hungered for books, new ways of looking and seeing. It was not a matter of believing or disbelieving what I read, but of feeling something new, of being affected by something that made the look of the world different.

As dawn broke I ate my pork and beans, feeling dopey, sleepy. I went to work, but the mood of the book would not die; it lingered, coloring everything I saw, heard, did. I now felt that I knew what the white men were feeling. Merely because I had read a book that had spoken of how they lived and thought, I identified myself with that book. I felt vaguely guilty. Would I, filled with bookish notions, act in a manner that would make the whites dislike me?

I forged more notes and my trips to the library became frequent. Reading grew into a passion. My first serious novel was Sinclair Lewis's *Main Street.* It made me see my boss, Mr.

Gerald, and identify him as an American type. I would smile when I saw him lugging his golf bags into the office. I had always felt a vast distance separating me from the boss, and now I felt closer to him, though still distant. I felt now that I knew him, that I could feel the very limits of his narrow life. And this had happened because I had read a novel about a mythical man called George F. Babbitt.

The plots and stories in the novels did not interest me so much as the point of view revealed. I gave myself over to each novel without reserve, without trying to criticize it; it was enough for me to see and feel something different. And for me, everything was something different. Reading was like a drug, a dope. The novels created moods in which I lived for days. But I could not conquer my sense of guilt, my feeling that the white men around me knew that I was changing, that I had begun to regard them differently.

Whenever I brought a book to the job, I wrapped it in newspaper—a habit that was to persist for years in other cities and under other circumstances. But some of the white men pried into my packages when I was absent and they questioned me.

"Boy, what are you reading those books for?"

"Oh, I don't know, sir."

"That's deep stuff you're reading, boy."

"I'm just killing time, sir."

"You'll addle your brains if you don't watch out."

I read Dreiser's *Jennie Gerhardt* and *Sister Carrie* and they revived in me a vivid sense of my mother's suffering; I was overwhelmed. I grew silent, wondering about the life around me. It would have been impossible for me to have told anyone what I derived from these novels, for it was nothing less than a sense of life itself. All my life had shaped me for the realism, the naturalism of the modern novel, and I could not read enough of them.

Steeped in new moods and ideas, I bought a ream of paper, and tried to write; but nothing would come, or what did come was flat beyond telling. I discovered that more than desire and feeling were necessary to write and I dropped the idea. Yet I still wondered how it was possible to know people sufficiently to write about them? Could I ever learn about life and people? To me, with my vast ignorance, my Jim Crow station in life, it seemed a task impossible of achievement. I now knew what being a Negro meant. I could endure the hunger. I had learned to live with hate. But to feel that there were feelings denied me, that the very breath of life itself was beyond my reach, that more than anything else hurt, wounded me. I had a new hunger.

In buoying me up, reading also cast me down, made me see what was possible, what I had missed. My tension returned, new, terrible, bitter, surging, almost too great to be contained. I no longer *felt* that the world about me was hostile, killing; I *knew* it. A million times I asked myself what I could do to save myself, and there were no answers. I seemed forever condemned, ringed by walls.

I did not discuss my reading with Mr. Falk, who had lent me his library card; it would have meant talking about myself and that would have been too painful. I smiled each day, fighting desperately to maintain my old behavior, to keep my disposition seemingly sunny. But some of the white men discerned that I had begun to brood.

"Wake up there, boy!" Mr. Olin said one day.

"Sir!" I answered for the lack of a better word.

"You act like you've stolen something," he said.

I laughed in the way I knew he expected me to laugh, but I resolved to be more conscious of myself, to watch my every act, to guard and hide the new knowledge that was dawning within me.

If I went north, would it be possible for me to build a new life then? But how could a man build a life upon vague, unformed yearnings? I wanted to write and I did not even know the English language. I bought English grammars and found them dull. I felt that I was getting a better sense of the language from novels than from grammars. I read hard, discarding a writer as soon as I felt that I had grasped his point of view. At night the printed page stood before my eyes in sleep.

Mrs. Moss, my landlady, asked me one Sunday morning:

"Son, what is this you keep on reading?"

"Oh, nothing. Just novels."

"What you get out of 'em?"

"I'm just killing time," I said.

"I hope you know your own mind," she said in a tone which implied that she doubted if I had a mind.

I knew of no Negroes who read the books I liked and I wondered if any Negroes ever thought of them. I knew that there were Negro doctors, lawyers, newspapermen, but I never saw any of them. When I read a Negro newspaper I never caught the faintest echo of my preoccupation in its pages. I felt trapped and occasionally, for a few days, I would stop reading. But a vague hunger would come over me for books, books that opened up new avenues of feeling and seeing, and again I would forge another note to the white librarian. Again I would read and wonder as only the naïve and unlettered can read and wonder, feeling that I carried a secret, criminal burden about with me each day.

That winter my mother and brother came and we set up housekeeping, buying furniture on the installment plan, being cheated and yet knowing no way to avoid it. I began to eat warm food and to my surprise found that regular meals enabled me to read faster. I may have lived through many illnesses and survived them, never suspecting that I was ill. My brother obtained a job and we began to save toward the trip north, plotting our time, setting tentative dates for departure. I told none of the white men on the job that I was planning to go north; I knew that the moment they felt I was thinking of the North they would change toward me. It would have made them feel that I did not like the life I was living, and because my life was completely conditioned by what they said or did, it would have been tantamount to challenging them.

I could calculate my chances for life in the South as a Negro fairly clearly now.

I could fight the southern whites by organizing with other Negroes, as my grandfather had done. But I knew that I could never win that way; there were many whites and there were but few blacks. They were strong and we were weak. Outright black rebellion could never win. If I fought openly I would die and I did not want to die. News of lynchings were frequent.

I could submit and live the life of a genial slave, but that was impossible. All of my life had shaped me to live by my own feelings and thoughts. I could make up to Bess and marry her and inherit the house. But that, too, would be the life of a slave; if I did that, I would crush to death something within me, and I would hate myself as much as I knew the whites already hated those who had submitted. Neither could I ever willingly present myself to be kicked, as Shorty had done. I would rather have died than do that.

I could drain off my restlessness by fighting with Shorty and Harrison. I had seen many Negroes solve the problem of being black by transferring their hatred of themselves to others with a black skin and fighting them. I would have to be cold to do that, and I was not cold and I could never be.

I could, of course, forget what I had read, thrust the whites out of my mind, forget them; and find release from anxiety and longing in sex and alcohol. But the memory of how my father had conducted himself made that course repugnant. If I did not want others to violate my life, how could I voluntarily violate it myself?

I had no hope whatever of being a professional man. Not only had I been so conditioned that I did not desire it, but the fulfillment of such an ambition was beyond my capabilities. Well-to-do Negroes lived in a world that was almost as alien to me as the world inhabited by whites.

What, then, was there? I held my life in my mind, in my consciousness each day, feeling at times that I would stumble and drop it, spill it forever. My reading had created a vast sense of distance between me and the world in which I lived and tried to make a living, and that sense of distance was increasing each day. My days and nights were one long, quiet, continuously contained dream of terror, tension, and anxiety. I wondered how long I could bear it.

THE ACCIDENTAL VISIT of Aunt Maggie to Memphis formed a practical basis for my planning to go north. Aunt Maggie's husband, the "uncle" who had fled from Arkansas in the dead of night, had deserted her; and now she was casting about for a living. My mother, Aunt Maggie, my brother, and I held long conferences, speculating on the prospects of jobs and the cost of apartments in Chicago. And every time we conferred, we defeated ourselves. It was impossible for all four of us to go at once; we did not have enough money.

Finally sheer wish and hope prevailed over common sense and facts. We discovered that if we waited until we were prepared to go, we would never leave, we would never amass enough money to see us through. We would have to gamble. We finally decided that Aunt Maggie and I would go first, even though it was winter, and prepare a place for my mother and brother. Why wait until next week or next month? If we were going, why not go at once?

Next loomed the problem of leaving my job cleanly, smoothly, without arguments or scenes. How could I present the fact of leaving to my boss? Yes, I would pose as an innocent boy; I would tell him that my aunt was taking me and my paralyzed mother to Chicago. That would create in his mind the impression that I was not asserting my will; it would block any expression of dislike on his part for my act. I knew that southern whites hated the idea of Negroes leaving to live in places where the racial atmosphere was different.

It worked as I had planned. When I broke the news of my leaving two days before I left—I was afraid to tell it sooner for fear that I would create hostility on the part of the whites with whom I worked—the boss leaned back in his swivel chair and gave me the longest and most considerate look he had ever given me.

"Chicago?" he repeated softly.

"Yes, sir."

"Boy, you won't like it up there," he said.

"Well, I have to go where my family is, sir," I said.

The other white office workers paused in their tasks and listened. I grew self-conscious, tense.

"It's cold up there," he said.

"Yes, sir. They say it is," I said, keeping my voice in a neutral tone.

He became conscious that I was watching him and he looked away, laughing uneasily to cover his concern and dislike.

"Now, boy," he said banteringly, "don't you go up there and fall into that lake."

"Oh, no, sir," I said, smiling as though there existed the possibility of my falling accidentally into Lake Michigan.

He was serious again, staring at me. I looked at the floor.

"You think you'll do any better up there?" he asked.

"I don't know, sir."

"You seem to've been getting along all right down here," he said.

"Oh, yes, sir. If it wasn't for my mother's going, I'd stay right here and work," I lied as earnestly as possible.

"Well, why not stay? You can send her money," he suggested.

He had trapped me. I knew that staying now would never do. I could not have controlled my relations with the whites if I had remained after having told them that I wanted to go north.

"Well, I want to be with my mother," I said.

"You want to be with your mother," he repeated idly. "Well, Richard, we enjoyed having you with us."

"And I enjoyed working here," I lied.

There was silence; I stood awkwardly, then moved to the door. There was still silence; white faces were looking strangely at me. I went upstairs, feeling like a criminal. The word soon spread through the factory and the white men looked at me with new eyes. They came to me.

"So you're going north, hunh?"

"Yes, sir. My family's taking me with 'em."

"The North's no good for your people, boy."

"I'll try to get along, sir."

"Don't believe all the stories you hear about the North."

"No, sir. I don't."

"You'll come back here where your friends are."

"Well, sir. I don't know."

"How're you going to act up there?"

"Just like I act down here, sir."

"Would you speak to a white girl up there?"

"Oh, no, sir. I'll act there just like I act here."

"Aw, no, you won't. You'll change. Niggers change when they go north."

I wanted to tell him that I was going north precisely to change, but I did not.

"I'll be the same," I said, trying to indicate that I had no imagination whatever.

As I talked I felt that I was acting out a dream. I did not want to lie, yet I had to lie to conceal what I felt. A white censor was standing over me and, like dreams forming a curtain for the safety of sleep, so did my lies form a screen of safety for my living moments.

"Boy, I bet you've been reading too many of them damn books."

"Oh, no, sir."

I made my last errand to the post office, put my bag away, washed my hands, and pulled on my cap. I shot a quick glance about the factory; most of the men were working late. One or two looked up. Mr. Falk, to whom I had returned my library card, gave me a quick, secret smile. I walked to the elevator and rode down with Shorty.

"You lucky bastard," he said bitterly.

"Why do you say that?"

"You saved your goddamn money and now you're gone."

"My problems are just starting," I said.

"You'll never have any problems as hard as the ones you had here," he said.

"I hope not," I said. "But life is tricky."

"Sometimes I get so goddamn mad I want to kill everybody," he spat in a rage.

"You can leave," I said.

"I'll never leave this goddamn South," he railed. "I'm always saying I am, but I won't . . . I'm lazy. I like to sleep too goddamn much. I'll die here. Or maybe they'll kill me."

I stepped from the elevator into the street, half expecting someone to call me back and tell me that it was all a dream, that I was not leaving.

This was the culture from which I sprang. This was the terror from which I fled.

The next day when I was already in full flight—aboard a northward bound train—I could not have accounted, if it had been demanded of me, for all the varied forces that were making me reject the culture that had molded and shaped me. I was leaving without a qualm, without a single backward glance. The face of the South that I had known was hostile and forbidding, and yet out of all the conflicts and the curses, the blows and the anger, the tension and the terror, I had somehow gotten the idea that life could be different, could be lived in a fuller and richer manner. As had happened when I had fled the orphan home, I was now running more away from something than toward something. But that did not matter to me. My mood was: I've got to get away; I can't stay here.

But what was it that always made me feel that way? What was it that made me conscious of possibilities? From where in this southern darkness had I caught a sense of freedom? Why was it that I was able to act upon vaguely felt notions? What was it that made me feel things deeply enough for me to try to order my life by my feelings? The external world of whites and blacks, which was the only world that I had ever known, surely had not evoked in me any belief in myself. The people I had met had advised and demanded submission. What, then, was I after? How dare I consider my feelings superior to the gross environment that sought to claim me?

It had been only through books—at best, no more than vicarious cultural transfusions—that I had managed to keep myself alive in a negatively vital way. Whenever my environment had failed to support or nourish me, I had clutched at books; consequently, my belief in books had risen more out of a sense of desperation than from any abiding conviction of their ultimate value. In a peculiar sense, life had trapped me in a realm of emotional rejection; I had not embraced insurgency through open choice. Existing emotionally on the sheer, thin margin of southern culture, I had felt that nothing short of life itself hung upon each of my actions and decisions; and I had grown used to change, to movement, to making many adjustments.

In the main, my hope was merely a kind of self-defense, a conviction that if I did not leave I would perish, either because of possible violence of others against me, or because of my possible violence against them. The substance of my hope was formless and devoid of any real sense of direction, for in my southern living I had seen no looming landmark by which I could, in a positive sense, guide my daily actions. The shocks of southern living had rendered my personality tender and swollen, tense and volatile, and my flight was more a shunning of external and internal dangers than an attempt to embrace what I felt I wanted.

It had been my accidental reading of fiction and literary

criticism that had evoked in me vague glimpses of life's possibilities. Of course, I had never seen or met the men who wrote the books I read, and the kind of world in which they lived was as alien to me as the moon. But what enabled me to overcome my chronic distrust was that these books—written by men like Dreiser, Masters, Mencken, Anderson, and Lewis—seemed defensively critical of the straitened American environment. These writers seemed to feel that America could be shaped nearer to the hearts of those who lived in it. And it was out of these novels and stories and articles, out of the emotional impact of imaginative constructions of heroic or tragic deeds, that I felt touching my face a tinge of warmth from an unseen light; and in my leaving I was groping toward that invisible light, always trying to keep my face so set and turned that I would not lose the hope of its faint promise, using it as my justification for action.

The white South said that it knew "niggers," and I was what the white South called a "nigger." Well, the white South had never known me—never known what I thought, what I felt. The white South said that I had a "place" in life. Well, I had never felt my "place"; or, rather, my deepest instincts had always made me reject the "place" to which the white South had assigned me. It had never occurred to me that I was in any way an inferior being. And no word that I had ever heard fall from the lips of southern white men had ever made me really doubt the worth of my own humanity. True, I had lied. I had stolen. I had struggled to contain my seething anger. I had fought. And it was perhaps a mere accident that I had never killed . . . But in what other ways had the South allowed me to be natural, to be real, to be myself, except in rejection, rebellion, and aggression?

Not only had the southern whites not known me, but, more important still, as I had lived in the South I had not had the chance to learn who I was. The pressure of southern living kept me from being the kind of person that I might have been. I had been what my surroundings had demanded, what my family—conforming to the dictates of the whites above them—had exacted of me, and what the whites had said that I must be. Never being fully able to be myself, I had slowly learned that the South could recognize but a part of a man, could accept but a fragment of his personality, and all the rest—the best and deepest things of heart and mind— were tossed away in blind ignorance and hate.

I was leaving the South to fling myself into the unknown, to meet other situations that would perhaps elicit from me other responses. And if I could meet enough of a different life, then, perhaps, gradually and slowly I might learn who I was, what I might be. I was not leaving the South to forget the South, but so that some day I might understand it, might come to know what its rigors had done to me, to its children. I fled so that the numbness of my defensive living might thaw out and let me feel the pain—years later and far away—of what living in the South had meant.

Yet, deep down, I knew that I could never really leave the South, for my feelings had already been formed by the South, for there had been slowly instilled into my personality and consciousness, black though I was, the culture of the South. So, in leaving, I was taking a part of the South to transplant in alien soil, to see if it could grow differently, if it could drink of new and cool rains, bend in strange winds, respond to the warmth of other suns, and, perhaps, to bloom . . . And if that miracle ever happened, then I would know that there was yet hope in that southern swamp of despair and violence, that light could emerge even out of the blackest of the southern night. I would know that the South too could overcome its fear, its hate, its cowardice, its heritage of guilt and blood, its burden of anxiety and compulsive cruelty.

With ever watchful eyes and bearing scars, visible and invisible, I headed North, full of a hazy notion that life could be lived with dignity, that the personalities of others should not be violated, that men should be able to confront other men without fear or shame, and that if men were lucky in their living on earth they might win some redeeming meaning for their having struggled and suffered here beneath the stars.

Joe Louis Uncovers Dynamite

It is not generally known that, like Theodore Dreiser and H. L. Mencken, whom he so greatly admired, Wright acquired some of his experience as a writer in newspaper offices. He served as a correspondent for the Harlem Bureau of the Daily Worker *(and, indeed, he often served as the whole Bureau all by himself) for the second half of 1937. Earlier still he had done reporting for* New Masses, *most notably on some fights of the boxer Joe Louis and on the meetings of the National Negro Congress and the John Reed Clubs Conference.*

"Joe Louis Uncovers Dynamite" (1935) is Wright's first published piece of journalistic reportage. It shows clearly that he had little to learn from the newspaper world in terms of craft. He brings to it excitement, a fresh sense of firsthand experience, a love for detail, and an effusion of creative imagination that belong properly to the novelist. These same characteristics later adorn his book-length reports on the birth of Ghana as an independent state and on the Bandung Conference.

"Joe Louis Uncovers Dynamite" originally appeared in *New Masses,* Vol. 17, Oct. 8, 1935.

WUN—TUH—THREE—fooo—fiiive—seex—seven—eight—
niine—thuun!"

"JOE LOUIS—THE WINNAH!"

On Chicago's South Side five minutes after these words
were yelled and Joe Louis' hand was hoisted as victor in his
four-round go with Max Baer, Negroes poured out of beer
taverns, pool rooms, barber shops, rooming houses and dingy
flats and flooded the streets.

"LOUIS! LOUIS! LOUIS!" they yelled and threw their hats
away. They snatched newspapers from the stands of astonished Greeks and tore them up, flinging the bits into the air.
They wagged their heads. Lawd, they'd never seen or heard
the like of it before. They shook the hands of strangers. They
clapped one another on the back. It was like a revival. Really,
there was a religious feeling in the air. Well, it wasn't exactly
a religious feeling, but it was *something,* and you could feel
it. It was a feeling of unity, of oneness.

Two hours after the fight the area between South Parkway
and Prairie Avenue on 47th Street was jammed with no less
than twenty-five thousand Negroes, joy-mad and moving to
they didn't know where. Clasping hands, they formed long
writhing snake-lines and wove in and out of traffic. They
seeped out of doorways, oozed from alleys, trickled out of
tenements, and flowed down the street; a fluid mass of joy.
White storekeepers hastily closed their doors against the tidal
wave and stood peeping through the plate glass with
blanched faces.

Something had happened, all right. And it had happened
so confoundingly sudden that the whites in the neighborhood were dumb with fear. They felt—you could see it in
their faces—that *something* had ripped loose, exploded.
Something which they had long feared and thought was
dead. Or if not dead, at least so safely buried under the
pretence of good-will that they no longer had need to fear it.
Where in the world did it come from? And what was worst
of all, how far would it go? Say, what's got into these Negroes?

And the whites and the blacks began to feel themselves. The blacks began to remember all the little slights, and discriminations and insults they had suffered; and their hunger too and their misery. And the whites began to search their souls to see if they had been guilty of something, some time, somewhere, against which this wave of feeling was rising.

As the celebration wore on, the younger Negroes began to grow bold. They jumped on the running boards of automobiles going east or west on 47th Street and demanded of the occupants:

"Who yuh fer—Baer or Louis?"

In the stress of the moment it seemed that the answer to the question marked out friend and foe.

A hesitating reply brought waves of scornful laughter. Baer, huh? That was funny. Now, hadn't Joe Louis just whipped Max Baer? Didn't think we had it in us, did you? Thought Joe Louis was scared, didn't you? Scared because Max talked loud and made boasts. We ain't scared either. We'll fight too when the time comes. We'll win, too.

A taxicab driver had his cab wrecked when he tried to put up a show of bravado.

Then they began stopping street cars. Like a cyclone sweeping through a forest, they went through them, shouting, stamping. Conductors gave up and backed away like children. Everybody had to join in this celebration. Some of the people ran out of the cars and stood, pale and trembling, in the crowd. They felt it, too.

In the crush a pocketbook snapped open and money spilled on the street for eager black fingers.

"They stole it from us, anyhow," they said as they picked it up.

When an elderly Negro admonished them, a fist was shaken in his face. Uncle Tomming, huh?

"Whut in hell yuh gotta do wid it" they wanted to know.

Something had popped loose, all right. And it had come from deep down. Out of the darkness it had leaped from its

34

coil. And nobody wanted to say. Blacks and whites were afraid. But it was a sweet fear, at least for the blacks. It was a mingling of fear and fulfillment. Something dreaded and yet wanted. A something had popped out of a dark hole, something with a hydra-like head, and it was darting forth its tongue.

You stand on the borderline, wondering what's beyond. Then you take one step and you feel a strange, sweet tingling. You take two steps and the feeling becomes keener. You want to feel some more. You break into a run. You know it's dangerous, but you're impelled in spite of yourself.

Four centuries of oppression, of frustrated hopes, of black bitterness, felt even in the bones of the bewildered young, were rising to the surface. Yes, unconsciously they had imputed to the brawny image of Joe Louis all the balked dreams of revenge, all the secretly visualized moments of retaliation, AND HE HAD WON! Good Gawd Almighty! Yes, by Jesus, it could be done! Didn't Joe do it? You see, Joe was the consciously-felt symbol. Joe was the concentrated essence of black triumph over white. And it comes so seldom, so seldom. And what could be sweeter than long-nourished hate vicariously gratified? From the symbol of Joe's strength they took strength, and in that moment all fear, all obstacles were wiped out, drowned. They stepped out of the mire of hesitation and irresolution and were free! Invincible! A merciless victor over a fallen foe! Yes, they had felt all that—for a moment . . .

And then the cops came.

Not the carefully picked white cops who were used to batter the skulls of white workers and intellectuals who came to the South Side* to march with the black workers to show their solidarity in the struggle against Mussolini's impending invasion of Ethiopia; oh, no, black cops, but trusted black

*George Martin's article about cops smashing an anti-war demonstration in Chicago. *New Masses,* September 17, 1935.

cops and plenty tough. Cops who knew their business, how to handle delicate situations. They piled out of patrols, swinging clubs.

"Git back! Gawddammit, git back!"

But they were very careful, very careful. They didn't hit anybody. They, too, sensed *something*. And they didn't want to trifle with it. And there's no doubt but that they had been instructed not to. Better go easy here. No telling what might happen. They swung clubs, but pushed the crowd back with their hands.

Finally, the street cars moved again. The taxis and automobiles could go through. The whites breathed easier. The blood came back to their cheeks.

The Negroes stood on the sidewalks, talking, wondering, looking, breathing hard. They had felt something, and it had been sweet—that feeling. They wanted some more of it, but they were afraid now. The spell was broken.

And about midnight down the street that feeling ebbed, seeping home—flowing back to the beer tavern, the pool room, the café, the barber shop, the dingy flat. Like a sullen river it ran back to its muddy channel, carrying a confused and sentimental memory on its surface, like water-soaked driftwood.

Say, Comrade, here's the wild river that's got to be harnessed and directed. Here's that *something*, that pent-up folk consciousness. Here's a fleeting glimpse of the heart of the Negro, the heart that beats and suffers and hopes—for freedom. Here's that fluid something that's like iron. Here's the real dynamite that Joe Louis uncovered!

Blueprint for Negro Writing

"Blueprint for Negro Writing" represents Wright's major attempt, as a Black Communist, to explore the relationship between literature and politics as well as that between class perspective and ethnic culture. The piece was written in 1938 and served to define the theoretical line of New Challenge, *a little left-wing magazine Wright helped edit in the summer of 1937. As an effort to bridge the gap between Marxism and Black nationalism, two often irreconcilable points of view, this ideological program for Afro-American writers was received with some reservations by the Communists at the time; more recently, Black cultural nationalists, like Addison Gayle, Jr., who included it in* The Black Aesthetic *(1970), have stressed its relevance to their own preoccupations.*

Although Wright's attitude toward the Communists greatly varied in later years, his attitude throughout his life never disowned one of the central points in this essay: "Negro writers," he said, "must accept the nationalist implications of their lives, but a nationalistic spirit in Negro writing means a nationalism carrying the highest possible pitch of social consciousness. It means a nationalism that is

"Blueprint for Negro Writing" originally appeared in *New Challenge*, II (Fall 1937).

aware of its origins, its limitations, that is aware of the dangers of its position . . ."

1. The Role of Negro Writing: Two Definitions

Generally speaking, Negro writing in the past has been confined to humble novels, poems, and plays, prim and decorous ambassadors who went a-begging to white America. They entered the Court of American Public Opinion dressed in the knee-pants of servility, curtsying to show that the Negro was not inferior, that he was human, and that he had a life comparable to that of other people. For the most part these artistic ambassadors were received as though they were French poodles who do clever tricks.

White America never offered these Negro writers any serious criticism. The mere fact that a Negro could write was astonishing. Nor was there any deep concern on the part of white America with the role Negro writing should play in American culture; and the role it did play grew out of accident rather than intent or design. Either it crept in through the kitchen in the form of jokes; or it was the fruits of that foul soil which was the result of a liaison between inferiority-complexed Negro "geniuses" and burnt-out white Bohemians with money.

On the other hand, these often technically brilliant performances by Negro writers were looked upon by the majority of literate Negroes as something to be proud of. At best, Negro writing has been something external to the lives of educated Negroes themselves. That the productions of their writers should have been something of a guide in their daily living is a matter which seems never to have been raised seriously.

Under these conditions Negro writing assumed two general aspects: (1) It became a sort of conspicuous ornamentation, the hallmark of "achievement." (2) It became the voice of the educated Negro pleading with white America for justice.

Rarely was the best of this writing addressed to the Negro himself, his needs, his sufferings, his aspirations. Through misdirection, Negro writers have been far better to others than they have been to themselves. And the mere recognition of this places the whole question of Negro writing in a new light and raises a doubt as to the validity of its present direction.

2. The Minority Outlook

Somewhere in his writings Lenin makes the observation that oppressed minorities often reflect the techniques of the bourgeoisie more brilliantly than some sections of the bourgeoisie themselves. The psychological importance of this becomes meaningful when it is recalled that oppressed minorities, and especially the petty bourgeois sections of oppressed minorities, strive to assimilate the virtues of the bourgeoisie in the assumption that by doing so they can lift themselves into a higher social sphere. But not only among the oppressed petty bourgeoisie does this occur. The workers of a minority people, chafing under exploitation, forge organizational forms of struggle to better their lot. Lacking the handicaps of false ambition and property, they have access to a wide social vision and a deep social consciousness. They display a greater freedom and initiative in pushing their claims upon civilization than even do the petty bourgeoisie. Their organizations show greater strength, adaptability, and efficiency than any other group or class in society.

That Negro workers, propelled by the harsh conditions of their lives, have demonstrated this consciousness and mobility for economic and political action there can be no doubt. But has this consciousness been reflected in the work of Negro writers to the same degree as it has in the Negro workers' struggle to free Herndon and the Scottsboro Boys, in the drive toward unionism, in the fight against lynching? Have they as creative writers taken advantage of their unique minority position?

The answer decidedly is *no*. Negro writers have lagged sadly, and as time passes the gap widens between them and their people.

How can this hiatus be bridged? How can the enervating effects of this longstanding split be eliminated?

In presenting questions of this sort an attitude of self-consciousness and self-criticism is far more likely to be a fruitful point of departure than a mere recounting of past achievements. An emphasis upon tendency and experiment, a view of society as something becoming rather than as something fixed and admired is the one which points the way for Negro writers to stand shoulder to shoulder with Negro workers in mood and outlook.

3. A Whole Culture

There is, however, a culture of the Negro which is his and has been addressed to him; a culture which has, for good or ill, helped to clarify his consciousness and create emotional attitudes which are conducive to action. This culture has stemmed mainly from two sources: (1) the Negro church; and (2) the folklore of the Negro people.

It was through the portals of the church that the American Negro first entered the shrine of western culture. Living under slave conditions of life, bereft of his African heritage, the Negroes' struggle for religion on the plantations between 1820–60 assumed the form of a struggle for human rights. It remained a relatively revolutionary struggle until religion began to serve as an antidote for suffering and denial. But even today there are millions of American Negroes whose only sense of a whole universe, whose only relation to society and man, and whose only guide to personal dignity comes through the archaic morphology of Christian salvation.

It was, however, in a folklore moulded out of rigorous and inhuman conditions of life that the Negro achieved his most indigenous and complete expression. Blues, spirituals, and folk tales recounted from mouth to mouth; the whispered words of a black mother to her black daughter on the ways of men, to confidential wisdom of a black father to his black son; the swapping of sex experiences on street corners from boy to boy in the deepest vernacular; work songs sung under blazing suns—all these formed the channels through which the racial wisdom flowed.

One would have thought that Negro writers in the last century of striving at expression would have continued and deepened this folk tradition, would have tried to create a more intimate and yet a more profoundly social system of artistic communication between them and their people. But the illusion that they could escape through individual achievement the harsh lot of their race swung Negro writers away from any such path. Two separate cultures sprang up: one for the Negro masses, unwritten and unrecognized; and the other for the sons and daughters of a rising Negro bourgeoisie, parasitic and mannered.

Today the question is: Shall Negro writing be for the Negro masses, moulding the lives and consciousness of those masses toward new goals, or shall it continue begging the question of the Negroes' humanity?

4. The Problem of Nationalism in Negro Writing

In stressing the difference between the role Negro writing failed to play in the lives of the Negro people, and the role it should play in the future if it is to serve its historic functions; in pointing out the fact that Negro writing has been addressed in the main to a small white audience rather than to a Negro one, it should be stated that no attempt is being made here to propagate a specious and blatant nationalism. Yet the nationalist character of the Negro people is unmistakable. Psychologically this nationalism is reflected in the whole of Negro culture, and especially in folklore.

In the absence of fixed and nourishing forms of culture, the Negro has a folklore which embodies the memories and hopes of his struggle for freedom. Not yet caught in paint or stone, and as yet but feebly depicted in the poem and novel, the Negroes' most powerful images of hope and despair still remain in the fluid state of daily speech. How many John Henrys have lived and died on the lips of these black people? How many mythical heroes in embryo have been allowed to perish for lack of husbanding by alert intelligence?

Negro folklore contains, in a measure that puts to shame more deliberate forms of Negro expression, the collective sense of Negro life in America. Let those who shy at the nationalist implications of Negro life look at this body of folklore, living and powerful, which rose out of a unified sense of a common life and a common fate. Here are those vital beginnings of a recognition of value in life as it is *lived*, a recognition that marks the emergence of a new culture in the shell of the old. And at the moment this process starts, at the moment when a people begin to realize a *meaning* in their suffering, the civilization that engenders that suffering is doomed.

The nationalist aspects of Negro life are as sharply manifest in the social institutions of Negro people as in folklore. There is a Negro church, a Negro press, a Negro social world, a Negro sporting world, a Negro business world, a Negro school system, Negro professions; in short, a Negro way of life in America. The Negro people did not ask for this, and deep down, though they express themselves through their institutions and adhere to this special way of life, they do not want it now. This special existence was forced upon them from without by lunch rope, bayonet and mob rule. They accepted these negative conditions with the inevitability of a tree which must live or perish in whatever soil it finds itself.

The few crumbs of American civilization which the Negro

has got from the tables of capitalism have been through these segregated channels. Many Negro institutions are cowardly and incompetent; but they are all that the Negro has. And, in the main, any move, whether for progress or reaction, must come through these institutions for the simple reason that all other channels are closed. Negro writers who seek to mould or influence the consciousness of the Negro people must address their messages to them through the ideologies and attitudes fostered in this warping way of life.

5. *The Basis and Meaning of Nationalism in Negro Writing*

The social institutions of the Negro are imprisoned in the Jim Crow political system of the South, and this Jim Crow political system is in turn built upon a plantation-feudal economy. Hence, it can be seen that the emotional expression of group-feeling which puzzles so many whites and leads them to deplore what they call "black chauvinism" is not a morbidly inherent trait of the Negro, but rather the reflex expression of a life whose roots are imbedded deeply in Southern soil.

Negro writers must accept the nationalist implications of their lives, not in order to encourage them, but in order to change and transcend them. They must accept the concept of nationalism because, in order to transcend it, they must *possess* and *understand* it. And a nationalist spirit in Negro writing means a nationalism carrying the highest possible pitch of social consciousness. It means a nationalism that knows its origins, its limitations; that is aware of the dangers of its position; that knows its ultimate aims are unrealizable within the framework of capitalist America; a nationalism whose reason for being lies in the simple fact of self-possession and in the consciousness of the interdependence of people in modern society.

For purposes of creative expression it means that the

Negro writer must realize within the area of his own personal experience those impulses which, when prefigured in terms of broad social movements, constitute the stuff of nationalism.

For Negro writers even more so than for Negro politicians, nationalism is a bewildering and vexing question, the full ramifications of which cannot be dealt with here. But among Negro workers and the Negro middle class the spirit of nationalism is rife in a hundred devious forms; and a simple literary realism which seeks to depict the lives of these people devoid of wider social connotations, devoid of the revolutionary significance of these nationalist tendencies, must of necessity do a rank injustice to the Negro people and alienate their possible allies in the struggle for freedom.

6. Social Consciousness and Responsibility

The Negro writer who seeks to function within his race as a purposeful agent has a serious responsibility. In order to do justice to his subject matter, in order to depict Negro life in all of its manifold and intricate relationships, a deep, informed, and complex consciousness is necessary; a consciousness which draws for its strength upon the fluid lore of a great people, and moulds this lore with the concepts that move and direct the forces of history today.

With the gradual decline of the moral authority of the Negro church, and with the increasing irresolution which is paralyzing Negro middle class leadership, a new role is devolving upon the Negro writer. He is being called upon to do no less than create values by which his race is to struggle, live and die.

By his ability to fuse and make articulate the experiences of men, because his writing possesses the potential cunning to steal into the inmost recesses of the human heart, because he can create the myths and symbols that inspire a faith in life, he may expect either to be consigned to oblivion, or to be recognized for the valued agent he is.

This raises the question of the personality of the writer. It means that in the lives of Negro writers must be found those materials and experiences which will create a meaningful picture of the world today. Many young writers have grown to believe that a Marxist analysis of society presents such a picture. It creates a picture which, when placed before the eyes of the writer, should unify his personality, organize his emotions, buttress him with a tense and obdurate will to change the world.

And, in turn, this changed world will dialectically change the writer. Hence, it is through a Marxist conception of reality and society that the maximum degree of freedom in thought and feeling can be gained for the Negro writer. Further, this dramatic Marxist vision, when consciously grasped, endows the writer with a sense of dignity which no other vision can give. Ultimately, it restores to the writer his lost heritage, that is, his role as a creator of the world in which he lives, and as a creator of himself.

Yet, for the Negro writer, Marxism is but the starting point. No theory of life can take the place of life. After Marxism has laid bare the skeleton of society, there remains the task of the writer to plant flesh upon those bones out of his will to live. He may, with disgust and revulsion, say *no* and depict the horrors of capitalism encroaching upon the human being. Or he may, with hope and passion, say *yes* and depict the faint stirrings of a new and emerging life. But in whatever social voice he chooses to speak, whether positive or negative, there should always be heard or *over*-heard his faith, his necessity, his judgement.

His vision need not be simple or rendered in primer-like terms; for the life of the Negro people is not simple. The presentation of their lives should be simple, yes; but all the complexity, the strangeness, the magic wonder of life that plays like a bright sheen over the most sordid existence, should be there. To borrow a phrase from the Russians, it should have a *complex simplicity*. Eliot, Stein, Joyce, Proust, Hemingway, and Anderson; Gorky, Barbusse, Nexo, and Jack London no less than the folklore of the Negro himself should form the heritage of the Negro writer. Every iota of gain in human thought and sensibility should be ready grist for his mill, no matter how far-fetched they may seem in their immediate implications.

7. The Problem of Perspective

What vision must Negro writers have before their eyes in order to feel the impelling necessity for an about face? What angle of vision can show them all the forces of modern society in process, all the lines of economic development converging toward a distant point of hope? Must they believe in some "ism"?

They may feel that only dupes believe in "isms"; they feel with some measure of justification that another commitment means only another disillusionment. But anyone destitute of a theory about the meaning, structure and direction of modern society is a lost victim in a world he cannot understand or control.

But even if Negro writers found themselves through some "ism," how would that influence their writing? Are they being called upon to "preach"? To be "salesmen"? To "prostitute" their writing? Must they "sully" themselves? Must they write "propaganda"?

No; it is a question of awareness, of consciousness; it is, above all, a question of perspective.

Perspective is that part of a poem, novel, or play which a writer never puts directly upon paper. It is that fixed point in intellectual space where a writer stands to view the struggles, hopes, and sufferings of his people. There are times when he may stand too close and the result is a blurred vision. Or he may stand too far away and the result is a neglect of important things.

Of all the problems faced by writers who as a whole have never allied themselves with world movements, perspective is the most difficult of achievement. At its best, perspective is a pre-conscious assumption, something which a writer takes for granted, something which he wins through his living.

A Spanish writer recently spoke of living in the heights of one's time. Surely, perspective means just *that*.

It means that a Negro writer must learn to view the life of a Negro living in New York's Harlem or Chicago's South Side with the consciousness that one-sixth of the earth surface belongs to the working class. It means that a Negro writer must create in his readers' minds a relationship between a Negro woman hoeing cotton in the South and the men who loll in swivel chairs in Wall Street and take the fruits of her toil.

Perspective for Negro writers will come when they have looked and brooded so hard and long upon the harsh lot of their race and compared it with the hopes and struggles of minority peoples everywhere that the cold facts have begun to tell them something.

8. The Problem of Theme

This does not mean that a Negro writer's sole concern must be with rendering the social scene; but if his conception of the life of his people is broad and deep enough, if the sense of the *whole* life he is seeking is vivid and strong in him, then his writing will embrace all those social, political, and economic forms under which the life of his people is manifest.

In speaking of theme one must necessarily be general and abstract; the temperament of each writer moulds and colors the world he sees. Negro life may be approached from a thousand angles, with no limit to technical and stylistic freedom.

Negro writers spring from a family, a clan, a class, and a

nation; and the social units in which they are bound have a story, a record. Sense of theme will emerge in Negro writing when Negro writers try to fix this story about some pole of meaning, remembering as they do so that in the creative process meaning proceeds *equally* as much from the contemplation of the subject matter as from the hopes and apprehensions that rage in the heart of the writer.

Reduced to its simplest and most general terms, theme for Negro writers will rise from understanding the meaning of their being transplanted from a "savage" to a "civilized" culture in all of its social, political, economic, and emotional implications. It means that Negro writers must have in their consciousness the foreshortened picture of the *whole,* nourishing culture from which they were torn in Africa, and of the long, complex (and for the most part, unconscious) struggle to regain in some form and under alien conditions of life a *whole* culture again.

It is not only this picture they must have, but also a knowledge of the social and emotional milieu that gives it tone and solidity of detail. Theme for Negro writers will emerge when they have begun to feel the meaning of the history of their race as though they in one life time had lived it themselves throughout all the long centuries.

9. Autonomy of Craft

For the Negro writer to depict this new reality requires a greater discipline and consciousness than was necessary for the so-called Harlem school of expression. Not only is the subject matter dealt with far more meaningful and complex, but the new role of the writer is qualitatively different. The Negro writers' new position demands a sharper definition of the status of his craft, and a sharper emphasis upon its functional autonomy.

Negro writers should seek through the medium of their craft to play as meaningful a role in the affairs of men as do other professionals. But if their writing is demanded to perform the social office of other professions, then the autonomy of craft is lost and writing detrimentally fused with other interests. The limitations of the craft constitute some of its greatest virtues. If the sensory vehicle of imaginative writing is required to carry too great a load of didactic material, the artistic sense is submerged.

The relationship between reality and the artistic image is not always direct and simple. The imaginative conception of a historical period will not be a carbon copy of reality. Image and emotion possess a logic of their own. A vulgarized simplicity constitutes the greatest danger in tracing the reciprocal interplay between the writer and his environment.

Writing has its professional autonomy; it should complement other professions, but it should not supplant them or be swamped by them.

10. The Necessity for Collective Work

It goes without saying that these things cannot be gained by Negro writers if their present mode of isolated writing and living continues. This isolation exists *among* Negro writers as well as *between* Negro and white writers. The Negro writers' lack of thorough integration with the American scene, their lack of a clear realization among themselves of their possible role, have bred generation after generation of embittered and defeated literati.

Barred for decades from the theater and publishing houses, Negro writers have been *made* to feel a sense of difference. So deep has this white-hot iron of exclusion been burnt into their hearts that thousands have all but lost the desire to become identified with American civilization. The Negro writers' acceptance of this enforced isolation and their attempt to justify it is but a defense-reflex of the whole special way of life which has been rammed down their throats.

This problem, by its very nature, is one which must be

approached contemporaneously from *two* points of view. The ideological unity of Negro writers and the alliance of that unity with all the progressive ideas of our day is the primary prerequisite for collective work. On the shoulders of white writers and Negro writers alike rest the responsibility of ending this mistrust and isolation.

By placing cultural health above narrow sectional prejudices, liberal writers of all races can help to break the stony soil of aggrandizement out of which the stunted plants of Negro nationalism grow. And, simultaneously, Negro writers can help to weed out these choking growths of reactionary nationalism and replace them with hardier and sturdier types.

These tasks are imperative in light of the fact that we live in a time when the majority of the most basic assumptions of life can no longer be taken for granted. Tradition is no longer a guide. The world has grown huge and cold. Surely this is the moment to ask questions, to theorize, to speculate, to wonder out of what materials can a human world be built.

Each step along this unknown path should be taken with thought, care, self-consciousness, and deliberation. When Negro writers think they have arrived at something which smacks of truth, humanity, they should want to test it with others, feel it with a degree of passion and strength that will enable them to communicate it to millions who are groping like themselves.

Writers faced with such tasks can have no possible time for malice or jealousy. The conditions for the growth of each writer depend too much upon the good work of other writers. Every first rate novel, poem, or play lifts the level of consciousness higher.

Letters

As his correspondence shows, Wright was a prolific letter writer. He seldom resisted the opportunity to express his feelings publicly, in open letters to the editor, whenever he believed an issue was important. He signed numerous calls and protests as a Communist, and then, after his break with the Communist Party, he did not hesitate to oppose it. Most often Wright took his stand as a Black American, or simply as a writer. His answers to the carping reviews of Native Son by critics Burton Rascoe and David Cohn, in 1940, are good instances of his indignation and satiric bent.

Wright's exchange with the South American engraver Antonio Frasconi took place on a different level and is included here as a lofty statement of Wright's firm belief in what literature could and should accomplish in relation to politics.

The review of *Native Son* by Burton Rascoe originally appeared in *American Mercury*, May 1940. Wright's response originally appeared in *American Mercury*, July 1940.

"The Negro Novel: Richard Wright" by David L. Cohn originally appeared in *Atlantic Monthly*, May 1940. Wright's response, "I Bite the Hand That Feeds Me," originally appeared in *Atlantic Monthly*, June 1940.

"Richard Wright and Antonio Frasconi: An Exchange of Letters" originally appeared in *Twice a Year*, No. 12–13, 1945.

Burton Rascoe: Review of *Native Son*

CONCERNING NO NOVEL in recent times, with the possible exception of *The Grapes of Wrath*, have the reviewers in general displayed a more utterly juvenile confusion of values than they have shown in their ecstatic appraisal of Richard Wright's *Native Son*. The only way I can account for the cataclysmic impact this novel made upon their brains is by deducing that they have kept themselves virginally aloof from the sort of reading which daily gives millions of us the stimulation and catharsis of pity and terror in the tabloids and in the magazine fiction professionally described as the "pulps." To this may be added the further deduction that, so hysterical have the strains of the times made many of us, these good people, the reviewers, go easily haywire about anything which looks to them like a social document exposing "conditions."

Sanely considered, it is impossible for me to conceive of a novel's being worse, in the most important respects, than *Native Son*. It has many technical excellences. They are such as any Street & Smith editor would applaud, or as Walter B. Pitkin, in his writing classes at Columbia, would grade as A–1. But the editors for Street & Smith, and Mr. Pitkin, would probably say very sensibly that there are faults in this novel which even a tyro in fiction should not be guilty of. Let me enumerate some of them:

(1) If there is a moral message to be emphasized, that message should be made implicit in the consistent action and dialogue of the novel. It should not be in the form of a running commentary by the author, particularly not when the author is very confused about what he wants to prove.

(2) If a character is conceived as being inarticulate and dumb about the economic and social forces which have (in your mind) been responsible for his social and moral delinquency, it is an artistic error to portray that character, at

times, as being fully conscious of the "conditions" which have mentally and emotionally crippled him. It is an elementary principle not only of art but of moral law, of legal principle, and of common sense, that, if you are aware of yourself and of the factors under which you live, you are, *yourself*, responsible for what you do and you must accept that responsibility. Mr. Wright has Bigger Thomas, the hero of his story, commit two murders on the appalling theory that he is justified in so doing because, as ecstatic reviewers assure us, "he knows religion as something meant to lull people into submission" and because Bigger feels "powerless and afraid of the white world, which exploits, condescends to, and in turn fears the race it has segregated." (The quotes are, respectively, from Milton Rugoff in the New York *Herald Tribune* and Margaret Marshall in the *Nation.*)

(3) It is a violation of a fundamental esthetic principle—sanctioned from Aristotle on down—to portray a character in speech, thought or action in a way not consistent with what you, the writer, might conceivably do in similar circumstances and in similar conditions.

Recently I witnessed a *reductio ad absurdum* of Mr. Wright's fundamental thesis in *Native Son.* Mr. Wright was a luncheon guest, in New York, of a club whose membership comprises men who have achieved a degree of importance in the creative arts—writers, musicians, painters, illustrators, engineers, editors, etc. Mr. Wright was introduced eulogistically by Mr. William Chenery, editor of *Collier's,* who dwelt upon the young novelist's accomplishment as a writer who had achieved best-sellerdom. There was no reference, condescending or otherwise, to the guest's color.

Mr. Wright had been told that, as the club's guest, he need not make any speech unless he felt like doing so. He is a handsome young man; his face is fine, kind and intelligent. It was a spontaneous tribute to him and to the success he had attained that the club gave him an ovation such as it has rarely given to anyone but artists like Pablo Casals and Jascha

Heifetz. Mr. Wright was, on this occasion (though he may not have realized it), an embodied refutation of his theme in *Native Son*. He was the only black man there, surrounded by white people. Yet they were all rejoicing in his success, eager to do him honor—even if there were many, of course, who had not read his book.

They were not, even unconsciously, trying to make things so difficult for Mr. Wright that he would have artistic or any other justification if he should choose to murder the first two debutantes he met after leaving the luncheon. Mr. Wright must have had some intimations of this anomaly—this contrast between himself and his fictional hero—when he arose to speak. In response to the spontaneous acclaim, he got up to say a few words. He was doubtless confused and embarrassed. Good writers, and Mr. Wright in his best vein is decidedly good, are rarely good speakers. He faltered, as most of us do who have not been trained to speak in public, and in his confusion he said, with the nicest air of camaraderie—as if to say "Come up and see me some time": "I hope you will all have a chance to meet Bigger Thomas."

I don't know what others who had read *Native Son* felt about the author's hope, but I for one shuddered. Bigger Thomas, in the novel, is a murderer because (so his creator tells us) he resents the white race. Bigger murders a rich white girl who is sentimentally interested in "the Negro problem" and whose family has contributed millions to alleviate conditions among the poor in the Negro quarters of Chicago. Bigger also murders his Negro mistress. He indulges in this slaughter not because of anything these poor, misguided women, white and black, have done to him, since they haven't harmed him at all, but because (Mr. Wright argues) all of us who happen to have white skins instead of black have made Bigger what he is.

In the midst of the hurrahing I rise to assert that I think the moral in *Native Son* is utterly loathsome and utterly insupportable as a "message." When I carefully examine all the evidence Mr. Wright offers to prove that Bigger Thomas should have become a murderer and that the guilt lies on our own heads, I remain emphatically unconvinced. I can't see that Bigger Thomas had anything more to contend with, in childhood and youth, than I had or than dozens of my friends had. Their lives and mine have not been velvety but we do not want to kill people because of this. And I have known fine priests, fine rabbis, fine Protestant ministers (black and white) whose "conditional environment" was even worse than this "conditional environment" which Mr. Wright would have us believe makes murderers out of Negro men.

Mr. Wright is as much an American as you are or I am. We Americans are constitutionally for the underdog, so long as it does not seriously interfere with the business at hand of getting along. It is quite the thing now, among our intellectuals, to contend that whites have given the Negroes a dirty deal, forgetting that whites have given themselves a dirty deal also. These intellectuals deplore Hitler, Stalin and Mussolini on psychopathic grounds, but they are unable to see that by their own logic Bigger Thomas is just a small-scale Negro Hitler. Or a Negro Stalin or Mussolini. The partiality of these dictators for bloodletting also can be traced to conditional environment. If I am supposed to start grieving over what I have done to Hitler and Stalin in their hard early life, I won't take any.

And the same applies to Bigger. This is also to serve notice that despite all the eloquence Bigger's lawyer and Wright's reviewers bring to Bigger's defense, if I were on the jury I would vote to hang Bigger. Bigger, I have been amply convinced, wouldn't hesitate two minutes to shoot me or his lawyer or his author, even if we were going about business and paying him no mind. I don't like the idea of being shot, even fictionally, just because my color is not like Bigger's. I wouldn't like it even if I knew that all the Bigger Thomases think I am somehow responsible because life hasn't been cushy for them. I'm just unreasonable in these matters of murder, where I'm the murderee.

Mr. Wright, one may note, is doing very well. A lot of white writers with talent doubtless are wishing they were making as much money as he is making. But they are not envious of him, nor do they begrudge his success in the least. They hope he prospers. For myself, I hope that now he has got *Native Son* out of his system, he will use his talents to more sensible ends. He is one of the two writers, white or black, who have ever had the ear to catch and transliterate Negro speech correctly. The other writer is Louis Paul, who is white.

Richard Wright: Reply to Burton Rascoe

SIR:

Mr. Burton Rascoe's review of my book, *Native Son*, under the heading *Negro Novel and White Reviewers*, certainly introduces some brand new and unheard of principles into American literary criticism. What in God's name has "He is a handsome young man; his face is fine and intelligent . . ." got to do with the merits or shortcomings of a novel? I had hoped that the *Mercury*'s review of *Native Son* would be as objective as my treatment of Bigger, but I suppose that's hoping for too much from the *Mercury* these days.

Mr. Rascoe hopes that now, with *Native Son* out of my system, I'll give some sweetness and light. No, not yet. I'll be dishing out this for quite some time to come. Understated in Mr. Rascoe's review is this attitude: "Why in the world does a Negro writer want to bother with such stuff when he can write differently and be liked for it and paid for it?" The answer is simply this: I don't choose to. I prefer to write out of the background of my experience in an imaginative fashion. I don't prefer to streamline my stuff to what the public will like. It is no fault of mine that *Native Son* is selling; it was not written to sell, but to convey in terms of words an American-Negro experience of life. Too often when a Negro writes something which wins a prize, or sells, and which carries in it a note of protest, a white reviewer rises to ask: "What is he yelling about? He's making money, isn't he?" Has the *Mercury* fallen that low?

Following his personal line, Mr. Rascoe implied that I tried to insult the members of the Dutch Treat Club. What rot! I don't think a single person in that audience misunderstood my remarks (not a speech!) to the extent that Mr. Rascoe did. When I attended that luncheon my book had been off the press for about two weeks; I knew that very few of those present had read it. I took the occasion to remark that I hoped that they would meet Bigger Thomas if they had the time; that is, I expressed my hope that they would read the book. Only a "Negro-baiter" could twist such a statement and make it mean something else.

As an artist I reserve the right to depict the actions of people I do not agree with, Aristotle to the contrary! After reading Mr. Rascoe's review, I wondered why he did not reprint Buckley's speech and let it stand as his view; it would have been more clean-cut and honest. Yes; while writing the book I realized that Max's speech would be "utterly loathsome" to many people. That is why Max said:

Of all things, men do not like to feel that they are guilty of wrong, and if you make them feel guilty, they will try desperately to justify it on any grounds; but failing that, and seeing no immediate solution that will set things right without too much cost to their lives and property, they will kill that which evoked in them the condemning sense of guilt. . . .

Does not this fall in line with Mr. Rascoe's statement that "We Americans are constitutionally for the underdog, so long as it does not seriously interfere with the business at hand of getting along"? I know that and that is why I wrote as I did. Max's speech anticipated every point raised by Mr. Rascoe.

Read the book again, Mr. Rascoe, and pay close attention to Max's speech, which was directed toward men of your attitude. And remember that the author wrote that book, in the words of Max, as "a test symbol" to determine if 100 per cent Americans would feel "utterly loathsome" when confronted with one of their own historical mistakes! *Mr. Rascoe ran true to form!*

David L. Cohn: Review of *Native Son*

RICHARD WRIGHT, a Mississippi-born Negro, has written a blinding and corrosive study in hate. It is a novel entitled *Native Son.* The race hatred of his hero, Bigger Thomas, is directed with equal malevolence and demoniac intensity toward *all* whites, whether they are Mary Dalton, the moony Negrophile whom he murdered, or the vague white men who seemed to bar his youthful ambition to become an aviator or join the navy. This book has far-reaching qualities of significance above and beyond its considerable virtues as a novel, because Mr. Wright elects to portray his hero not as an individual merely but as a symbol of twelve million American Negroes.

Bigger is very young. His exact age is not stated, but we are told he is too young to vote, and he is therefore under twenty-one. Although his life has hardly begun, his career and hopes for the future have been blasted by the Negro-hating whites of Chicago. On page 14 of *Native Son,* Bigger and his friend Gus are watching an airplane above the city. 'I *could* fly a plane if I had a chance,' Bigger says. 'If you wasn't black and if you had some money and if they'd let you go to that aviation school, you *could* fly a plane,' Gus answers. And time after time, throughout the length of this book, Bigger bitterly complains that he is denied access to the broad, glittering world which the whites monopolize for themselves to the exclusion of Negroes. Toward the end of the novel (p. 302), Bigger, in jail for murdering a white girl and his Negro mistress, says: 'I ain't asking nobody to be sorry for me . . . I'm black. *They don't give black people a chance*' (my italics). Bigger's crimes and his fate in the electric chair, the author makes clear to us, are consequently to be laid at the door of white society.

In the speech of Bigger's lawyer at his trial, one finds the fullest summation of Mr. Wright's point of view toward the Negro question in America, and the most explicit statement of his use of Bigger as a symbol of the oppressed Negro. 'This boy,' says lawyer Max, 'represents but a tiny aspect of the problem whose reality sprawls over a third of a nation. . . . Multiply Bigger Thomas twelve million times, allowing for environmental and temperamental variations . . . and you have the psychology of the Negro people. . . . Taken collectively, they are not simply twelve million; in reality they constitute a separate nation, stunted, stripped, and held captive *within* this nation, devoid of political, social, economic and property rights.'

Mr. Wright might have made a more manly and certainly more convincing case for his people if he had stuck to fact. In all of the non-Southern states, Negroes have complete political rights, including the suffrage, and even in the South Negro suffrage is constantly being extended. So powerful, indeed, is the Negro vote, and so solidly is it cast en bloc in Negro-populous Eastern and Midwestern states, that in closely contested Presidential elections the Negro vote may decide who shall become President of the United States. Hence the scramble of both parties for the Negro vote. Nowhere in America save in the most benighted sections of the South, or in times of passion arising from the committing of atrocious crime, is the Negro denied the equal protection of the laws. If he is sometimes put in jail for no reason at all in Memphis, so too are whites put in jail for no reason at all in Pittsburgh. This is the unjust fate, not of the Negro alone, but of the poor, the obscure, and the inarticulate everywhere, regardless of pigmentation. The ownership, also, of more than a billion dollars' worth of property by Negroes in the South alone, and the presence of prosperous Negro business concerns throughout the country, are some refutation of the sweeping statement that Negroes are denied property rights in this country.

Through the mouth of Bigger's lawyer we are told in unmistakable terms that the damming up of the Negro's aspirations, and the denial to him of unrestricted entry into the whole environment of the society in which he is cast, may lead Negroes, in conjunction with others, toward a new civil war in America. Mr. Wright seems to have completely forgotten the unparalleled phenomenon—unique in the world's history—of the *first* American Civil War, in which millions of white men fought and killed one another over the issue of the black slave. If it be granted that the original enslavement of Negroes was a crime against justice, then it must also be granted that its bloody expiation was filled with enough death and destruction to satisfy even the most hate-consumed Negro. But it doesn't seem to satisfy Mr. Wright. A second civil war must begin where the first one left off in order to bring about the eventual freeing of the Negro minority, even if it means the destruction of the society of the majority. Justice and understanding are to come through the persuasive snouts of machine guns.

Bigger's lawyer is a Jew. As a member of a race which has known something of oppression—not for three centuries, the length of the Negro's residence in America, but for more than twenty centuries in nearly every country of the world —he pleads extenuation for his client both on broad grounds of justice and on the ground that white society drove Bigger to crime by repressing him. If repression of the members of a minority drives them to slay members of the majority, it would follow that the principal occupation of Jews in Tsarist Russia, Poland, Rumania, and other bitterly anti-Semitic countries would have been to use their oppressors as clay pigeons. Jewish revolutionists there have been, indeed, but over the whole sweep of two thousand years of dark Jewish history the mass of these people, enduring greater oppression than Negroes knew here even in slavery, created within the walls of their ghettos an intense family and communal life and constructed inexhaustible wells of spiritual resource. They used their talents and energies as best they could, serene in the belief either that a Messiah would ultimately come and deliver them out of bondage into the Promised Land or that justice would ultimately triumph. Mr. Wright uses a Jewish lawyer as his mouthpiece, but he has learned nothing from Jewish history, nor gleaned anything of the spirit of that group whom Tacitus called 'a stubborn people.'

It is beyond doubt that Negroes labor under grave difficulties in America; that economic and social discrimination is practised against them; that opportunities open to whites are closed to blacks. It is also beyond doubt that the position, if not the status, of the Negro is constantly improving in the United States. The evidence on this point is overwhelming. But there is one hard and inescapable fact which must be courageously faced. The social structure of America, despite many racial admixtures, is Anglo-Saxon. And nowhere on earth—save in isolated instances—do whites and Negroes in Anglo-Saxon communities intermingle socially or intermarry. And so long as this is a fact, neither the Negro—and this is what completely escapes Mr. Wright—*nor the white man* will function as a full-fledged personality. It could easily be demonstrated that Southern whites living in the presence of masses of Negroes, and maintaining at least tolerable racial relations through the exercise of exquisite, intuitive tact on both sides, suffer aberrations and distortions of the spirit only slightly less severe than those suffered by Negroes.

It is no fault of the Negro or of the present generation of whites that the Negro is here. But the preaching of Negro hatred of whites by Mr. Wright is on a par with the preaching of white hatred of Negroes by the Ku Klux Klan. The position, moreover, of a minority struggling toward the sun must be gauged at any given time by its relative rather than its absolute state, and in accordance with this postulate it is clear that the Negro's lot in America is constantly being ameliorated.

It is highly significant of the whole hate-headlong point of view of Mr. Wright that he has chosen to make his hero so hopelessly despairing of making a good life for himself because of white repressions, that he drives him to crime and execution when his adult life has hardly begun. Contrast this with the experience of the Jews in England, who were first granted full civil rights only after five centuries of living in the country.

Mr. Wright obviously does not have the long view of history. He wants not only complete political rights for his people, but also social equality, and he wants them now. Justice demands that every right granted to others shall be granted to Negroes, but men are not gods. A hard-headed people will be conscious of the Pauline law of expedience: 'All things are lawful unto me, but all things are not expedient.'

Justice or no justice, the whites of America simply will not grant to Negroes at this time those things that Mr. Wright demands. The Negro problem in America is actually insoluble; all profound, complex social problems are insoluble, and only a politically naïve people will believe otherwise. In the meanwhile, recognition by both sides that the question is insoluble, followed by tempered, sincere efforts to make the best of the situation within its frame of reference, will produce the most equitable results for both. Hatred, and the preaching of hatred, and incitement to violence can only make a tolerable relationship intolerable.

Even Abraham Lincoln did not envisage a time when the Negro question would be solved upon Mr. Wright's terms. In 1862 he said to a Negro delegation who called on him:

You and we are different races. . . . But even when you cease to be slaves you are yet far from being placed on an equality with the white race. . . . The aspiration of men is to enjoy equality with the best when free, but on this continent not a single man of your race is made the equal of a single man of ours. . . . Go where you are treated best, and the ban is still upon you.

And Mr. Wright's hero kills and dies in Mr. Lincoln's state of Illinois.

Richard Wright: Reply to David L. Cohn

I WANT TO REPLY to Mr. David L. Cohn, whose article criticized my novel, *Native Son*, in the May issue of the *Atlantic Monthly*. In the eyes of the average white American reader, his article made it more difficult for a Negro (child of slaves and savages!) to answer a cultured Jew (who had two thousand years of oppression to recommend him in giving advice to other unfortunates!) than an American white. Indeed, Mr. Cohn writes as though he were recommending his 'two thousand years of oppression' to the Negroes of America! No, thank you, Mr. Cohn. I don't think that we Negroes are going to have to go through with it. We might perish in the attempt to avoid it; if so, then death as men is better than two thousand years of ghetto life and seven years of Herr Hitler.

The Negro problem in America is *not* beyond solution. (I write from a country—Mexico—where people of all races and colors live in harmony and without racial prejudices or theories of racial superiority. Whites and Indians live and work and die here, always resisting the attempts of Anglo-Saxon tourists and industrialists to introduce racial hate and discrimination.) Russia has solved the problem of the Jews and that of all her other racial and national minorities. Probably the Soviet solution is not to Mr. Cohn's liking, but I think it is to the liking of the Jews in Russia and Biro-Bidjan. I accept the Russian solution. I am proletarian and Mr. Cohn is bourgeois; we live on different planes of social reality, and we see Russia differently.

'He [Wright] wants not only complete political rights for his people, but also social equality, and he wants them now.' Certainly I want them now. And what's wrong with my wanting them now? What guarantee have we Negroes, if we were 'expedient' for five hundred years, that America would extend to us a certificate stating that we were civilized? I am proud to declaim—as proud as Mr. Cohn is of his two thousand years of oppression—that at no time in the history of American politics has a Negro stood for anything but the untrammeled rights of human personality, *his* and *others*.

Mr. Cohn implies that as a writer I should look at the state of the Negro through the lens of relativity, and not judge his plight in an absolute sense. That is precisely what, as an artist, I try *not* to do. My character, Bigger Thomas, lives and suffers in the real world. Feeling and perception, from moment to moment, are absolute, and if I dodged my responsibility as an artist and depicted them as otherwise I'd be a traitor, not to my race alone, but to *humanity*. An artist deals with aspects of reality different from those which a scientist sees. My task is not to abstract reality, but to enhance its value. In the process of objectifying emotional experience in words— paint, stone, or tone—an artist uses his feelings, in an immediate and absolute sense. To ask a writer to deny the validity of his sensual perceptions is to ask him to be 'expedient' enough to commit spiritual suicide for the sake of politicians. And that I'll *never* consent to do. No motive of 'expediency' can compel me to elect to justify the ways of white America to the Negro; rather, my task is to weigh the effects of our civilization upon the personality, as it affects it *here* and *now*. If, in my weighing of those effects, I reveal rot, pus, filth, hate, fear, guilt, and degenerate forms of life, must I be consigned to hell? (Yes, Bigger Thomas hated, but he hated because he *feared*. Carefully, Mr. Cohn avoided all mention of that fact. Or does Mr. Cohn feel that the 'exquisite, intuitive' treatment of the Negro in America does not inspire fear?) I wrote *Native Son* to show what manner of men and women our 'society of the majority' breeds, and my aim was to depict a character in terms of the living tissue and texture of daily consciousness. And who is responsible for his feelings, anyway?

Mr. Cohn, my view of history tells me this: *Only the strong are free.* Might may not make right, but there is no 'right' nation without might. That may sound cynical, but it is nevertheless true. If the Jew has suffered for two thousand years, then it is mainly because of his religion and his other-worldliness, and he has only himself to blame. The Jew had a choice, just as the Negro in America has one. We Negroes prefer to take the hint of that great Jewish revolutionist, Karl Marx, and look soberly upon the facts of history, and organize, ally ourselves, and fight it out. Having helped to build the 'society of the majority,' we Negroes are not so dazzled by its preciousness that we consider it something holy and beyond attack. We know our weakness and we know our strength, and we are not going to fight America *alone.* We are not so naïve as that. The Negro in America became politically mature the moment he realized that he could not fight the 'society of the majority' alone and organized the National Negro Congress and threw its weight behind John L. Lewis and the CIO!

I urge my race to become strong through *alliances,* by joining in common cause with other oppressed groups (and there are a lot of them in America, Mr. Cohn!), workers, *sensible* Jews, farmers, declassed intellectuals, and so forth. I urge them to master the techniques of political, social, and economic struggle and cast their lot with the millions in the world today who are fighting for freedom, crossing national and racial boundaries if necessary.

The unconscious basis upon which most whites excuse Negro oppression is as follows: (1) the Negro did not have a culture when he was brought here; (2) the Negro was physically inferior and susceptible to diseases; (3) the Negro did not resist his enslavement. These three falsehoods have been woven into an ideological and moral principle to justify whatever America wants to do with the Negro, and, whether Mr. Cohn realizes it or not, they enable him to say 'the Negro problem in America is actually insoluble.'

But there is not one ounce of history or science to support oppression based upon these assumptions.

The Negro (just as the Mexican Indian today) possessed a rich and complex culture when he was brought to these alien shores. He resisted oppression. And the Negro, instead of being physically weak, is tough and has withstood hardships that have cracked many another people. This, too, is history. Does it sound strange that American historians have distorted or omitted hundreds of records of slave revolts in America?

We Negroes have no religion that teaches us that we are 'God's chosen people'; our sorrows cannot be soothed with such illusions. What culture we did have when we were torn from Africa was taken from us; we were separated when we were brought here and forbidden to speak our languages. We possess no remembered cushion of culture upon which we can lay our tired heads and dream of our superiority. We are driven by the nature of our position in this country into the thick of the struggle, whether we like it or not.

In *Native Son* I tried to show that a man, bereft of a culture and unanchored by property, can travel but one path if he reacts positively but unthinkingly to the prizes and goals of civilization; and that one path is emotionally blind rebellion. In *Native Son* I did not defend Bigger's actions; I explained them through depiction. And what alarms Mr. Cohn is not what I say Bigger *is*, but what I say *made* him what he is. Yes, white boys commit crimes, too. But would Mr. Cohn deny that the social pressure upon Negro boys is far greater than that upon white boys? And how does it materially alter the substance of my book if white boys do commit murder? Does not Mr. Cohn remember the Jewish boy who shot the Nazi diplomat in Paris a year or two ago? No Jewish revolutionist egged that boy to do that crime. Did not the Soviet officials, the moment they came into power, have to clean up the roaming bands of Jewish and Gentile youth who lived outside of society by crime, youth spawned by the Czar's holy belief that social, racial, and economic problems were 'actually insoluble'?

Now, let me analyze more closely just how much and what kind of hate is in *Native Son*. Loath as I am to do this, I have no choice. Mr. Cohn's article, its tone and slant, convince me more than anything else that I was *right* in the way I handled Negro life in *Native Son*. Mr. Cohn says that the burden of my book was a preachment of hate against the white races. It was not. No *advocacy* of hate is in that book. *None!* I wrote as objectively as I could of a Negro boy who hated and feared whites, hated them because he feared them. What Mr. Cohn mistook for my advocacy of hate in that novel was something entirely different. In every word of that book are *confidence, resolution,* and the *knowledge* that the Negro problem can and will be solved *beyond* the frame of reference of thought such as that found in Mr. Cohn's article.

Further in his article Mr. Cohn says that I do not understand that oppression has harmed whites as well as Negroes. Did I not have my character, Britten, exhibit through page after page the aberrations of whites who suffer from oppression? Or, God forbid, does Mr. Cohn *agree* with Britten? Did I not make the mob as hysterical as Bigger Thomas? Did I not ascribe the hysteria to the same origins? The entire long scene in the furnace room is but a depiction of how warped the whites have become through their oppression of Negroes. If there had been *one* person in the Dalton household who viewed Bigger Thomas as a human being, the crime would have been solved in half an hour. Did not Bigger himself know that it was the denial of his personality that enabled him to escape detection so long? The one piece of incriminating evidence which would have solved the 'murder mystery' was Bigger's humanity, and the Daltons, Britten, and the newspaper men could not see or admit the living clue of Bigger's humanity under their very eyes! More than two thirds of *Native Son* is given over to depicting the very thing which Mr. Cohn claims 'completely escapes' me. I wonder how much of my book escaped *him*.

Mr. Cohn says that Bigger's age is not stated. It is. Bigger himself tells his age on page 42. On page 348 it is stated again in the official death sentence.

Mr. Cohn wonders why I selected a Negro *boy* as my protagonist. To any writer of fiction, or anyone acquainted with the creative process, the answer is simple. Youth is the turning point in life, the most sensitive and volatile period, the state that registers most vividly the impressions and experiences of life; and an artist likes to work with sensitive material.

Antonio Frasconi/Richard Wright Letters

Montevideo, Uruguay
November 1, 1944

Dear Richard Wright:

I write this letter to obtain your valuable and unauthorized opinion, the communication of which I will appreciate; of course, if it does not cause you any trouble or inconvenience.

A Uruguayan painter and engraver, I have for many years belonged to the group of those that defend and fight for the ideals of a democracy and a real human equality; and my most profound sympathy is especially inclined to a clearer understanding of the Negro problem, to which I dedicate my intellectual and artistic efforts.

Therefore, I am thinking of editing and publishing an album that will consist of a series of wood cuts, conceived in

68

this subject, and in which I will deal in my manner—that of
an engraver—with the present conflict and its future solu-
tions. (Let me remind you of the series of the Belgian engraver Frans Masserel: History of a Rebel.)

The reason why I am taking the liberty of bothering you,
is the following:

You probably imagine the difficulty in determining the
proportions of this problem, specifically North American,
from Uruguay. While some friends are enthusiastic adher-
ents of this idea, others, on the contrary, judge that the actual
moment, when more than ever it is necessary to maintain the
unity forced by the anti-fascist war, is not propitious for such
a publication, as in the wood cuts and prologue, certain objections and allusions to the American democracy will be
inevitable, for example, I am referring to the events in Detroit in 1943 and which, in parenthesis, constitute the leit-
motiv of the series of engravings.

Being then, the opinions concerning this matter, so hetero-
geneous, the idea occurred to me to expose it to you and
inquire which is the tactic I should follow, and, of course, I
shall be pending on your answer to take the final decision.

Waiting for your prompt reply,

Cordially yours,
Antonio R. Frasconi

Brooklyn, N.Y.
November, 1944

DEAR SEÑOR FRASCONI:

I have just read your letter of November 1 with great
concern, and I want to tell you at once that I sympathize with
the perplexity which moved you to appeal to me for advice
across such a vast geographical and psychological distance.
The question you pose and the nature of your choice are not
new, and the situation in which you find yourself is common

among the artists of my own country today. To me, the fact that you did not make a quick, careless judgment; that you felt unwilling to accept the easy counsel of your friends; and that you tried to weigh all the values of the factors involved, seems to imply that you feel the Negro's situation in the world today very keenly. And, in my opinion, that is how an artist should feel it.

But I regret to say that I cannot tell you exactly what to do in terms of your concrete political situation. I'm ignorant of the language and culture of South America, of its economics, and of the currents of political pressure that may be influencing you and those who surround you. Hence, my presumptuous words of counsel cannot be too specific; and, in order to make my attitude clear, I must assume that we share a common sense of life, a sense of life out of which we both are trying to create.

You ask me if the "moment is propitious" for presenting the plight of the Negro in your art, and if the presentation of that plight will damage the "unity forced by the anti-fascist war," and you imply that some of your friends, motivated by political fears, urged you to abandon your project lest it comfort the enemy and render more difficult the task of the soldiers of the United Nations.

Is there not something very dubious in the way in which this question is posed? What is the basis for the assumption that artistic representation of the plight of the Negro would make our victory over the fascists more difficult? Is it assumed that the basis of our morale rests upon the conviction that there is no injustice in North and South America? I do not believe that any such conviction honestly exists in a wide degree in the whole of the New World. Then, why are people anxious today to conceal the facts of Negro life? What has North and South America let happen to Negroes that has evoked such a wide belief that if the truth of Negro life were known it would hinder the march of our armies?

Are we not confronted here with the attitude of "moral

slackers," "moral dodgers," who, wanting to conquer the fascist enemy, do not want to rid their lives of the fascist-like practices of which they have grown so profitably fond? The whole question, when looked at from this point of view, is wrapped and lost in the subjective fears of politicians.

I do not believe that the truth of Negro life, when expressed either artistically or factually, will harm the cause of the United Nations. On the contrary, I believe that the opposite is true. Might it not be that the expression of the truth of Negro life might clarify the issues for which we are fighting this war? Of course, it is commonly said that the fascist propagandists make great use of our acts of injustice; and, if this is so, I propose that we forthwith divest such facts of any advantage they might contain for fascists by removing injustice from our midst. I propose that we deliberately exhibit all those social cancers whose removal would facilitate and strengthen our morale and conviction in this war.

But I must admit that my above arguments are pure speculation; I allowed myself the indulgence of expressing them to show that the OPINIONS OF POLITICIANS CAN BE WRONG. There is, however, beyond the boundaries of imperious politics, a common ground upon which we can stand and see the truth of this problem. And that ground can be ours if I rephrase your question in more general terms: Out of what vision must an artist create? The question seems vague, but when it is conceived in terms of political pressure from Left or Right, it has vital meaning. Must an artist's vision—that complex condition of perception that compels him to express himself—stem on the whole from the pronouncements of political leaders, or must the artist accept mainly the evidence of his sensibilities to lead him?

I hold that, in the last analysis, the artist must bow to the monitor of his own imagination; must be led by the sovereignty of his own impressions and perceptions; must be guided by the tyranny of what troubles and concerns him personally; and that he must learn to trust the impulse, vague and compulsive as it may be, which moves him in the first instance toward expression. There is no other true path, and the artist owes it to himself and to those who live and breathe with him to render unto reality that which is reality's.

Your question implies that some of your advisers feel that your artistic representations of the Negro will create disunity; if that is so, then I would question seriously the kind of human unity that some of your advisers are striving to build. I, of course, take it for granted that your art is seeking passionately to render an honest reaction to the problem of the Negro in North and South America; and, if so, then your expression of that reaction in terms of images that kindle feeling will create the deepest sense of unity between the Negro, in North or South America, and other oppressed men, black or white, wherever they are found on earth, a sense of unity that will make men feel that they are brothers!

Paint, draw, engrave, and let all facts that impinge upon your sensibilities be your subject matter, and let your heart strike the hour as to when you should give what you have said to others! And I assure you that in answering your letter I have not looked at the clock in my room to see what hour of the day it is; I have not consulted the calendar to determine the day of the month; I have not examined a map to see where our armies are standing; in short, I have not tried to give you advice conditioned or limited by expediency or fear. Instead, I sat right down and wrote you what was in my heart; and my heart is full of this: There are 13,000,000 black people in the United States who practically have no voice in the government that governs them; who must fight in the United States Army under Jim Crow conditions of racial humiliation; who literally have the blood, which they so generously offer out of their veins to wounded soldiers, segregated in blood (plasma) banks of the American Red Cross, as though their blood were the blood of subhumans; who, on the whole, live lives that are possessed of but a few rights which others respect; who, daily and hourly, are restricted in their behavior to an orbit branded as inferior; who must, for the most part, live their lives in artificially marked-off, ghetto-like areas of our cities and countryside; and whose manliness and self-assertion generally warrant instant reprisal!

Can you know this and hesitate to speak or act? What I have described above is not only a picture of the plight of Negroes in the United States; it is a picture of the majority of mankind in the world today, colored and white. And if your art can further a popular unity of feeling based upon the common experiences of these oppressed, would you withhold that art?

If you reject my plea, then, pray, tell me, how will you finally determine when to express yourself? Will you wait until those who say that your artistic expression must be guided by global political issues grant permission? And who is qualified to give you the signal to begin? It might happen that when you are in the very throes of creation the "line" will change! Or that an entirely new "line" will have come into being! Or that, when your work is done, you will be criticized for not having expressed yourself with enough militancy, for not having been soft enough, subtle or tender enough in the light of a "new" political situation. Who knows?

I really believe that it would be far wiser for you to willingly and honestly hire yourself out to the business firms of your native country as an advertising copy writer than to try to reduce your artistic expression to another kind of advertising under the mistaken illusion that you are helping mankind by so doing. But, really, must you hire yourself out to anybody? Must we artists have bosses, Left or Right? Cannot our art be a guide to all men of good-will who want to know the truth of our time? Cannot we artists speak in a tone of authority of our own? A tone of authority that will depict the tissue, the texture, the quality, and value of experience?

It is imperative that we artists seek and find a simpler, a more elementary, and a more personal guide to the truth of experience and events than those contained in the mandates of frenzied politicians; and I say that we shall find it where artists have always found it: in the visions which our eyes create out of the insistent welter of reality, and out of the surging feelings which those visions evoke in our hearts.

Life is sufficient unto life if it is lived and felt directly and deeply enough; and I would warn that we must beware of those who seek, in words no matter how urgent or crisis-charged, to interpose an alien and dubious curtain of reality between our eyes and the crying claims of a world which it is our lot to see only too poignantly and too briefly.

Fraternally yours,
Richard Wright

Review
Wars I Have Seen
Gertrude Stein

Out of a score of book reviews written by Richard Wright, the following one has a special history. The prose of Gertrude Stein was an important early influence on Wright's own sense of language and use of the rhythms of popular speech. The naturalness of the dialogue Stein used in "Melanctha," the story of a black servant, astonished Wright and gave him an example to emulate. Therefore, when his friend Roger Pipett, an editor at P.M., asked him to review Wars I Have Seen, *he was so enthusiastic and became so deeply engrossed in his reminiscences that he offered a long piece, significantly entitled "Memories of My Grandmother," in which he linked his reading of Stein's "Melanctha" with the religious outlook and vernacular of his own family and explored the surrealistic aspects of Black talk and jazz.*

"I had heard my grandmother speak ever since I can remember, so that I was conscious of anything particularly distinctive in her speech. Then I read a sketch of Negro life by Gertrude Stein and suddenly it was as if I were listening to my grandmother for the first time, so fresh was the feeling it gave me," he remarked.

The review presented here is the portion of "Memories of

This review of *Wars I Have Seen* by Gertrude Stein originally appeared in *P.M. Magazine,* March 11, 1945.

My Grandmother" that P.M. *published in March 1945. Gertrude Stein considered this piece the best ever written about her book and immediately asked Carl Van Vechten to contact the young black writer for her. This led to an exchange of letters and a close literary friendship between the two writers.*

Stein advised and in 1946 helped Wright to get to Paris, where he saw much of her before her death later that year. He always ranked her among the leading writers of the twentieth century, and her books were the only ones he ever systematically collected.

GERTRUDE STEIN has laid the 19th century by its heels. For years she has been chasing that proud, stubborn century, mocking it, lying in ambush for it, trying to kill it. Well, at last she has done it. And now she trumpets forth that hope, idealism, aspiration, the sense of the future, high-blown metaphysics and all the big, vague, emotional words of our time have gone down the drain of World War II.

But, you might ask, why do I, a Negro, read the allegedly unreadable books of Gertrude Stein? It's all very simple, innocent even. Years ago, I stumbled upon her books without the guidance of those critics who hint darkly of "the shock of recognition."

Prompted by random curiosity while I was browsing one day in a Chicago public library, I took from the open shelves a tiny volume called *Three Lives* and looked at a story in it, entitled "Melanctha." The style was so insistent and original and sang so quaintly that I took the book home.

As I read it, my ears were opened for the first time to the magic of the spoken word. I began to hear the speech of my grandmother, who spoke a deep, pure Negro dialect and with whom I had lived for many years.

All of my life I had been only half hearing, but Miss Stein's struggling words made the speech of the people around me vivid. From that moment on, in my attempts at writing, I was able to tap at will the vast pool of living words that swirled around me.

But, in the midst of my delight, I was jolted. A left-wing literary critic, whose judgment I had been led to respect, condemned Miss Stein in a sharply-worded newspaper article, implying that she spent her days reclining upon a silken couch in Paris smoking hashish, that she was hopeless prey to hallucinations and that her tortured verbalisms were throttling the Revolution. I was disturbed. Had I duped myself into worshiping decadence?

Believing in direct action, I contrived a method to gauge the degree to which Miss Stein's prose was tainted with the spirit of counter-revolution. I gathered a group of semi-literate Negro stockyard workers—"basic proletarians with the instinct for revolution" (am I quoting right?)—into a Black Belt basement and read "Melanctha" aloud to them. They understood every word. Enthralled, they slapped their thighs, howled, laughed, stomped and interrupted me constantly to comment upon the characters.

My fondness for Steinian prose never distressed me after that.

Her latest book, *Wars I Have Seen,* begins in the usual Steinian manner of evoking her on-the-spot consciousness in repetitive rhythms about life and memory and books, about the 19th century as opposed to the 20th. But soon the war intrudes, and her narrative becomes drenched in the horror of Hitler's brutality in France.

With the exception of Jack Belden's *Still Time to Die,* I know of no current war book that conveys a more awful sense of the power of war to kill the soul, of the fear, the rumor, the panic and the uncertainty of war.

Indeed, Miss Stein possesses a great, perhaps even unfair advantage over other writers about the war, for she exultingly admits that she loves confusion, that she finds no real difference between peace and war and life in general. Boasting cynically, she says: "I do not like to fish in troubled waters but I do like to see the troubled water and the fish and the fishermen . . . "

The long wait for Eisenhower's landing in Normandy is dug up out of the unconscious of the French people and given voice (try reading this and the following quotations with your ear or punctuate with your eyes or read Miss Stein's *Narration* or practice by reading the Old Testament or Hemingway): "To be sure when there is a war the years are longer that is to say the days are longer the months are longer the years are much longer but the weeks are shorter that is what makes a war."

The constant sense of impending death is rendered thus: "the air at night, when the moon is bright is full of them going over to Italy to do their bombing and the mountain makes a reverberation as a woman said to me like being inside a copper cooking utensil well when you keep on thinking how quickly anybody can get killed, just as quickly as just very quickly, more quickly even than in a book . . . "

She explains why statesmen blunder into wars: "they are still believing what they are supposed to believe nobody else believes it, not even all their families believe it but believe it or not, they still do believe it, believe what they are supposed to believe. And so naturally they believing what they are supposed to believe make it possible for the country to think they can win a war . . . "

Miss Stein is much clearer about peace terms than are many of our Senators. She says: "if the winner wins, then the vanquished should give in, and why ask for terms beforehand, if the winner is going to be generous he is going to be generous and if he is not going to be generous he is not going to be generous. . . . Unconditional Surrender and then let them be generous or not."

Miss Stein, whose defiant prose was forged out of her fight against the foggy logic of the 19th century, declares: "In the

19th century, there is the feeling that one is justified in being angry, in being right, in being justified. In the 20th century it is not that it is right but that what happens truly happens." And: "I suppose that is the reason that I so naturally had my part in killing the 19th century and killing it dead, quite like a gangster with . . . a tommy gun."

Her view of civilization is bleak: "Really and truly this time nobody in their hearts really believes that everybody that anybody will be peaceful and happy, not anybody, not even the immense majority believe any such thing . . . "

Commenting upon the complexity of French politics, she describes a doctor who was "anti-Russian he was anti-Anglo-American he was anti-German, he was anti-DeGaulle he was anti-Vichy he was anti-Pétain he was anti-Maquis he was anti-persecutions he was anti-collabo, he was anti-bombardments he was anti-militia he was anti-monarchy he was anti-communist he was anti-everything."

Other Steinian propositions are: Only a foreigner like Hitler could be so bent upon destroying Germany. When a German is not winning, he runs like a rabbit. The Maquis were "not too favorably regarded by their own countrymen, it was a kind of Valley Forge with no George Washington." And if you beat the white of an egg in a cup of water, and drink it, diarrhea will stop.

Her description of how she welcomed the American troops sounds like a steal from Father Divine (who is definitely 11th century): "wonderful that is all I can say about it wonderful, and I said you are going to sleep in the beds where German officers slept six weeks ago wonderful my gracious perfectly wonderful."

Wouldn't it be strange if, in 1988, our colleges made the reading of *Wars I Have Seen* mandatory, so that our grandchildren might learn how men felt about war in our time? Wouldn't it be simply strange if Miss Stein's grammarless prose was destined for such a strange destiny? Would it not be strange if anything strange like that did happen?

There's Always Another Café

Unlike James Baldwin, Wright made comparatively little use of the European setting in which he lived, and he seldom emphasized the cultural differences about which he had sometimes been disturbed at the outset of his exile in Paris. His silence probably stems from the fact that by that time he had already acquired the emotional and intellectual baggage that was to be his, while Baldwin had gone to France in search of his own identity as a Black American. Yet Wright always was a mature and penetrating observer of foreign customs and a critical commentator on American behavior abroad, especially during the era of the Cold War and McCarthyism. The atmosphere of the cafés he depicts in "There's Always Another Café" he knew quite well, since the Flore, the Deux Magots, the Tournon, the Monaco were, successively, his favorite haunts. He used them as a background for his unpublished novel, "Island of Hallucinations," which deals with Afro-American exiles in Paris in the Fifties.

Pinioned in the straitened confines of a Paris hotel, a restive American soon finds the answer to a question which has

"There's Always Another Café" originally appeared in *Kiosk*, No. 10, 1953.

perhaps slumbered teasingly in the back of his mind since the days when he'd gazed at exotic Paris scenes in the rotogravure section of his Sunday newspaper, and that question is: Why do Frenchmen spend so much of their time in cafés? Donning his adopted beret and pulling on his coat, the American descends the highly-waxed wooden stairway, seeking, like his French brother, a café—preferring the spaciousness, the bustle and the cacophony of voices to the bleak, blank walls of his hotel room . . .

On a salary of twenty or thirty thousand francs a month, a Frenchman cannot afford a living room; indeed, he's lucky if he has an apartment at all. And if he ever invites a foreigner to his tiny, drab flat, it's a signal that he's sure that his guest will not judge his moral or intellectual capacity by the low standard of his plumbing. Your French host, feeling that he is on trial, will outdo any American in laying out the carpet of welcome for you (even if he has to pawn the family silverware!).

But usually it's in a café that you'll meet your French friend. He rises, shakes your hand, inquires after your health, insists that you sit so that you'll have a view of the street, and hovers helpfully while you try to decide which drink, among the hundreds of French beverages, you'll take . . .

. . . In terms of visibility Paris seems composed only of cafés which, in the mornings, at noon, and in the evenings, burst with clients from whom café owners reap a stupendous profit. You'd scarcely recognize the harassed little proprietor of your favorite café if you met him, of a Sunday afternoon, strolling with his family down the Champs-Elysées, for his garb would make him look like a stockbroker.

In Paris there are cafés and cafés: some are called *bistros* and are located in the dingier quarters (they sometimes sell coal and wood as a sideline!). There are cafés for frowzy housewives who play the horses, students, graying bank clerks, government workers, artists, writers, demi-monde, lesbians, homosexuals, and, lastly, that queer, gray cloud of foreigners who, despite fierce French chauvinism, live in Paris the year around.

At the outset of his sojourn in Paris a foreigner does not at once select his favorite café. The determination of a café in which to spend one's hours of relaxation is a delicate problem, a matter of trial and error, tasting, testing the nature and quality of the café's atmosphere. Café façades that invitingly strike the eye are not always what they seem. You may prefer the crowded Deux Magots, or you may find that a quiet café in a side street is more to your liking.

My first Paris café, though commanded by a friendly *patron*, had an atmosphere that did not permit me to relax. The chairs were too stiff, the neon lights were too garish, the sun did not strike the terrace at the right hours, and a cold draft swept down my neck when a customer entered. . . .

The spiritual conditions of my next café were just right, but, to my chagrin, the *patron* turned out to be dirty, serving drinks in glasses that bore the imprint of lipstick. . . . And he was slightly avaricious to boot.

In my search for a café I strayed into the Deux Magots, the Flore, the Montana, the Reine Blanche, Lipps, the Royal St. Germain. . . . It was no go—too many tourists, too many tense characters on the make. . . . One could not sit a quarter of an hour without somebody violating that most sacred rule of café life: leave your neighbor alone. . . . Wishing to speak to a stranger in a Paris café, you'd best ask your *garçon* to deliver a discreet note requesting an audience. Forty-five million Frenchmen, crowded into an area smaller than Texas, have devised means of living without getting on one another's nerves!

I finally found my favorite bistro by straying one day into the Monaco, just off the Carrefour de l'Odéon. The *patron*, his wife, and daughter (French cafés are generally family businesses) were smiling, polite, but reserved. One end of the Monaco is occupied by the usual Parisien belote—and "421" players—apéritifs at elbows, berets slanted down over the eyes, cigarettes dangling limply from lips. . . .

The other end of the Monaco, near the windows, is crowded by Americans, Swedes, Danes, Dutch, Canadians, Swiss, Norwegians, and other English-speaking aliens. English is spoken in a dozen accents. They are bourgeois, middle class, working class, bohemian, and right on down to just plain lumpenproletariat. . . . Some are white, some black, some African with tribal scars decorating their cheeks, and some have lisping accents signaling that they are from Princeton. . . . Most of them were born since 1914 and cannot be numbered in that category of the "Condemned Generation" that Senator McCarthy is hunting down. They are, for the most part, passive, vague, sweet, fun-loving, devoid of conviction and would rather die than be caught entertaining such horrible things as "ideas."

Some of the young men, having caught fire from Hemingway, have sprouted beards and are groping for new ways in which to say, "I'm lonely." The others are having their "fling." Gangly in physique, the Americans affect T-shirts and blue denim trousers; the Scandinavian girls are distinguished by the color and dash of their clothes.

I used to sit at the Monaco in a corner and listen to American GIs discuss American foreign policy; the reality of Paris would fall away from me. Psychologically, I'd be transported back to New York and Chicago.

Listening to students and GIs, I kept in touch with my homeland's heartbeat. I discovered that transplanted Americans are uncontaminated with the daring French philosophical ideas that swirl about them, and their intellectual manifestations are projected against an alien background that throws their attitudes into relief, indicating two vastly different worlds of values: French and non-French.

I've gained much insight into America by frequenting the Monaco and observing the behavior of the American boys and girls who live in but not of Paris. For example, I recall a quiet, family boy from Brooklyn whom we'll dub X. X yearned for a personal freedom which his church, school and Brooklyn neighborhood had stifled by holding him to a rigorous stance of moral rectitude. Why, then, did X go to pieces so quickly in Paris? Why did he end up in the arms of the police? He was definitely not a criminal type. Was it because he did not have to fear the reactions of his French neighbors to his behavior? That morning at 3 A.M. when X was drunk and yelling in the middle of the Rue Monsieur-le-Prince—would he have dared do that on Eastern Parkway in Brooklyn?

And what of that disturbed, sensitive Jewish boy from Upstate New York whose values were shattered by French standards . . . ? Why did he weep when time came for him to go home? Why did he say that he'd miss the food, the wine, the talk, the tranquility of Paris? Did he take home a detached attitude toward America? Is he feeling guilty now because he allowed himself to be so seduced by an alien atmosphere?

One morning when the Monaco was partly empty of foreigners, the *patron* came and sat beside me.

"Tell me," he asked, "what are my American clients always talking about? I hear the word race. That's *race*, isn't it?"

I could see that he was baffled; he knew most of his American clients by their first names, but he didn't know what their ideas or feeling were.

"They talk about everything," I told him. "Politics, race, culture, life . . . "

"And race? I hear them talking about race all the time. "Why?"

"They've encountered new ideas and notions in France," I said cautiously.

"They laugh a lot," the proprietor said. "But they don't seem to be really happy. . . . "

"No; they're not really happy," I agreed, amazed that he had sensed it. "They don't really feel at home here."

"Do they love their country?" he asked.

"Sure, they do," I replied. I could feel that there were other questions he wanted to pose; his eyes had a faraway look.

The proprietor said wistfully: "I don't understand why Americans travel so much."

He was not angry; he was not anti-American; he was not resentful; he was just puzzled.

In the Monaco the Americans cling together for mutual protection against an alien world; they develop a communal cohesion that they would never need to develop at home; they share their food, clothes, their girl friends, aid one another in things both small and great. In their hearts lurk a fear of France and its complicated history. They'd like to see an industrialized, simple, modernized, efficient France, yet they inhibit their judgment, for they know that the French are a proud people.

One can get a good notion of what is happening back home by observing the newcomers fresh from the transatlantic liners. I was able to predict confidently Eisenhower's victory over Stevenson by listening to American remarks that were far removed from politics.

The vantage point of a café terrace is the boon of a Paris spring. Never select a café that is not lucky enough to possess enough sidewalk space to allow chairs to be placed for clients, for it is here that you can loll with your *fine* or *café crème* and watch the world go by. And I mean literally the *world*. For Paris is the crossroads of the earth and sooner or later all folks with enough gumption to travel will pass through.

And what a world Paris offers to the eye: bearded youths who seem to be barricading themselves behind a jungle of hair; girls in trousers with too-big breasts and buttocks and with horse-tail coiffures dangling behind them; middle-class Frenchmen who, though it be August, are buttoned to the neck in tweed coats, spatted, hatted, gloved, and swinging huge briefcases; and Arabs with carpets slung over their shoulders, selling bracelets, leather billfolds, peanuts, and "feelthy pictures" which, upon examination in the privacy of your hotel room, will turn out to be harmless nudes from classic paintings in the Louvre.

To see the thousands of Sorbonne students, it's necessary to choose a café on Boul' Mich', Dupont, La Source, etc., and through your sunglasses, you'll witness France's next generation gambolling in motley attire. . . .

There comes to my mind the experience of an ebullient student. Y was from Tulsa and to him Paris was like wine. He was a first-year medical student at the Sorbonne where freshmen are compelled to specialize in anatomy. Y was night and day in the company of Swedish, Danish, Norwegian, and English girls and, consequently, when he took his finals in anatomy, he failed. He tried desperately to blame his failure on his imperfect grasp of the language, on the alleged anti-American attitude of his Sorbonne instructors, on the state of his health (he *had* lost some fifteen pounds during the school term!). But, in the end, he had to confess that, trying to make up for his quiet Tulsa days, he had simply concentrated upon studying alien anatomies, especially those of the female variety. . . . This year Y is off to continue his medical studies in the mountain fastness of Switzerland, where puritanical mores will prove less of a distraction. . . .

All Paris cafés are not like the Monaco. A café derives its atmosphere from its clientele. If you are searching for a café to suit your temperament and fail to find it, take heart and search on, for there's always, in Paris, another café.

Black Power

Eager to visit Africa, the land of his remote ancestors, Wright tried several times to go there before actually reaching its shores in the summer of 1953. He spent several months in the Gold Coast at a time when this British colony had not been granted independence. His travel diary is a fascinating record of his impressions, reactions, and interpretations of the reality around him: poverty and disease, economic exploitation and colonial oppression, strange rites and baffling tribal customs and a new pride and a passionate desire for freedom under the strong impulse of Prime Minister Kwame Nkrumah. When Black Power, subtitled "A Record of Reactions in a Land of Pathos," was published in 1954, the British press reproached Wright with being unfair to the British colonial rule in Africa, while a few Africans were incensed at Wright's having viewed their ancestors as the men who had sold their people to the slave traders. With the passing of years, this firsthand report on an important step of the "African revolution" appears to have been written with a humor and an understanding not well appreciated at the time.

For lack of space, we have selected a fine analysis of the effects of an English, French or American education in mold-

Black Power was published by Harper & Brothers in 1954.

ing the reactions of an African and Wright's letter of advice
to Nkrumah, calling for the militarization of African life in
order to resist neo-colonialism. This letter has sometimes
been called "arrogant" by white critics, and Wright has been
accused of playing God to the dark continent, yet political
changes and the ousting of Nkrumah justify the novelist's
direst predictions.

TO FIND OPINIONS on these questions, I sought to talk to Dr.
K. A. Busia, one of Africa's foremost social scientists. He was
with the opposition, but he had indisputable facts in his
grasp.

I called at his office in the Department of Social Sciences
at Achimota University. Dr. Busia turned out to be a short,
medium-sized, affable man who had about him a slightly
worried and puzzled air. He was the author of *The Position*
of the Chief in the Modern Political System of Ashanti and
Social Survey Sekondi-Takoradi. I could tell at once that he
was orientated and could express himself with ease.

"Dr. Busia, to just what degree are the traditional rituals
and ceremonies of the Akan people still intact?" I asked him.

"They are completely intact," he told me. "The people
hide them from the West, and they make peripheral conces-
sions to Western opinion. But the central body of our beliefs
and practices still functions and is a working frame of reference from day to day."

"You are with the opposition, are you not?"

"I am."

"Do tribal rituals play a part in the Convention People's
Party?"

"They most certainly do," he snapped.

"Why has not this been pointed out before? Why has no
one shown the vital link between modern politics in Africa
and the religious nature of tribal life?"

"Westerners who approach tribal life always pick out those manifestations which most resemble their own culture and ignore the rest," he said. "That which they recognize as Western, they call progress."

"What is the significance of the oath-taking and libation pouring at Convention People's Party's rallies?"

"It's to bind the masses to the party," he said. "Tribal life is religious through and through. An oath is a great thing to an African. An oath links him with the past, allies him with his ancestors. That's the deepest form of loyalty that the tribal man knows. The libation pouring means the same thing. Now, these things, when employed at a political meeting, insure, with rough authority, that the masses will follow and accept the leadership. That is what so-called mass parties need. . . . The leaders of the Convention People's Party use tribal methods to enforce their ends."

"I take it that *you* wouldn't use such methods?"

"I'm a Westerner," he said, sucking in his breath. "I was educated in the West."

I had the feeling that he was speaking sincerely, that he could not conceivably touch such methods, that he regarded them with loathing, and that he did not even relish thinking that anybody else would. My personal impression was that Dr. Busia was not and could never be a politician, that he lacked that innate brutality of force and drive that makes a mass leader. He was too analytical, too reflective to even want to get down into the muck of life and organize men. I sensed, too, that maybe certain moral scruples would inhibit him in acting. . . .

"What has been the influence of Christianity?"

"Despite all the efforts of the missionaries, the Akan people have not changed their center of cultural gravity. Where you do find changes, they are mainly due to the church and the factor of urbanization. But even there you find a curious overlapping, a mixture. You have literate chiefs, for example, who practice an unwritten religion; you have lawyers trained in England who feel a tie to the tribal legal conceptions of their people. Such mixtures go right through the whole of our society. It's not simple."

"Have any psychological examinations been done to determine how this mixture is reflected in the minds of the people?"

"Nothing has been done in that direction," he said.

I next inquired of Dr. Busia the reasons for the low population level of the Gold Coast. I pointed out to him that the geographical area of the Gold Coast was more or less the same as that of England, but the Gold Coast had less than one-tenth of England's population. . . .

"Two things have kept the population level low," he said. "The lack of water and the tsetse fly. Seventy-five per cent of our population live in the forest area. If we could banish the tsetse fly from that area, we'd have horses to draw our carts and cows for meat and dairy products. Now, in the Northern Territories there is no water; it's filled with scrubland that can barely support its meager population."

"Dr. Busia, if you don't want to commit yourself on the question I'm going to ask, you can just tell me," I told him. "How do you, a British-trained social scientist, feel about the British recognizing the Convention People's Party . . . ?"

"Sure; I'll tell you," he said readily. "I'll tell you exactly what I told Sir Arden-Clarke, the Governor of this Colony. . . . The British here care nothing for our people; they are concerned with their political power which enables them to defend their financial interests. They sided with the Convention People's Party in order to protect those interests. It's that simple. We educated Africans looked to the British for but one thing: the maintenance of standards. Now that they have let that drop, what are they good for?"

Again I heard the echo of pathos. . . . A scientist had been trained by Britain to expect certain kinds of behavior from Britishers; now British behavior had turned out to be something that even their best pupils found some-what nauseating. . . .

"The British call such abrupt changes 'flexibility,' do they not, Dr. Busia?"

Dr. Busia laughed ruefully.

"But tell me . . . In your book, *Social Survey Sekondi-Takoradi*, you show pretty clearly the disintegrating forces of urbanization at work in the cities of the Gold Coast. Now, is there any widespread awareness of this?"

"No," he said.

"Is there any plan to see that the growth of your cities can take a new direction?"

"There is no plan," he said.

"I feel, from reading your book, that when tribal life and rituals break down under the impact of urbanization, and when no new sense of direction takes the place of what tribal culture gave, you will find a new kind of pagan among you: a pagan who feels no need to worship. . . . "

"The germs of that are making their appearance in our country," he admitted. "It's not widespread as yet; but it's evident."

"Do you think that Nkrumah can easily wipe out the old habits of the people—?"

"The African will react in that matter just as all people react," he said. "In the crucial moments of life, people fall back upon the deepest teachings of their lives; hence, in matters like politics, death, childbirth, etc., it's the teachings and beliefs of the tribe that all people—even those who are literate—turn to, give support to and trust. . . . "

There were other questions that I wanted to ask Dr. Busia, but I felt that they were too delicate. Had I not been afraid of wounding his feelings, I'd have asked him how was it that he, a social scientist, who saw so clearly the forces that were breaking down tribal life, could oppose those forces? If those forces had given way under the impact of industrialization in other countries, would they not do so in the Gold Coast? And, knowing that, why did he take his stand with the opposition? But I'd been told that Dr. Busia came of royal stock, that his brother was a chief, that he too might possibly some day be a chief. . . .

I'd now talked to enough educated Africans of the Gold Coast for there to emerge in my mind a dim portrait of an African character that the world knew little or nothing about. . . . I could imagine a young boy being born in a tribe, taking his mother's name, belonging to the blood-clan of his mother, but coming under the daily authority of his father, starting life by following his father's trade. I could well imagine this boy's father's coming in contact with missionaries who would tell him that his religion was crude, primitive, that he ought to bring his family into the church of the One and Living God. . . .

I could imagine that family's trying to change its ways; I could sense conflicts between husband and wife, between the father's family and the mother's family over the issue of Christianity; and I could readily picture the father, in the end, winning his argument on the basis of his superior earning power gained from working for Christian Europeans.

Let us assume, then, that the boy is the first child that the family has consented to send to the mission school. . . . There, he learns how "bad" is the life of his tribe; he's taught to know what power the outside world has, how weak and fragile is his country in comparison to the might of England, America, or France. Slowly he begins to feel that the communal life under the various stools is a childlike and primitive thing, and that the past of his tribe reeks of human sacrifice.

He now begins to identify himself with his mentors; they teach him to eat a balanced diet; he becomes ashamed to go about half nude; he feels that painting the body with lurid colors signifies nothing; he grows to loathe the mumbo-jumbo of the chiefs and the incessant beating of those infernal drums of state; and, above all, he squirms in the grip of the sticky compound life where every man is his brother and every woman is his sister or mother and can lay claims upon him which, if he refuses to honor them, can make him an outlaw. . . .

He develops a sense of his own individuality as being different and unique and he comes to believe that he has a destiny, a personality that must not be violated by others. He cringes in his heart at the memory that he once had to obey orders but confusedly heard and dimly understood from the shades where his ancestors dwelt.

Christ is offered and he accepts the way of the Cross. He now has a stake in the divine; he has a soul to save, and there seeps into his young and yearning heart that awful question: Where will I spend Eternity? The future looms before him in terms of a romantic agony: he can either live forever or be consigned to a lake of fire that never ceases to burn those whose sins have found them out. . . .

Yes, he must redeem himself; he must change; he must have a career. He reads of the exploits of the English and the Americans and the French, and he is told that they are strong and powerful because they believe in God. Therefore, finishing his mission studies, he elects to go to England or France or America to study. . . . He is baptized and his name is changed from Kojo or Kwame or Kobina or Kofi or Akufo or Ako or Kwesi, to Luke or Peter or Matthew or Paul or Mark or John. . . . He adopts a Western style of dress, even if it does not fit his needs or the climate. He no longer eats with his brothers, squatting on the floor about a common dish and lifting the food with his fingers; he insists upon sitting at a table and using a knife and fork.

If he goes to America to continue his studies, he is elated upon arrival. What a country! What a people! The seeming openness, the lavish kindness, the freedom of the individual, and the sense that one can change one's lot in life, the light-heartedness, the almost seeming indifference with which religion is taken, the urban manner of Negro living and what the Negroes have achieved against great odds—all of this

contrasts with the bleak mud huts and the harsh life of the
African compounds. For the first time in his life he sees black
men building and operating their own institutions in a Western manner, and a sense of social romance is disclosed to him,
and he yearns to emulate it. . . . All of this makes him apply
himself to the study of his chosen subjects with a zeal that is
second only to the religion that he'd been taught back in his
African mission school. But . . .

He begins, as the years pass, to detect that the Americans
are not a happy or contented people. He learns how to be
afraid, how to decipher the looks of desperation on the
American faces about him. He learns how it feels to be
related to nobody. What at first had seemed a great romance
now seems like a panting after money with a hotness of
emotion that leaves no time to relax. And he begins to wonder what would happen to him in such a life. . . .

And he learns the meaning of the word "race." What he
had failed to notice before now strikes home: he is free, but
there are certain things he cannot do, certain places where
he cannot go, all because he's black. A chronic apprehension
sets up in him; the "person" in him that the missionaries had
told him to develop is reduced, constricted. He'd never
thought of being rich, and now he knows that if he is not rich
in this land, he's lost, a shameful thing. . . .

That sense of poetry in him that even religion had not
dulled makes him ask himself if he wants to be defined in
terms of production and consumption. The feeling of security he had first felt is gone; the more he comes to know
America, the more he, stammeringly at first and more forth-
rightly later on, begins to ask himself: "Where's it all going?
What's it all for?"

And the only answers that make sense to him are heard in
Union Square or Washington Park. Yes; he'd go back home
and try to change things, to fight for freedom. . . .

And if he went to England for his education, his sense of
alienation would be the same, but differently arrived at. In-

deed, his blackness is swallowed up in the vast grayness of London. Perhaps he might have difficulty getting a room in which to live because of his blackness, but he soon meets another Englishman who feels free to do what he likes with his own home. But what puzzles him is the English assumption that everything that is done in England is right, that the English way is the only way to do it. He sees that no black man could ever sit in the House of Commons, that he is not expected to participate in English life on any level except that of a doctor. It seems that the English entertain a quaint notion that all Africans have sensitive hands that can heal the sick!

At Oxford or Cambridge he is far from the world of "race." He is a black gentleman in a graded hierarchy of codes of conduct in which, if he learns them, he can rise. He can, even though black, become a Sir. . . . The more he learns, the more Africa fades from his mind and the more shameful and bizarre it seems. But, finally, he begins to gag. The concepts that are being fed to him insult him. Though he will have a place of honor, that place will be with the lower and subject races. . . . Every book he reads reveals how England won her empire and this begins to clash in his mind with the codes of honor that he's learning so skillfully to practice. Soon he knows that he has to avoid saying certain things; for example, if it's known that he's a nationalist, he will surely not pass his bar examinations. Inhibition sets in and he has to choose whether he's to be among the favored or the scorned.

He learns that his blackness can be redeemed by service, but this service is not in the interests of his people; it's against them. . . . He begins to wonder why his missionary teachers never hinted at all about this. Were they parties to this deception? At the bottom of English society he sees servility and suffering and he senses that what has ensnared the people of his country has also ensnared these poor whites, and the first blow to his confidence is received. He could have been like those drab and colorless millions of London's slums;

indeed, his mother and father are like that in far-off Africa.
. . . He becomes afraid of his choice, and slowly he begins to
sympathize with the fear and insecurity of the poor whites
around him and, in the end, he begins to identify himself
with them. It's not in the schoolrooms or the churches that
he can hear moral preachments denouncing what is being
done to his country; he hears it only in Hyde Park. But he's
too afraid as yet to agree with what he hears; it sounds too
violent, too drastic; it offends those delicate feelings that the
missionaries instilled in him.

His first clumsy criticisms are addressed to religious people
and he's disturbed that they defend the system as it is. He's
secretly enraged that the English do not feel that he is being
dishonored. Just as the missionaries taught him just so much
and no more, he finds that the English accept him just so
much and no more. He's praised when he's like the English,
but he sees that the English are careful to make sure that he's
kept at arm's length and he begins to feel that he's a fish out
of water—he's not English and he's not African. . . .

If he chooses to go to France, he will encounter the same
theme, but with even subtler variations. Indeed, in France
he'll need all of his will power to keep from being completely
seduced by the blandishments of French culture. None of the
blatant American racism or that vague social aloofness which
so often prevails in England will meet him in Paris. Instead,
he'd be eagerly received everywhere, but . . .

He senses that the Frenchmen he meets are sounding him
out about the national liberation movement in his country.
If he makes the mistake of being forthright about his country's demand for freedom, he'll encounter no overt racial
discrimination; he'll simply find everything suddenly becoming extremely difficult. He'll learn, as he talks to animated
and polite Frenchmen, that they feel that they have worked
out, in the last two thousand years, just about the most civilized attitude on earth; he'll be obliquely but constantly dis-
couraged to think in any terms save those of extreme individualism.

Suppose he discovers that the French know nothing of his country and its culture, and, to remedy this lack, suppose he tells his French friends that he plans to launch a magazine in which young Africans can express themselves to the people of the Western world . . . ? A good idea! But, *mon ami*, you don't need to create a new magazine! You have the freedom to contribute to any magazine published in Paris! In fact, *mon vieux*, we'd welcome any contribution you might make. By the way, we'd like to make you a co-editor of our review!

The more intelligent the French think he is, the more he'll be watched; but this surveillance is not done in terms of crude spying, not yet—but in terms of social cultivation. He'll hear his professors in the classrooms constantly asking him: "What do you intend to do when you get your degree?" And if he says he's seriously thinking of settling down in France and pursuing his profession, marrying, no matter what woman of what race, his professors nod and smile their encouragement. But if he says that he wishes to return to his homeland and fight to lift up the standards of living, to free his country from foreign rule, from French domination, he feels a coolness of attitude that, in time, will change to freezing. . . .

He sees that many of his fellow blacks are obtaining university degrees and that almost all of them are at once put into civil service where they can be effectively controlled!

The black colonial Frenchman in Paris, like his counterpart in London or New York, will encounter the men on soapboxes preaching revolution, but, to his surprise, he'll find that the French are fairly indulgent toward his budding interest in Marxism! It's only upon nationalism that they frown. . . . He'll find, in Paris as in the colonies proper, that the French will prefer his becoming a Communist rather than his embracing the cause of his homeland. In time he sees that the French have a great deal of experience in dealing with Communists, but that they shy off in a state of terror when confronted with nationalists.

He learns that in French eyes nationalism implies a rejection of French culture, whereas they regard Communism as a temporary aberration of youth. Let him yell for revolution all he can; he might find a few French millionaires at his side, helping to spur him on . . . !

Alone in Paris, he'll take up with some French girl and she'll sympathize with him, but will tactfully point out how hard and long will be his fight, that there are so many pleasures to be savored, and he'll be lucky if he does not yield. He sees that many of his black brothers who came to France are sophisticated, successful black *Frenchmen!*

Still thirsting for self-redemption, thwarted in pride, he dreams of showing the French that he too can build a nation. He realizes now that his resolution to do this must be ten times as strong as that of an African in New York or London; also he begins to realize that the culture of France is so profound that it can absorb even Communism and pat its stomach. . . .

It's a desperate young black French colonial who resolves to return to his homeland and face the wrath of white Frenchmen who'll kill him for his longing for the freedom of his own nation, but who'll give him the *Legion d'honneur* for being French. . . . Through books he finds that other men have forged weapons to defend themselves from the domination of the West; he learns that the Russians, the Chinese, the Indians, and the Burmese saved themselves and he begins to master the theories of how they did it.

Strangely, he now yearns to build a land like France or England or America. Only such a deed will assuage his feelings of shame and betrayal. He too can be like they are. That's the way to square the moral outrage done to his feelings. Whether America or France or England have built societies to the liking of his heart no longer concerns him; he must prove his worth in terms that they have taught him.

But when he arrives in his tropical homeland, he is dismayed to find that he's almost alone. The only people who are solidly against the imperialists are precisely those whose words and manner of living had evoked in him that sense of shame that made him want to disown his native customs. They want national freedom, but, unlike him, they do not want to "prove" anything. Moreover, they don't know how to organize. They are willing to join him in attempting to drive out the invaders; they are willing, nay, anxious, on the oaths of their ancestors, to die and liberate their homeland. But they don't want to hear any talk of ideas beyond that. . . .

So, the young man who spurned the fetish religion of his people returns and finds that that religion is the only thing that he has to work with; it's muck, but he must *use* it. . . . So, not believing in the customs of his people, he rolls up his sleeves and begins to organize that which he loathes. . . . Feeling himself an outsider in his native land, watching the whites take the gold and the diamonds and the timber and the bauxite and the manganese, seeing his fellow blacks who were educated abroad siding with the whites, seeing his culture shattered and rendered abhorrent, seeing the tribes turned into pawns that float about the harbor towns, stealing, begging, killing—seeing that the black life is detribalized and left to rot, he finally lifts his voice in an agonized cry of nationalism, *black* nationalism!

He's the same man whom the missionaries educated; he's acting on the impulses that they evoked in him; his motives are really deeply moral, but pitched on a plane and in a guise that the missionaries would not recognize. . . . And almost the only ones who answer his cry of nationalism-at-any-price, nationalism as a religion, are the tribes who are sick of the corrupt chiefs, the few who share his emotional state, the flotsam and jetsam of the social order! But, things being as they are, there's no other road for him; and he resolves: "So be it. . . . "

The strange soil of the Western world, composed as it is of individualism, hunger for a personal destiny, a romantic sense of self redemption, gives birth to fantastic human plants that it is ashamed of!

. . . DEAR KWAME NKRUMAH:

My journey's done. My labors in your vineyard are over. The ship that bears me from Africa's receding shore holds a heart that fights against those soft, sentimental feelings for the sufferings of our people. The kind of thinking that must be done cannot be done by men whose hearts are swamped with emotion.

While roaming at random through the compounds, market places, villages, and cities of your country, I felt an odd kind of at-homeness, a solidarity, that stemmed not from ties of blood or race, or from my being of African descent, but from the quality of deep hope and suffering embedded in the lives of your people, from the hard facts of oppression that cut across time, space, and culture. I must confess that I, an American Negro, was filled with consternation at what Europe has done to this Africa. . . .

Yet, as grim as the picture is, its grimness is somewhat relieved by the fact that African conditions are not wholly unique. The suffering that your people bear has been born triumphantly before, and your fellow countrymen have shared that burdensome experience of having had their destinies dictated by alien powers, from above, an experience that has knit together so many of the world's millions in a common consciousness, a common cause.

Kwame, let me put it bluntly: Western lay and academic circles utter many a hard saying against Africa. In defending their subjugation of Africa, they contend that Africa has no culture, no history, no background, etc. I'm not impressed by these gentlemen, lay or academic. In matters of history they have been more often wrong than right, and even when they have been right, it has been more by accident than design, or they have been right only after facts have already been so clearly established that not even a fool could go wrong.

I found only one intangible but vitally important element in the heritage of tribal culture that militated against cohesiveness of action: African culture has not developed the personalities of the people to a degree that their egos are stout, hard, sharply defined; there is too much cloudiness in the African's mentality, a kind of sodden vagueness that makes for lack of confidence, an absence of focus that renders that mentality incapable of grasping the workaday world. And until confidence is established at the center of African personality, until there is an inner reorganization of that personality, there can be no question of marching from the tribal order to the twentieth century.... At the moment, this subjective task is more important than economics!

Manifestly, as in all such situations, the commencement of the injection of this confidence must come from without, but it *cannot* and *will* not come from the West. (Let's hope I'm wrong about that!)

Have no illusions regarding Western attitudes. Westerners, high and low, feel that their codes, ideals, and conceptions of humanity do not apply to black men. If until today Africa was static, it was because Europeans deliberately wanted to keep her that way. They do not even treat the question of Africa's redemption seriously; to them it is a source of amusement; and those few Europeans who do manage to become serious about Africa are more often prompted by psychological reasons than anything else. The greatest millstone about the neck of Africa for the past three hundred years has been the psychologically crippled white seeking his own perverse personal salvation. . . .

Against this background one refrain echoes again and again in my mind: *You must be hard!* While in Africa one question kept hammering at me: Do the Africans possess the necessary hardness for the task ahead?

If the path that you and your people had to tread were an old and tried one, one worn somewhat smooth by the past

trampings of many people; had Europe, during the past centuries, dealt with Africans differently, had they laid the foundations of the West so securely that the Africans could now
hold Western values as basic assumptions—had all this happened, the question of "hardness" would not have presented
itself to me. (I know that some Europeans are going to say:
"Ah, look, a black man advocates stern measures for Africa!
Didn't we tell you that they needed such as that?") But
Kwame, the truth is that nothing could have been more
brutally horrible than the "slow and sound" educational development that turned into a kind of teasing torture, which
Europe has imposed so profitably upon Africa since the
fifteenth century. . . .

The accomplishment of this change in the African attitude
would be difficult under the best of circumstances; but to
attain that goal in an Africa beset with a gummy tribalism
presents a formidable problem: the psychological legacy of
imperialism that lingers on represents the antithesis of the
desired end; unlike the situations attending the eruptions of
the masses in Russia, China, and India, you do not have the
Western-educated Africans with you; in terms of mechaniza-
tion, you must start from scratch; you have a populace ridden
with a 90 per cent illiteracy; communication and transportation are poor. . . .

Balancing these drawbacks are some favorable features:
West Africa, thanks to climate, is predominantly *black!* You
can pour a libation to the nameless powers that there are no
white settlers to be driven out, no knotty land problem to be
solved by knocking together the heads of a landed black
bourgeoisie. And, though the cultural traditions of the people
have been shattered by European business and religious interests, they were so negatively shattered that the hunger to
create a *Weltanschauung* is still there, virginal and unim-
paired.

If, amidst such conditions, you elect, at this late date in
world's history, to follow the paths of social and political

evolution such as characterized the history of the institutions of the Western powers, your progress will go at a snail's pace and both of your flanks will be constantly exposed and threatened.

On the one hand, just as you organized against the British, so will other Nkrumahs organize against you. What Nkrumah has done, other Nkrumahs can do. You have made promises to the masses; in your heart of hearts I know that you wish hotly to keep those promises, for you are sincere. . . . But suppose the Communists outbid you! Suppose a sullen mood sets in? Would not that give the Communists *their* opportunity?

On the other hand, I cannot, as a man of African descent brought up in the West, recommend with good faith the agitated doctrines and promises of the hard-faced men of the West. Kwame, until they have set their own houses in order with their own restless populations, until they have solved their racial and economic problems, they can never—no matter *what* they may say to you at any *given* moment!— deal honestly with you. Given the opportunity, they'll pounce at any time upon Africa to solve their own hard-pressing social and political problems, just as you well know that they have pounced in the past. And, also, I'm convinced that the cultural conditioning of the Africans will make it difficult for them to adjust quickly to values that are solely Western, values that have mocked and shamed them so much in the past, values that go against the grain of so much in the African heart. . . . After all, you have already been down that road.

Your safety, your security lie in plunging full speed ahead!

But, how? What methods? Means? What instrumentalities? Ah, there's the rub. . . . The neurotically fluttering attempts of missionaries, the money lust of businessmen, the cool contempt of European soldiers and politicians, the bungling cynicism of statesmen splitting up families and cultures and indigenous national groupings at their pleasure—all of these have left the task of the redemption of Africa to you and yours, to us . . . And what a task! What a challenge! What an opportunity for creation . . . !

One simple conviction stands straight up in me: Our people must be made to walk, forced draft, into the twentieth century! The direction of their lives, the duties that they must perform to overcome the stagnancy of tribalism, the sacrifices that must yet be made—all of this must be placed under firm social discipline!

I say to you publicly and frankly: The burden of suffering that must be borne, impose it upon *one* generation! Do not, with the false kindness of the missionaries and businessmen, drag out this agony for another five hundred years while your villages rot and your people's minds sink into the morass of a subjective darkness. . . . Be merciful by being stern! If I lived under your regime, I'd ask for this hardness, this coldness. . . .

Make no mistake, Kwame, they are going to come at you with words about democracy; you are going to be pinned to the wall and warned about decency; plump-faced men will mumble academic phrases about "sound" development; gentlemen of the cloth will speak unctuously of values and standards; in short, a barrage of concentrated arguments will be hurled at you to persuade you to temper the pace and drive of your movement. . . .

But you know as well as I that the logic of your actions is being determined by the conditions of the lives of your people. If, for one moment, you take your eyes off that fact, you'll soon be just another African in a cloth on the streets of Accra! You've got to find your *own* paths, your *own* values. . . . Above all, feel free to *improvise!* The political cat can be skinned in many fashions; the building of that bridge between tribal man and the twentieth century can be done in a score of ways. . . .

You might offer ideology as an instrument of organization; but, evidently, you have no basis for that in Africa at this

time. You might, by borrowing money from the West, indus-
trialize your people in a cash-and-carry system, but, in doing
so, you will be but lifting them from tribal to industrial slavery, for tied to Western money is Western control, Western
ideas. . . . Kwame, there is nothing on earth more afraid than
a million dollars; and, if a million dollars means fear, a billion
dollars is the quintessence of panic. . . .

Russia will not help you, unless you accept becoming an
appendage of Moscow; and why should you change one set
of white masters for another . . . ?

There is but one honorable course that assumes and answers the ideological, traditional, organizational, emotional,
political, and productive needs of Africa at this time:

AFRICAN LIFE MUST BE MILITARIZED!

. . . not for war, but for peace; not for destruction, but for
service; not for aggression, but for production; not for despotism, but to free minds from mumbo-jumbo.

I'm not speaking of a military dictatorship. You know that.
I need not even have to say that to you, but I say it for the
sake of others who will try to be naïve enough to misconstrue
my words. I'm speaking simply of a militarization of the daily,
social lives of the people; I'm speaking of giving form, organization, direction, meaning, and a sense of justification
to those lives. . . . I'm speaking of a temporary discipline
that will unite the nation, sweep out the tribal cobwebs, and
place the feet of the masses upon a basis of reality. I'm not
speaking of guns or secret police; I'm speaking of a method
of taking people from one order of life and making them
face what men, all men everywhere, must face. What the
Europeans failed to do, didn't want to do because they feared disrupting their own profits and global real estate, you
must do.

Above all, Africans must be regimentalized for the "long
pull," for what will happen in Africa will spread itself out
over decades of time and a continent of space. . . . You know
as well as I that what has happened in the Gold Coast is just

the beginning; and there will be much marching to and fro; there will be many sunderings and amalgamations of people; there will be many shiftings and changes of aims, perspectives, and ideologies—there will be much confusion before the final redemption of Africa is accomplished.

Do I sound gratuitously hard, cruel? How I wished I did not have to think of such measures! Yet, what could make such measures unnecessary? Only a West that could come forth and admit that it didn't do the job, that the job has to be done, and that it was willing to help you to do it. . . . Yet, I cannot conceive of the West acting in that manner, even though all the common sense of history, moral and material, is in favor of it. In its fight against Communism, Europe could bind Africa to her by such an act of help and understanding. . . . Of course, when this is pointed out to Westerners, they shrug their shoulders and say that they have timed African development according to their conceptions of what Africans can do; but, in saying this, they forget that they are not free to indulge in such fantasies. Western time today is being timed by another time: *Communist* time! It would seem that the issue of self-preservation alone would jolt Europeans out of their infantile dreams about Africa. . . .

And in exchange for aiding honest Africans to shake their people loose from their tribal moorings, the West could have all the raw materials it wanted, a larger market for its products. . . . And an Africa deliberately shaken loose from its traditional past would, for a time, be a more dependent Africa than the angry, aimless Africa of the present day. Such an Africa could menace nobody.

Why do I bring up the question of "menace"? Because the mere thought of a free Africa frightens many Europeans. Europeans do not and cannot look upon Africa objectively. Back of their fear of African freedom lies an ocean of *guilt!* In their hearts they know that they have long tried to murder Africa. . . . And this powerful Europe, with atom bombs in its hands, is haunted by visions of an eventual black revenge that has no basis in reality. It is this subjective factor, among others, that makes the West brutally determined to keep Africa on a short chain. . . .

Will the West come forward and head up these nationalist revolutions in Africa? No; it's a dream. If it comes true, I'd be the first to hail it. But since we cannot wait for dreams, let us turn to reality. . . . That is, the militarization of African life.

The basis, concrete and traditional, for the militarization of African life is there already in the truncated tribal structure. The ideological justification for such measures is simple survival; the military is but another name for fraternalization, for cohesiveness. And a military structure of African society can be used eventually for defense. Most important of all, a military form of African society will atomize the fetish-ridden past, abolish the mystical and nonsensical family relations that freeze the African in his static degradation; it will render impossible the continued existence of those parasitic chiefs who have too long bled and misled a naïve people; it is the one and only stroke that can project the African immediately into the twentieth century!

Over and above being a means of production, a militarized social structure can replace, for a time, the political; and it contains its own form of idealistic and emotional sustenance. A military form of life, of social relations, used as a deliberate bridge to span the tribal and the industrial ways of life, will free you, to a large extent, from begging for money from the West, and the degrading conditions attached to such money. A military form of life will enable you to use *people* instead of money for many things and on many occasions! And if your people knew that this military regime was for their freedom, for their safety, for the sake of their children escaping the domination of foreigners, they will make all the sacrifices called for.

Again I say: Would that Western understanding and generosity make these recommendations futile. . . . But if the choice is between traditional Western domination and this hard path, take the hard path!

Beware of a Volta Project built by foreign money. Build your own Volta, and build it out of the sheer lives and bodies of your people! With but limited outside aid, your people can rebuild your society with their bare hands. . . . Africa needs this hardness, but only from Africans.

You know as well as I know that politics alone is not enough for Africa. Keep the fires of passion burning in your movement; don't let Westerners turn you away from the only force that can, at this time, knit your people together. It's a secular religion that you must slowly create; it's that, or your edifice falls apart.

There will be those who will try to frighten you by telling you that the organization you are forging looks like Communism, Fascism, Nazism; but, Kwame, the form of organization that you need will be dictated by the needs, emotional and material, of your people. The content determines the form. Never again must the outside world decide what is good for you.

Regarding corruption: use fire and acid and cauterize the ranks of your party of all opportunists! *Now!* Corruption is the one single fact that strikes dismay in the hearts of the friends of African freedom. . . .

In your hands lies the first bid for African freedom and independence. Thus far you have followed an *African* path. I say: *So be it!* Whatever the West or East offers, take it, but don't let them take you. You have taken Marxism, that intellectual instrument that makes meaningful the class and commodity relations in the modern state; but the moment that that instrument ceases to shed meaning, drop it. Be on top of theory; don't let theory be on top of you. In short, be *free,* be a living embodiment of what you want to give your people. . . .

You and your people need no faraway "fatherland" in either England or Russia to guide and spur you on; let your own destiny claim your deepest loyalty. You have escaped one form of slavery; be chary of other slaveries no matter in what guise they present themselves, whether as glittering ideas, promises of security, or rig mortgages upon your future.

There will be no way to avoid a degree of suffering, of trial, of tribulation; suffering comes to all people, but you have within your power the means to make the suffering of your people meaningful, to redeem whatever stresses and strains may come. None but Africans can perform this for Africa. And, as you launch your bold programs, as you call on your people for sacrifices, you can be confident that there are free men beyond the continent of Africa who see deeply enough into life to know and understand what you *must* do, what you *must* impose. . . .

You have demonstrated that tribes can be organized; you must now show that tribes can march socially! And remember that what you build will become a haven for other black leaders of the continent who, from time to time, long for rest from their tormentors. Gather quickly about you the leaders of Africa; you need them and they need you. Europe knows clearly that what you have achieved so far is not confined to the boundaries of the Gold Coast alone; already it has radiated outward and as long as the influence of your bid for freedom continues to inspire your brothers over the teeming forests of West Africa, you can know that the ball of freedom that you threw still rolls. . . .

With words as our weapons, there are some few of us who will stand on the ramparts to fend off the evildoers, the slanderers, the greedy, the self-righteous! You are not alone. . . .

Your fight has been fought before. I am an American and my country too was once a colony of England . . . It was old Walt Whitman who felt what you and your brother fighters are now feeling when he said:

Suddenly, out of its stale and drowsy lair, the lair of
*   slaves,*
Like lightning it le'pt forth, half startled at itself,
Its feet upon the ashes and rags—its hands tight to the
*   throats of kings.*

O hope and faith!
O aching close of exiled patriots' lives!
O many a sicken'd heart!
Turn back unto this day, and make yourself afresh.
And you, paid to defile the People! you liars, mark!
Not for numberless agonies, murders, lusts,
For court thieving in its manifold mean forms, worming
*   from his simplicity the poor man's wages,*
For many a promise sworn by royal lips, and broken and
*   laugh'd at in the breaking.*
Then in their power, not for all these, did the blows strike
*   revenge, or the heads of nobles fall;*
The People scorn'd the ferocity of kings.

Pagan Spain

In 1954–1955 Wright spent several months in Spain seeking answers to why his ancestors were enslaved by Western civilization. The book Pagan Spain *is the culmination of Wright's search. He explores the people and place which to his mind best explained why the West sought and needed the Black and how it was ultimately trapped by its own traditions. Wright's own words on the jacket of the British edition probably afford the most accurate introduction:*

I'm a self-conscious Negro and I'm the product of Western culture, living with white people far from my racial origins. I began to ask myself how did I get there, who brought me there and why? What kind of people were they who dared the oceans to get slaves and sell them? It was in Spain, where tradition has not changed, that I found my answers. In Seville I saw the kind of men, idle and useless, rejected by the Church and State, who followed Columbus across the Atlantic . . .

But my going to Spain had yet another and deeper meaning, a meaning that I did not know until I got there. I found myself a man freed of traditions, uprooted from my own racial heritage, looking at white people who were still caught in their age-old traditions. The white man had un-

Pagan Spain was published by Harper & Brothers in 1957. This selection is chapters 16–22, 25, and 26 of the original work.

knowingly freed me of my traditional, backward culture,
but had clung fiercely to his own. This is the point of *Pagan
Spain*.

*Wright deals mainly with people and customs, not with
institutions. He believes that the central paradox of Spain is
a religious one. In this Catholic country, worship, festivals,
even the bull-ring assert a faith that is a mixture of Christianity with the primitive and the pagan. Hence the title of the
book. Hence our choice of Wright's description of a bullfight,
which vies with Ernest Hemingway's best in narrative power
and certainly goes deeper in social analysis.*

TALK OF BULLS and bullfighters swamped a long, heavy
luncheon that swam in olive oil. The afternoon was torrid
and, though we were in our shirt sleeves, I sweated as I ate.
Spain being a man's world, we men were served first by
André's mother; the women had to wait meekly for their
turn. No nonsense here about the priority of women, of the
mothers of the race, not even if they were certified virgins.
The women ate silently, with one eye cocked in the direction
of their men, ready at a moment's notice to drop their knives
and forks and refill the half-empty masculine plates.

At four o'clock we left and, as we came in sight of the
arena, even I began to succumb to the contagion of bull-
fever. One glance at the straggling throngs converging upon
the circular stadium was sufficient to disclose that all social,
class, and political lines were melted here; but, wherever I
looked, I saw armed members of the Civil Guard, their machine guns ready.

The yokels from the hinterland wearing dull brogans and
willowy, crumpled trousers mingled with the sleek members
of the nobility, and one could see the absoluteness that

cleaved Spanish society, the working class and the nobility, in twain. I was quickly hemmed in by men wishing to sell booklets in English describing bullfighting, photos of matadors, and brochures detailing their exploits. Others peddled combs, cigarettes, canaries in cages, paper hats of many colours to shade the head from the sun, pocket-knives, wristwatch bands, dolls, rings, and a sprawling welter of other cheap and vulgar trinkets. Beggars were universal, eagerly exhibiting the stumps of arms and legs, their outstretched palms beseeching centavos; they would follow you for minutes, jabbering plaintively, their eyes humble and desperate.

Suppressed emotion filled the air; all about me eyes glittered with the expectation of seeing something loved and believed in. Several working-class women carried tiny babies in their arms; in a quiet, shaded nook of the stadium wall one young woman was giving her swollen, veined teat to her infant and crumbly milk drooled from the tiny mouth as it suckled, and the mother, her eyes dreamy and vacant, stood oblivious of passers-by. To me she was a spectacle far more moving and beautiful than the ancient, wooden Black Virgin seated among the rearing stones of Montserrat.

I surrendered my ticket and followed the stream inside, renting a tiny pillow that was thrust upon me, the significance of which I did not appreciate until I saw the bare slab of concrete that was to be my seat for more than two hours. Up a short flight of steps and some thirty thousand people magically appeared in a vast sun-drenched circle, the tiers of faces rising like a wall towards the hot blue sky. The scene leaped with colour and noise. The heat was like steam and there was scarcely room to move. I was jostled in front, in back, and from both sides by pushing, sweating, panting people. An usher grabbed the stub of my ticket and beckoned me to follow him; he pointed to a seat in the shade of the barrier, with no one directly blocking my view of the wide circle of red sand that formed the bullring. But, when the usher indicated a span of bleak concrete ten inches wide and jammed in between two other people, I thought that surely a mistake had been made. But, no. . . . That was my seat. In order to possess it, I had to straddle my legs so that my kneecaps, when I eased down into a sitting position, touched both of the hips of a fat woman sitting directly ahead of me on a lower tier; and I could feel the fleshy legs of a woman behind me cushioning my back. I could not crook my elbow or reach for my pack of cigarettes without colliding intimately with female anatomy.

Momently the crowd thickened. The bullfighters and their assistants began to make their appearance in the space, about a yard wide, between the barrier and the bullring. The matadors were dressed in flashy, tight-fitting costumes that were known as 'suits of lights'; their aides were less gaudily clad. Reporters and photographers began to circulate among the bullfighters who went about arranging their capes and swords and other paraphernalia in a tight-lipped, matter-of-fact manner. Their faces were drawn, their eyes held dull glints of apprehension.

THE TEMPO OF EVENTS quickened. As with one prompting, everybody now turned towards the ornately decorated presidential box where sat the president of the bullring and official referee of the deadly actions that were about to transpire. His signal for the commencement of the drama came when his fluttering white handkerchief showed over the top railing of his box, and a highly synchronized, dazzling, and bloody game got under way.

A bugle sang a clear, golden note and the band began to play the dolorously lively bullfighter's *pasodoble.* From out of a wide opening on the far side of the blindingly bright red ring a score or more of brilliantly costumed men, led by a lone black figure astride a gracefully prancing horse, fanned out slowly and evenly over the scarlet sand and advanced with solemn steps towards the presidential box, looking like glowing pawns as they moved in the sunlight. They halted, facing the presidential box, and lifted their dark eyes grimly upwards. The lone, mounted black figure now doffed his hat to the president; the others—the matadors, banderilleros, and picadors; then, following tradition, they pressed their black hats firmly upon their heads, waiting. The president now rose and tossed a key that traced a swift downward arc and fell into the hat of the black, horse-mounted figure who, whirling his horse, galloped across the ring of sand and handed the key to the doorkeeper of the bull pen. Meanwhile, the matadors and their entourage were bowing to the president, then, with hurried, tense steps, they scampered behind wooden, protective barriers at three points in the circumference of the ring.

Again came the sound of a bugle, higher, clearer. A huge gate was thrown open by a man who fled to safety. A gaping black hole yawned and all eyes peered expectantly into it. Then out thundered a wild, black, horned beast, his eyes ablaze, his nostrils quivering, his open mouth flinging foam, his throat emitting a bellow. He halted for a second, amazed, it seemed, at the spectacle confronting him, then he settled squarely and fearlessly on his four hoofs, ready to lower his head and charge at the least sign of movement, his sharp horns carrying the threat of death, his furious tenacity swollen with a will that would brook no turning aside until all movement about him had been struck down, stilled, and he alone was left lord and master of the bloody field.

FROM BEHIND THE THREE wooden, protective barriers of the ring, the bullfighters now ventured cautiously out into the sandy arena, each group converging from a different angle, waving their scarlet capes to lure the bull into making repeated charges so that they might study his modes of attack, his manner of hooking with his horns, his predilection for tossing his head to left or right; in brief, in a frantically short space of time they had to familiarize themselves with the aggressive tendencies of that restless beast.

And that crashing hump of a black bull that they had sworn to kill was deeply loved; no mistake must be made about that. The long, secluded, and attentive rearing that had been lavished upon him to bring him into this ring virginal and pure in terms of his having had no previous experience in fighting men afoot had been much too expensive and elaborate to fit merely into a design of assuaging the desire to kill for the sake of killing. That bull had been so tended, fed, supervised that he was beautifully, wonderfully, innocently, and miraculously bad, evil, ungovernable—the hallucinatory image of the lust to kill.

That starting black hair, that madly slashing tail, that bunched and flexed mountain of neck and shoulder muscle, that almost hoglike distension of the wet and inflated and dripping nostrils, that defiant and careless lack of control of the anal passage, that continuous throbbing of the thin, trembling flanks, that open-mouthed panting that was so rapid that it resembled a prolonged shivering, that ever-ready eagerness to attack again and again that was evident by those shiftings of his massive and mobile weight from hoof to hoof, those unreserved lunges that sometimes carried him far past the elusive capes and sent him pitching and sprawling into the dirt until his flaring nostrils scooped up sand, that single-mindedness of concentration that would never allow his turning his head away from his enemy, that instinctive, imperious pride that told him that he and he alone was right, that superb self-forgetfulness that made him make of his body an expendable projectile to hurl at and annihilate his adversaries, that unheard-of ability to fight on even when rigor mortis was slowly engulfing the tottering limbs, that total and absolute dedication of life to defend life at any cost —all of these qualities made of that murderously leaping monster in that red ring a bull that was obviously something more than a bull. He was a substitutive instinct, a careening impulse, a superhuman image to contemplate for an awful hour in the hot sun buttressed by the supporting presence of one's neighbours—something to look at and then forget with a sigh—something to be pushed down into the underground of one's feelings till the overmastering need to experience it again would arise. Yes, the mystery and the miracle were here: the mystery resided in why the human heart hungered for this strange need; and the miracle was in the heart's finding that a rampaging bull so amply satisfied that need.

The matadors worked tensely with their capes. This beast had to be known, tamed—that proud and insurgent head had to be lowered—that wild lunging had to be calmed—in sum, this beast had to be educated quickly, so that he could serve human ends, human purposes. The bull's desire to kill had to be harnessed so that those sharp horns could, when guided by the skillfully held cape in the hands of a man who was master of his fear, graze the chest with an inch to spare and death would not come! *Death must serve as a secular baptism of emotion to wash the heart clean of its illegal dirt.* . . . And the matador in his bright 'suit of lights' was a kind of lay priest offering up the mass for thirty thousand guilty penitents.

JOYOUS CRIES OF admiration for the bull now filled the stadium. It could be seen at once that he was a fighting bull, the ever-charging kind, the sort that moved as though he had rails under him to make him come at you like a thundering train. Once again the bugle sounded through the hot, golden afternoon sunshine. The bull had now been satisfactorily observed by the matador and his assistants and the moment had come to attack the beast directly by the picador's jabbing picks of steel deep into the centre of the mound of the knotted muscle on the hump of his monstrous neck, the ultimate object being to wear him down, to tire him and make him lower his defiant head so that, at the moment of killing, the matador could, while luring the bull in one direction, move his body in another and reach across those ever-moving horns and plunge the sword hilt-deep into the vital area of his body.

Also the matador had to check the beast's leaping lunges, had to slow down his unearthly pace so that he could be played with the *muleta,* the small, yard-wide, yard-long stretch of red cloth attached to a stick which the matador would use in his final and finest stages of playing the bull. The bull had to be so conditioned that, when he chased the *muleta* guided by the supple wrist of the matador, his horns would sweep past the back, the side, the stomach, or the chest of the matador with but an inch or a fraction of an inch to spare, sometimes leaving smears of blood from the bull's sticky mane on the matador's uniform. This was the dreadful, delightful climax that could evoke the scent of death in the nostrils, the taste of death on the tongue, and the feel of death in the blood—which was a way of experiencing death vicariously.

The goriest part of the gory drama was undoubtedly the work of the picador. Swathed in protective material and straddling a padded, blinded old horse, the picador was led forward by two assistants alongside the wooden barrier. He carried on his arm a long pole whose shiny steel tip resembled an enormous fish-hook. The bull, spotting the picador and his horse, twisted his gigantic body in a swift arc almost in mid-air and went on the attack. Three times the beast charged the picador and his horse and three times, with facial muscles distorted with physical effort, the picador rammed the steel-tipped pick with brute force deep into the bristling hump on the back of the bull's neck, each thrust of the pick shredding flesh and tendons and producing tiny geysers of blood jutting two inches high in the bright sun and coagulating in irregular lumps on the bull's flanks—a punishment which tired and slowed the rearing animal and compelled him to lower his head. The crowd began to howl protestingly, fearing that the beast was being punished too much, and, as thousands rose to their feet, the bugle sounded, signalling the end of the picador's work and the beginning of the artful and colourful drama of the bull and the banderilleros.

The matador and his assistants now took up positions to be ready in case they were needed to coax the bull with their capes into a stance where the banderillero could make his approach and jab home the darts of steel. The panting bull now stood alone, looking from man to man, waiting for some move, not knowing from what direction action would come first. Then, on the far side of the ring, from behind a protective, wooden barrier, a man stepped forth and stood erect, bold, holding a stick about two feet long in each hand. The sticks were gaily decorated with frizzily cut, coloured paper and were made of slender rods of hard wood tipped with sharp, short spears of steel barbed and forged like fish-hooks. Once sunk into the body, they could not be withdrawn without shredding the flesh.

The bull and the man were now alone in the red ring. The stadium was silent. The sun beat down pitilessly. The man now proudly lifted the brightly-coloured banderillas high above his head, straightened his shoulders and stood poised, then began to ready himself by flexing his muscles as he lifted his body repeatedly on his toes. The bull watched, then slowly began to move closer to the man. Man and bull were still far apart and the distance between them burned with tension. Still lifting and lowering his body on toes, the banderillero began brandishing the sticks at the bull, shouting hoarsely with full lungs, his pelvis jutting forward, his chest reared back:

'Ha! Ha! Ha!'

The bull lowered his horns for attack. The banderillero began advancing, step by step, teasingly twisting his body from side to side, all the time nearing the bull. The bull advanced. The man advanced. Now both quickened their pace. Then man and beast rushed headlong at each other, both on a dead run. The bull had reached the speed of an express train, his horns lowered and aimed at the man's stomach. The banderillerò held his barbed sticks high, slanting a bit downward, and his body was leaning forward at an angle, the steel tips in his hands ready to fly over the onrushing horns to the hump of neck of the black, hurtling body. Then, at the point of what seemed an inevitably bloody juncture of man and beast, the man swerved to one side and leaped into the air, and, at the same time, plunged the steel darts home into the hot, bloody, quivering flesh of the back of the bull's knotted neck, then skipped aside, avoiding the seeking horns, leaving the sticks dangling and flopping as the bull still moved. The man escaped and the bull now stopped in his tracks, searching for the missed target and feeling searing fire blazing in his gashed flesh.

A quick sigh went up from the audience. There was some handclapping. Then came cries of:

'Muy bien! Muy bien!' *'Bravo hombre! Bravo hombre!'*

The bull galloped in circles, heaving his massive shoulders, trying to dislodge the steel hooks that ripped him the more he moved. His target had eluded him and now he sought it again, determined, undaunted. He trotted this way and that, thrashing his gigantic body about to rid himself of those hooks in his flesh, and the candy-looking sticks bobbed and flapped like circus pennants waving in the wind, shaving the tissues anew, causing tiny streaks of scarlet to ooze down his forelegs each step he took.

As though crazed, the bull loped into the centre of the ring, snorting, flinging his body to toss away those splinters of steel that bit ever deeper into his muscles and the red streaks of blood turned to broad, gleaming patches of scarlet that matted the black hair of his back.

Then, to his right, another man appeared. The bull turned to face his adversary, settling solidly on his four hoofs, then advanced. The man advanced, holding two more red and green and white sticks tipped with steel. Pained, the bull pawed the sand, lowered his horns, sighting his target, and moved forward with quicker momentum, and the two steel tips tore and widened the gash in his neck. On he came and on came the man, and, at the point of meeting, when the horns of the bull seemed about to gore the intestines and you could hear the bull's vast lungs expelling a mighty breath, the man rose into the air, shooting the steel-tipped darts downward and into the gaping, bloody wound. The man was in the air when the sticks left his hands and, upon his landing lightly upon the sand, he leaped aside, veering from the searching horns, escaping to safety.

The bull now stood and lifted his head and bellowed, raging, looking about for the vanished target, heaving his vast black shoulders and feeling the steel slashing his flesh and the streaks of blood now turned to rivulets. The peak of muscle back of his neck gushed blood. That was the way it had been planned. The means were cruel; the ends were cruel; the beast was cruel; and the men who authored the bloody drama were cruel. . . . The whirlpool of discordant instincts out of which this sodden but dazzling drama had been projected hinted at terrible torments of the heart. . . . Anyway, the results were being attained; the bull was now forced to hold his head a bit lower.

The goaded animal now careened into the middle of the sandy ring, bellowing, whirling his head in agony, his glaring eyes seeking vainly for a moving target. It appeared; the banderillero stood arrogantly some distance from him, again waving two more beautifully deadly bright sticks capped with hooks of shining steel, making dainty, capering steps, yelling disdainfully:

'Ha! Ha! Ha!'

The bull studied the target. The man advanced mincingly, edging closer. Slowly, head down, horns ready, the bull came shaking his body to lose those four arrows of steel that had now built a roaring fire in the muscle back of his neck; he came, dripping blood, his mouth shedding viscous gobs of white foam and saliva, his anal passage emptying, his urine spraying the red sand. The man stopped and motioned the two sticks at the bull, then stepped forward again. Then they both rushed at each other; the man again left the earth, his arms outstretched, his feet close together, and then he flung his arms forward, the pointed steel tips shooting downward and sinking into the shaking flesh as the horns passed an inch away from the stomach and the man skipped off to freedom. Maddened, the bull charged about the ring at random, his eyes hunting something to hurt, to kill, the sticks flinging limply about his bloody shoulders. He lifted his head and bellowed to the hot and empty skies.

The bugle sounded yet again as the ritual of blood and fear marched relentlessly on. I sighed and settled back to watch the work of the lonely matador. The drama had now reached its third and climactic phase. A stylized death was about to be enacted in the hot sun.

THE MATADOR was Chamaco. The bull now stood in the centre of the ring, winded, his head down, his eyes balefully watching the vague movements of the men at the barrier. Across the red sand came a slender figure carrying a *muleta* and a sword under his left arm. The sun glinted softly on his 'suit of lights' and his step was solemn, slow. With his chin almost on his chest, he walked towards the presidential box, stopped, looked up, bowed, then, following tradition, tossed his black hat to the red sand, and turned. He strode slowly along the barrier, his assistants following at a respectful distance.

Many people stood to get a full view of him. There was some handclapping. He gave a swift, enigmatic glance at the circular wall of faces and I was stupefied to see how young he really was; the contours of adolescence were still upon his dark, brooding face. Impulsively, I turned to the man who sat on my left and asked him in French:

'Quel age a-t-il?'
'Dix-neuf,' he said.
'C'est un enfant,' I said.
'Oui. Mais il est brave,' the man said. He smiled at me. 'That boy comes from a poor section of Spain, a town called Huelva, in Andalusia. He has a large family, many brothers and sisters. Two years ago he was starving; now he is almost rich.'

I resumed watching Chamaco, who was now strolling with downcast head towards the bull. The bull turned and faced him, eyeing him, immobile. I had seen the boy Chamaco rushing about the ring with the others; I had even noticed that he wore a 'suit of lights,' but I had refused to believe that one so young was a full-fledged bullfighter. (In fact, technically speaking, Chamaco was not a full-fledged bullfighter. He was what was called a *novillero,* that is, a fighter of young bulls. But he had been fighting full-grown bulls for a long time now and he was slated to take his *alternativa,* that is, his formal inauguration as a regular bullfighter, in the ring in Madrid.)

He strode across the bloody sand and stopped at a spot about ten yards from the bull who regarded him tensely, not moving. Then, without once glancing at the bull, Chamaco unfolded his *muleta* and took out his sword, as though he were at home pulling off his hat and coat to hang them up. He put the end of the spread *muleta* between his thighs, like a boy straddling a broomstick, making believe that it was a horse. The other end of the *muleta* now extended out, about a yard from his knees, the red folds dangling. His right hand held the sword which he now inserted under the cloth so that the tip of the sword terminated at the point where the *muleta* ended and fell towards the sand. Until that moment he had been facing the bull; now he turned his left side to the bull and stared straight ahead, acting as though the bull did not exist.

The thousands of onlookers were profoundly quiet, watching. The bull advanced a step, lifting his head imperceptibly, studying the new phenomenon. Then, for the first time, Chamaco looked at the bull, his chin still on his chest. The bull trotted closer, looking, watching for a movement. Chamaco's right hand now jiggled the sword ever so lightly and the outer fringes of the *muleta* fluttered a bit.

The bull was at Chamaco's left. Chamaco was fronting the crowded stands, his slight figure draped in an attitude of indifference. Once more he twitched the far end of the *muleta* with the sword, making the folds in the cloth tremble. Chamaco was sighting the bull's left eye, and was so gauging and calculating the bull's angle of attack that he knew exactly where the bull's right horn would pass and how deadly close.

The bull charged ahead full tilt. As he thundered forward, Chamaco moved the far end of the *muleta* slowly, slightly, lifting it, and the bull's right horn swept past, within inches of Chamaco's chest, his body rearing, and, as the *muleta* continued to float upward into the air, the bull finished his wild lunge with his head high, horns pointing skyward, both of his front legs extended, slanting upwards in mid-air, and his entire mass was one vast ensemble of taut black muscle covered with bristling hair. Other than the lifting of his arms to raise the *muleta*, Chamaco had not moved.

As with one voice, thirty thousand throats sang out in a soft slow burst:

'*Olé!*'

The bull's wild leap finished and he settled to earth, turned; he now stood to Chamaco's right. Chamaco, without moving from his tracks, held the *muleta* in his right hand, waist high, about two feet from him, and the bull, without ceasing to move, came in for another charge, his horns this time sweeping past Chamaco's stomach and, following the *muleta*, the bull rose the height of Chamaco's shoulder, the force of the beast's effort making his forelegs shoot into the air while the *muleta* floated above his head.

'*Olé!*' the crowd sang with bated breath.

Man and beast had now become fused into one plastic, slow-moving, terrible, delicate dance of death, the outcome of which hung upon the breadth of a split second. The bull, now to Chamaco's left again, was turning, his tail swishing, readying himself to resume attack. Chamaco, still rooted to the spot, lowered the *muleta* till it dragged in the sand, the handle of the stick of the *muleta* being held close to his thigh. He held the *muleta* this time in his right hand and, as the bull came in, he swept it gently, slowly backwards, round to his side. The bull, head down, hypnotized by the cloth, followed, hooking his horns past Chamaco's kneecaps. While the bull was in this low charge, Chamaco, pivoting slowly, advancing his left foot and pulling back his right, turned, still moving the *muleta* ahead of the bull's nose, luring the beast around him so that, when he whipped the *muleta* out of range of the bull's vision, the bull's horns were almost touching his knees, the beast having made a full circle around the man.

'*Olé!*' the mass chanted with fearful glee.

There was a dramatic pause. Chamaco hid the *muleta* behind him; he was now two feet from the bull, looking directly down at the bull not moving, his right hand lifted high into the air. The bull stared, baffled, outwitted.

Chamaco now stepped aside, disclosing the *muleta* which he now held in his left hand. The bull lowered his head, then looked at Chamaco, then at the cloth, at Chamaco, then at the cloth. . . .

The stadium filled with murmurs. Everyone knew that the bull was now trying to choose between the man and the cloth. Had the beast learnt the difference so quickly? Then the bull hurled himself at the cloth and a sigh went up. Chamaco swept the cloth gently around him until he was facing the middle of the bull's body, while the bull rushed until his horns were in the back of the man. Chamaco shifted the cloth from his left to his right hand, and the bull was bound to his waist, still whirling, and at last his horns were almost scraping the back of Chamaco's calves.

'*Olé!*' the crowd whispered its reaction, waiting.

Two feet out of line with the bull, Chamaco now stood with his back to the bull's horns. The *muleta* was held in his right hand, about a foot from his body. The bull moved. The cloth moved. Head and horns lifted violently, viciously, sweeping under Chamaco's elbow and into the air.

'*Olé!*' rolled from the tiers of jammed seats.

Chamaco now draped the cloth over the bull's nose and lured the beast towards his feet, then, as the bull, head down, followed, the cloth moved to the side and then to the rear of Chamaco. Chamaco's left hand now reached behind him, taking the cloth from his right hand, keeping it moving all the while, and the bull circled him once more, his head and horns at Chamaco's feet.

'*Olé!*' It was barely heard now.

With the *muleta* still in his left hand, Chamaco drew the bull round past him, floating the cloth, his back leaning backward over the bull's back. The bull's horns, ever seeking the cloth, now thrust past the retreating cloth and into the blinding sun, rushing past Chamaco's chest and his lifted arm—the beast's forelegs kicking skyward and his eyes round pools of frustrated fury.

'*Olé!*' It came crisp now; the crowd was sure that the man had mastered the bull.

Chamaco faced the bull, planted his feet in the sand, holding the *muleta* at his left side. The bull brushed past his left hip, his lunging head and horns lifting the *muleta*, his forelegs pawing the air.

'*Olé!*' The crowd sang.

The bull turned, always charging. Chamaco now extended his right arm behind his body so that the *muleta* jutted out from his left side. The bull leaped at it again, its horns grazing Chamaco's left side, rising in the air past Chamaco's shoulder, and the man stood gazing calmly at the madly lashing tail of the bull which was now directly under his eyes.

'*Olé!*' The voices now sounded like a prolonged sob.

Man and beast confronted each other. Chamaco, holding the *muleta* in his right hand, began a kind of slow, creeping movement with his feet, standing upright all the while, one foot thrusting out before the other, then the other. Standing still, the bull turned his head, his eyes following the ever-elusive cloth. Chamaco, shuffling one foot ahead of the other, completed half a circle about the bull, and his back was now to the barrier. Had the bull charged, he would have been killed, for he could not have escaped.

A sigh swept the stands. Men closed their eyes and moaned:

'*Bravo hombre . . .*!

On and on Chamaco turned, shuffling his feet in the sand; and the bull's eyes followed the cloth, his massive black and bleeding body turning. Chamaco returned to the original spot from which he had begun his creeping movement. The bull was mastered.

Soft handclapping swept the stands.

The bull now stood facing Chamaco, his eyes dazed, his four feet directly in line with his vast, heaving body, his head down. Chamaco was about six feet away. Suddenly you knew that the moment for the kill had come.

Chamaco's left hand now grasped the *muleta* firmly; he turned away from the bull, looking at him sideways, letting the red cloth drop below his left knee. He now lifted his gleaming sword chin-high and sighted along the length of it, pointing its sharp, steel tip at the tormented and bloody mound of wounds on the bull's back. Chamaco's left hand twitched the cloth, sighting the bull. The bull saw it and charged. Chamaco charged, meeting the bull. But, as he moved towards the bull, his left hand swung the *muleta* farther leftwards and his feet moved sharply to the right. The bull's horns rushed past his stomach as Chamaco tiptoed, leaning in and over the driving horns, and sent the sword to its hilt into the correct spot in the bull's body.

The bull halted, swayed. Chamaco stood watching him, gazing gently, sadly it seemed, into the bull's glazed and shocked eyes.

An uproar broke out in the stands. Almost everybody stood up, pulled out white pocket handkerchiefs and waved them, making the looming, circular stadium resemble a ripe cotton field being whipped by wind.

I watched the bull. He sagged, his eyes on his tormentor. He took an uncertain, hesitant step forward, and then was still. Chamaco lifted his right hand high above the bull's dying head; it was a gesture that had in it a mixture of triumph and compassion. The bull now advanced a few feet more on tottering legs, then his back legs folded and his hind part sank to the sand, his forelegs bent at the knees. And you saw the split second when death gripped him, for his head nodded violently and dropped forward, still. A heave shook his body as he gave up his breath and his eyes went blank. He slid slowly forward, resting on his stomach in the sand, his legs stretching straight out. He rolled over on his back; his four legs, already stiffening in death, shot up into the air.

BUT WHAT IS THIS mysterious 'spiritual exercise' of which Juan Belmonte, perhaps the most intelligent, courageous, and perceptive of all the men who ever entered a ring to kill a bull, speaks? Is there something hidden here? If there is something hidden, why are bullfights enacted out in the open, before thousands of spectators? The answer is so simple that it is not often recognized even when one is directly confronted with it. It is the conquering of fear, the making of a religion of the conquering of fear. Any man with enough courage to stand perfectly still in front of a bull will not be attacked or killed by that bull. It has been known for a man to sit in the bullring in a chair reading a newspaper in front of the bull pen gate. The gate was thrown open; the bull thundered out, stopped, gazed at the seated man, and trotted away. But to remain immobile when a beast of more than a thousand pounds is hurtling towards you is usually beyond human capacity.

And that was why I had heard the phrase, *bravo hombre,* so often on the lips of the spectators in the stadium. They knew well that the ability to master one's feelings of fear in the presence of that which immediately and dramatically threatened one's life was the cardinal quality that made the bullfight the gripping emotional spectacle that it was. As an American, a man from a world that valued and eulogized intelligence, responsibility, industrial processes, social-mindedness, property, etc., it was indeed odd to hear personal bravery extolled so highly. But Spain was another world with other values.

WHEN I EMERGED from my room it was night. I wandered about awhile, then stopped at a kiosk exhibiting photos of Chamaco. I bought one and went into a bar and studied it. That photo gave me the creeps. That a boy of nineteen should be so intimately acquainted with fear, death, and sacrifice violated something in me.

Later I strolled about the streets of the working-class quarter, glancing into bars, pausing to scan the huge variety of gaudy Spanish comic books that were on sale at news stands and in the windows of stationery stores. Suddenly I saw ahead of me a hauntingly familiar face reflecting itself in the dim beams of a street lamp. My God. . . . *It was Chamaco!* I quickened my steps and overtook him. He was walking slowly, alone, his head down; he was coatless and his shirt collar was open. There was nothing in his manner that would have distinguished him from the hundreds of other young men upon the sidewalk.

I should have thought that a fairly wealthy young bullfighter like Chamaco would have been spending his hours of relaxation in some expensive night club, surrounded by flamenco singers, dancers, and bottles of iced champagne.

But, no; here he was in these cluttered, dirty, tenement lanes where the prostitutes whisperingly hawked their soiled wares. Perhaps he was walking amidst these poor people from whom he had sprung to convince himself that his choice of risking his life to make money had been the right one . . . ?

I came abreast of him and called softly:

'Señor Chamaco?'

He turned his head and looked at me without smiling, then he nodded and at once a crowd began to collect. My stopping him had made others recognize him. I extended his photo and requested:

'Autograph, please.'

He understood. He took the photo and looked at me and shook his head. I thought that he was refusing. No; he simply did not have a fountain pen. Before I could proffer mine, somebody in the crowd had given him theirs. Chamaco tried to sign the photo while holding it in one hand and writing with the other, an awkward thing to do. It was clear that he was in difficulty. A brightly smiling youngster stepped forward and turned his back and let Chamaco rest the photo against his shoulder blades. Chamaco signed it, handed it to me and smiled slightly for the first time.

'*Gracias,*' I murmured.

'*Nada,*' he almost whispered.

'*Yo,*' I stammered, pointing elaborately to myself, '*Americano.*'

'*Si,*' he said.

'*Yo Ustéd* interview,' I said; my Spanish was a crime, but he understood.

'What do you wish to ask him?' a young man asked me. 'I speak English.'

A crowd of men and women, their eyes round with awe and respect, was now blocking the sidewalk and Chamaco was forced to back into the entrance of a store.

'Thank you,' I told my interpreter, glad that I had a chance

to communicate. 'Ask him why do the Spanish love bullfighting so much.'

The question was put and there was an outburst of laughter in the crowd. I heard someone murmur: *'Americano.'*
Then another whispered: *'Simpático.'* Chamaco smiled
wryly, then shrugged his shoulders. He was a god to these
people; he had publicly offered his life to a wild animal, had
killed that animal according to the most stringent rules, and
was alive and upon the streets. He had gone 'through the
valley of the shadow of death' and had come out alive, while
they lived in hunger and fear and trembling. But the young
dark god had no answer.

'Do you love the bulls?' I asked him.

The question was posed and he grew serious and answered
with a vigorous nod of the head:

'Si, si, si.'

'Why?'

'They are beautiful, Señor,' he explained. 'They are brave.
They know no fear.'

I wanted to ask him for a definition of that kind of beauty,
but I felt that my question would have been too abstruse.

'Tell him that I saw him fight today. I want to know if he
was afraid,' I asked.

That question agitated the crowd. But my interpreter
quickly restored quiet, put the question and got an answer.

'Yes. In a way, yes. I'm always afraid when I'm in the ring.
But my job is to kill the bull. I killed him,' he said proudly.

'Have you been gored often?' I asked.

'Yes. I've been gored several times,' he admitted readily.

The young man serving as a translator voluntarily informed me that Chamaco had already lost one testicle.

'I've heard some cynic say that the only wild beast in the
arena is the audience,' I told him. 'What do you think of that?'

Chamaco's expression indicated that he knew exactly what
I meant; he stared at me for a moment and then came nearer
to laughing than I had ever seen him do. But he shook his

head and refused to answer. He knew the answer, all right, but he did not wish to commit himself publicly. The people about us were silent. Chamaco was silent. And, suddenly, I saw a detached, withdrawing look come into his eyes. Something urged me not to question him any more. I could feel that he was hiding a consciousness of death; there was in him the presence of death; he was a bridegroom-to-be of death. . . . He would still fight and kill bulls; he would still risk his life for money, knowing that any day might be his last, but he did not wish to speak of it. He knew that he was selling his desperate courage to emotionally starved people, just as a woman sells her body on the night streets. He knew something of the human heart about which he thought it best to remain silent.

I shook his hand, wished him luck, and left, convinced that he instinctively understood the role he played in the complex psychological drama that took place between him, the bull, and the avid audience under the hot skies. . . . Would I be able to talk to a bullfighter who knew the role he played and could express it? I doubted it. (As usual, I was much too pessimistic; I did finally meet and talk to bullfighters who could express themselves, perhaps not as freely as I wanted, but enough. But that was later, in Madrid, and under totally different circumstances.)

THERE WAS NO vast, black, girting belt of tumbling industrial suburbs circling Madrid that one had to traverse before entering the city proper—sooty, smoky suburbs such as too often mar the approach to so many great world capitals. From Guadalajara one streaked over a smooth macadam highway past barren and dusty stretches of red and yellow clay and then suddenly one saw tall apartment buildings of reinforced concrete, new, glistening structures shaped modernistically, all angles and clean, plunging lines, six and seven stories high, their façades tan, yellow, blue—running the gamut of pastel shades.

The sun, a seething disc of brass, blazed brutally down from a sky shorn of all clouds. It was a kind of sky that made one thoughtful; I had never seen a sky whose infinite immensity so dominated the finiteness of human dwellings. I cruised through magnificent, tree-guarded, flower-bordered boulevards that were lined with roomy mansions whose metal shutters were already closed—it was nearing noon—against the dry and searing heat. The tyres of my car made a soft, whirring hum that seemed to blend with the air of an arrogantly restrained bourgeois Madrid.

This city surpassed Barcelona in the sumptuousness and splendour of its imposing ministries, its quiet, gleaming museums, its bubbling fountains, and its proud ornate monuments; but, as in Barcelona, I had to exercise caution to keep from running down chickens, goats, and sheep in the centre of the city just a few blocks from some of the world's most luxurious hotels. I passed four slovenly-dressed young men sauntering abreast down the middle of one of the main, busy streets carolling flamenco songs at the top of their tremulous voices to the accompaniment of a twanging guitar, and I was surprised because no one else seemed surprised.

Shoeshine boys, those inevitable heralds of endemic poverty, clogged the sidewalks. I could see no sign whatever of factories, of mills, of industrial activity. I discovered later that Madrid had no real *raison d'être*, that it had been designated as the capital centuries earlier merely because of its central location. It was not really a city at all, but an enforced conglomeration of bureaux of the Army, the Church, the State, and the Falange—an administrative unit out from which the main arteries of the nation fanned to distant hamlets, like the spokes of a wheel radiating out from its hub.

I chose a typical pension midway between the slum section and midtown, then set out to see acquaintances at the British-American Club, which was located in the heart of the city's café and night-life area. My first contact was with P.H., a soft-spoken, shyly affable, curly-haired young man from Arkansas.

'You know any bullfighters?' I asked him.

'Yeah. One,' he said offhandedly. 'But this one's an American.'

'When can I see him?'

'I'll have him here for you right after lunch,' P.H. said.

An opportunity to talk to an American bullfighter was more than I had hoped for. Perhaps this man would, in some respects, aid me in bridging that gap that separated the Spanish and the American spheres of value. I lunched at the club, then browsed among the newspapers in the library to find out what had been happening in the rest of the world since I had been in Spain. At a few minutes past two P.H. entered with a tall, blond chap.

'This is the bullfighter, Harry Whitney,' P.H. said.

Whitney was a six-foot, lanky young man with wide-apart blue eyes, a grave manner, a firm, almost tight mouth and a somewhat diffident air that concealed a great reserve of volatile emotion. He was neatly dressed in a dark suit. He sat down a little self-consciously and looked straight at me, calmly, evenly.

'So you're a bullfighter?' I asked him.

'Yes. I'm trying to be one,' he said modestly.

He told me that he was twenty-eight, had been to University, and had fought as a bomber pilot in the war.

'When did you come to Spain?' I said.

'Two years ago.'

'Why?'

'To learn bullfighting.'

'Do you like Spain?'

'Very much.'

'How long are you going to stay?'

'I've no plans,' he said.

'Huh-huh.... Now, brother, just lean back and tell me why you fight bulls,' I asked him.

It was a hard question, but I felt that he was intelligent, perceptive, and could take it. I expected a strong reaction and it came. He sighed and his eyes wandered. He was a direct person and I could feel that his mind was fumbling for answers. My asking him why he fought bulls was asking him the meaning of his life. Slowly he brushed his right hand over his wavy, blond hair and said in a low voice:

'I feel the bullfight deeply. Only a few people have really understood it. Hemingway has described the technical side of it, but not the emotional . . . There's one man who knows what it's all about: He's Juan Belmonte, in Seville——'

'I've read him,' I said. 'You think he's right?'

'Yes; definitely.'

'What do you feel out there in the ring?' I asked.

'When I'm out there facing a charging bull and hearing the crowd yell: *"Olé!"* I could stand still and let that bull gore me—'

'Stand still and *let* it happen?'

'Yes,' he said emphatically. 'You become sort of drunk with it. You feel the bull in your power. . . . That's how many bullfighters get killed. . . .'

'Many people think that bullfighting is something like ballet dancing,' I told him.

He doubled over with a burst of laughter.

'A ballet dancer would be killed in thirty seconds in a bullring. . . . People get things mixed up. Out of the thousands watching a bullfight, only a few really know what is going on. *Ballet dancers?'* He laughed again, cocked his head and stared off, deeply amused. 'Maybe it's because the bullfighter wears a tight-fitting uniform, like the ballet dancer. . . . But that's a superficial likeness. I don't know why ballet dancers wear tight-fitting costumes, but we bullfighters wear tight-fitting uniforms for protection. They are made of silk and silk is tough. Silk won't keep a bull from goring you, but many times the bull's horns will glide off and not penetrate. . . .

'Listen, we bullfighters do not make ourselves move like ballet dancers. We are not consciously seeking graceful movements. All of our movement is dictated by the bull and the bull only. The essence of the bullfight is not in moving around, but in standing still . . . and that is a hard thing to do in the ring. Look, you're holding the *muleta;* the bull charges towards you; your instinct will make you want to hold that *muleta* in front of you for protection; and, if you do, you're dead. The real moves in the bullfight cannot be seen; those moves are *courage.* . . . You must plant your feet in the sand and face death. If you run, you'll be killed. A fresh bull can outrun a racehorse, and, for the first fifty yards, can outrun an express train. . . . The slow, concealed movements in the ring are designed *not* to attract the attention of the bull; they are *not* for the spectators. . . . Ha! Ha! If people only knew. . . .'

'With whom does the spectator identify when he's watching a bullfight?' I asked him.

'I don't know the identifications they *do* make,' he said. 'But I do know what they *ought* to make. . . . There are two sets of identifications for the spectator: one is with the bull and the other is with the matador. It is only when the spectator can make the two identifications at once, jumping from the bull to the matador and back again, that the bullfight is really experienced—'

'You are acting *for* the spectators?' I asked.

'In a way, yes.'

'And who is the bull acting for?'

'Himself, I guess,' he said.

'Has it ever occurred to you that your bullfight costume is very much similar to the vestments of the priest?' I asked.

He became agitated and rose and walked nervously a few feet.

'You're getting close to it,' he said. 'The bullfight is on the level and intensity of religious emotion.'

'The matador exorcises the bull,' I said, urging him on.

'Why? What does the bull represent?'

'I ᴄon't know,' he admitted. 'All I know is that you offer your life to the bull.' He groped for words. 'Without that, there is no bullfight.'

'You surrender yourself to the bull and you overcome him,' I said.

'That's another way of saying it,' he said.

'Harry, why bullfighting at all?' I asked him.

'That's a good question,' he said, 'because football is replacing bullfighting, especially in the cities. Bullfighting is slowly dying out.'

'Would you say that bullfighting is a rural or a city thing?'

'I'd say that it's not a modern thing,' he explained. 'It comes from the slums of both the city and the country.'

'Out of a world that is different from the kind that you and I know?'

'Distinctly.'

'Tell me a little about the world that produces bullfighters,' I asked him.

'You have asked the *big* question now,' he said. 'Often what happens outside of the ring is more interesting than what happens in the ring. If you think that what goes on in the ring is awful, then what happens before one gets into the ring is indescribable. It has never been written about. Novels have romanticized the lives of bullfighters. Their lives are sheer misery, hunger. Most of those who want to fight bulls never reach the bullring; they starve. . . .'

'How do they live?'

'From hand to mouth,' he said. 'We are not supposed to drink or bother with women. That is not to help you in fighting the bull. Fighting bulls does not require a lot of strength. That is not why you are urged to leave women and liquor alone. To live well and clean is to help you to keep in condition to recuperate when you are gored. . . . And, make no mistake, you *will* be gored. . . . That is certain. I was gored soon after I started fighting and I'm glad it happened, for now I know what it feels like. . . .

'Oh, that first time before a bull! They are huge, strong, powerful, quick, *so* quick. . . . You are standing still with that cape or *muleta*. . . . One false move and you are dead. You've got to master yourself; death is there, right before you, two feet away. . . .'

'Do bulls dislike red?' I asked.

'That's a myth,' he said. 'Bulls will charge the nearest moving object. They are colour blind.'

'Do they shut their eyes when they charge?'

'God, I wish they did! Their eyes are wide open and they see what they want to kill. They follow that moving cloth and your business is to see that you are not behind it; if you are, the bull has got you.

'Now, here is what makes bullfighting hard as a profession. Of the nine hundred and eighty bullfighters, there are about sixty famous ones. The public naturally wants to see these famous ones continually in action. Now, if each of the nine hundred and eighty bullfighters got their fair share of the three thousand and five hundred bullfights, they would fight about three and one-half times a year. But what really happens? The sixty famous bullfighters actually fight one thousand and eight hundred times, which leaves one thousand seven hundred bullfights to be scattered among nine hundred and twenty bullfighters. . . . A young man aspiring to be a bullfighter, no matter how zealously he is trying to toss his life away, has almost got to starve to do so.'

'Tell me more of the life outside the bullring,' I suggested.

'We starve and live sordid lives,' he said candidly. 'Of the young bullfighters, about fifteen or twenty make enough to live on. There are about thirty matadors who make money. The bullfighter is more hungry for food than fame. . . .

'After the season is over in October, we relax and do what we couldn't do during the season; we make up for denying ourselves. We go to Seville or Salamanca and we drink and have as much fun as we can, but we do try to keep in shape.

'Bullfighting life is dull. You live for Sunday to come so you can be in the ring. . . . You fight on Sunday, and on Monday you are in the bullfighting cafés where business is done. . . .

'Learning to fight bulls is easy; it takes about a month to learn to use the cape and *muleta*. But unless you were born around bulls, you can't learn to know them in a month. That takes years and that's what I've not got. I depend upon my aides. These Spanish boys can look at a bull for thirty seconds and they will know exactly what that bull will do. It takes me five minutes to know what the bull will do, and five minutes is too long a time; that bull can kill me during that time. . . .'

'And who is really the wild beast in the ring?' I asked him at last.

'It's the audience,' he confessed. 'There's no doubt about that. Bulls don't kill bullfighters. It's the public clamouring for more and more danger. Your public builds up a great legend about you. More and more, when you are in the ring, you are not fighting the bull; you are trying to live up to the expectations of the public. They ask for risks; they boo you when you refuse to take them. When the bullfighter believes in his legend and tries to obey the crowd, he is on his way to the graveyard. . . .'

'I'm told that bullfights in little villages are interesting,' I said.

'Would you like to see one? There's one tomorrow.'

'It's a deal,' I said.

NEXT DAY, directly after lunch, I sat in my car in front of the British-American Club and waited for Harry. The insistent honking of an auto horn attracted my attention; it was Harry, leaning out of the window of another car, beckoning to me to follow. I pulled into the stream of heavy traffic, keeping as much as possible directly behind him as he led me down narrow streets to a dilapidated tenement in front of which we stopped. A young man emerged and got into the car with Harry. Again I trailed them, this time to an apartment building on the outskirts of the city where three other men were waiting upon the sidewalk beside huge, clumsy bundles containing bullfighting gear. Harry introduced me to the men.

The bullfight team was composed of father and son, both well-known matadors. There were two banderilleros. Harry was going along to substitute for one of the others should an accident occur. There was no picador; small villages could not afford to engage them. They were an affable, polite lot, deferential yet poised towards a visiting stranger. Their mode of expressing themselves indicated that they thought in terms of images, that the world of ideas was far away. But it was clear that the pending fight had made them tense, and, though they smiled readily enough, they did not wish to do much talking. They were, as I later discovered, ridden with the most outlandish superstitions. They were dressed in casual sports clothes and each had a medallion of the Virgin dangling in the V of his opened shirt collar.

'Harry,' I asked as we prepared to get under way, 'are you religious?'

'No,' he answered, smiling.

'What do these boys think of your lack of religion?'

'At first they couldn't believe it,' he told me. 'But when they found that I would share their lives, they accepted it. They think I'm a little boy who will finally grow up some day; and, of course, when I grow up, they think that I'll naturally be Catholic. They can't conceive of anything else.'

We came to a stop in the middle of a village square covered with yellow sand. At once hundreds of astonished peasants poured, shouting and screaming, out of their homes, cafés, and bars to stare at us, the demigod bullkillers from another world. Amidst these naïve yokels I became something that I had never been before, an object that was neither human nor animal, my dark skin and city clothes attracting more attention than even the bullfighters, their beloved lay priests. I was stared at with a kind of fearful, blank, absorbed curiosity that one reserved for the unheard-of, the unnatural, the fantastic. The squat, big-breasted, broad-hipped young women seemed especially struck by me, gazing as though hypnotized at my face, nudging their friends in the ribs with their elbows as their lips sagged apart.

The sandy village square had obviously been built some centuries before with but one thought in mind: bulls. . . . For that square was really only a kind of crude, permanent bullring. Numerous thick, hand-hewn beams of heavy hardwood had been driven like stakes down through the yellow sand and into the clay, forming a rough blockade on the square's four sides, obscuring the dingy façades of the meat markets, wine shops, grocery stores, and even the delicate Gothic entrance of the local church. This was indeed a bull-conscious village, its life having been overtly organized around the compulsively ceremonious slaying of that totem animal. The heavy beams had been spaced some eighteen inches or so apart so that the body of a normal-sized man could easily squeeze through, but the spaces were small enough to keep out the body of an enraged and charging bull.

In the afternoon heat coloured pennants hung limp from the façade of the city hall and the fronts of stores and houses were decked out in gay bunting. Flies as big as the thumb buzzed and sang everywhere, alighting on the bloody bullfighting capes, trying to suck nourishment from the dried blood clots. Franco's Civil Guards, an organic part of the Spanish landscape, were planted at intervals with their efficient machine guns.

Almost everybody was wearing black or green or red paper hats. Little girls stalked to and fro in their starched dresses, waving wooden rattles that made a throbbing sound. Little boys blew whistles, setting off a hurricane of noise. The older men sat on café terraces playing cards or dominoes or drinking beer. The women, dressed in black, sat in seats high above the bullring, fanning themselves, waiting for the commencement of the excitement of blood and death. Amidst all of this strode the men of the Church, carrying their unquestioned authority and power proudly, huge silver crosses bobbing on their black-robed chests. And from a spot high on the front of the city hall a gigantic photo of the ever-watching Franco, now somewhat benign of visage, surveyed his quaint domain.

We entered a café to wash the dust out of our throats; I drank beer, but the bullfighters sipped only a little water, observing a tradition that stipulated that they could not eat or drink until after they had killed their bulls. The blaring music of a band made us rise and rush out. Musicians clad in dark blue were marching into the bullring and children followed them, clapping their hands, laughing, rolling their eyes, and cutting capers with their naked feet in the sand.

The time had come for the bullfighters to don their complicated 'suits of light' and I was honoured by being invited to watch them. Harry warned me in a whisper:

'This is a serious moment. Just sit, look, and say nothing.'

A 'dressing-room' had been set aside for them on the first floor of the city hall. The 'suits of light' were elaborate, traditional affairs. Five men were dressing and they had to pause frequently to help one another, for it was impossible for them to dress alone, so heavy and tight-fitting was the gear. They stripped down to their underwear and I saw that their bodies were a mass of mangled tissue, scars and gashes from previous gorings. First, they struggled into narrow-legged trousers of raw silk brocaded with gold and adorned with tassels. Next they buttoned pleated and ruffled white shirts and tied little black bow ties. Then came pink silk stockings, two pairs of them, one being put on over the other in the hope that a bull's horn would glide harmlessly off the leg.

'You'll notice,' Harry whispered to me, 'that we follow a strict routine in dressing. We always put on our suits of clothes in the order that you have observed.'

'Why?' I wanted to know.

'Custom,' he said. 'Superstition.'

'What happens if a bullfighter is wounded?' I asked him. 'You are laced and dressed like a knight of the Middle Ages,' I told him. 'How on earth could a doctor get at a wound with all that regalia strapped on to the body?'

'A doctor'd have to cut this stuff off us if we were wounded,' he said. 'If he tried to undress us, we would bleed to death before he could get to the wound. . . .'

It took them more than an hour and a half to put on the heavy silk suits and, when they were finished, they were forced to move about with stiff, almost slow movements, so laced and buckled were they. Then, from out of a box, they took a flat package done up in crumpled, brown wrapping paper; they untied it and spread out a three-flapped photo which, when perched upon a table, proved to be a coloured image of the Virgin. One by one, they all, excepting Harry, went and knelt before it, closing their eyes and praying silently. They crossed themselves, then rose. Without a word being uttered, they gathered up their capes, *muletas,* and swords and marched directly towards the bullring. I ran to the balcony to see them enter.

It was not an emotional bullfight, but some odd and revealing things did occur. The bulls were not good and they had to be run and played long and violently to get them to lower their heads, for they had no picadors to punish the humps of muscle in the bulls' powerful necks.

The first bull bounded into the ring to wild cheers. He was an unruly beast, often refusing to charge and, when he did charge, he did so at the wrong times, hooking viciously. When the matador finally killed him, hundreds of men and boys squeezed through the spaces in the stockade and swarmed on to the sand of the ring and converged upon the dead bull's carcass. Then something happened that made my lips part in utter astonishment. The crowd went straight to the dead bull's testicles and began kicking them, stamping them, spitting at them, grinding them under their heels, while their eyes held a glazed and excited look of sadism. They mutilated the testicles of the dead bull for more than ten minutes, until the dead bull's carcass was hauled away.

And the same strange, sadistic ceremony was inflicted by the excited crowd upon the second dead bull's testicles—there were only three bulls killed that afternoon—and they did not cease until the dead bull's carcass had been taken from them. One would have to be psychologically blind to miss the meaning of that. That dead bull had been a proud, sireing, fighting, lascivious sexual machine and now, having been ceremoniously slain, they went straight to the real object on that dead bull's body that the bull had symbolized for them and poured out the hate and frustration and bewilderment of their troubled and confused consciousnesses.

I was later told that in some backward villages the men and the women smeared their faces and bodies with the blood of the dead bull, hoping thereby to gain potency or be cured of various diseases, particularly tuberculosis. In many backward areas the meat of the ceremoniously slain bull commanded a higher price than that of ordinary beef.

12 Million Black Voices

A Folk History of the Negro in the U.S.

On the heels of the success of Native Son, *Wright worked simultaneously on the stage adaptation of that novel with Paul Green and collaborated with photographer Edwin Rosskam on a "folk history of the Negro in the United States." Although Rosskam used some of his own photographs in the book, he mainly selected other photographers' works from the Farm Security Administration (FSA) picture collection for this project. Wright's accompanying text evolved from his friend Horace Cayton's extensive files on the Black migrant in Chicago (these files were later used in* Black Metropolis). *He was able to develop from Cayton's information a complex sociological and historical frame with a generally Marxist perspective. Yet the sheer beauty of* 12 Million Black Voices *results largely from the mastery with which his prose clothed this conceptual framework in poetic images without ever detracting from the suggestive visual beauty of the photographs themselves.*

This book was important to Wright; it represented one of his major preoccupations, namely, to retrace through the generations the whole story of the Negro in America, which he regarded as emblematic of that of the Third World and of modern man at large. The tale of the Black migrants,

12 Million Black Voices was first published by Viking Press in 1941. Some of the original pictures used in this work have been deleted for this edition.

illuminated by the heritage of slavery and dominated by economic exploitation in the post-Reconstruction South, forms the motif of this saga. It is told in a poetic prose style which Arna Bontemps accurately describes as belonging to the authentic tradition of the blues and spirituals. But the final section does not end on a blues note. It is a defiant, triumphant challenge to racist America, which not only heralds the militancy of the Civil Rights Movement but foreshadows more revolutionary contemporary attitudes.

1. Our Strange Birth

EACH DAY when you see us black folk upon the dusty land of the farms or upon the hard pavement of the city streets, you usually take us for granted and think you know us, but our history is far stranger than you suspect, and we are not what we seem. Our outward guise still carries the old familiar aspect which three hundred years of oppression in America have given us, but beneath the garb of the black laborer, the black cook, and the black elevator operator lies an uneasily tied knot of pain and hope whose snarled strands converge from many points of time and space.

We millions of black folk who live in this land were born into Western civilization of a weird and paradoxical birth. The lean, tall, blond men of England, Holland, and Denmark, the dark, short, nervous men of France, Spain, and Portugal, men whose blue and gray and brown eyes glinted with the light of the future, denied our human personalities, tore us from our native soil, weighted our legs with chains, stacked us like cord-wood in the foul holes of clipper ships, dragged us across thousands of miles of ocean, and hurled us into another land, strange and hostile, where for a second time we felt the slow, painful process of a new birth amid conditions harsh and raw.

The immemorial stars must have gazed down in amazement at the lowly of England and Europe, who, with
hearts full of hope, pushed out to sea to urge rebellion
against tyranny and then straightway became engaged in
the slave trade, in the buying and selling of our human
bodies. And those same stars must have smiled when, following the War of Independence, the Lords of the Land
in the South relaxed their rigid slave code ever so little to

square their guilty conscience with the lofty ideals of the rights of man for which they had fought and died; but never did they relax their code so much as to jeopardize their claim of ownership of us.

Our captors were hard men, brutal men; yet they held locked somewhere within their hearts the fertile seeds that were to sprout into a new world culture, that were to blossom into a higher human consciousness. Escaping from the fetid medieval dens, angrily doffing the burial sheets of feudal religion, and flushed with a new and noble concept of life, of its inherent dignity, of its unlimited possibilities, of its natural worth, these men leaped upon the road of progress; and their leap was the windfall of our tragedy. Their excessive love of life wove a deadly web of slavery that snared our naked feet. Their sense of the possibility of building a more humane world brought devastation and despair to our pointed huts on the long, tan shores of Africa. We were an unlucky people; the very contours and harbors of our native land conspired against our freedom. The coastline of our Africa was long and flat and easy to invade; we had no mountains to serve as natural forts from behind which we could fight and stave off the slave traders.

We had our own civilization in Africa before we were captured and carried off to this land. You may smile when we call the way of life we lived in Africa "civilization," but in numerous respects the culture of many of our tribes was equal to that of the lands from which the slave captors came. We smelted iron, danced, made music, and recited folk poems; we sculptured, worked in glass, spun cotton and wool, wove baskets and cloth; we invented a medium of exchange, mined silver and gold, made pottery and cutlery; we fashioned tools and utensils of brass, bronze, ivory, quartz, and granite; we had our own literature, our own systems of law, religion, medicine, science, and education; we painted in color upon rocks; we raised cattle, sheep, and goats; we planted and harvested grain—in short, centuries before the Romans ruled, we lived as men.

Our humanity, however, did not save us; the New England Puritans and the imperialists of Europe erected the traffic in our bodies into the "big business" of the eighteenth century, and but few industries the world has ever known have yielded higher profits. There were "tricks of the trade" then as now; the slave traders, operators of fleets of stench-ridden sailing vessels, were comparable to our contemporary "captains of industry" and "tycoons of finance," and the Union Jack and the Stars and Stripes fluttered from the masts of men-of-war as the ensign of protection for "free trade" in our bodies. It was mainly the kings of vast rum distilleries who owned the ships that scoured the seven seas in search of our bodies. Jew as well as Gentile took part in these voyages of plunder. Nation waged war against nation for the right to buy and sell us, just as today they fight for "markets and raw materials." To Africa the traders brought rum and swapped it to corrupt chiefs for our bodies; we were then taken to the colonies, the West Indies, Cuba, and Brazil and used as currency to buy molasses; the molasses in turn was taken to the distilleries of New England and bartered for rum, which formed the basis for another slave voyage.

The slave ships, equipped for long voyages, were floating brothels for the slave traders of the seventeenth and eighteenth centuries. Bound by heavy chains, we gazed impassively upon the lecherous crew members as they vented the pent-up bestiality of their starved sex lives upon our sisters and wives. This was a peculiar practice which, as the years flowed past, grew into a clandestine but well-established institution which the owners of cotton and tobacco plantations upheld, and which today, in large measure, accounts for the widespread mulatto population in the United States. Indeed, there were slave-breeding farms. Slaves were valuable; cotton meant cash, and each able-bodied slave could be depended upon to produce at least 5000 pounds of cotton each year.

The *Mayflower's* nameless sister ship, presumably a Dutch vessel, which stole into the harbor of Jamestown in 1619 and unloaded her human cargo of 20 of us, was but the first such ship to touch the shores of this New World, and her arrival signalized what was to be our trial for centuries to come. More than 14,000,000 of us were brought to America alone. For every 100 of us who survived the terrible journey across the Atlantic, the so-called "middle passage" of these voyages,

400 of us perished. During three hundred years—the seventeenth, eighteenth, and nineteenth centuries—more than 100,000,000 of us were torn from our African homes. Until the dawn of the nineteenth century, slavery was legal the world over.

Laid out spoon-fashion on the narrow decks of sailing ships, we were transported to this New World so closely packed that the back of the head of one of us nestled between the legs of another. Sometimes 720 of us were jammed into a space 20 feet wide, 120 feet long, and 5 feet high. Week after week we would lie there, tortured and gasping, as the ship heaved and tossed over the waves. In the summer, down in the suffocating depths of those ships, on an eight- or ten-week voyage, we would go crazed for lack of air and water, and in the morning the crew of the ship would discover many of us dead, clutching in rigor mortis at the throats of our friends, wives, or children.

During the seventeenth century, to protect themselves against the overwhelming influx of us, some governments launched numerous men-of-war to track down and seize the slave ships. We captives did not know whether to feel dread or joy when a man-of-war was sighted, for the captain would command that a few of us be pitched alive into the sea as moral bait to compel the captain of the pursuing ship to desist from his duty. Every mile or so one of us would be bound fast to a cask or spar and tossed overboard with the hope that the sight of our forlorn struggle against the sea would stir such compassion in the heart of the captain of the man-of-war that he would abandon pursuit, thereby enabling the slave ships to escape.

At other times, when we were sick, we were thrown alive into the sea and the captain, pilgrim of progress, would studiously enter into the ship's log two words that would balance all earthly accounts: "jettisoned cargo."

At still other times we went on hunger strikes; but the time allotted us to starve to death was often too short, and the ship would arrive in port before we had outwitted the slave traders. The more ambitious slavers possessed instruments with which to pry our teeth apart and feed us forcibly. Whenever we could we leaped into the sea.

To quench all desire for mutiny in us, they would sometimes decapitate a few of us and impale our black heads upon the tips of the spars, just as years later they impaled our heads upon the tips of pine trees for miles along the dusty highways of Dixie to frighten us into obedience.

Captivity under Christendom blasted our lives, disrupted our families, reached down into the personalities of each one of us and destroyed the very images and symbols which had guided our minds and feelings in the effort to live. Our folkways and folk tales, which had once given meaning and sanction to our actions, faded from consciousness. Our gods were dead and answered us no more. The trauma of leaving our African home, the suffering of the long middle passage, the thirst, the hunger, the horrors of the slave ship—all these hollowed us out, numbed us, stripped us, and left only physiological urges, the feelings of fear and fatigue.

Against the feudal background of denials of love and happiness, the trade in our bodies bred god-like men who exalted honor, enthroned impulse, glorified aspiration, celebrated individuality, and fortified the human heart to strive against the tyrannical forms of nature and to bend obstreperous materials closer to a mold that would slake human desire. As time elapsed, these new men seized upon the unfolding discoveries of science and invention, and, figuratively, their fingers became hot as fire and hard as steel. Literature, art, music, and philosophy set their souls aflame with a desire for the new mode of living that had come into the world. Exploration opened wide the entire surface of the earth as a domain of adventure.

Window glass, drugs to dull pain, printing presses, larger ships, bigger and more powerful guns—these and a thousand other commodities began to spread across the area of man's living and give it a new quality. Never before had human life on earth felt more confident; human feelings grew sensitive and complex, and human sentiment, pouring from the newly released human organism, wrapped itself about the whole world, each man and object in it, creating an all-powerful atmosphere of ambition and passion in which we black slaves were the main objects of exploitation.

Sustained by an incredible hope such as the world had never felt before, the slavers continued to snatch us by the millions from our native African soil to be used as tools to till the tobacco, rice, sugar-cane, and cotton plantations; they built powerful empires, replete with authority and comfort, and, as a protecting superstructure, they spun tight ideological webs of their right to domination. Daily these eager men slashed off the rotting trappings of feudal life, a life which for centuries had endowed man with a metaphysical worth, rank, use, and order; and, in its stead, they launched the foundations of a new dispensation to prove that man could step beyond the boundaries of ignorance and superstition and live by reason. And they shackled millions of us to labor for them, to give them the instrumentalities.

But as we blacks toiled, millions of poor free whites, against whom our slave labor was pitted, were rendered indigent and helpless. The gold of slave-grown cotton concentrated the political power of the Old South in the hands of a few Lords of the Land, and the poor whites decreased in number as we blacks increased. To protect their delicately balanced edifice of political power, the Lords of the Land proceeded to neutralize the strength of us blacks and the growing restlessness of the poor whites by dividing and ruling us, by inciting us against one another. But, complementing this desire for safety, there was the growth of the hunger for more wealth, and the Lords of the Land increased their importations of us, and in turn we blacks continued to squeeze the poor whites to lower levels of living. Fear became the handmaid of cotton culture, spreading and deepening; but the slave ships sailed on, bringing thousands of us yearly to the New World.

The beginning of the eighteenth century marked the rise of a fully developed anti-slavery sentiment in the North. Tardily, the French Revolution captured to some degree the imagination of the New England Puritans, and again there sounded a passionate, humanitarian belief in the rights of man; and, overlapping this, there came the religious exhortations of the Quakers, with their mystical belief in the Golden Rule. And we black tools responded as fervently as did the rest of mankind to the call of Liberty, Equality, and Fraternity, to the expressed conviction that all men were equal in the sight of God. Fury swept the hearts of the Lords of the Land who heard spilling from the thick, black lips of their tools the first broken syllables of freedom, the first stammered assertions of manhood. The foundations of their world trembled and they turned their eyes to God, seized whips, knives, or guns, and rushed forth, bellowing to set aright the order of the universe.

In the latter part of the eighteenth century, however, the conduct of most of the Lords of the Land began to alter toward us. To evade the prevailing Christian injunction that all baptized men are free, and to chcck our growing record of revolt, they culled from the Bible a thousand quotable verses admonishing us slaves to be true to our masters. Thereupon they felt that they had squared conscience with practice, and they extended Christian salvation to us without granting the boon of freedom. This dual attitude, compounded of a love of gold and God, was the beginning of America's paternalistic code toward her black maid, her black industrial worker, her black stevedore, her black dancer, her black waiter, her black sharecropper; it was a code of casual cruelty, of brutal kindness, of genial despotism, a code which has survived, grown, spread, and congealed into a national tradition that dominates, in small or large measure, all black and white relations throughout the nation until this day.

How did this paradoxical amalgam of love and cruelty come to be? Well, men are many and each has his work to do. A division of labor among men, splitting them up into groups and classes, enables whole segments of populations to be so influenced by their material surroundings that they see

The black maid

The black industrial worker

The black stevedore

The black dancer

The black sharecropper

The black waiter

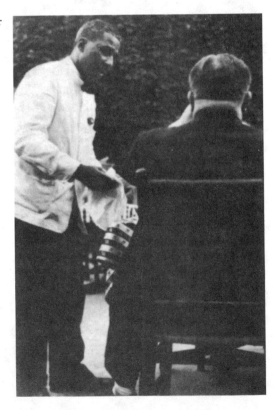

but a little phase of the complex process of their lives and the whole is obscured from them, thereby affording them the unfortunate opportunity to move and work at cross-purposes with one another, even though in their hearts they may feel that they are engaged in a crusade of common hope.

So our bent backs continued to give design and order to the fertile plantations. Stately governmental structures and vast palatial homes were reared by our black hands to reflect the genteel glory of the new age. And the Lords of the Land created and administered laws in the belief that *their* God ruled in Heaven, that He sanctioned this new day. After they had amassed mountains of wealth, they compared the wretchedness of our lives with the calm gentility of theirs and felt that they were truly the favored of God. The lyrical mantle of prayer and hymn, accordingly, justified and abetted our slavery; and whenever we murmured against the degradation of the plantation, the Lords of the Land acted against us with whips and hate to protect their God-sanctioned civilization.

Our black bodies were good tools that had to be kept efficient for toil. Therefore, when schools were built, it was decreed that we must not partake of the teaching in them. When praises were sung to God, it was decided that we must not lift our voices in common hymn. Time and again we rose and struck angrily for freedom; sometimes we revolted in two's and three's; at other times we rose by the thousands, trying to break through the white wall that hemmed us in.

Convinced now at last of peril, the Lords of the Land began to drape their possessions in the protective hues of rationalism, to write and preach of their humanity and justice, but they found that the lash and the mob were needed to keep their positions of power, and soon these twin serpents of terror were organically entwined about the columns of legal government.

The eyes of the Lords of the Land grew challenging; but, blinded by the glittering prize they sought to keep, they could not detect the stealthy forces at work in the world, forces which were destined to wreck their empire and disperse us black men like whirling atoms upon the face of the earth.

The hope which had lured millions of restless men into the New World still lived precariously in many hearts, untouched by the fever of possession and the seduction of power. From English and Yankee brains there came in quick succession the spinning jenny, the spinning mule, and the application of steam power. There began to crawl across the landscape lumbering machines that magically threatened to turn millions of our black fingers idle. And the generous earth, once so green and so new, began to rot the seed and stunt the plant, forcing the Lords of the Land, in their search for new soil, to migrate westward, where they clashed with free men to whom the slave ethic was useless and obnoxious.

Eastern industry, which had begun to flood the nation with commodities, was owned by men who wielded a new type of authority. Free white labor of the North and West built thousands upon thousands of buildings—dwellings, shops, factories, mills, and foundries—and the Bosses of the Buildings, the bankers, foresaw that the day was coming when we slaves would not be worth the food we ate. These men grew alarmed over the fate of their nation and over their own ultimate racial identity in face of the black tide of us who were being poured out of the clipper ships.

The opinion of the nation divided into two opposing constellations: a world of machines and a world of slaves. Two groups of leaders sprang up: the Bosses of the Buildings and the Lords of the Land. As the full consequences of the two divergent ways of life became manifest, millions began an impassioned questioning of the basis of the ideas which they had sought to make operative in the New World. A small minority, both north and south, felt outraged at a system of human bondage that nullified all they had so ardently striven to build, and many sensitive men grew violent against *all* government and went up and down the land propounding the principles of passive resistance and civil disobedience.

In an atmosphere of such tension, the whites began to distrust each other. Therefore, when the Bosses of the Buildings suggested that we blacks be deported and colonized, the Lords of the Land rose and threatened to resort to a wholesale breeding of slaves in order not to be deprived of our living bodies. And, on the other hand, when the Lords of the Land, afraid of our growing numbers and increasing rebelliousness, suggested that the entire nation be taxed to raise money to deport us, the Bosses of the Buildings declared that such a course would destroy the capital of the nation, stifle productivity, and crush the poor whites, who were already being smothered in the slave atmosphere. But as we blacks continued to multiply and spread, the Lords of the Land sought to distribute us on the plantations so that our population would never exceed that of the whites or grow so great in any one area as to constitute an insurrectionary danger.

To enjoy a spell more of time in their cool mansions, the majority of the Lords of the Land disciplined the animal panic in their hearts and decided to hang on; they declared their independence, and war was waged for new lands to expand in, for the right to import more of us to raise cotton. And the Bosses of the Buildings, eager to manufacture and sell their commodities, stood against them in four years of battle to protect themselves, their future, and their hope of an industrial civilization.

We were freed because of a gnawing of some obscure sense of guilt, because of a cloudy premonition of impending disaster, because of a soil becoming rapidly impoverished, because of the hunger for fresh land, because of the new logic of life that came in the wake of clanking machines—it was all these things, and not the strength of moral ideals alone, that lessened the grip of the Lords of the Land upon us.

We black men and women in America today, as we look back upon scenes of rapine, sacrifice, and death, seem to be children of a devilish aberration, descendants of an interval of nightmare in history, fledglings of a period of amnesia on the part of men who once dreamed a great dream and forgot.

2. Inheritors of Slavery

THE WORD "NEGRO," the term by which, orally or in print,
we black folk in the United States are usually designated, is
not really a name at all nor a description, but a psychological
island whose objective form is the most unanimous fiat in all
American history; a fiat buttressed by popular and national
tradition, and written down in many state and city statutes;

a fiat which artificially and arbitrarily defines, regulates, and limits in scope of meaning the vital contours of our lives, and the lives of our children and our children's children.

This island, within whose confines we live, is anchored in the feelings of millions of people, and is situated in the midst of the sea of white faces we meet each day; and, by and large, as three hundred years of time has borne our nation into the twentieth century, its rocky boundaries have remained unyielding to the waves of our hope that dash against it.

The steep cliffs of this island are manifest, on the whole, in the conduct of whites toward us hour by hour, a conduct which tells us that we possess no rights commanding respect, that we have no claim to pursue happiness in our own fashion, that our progress toward civilization constitutes an insult, that our behavior must be kept firmly within an orbit branded as inferior, that we must be compelled to labor at the behest of others, that as a group we are owned by the whites, and that manliness on our part warrants instant reprisal.

Three hundred years are a long time for millions of folk like us to be held in such subjection, so long a time that perhaps scores of years will have to pass before we shall be able to express what this slavery has done to us, for our

personalities are still numb from its long shocks; and, as the numbness leaves our souls, we shall yet have to feel and give utterance to the full pain we shall inherit.

More than one-half of us black folk in the United States are tillers of the soil, and three-fourths of those of us who till the soil are sharecroppers and day laborers.

The land we till is beautiful, with red and black and brown clay, with fresh and hungry smells, with pine trees and palm trees, with rolling hills and swampy delta—an unbelievably fertile land, bounded on the north by the states of Pennsylvania, Ohio, Illinois, and Indiana, on the south by the Gulf of Mexico, on the west by the Mississippi River, and on the east by the Atlantic Ocean.

Our southern springs are filled with quiet noises and scenes of growth. Apple buds laugh into blossom. Honeysuckles creep up the sides of houses. Sunflowers nod in the hot fields. From mossy tree to mossy tree—oak, elm, willow, aspen, sycamore, dogwood, cedar, walnut, ash, and hickory—bright green leaves jut from a million branches to form an awning

that tries to shield and shade the earth. Blue and pink kites of small boys sail in the windy air.

In summer the magnolia trees fill the countryside with sweet scent for long miles. Days are slumberous, and the skies are high and thronged with clouds that ride fast. At midday the sun blazes and bleaches the soil. Butterflies flit through the heat; wasps sing their sharp, straight lines; birds fluff and flounce, piping in querulous joy. Nights are covered with canopies sometimes blue and sometimes black, canopies that sag low with ripe and nervous stars. The throaty boast of frogs momentarily drowns out the call and counter-call of crickets.

In autumn the land is afire with color. Red and brown leaves lift and flutter dryly, becoming entangled in the stiff grass and cornstalks. Cotton is picked and ginned; cane is crushed and its juice is simmered down into molasses; yams are grubbed out of the clay; hogs are slaughtered and cured in lingering smoke; corn is husked and ground into meal. At twilight the sky is full of wild geese winging ever southward, and bats jerk through the air. At night the winds blow free.

In winter the forests resound with the bite of steel axes eating into tall trees as men gather wood for the leaden days of cold. The guns of hunters snap and crack. Long days of rain come, and our swollen creeks rush to join a hundred rivers that wash across the land and make great harbors where they feed the gulf or the sea. Occasionally the rivers leap their banks and leave new thick layers of silt to enrich the earth, and then the look of the land is garish, bleak, suffused with a first-day stillness, strangeness, and awe.

But whether in spring or summer or autumn or winter, time slips past us remorselessly, and it is hard to tell of the iron that lies beneath the surface of our quiet, dull days.

To paint the picture of how we live on the tobacco, cane, rice, and cotton plantations is to compete with mighty artists: the movies, the radio, the newspapers, the magazines, and even the Church. They have painted one picture: charming, idyllic, romantic; but we live another: full of the fear of the Lords of the Land, bowing and grinning when we meet white faces, toiling from sun to sun, living in unpainted wooden shacks that sit casually and insecurely upon the red clay.

In the main we are different from other folk in that, when an impulse moves us, when we are caught in the throes of inspiration, when we are moved to better our lot, we do not ask ourselves: "Can we do it?" but: "Will they let us do it?" Before we black folk can move, we must first look into the white man's mind to see what is there, to see what he is thinking, and the white man's mind is a mind that is always changing.

In general there are three classes of men above us: the Lords of the Land—operators of the plantations; the Bosses of the Buildings—the owners of industry; and the vast numbers of poor white workers—our immediate competitors in the daily struggle for bread. The Lords of the Land hold sway over the plantations and over us; the Bosses of the Buildings lend money and issue orders to the Lords of the Land. The Bosses of the Buildings feed upon the Lords of the Land, and the Lords of the Land feed upon the 5,000,000 landless poor whites and upon us, throwing to the poor whites the scant solace of filching from us 4,000,000 landless blacks what the poor whites themselves are cheated of in this elaborate game.

Back of this tangled process is a long history. When the Emancipation Proclamation was signed, there were some 4,000,000 of us black folk stranded and bewildered upon the land which we had tilled under compulsion for two and a half centuries. Sundered suddenly from the only relationship with Western civilization we had been allowed to form since our captivity, our personalities blighted by two hundred and fifty years of servitude, and eager to hold our wives and husbands and children together in family units, some of us turned back to the same Lords of the Land who had held us as slaves and begged for work, resorted to their advice; and there began for us a new kind of bondage: sharecropping.

Glad to be free, some of us drifted and gave way to every vagary of impulse that swept through us, being held in the line of life only by the necessity to work and eat. Confined for centuries to the life of the cotton field, many of us possessed no feelings of family, home, community, race, church, or progress. We could scarcely believe that we were free, and our restlessness and incessant mobility were our naïve way of testing that freedom. Just as a kitten stretches and yawns after a long sleep, so thousands of us tramped from place to place for the sheer sake of moving, looking, wondering, landless upon the land. Arkansas, Missouri, Tennessee, Kentucky, North Carolina, South Carolina, Louisiana, Alabama, Mississippi, Georgia, Virginia, and West Virginia became the home states of us freed blacks.

In 1890 many white people predicted that we black folk would perish in a competitive world; but in spite of this we left the land and kept afloat, wandering from Natchez to New Orleans, from Mobile to Montgomery, from Macon to Jacksonville, from Birmingham to Chattanooga, from Nashville to Louisville, from Memphis to Little Rock—laboring in the sawmills, in the turpentine camps, on the road jobs; working for men who did not care if we lived or died, but who did not want their business enterprises to suffer for lack of labor. During the first decade of the twentieth century, more than one and three-quarter millions of us abandoned the plantations upon which we had been born; more than a million of us roamed the states of the South and the remainder of us drifted north.

Our women fared easier than we men during the early days of freedom; on the whole their relationship to the world was more stable than ours. Their authority was supreme in most of our families inasmuch as many of them had worked in the "Big Houses" of the Lords of the Land and had learned manners, had been taught to cook, sew, and nurse. During slave days they did not always belong to us, for the Lords of the Land often took them for their pleasure. When a gang of us was sold from one plantation to another, our wives would sometimes be kept by the Lords of the Land and we men would have to mate with whatever slave girl we chanced upon. Because of their enforced intimacy with the Lords of the Land, many of our women, after they were too old to work, were allowed to remain in the slave cabins to tend generations of black children. They enjoyed a status denied us men, being called "Mammy"; and through the years they became symbols of motherhood, retaining in their withered bodies the burden of our folk wisdom, reigning as arbiters in our domestic affairs until we men were freed and had moved to cities where cash-paying jobs enabled us to become the heads of our own families.

The economic and political power of the South is not held in our hands; we do not own banks, iron and steel mills, railroads, office buildings, ships, wharves, or power plants. There are some few of us who operate small grocery stores, barber shops, rooming houses, burial societies, and undertaking establishments. But none of us owns any of the basic industries that shape the course of the South, such as mining, lumber, textiles, oil, transportation, or electric power. So, in the early spring, when the rains have ceased and the ground is ready for plowing, we present ourselves to the Lords of the Land and ask to make a crop. We sign a contract—usually our contracts are oral—which allows us to keep one-half of the harvest after all debts are paid. If we have worked upon these plantations before, we are legally bound to plant, tend, and harvest another crop. If we should escape to the city to avoid paying our mounting debts, white policemen track us down and ship us back to the plantation.

The Lords of the Land assign us ten or fifteen acres of soil already bled of its fertility through generations of abuse. They advance us one mule, one plow, seed, tools, fertilizer, clothing, and food, the main staples of which are fat hog meat, coarsely ground corn meal, and sorghum molasses. If we have been lucky the year before, maybe we have saved a few dollars to tide us through the fall months, but spring finds us begging an "advance"—credit—from the Lords of the Land.

From now on the laws of Queen Cotton rule our lives. (Contrary to popular assumption, cotton is a *queen,* not a king. Kings are dictatorial; cotton is not only dictatorial but self-destructive, an imperious woman in the throes of constant childbirth, a woman who is driven by her greedy passion to bear endless bales of cotton, though she well knows that she will die if she continues to give birth to her fleecy children!) If we black folk had only to work to feed the Lords of the Land, to supply delicacies for their tables—as did the slaves of old for their masters—our degradation upon the

168

plantations would not have been the harshest form of human servitude the world has ever known. But we had to raise cotton to clothe the world; cotton meant money, and money meant power and authority and prestige. To plant vegetables for our tables was often forbidden, for raising a garden narrowed the area to be planted in cotton. The world demanded cotton, and the Lords of the Land ordered more acres to be planted—planted right up to our doorsteps!—and the ritual of Queen Cotton became brutal and bloody.

Because they feel that they cannot trust us, the Lords of the Land assign a "riding boss" to go from cotton patch to cotton patch and supervise our work. We pay for the cost of this supervision out of our share of the harvest; we pay interest on the cost of the supplies which the Lords of the Land advance to us; and, because illness and death, rain and sun, boll weevil and storms, are hazards which might work to the detriment of the cotton crop, we agree to pay at harvest a

The laws of Queen Cotton rule our lives

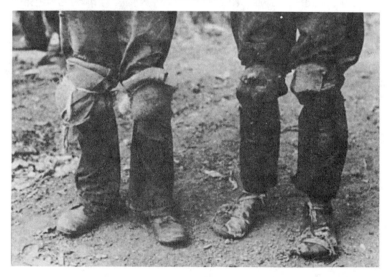

"time price," a sum payable in cotton, corn, or cane, which the Lords of the Land charge us to cover a probable loss on their investment in us.

We who have followed the plow in this fashion have developed a secret life and language of our own. When we were first brought here from our innumerable African tribes, each of us spoke the language of his tribe. But the Lords of the Land decreed that we must be distributed upon the plantations so that no two of us who spoke a common tongue would be thrown together, lest we plot rebellion. So they shackled one slave to another slave of an alien tribe. Our eyes would look wistfully into the face of a fellow-victim of slavery, but we could say no word to him. Though we could hear, we were deaf; though we could speak, we were dumb!

We stole words from the grudging lips of the Lords of the Land, who did not want us to know too many of them or their meaning. And we charged this meager horde of stolen sounds with all the emotions and longings we had; we proceeded to build our language in inflections of voice, through tonal variety, by hurried speech, in honeyed drawls, by rolling our eyes, by flourishing our hands, by assigning to common, simple words new meanings, meanings which enabled us to speak of revolt in the actual presence of the Lords of the Land without their being aware! Our secret language extended our understanding of what slavery meant and gave us the freedom to speak to our brothers in captivity; we polished our new words, caressed them, gave them new shape and color, a new order and tempo, until, though they were the words of the Lords of the Land, they became *our* words, *our* language.

The steady impact of the plantation system upon our lives created new types of behavior and new patterns of psychological reaction, welding us together into a separate unity with common characteristics of our own. We strove each day to maintain that kind of external behavior that would best allay the fear and hate of the Lords of the Land, and over a period of years this dual conduct became second nature to us and we found in it a degree of immunity from daily oppression. Even when a white man asked us an innocent question, some unconscious part of us would listen closely, not only to the obvious words, but also to the intonations of voice that indicated what kind of answer he wanted; and, automatically, we would determine whether an affirmative or negative reply was expected, and we would answer, not in terms of objective truth, but in terms of what the white man wished to hear.

If a white man stopped a black on a southern road and asked: "Say, there, boy! It's one o'clock, isn't it?" the black man would answer: "Yessuh."

If the white man asked: "Say, it's not one o'clock, is it, boy?" the black man would answer: "Nawsuh."

And if the white man asked: "It's ten miles to Memphis, isn't it, boy?" the black man would answer: "Yessuh."

And if the white man asked: "It isn't ten miles to Memphis, is it, boy?" the black man would answer: "Nawsuh."

Always we said what we thought the whites wanted us to say.

So our years pass within the web of a system we cannot beat. Years of fat meat and corn meal and sorghum molasses, years of plowing and hoeing and picking, years of sun and wind and rain—these are the years that do with us what they will, that form our past, shape our present, and loom ahead as the outline of our future.

Most of the flogging and lynchings occur at harvest time, when fruit hangs heavy and ripe, when the leaves are red and gold, when nuts fall from the trees, when the earth offers its best. The thought of harvest steals upon us with a sense of an inescapable judgment. It is time now to settle accounts with the Lords of the Land, to divide the crops and pay old debts, and we are afraid. We have never grown used to confronting the Lords of the Land when the last of the cotton is ginned and baled, for we know beforehand that we have

lost yet another race with time, that we are deeper in debt. When word reaches us that the Lords of the Land are bent over the big books down at the plantation commissary, we lower our eyes, shake our heads, and mutter:

> *A naught's a naught,*
> *Five's a figger;*
> *All for the white man,*
> *None for the nigger. . . .*

If the Lord of the Land for whom we are working happens to be a foreigner who came to the United States to escape oppression in Europe, and who has taken to the native way of cheating us, we spit and mutter:

> *Red, white, and blue,*
> *Your daddy was a Jew,*
> *Your ma's a dirty dago,*
> *Now what the hell is you? . . .*

And after we have divided the crops we are still entangled as deeply as ever in this hateful web of cotton culture. We are older; our bodies are weaker; our families are larger; our clothes are in rags; we are still in debt; and, worst of all, we face another year that holds even less hope than the one we have just endured. We know that this is not right, and dark thoughts take possession of our minds. We know that to tread this mill is to walk in days of slow death. When alone, we

The law is white

stand and look out over the green, rolling fields and wonder why it is that living here is so hard. Everything seems to whisper of the possibility of happiness, of satisfying experiences; but somehow happiness and satisfaction never come into our lives. The land upon which we live holds a promise, but the promise fades with the passing seasons.

And we know that if we protest we will be called "bad niggers." The Lords of the Land will preach the doctrine of "white supremacy" to the poor whites who are eager to form mobs. In the midst of general hysteria they will seize one of us—it does not matter who, the innocent or guilty—and, as a token, a naked and bleeding body will be dragged through the dusty streets. The mobs will make certain that our token-death is known throughout the quarters where we black folk live. Our bodies will be swung by ropes from the limbs of trees, will be shot at and mutilated.

And we cannot fight back; we have no arms; we cannot vote; and the law is white. There are no black policemen, black justices of the peace, black judges, black juries, black jailers, black mayors, or black men anywhere in the government of the South. The Ku Klux Klan attacks us in a thousand ways, driving our boys and girls off the jobs in the cities and keeping us who live on the land from protesting or asking too many questions.

This is the way the Lords of the Land keep their power. For them life is a continuous victory; for us it is simply trouble in the land. Fear is with us always, and in those areas where we black men equal or outnumber the whites fear is at its highest. Two streams of life flow through the South, a black stream and a white stream, and from day to day we live in the atmosphere of a war that never ends. Even when the sprawling fields are drenched in peaceful sunshine, it is war. When we grub at the clay with our hoes, it is war. When we sleep, it is war. When we are awake, it is war. When one of us is born, he enters one of the warring regiments of the South. When there are days of peace, it is a peace born of a victory over us; and when there is open violence, it is when we are trying to push back the encroachments of the Lords of the Land.

Sometimes, fleetingly, like a rainbow that comes and vanishes in its coming, the wan faces of the poor whites make us think that perhaps we can join our hands with them and lift the weight of the Lords of the Land off our backs. But, before new meanings can bridge the chasm that has been long created between us, the poor whites are warned by the Lords of the Land that they must cast their destiny with their own color, that to make common cause with us is to threaten the foundations of civilization. Fear breeds in our hearts until each poor white face begins to look like the face of an enemy soldier. We learn that almost all white men feel it is their duty to see that we do not go beyond the prescribed boundaries. And so both of us, the poor black and the poor white, are kept poor, and only the Lords of the Land grow rich. When we black folk are alone together, we point to the poor whites and croon with vindictiveness:

> *I don't like liver*
> *I don't like hash*
> *I'd rather be a nigger*
> *Than poor white trash. . . .*

And then, conversely, when we compare our hopelessness with the vast vistas of progress about us, when we feel self-disgust at our bare lot, when we contemplate our lack of courage in the face of daily force, we are seized with a desire to escape our shameful identification; and, overwhelmed emotionally, we seek to become protectively merged with the least-known and farthest removed race of men we know; yes, when we weigh ourselves and find ourselves wanting, we say with a snicker of self-depreciation:

> *White folks is evil*
> *And niggers is too*
> *So glad I'm a Chinaman*
> *I don't know what to do. . . .*

There is something "funny" about the hate of the poor whites for us and our hate for them. Our minds fight against it, but external reality freezes us into stances of mutual resistance. And the irony of it is that both of us, the poor white and the poor black, are spoken of by the Lords of the Land as "our men." When they stride along and see us working their fields, they point to us and speak of us as though they owned us, saying: "There are our men." Jobs are few and the Lords of the Land know it, and when they refer to us, black or white, we are always "somebody's men."

So we stay fixed in attitudes of opposition, as though the Lords of the Land had waved a magic wand and cast a spell upon us, a spell from which we cannot awaken. And we blacks and whites ride down the years as the plantation system gnaws at the foundations of our characters. The plantation warps us so that some say we black and white upon the land cannot learn to live as other men do. But we know otherwise; we can learn. The Lords of the Land stand in our way; they do not permit the poor whites to make common union with us, for that would mean the end of the Lords' power. To ask questions, to protest, to insist, to contend for a secure institutional and political base upon which to stand and fulfill ourselves is equivalent to a new and intensified declaration of war.

Sometimes a few of us escape the sharecropping system and become home-owners. But gray and blue eyes watch us and if we do not help them in their game of "keeping the niggers down," if we do not ally ourselves with them and partake of their attitudes toward our own black folk, they find fault with us and drive us from our homes. An independent and prosperous black family flourishing amid a vast area of poverty is in itself a powerful enough symbol of aspiration to be a source of trouble, for that black family's mere well-being prods the black thousands, who, if they moved, would disrupt the delicately balanced forces of racial and economic power in the South.

But in spite of this, how eagerly have we taken to the

culture of this new land when opportunity was open to us! Knowing no culture but this, what can we do but live in terms of what we see before our eyes each day? From the simple physiological reactions of slave days, from casual relations and sporadic hope, we learn to live the way of life of the Western world. Behind our pushing is the force of life itself, as strong in black men as in white, as emergent in us as in those who contrive to keep us down.

We hear men talk vaguely of a government in far-away Washington, a government that stands above the people and desires the welfare of all. We do not know this government; but the men it hires to execute its laws are the Lords of the Land whom we have known all our lives. We hear that the government wants to help us, but we are too far down at the bottom of the ditch for the fingers of the government to reach us, and there are too many men—the Lords of the Land and the poor whites—with their shoulders pressing tightly together in racial solidarity, forming a wall between us and the government. More to keep faith alive in our hearts than from any conviction that our lot will be bettered, we cling to our hope that the government would help us if it could. But for three hundred years we have been forced to accept the word of men instead of written contracts, for three hundred years we have been forced to rely upon the whimsical kindness of others rather than upon legal agreements; and all this has grown into hallowed tradition, congealed into reflex habit, hardened into a daily ritual, backed by rope and fagot.

When you, your father, and your father's father have lived under a system that permits others to organize your life, how can you get a check the government sends you? The Lords of the Land receive your mail and when you go to the Big House to ask for your check, they look at you and say: "Boy, get back in the field and keep working. We'll take care of your check. Here, you'd better make your mark on it so's we can cash it. We'll feed you until it is used up." Ordinarily you are so deep in debt when you receive a check from the government that you sign it entirely over to the Lords of the Land and forget about it.

Our days are walled with cotton; we move casually among the whites and they move casually among us; our speech is drawled out with slow smiles; there are no loud arguments; no voices are raised in contention; no shouts of passion betray the desire of one to convince the other. It is impossible to debate or maneuver for advantage without colliding; then blood is spilt. Trapped by the plantation system, we beg bread of the Lords of the Land and they give it to us; they need us to work for them. Although our association partakes of an odd sort of father-child relationship, it is devoid of that affinity of blood that restrains the impulse to cruelty, empty of that sense of intimate understanding born of a long proximity of human lives.

We plow, plant, chop, and pick the cotton, working always toward a dark, mercurial goal. We hear that silk is becoming popular, that jute is taking the place of cotton in many lands, that factories are making clothing out of rayon, that scientists have invented a substance called nylon. All these are blows to the reign of Queen Cotton, and when she dies we do not know how many of us will die with her. Adding to our confusion is the gradual appearance of machines that can pick more cotton in one day than any ten of us. How can we win this race with death when our thin blood is set against the potency of gasoline, when our weak flesh is pitted against the strength of steel, when our loose muscles must vie with the power of tractors?

Through the years rumor filters down to us of cotton being grown in Egypt, Russia, Japan, India, in lands whose names we cannot pronounce. We black folk are needed no longer to grow cotton to clothe the world. Moreover, we cannot imagine that there will be so many factories erected in the South—since there are thousands already manufacturing more goods than can be bought—that those of us who cannot earn our bread by growing cotton will get jobs in them. Our future on the plantation is a worry.

Our lives are walled with cotton

We plow and plant cotton

We chop cotton

We pick cotton

When Queen Cotton dies . . .

how many of us will die with her?

Of a summer night, sitting on our front porches, we discuss how "funny" it is that we who raise cotton to clothe the nation do not have handkerchiefs to wipe the sweat from our brows, do not have mattresses to sleep on; we need shirts, dresses, sheets, drawers, tablecloths. When our cotton returns to us—after having been spun and woven and dyed and wrapped in cellophane—its cost is beyond our reach. The Bosses of the Buildings, owners of the factories that turn out the mass of commodities we yearn to buy, have decided that no cheap foreign articles can come freely into the country to undersell the products made by "their own workers."

The years glide on and strange things come. The Lords of the Land, as the cotton market shrinks and prices fall, grow poor and become riding bosses, and the riding bosses grow poor and become tenant farmers, and the tenant farmers grow poor and become sharecroppers, and the sharecroppers grow poor and become day laborers, migrants upon the land whose home is where the next crop is. We ask how such things can happen and we are told that the South is "broke," that it has to borrow money from the Bosses of the Buildings, that it must pay dearly for this hired gold, and that the soil is yielding less because of erosion. As plantation after plantation fails, the Bosses of the Buildings acquire control and send tractors upon the land, and still more of us are compelled to search for "another place." The Bosses of the Buildings now own almost one-third of the plantations of the South, and they are rapidly converting them into "farm factories."

When we grumble about our hard life, the Lords of the Land cry: "Listen, I've borrowed money on my plantation and I'm risking my *land* with you folks!" And we, hungry and barefoot, cry: "And we're risking our *lives* with you!" And that is all that can be said; there is no room for idle words. Everything fits flush, each corner fitting tight into another corner. If you act at all, it is either to flee or to kill; you are either a victim or a rebel.

Days come and days go, but our lives upon the land remain without hope. We do not care if the barns rot down; they do not belong to us, anyway. No matter what improvement we may make upon the plantation, it would give us no claim upon the crop. In cold weather we burn everything in sight to keep us warm; we strip boards from our shacks and palings from the straggling fences. During long winter days we sit in cabins that have no windowpanes; the floors and roofs are made of thin planks of pine. Out in the backyard, over a hole dug in the clay, stands a horizontal slab of oak with an oval opening in it; when it rains, a slow stink drifts over the wet fields.

To supplement our scanty rations, we take our buckets and roam the hillsides for berries, nuts, or wild greens; sometimes we fish in the creeks; at other times our black women tramp the fields looking for bits of firewood, piling their aprons high, coming back to our cabins slowly, like laden donkeys.

If our shacks catch fire, there is nothing much we can do but to snatch our children and run to a safe place and watch the flames eat the dry timbers. There is no fire wagon and there is but little water. Fire, like other things, has its way with us.

Lord, we *know* that this is a hard system! Even while we are hating the Lords of the Land, we know that if they paid us a just wage for all the work we do in raising a bale of cotton, the fleecy strands would be worth more than their weight in gold! Cotton is a drug, and for three hundred years we have taken it to kill the pain of hunger; but it does not ease our suffering. Most people take morphine out of choice; we take cotton because we must. For years longer than we remember, cotton has been our companion; we travel down the plantation road with debt holding our left hand, with credit holding our right, and ahead of us looms the grave, the final and simple end.

We move slowly through sun and rain, and our eyes grow dull and our skin sags. For hours we sit on our porches and stare out over the dusty land, wondering why we are so tired. In the fall the medicine men come and set up their tents, light gas flares, and amuse us with crude jokes. We take the pennies out of the tin can under a plank in the barn and buy patent medicine for Grandpa's malaria-like feeling, for Grandma's sudden chills, for Susie's spasms of hotness, for the strange and nasty rash that eats at Rosa's skin, for Bob's hacking cough that will not leave, for the pain that gnaws the baby's stomach day and night.

Yet we live on and our families grow large. Some people wag their heads in amusement when they see our long lines of ragged children, but we love them. If our families are large, we have a chance to make a bigger crop, for there are more hands to tend the land. But large families eat more, and, although our children lighten the burden of toil, we finish the year as we were before, hungry and in debt. Like black buttercups, our children spring up on the red soil of the plantations. When a new one arrives, neighbors from miles around come and look at it, speculating upon which parent it resembles. A child is a glad thing in the bleak stretches of the cotton country, and our gold is in the hearts of the people we love, in the veins that carry our blood, upon those faces where we catch furtive glimpses of the shape of our humble souls.

Our way of life is simple and our unit of living is formed by the willingness of two or more of us to organize ourselves

184

voluntarily to make a crop, to pool our labor power to wrest
subsistence from the stubborn soil. We live just as man lived
when he first struggled against this earth. After having been
pulverized by slavery and purged of our cultural heritage,
we have been kept so far from the sentiments and ideals of
the Lords of the Land that we do not feel their way of life
deeply enough to act upon their assumptions and motives.
So, living by folk tradition, possessing but a few rights which
others respect, we are unable to establish our family groups
upon a basis of property ownership. For the most part our
delicate families are held together by love, sympathy, pity,
and the goading knowledge that we must work together to
make a crop.

That is why we black folk laugh and sing when we are
alone together. There is nothing—no ownership or lust for
power—that stands between us and our kin. And we reckon
kin not as others do, but down to the ninth and tenth cousin.
And for a reason we cannot explain we are mighty proud
when we meet a man, woman, or child who, in talking to us,
reveals that the blood of our brood has somehow entered his
veins. Because our eyes are not blinded by the hunger for
possessions, we are a tolerant folk. A black mother who
stands in the sagging door of her gingerbread shack may

weep as she sees her children straying off into the unknown world, but no matter what they may do, no matter what happens to them, no matter what crimes they may commit, no matter what the world may think of them, that mother always welcomes them back with an irreducibly human feeling that stands above the claims of law or property. Our scale of values differs from that of the world from which we have been excluded; our shame is not its shame, and our love is not its love.

Our black children are born to us in our one-room shacks, before crackling log fires, with rusty scissors boiling in tin pans, with black plantation midwives hovering near, with pine-knot flames casting shadows upon the wooden walls, with the sound of kettles of water singing over the fires in the hearths. . . .

As our children grow up they help us day by day, fetching pails of water from the springs, gathering wood for cooking, sweeping the floors, minding the younger children, stirring the clothes boiling in black pots over the fires in the backyards, and making butter in the churns. . . .

Sometimes there is a weather-worn, pine-built schoolhouse for our children, but even if the school were open for the full term our children would not have the time to go. We cannot let them leave the fields when cotton is waiting to be picked. When the time comes to break the sod, the sod must be broken; when the time comes to plant the seeds, the seeds must be planted; and when the time comes to loosen the red clay from about the bright green stalks of the cotton plants, that, too, must be done even if it is September and school is open. Hunger is the punishment if we violate the laws of Queen Cotton. The seasons of the year form the mold that shapes our lives, and who can change the seasons?

Deep down we distrust the schools that the Lords of the Land build for us and we do not really feel that they are ours. In many states they edit the textbooks that our children study, for the most part deleting all references to government, voting, citizenship, and civil rights. Many of them say that French, Latin, and Spanish are languages not for us, and they become angry when they think that we desire to learn more than they want us to. They say that "all the geography a nigger needs to know is how to get from his shack to the plow." They restrict our education easily, inasmuch as their laws decree that there must be schools for our black children and schools for the white, churches for our black folk and churches for the white, and in public places their signs read: FOR COLORED and FOR WHITE. They have arranged the

order of life in the South so that a different set of ideals is
inculcated in the opposing black and white groups.

Yet, in a vague, sentimental sort of way we love books
inordinately, even though we do not know how to read them,
for we know that books are the gateway to a forbidden world.
Any black man who can read a book is a hero to us. And we
are joyful when we hear a black man speak like a book. The
people who say how the world is to be run, who have fires
in winter, who wear warm clothes, who get enough to eat,
are the people who make books speak to them. Sometimes
of a night we tell our children to get out the old big family

Bible and read to us, and we listen wonderingly until, tired from a long day in the fields, we fall asleep.

The Lords of the Land have shown us how preciously they regard books by the manner in which they cheat us in erecting schools for our children. They tax black and white equally throughout the state, and then they divide the money for education unequally, keeping most of it for their own schools, generally taking five dollars for themselves for every dollar they give us. For example, in the state of Mississippi, for every $25 a year that is spent to educate a white child, only $5 a year is spent to educate a black child. In many counties there is no school at all, and where there is one, it is old, with a leaky roof; our children sit on wooden planks made into crude benches without backs. Sometimes seventy children, ranging in age from six to twenty, crowd into the one room which comprises the entire school structure; they are taught by one teacher whose wage is lower and whose conditions of work are immeasurably poorer than those of white teachers.

Many of our schools are open for only six months a year, and allow our children to progress only to the sixth grade. Some of those who are lucky enough to graduate go back as teachers to instruct their brothers and sisters. Many of our children grow to feel that they would rather remain upon the plantations to work than attend school, for they can observe so few tangible results in the lives of those who do attend.

The schoolhouse is usually far away; at times our children must travel distances varying from one to six miles. Busses are furnished for many white children, but rarely for ours. The distances we walk are so legendary that often the measure of a black man's desire to obtain an education is gauged by the number of miles he declares he walked to school when a child.

Sunday is always a glad day. We call all our children to us and comb the hair of the boys and plait the hair of the girls; then we rub their heads with hog fat to make their hair shine. We wrap the girls' hair in white strings and put a red ribbon upon their heads; we make the boys wear stocking caps, that is, we make them pull upon their heads the tops of our stockings, cut and stretched taut upon their skulls to keep their hair in place. Then we rub the hog fat upon their faces to take that dull, ashy look away from skins made dry and rough from the weather of the fields. In clean clothes ironed stiff with starch made from flour, we hitch up the mule to the wagon, pile in our Bibles and baskets of food—hog meat and greens—and we are off to church.

The preacher tells of days long ago and of a people whose sufferings were like ours. He preaches of the Hebrew children and the fiery furnace, of Daniel, of Moses, of Solomon,

and of Christ. What we have not dared feel in the presence of the Lords of the Land, we now feel in church. Our hearts and bodies, reciprocally acting upon each other, swing out into the meaning of the story the preacher is unfolding. Our eyes become absorbed in a vision. . . .

. . . a place eternal filled with happiness where dwell God and His many hosts of angels singing His praises and glorifying His name and in the midst of this oneness of being there arises one whose soul is athirst to feel things for himself and break away from the holy band of joy and he organizes revolt in Heaven and preaches rebellion and aspires to take the place of God to rule Eternity and God condemns him from Heaven and decrees that he shall be banished

*and this Rebel this Satan this Lucifer persuades one-third of all the
many hosts of angels in Heaven to follow him and build a new
Heaven and down he comes with his angels whose hearts are black
with pride and whose souls are hot with vengeance against God
who decides to make Man and He makes Man in His own image and
He forms him of clay and He breathes the breath of life into him
but He warns him against the Rebel the Satan the Lucifer who had
been banished from Heaven for his pride and envy and Man lives
in a garden of peace where there is no Time no Sorrow and no Death
and while Man lives in this happiness there comes to him the Rebel
the Satan the Lucifer and he tempts Man and drags him down the
same black path of rebellion and sin and God seeing this decrees
that Man shall live in the Law and not Love and must endure Toil
and Pain and Death and must dig for his bread in the stony earth
but while Man suffers God's compassion is moved and God Himself
assumes the form of Man's corrupt and weak flesh and comes down*

*and lives and suffers and dies upon a cross to show Man the way
back up the broad highway to peace and thus Man begins to live
for a time under a new dispensation of Love and not Law and the
Rebel the Satan the Lucifer still works rebellion seducing persuading falsifying and God through His prophets says that He will come
for a second time bringing not peace but a sword to rout the powers
of darkness and build a new Jerusalem and God through His prophets says that the final fight the last battle the Armageddon will be
resumed and will endure until the end of Time and of Death. . . .*

. . . and the preacher's voice is sweet to us, caressing and
lashing, conveying to us a heightening of consciousness that
the Lords of the Land would rather keep from us, filling us
with a sense of hope that is treasonable to the rule of Queen
Cotton. As the sermon progresses, the preacher's voice increases in emotional intensity, and we, in tune and sympathy
with his sweeping story, sway in our seats until we have lost
all notion of time and have begun to float on a tide of passion.
The preacher begins to punctuate his words with sharp
rhythms, and we are lifted far beyond the boundaries of our
daily lives, upward and outward, until, drunk with our enchanted vision, our senses lifted to the burning skies, we do
not know who we are, what we are, or where we are. . . .

We go home pleasantly tired and sleep easily, for we know
that we hold somewhere within our hearts a possibility of

inexhaustible happiness; we know that if we could but get our feet planted firmly upon this earth, we could laugh and live and build. We take this feeling with us each day and it drains the gall out of our years, sucks the sting from the rush of time, purges the pain from our memory of the past, and banishes the fear of loneliness and death. When the soil grows poorer, we cling to this feeling; when clanking tractors uproot and hurl us from the land, we cling to it; when our eyes behold a black body swinging from a tree in the wind, we cling to it. . . .

Some say that, because we possess this faculty of keeping alive this spark of happiness under adversity, we are children. No, it is the courage and faith in simple living that enable us to maintain this reservoir of human feeling, for we know that there will come a day when we shall pour out our hearts over this land.

Neither are we ashamed to go of a Saturday night to the crossroad dancehall and slow drag, ball the jack, and Charleston to an old guitar and piano. Dressed in starched jeans, an old silk shirt, a big straw hat, we swing the girls over the plank floor, clapping our hands, stomping our feet, and singing:

> *Shake it to the east*
> *Shake it to the west,*
> *Shake it to the one*
> *You love the best. . . .*

It is what makes our boys and girls, when they are ten or twelve years of age, roam the woods, bareheaded and bare-foot, singing and whistling and shouting in wild, hilarious chorus a string of ditties that make the leaves of the trees shiver in naked and raucous laughter.

> *I love you once*
> *I love you twice*
> *I love you next to*
> *Jesus Christ . . .*

And it is this same capacity for joy that makes us hymn:

> *I'm a stranger*
> *Don't drive me away*
> *I'm a stranger*
> *Don't drive me away*
> *If you drive me away*
> *You may need me some day*
> *I'm a stranger*
> *Don't drive me away. . . .*

But there are times when we doubt our songs; they are not enough to unify our fragile folk lives in this competitive world. As our children grow older, they leave us to fulfill the sense of happiness that sleeps in their hearts. Unlike us, they have been influenced by the movies, magazines, and glimpses of town life, and they lack the patience to wait for the consummation of God's promise as we do. We despair to see them go, but we tell them that we want them to escape the deadening life of the plantation. Our hearts are divided: we want them to have a new life, yet we are afraid if they challenge the Lords of the Land, for we know that terror will assail them. As our children learn what is happening on other plantations and up north, the casual ties of our folk families begin to dissolve.

Vast changes engulf our lives. We sit on our front porches, fanning the flies away, and watch the men with axes come through the Southland, as they have already gone through

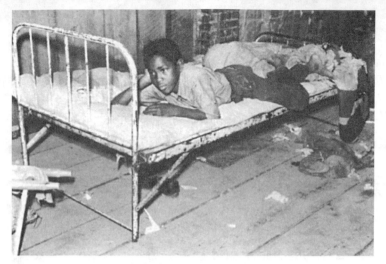

There are times when we doubt our songs

the Northland and the Westland, and whack down the pine, oak, ash, elm, and hickory trees, leaving the land denuded as far as the eye can see. And then rain comes in leaden sheets to slant and scour at the earth until it washes away rich layers of top soil, until it leaves the land defenseless, until all vegetation is gone and nothing remains to absorb the moisture and hinder the violent spreading floods of early spring.

Cotton crops have sapped the soil of its fertility; twenty or thirty years of good cotton farming are enough to drain the land and leave it a hard, yellow mat, a mockery to the sky and a curse to us.

On top of this there come, with a tread as of doom, more and more of the thundering tractors and cotton-picking machines that more and more render our labor useless. Year by year these machines grow from one odd and curious object to be gaped at to thousands that become so deadly in their impersonal labor that we grow to hate them. They do our work better and faster than we can, driving us from plantation to plantation. Black and white alike now go to the pea, celery, orange, grapefruit, cabbage, and lemon crops. Sometimes we walk and sometimes the bosses of the farm factories send their trucks for us. We go from the red land to the brown land, from the brown land to the black land, working our way eastward until we reach the blue Atlantic. In spring we chop cotton in Mississippi and pick beans in Florida; in summer we labor in the peach orchards of Georgia and tramp on to the tobacco crop in North Carolina; then we trek to New Jersey to dig potatoes. We sleep in woods, in barns, in wooden barracks, on sidewalks, and sometimes in jail. Our dog-trot, dog-run, shotgun, and gingerbread shacks fill with ghosts and tumble down from rot.

News comes that there are better places to go, but we know that the next place will be as bad as the last one. Yet we go. Our drifting is the expression of our hope to improve our lives. Season after season the farm factories pass before

We labor in the farm factories

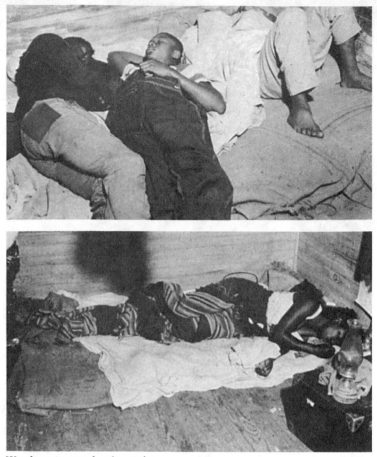

We sleep in wooden barracks

our eyes, and at the end of the long journey we are filled with nostalgic melancholy, a blurred picture of many places seen and suffered in, a restlessness which we cannot appease.

In 1914, out of the unknown, comes the news that a war is in progress to hold back the Germans, who are determined to wrest markets and lands away from other countries. We hear that the government has decided to keep alien labor out of the country, and a call is made to us to come north and help turn the wheels of industry. At the thought of leaving our homes again, we cry: "What a life it is we live! Our roots are nowhere! We have no home even upon this soil which formed our blood and bones!" But hundreds of thousands of us get on the move once more.

The Lords of the Land pause now and speak kind words to us; they want us to remain upon the plantations. They tell us that they are our best friends; we smile and say nothing. As we abandon the land, odd things happen to us. If one of us should run afoul of the law at harvest time, the Lords of the Land will speak a good word to the sheriff for "his niggers." The law listens and turns us over to the Lords of the Land who pay our fines. Then we labor upon the plantation to pay the debt! But as long as we merely drift from plantation to plantation, the Lords of the Land do not really care. They say: "Niggers don't know what they want. Niggers come and niggers go, but we'll always have the niggers. Only it's hard to keep the books with them moving all the time."

Soon, however, they take a more serious attitude toward us, for the Bosses of the Buildings send men with fair words down from the North, telling us how much money we can make digging in the mines, smelting ore, laying rails, and killing hogs. They tell us that we will live in brick buildings, that we will vote, that we will be able to send our children to school for nine months of the year, that if we get into trouble we will not be lynched, and that we will not have to grin, doff our hats, bend our knees, slap our thighs, dance, and laugh when we see a white face. We listen, and it sounds like religion. Is it really true? Is there not a trick somewhere? We have grown to distrust all white men. Yet they say: "Listen, we need you to work. We'll hire trains to take you away." Then the weekly Negro newspapers supplement their pleas; the Chicago *Defender,* the Pittsburgh *Courier,* the Baltimore *Afro-American,* and many other newspapers paint the North as a land of promise. We cannot help but believe now. We cannot work the cotton fields for thinking of it; our minds are paralyzed with the hope and dread of it. Not to go means lingering here to live out this slow death; to go means facing the unknown. But, strangely, life has already prepared us for moving and drifting. Have we not already roamed the South? Yes, we will go and see. But we do not move. We are scared.

Who will go first? Then, suddenly, a friend leaves and we whisper to him to write and tell us if the dream is true. We wait. Word comes. It *is* true! "Come on!" the letters tell us. We go.

It is like this: suddenly, while we are chopping at the clods of clay with a heavy hoe, the riding boss gallops up and says: "Hurry up there, nigger!"

Perhaps for the first time in our lives we straighten our backs, drop the hoe, give a fleeting glance at the white man's face, and walk off.

"Hey, where the hell you going, nigger?"

"I'm shaking the dust of the South off my feet, white man."

"You'll starve up north, nigger."

"I don't care. I'm going to die some day anyhow."

But so many of us are leaving that the Lords of the Land begin to worry.

"Don't go," they say.

"We're already going," we say, and keep leaving.

If we have no money, we borrow it; if we cannot borrow it, we beg it. If the Bosses of the Buildings do not furnish us with a train, we walk until we reach a railroad and then we swing onto a freight. There develops such a shortage of labor in the South that the Lords of the Land order us rounded up and threatened with jail sentences unless we consent to go to the fields and gather the waiting crops. Finally they persuade men of our own race to talk to us.

"Let down your buckets where you are," our black leaders say.

"We're leaving," we answer.

"The white man of the South is your friend," they say.

"How much are they paying you to say that?" we ask.

"You'll freeze up north."

"We don't care."

The Lords of the Land say: "You niggers are going north because you think you'll mix with whites."

"Look at all the half-white boys and girls on the plantations," we answer. "We black men did not do that."

"Don't talk fresh, nigger!"

"We ain't talking; we're leaving!"

"Come on; we'll build you a big school!"

"We'd rather be a lamppost in Chicago than the president of Dixie!"

While we are leaving, our black boys come back from Flanders, telling us of how their white officers of the United States Army had treated them, how they had kept them in labor battalions, how they had jim-crowed them in the trenches even when they were fighting and dying, how the white officers had instructed the French people to segregate them. Our boys come back to Dixie in uniform and walk the streets with quick steps and proud shoulders. They cannot help it; they have been in battle, have seen men of all nations and races die. They have seen what men are made of, and now they act differently. But the Lords of the Land cannot understand them. They take them and lynch them while they are still wearing the uniform of the United States Army.

Our black boys do not die for liberty in Flanders. They die in Texas and Georgia. Atlanta is our Marne. Brownsville, Texas, is our Château-Thierry.

It is a lesson we will never forget; it is written into the pages of our blood, into the ledgers of our bleeding bodies, into columns of judgment figures and balance statements in the lobes of our brains.

"Don't do this!" we cry.

"Nigger, shut your damn mouth!" they say.

"Don't lynch us!" we plead.

"You're not white!" they say.

"Why don't somebody say something?" we ask.

"We told you to shut your damn mouth!"

We listen for somebody to say something, and we still travel, leaving the South. Our eyes are open, our ears listening for words to point the way.

From 1890 to 1920, more than 2,000,000 of us left the land.

3. Death on the City Pavements

LORD IN HEAVEN! Good God Almighty! Great Day in the Morning! It's here! Our time has come! We are leaving! We are angry no more; we are leaving! We are bitter no more; we are leaving! We are leaving our homes, pulling up stakes to move on. We look up at the high southern sky and remember all the sunshine and the rain and we feel a sense of loss, but we are leaving. We look out at the wide green fields which our eyes saw when we first came into the world and we feel full of regret, but we are leaving. We scan the kind black faces we have looked upon since we first saw the light of day, and, though pain is in our hearts, we are leaving. We take one last furtive look over our shoulders to the Big House —high upon a hill beyond the railroad tracks—where the Lord of the Land lives, and we feel glad, for we are leaving....

For a long time now we have heard tell that all over the world men are leaving the land for the streets of the city, so we are leaving too. As we leave we see thousands of the poor whites also packing up to move to the city, leaving the land that will not give life to her sons and daughters, black or white. When a man lives upon the land and is cold and hungry and hears word of the great factories going up in the cities, he begins to hope and dream of a new life, and he leaves.

In 1890 there were 1,500,000 of us black men and women in the cities of the nation, both north and south. In 1900 there were 2,000,000 of us. In 1920 there were 3,500,000 of us in the cities of the nation and we were still going, still leaving the land. So many of us crowded into New York City that Harlem's black population doubled between 1900 and 1920. In Philadelphia our influx increased the number of black people by one-third in a few years. In Chicago our endless trek inflated the Black Belt population by more than 125,000 from 1920 to 1930. And our tide continued to roll from the farm to the factory, from the country to the city.

Perhaps never in history has a more utterly unprepared folk wanted to go to the city; we were barely born as a folk when we headed for the tall and sprawling centers of steel and stone. We, who were landless upon the land; we, who had barely managed to live in family groups; we, who needed the ritual and guidance of institutions to hold our atomized lives together in lines of purpose; we, who had known only relationships to people and not relationships to things; we who had never belonged to any organizations except the church and burial societies; we, who had had our personalities blasted with two hundred years of slavery and had been turned loose to shift for ourselves—we were such a folk as this when we moved into a world that was destined to test all we were, that threw us into the scales of competition to weigh our mettle. And how were we to know that, the moment we landless millions of the land—we men who were struggling to be born—set our awkward feet upon the pavements of the city, life would begin to exact of us a heavy toll in death?

We did not know what would happen, what was in store for us. We went innocently, longing and hoping for a life that the Lords of the Land would not let us live. Our hearts were high as we moved northward to the cities. What emotions, fears, what a complex of sensations we felt when, looking out of a train window at the revolving fields, we first glimpsed the sliding waters of the gleaming Ohio! What memories that river evoked in us, memories black and gloomy, yet tinged with the bright border of a wild and desperate hope! The Ohio is more than a river. It is a symbol, a line that runs through our hearts, dividing hope from despair, just as once it bisected the nation, dividing freedom from slavery. How many desperate scenes have been enacted upon its banks! How many grim dramas have been played out upon its bosom! How many slave hunters and Abolitionists have clashed here with fire in their eyes and deep convictions in their hearts! This river has seen men whose beliefs were so strong that the rights of property meant nothing, men whose feelings were so mighty that the laws of the land meant nothing, men whose passions were so fiery that only human life and human dignity mattered.

The train and the auto move north, ever north, and from 1916 to 1928, 1,200,000 of us were moving from the South to the North and we kept leaving. Night and day, in rain and in sun, in winter and in summer, we leave the land. Already, as we sit and look broodingly out over the turning fields, we notice with attention and hope that the dense southern swamps give way to broad, cultivated wheat farms. The spick-and-span farmhouses done in red and green and white crowd out the casual, unpainted gingerbread shacks. Silos take the place of straggling piles of hay. Macadam highways now wind over the horizon instead of dirt roads. The cheeks of the farm people are full and ruddy, not sunken and withered like soda crackers. The slow southern drawl, which in legend is so sweet and hospitable but which in fact has brought down on our black bodies suffering untold, is superseded by clipped Yankee phrases, phrases spoken with such rapidity and neutrality that we, with our slow ears, have difficulty in understanding. And the foreigners—Poles, Germans, Swedes, and Italians—we never dreamed that there were so many in the world! Yes, coming north for a Negro sharecropper involves more strangeness than going to another country. It is the beginning of living on a new and terrifying plane of consciousness.

We see white men and women get on the train, dressed in expensive new clothes. We look at them guardedly and wonder will they bother us. Will they ask us to stand up while they sit down? Will they tell us to go to the back of the coach? Even though we have been told that we need not be afraid, we have lived so long in fear of all white faces that we cannot help but sit and wait. We look around the train and we do not see the old familiar signs: FOR COLORED and FOR WHITE. The train speeds north and we cannot sleep. Our heads sink in a doze, and then we sit bolt-upright, prodded by the thought that we must watch these strange surroundings. But nothing happens; these white men seem impersonal and their very neutrality reassures us—for a while. Almost against our deeper judgment, we try to force ourselves to relax, for these brisk men give no sign of what they feel. They are indifferent. O sweet and welcome *indifference!*

The miles click behind us. Into Chicago, Indianapolis, New York, Cleveland, Buffalo, Detroit, Toledo, Philadelphia, Pittsburgh, and Milwaukee we go, looking for work. We feel freer than we have ever felt before, but we are still a little scared. It is like a dream. Will we wake up suddenly and find that none of this is really true, that we are merely daydreaming behind the barn, snoozing in the sun, waiting to hear the hoarse voice of the riding boss saying: "Nigger, where do you think you are? Get the hell up from there and move on!"

Timidly, we get off the train. We hug our suitcases, fearful of pickpockets, looking with unrestrained curiosity at the great big brick buildings. We are very reserved, for we have been warned not to act "green," that the city people can spot a "sucker" a mile away. Then we board our first Yankee street car to go to a cousin's home, a brother's home, a sister's home, a friend's home, an uncle's home, or an aunt's home. We pay the conductor our fare and look about apprehensively for a seat. We have been told that we can sit where we please, but we are still scared. We cannot shake off three hundred years of fear in three hours. We ease into a seat and look out of the window at the crowded streets. A white man or a white woman comes and sits beside us, not even looking at us, as though this were a normal thing to do. The muscles of our bodies tighten. Indefinable sensations crawl over our skins and our blood tingles. Out of the corners of our eyes we try to get a glimpse of the strange white face that floats but a few inches from ours. The impulses to laugh and to cry clash in us; we bite our lips and stare out of the window.

There are so many people. For the first time in our lives we feel human bodies, strangers whose lives and thoughts are unknown to us, pressing always close about us. We cannot see or know a *man* because of the thousands upon thousands of *men*. The apartments in which we sleep are crowded and noisy, and soon enough we learn that the brisk, clipped men of the North, the Bosses of the Buildings, are not at all *indifferent*. They are deeply concerned about us, but in a new way. It seems as though we are now living inside of a machine; days and events move with a hard reasoning of their own. We live amid swarms of people, yet there is a vast distance between people, a distance that words cannot bridge. No longer do our lives depend upon the soil, the sun, the rain, or the wind; we live by the grace of jobs and the brutal logic of jobs. We do not know this world, or what makes it move. In the South life was different; men spoke to you, cursed you, yelled at you, or killed you. The world moved by signs we knew. But here in the North cold forces hit you and push you. It is a world of *things*.

Our defenseless eyes cloud with bewilderment when we learn that there are not enough houses for us to live in. And competing with us for shelter are thousands of poor migrant whites who have come up from the South, just as we have come. The cost of building a house is high, and building activities are on the downgrade. It is wartime; no new labor is coming in from the old countries across the seas. The only district we can live in is the area just beyond the business belt, a transition area where a sooty conglomeration of factories and mills belches smoke that stains our clothes and lungs.

We black folk are not the only ones who move into this so-called transition area; it is the first port of call for that incoming horde of men who float continuously into cities. The tenements we live in are old; they are rarely repaired or

replaced. On most of our buildings are signs: THIS PROPERTY IS FOR SALE. Any day we can be told to move, that our home is to be torn down to make way for a new factory or a new mill.

So, under the black mourning pall of smoke from the stacks of American industry, our observing Negro eyes watch a thousand rivulets of blood melt, fuse, blend, and flow in a common stream of human unity as it merges with the great American tide. But we never mix with that stream; we are not allowed to. For years we watch the timid faces of poor white peasants—Turks, Czechs, Croats, Finns, and Greeks—pass through this curtain of smoke and emerge with the sensitive features of modern men. But our faces do not change. Our cheek-bones remain as unaltered as the stony countenance of the Sphinx.

From this transition area we watch many of the immigrants move on to the rooming-house district which almost always borders the transition area of the big industrial city; later many of them move from the rooming-house area into the apartment-house district. After that the only news we hear of some of them is what we read in the newspapers. Of a morning, years later, we pick up the Chicago *Daily Tribune*, or the Cleveland *Plain Dealer*, or the Detroit *Free Press*, or the Philadelphia *Inquirer*, or the New York *Times*, and see that some former neighbors of ours, a Mr. and Mrs. Klein or Murphy or Potaci or Pierre or Cromwell or Stepanovich and their children—kids we once played with upon the slag piles —are now living in the suburban areas, having swum upstream through the American waters of opportunity into the professional classes.

Times without number our eyes witness this drama. The gigantic American companies will not employ our daughters in their offices as clerks, bookkeepers, or stenographers; huge department stores will not employ our young women, fresh from school, as saleswomen. The engineering, aviation, mechanical, and chemical schools close their doors to our sons, just as the great corporations which make thousands of commodities refuse to employ them. The Bosses of the Buildings decree that we must be maids, porters, janitors, cooks, and general servants.

We remain to live in the clinging soot just beyond the factory areas, behind the railroad tracks, near the river banks, under the viaducts, by the steel and iron mills, on the edges of the coal and lumber yards. We live in crowded, barn-like rooms, in old rotting buildings where once dwelt rich native whites of a century ago. Because we are black, because our love of life gives us many children, because we do not have quiet ways of doing things, because the outdoor boisterousness of the plantation still clings to us, because we move slowly and speak slowly, white people say that we are destructive and therefore do not want us in their neighborhoods. When we return home at night from our jobs, we are afraid to venture into other sections of the city, for we fear that the white boys will gang up and molest us. When we do go out into white neighborhoods, we always go in crowds, for that is the best mode of protection.

White people say that they are afraid of us, and it often

makes us laugh. When they see one of us, they either smile with contempt or amusement. When they see *two* or us, they treat us as though some grave thought were on their minds. When they see *four* of us, they are usually silent. When they see *six* of us, they become downright apprehensive and alarmed. And because they are afraid of us, we are afraid of them. Especially do we feel fear when we meet the gangs of white boys who have been taught—at home and at school—that we black folk are making their parents lose their homes and life's savings because we have moved into their neighborhoods.

They say our presence in their neighborhoods lowers the value of their property. We do not understand why this should be so. We are poor; but they were once poor, too. They make up their minds, because others tell them to, that they must move at once if we rent an apartment near them. Having been warned against us by the Bosses of the Buildings, having heard tall tales about us, about how "bad" we are, they react emotionally as though we had the plague when we move into their neighborhoods. Is it any wonder, then, that their homes are suddenly and drastically reduced in value? They hastily abandon them, sacrificing them to the Bosses of the Buildings, the men who instigate all this for whatever profit they can get in real-estate sales. And in the end we are the "fall guys." When the white folks move, the Bosses of the Buildings let the property to us at rentals higher than those the whites paid.

And the Bosses of the Buildings take these old houses and convert them into "kitchenettes," and then rent them to us at rates so high that they make fabulous fortunes before the houses are too old for habitation. What they do is this: they take, say, a seven-room apartment, which rents for $50 a month to whites, and cut it up into seven small apartments, of one room each; they install one small gas stove and one small sink in each room. The Bosses of the Buildings rent these kitchenettes to us at the rate of, say, $6 a week. Hence, the same apartment for which white people—who can get jobs anywhere and who receive higher wages than we—pay $50 a month is rented to us for $42 a week! And because there are not enough houses for us to live in, because we have been used to sleeping several in a room on the plantations in the South, we rent these kitchenettes and are glad to get them. These kitchenettes are our havens from the plantations in the South. We have fled the wrath of Queen Cotton and we are tired.

Sometimes five or six of us live in a one-room kitchenette, a place where simple folk such as we should never be held captive. A war sets up in our emotions: one part of our feelings tells us that it is good to be in the city, that we have a chance at life here, that we need but turn a corner to become a stranger, that we no longer need bow and dodge at the sight of the Lords of the Land. Another part of our feelings tells us that, in terms of worry and strain, the cost of living in the kitchenettes is too high, that the city heaps too much responsibility upon us and gives too little security in return.

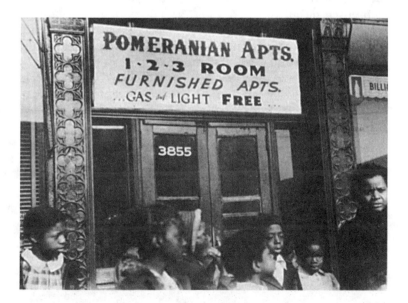

The kitchenette is the author of the glad tidings that new suckers are in town, ready to be cheated, plundered, and put in their places.

The kitchenette is our prison, our death sentence without a trial, the new form of mob violence that assaults not only the lone individual, but all of us, in its ceaseless attacks.

The kitchenette, with its filth and foul air, with its one toilet for thirty or more tenants, kills our black babies so fast that in many cities twice as many of them die as white babies.

The kitchenette is the seed bed for scarlet fever, dysentery, typhoid, tuberculosis, gonorrhea, syphilis, pneumonia, and malnutrition.

The kitchenette scatters death so widely among us that our death rate exceeds our birth rate, and if it were not for the trains and autos bringing us daily into the city from the plantations, we black folks who dwell in northern cities would die out entirely over the course of a few years.

The kitchenette, with its crowded rooms and incessant bedlam, provides an enticing place for crimes of all sort—crimes against women and children or any stranger who

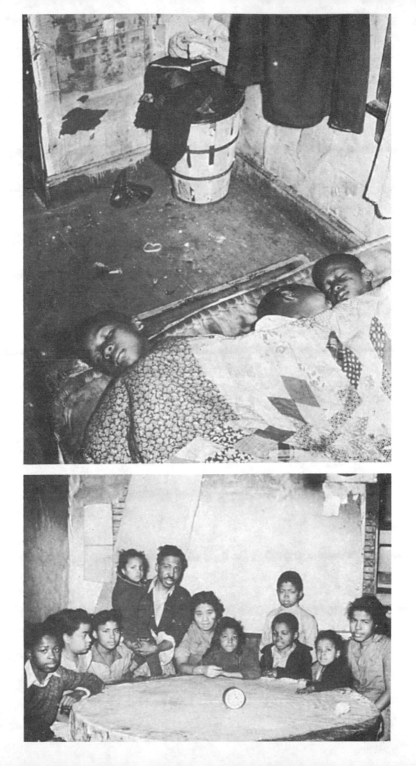

happens to stray into its dark hallways. The noise of our living, boxed in stone and steel, is so loud that even a pistol shot is smothered.

The kitchenette throws desperate and unhappy people into an unbearable closeness of association, thereby increasing latent friction, giving birth to never-ending quarrels of recrimination, accusation, and vindictiveness, producing warped personalities.

The kitchenette injects pressure and tension into our individual personalities, making many of us give up the struggle, walk off and leave wives, husbands, and even children behind to shift as best they can.

The kitchenette creates thousands of one-room homes where our black mothers sit, deserted, with their children about their knees.

The kitchenette blights the personalities of our growing children, disorganizes them, blinds them to hope, creates problems whose effects can be traced in the characters of its child victims for years afterward.

The kitchenette jams our farm girls, while still in their teens, into rooms with men who are restless and stimulated by the noise and lights of the city; and more of our girls have bastard babies than the girls in any other sections of the city.

The kitchenette fills our black boys with longing and restlessness, urging them to run off from home, to join together with other restless black boys in gangs, that brutal form of city courage.

The kitchenette piles up mountains of profits for the Bosses of the Buildings and makes them ever more determined to keep things as they are.

The kitchenette reaches out with fingers full of golden bribes to the officials of the city, persuading them to allow old firetraps to remain standing and occupied long after they should have been torn down.

The kitchenette is the funnel through which our pulverized lives flow to ruin and death on the city pavements, at a profit. . . .

A few of our black boys save enough from their weekly wages to make payments on homes. But they discover that white home-owners refuse to sell to them and stand solid against any extension of the Black Belt. Meanwhile we continue to pour in from the South, swelling our numbers that live in these locked-in quarters. And then one day some shrewd white man, eager for a high profit, decides to sell his home to a black buyer, and for the first time a black family "invades" a white neighborhood and is greeted with violence. When our black fathers go to work in the mornings, they hear the muttered insults of their white neighbors. Bricks are hurled through the windows of our homes; garbage is tossed at our black children when they go to school; and finally bombs explode against our front doors. But whenever we can escape the terrors and limitations of the Black Belt, we move into the white area, disdainful of reprisal.

Grudgingly, the white population falls back, street by street, leaving its homes empty. Sometimes the members of a white family will board up their old homestead and move away, but not before they have cautioned their real-estate broker that no black folk should be allowed to purchase their property. The white families do not want black strangers to dwell within the walls of rooms made sacred to them through long years of intimate living.

With rows of empty houses at their disposal, the Bosses of the Buildings step in with the smiles of salesmanship. They purchase the abandoned properties, promising to respect the wishes of the owners, and then they immediately hang up placards, saying: NOW OPEN TO COLORED TENANTS. And we black folk, glad at long last to find living space, rush to sign leases at exorbitant rentals. In this manner we force the whites back year by year until the tide of our black life, pushing irresistibly outward, reaches the border of some restricted middle-class neighborhood, and then the warfare begins anew. Encouraged by powerful real-estate boards and business interests, home-owners hurriedly create property-owning associations to stem our black "invasion." If the situation is acute and feeling is running high, local vigilante groups will spring into action; but usually a more routine course is followed: long, grim "legal" documents are drawn up covering agreements among wide groups of white homeowners who pledge not to sell their property to us blacks under any circumstances. They call these agreements "restrictive covenants," and in time they grow to be as powerful a detriment to us as had been the policies of the Lords of the Land in the South. In many of the large cities of the United States these agreements affect 80 per cent of all real estate, and they are hailed by the Bosses of the Buildings as the "solution," and the real-estate profits which accrue from our kitchenettes are thereby guaranteed.

Though the United States Supreme Court has so far adroitly avoided rendering a direct decision as to the constitutionality of these restrictive covenants, almost all state, county, and city courts invariably pronounce them "legal." Sometimes ponderous judges point out to us black folk that the real justice of their judgment lies in the fact that we black folk can organize our own property-owning associations and exclude white folk, if we so desire! The courts therefore juggle words so that these restrictive covenants are always "constitutional" and in defense of public policy, thereby assuming the role of policemen in enforcing residential segregation. Newspapers, radios, Protestant and Catholic churches, Jewish synagogues, clubs, civic groups, fraternities, sororities, leagues, and universities bring their moral precepts to bolster their locking-in of hundreds of thousands of us black folk in single, constricted areas. Once again the evils which we thought we had fled forever come back; once again educational appropriations for our black children are curtailed. Local boards of education twist the boundary lines of school districts in such fashion that our boys and girls are legally jim-crowed. The inventive Yankee Bosses of the Buildings go further and contrive even new practices: they reduce the

services of the city in our districts; many of our streets remain unlighted at night; violations of fire laws go unpunished; garbage piles up in our alleyways; pavements fall into disrepair; merchants dump tons of their stale and rotten food into the stores and shops of our Black Belts and exact prices as high for these damaged goods as first-rate and grade-A commodities sell for in other sections of the city. Even in times of peace some of the neighborhoods in which we live look as though they had been subjected to an intensive and prolonged aerial bombardment.

Because we are eager to escape these marked-off areas of life, we usually pay more for our homes than whites pay for those of similar value. The Bosses of the Buildings increase their selling prices when they see our black faces. We pay the first installment and then, usually, every member of our family who is able-bodied must work in order to help meet future payments, for our wages are low and our jobs are restricted. Often we move into one room of our new home and rent the remaining rooms to lodgers. Buying homes is a gamble for us black folk in northern cities; completing the purchase depends upon a lot of factors far beyond our control. A depression may throw us out of our low-paying jobs and then we lose our property. Or the health of one or more of the members of our family may fail in the hard grind of a city life that is still new and strange to us.

The Bosses of the Buildings seldom repair the kitchenettes in which we live, and day after day our children romp and play in the hallways and on the stairways until the old buildings sway and creak as though ready to fall in the first high wind. Often the Bosses of the Buildings refuse to pay taxes to the city on Black Belt property, for they know that the amount of accumulated taxes will soon exceed the actual value of the buildings. After they have wrung from us the last bit of profit, they allow the city to assume control of the dilapidated property. And when whole areas of our Black Belt have become filled with condemned buildings which are dangerous for human habitation, the officials of the city will decide that it is unwise to demolish them, for the majority of us black folk would be without shelter, inasmuch as the rest of the city is barred against us.

If you want to see how crowdedly we live, if you want to know how our meager incomes force our families to "double up" to save space, visit a kitchenette building in some Black Belt and look at the long list of American names under our mail boxes: Jackson, Jefferson, Harrison, Grant, Adams, Johnson, Wilson, Madison, Washington, Taylor. . . . So many of us are forced to live in one building that you would think you were reading a crude telephone directory or a clumsy census report when you see our names scrawled on the walls of a thousand dingy vestibules.

Because the Lords of the Land did not build schools for us, many of us know no trades. When applying for a job, we are asked: "What can you do?"

We reply simply and naïvely: "Anything."

What we mean, of course, is that we know nothing but manual labor. Hence, while the Irishman, the Scot, the Croat, the Welshman, the Frenchman, the Spaniard, to whom opportunities are open, merge with the river of American life, we black folk remain out of touch with the quickening fluids of American hope.

In the main, we black folk earn our living in two ways in the northern cities: we work as domestics or as laborers. Our work inside the homes of the Bosses of the Buildings does not differ greatly from the work we did in the homes of the Lords of the Land. But it is in industry that we encounter experiences that tend to break down the structure of our folk characters and project us toward the vortex of modern urban life. It is when we are handling picks rather than mops, it is when we are swinging hammers rather than brooms, it is when we are pushing levers rather than dust-cloths that we are gripped and influenced by the world-wide forces that shape and mold the life of Western civilization. We load and unload the ships and trains, demolish and erect buildings, wheel barrows of cement and sand, pound steel spikes into miles of railroad track, lay brick, drive heavy trucks of lumber and gravel, butcher hogs and sheep and cattle, dig ore, and mine coal.

During the First World War we find plenty of jobs. We are hired at low wages and perform the heavy and dirty work, work which the poor white workers call "nigger work." Our choice is a hard and narrow one, but we make it. Our choice is between eating and starving, and we choose to eat. Mainly our jobs in industry come to us through two routes: (1) strike-breaking and (2) when factories and mills expand so rapidly that not enough white workers can be found to work in them.

Here is how it happens: the white workers, the majority of whom will not admit us to membership in their powerful trade unions, go out on strike against the wage cuts and long hours imposed by the Bosses of the Buildings, to whom color is of less significance than profits. To break the strike, the Bosses of the Buildings appeal to us black folk to work; they send labor agents into the South to fetch us north; they promise us "protection"; they tell us that they are our "best friends." We are hungry and eager to work, and yet we know that if we work we will be taking the jobs of other men, and we do not want to do that. We do not want to be scabs; we do not want to be strike-breakers; we do not want to snatch food from the tables of poor white children, for we, of all people, really know how hungry children can be. But, again, we say that we have no choice, and the white workers are emphatic in drawing the color line against us. So, trembling and scared, we take spikes, knives, guns, and break the picket lines and work for the Bosses of the Buildings for our daily bread. And when the work day is over, we find ourselves fighting mobs of white workers in the city streets. After scores of such battles in many cities, after much blood is shed, we black folk gain a precarious foothold in the industries of the North.

But even after we are steadily employed in these industries, the Bosses of the Buildings arrange our lives so that we remain a constant threat to the poor white union workers, who now hate us more than ever for having broken their strike and driven down their wages. But still they refuse to admit us to union membership. Surreptitiously, the Bosses of the Buildings counsel us black folk to have nothing to do with the white workers; they tell us that "good white people" have given us our jobs and we can retain them only if we keep to ourselves. They help us to build churches; they make donations to our institutions; they generally ingratiate themselves as benefactors. And to us, men with simple folk minds, men who have been long used to dealing with other men and not with organizations, this seems sensible and right. So we follow the lead of the Bosses of the Buildings.

The Bosses of the Buildings are much shrewder than the white workers; they place us black folk in the most strategic positions in their plants; they create entire departments for us and place black straw-bosses over us to tell us what to do.

And we feel proud, for we know that the trade unions of the white workers will not sanction such advances as this for us. Yet, deep down, we know the motives that prompt the Bosses of the Buildings to do this for us; in fact, they tell us quite frankly: "Listen, you boys, we are making you boss of this whole department, but we want you to keep away from the white boys, see? We're paying you higher wages than they get, and when they go out on strike we want you boys to carry on."

And we say: "Yes, sir. Thank you, sir."

The white workers, in turn, are wary of us. For generations our labor has been pitted against theirs and their living standards have in many instances been dragged down below even ours. It is an old, sore problem that evokes unreasonable attitudes when it is discussed. Guilty feelings on both sides

make it difficult for us to work alongside one another in the mills and factories. We strive for trade-union membership, but the white workers bar us. So we turn to the Bosses of the Buildings, just as in the South we turned to the Lords of the Land, and beg for help. And we get help, but at what a price!

To divide and exploit us still further, the Bosses of the Buildings send their "mouthpieces," their gangster-politicians, to us to preach a gospel that sounds good. They tell us that old Abe Lincoln's party, the Grand Old Party, the Republican Party, is "a ship and all else is the sea"; they explain to us that the Republican Party freed us and is therefore our "natural friend," and that we would be "selling our birthright for a mess of pottage" if we voted for any other party. Our naïve folk minds become lost in the labyrinth of this reasoning. For centuries we have had to rely on the word of others instead of on our own judgment and organized strength; so, with the memory of the Lords of the Land still vivid in our minds, with the image of the hard face of the riding boss still lingering before our eyes, we are swept by our simple fears and hopes into the toils of the gangster-politicians.

Innocently, we vote into office men to whom the welfare of our lives is of far less concern than yesterday's baseball score. The gangster-politicians play a tricky game. In the realm of politics, just as in the realm of jobs, the Bosses of the Buildings pit us against the prejudiced white population and in turn pit them against us. It operates somewhat like this: they make us afraid and then offer to save us. During election campaigns the gangster-politicians come into black neighborhoods and inform us that the whites are planning to attack us, and they tell us that they, and they alone, are our friends and will protect us if we vote for them. Then they go to the bewildered whites and tell them that we black folk plan to attack them; and then they pose as the friends of the whites and propose to protect *them* against *us*. They ask our black boys to work for them, to become precinct captains, and our boys consent, for here is the promise of a job behind a desk, the kind of job that the white population does not want us to have. In exchange for our vote the gangster-politicians sometimes give us so many petty jobs that the white newspapers in certain northern cities contemptuously refer to their city hall as "Uncle Tom's Cabin."

Usually our voting strength constitutes the balance of power in those northern cities where the population is divided by the artificially stimulated animosities of many races, and the gangster-politicians, once our vote has established them in the power of office, grant a free hand to the Bosses of the Buildings to proceed with a policy of dishonesty against *all* the citizens of the city.

Yet through the years our loyalty to these gangster-politicians remains stanch because they are almost the only ones who hold out their hands to help us, whatever their motives. They induce enduring sentiments of gratitude among us simple folk. It is the gangster-politician who distributes baskets of food to our poor black families at Christmas time; it is the gangster-politician who advises the distraught black homeowner who is about to become a victim of a mortgage foreclosure; it is the gangster-politician who directs the black plantation-born grandmother to a dentist to have her teeth pulled; it is the gangster-politician who bargains our black boys out of jail when they clash with the law. The Bosses of the Buildings declare that they will not be taxed to build social agencies among us black folk, and the gangster-politicians, passionate seekers of political power, are thereby enabled to perform the function that the social consciousness of the city should perform, granting favors to us in return for votes that place them in political office. The most paradoxical gift ever tendered to us black folk in the city is aid from the underworld, from the gangster, from the political thief. The law says that we are *all* free, but the Bosses of the Buildings say that only *they* are free. We are caught in a tangle of conflicting ideals; we must either swap our votes for bread or starve.

The white workers come to feel that the gangster-politicians are taking their wages from them in the form of high taxes, and they blame us black folk for voting them into power. The white workers charge that we black folk corrupt the life of the city, menace their wages, lengthen their hours of work, decrease the value of their very homes in the neighborhoods where we both live. Of course all this is only relatively true, but the Bosses of the Buildings have so ordered the structure of the lives of both black and white that it is only through a heroic effort of will that either of us can cast off this spell of make-believe and see how artificial and man-made is this enmity between us, to see that our common lives are bound by a common cause.

The majority of both black and white, however, live under the spell wrought by the Bosses of the Buildings. During the years following the First World War a depression grips the nation and the poor white workers, frantic and embittered, begin to push us out of our jobs. We can be waiters no longer, for the Bosses of the Buildings, to appease the unrest of the white workers, grant them the honor of serving tables in many hotels and cafés. They feel that it is wiser to give them our jobs than to let them go idle and think and organize. In many cities, where there was a black porter there is now a white porter. In many apartments white cooks replace black cooks. As our unemployment increases, the Bosses of the Buildings pay more taxes to feed us and we sit in our kitchenettes and wonder.

Bloody riots break forth over trifling incidents that would ordinarily be forgotten in the routine of daily living. Throughout the North tension mounts. The atmosphere grows ripe for violence. We feel it coming. Still we go to the scab jobs for bread. Then, suddenly, over anything, over an imagined insult, over an altercation between a black boy and a white boy on a beach, over the wild rumor that a white man has slapped a black boy in a store, over the whispered tale that some white man has spoken improperly to a black girl, over the fact that a black man has accidentally stepped on a white woman's foot, over the gossip that a black woman has talked back to a white woman—it matters not what the pretext is!—street-fighting, protracted, bitter, sanguine, flares in Pittsburgh, Chicago, Washington, New York, Atlanta, and East St. Louis. They kill us and we kill them. We both feel that we are right. This is what life comes to when men's minds are snared in darkness and confusion. . . .

State troops come and impose order. When the fighting is over, we bind up our wounds and count our dead, and another day finds us still marching forward for jobs. Again we say, of the North as of the South, that life for us is daily warfare and that we live hard, like soldiers. We are set apart from the civilian population; our kitchenettes comprise our barracks; the color of our skins constitutes our uniforms; the streets of our cities are our trenches; a job is a pill-box to be captured and held; and the unions of white workers for a long time have formed the first line of resistance which we encounter. The gangster-politicians are our captains, the men who lead us into the immediate assault. The Bosses of the Buildings are the generals who decree the advance or retreat. We are always in battle, but the tidings of victory are few.

When off duty after a hard day of fighting, we are like spent troops, ready to plunge into pleasure to obliterate the memory of this slow death on the city pavements. Just as in the South, in spite of the Lords of the Land, we managed to keep alive deep down in us a hope of what life could be, so now, with death ever hard at our heels, we pour forth in song and dance, without stint or shame, a sense of what our bodies want, a hint of our hope of a full life lived without fear, a whisper of the natural dignity we feel life can have, a cry of hunger for something new to fill our souls, to reconcile the ecstasy of living with the terror of dying. . . .

It is when we seek to express ourselves that the paradoxical cleavage in our lives shows most. Day after day we labor in the gigantic factories and mills of Western civilization, but we have never been allowed to become an organic part of this civilization; we have yet to share its ultimate hopes and expectations. Its incentives and perspectives, which form the core of meaning for so many millions, have yet to lift our personalities to levels of purpose. Instead, after working all day in one civilization, we go home to our Black Belts and live, within the orbit of the surviving remnants of the culture of the South, our naïve, casual, verbal, fluid folk life.

Alone together with our black folk in the towering tenements, we play our guitars, trumpets, and pianos, beating out rough and infectious rhythms that create an instant appeal among all classes of people. Why is our music so contagious? Why is it that those who deny us are willing to sing our songs? Perhaps it is because so many of those who live in cities feel deep down just as we feel. Our big brass horns, our huge noisy drums and whirring violins make a flood of melodies whose poignancy is heightened by our latent fear and uneasiness, by our love of the sensual, and by our feverish hunger for life. On the plantations our songs carried a strain of other-worldly yearning which people called "spiritual"; but now our blues, jazz, swing, and boogie-woogie are our "spirituals" of the city pavements, our longing for freedom and opportunity, an expression of our bewilderment and despair in a world whose meaning eludes us. The ridiculousness and sublimity of love are captured in our blues, those sad-happy songs that laugh and weep all in one breath, those mockingly

tender utterances of a folk imprisoned in steel and stone. Our thirst for the sensual is poured out in jazz; the tension of our brittle lives is given forth in swing; and our nervousness and exhaustion are pounded out in the swift tempo of boogie-woogie.

We lose ourselves in violent forms of dances in our ball-rooms. The faces of the white world, looking on in wonder and curiosity, declare: *"Only* the Negro can play!" But they are wrong. They misread us. We are able to play in this fashion because we have been excluded, left behind; we play in this manner because all excluded folk play. The English say of the Irish, just as America says of us, that only the Irish can play, that they laugh through their tears. But every pow-erful nation says this of the folk whom it oppresses in justifica-tion of that oppression. And, ironically, they are angered by the exhibition of any evidence to the contrary, for it disturbs their conscience with vague and guilty doubts. They smile with cold disdain when we black folk say that our thirst can be slaked in art, that our tensions can be translated into industry, that our energies can be applied to finance, that our delight in the world can be converted into education, that our love of adventure can find fulfillment in aviation. But in one way or another, the white folk deny us these pursuits, and our hunger for expression finds its form in our wild, raw

music, in our invention of slang that winds its way all over America. Our adoration of color goes not into murals, but into dress, into green, red, yellow, and blue clothes. When we have some money in our pockets on payday, our laughter and songs make the principal streets of our Black Belts—Lenox Avenue, Beale Street, State Street, South Street, Second Street, Auburn Avenue—famous the earth over.

The Bosses of the Buildings would have the world believe that we black folk, after these three hundred years, have locked in our veins blood of a queer kind that makes us act in this "special pattern." In their classrooms and laboratories they attempt to harness science in defense of their attitudes and practices, and never do they so vigorously assail us as "trouble-makers" as when we say that we are "this way" because we are made to live "this way." They say we speak treasonably when we declare that human life is plastic, that human nature is malleable, that men possess the dignity and meaning of the environmental and institutional forms through which they are lucky or unlucky enough to express themselves. They solemnly assert that we seek to overthrow the government by violence when we say that we live in this manner because the Black Belt which cradles our lives is created by the hands and brains of men who have decreed that we must live differently. They brand us as revolutionists when we say that we are not allowed to react to life with an honest and frontal vision.

We live on, and our music makes the feet of the whole world dance, even the feet of the children of the poor white workers who live beyond the line that marks the boundary of our lives. Where we cannot go, our tunes, songs, slang, and jokes go. Some of the white boys and girls, starved prisoners of urban homes, even forget the hatred of their parents when they hear our sensual, wailing blue melodies. The common people of the nation grow to love our songs so much that a few of us make our living by creating a haven of song for those who are weary of the barren world of steel and stone reared by the Bosses of the Buildings. But only a few of those who dance and sing with us suspect the rawness of life out of which our laughing-crying tunes and quick dance-steps come; they do not know that our songs and dances are our banner of hope flung desperately up in the face of a world that has pushed us to the wall.

Despite our new worldliness, despite our rhythms, our colorful speech, and our songs, we keep our churches alive. In fact, we have built more of them than ever here on the city pavements, for it is only when we are within the walls of our churches that we are wholly ourselves, that we keep alive a sense of our personalities in relation to the total world in which we live, that we maintain a quiet and constant communion with all that is deepest in us. Our going to church of a Sunday is like placing one's ear to another's chest to hear the unquenchable murmur of the human heart. In our collective outpourings of song and prayer, the fluid emotions of others make us feel the strength in ourselves. We build great churches, some of the greatest in terms of membership— some of our churches have more than 20,000 members— ever built in the history of Western civilization. Our churches are where we dip our tired bodies in cool springs of hope, where we retain our wholeness and humanity despite the blows of death from the Bosses of the Buildings.

Our churches are centers of social and community life, for we have virtually no other mode of communion and we are usually forbidden to worship God in the temples of the Bosses of the Buildings. The church is the door through which we first walked into Western civilization; religion is the form in which America first allowed our personalities to be expressed. Our churches provide social activities for us, cook and serve meals, organize baseball and basketball teams, operate stores and businesses, and conduct social agencies. Our first newspapers and magazines are launched from our churches.

In the Black Belts of the northern cities, our women are

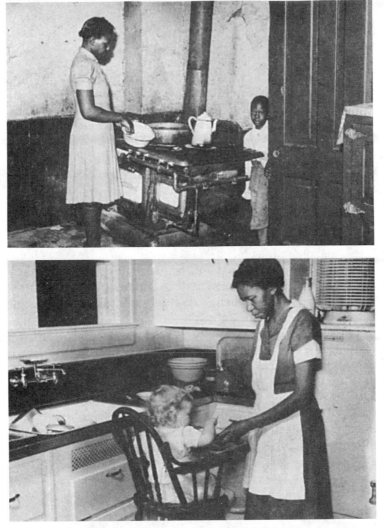

From the kitchenette to the white folk's kitchen

the most circumscribed and tragic objects to be found in our lives, and it is to the churches that our black women cling for emotional security and the release of their personalities. Because their orbit of life is narrow—from their kitchenette to the white folk's kitchen and back home again—they love the church more than do our men, who find a large measure of

232

the expression of their lives in the mills and factories. Surrounding our black women are many almost insuperable barriers: they are black, they are women, they are workers; they are triply anchored and restricted in their movements within and without the Black Belts.

So they keep thousands of Little Bethels and Pilgrims and Calvarys and White Rocks and Good Hopes and Mount Olives going with their nickels and dimes. Nurtured in the close and intimate folk culture of the South, where each person knew the others, where the basic emotions of life were shared by all, many of them sometimes feel that the elaborate ritual of our big churches is too cold and formal for them. To retain the ardent religious emotionalism of which they are so fond, many of them will group themselves about a lonely young black preacher and help him to establish what is called a "store front" church, in which they are still able to perform their religious rituals on the fervid levels of the plantation revival. Sometimes, even in crowded northern cities, elderly black women, hungry for the South but afraid to return, will cultivate tiny vegetable gardens in the narrow squares of ground in front of their hovels. More than even that of the American Indian, the consciousness of vast sections of our black women lies beyond the boundaries of the modern world, though they live and work in that world daily.

Outside of the church, many of our black women drift to ruin and death on the pavements of the city; they are sold, by white men as well as by black, for sex purposes. As a whole, they must go to work at an earlier age than any other section of the nation's population. For every 5 white girls between the ages of ten and fifteen who must work, 25 of our black girls must work; for every 5 white mothers who must leave their children unattended at home in order to work, 25 of our black mothers must leave their children unattended at home in order to work. As modernity and complexity spread through the cities, our black women find that their jobs grow fewer. Many white folk send their soiled clothes to the laundry and hire Japanese, Chinese, and Filipinos as servants to do their domestic work.

Many of our children scorn us; they say that we still wear the red bandanna about our heads, that we are still Uncle Toms. We lean upon our God and scold our children and try to drag them to church with us, but just as we once, years ago, left the plantation to roam the South, so now they leave us for the city pavements. But deep down in us we are glad that our children feel the world hard enough to yearn to wrestle with it. We, the mothers and fathers of the black children, try to hold them back from death, but if we persuade them to stay, or if they come back because we call them, we will pour out our pity upon them. Always our deepest love is toward those children of ours who turn their backs upon our way of life, for our instincts tell us that those brave ones who struggle against death are the ones who bring new life into the world, even though they die to do so, even though our hearts are broken when they die.

We watch strange moods fill our children, and our hearts swell with pain. The streets, with their noise and flaring lights, the taverns, the automobiles, and the poolrooms claim them, and no voice of ours can call them back. They spend their nights away from home; they forget our ways of life, our language, our God. Their swift speech and impatient eyes make us feel weak and foolish. We cannot keep them in

234

school; more than 1,000,000 of our black boys and girls of high school age are not in school. We fall upon our knees and pray for them, but in vain. The city has beaten us, evaded us; but they, with young bodies filled with warm blood, feel bitter and frustrated at the sight of the alluring hopes and prizes denied them. It is not their eagerness to fight that makes us afraid, but that they go to death on the city pavements faster than even disease and starvation can take them. As the courts and the morgues become crowded with our lost children, the hearts of the officials of the city grow cold toward us. As our jobs begin to fail in another depression, our lives and the lives of our children grow so frightful that even some of our educated black leaders are afraid to make known to the nation how we exist. They become ashamed of us and tell us to hide our wounds. And many white people who know how we live are afraid of us, fearing that we may rise up against them.

The sands of our simple folk lives run out on the cold city pavements. Winter winds blow, and we feel that our time is nearing its end. Our final days are full of apprehension, for our children grapple with the city. We cannot bear to look at them; they struggle against great odds. Our tired eyes turn away as we hear the tumult of battle. . . .

Strange moods fill our children

The streets claim our children

4. Men in the Making

WE ARE THE CHILDREN of the black sharecroppers, the first-born of the city tenements.

We have tramped down a road three hundred years long. We have been shunted to and fro by cataclysmic social changes.

We are a folk born of cultural devastation, slavery, physical suffering, unrequited longing, abrupt emancipation, migration, disillusionment, bewilderment, joblessness, and insecurity—all enacted within a *short* space of historical time!

There are millions of us and we are moving in all directions. All our lives we have been catapulted into arenas where, had we thought consciously of invading them, we

would have hung back. A sense of constant change has stolen silently into our lives and has become operative in our personalities as a law of living.

There are some of us who feel our hurts so deeply that we find it impossible to work with whites; we feel that it is futile to hope or dream in terms of American life. Our distrust is so great that we form intensely racial and nationalistic organizations and advocate the establishment of a separate state, a forty-ninth state, in which we black folk would live.

There are even today among us groups that forlornly plan a return to Africa.

There are others of us who feel the need of the protection of a strong nation so keenly that we admire the harsh and imperialistic policies of Japan and ardently hope that the Japanese will assume the leadership of the "darker races."

As our consciousness changes, as we come of age, as we shed our folk swaddling-clothes, so run our lives in a hundred directions.

Today, all of us black folk are not poor. A few of us have money. We make it as the white folk make theirs, but our money-making is restricted to our own people. Many of us black folk have managed to send our children to school, and a few of our children are now professional and business men whose standards of living approximate those of middle-class whites. Some of us own small businesses; others devote their lives to law and medicine.

But the majority of us still toil on the plantations, work in heavy industry, and labor in the kitchens of the Lords of the Land and the Bosses of the Buildings.

The general dislocation of life during the depression caused many white workers to learn through chronic privation that they could not protect their standards of living so long as we blacks were excluded from their unions. Many hundreds of thousands of them found that they could not fight successfully for increased wages and union recognition unless we stood shoulder to shoulder with them. As a consequence, many of us have recently become members of steel, auto, packing, and tobacco unions.

In 1929, when millions of us black folk were jobless, many unemployed white workers joined with us on a national scale to urge relief measures and adequate housing. The influence of this united effort spread even into the South where black and white sharecroppers were caught in the throes of futile conflict.

The fears of black and white lessened in the face of the slowly widening acceptance of an identity of interests. When the depression was at its severest, the courts of many cities, at the instigation of the Bosses of the Buildings, sent armed marshals to evict our jobless black families for their inability to pay rent for the rotting kitchenettes. Organized into groups, we black folk smashed the marshals' locks, picked up the paltry sticks of furniture, and replaced the evicted families. Having hurdled fear's first barrier, we found that many white workers were eager to have us in their organizations, and we were proud to feel that at last our strength was sufficient to awaken in others a desire to work with us. These men differed from those whom we had known on the plantations; they were not "po' white trash." We invited them into our homes and broke our scanty bread with them, and this was our supreme gesture of trust. In this way we encountered for the first time in our lives the full effect of those forces that tended to reshape our folk consciousness, and a few of us stepped forth and accepted within the confines of

our personalities the death of our old folk lives, an acceptance of a death that enabled us to cross class and racial lines,
a death that made us free.

Not all black folk, however, reacted to the depression in
this manner. There were hundreds of thousands of us who
saw that we bought our groceries from white clerks, that we
paid our insurance to white agents, that we paid our rent to
white realtors, that our children were taught in school by
white teachers, that we were served in hospitals by white
doctors, that we asked jobs of white bosses, that we paid our
fares on busses and street cars to white conductors; in short,
that we had no word to say about anything that happened in
our lives. In 1935, inarticulate black men and women, filled
with a naïve, peasant anger, rioted in Harlem's business district and wrought a property damage of more than $2,000,-
000!

But our most qualitatively significant progress was organized and conducted through peaceful channels. In many
large cities there were sturdy minorities of us, both black and
white, who banded together in disciplined, class-conscious
groups and created new organs of action and expression. We
were able to seize nine black boys in a jail in Scottsboro,
Alabama, lift them so high in our collective hands, focus such
a battery of comment and interpretation upon them, that
they became symbols to all the world of the plight of black
folk in America.

If we had been allowed to participate in the vital processes
of America's national growth, what would have been the
texture of our lives, the pattern of our traditions, the routine
of our customs, the state of our arts, the code of our laws, the
function of our government! Whatever others may say, we
black folk say that America would have been stronger and
greater!

Standing now at the apex of the twentieth century, we look
back over the road we have traveled and compare it with the
road over which the white folk have traveled, and we see
that three hundred years in the history of our lives are equiv-

alent to two thousand years in the history of the lives of whites! The many historical phases which whites have traversed voluntarily and gradually during the course of Western civilization we black folk have traversed through swift compulsion. During the three hundred years we have been in the New World, we have experienced all the various types of family life, all the many adjustments to rural and urban life, and today, weary but still eager, we stand ready to accept more change.

Imagine European history from the days of Christ to the present telescoped into three hundred years and you can comprehend the drama which our consciousness has experienced! Brutal, bloody, crowded with suffering and abrupt transitions, the lives of us black folk represent the most magical and meaningful picture of human experience in the Western world. Hurled from our native African homes into the very center of the most complex and highly industrialized civilization the world has ever known, we stand today with a consciousness and memory such as few people possess.

We black folk, our history and our present being, are a mirror of all the manifold experiences of America. What we want, what we represent, what we endure is what America *is*. If we black folk perish, America will perish. If America has forgotten her past, then let her look into the mirror of our consciousness and she will see the *living* past living in the present, for our memories go back, through our black folk of today, through the recollections of our black parents, and through the tales of slavery told by our black grandparents, to the time when none of us, black or white, lived in this fertile land.

The differences between black folk and white folk are not blood or color, and the ties that bind us are deeper than those that separate us. The common road of hope which we all have traveled has brought us into a stronger kinship than any words, laws, or legal claims.

Look at us and know us and you will know yourselves, for

we are *you,* looking back at you from the dark mirror of our lives!

What do we black folk want?

We want what others have, the right to share in the upward march of American life, the only life we remember or have ever known.

The Lords of the Land say: "We will not grant this!"

We answer: "We ask you to grant us nothing. We are winning our heritage, though our toll in suffering is great!"

The Bosses of the Buildings say: "Your problem is beyond solution!"

We answer: "Our problem is being solved. We are crossing the line you dared us to cross, though we pay in the coin of death!"

The seasons of the plantation no longer dictate the lives of many of us; hundreds of thousands of us are moving into the sphere of conscious history.

We are with the new tide. We stand at the crossroads. We watch each new procession. The hot wires carry urgent appeals. Print compels us. Voices are speaking. Men are moving! And we shall be with them. . . .

Poetry

It should be remembered that Wright became known in left-wing circles as a poet and that it is through his revolutionary verse, published in Anvil, Left Front, *and* New Masses, *that he first tried "to link white life with black, to merge two streams of common experience." The score of poems he published between 1935–40 are free-verse pieces dealing with political themes, the life of the poor or the plight of Black people in America. These early poems reflect such diverse influences as those of black folklore, Langston Hughes, Walt Whitman, Carl Sandburg, or T. S. Eliot. Yet most of them have distinct originality, like "I Have Seen Black Hands" (1934) and "Between the World and Me" (1935).*

Later, Wright devoted more time to the blues, of which his "Red Clay Blues" (1939), written in collaboration with Langston Hughes, is an example. "Joe Louis Blues," his lyrics in praise of the black champion, was sung by Paul Robeson and recorded in 1941 by Count Basie's orchestra. When he

---

"I Have Seen Black Hands" originally appeared in *New Masses*, Vol. 11, June 26, 1934.
"Between the World and Me" originally appeared in *Partisan Review*, Vol. 2, July–August 1935.
"Red Clay Blues" originally appeared in *New Masses*, Vol. 32, August 1, 1939.
"The FB Eye Blues" originally was published as an unauthorized leaflet in New York, ca. 1949.

returned to the United States during the Cold War on his way to Argentina, he even wrote a satirical "F. B. Eye Blues."

In 1959, Wright discovered the Japanese haiku. He was entranced by the 17-syllable form and jotted down several thousands of the brief poems, mostly during his treatment at the hospital. "Maybe I'm fooling around with these tiny little poems, but I could not let them go. I was possessed by them," he wrote a friend in May 1960, just six months before his death. While keeping as closely as possible to the original genre, respecting not only the pattern and number of syllables but even the kireji, *or "mood word," Wright was able to inject a deeply personal tone to these pieces. They represent some of his best efforts at writing poetry.*

The distance separating the revolutionary poems of the Thirties, vibrant with generous indignation and bristling with crude imagery, from the disciplined haikus may seem great, but the road traveled from the enthusiasm of the young Communist to the more serene mastery of the mature artist is no evidence of a lessening militancy. Wright simply confined the political statements of his later years to prose. There remains a definite separation between the ideological essays of White Man Listen *(1957) and the sensitive lyricism of this intimate poetry.*

I Have Seen Black Hands

*I am black and I have seen black hands, millions and
    millions of them—
Out of millions of bundles of wool and flannel tiny black
    fingers have reached restlessly and hungrily for life.*

Reached out for the black nipples at the black breasts of
    black mothers,
And they've held red, green, blue, yellow, orange, white,
    and purple toys in the childish grips of possession.
And chocolate drops, peppermint sticks, lollypops,
    wineballs, ice cream cones, and sugared cookies in
    fingers sticky and gummy,
And they've held balls and bats and gloves and marbles
    and jack-knives and sling-shots and spinning tops in
    the thrill of sport and play,
And pennies and nickels and dimes and quarters and
    sometimes on New Year's, Easter, Lincoln's Birthday,
    May Day, a brand new green dollar bill,
They've held pens and rulers and maps and tablets and
    books in palms spotted and smeared with ink,
And they've held dice and cards and half-pint flasks and
    cue sticks and cigars and cigarettes in the pride of
    new maturity . . .

II

I am black and I have seen black hands, millions and
    millions of them—
They were tired and awkward and calloused and grimy
    and covered with hangnails,
And they were caught in the fast-moving belts of
    machines and snagged and smashed and crushed,
And they jerked up and down at the throbbing machines
    massing taller and taller the heaps of
    gold in the banks of bosses,
And they piled higher and higher the steel, iron, the
    lumber, wheat, rye, the oats, corn, the cotton, the
    wool, the oil, the coal, the meat, the fruit, the glass,
    and the stone until there was too much to be used,
And they grabbed guns and slung them on their
    shoulders and marched and groped in trenches and

fought and killed and conquered nations who were
customers for the goods black hands had made.
And again black hands stacked goods higher and higher
until there was too much to be used,
And then the black hands held trembling at the factory
gates the dreaded lay-off slip,
And the black hands hung idle and swung empty and
grew soft and got weak and bony from
unemployment and starvation,
And they grew nervous and sweaty, and opened and
shut in anguish and doubt and hesitation and
irresolution . . .

III

I am black and I have seen black hands, millions and
millions of them—
Reaching hesitantly out of days of slow death for the
goods they had made, but the bosses warned that
the goods were private and did not belong to them,
And the black hands struck desperately out in defence of
life and there was blood, but the enraged bosses
decreed that this too was wrong,
And the black hands felt the cold steel bars of the prison
they had made, in despair tested their strength and
found that they could neither bend nor break them,
And the black hands lifted palms in mute and futile
supplication to the sodden faces of mobs wild in
the revelries of sadism,
And the black hands strained and clawed and struggled
in vain at the noose that tightened about the black
throat,
And the black hands waved and beat fearfully at the tall
flames that cooked and charred the black flesh . . .

IV

I am black and I have seen black hands
Raised in fists of revolt, side by side with the white fists
*   of white workers,*
And some day—and it is only this which sustains me—
Some day there shall be millions and millions of them,
On some red day in a burst of fists on a new horizon!

Between the World and Me

And one morning while in the woods I stumbled
*   suddenly upon the thing,*
Stumbled upon it in a grassy clearing guarded by scaly
*   oaks and elms.*
And the sooty details of the scene rose, thrusting
*   themselves between the world and me. . . .*

There was a design of white bones slumbering forgottenly
*   upon a cushion of ashes.*
There was a charred stump of a sapling pointing a blunt
*   finger accusingly at the sky.*
There were torn tree limbs, tiny veins of burnt leaves, and
*   a scorched coil of greasy hemp;*
A vacant shoe, an empty tie, a ripped shirt, a lonely hat,
*   and a pair of trousers stiff with black blood.*
And upon the trampled grass were buttons, dead matches,
*   butt-ends of cigars and cigarettes, peanut shells, a*
*   drained gin-flask, and a whore's lipstick;*
Scattered traces of tar, restless arrays of feathers, and the
*   lingering smell of gasoline.*
And through the morning air the sun poured yellow
*   surprise into the eye sockets of a stony skull. . . .*

And while I stood my mind was frozen with a cold pity
for the life that was gone.
The ground gripped my feet and my heart was circled by
icy walls of fear—
The sun died in the sky; a night wind muttered in the
grass and fumbled the leaves in the trees; the woods
poured forth the hungry yelping of hounds; the
darkness screamed with thirsty voices; and the
witnesses rose and lived:
The dry bones stirred, rattled, lifted, melting themselves
into my bones.
The grey ashes formed flesh firm and black, entering into
my flesh.

The gin-flask passed from mouth to mouth; cigars and
cigarettes glowed, the whore smeared the lipstick red
upon her lips,
And a thousand faces swirled around me, clamoring that
my life be burned. . . .

And then they had me, stripped me, battering my teeth
into my throat till I swallowed my own blood.
My voice was drowned in the roar of their voices, and my
black wet body slipped and rolled in their hands as
they bound me to the sapling.
And my skin clung to the bubbling hot tar, falling from
me in limp patches.
And the down and quills of the white feathers sank into
my raw flesh, and I moaned in my agony.
Then my blood was cooled mercifully, cooled by a
baptism of gasoline.
And in a blaze of red I leaped to the sky as pain rose like
water, boiling my limbs.
Panting, begging I clutched childlike, clutched to the hot
sides of death.
Now I am dry bones and my face a stony skull staring in
yellow surprise at the sun.. . .

Red Clay Blues

I miss that red clay, Lawd, I
Need to feel it on my shoes.
Says miss that red clay, Lawd, I
Need to feel it on my shoes.
I want to see Georgia, cause I
Got them red clay blues.

Pavement's hard on my feet. I'm
Tired o'this concrete street.
Pavement's hard on my feet, I'm
Tired o'this city street.
Goin' back to Georgia where
That red clay can't be beat.

I want to tramp in the red mud, Lawd, and
Feel the red clay round my toes.
I want to wade in the red mud,
Feel that red clay suckin' at my toes.
I want my little farm back and I
Don't care where that landlord goes.

I want to be in Georgia, when the
Big storms start to blow.
Yes I want to be in Georgia when that
Big storm starts to blow.
I want to see the landlords runnin' cause I
Wonder where they gonna go!

I got them red clay blues.

The FB Eye Blues

That old FB eye
Tied a bell to my bed stall
Said old FB eye
Tied a bell to my bed stall
Each time I love my baby, gover'ment knows it all.

Woke up this morning
FB eye under my bed
Said I woke up this morning
FB eye under my bed
Told me all I dreamed last night, every word I said.

Everywhere I look, Lord
I see FB eyes
Said everywhere I look, Lord
I find FB eyes
I'm getting sick and tired of gover'ment spies.

My mama told me
A rotten egg'll never fry
Said my mama told me
A rotten egg'll never fry
And everybody knows a cheating dog'll never thrive.

Got them blues, blues, blues
Them mean old FB eye blues
Said I got them blues, blues, blues
Them dirty FB eye blues
Somebody tell me something, some good news.

If he'd been a snake, Lord
He'd a jumped up and bit me
Said if he'd been a snake, Lord
He'd a jumped up and bit me
But old FB eye just hauled off and hit me.

Now kittens like milk
and rats love cheese
Said kittens like milk
And rats sure love their cheese
Wonder what FB eye loves crawling on his knees?

Grasshopper likes to spit
In a bloodhound's eye
Said grasshopper likes to spit
In a bloodhound's eye.
Lord, let that grasshopper meet the FB eye.

Breaks my heart in two, Lord
And I just can't forget
Said it breaks my heart, Lord
And I just can't forget
Old jealous FB eye ain't ended yet.

Haikus

For you, O gulls
I order slaty waters
and this leaden sky

I would like a bell
Tolling in this soft twilight
Over willow trees

The dog's violent sneeze
Fails to rouse a single fly
On his mangy back

An autumn sunset
A buzzard sails slowly past
Not flapping its wings

Merciful autumn
Tones down the shabby curtains
Of my rented room

Winter rain at night
Sweetening the taste of bread
And spicing the soup

Coming from the woods
A bull has a lilac sprig
Dangling from a horn

An empty sickbed
An indented white pillow
In weak winter sun

From across the lake
Past the black winter trees
Faint sounds of a flute

Just enough of rain
To bring the smell of silk
From umbrellas

Why is hail so wild
Bouncing so frighteningly
Only to lie so still

Standing in the field
I hear the whispering of
Snowflake to snowflake

The green cockleburs
Caught in the thick wooly hair
Of the black boy's head

A balmy spring wind
Reminding me of something
I cannot recall

I am nobody
A red sinking autumn sun
Took my name away

Make up your mind snail!
You are half inside your house
And halfway out!

In the falling snow
A laughing boy holds out his palms
Until they are white

Keep straight down this block
Then turn right where you will find
A peach tree blooming

With a twitching nose
A dog reads a telegram
On a wet tree trunk

The spring lingers on
In the scent of a damp log
Rotting in the sun

Whose town did you leave
O wild and drowning spring rain
And where do you go?

The crow flew so fast
That he left his lonely caw
Behind in the fields

It is September
The month when I was born
And I have no thoughts

FICTION

Long Black Song

"Long Black Song" was written while Wright was employed on the Federal Writers' Project in Chicago in 1935. He later acknowledged that his style and language had been strongly influenced by those of Gertrude Stein, in Three Lives *and "Melanctha," but he also declared in 1938:*

> *Practically all of us, young writers, were influenced by Ernest Hemingway. We liked the simple, direct way in which he wrote, but a great many of us wanted to write about social problems. The question came up: how could we write about social problems and use a simple style? Hemingway's style is so concentrated on naturalistic detail that there is no room for social comment. One boy said that one way was to dig deeper into the character and try to get something that will live. I decided to try it. I took a very simple Negro woman living in the Northern hills of Mississippi and tried to construct a story about her. In order to make an implied social comment about her, I tried to conceive of a simple peasant woman, whose outlook upon life was influenced by natural things, and to contrast her with a white salesman selling phonographs and records.*

In the arrangement of his collection of novellas, Uncle Tom's Children *(1938), this third story offered an even bleaker ending than "Big Boy Leaves Home" and "Down by*

"Long Black Song" originally appeared in *Uncle Tom's Children*, a collection of short stories, published by Harper & Brothers in 1938.

the Riverside," which preceded it. "Far more disgruntled," Wright was also, he admitted "far more pleased" with this story, since the redemption of the protagonist Silas, although a private affair, was the outcome of his determination to fight his oppressors with their own weapons. Hopelessly outnumbered in his fight, Silas dies in the charred ruins of his house, beaten but with dignity intact. Silas was the first of Wright's characters to set an example of black resistance but the theme reappeared soon after with larger social significance through the character Reverend Taylor in "Fire and Cloud."

> Go t sleep, baby
> Papas gone t town
> Go t sleep, baby
> The suns goin down
> Go t sleep, baby
> Yo candys in the sack
> Go t sleep, baby
> Papas comin back . . .

OVER AND OVER she crooned, and at each lull of her voice she rocked the wooden cradle with a bare black foot. But the baby squalled louder, its wail drowning out the song. She stopped and stood over the cradle, wondering what was bothering it, if its stomach hurt. She felt the diaper; it was dry. She lifted it up and patted its back. Still it cried, longer and louder. She put it back into the cradle and dangled a string of red beads before its eyes. The little black fingers clawed them away. She bent over, frowning, murmuring: "Whuts the mattah, chile? Yuh wan some watah?" She held a dripping gourd to the black lips, but the baby turned its head and kicked its legs. She stood a moment, perplexed. Whuts wrong wid that chile? She ain never carried on like this this tima day. She picked it up and went to the open door. "See the sun, baby?" she asked, pointing to a big ball of red dying between the branches of trees. The baby pulled back and strained its round black arms and legs against her stomach and shoulders. She knew it was tired; she could tell by the halting way it opened its mouth to draw in air. She sat on a wooden stool, unbuttoned the front of her dress, brought the baby closer and offered it a black teat.

"Don baby wan suppah?" It pulled away and went limp, crying softly, piteously, as though it would never stop. Then it pushed its fingers against her breasts and wailed. Lawd, chile, what yuh wan? Yo ma cant hep yuh less she knows whut yuh wan. Tears gushed; four white teeth flashed in red gums; the little chest heaved up and down and round black fingers stretched floorward. Lawd, chile, whuts wrong wid yuh? She stooped slowly, allowing her body to be guided by the downward tug. As soon as the little fingers touched the floor the wail quieted into a broken sniffle. She turned the baby loose and watched it crawl toward a corner. She followed and saw the little fingers reach for the tail-end of an old eight-day clock. "Yuh wan tha ol clock?" She dragged the clock into the center of the floor. The baby crawled after it, calling, "Ahh!" Then it raised its hands and beat on the top of the clock Bink! Bink! Bink! "Naw, yuhll hurt yo hans!" She held the baby and looked around. It cried and struggled. "Wa t, baby!" She fetched a small stick from the top of a rickety dresser. "Here," she said, closing the little fingers about it. "Beat wid this, see?" She heard each blow landing squarely on top of the clock. Bang! Bang! Bang! And with each bang the baby smiled and said, "Ahh!" Mabbe thall keep yuh quiet erwhile. Mabbe Ah kin git some res now. She stood in the doorway. Lawd, tha chiles a pain! She mus be teethin. Er something . . .

She wiped sweat from her forehead with the bottom of her dress and looked out over the green fields rolling up the hillsides. She sighed, fighting a feeling of loneliness. Lawd, its sho hard t pass the days wid Silas gone. Been mos a week now since he took the wagon outta here. Hope ain nothin wrong. He must be buyin a heapa stuff there in Colwatah t be stayin all this time. Yes; maybe Silas would remember and bring that five-yard piece of red calico she wanted. Oh, Lawd! Ah *hope* he don fergit it!

She saw green fields wrapped in the thickening gloam. It was as if they had left the earth, those fields, and were floating slowly skyward. The afterglow lingered, red, dying, somehow tenderly sad. And far away, in front of her, earth and sky met in a soft swoon of shadow. A cricket chirped, sharp and lonely; and it seemed she could hear it chirping long after it had stopped. Silas oughta c mon soon. Ahm tireda staying here by mahsef.

Loneliness ached in her. She swallowed, hearing Bang! Bang! Bang! Tom been gone t war mos a year now. N tha ol wars over n we ain heard nothing yit. Lawd, don let Tom be dead! She frowned into the gloam and wondered about that awful war so far away. They said it was over now. Yeah, Gawd had t stop em fo they killed everybody. She felt that merely to go so far away from home was a kind of death in itself. Just to go that far away was to be killed. Nothing good could come from men going miles across the sea to fight. N how come they wanna kill each other? How come they wanna make blood? Killing was not what men ought to do. Shucks! she thought.

She sighed, thinking of Tom, hearing Bang! Bang! Bang! She saw Tom, saw his big black smiling face; her eyes went dreamily blank, drinking in the red afterglow. Yes, God; it could have been Tom instead of Silas who was having her now. Yes; it could have been Tom she was loving. She smiled and asked herself, Lawd, Ah wondah how would it been wid Tom? Against the plush sky she saw a white bright day and a green cornfield and she saw Tom walking in his overalls and she was with Tom and he had his arm about her waist. She remembered how weak she had felt feeling his fingers sinking into the flesh of her hips. Her knees had trembled and she had had a hard time trying to stand up and not just sink right there to the ground. Yes; that was what Tom had wanted her to do. But she had held Tom up and he had held her up; they had held each other up to keep from slipping to the ground there in the green cornfield. Lawd! Her breath went and she passed her tongue over her lips. But that was not as exciting as that winter evening when the grey skies were sleeping and she and Tom were coming home from church down dark Lover's Lane. She felt the tips of her teats tingling and touching the front of her dress as she remembered how he had crushed her against him and hurt her. She had closed her eyes and was smelling the acrid scent of dry October leaves and had gone weak in his arms and had felt she could not breathe any more and had torn away and run, run home. And the sweet ache which had frightened her then was stealing back to her loins now with the silence and the cricket calls and the red afterglow and Bang! Bang! Bang! Lawd, Ah wondah how would it been wid Tom?

She stepped out on the porch and leaned against the wall of the house. Sky sang a red song. Fields whispered a green prayer. And song and prayer were dying in silence and shadow. Never in all her life had she been so much alone as she was now. Days were never so long as these days; and nights were never so empty as these nights. She jerked her head impatiently, hearing Bang! Bang! Bang! Shucks! she thought. When Tom had gone something had ebbed so slowly that at first she had not noticed it. Now she felt all of it as though the feeling had no bottom. She tried to think just how it had happened. Yes; there had been all her life the long hope of white bright days and the deep desire of dark black nights and then Tom had gone. Bang! Bang! Bang! There had been laughter and eating and singing and the long gladness of green cornfields in summer. There had been cooking and sewing and sweeping and the deep dream of sleeping grey skies in winter. Always it had been like that and she had been happy. But no more. The happiness of those days and nights, of those green cornfields and grey skies had started to go from her when Tom had gone to war. His leaving had left an empty black hole in her heart, a black hole that Silas had come in and filled. But not quite. Silas had not quite filled that hole. No; days and nights were not as they were before.

She lifted her chin, listening. She had heard something, a dull throb like she had heard that day Silas had called her outdoors to look at the airplane. Her eyes swept the sky. But there was no plane. Mabbe its behin the house? She stepped into the yard and looked upward through paling light. There were only a few big wet stars trembling in the east. Then she heard the throb again. She turned, looking up and down the road. The throb grew louder, droning; and she heard Bang! Bang! Bang! There! A car! Wondah whuts a car doin coming out here? A black car was winding over a dusty road, coming toward her. Mabbe some white mans bringing Silas home wida loada goods? But, Lawd, Ah *hope* its no trouble! The car stopped in front of the house and a white man got out. Wondah whut he wans? She looked at the car, but could not see Silas. The white man was young; he wore a straw hat and had no coat. He walked toward her with a huge black package under his arm.

"Well, howre yuh today, Aunty?"

"Ahm well. How yuh?"

"Oh, so-so. Its sure hot today, hunh?"

She brushed her hand across her forehead and sighed.

"Yeah; it is kinda warm."

"You busy?"

"Naw, Ah ain doin nothin."

"Ive got something to show you. Can I sit here, on your porch?"

"Ah reckon so. But, Mistah, Ah ain got no money."

"Haven't you sold your cotton yet?"

"Silas gone t town wid it now."

"Whens he coming back?"

"Ah don know. Ahm waitin fer im."

She saw the white man take out a handkerchief and mop his face. Bang! Bang! Bang! He turned his head and looked through the open doorway, into the front room.

"Whats all that going on in there?"

She laughed.

"Aw, thas jus Ruth."

"Whats she doing?"

"She beatin tha ol clock."

"Beating a *clock?*"

She laughed again.

"She wouldn't go t sleep so Ah give her tha ol clock t play wid."

The white man got up and went to the front door; he stood a moment looking at the black baby hammering on the clock. Bang! Bang! Bang!

"But why let her tear your clock up?"

"It ain no good."

"You could have it fixed."

"We ain got no money t be fixin' no clocks."

"Haven't you got a clock?"

"Naw."

"But how do you keep time?"

"We git erlong widout time."

"But how do you know when to get up in the morning?"

"We jus git up, thas all."

"But how do you know what time it is when you get up?"

"We git up wid the sun."

"And at night, how do you tell when its night?"

"It gits dark when the sun goes down."

"Haven't you ever had a clock?"

She laughed and turned her face toward the silent fields. "Mistah, we don need no clock."

"Well, this beats everything! I don't see how in the world anybody can live without time."

"We just don need no time, Mistah."

The white man laughed and shook his head; she laughed

and looked at him. The white man was funny. Jus like lil boy. Astin how do Ah know when t git up in the mawnin! She laughed again and mused on the baby, hearing Bang! Bang! Bang! She could hear the white man breathing at her side; she felt his eyes on her face. She looked at him; she saw he was looking at her breasts. Hes jus lika lil boy. Acks like he cant understand *nothin!*

"But you need a clock," the white man insisted. "Thats what Im out here for. I'm selling clocks and graphophones. The clocks are made right into the graphophones, a nice sort of combination, hunh? You can have music and time all at once. Ill show you . . ."

"Mistah, we don need no clock!"

"You dont have to buy it. It wont cost you anything just to look."

He unpacked the big black box. She saw the strands of his auburn hair glinting in the afterglow. His back bulged against his white shirt as he stooped. He pulled out a square brown graphophone. She bent forward, looking. Lawd, but its pretty! She saw the face of a clock under the horn of the graphophone. The gilt on the corners sparkled. The color in the wood glowed softly. It reminded her of the light she saw sometimes in the baby's eyes. Slowly she slid a finger over a beveled edge; she wanted to take the box into her arms and kiss it.

"Its eight o'clock," he said.

"Yeah?"

"It only costs fifty dollars. And you dont have to pay for it all at once. Just five dollars down and five dollars a month."

She smiled. The white man was just like a little boy. Jus like a chile. She saw him grinding the handle of the box.

There was a sharp, scratching noise; then she moved nervously, her body caught in the ringing coils of music.

When the trumpet of the Lord shall sound . . .

She rose on circling waves of white bright days and dark black nights.

. . . and time shall be no more . . .

Higher and higher she mounted.

And the morning breaks . . .

Earth fell far behind, forgotten.

. . . eternal, bright and fair . . .

Echo after echo sounded.

When the saved of the earth shall gather . . .

Her blood surged like the long gladness of summer.

. . . over the other shore . . .

Her blood ebbed like the deep dream of sleep in winter.

And when the roll is called up yonder . . .

She gave up, holding her breath.

I'll be there . . .

A lump filled her throat. She leaned her back against a post, trembling, feeling the rise and fall of days and nights, of summer and winter; surging, ebbing, leaping about her, beyond her, far out over the fields to where earth and sky lay folded in darkness. She wanted to lie down and sleep, or else leap up and shout. When the music stopped she felt herself coming back, being let down slowly. She sighed. It was dark now. She looked into the doorway. The baby was sleeping on the floor. Ah gotta git up n put tha chile t bed, she thought.

"Wasnt that pretty?"

"It wuz pretty, awright."

"When do you think your husbands coming back?"

"Ah don know, Mistah."

She went into the room and put the baby into the cradle. She stood again in the doorway and looked at the shadowy box that had lifted her up and carried her away. Crickets called. The dark sky had swallowed up the earth, and more stars were hanging, clustered, burning. She heard the white man sigh. His face was lost in shadow. She saw him rub his palms over his forehead. *Hes just lika lil boy.*

"Id like to see your husband tonight," he said. "Ive got to be in Lilydale at six o'clock in the morning and I wont be back through here soon. I got to pick up my buddy over there and we're heading North."

She smiled into the darkness. He was just like a little boy. A little boy selling clocks.

"Yuh sell them things alla time?" she asked.

"Just for the summer," he said. "I go to school in winter. If I can make enough money out of this Ill go to Chicago to school this fall . . ."

"Whut yuh gonna be?"

"*Be?* What do you mean?"

"Whut yuh goin to school fer?"

"Im studying science."

"Whuts tha?"

"Oh, er . . ." He looked at her. "Its about why things are as they are."

"Why things is as they *is?*"

"Well, its something like that."

"How come yuh wanna study tha?"

"Oh, you wouldnt understand."

She sighed.

"Naw, Ah guess Ah wouldnt."

"Well, I reckon Ill be getting along," said the white man. "Can I have a drink of water?"

"Sho. But we ain got nothin but well-watah, n yuhll have t come n git."

"Thats all right."

She slid off the porch and walked over the ground with bare feet. She heard the shoes of the white man behind her, falling to the earth in soft whispers. It was dark now. She led him to the well, groped her way, caught the bucket and let it down with a rope; she heard a splash and the bucket grew heavy. She drew it up, pulling against its weight, throwing one hand over the other, feeling the cool wet of the rope on her palms.

"Ah don git watah outa here much," she said, a little out of breath. "Silas gits the watah mos of the time. This buckets too heavy fer me."

"Oh, wait! Ill help!"

His shoulder touched hers. In the darkness she felt his warm hands fumbling for the rope.

"Where is it?"

"Here."

She extended the rope through the darkness. His fingers touched her breasts.

"Oh!"

She said it in spite of herself. He would think she was thinking about that. And he was a white man. She was sorry she had said that.

"Wheres the gourd?" he asked. "Gee, its dark!"

She stepped back and tried to see him.

"Here."

"I cant see!" he said, laughing.

Again she felt his fingers on the tips of her breasts. She backed away, saying nothing this time. She thrust the gourd out from her. Warm fingers met her cold hands. He had the gourd. She heard him drink; it was the faint, soft music of water going down a dry throat, the music of water in a silent night. He sighed and drank again.

"I was thirsty," he said. "I hadnt had any water since noon."

She knew he was standing in front of her; she could not see him, but she felt him. She heard the gourd rest against the wall of the well. She turned, then felt his hands full on her breasts. She struggled back.

"Naw, Mistah!"

"Im not going to hurt you!"

White arms were about her, tightly. She was still. But hes

a *white* man. A *white* man. She felt his breath coming hot on her neck and where his hands held her breasts the flesh seemed to knot. She was rigid, poised; she swayed backward, then forward. She caught his shoulders and pushed.

"Naw, naw . . . Mistah, Ah cant do that!"

She jerked away. He caught her hand.

"Please . . ."

"Lemme go!"

She tried to pull her hand out of his and felt his fingers tighten. She pulled harder, and for a moment they were balanced, one against the other. Then he was at her side again, his arms about her.

"I wont hurt you! I wont hurt you . . ."

She leaned backward and tried to dodge his face. Her breasts were full against him; she gasped, feeling the full length of his body. She held her head far to one side; she knew he was seeking her mouth. His hands were on her breasts again. A wave of warm blood swept into her stomach and loins. She felt his lips touching her throat and where he kissed it burned.

"Naw, naw . . ."

Her eyes were full of the wet stars and they blurred, silver and blue. Her knees were loose and she heard her own breathing; she was trying to keep from falling. But hes a *white* man! A *white* man! Naw! Naw! And still she would not let him have her lips; she kept her face away. Her breasts hurt where they were crushed against him and each time she caught her breath she held it and while she held it it seemed that if she would let it go it would kill her. Her knees were pressed hard against his and she clutched the upper parts of his arms, trying to hold on. Her loins ached. She felt her body sliding.

"Gawd . . ."

He helped her up. She could not see the stars now; her eyes were full of the feeling that surged over her body each time she caught her breath. He held her close, breathing into her ear; she straightened, rigidly, feeling that she had to straighten or die. And then her lips felt his and she held her breath and dreaded ever to breathe again for fear of the feeling that would sweep down over her limbs. She held tightly, hearing a mountain tide of blood beating against her throat and temples. Then she gripped him, tore her face away, emptied her lungs in one long despairing gasp and went limp. She felt his hand; she was still, taut, feeling his hand, then his fingers. The muscles in her legs flexed and she bit her lips and pushed her toes deep into the wet dust by the side of the well and tried to wait and tried to wait until she could wait no longer. She whirled away from him and a streak of silver and blue swept across her blood. The wet ground cooled her palms and knee-caps. She stumbled up and ran, blindly, her toes flicking warm, dry dust. Her numbed fingers grabbed at a rusty nail in the post at the porch and she pushed ahead of hands that held her breasts. Her fingers found the door-facing; she moved into the darkened room, her hands before her. She touched the cradle and turned till her knees hit the bed. She went over, face down, her fingers trembling in the crumpled folds of his shirt. She moved and moved again and again, trying to keep ahead of the warm flood of blood that sought to catch her. A liquid metal covered her and she rode on the curve of white bright days and dark black nights and the surge of the long gladness of summer and the ebb of the deep dream of sleep in winter till a high red wave of hotness drowned her in a deluge of silver and blue and boiled her blood and blistered her flesh *bangbangbang* . . .

"YUH BETTAH GO," she said.

She felt him standing by the side of the bed, in the dark. She heard him clear his throat. His belt-buckle tinkled.

"Im leaving that clock and graphophone," he said.

She said nothing. In her mind she saw the box glowing

softly, like the light in the baby's eyes. She stretched out her legs and relaxed.

"You can have it for forty instead of fifty. Ill be by early in the morning to see if your husbands in."

She said nothing. She felt the hot skin of her body growing steadily cooler.

"Do you think hell pay ten on it? Hell only owe thirty then."

She pushed her toes deep into the quilt, feeling a night wind blowing through the door. Her palms rested lightly on top of her breasts.

"Do you think hell pay ten on it?"

"Hunh?"

"Hell pay ten, wont he?"

"Ah don know," she whispered.

She heard his shoe hit against a wall; footsteps echoed on the wooden porch. She started nervously when she heard the roar of his car; she followed the throb of the motor till she heard it when she could hear it no more, followed it till she heard it roaring faintly in her ears in the dark and silent room. Her hands moved on her breasts and she was conscious of herself, all over; she felt the weight of her body resting heavily on shucks. She felt the presence of fields lying out there covered with night. She turned over slowly and lay on her stomach, her hands tucked under her. From somewhere came a creaking noise. She sat upright, feeling fear. The wind sighed. Crickets called. She lay down again, hearing shucks rustle. Her eyes looked straight up in the darkness and her blood sogged. She had lain a long time, full of a vast peace, when a far away tinkle made her feel the bed again. The tinkle came through the night; she listened, knowing that soon she would hear the rattle of Silas' wagon. Even then she tried to fight off the sound of Silas' coming, even then she wanted to feel the peace of night filling her again; but the tinkle grew louder and she heard the jangle of a wagon and the quick trot of horses. Thas Silas! She gave up and waited.

She heard horses neighing. Out of the window bare feet whispered in the dust, then crossed the porch, echoing in soft booms. She closed her eyes and saw Silas come into the room in his dirty overalls as she had seen him come in a thousand times before.

"Yuh sleep, Sarah?"

She did not answer. Feet walked across the floor and a match scratched. She opened her eyes and saw Silas standing over her with a lighted lamp. His hat was pushed far back on his head and he was laughing.

"Ah reckon yuh thought Ah waznt never comin back, hunh? Cant yuh wake up? See, Ah got that red cloth yuh wanted . . ." He laughed again and threw the red cloth on the mantel.

"Yuh hongry?" she asked.

"Naw, Ah kin make out till mawnin." Shucks rustled as he sat on the edge of the bed. "Ah got two hundred n fifty fer mah cotton."

"Two hundred n fifty?"

"Nothin different! N guess whut Ah done?"

"Whut?"

"Ah bought ten mo acres o lan. Got em from ol man Burgess. Paid im a hundred n fifty dollahs down. Ahll pay the rest next year ef things go erlong awright. Ahma have t git a man t hep me nex spring . . ."

"Yuh mean hire somebody?"

"Sho, hire somebody! Whut yuh think? Ain tha the way the white folks do? Ef yuhs gonna git anywheres yuhs gotta do just like they do." He paused. "Whut yuh been doin since Ah been gone?"

"Nothin. Cookin, cleanin, n . . ."

"How Ruth?"

"She awright." She lifted her head. "Silas, yuh git any lettahs?"

"Naw. But Ah heard Tom wuz in town."

"In *town?*"

She sat straight up.

"Yeah, thas whut the folks wuz sayin at the sto."

"Back from the war?"

"Ah ast erroun t see ef Ah could fin im. But Ah couldnt."

"Lawd, Ah wish hed c mon home."

"Them white folks shos glad the wars over. But things wuz kinda bad there in town. Everywhere Ah looked wuznt nothin but black n white soljers. N them white folks beat up a black soljer yestiddy. He was jus in from France. Wuz still wearin his soljers suit. They claimed he sassed a white wo-man . . ."

"Who wuz he?"

"Ah don know. Never saw im befo."

"Yuh see An Peel?"

"Naw."

"Silas!" she said reprovingly.

"Aw, Sarah, Ah jus couldnt git out there."

"Whut else yuh bring sides the cloth?"

"Ah got yuh some high-top shoes." He turned and looked at her in the dim light of the lamp. "Woman, ain yuh glad Ah bought yuh some shoes n cloth?" He laughed and lifted his feet to the bed. "Lawd, Sarah, yuhs sho sleepy, ain yuh?"

"Bettah put tha lamp out, Silas . . ."

"Aw . . ." He swung out of the bed and stood still for a moment. She watched him, then turned her face to the wall.

"Whuts that by the windah?" he asked.

She saw him bending over and touching the graphophone with his fingers.

"Thasa graphophone."

"Where yuh git it from?"

"A man lef it here."

"When he bring it?"

"Today."

"But how come he t leave it?"

"He says hell be out here in the mawnin t see ef yuh wans t buy it."

He was on his knees, feeling the wood and looking at the gilt on the edges of the box. He stood up and looked at her.

"Yuh ain never said yuh wanted one of these things."

She said nothing.

"Where wuz the man from?"

"Ah don know."

"He white?"

"Yeah."

He put the lamp back on the mantel. As he lifted the globe to blow out the flame, his hand paused.

"Whos hats this?"

She raised herself and looked. A straw hat lay bottom upwards on the edge of the mantel. Silas picked it up and looked back to the bed, to Sarah.

"Ah guess its the white mans. He must a lef it . . ."

"Whut he doin *in our room?*"

"He wuz talkin t me bout that graphophone."

She watched him go to the window and stoop again to the box. He picked it up, fumbled with the price-tag and took the box to the light.

"Whut this thing cos?"

"Forty dollahs."

"But its marked fifty here."

"Oh, Ah means he said fifty . . ."

He took a step toward the bed.

"Yuh lyin t me!"

"Silas!"

He heaved the box out of the front door; there was a smashing, tinkling noise as it bounded off the front porch and hit the ground. "Whut in hell yuh lie t me fer?"

"Yuh broke the box!"

"Ahma break yo Gawddam neck ef yuh don stop lyin t me!"

"Silas, Ah ain lied t yuh!"

"Shut up, Gawddammit! Yuh did!"

He was standing by the bed with the lamp trembling in his

hand. She stood on the other side, between the bed and the wall.

"How come yuh tell me that thing cos *forty* dollahs when it cos *fifty?*"

"Thas whut he tol me."

"How come he take *ten* dollars off fer yuh?"

"He ain took nothin off fer me, Silas!"

"Yuh lyin t me! N yuh lied t me bout Tom, too!"

She stood with her back to the wall, her lips parted, looking at him silently, steadily. Their eyes held for a moment. Silas looked down, as though he were about to believe her. Then he stiffened.

"Whos this?" he asked, picking up a short, yellow pencil from the crumpled quilt.

She said nothing. He started toward her.

"Yuh wan me t take mah raw-hide whip n make yuh talk?"

"Naw, naw, Silas! Yuh wrong! He wuz figgerin wid tha pencil!"

He was silent a moment, his eyes searching her face.

"Gawddam yo black soul t hell, don yuh try lyin t me! Ef yuh start layin wid white men Ahll hosswhip yuh t a incha yo life. Shos theres a Gawd in Heaven Ah will! From sunup t sundown Ah works mah guts out t pay them white trash bastards whut Ah owe em, n then Ah comes n fins they been in mah house! Ah cant go into their houses, n yuh know Gawddam well Ah cant! They don have no mercy on no black folks; wes jus like dirt under their feet! Fer ten years Ah slaves lika dog t git mah farm free, givin ever penny Ah kin t em, n then Ah comes n fins they been in mah house . . ." He was speechless with outrage. "If yuh wans t eat at mah table yuhs gonna keep them white trash bastards out, yuh hear? Tha white ape kin come n git tha damn box n Ah ain gonna pay im a cent! He had no bisness leavin it here, n yuh had no bisness lettin im! Ahma tell tha sonofabitch something when he comes out here in the mawnin, so hep me Gawd! Now git back in tha bed!"

She slipped beneath the quilt and lay still, her face turned to the wall. Her heart thumped slowly and heavily. She heard him walk across the floor in his bare feet. She heard the bottom of the lamp as it rested on the mantel. She stiffened when the room darkened. Feet whispered across the floor again. The shucks rustled from Silas' weight as he sat on the edge of the bed. She was still, breathing softly. Silas was mumbling. She felt sorry for him. In the darkness it seemed that she could see the hurt look on his black face. The crow of a rooster came from far away, came so faintly that it seemed she had not heard it. The bed sank and the shucks cried out in dry whispers; she knew Silas had stretched out. She heard him sigh. Then she jumped because he jumped. She could feel the tenseness of his body; she knew he was sitting bolt upright. She felt his hands fumbling jerkily under the quilt. Then the bed heaved amid a wild shout of shucks and Silas' feet hit the floor with a loud boom. She snatched herself to her elbows, straining her eyes in the dark, wondering what was wrong now. Silas was moving about, cursing under his breath.

"Don wake Ruth up!" she whispered.

"Ef yuh say one mo word t me Ahma slap yuh inter a black spasm!"

She grabbed her dress, got up and stood by the bed, the tips of her fingers touching the wall behind her. A match flared in yellow flame; Silas' face was caught in a circle of light. He was looking downward, staring intently at a white wad of cloth balled in his hand. His black cheeks were hard, set; his lips were tightly pursed. She looked closer; she saw that the white cloth was a man's handkerchief. Silas' fingers loosened; she heard the handkerchief hit the floor softly, damply. The match went out.

"Yuh little bitch!"

Her knees gave. Fear oozed from her throat to her stomach. She moved in the dark toward the door, struggling with the dress, jamming it over her head. She heard the thick skin of Silas' feet swish across the wooden planks.

"Ah got mah raw-hide whip n Ahm takin yuh t the barn!"

She ran on tiptoe to the porch and paused, thinking of the baby. She shrank as something whined through the air. A red streak of pain cut across the small of her back and burned its way into her body, deeply.

"Silas!" she screamed.

She grabbed for the post and fell in dust. She screamed again and crawled out of reach.

"Git t the barn, Gawddammit!"

She scrambled up and ran through the dark, hearing the baby cry. Behind her leather thongs hummed and feet whispered swiftly over the dusty ground.

"C mere, yuh bitch! C mere, Ah say!"

She ran to the road and stopped. She wanted to go back and get the baby, but she dared not. Not as long as Silas had that whip. She stiffened, feeling that he was near.

"Yuh jus as well c mon back n git yo beatin!"

She ran again, slowing now and then to listen. If she only knew where he was she would slip back into the house and get the baby and walk all the way to Aunt Peel's.

"Yuh ain comin back in mah house till Ah beat yuh!"

She was sorry for the anger she knew he had out there in the field. She had a bewildering impulse to go to him and ask him not to be angry; she wanted to tell him that there was nothing to be angry about; that what she had done did not matter; that she was sorry; that after all she was his wife and still loved him. But there was no way she could do that now; if she went to him he would whip her as she had seen him whip a horse.

"Sarah! Sarah!"

His voice came from far away. Ahm goin git Ruth. Back through dust she sped, going on her toes, holding her breath.

"Saaaarah!"

From far off his voice floated over the fields. She ran into the house and caught the baby in her arms. Again she sped through dust on her toes. She did not stop till she was so far away that his voice sounded like a faint echo falling from the sky. She looked up; the stars were paling a little. Mus be gittin near mawnin. She walked now, letting her feet sink softly into the cool dust. The baby was sleeping; she could feel the little chest swelling against her arm. She looked up again; the sky was solid black. Its gittin near mawnin. Ahma take Ruth t An Peels. N mabbe Ahll fin Tom . . . But she could not walk all that distance in the dark. Not now. Her legs were tired. For a moment a memory of surge and ebb rose in her blood; she felt her legs straining, upward. She sighed. Yes, she would go to the sloping hillside back of the garden and wait until morning. Then she would slip away. She stopped, listened. She heard a faint, rattling noise. She imagined Silas' kicking or throwing the smashed graphophone. Hes mad! Hes sho mad! Aw, Lawd! . . . She stopped stock still, squeezing the baby till it whimpered. What would happen when that white man came out in the morning? She had forgotten him. She would have to head him off and tell him. Yeah, cause Silas jus mad ernuff t kill! Lawd, hes mad ernuff t kill!

SHE CIRCLED the house widely, climbing a slope, groping her way, holding the baby high in her arms. After awhile she stopped and wondered where on the slope she was. She remembered there was an elm tree near the edge; if she could find it she would know. She groped farther, feeling with her feet. Ahm gittin los! And she did not want to fall with the baby. Ahma stop here, she thought. When morning came she would see the car of the white man from this hill and she would run down the road and tell him to go back; and then there would be no killing. Dimly she saw in her mind a picture of men killing and being killed. White men killed the black and black men killed the white. White men killed the black men because they could, and the black men killed the white men to keep from being killed. And killing was blood. Lawd, Ah wish Tom wuz here. She shuddered, sat on the ground and watched the sky for signs of morning. Mabbe Ah oughta walk on down the road? Naw . . . Her legs were tired. Again she felt her body straining. Then she saw Silas holding the white man's handkerchief. She heard it hit the floor, softly, damply. She was sorry for what she had done. Silas was as good to her as any black man could be to a black woman. Most of the black women worked in the fields as croppers. But Silas had given her her own home, and that was more than many others had done for their women. Yes, she knew how Silas felt. Always he had said he was as good as any white man. He had worked hard and saved his money and bought a farm so he could grow his own crops like white men. Silas hates white folks! Lawd, he sho hates em!

The baby whimpered. She unbuttoned her dress and nursed her in the dark. She looked toward the east. There! A tinge of grey hovered. It wont be long now. She could see ghostly outlines of trees. Soon she would see the elm, and by the elm she would sit till it was light enough to see the road.

The baby slept. Far off a rooster crowed. Sky deepened. She rose and walked slowly down a narrow, curving path and came to the elm tree. Standing on the edge of a slope, she saw a dark smudge in a sea of shifting shadows. That was her home. Wondah how come Silas didnt light the lamp? She shifted the baby from her right hip to her left, sighed, struggled against sleep. She sat on the ground again, caught the baby close and leaned against the trunk of a tree. Her eye-lids drooped and it seemed that a hard, cold hand caught hold of her right leg or was it her left leg—she did not know which —and began to drag her over a rough litter of shucks and when she strained to see who it was that was pulling her no one was in sight but far ahead was darkness and it seemed that out of the darkness some force came and pulled her like a magnet and she went sliding along over a rough bed of screeching shucks and it seemed that a wild fear made her want to scream but when she opened her mouth to scream she could not scream and she felt she was coming to a wide black hole and again she made ready to scream and then it was too late for she was already over the wide black hole falling falling falling . . .

She awakened with a start and blinked her eyes in the sunshine. She found she was clutching the baby so hard that it had begun to cry. She got to her feet, trembling from fright of the dream, remembering Silas and the white man and Silas' running her out of the house and the white man's coming. Silas was standing in the front yard; she caught her breath. Yes, she had to go and head that white man off! Naw! She could not do that, not with Silas standing there with that whip in his hand. If she tried to climb any of those slopes he would see her surely. And Silas would never forgive her for something like that. If it were anybody but a white man it would be different.

Then, while standing there on the edge of the slope looking wonderingly at Silas striking the whip against his overall-leg—and then, while standing there looking—she froze. There came from the hills a distant throb. Lawd! The baby whimpered. She loosened her arms. The throb grew louder, droning. Hes comin fas! She wanted to run to Silas and beg him not to bother the white man. But he had that whip in his hand. She should not have done what she had done last night. This was all her fault. Lawd, ef anything happens t im its mah blame . . . Her eyes watched a black car speed over the crest of a hill. She should have been out there on the road instead of sleeping here by the tree. But it was too late now. Silas was standing in the yard; she saw him turn with a nervous jerk and sit on the edge of the porch. He was holding the whip stiffly. The car came to a stop. A door swung open. A white man got out. Thas im! She saw another white man in the front seat of the car. N thats his buddy . . . The white man who had gotten out walked over the ground, going to Silas. They faced each other, the white man standing up and Silas sitting down; like two toy men they faced each other. She saw Silas point the whip to the smashed graphophone. The white man looked down and took a quick step backward. The white man's shoulders were bent and he shook his head from left to right. Then Silas got up and they faced each other again; like two dolls, a white doll and a black doll, they faced each other in the valley below. The white man pointed his finger into Silas' face. Then Silas' right arm went up; the whip flashed. The white man turned, bending, flinging his hands to shield his head. Silas' arm rose and fell, rose and fell. She saw the white man crawling in dust, trying to get out of reach. She screamed when she saw the other white man get out of the car and run to Silas. Then all three were on the ground, rolling in dust, grappling for the whip. She clutched the baby and ran. Lawd! Then she stopped, her mouth hanging open. Silas had broken loose and was running toward the house. She knew he was going for his gun.

"Silas!"

Running, she stumbled and fell. The baby rolled in the dust and bawled. She grabbed it up and ran again. The white men were scrambling for their car. She reached level ground, running. Hell be killed! Then again she stopped. Silas was on the front porch, aiming a rifle. One of the white men was climbing into the car. The other was standing, waving his arms, shouting at Silas. She tried to scream, but choked; and she could not scream till she heard a shot ring out.

"Silas!"

One of the white men was on the ground. The other was in the car. Silas was aiming again. The car started, running in a cloud of dust. She fell to her knees and hugged the baby close. She heard another shot, but the car was roaring over the top of the southern hill. Fear was gone now. Down the slope she ran. Silas was standing on the porch, holding his gun and looking at the fleeing car. Then she saw him go to the white man lying in dust and stoop over him. He caught one of the man's legs and dragged the body into the middle of the road. Then he turned and came slowly back to the house. She ran, holding the baby, and fell at his feet.

"Silas!"

"GIT UP, SARAH!"

His voice was hard and cold. She lifted her eyes and saw blurred black feet. She wiped tears away with dusty fingers and pulled up. Something took speech from her and she stood with bowed shoulders. Silas was standing still, mute; the look on his face condemned her. It was as though he had gone far off and had stayed a long time and had come back changed even while she was standing there in the sunshine before him. She wanted to say something, to give herself. She cried.

"Git the chile up, Sarah!"

She lifted the baby and stood waiting for him to speak, to tell her something to change all this. But he said nothing. He walked toward the house. She followed. As she attempted to go in, he blocked the way. She jumped to one side as he threw the red cloth outdoors to the ground. The new shoes came next. Then Silas heaved the baby's cradle. It hit the porch and a rocker splintered; the cradle swayed for a second, then fell to the ground, lifting a cloud of brown dust against the sun. All of her clothes and the baby's clothes were thrown out.

"Silas!"

She cried, seeing blurred objects sailing through the air and hearing them hit softly in the dust.

"Git yo things n go!"

"Silas!"

"Ain no use yuh sayin *nothin* now!"

"But theyll kill yuh!"

"There ain nothin Ah kin do. N there ain nothin yuh kin do. Yuh done done too Gawddam much awready. Git yo things n go!"

"Theyll kill yuh, Silas!"

He pushed her off the porch.

"GIT YO THINGS N GO T AN PEELS!'"

"Les *both* go, Silas!"

"Ahm stayin here till they come back!"

She grabbed his arm and he slapped her hand away. She dropped to the edge of the porch and sat looking at the ground.

"Go way," she said quietly. "Go way fo they comes. Ah didnt mean no harm . . ."

"Go way fer whut?"

"Theyll *kill* yuh . . ."

"It don make no difference." He looked out over the sunfilled fields. "Fer ten years Ah slaved mah life out t git mah farm free . . ." His voice broke off. His lips moved as though a thousand words were spilling silently out of his mouth, as though he did not have breath enough to give them sound. He looked to the sky, and then back to the dust. "Now, its all gone. *Gone* . . . Ef Ah run erway, Ah ain got nothin. Ef Ah stay n fight, Ah ain got nothin. It dont make no difference which way Ah go. Gawd! Gawd, Ah wish all them white folks wuz dead! *Dead*, Ah tell yuh! Ah wish Gawd would kill em *all!"*

She watched him run a few steps and stop. His throat swelled. He lifted his hands to his face; his fingers trembled. Then he bent to the ground and cried. She touched his shoulders.

"Silas!"

He stood up. She saw he was staring at the white man's body lying in the dust in the middle of the road. She watched him walk over to it. He began to talk to no one in particular; he simply stood over the dead white man and talked out of his life, out of a deep and final sense that now it was all over and nothing could make any difference.

"The white folks ain never gimme a chance! They ain never give no black man a chance! There ain nothin in yo whole life yuh kin keep from em! They take yo lan! They take

yo freedom! They take yo women! N then they take yo life!"
He turned to her, screaming. "N then Ah gits stabbed in the
back by mah own blood! When mah eyes is on the white folks
to keep em from killin me, mah own blood trips me up!" He
knelt in the dust again and sobbed; after a bit he looked to
the sky, his face wet with tears. "Ahm gonna be hard like
they is! So hep me, Gawd, Ah'm gonna be *hard!* When they
come fer me Ahm gonna *be here!* N when they git me outta
here theys gonna *know* Ahm gone! Ef Gawd lets me live
Ahm gonna make em *feel* it!" He stopped and tried to get his
breath. "But, Lawd, Ah don wanna be this way! I don mean
nothin! Yuh die ef yuh fight! Yuh die ef yuh don fight! Either
way yuh die n it don mean nothin . . ."

He was lying flat on the ground, the side of his face deep
in dust. Sarah stood nursing the baby with eyes black and
stony. Silas pulled up slowly and stood again on the porch.

"Git on t An Peels, Sarah!"

A dull roar came from the south. They both turned. A long
streak of brown dust was weaving down the hillside.

"Silas!"

"Go on cross the fields, Sarah!"

"We kin *both* go! Git the hosses!"

He pushed her off the porch, grabbed her hand, and led
her to the rear of the house, past the well, to where a path
led up a slope to the elm tree.

"Silas!"

"Yuh git on fo they ketch yuh too!"

Blind from tears, she went across the swaying fields, stumbling over blurred grass. It ain no use! She knew it was now
too late to make him change his mind. The calves of her legs
knotted. Suddenly her throat tightened, aching. She stopped,
closed her eyes and tried to stem a flood of sorrow that
drenched her. Yes, killing of white men by black men and
killing of black men by white men went on in spite of the
hope of white bright days and the desire of dark black nights
and the long gladness of green cornfields in summer and the

deep dream of sleepy grey skies in winter. And when killing started it went on, like a river flowing. Oh, she felt sorry for Silas! Silas. . . . He was following that long river of blood. Lawd, how come he wans t stay there like tha? And he did not want to die; she knew he hated dying by the way he talked of it. Yet he followed the old river of blood, knowing that it meant nothing. He followed it, cursing and whimpering. But he followed it. She stared before her at the dry, dusty grass. Somehow, men, black men and white men, land and houses, green cornfields and grey skies, gladness and dreams, were all a part of that which made life good. Yes, somehow, they were linked, like the spokes in a spinning wheel. She felt they were. She knew they were. She felt it when she breathed and knew it when she looked. But she could not say how; she could not put her finger on it and when she thought hard about it it became all mixed up, like milk spilling suddenly. Or else it knotted in her throat and chest in a hard, aching lump, like the one she felt now. She touched her face to the baby's face and cried again.

There was a loud blare of auto horns. The growing roar made her turn round. Silas was standing, seemingly unafraid, leaning against a post of the porch. The long line of cars came speeding in clouds of dust. Silas moved toward the door and went in. Sarah ran down the slope a piece, coming again to the elm tree. Her breath was slow and hard. The cars stopped in front of the house. There was a steady drone of motors and drifting clouds of dust. For a moment she could not see what was happening. Then on all sides white men with pistols and rifles swarmed over the fields. She dropped to her knees, unable to take her eyes away, unable, it seemed, to breathe. A shot rang out. A white man fell, rolling over, face downward.

"Hes gotta gun!"
"Git back!"
"Lay down!"
The white men ran back and crouched behind cars. Three

more shots came from the house. She looked, her head and eyes aching. She rested the baby in her lap and shut her eyes. Her knees sank into the dust. More shots came, but it was no use looking now. She knew it all by heart. She could feel it happening even before it happened. There were men killing and being killed. Then she jerked up, being compelled to look.

"Burn the bastard out!"

"Set the sonofabitch on fire!"

"Cook the coon!"

"Smoke im out!"

She saw two white men on all fours creeping past the well. One carried a gun and the other a red tin can. When they reached the back steps the one with the tin can crept under the house and crept out again. Then both rose and ran. Shots. One fell. A yell went up. A yellow tongue of fire licked out from under the back steps.

"Burn the nigger!"

"C mon out, nigger, n git yos!"

She watched from the hill-slope; the back steps blazed. The white men fired a steady stream of bullets. Black smoke spiraled upward in the sunshine. Shots came from the house. The white men crouched out of sight, behind their cars.

"Make up your mind, nigger!"

"C mon out er burn, yuh black bastard!"

"Yuh think yuhre white now, nigger?"

The shack blazed, flanked on all sides by whirling smoke filled with flying sparks. She heard the distant hiss of flames. White men were crawling on their stomachs. Now and then they stopped, aimed, and fired into the bulging smoke. She looked with a tense numbness; she looked, waiting for Silas to scream, or run out. But the house crackled and blazed, spouting yellow plumes to the blue sky. The white men shot again, sending a hail of bullets into the furious pillars of smoke. And still she could not see Silas running out, or hear his voice calling. Then she jumped, standing. There was a loud crash; the roof caved in. A black chimney loomed amid crumbling wood. Flames roared and black smoke billowed, hiding the house. The white men stood up, no longer afraid. Again she waited for Silas, waited to see him fight his way out, waited to hear his call. Then she breathed a long, slow breath, emptying her lungs. She knew now. Silas had killed as many as he could and stayed on to burn, had stayed without a murmur. She filled her lungs with a quick gasp as the walls fell in; the house was hidden by eager plumes of red. She turned and ran with the baby in her arms, ran blindly across the fields, crying, "Naw, Gawd!"

Fire and Cloud

Dissatisfied as he was with the bleak ending of "Long Black Song" in terms of the hero's resistance to oppression, Wright immediately started to look for another solution. But, he confides in a June 1936 report of the genesis of Uncle Tom's Children:

Nowhere in the literary education of the majority of Negroes do even ordinary human actions find themselves clothed in terms of daily Negro life. Always it is in something faraway in the white world, sometimes bound up with ways of life and social actions forbidden and prohibited upon penalty to the Negro in America. What I wanted was to see these things come into Negro life, dressed in Negro clothes, speaking Negro language. . . . In casting about for another character, I was drawn to the "old Negro," the Negro close to the soil, the Negro whose staunch will four centuries of arduous oppression has not broken. And especially was I drawn toward the religious expression of the "old Negro." And I made the startling discovery—no doubt a naïve one, but after all it was mine, a Negro's—that the images, symbols and attitudes of Christianity were the highest crystallizations of the Negro's will to live he has made in this country. . . . In "Fire and Cloud," Taylor, who unconsciously identifies his will with that of

"Fire and Cloud" originally appeared in *Story Magazine*, Vol. 12, March 1938. It was included in *Uncle Tom's Children*, a collection of short stories, published by Harper & Brothers in 1938.

God—a common thing among Negroes (else how could they have lived so long under oppression without any tradition of their own to buttress and sustain them?)—as I say, the religious Taylor is set among conditions calling for a struggle which is essentially a class one. In other words, he is called upon to do class battle with the only spiritual weapons he has, a belief in his right to the earth.

The balance between ideology and symbolic pattern, between message and medium was so nicely struck in "Fire and Cloud" that the jury of the 1938 Story Magazine *contest awarded it a first prize over four hundred entries. This was the beginning of Wright's "luck" with American publishers: Harper's gave him a contract for his first volume of novellas,* Uncle Tom's Children, *which attracted national attention.*

"A NAUGHTS A NAUGHT . . ."

As he walked his eyes looked vacantly on the dusty road, and the words rolled without movement from his lips, each syllable floating softly up out of the depths of his body.

"N five a figger . . ."

He pulled out his pocket handkerchief and mopped his brow without lessening his pace.

"All fer the white man . . ."

He reached the top of the slope and paused, head down.

"N none fer the nigger. . . ."

His shoulders shook in half-laugh and half-shudder. He finished mopping his brow and spat, as though to rid himself of some bitter thing. He thought. Thas the way its awways been! Wistfully he turned and looked back at the dim buildings of the town lying sprawled mistily on the crest of a far hill. Seems like the white folks jus erbout owns this whole worl! Looks like they done conquered *everything.* We black folks is jus los in one big white fog. . . . With his eyes still on the hazy buildings, he flexed his lips slowly and spoke under his breath:

"They could do something! They could do *something,* awright! Mabbe ef fiv er six thousan of us marched downtown we could *scare* em inter doin something! Lawd, mabbe them Reds *is* right!"

He walked again and tucked his handkerchief back into his pocket. He could feel the heat of the evening over all his body, not strongly, but closely and persistently, as though he were holding his face over a tub of steaming suds. Far below him at the bottom of the valley lay a cluster of bleak huts with window panes red-lit from dying sunlight. Those huts were as familiar to his eyes as a nest is to the eyes of a bird, for he had lived among them all his life. He knew by sight or sound every black man, woman and child living within those huddled walls. For a moment an array of soft black faces hovered before his eyes. N whut kin Ah tell em? Whut kin Ah say t em? He stopped, looked at the ground and sighed. And then he saw himself as he had stood but a few moments ago, facing the white woman who sat behind the brown, gleaming desk: her arms had been round, slender, snow-white, like cold marble; her hair had been the color of flowing gold and had glinted in the sunlight; her eyes had been wide and grey behind icily white spectacles. It seemed he could hear her saying in her dry, metallic voice: I'm sorry, Taylor. You'll just have to do the best you can. Explain it to them, make them understand that we cant do anything. Everybodys hongry, and after all, it's no harder on your people than it is on ours. Tell them they'll just have to wait. . . .

He wagged his head and his lips broke in a slow, sick smile. Whut she know erbout being hongry? Whut she know erbout it? He walked again, thinking, Here Ah is a man called by Gawd t preach n whut kin Ah do? Hongry folks lookin t me fer hep n whut kin Ah do? Ah done tried everything n cant do *nuthin!* Shucks, mabbe Hadley n Greens right? They *might* be right. Gawd knows, they *might* be right.

He lifted his head and saw the wide fields plunging before him, down the hillside. The grass was dark and green. All this! he thought. All *this* n folks hongry! Good Gawd, whuts *wrong!* He saw the road running before him, winding, vanishing, the soft yellow dust filled with the ruts of wagon wheels and tiny threads of auto tires. He threw back his head and spoke out loud:

"The good Lawds gonna clean up this ol worl some day! Hes gonna make a new Heaven n a new Earth! N Hes gonna do it in a eye-twinkle change; Hes gotta do it! Things cant go on like this ferever! Gawd knows they cant!" He pulled off his coat and slung it under his left arm. "Waal, there ain nothing t do but go back n tell em. . . . Tell em the white folks wont let em eat. . . ."

The road curved, descending among the green fields that tumbled to a red sky. This was the land on which the Great God Almighty had first let him see the light of His blessed day. This was the land on which he had first taken unto himself a wife, leaving his mother and father to cleave to her. And it was on the green slopes of these struggling hills that his first-born son, Jimmy, had romped and played, growing to a strong, upright manhood. He wagged his head, musing: Lawd, them wuz the good ol days. . . . There had been plenty to eat; the blessings of God had been overflowing. He had toiled from sunup to sundown, and in the cool of the evenings his wife, May, had taught him to read and write. Then God had spoken to him, a quiet, deep voice coming out of the black night; God had called him to preach His word, to spread it to the four corners of the earth, to save His black people. And he had obeyed God and had built a church on a rock which the very gates of Hell could not prevail against. Yes, he had been like Moses, leading his people out of the wilderness into the Promised Land. He sighed, walking and taking his coat from his left arm and tucking it under his right. Yes, things had been clear-cut then. In those days there had stretched before his eyes a straight and narrow path and he had walked in it, with the help of a Gracious God. On Sundays he had preached God's Word, and on Mondays and Tuesdays and Wednesdays and Thursdays and Fridays and Saturdays he had taken old Bess, his mule, and his plow and had broke God's ground. For a moment while walking through the dust and remembering his hopes of those early years he seemed to feel again the plow handles trembling in his calloused hands and hear the earth cracking and breaking open, black, rich and damp; it seemed he could see old Bess straining forward with the plow, swishing her tail and tossing her head and snorting now and then. Yes, there had been something in those good old days when he had walked behind his plow, between the broad green earth and a blue sweep of sunlit sky; there had been in it all a surge of will, clean, full, joyful; the earth was his and he was the earth's; they were one; and it was that joy and will and oneness in him that God had spoken to when He had called him to preach His word, to save His black people, to lead them, to guide them, to be a shepherd to His flock. But now the whole thing was giving way, crumbling in his hands, right before his eyes. And every time he tried to think of some way out, of some way to stop it, he saw wide grey eyes behind icily white spectacles. He mopped his brow again. Mabbe Hadley n Greens right. . . . Lawd, Ah don know whut t do! Ef Ah fight fer things the white folk say Ahma bad nigger stirrin up trouble. N ef Ah don do nothin, we starve. . . . But somethings *gotta* be done! Mabbe ef we had a demonstration like Hadley n Green said, we could *scare* them white folks inter doin something. . . .

He looked at the fields again, half wistfully, half curiously. Lawd, we could make them ol fields bloom ergin. We could make em feed us. Thas whut Gawd put em there fer. Plows could break and hoes could chop and hands could pick and arms could carry. . . . On and on that could happen and people could eat and feel as he had felt with the plow handles trembling in his hands, following old Bess, hearing the earth cracking and breaking because he wanted it to crack and break; because he willed it, because the earth was his. And they could sing as he had sung when he and May were first married; sing about picking cotton, fishing, hunting, about sun and rain. They could. . . . But whuts the usa thinkin erbout stuff like this? Its all gone now. . . . And he had to go and tell his congregation, the folks the Great God Almighty had called him to lead to the Promised Land—he had to tell them that the relief would give them no food.

That morning he had sent a committee of ten men and women from his congregation to see the mayor. Wondah how they come out? The mayor tol em something, sho! So fer hes been pretty wid me even if he is a white man. As his feet sank softly into the dust he saw Mayor Bolton; he saw the red chin that always had a short, black stubble of beard; he saw the cigar glowing red in front of a pink, fat face. But he needs something t scare im now, he thought. Hes been running over us too long. . . .

He reached the bottom of the slope, turned into a cinder path, and approached the huts. N Lawd, when Ah do try t do somethin mah own folks wont stan by me, wont stick wid me. Theres old Deacon Smith a-schemin n a-plottin, just a-watchin me lika hawk, just a-waitin fer me t tak mah eyes off the groun sos he kin trip me up, sos he kin run t the white folks n tell em Ahm doin something wrong! A black snake in the grass! A black Judas! Thas all he is! Lawd, the Devils sho busy in this world. . . .

He was walking among the crowded huts now.

hello reveren

"How yuh tonight, sonny!" Let ol Deacon Smith tell it, no matter whut Ah *do*, Ahm wrong. . . .

good evenin reveren

"Good evenin, Sistah!" Hes been a-tryin t cheat me outta mah church ever since hes been erroun here. . . .

how yuh tonight reveren Taylor

"Jus fine. N how yuh tonight, Brother?" Hes awways awhisperin berhin mah back, a-tryin t take mah congregation erway from me. . . . N when he ain doin that hes a-tryin his best t give me wrong advice, jus like the Devil a-tryin t tempt Jesus. But Ahm gonna march on wida hepa Gawd. . . . Yeah, Ah might preach a sermon erbout tha nex Sunday.

As he turned into the street leading to his home and church he saw a tall brown-skinned boy hurrying towards him. Here comes Jimmy! Ah bet hes lookin fer me. . . . Lawd, Ah hope ain nothin wrong. . . .

"PA!" SAID JIMMY breathlessly when he was some twenty feet away.

Taylor stopped.

"Whuts the mattah, son?"

Jimmy came close.

"The mayors at home, waitin t see yuh," he whispered.

"The *mayor?*"

"Yeah, n two mo white men. One of em is the Chiefa Police."

"They there *now?*"

"Yeah; in the parlor."

"How long they been there?"

"Bout two-three minutes, Ah reckon. N lissen, Pa . . . Sam wuz by jus now. He say the white folks is ridin up n down the streets in their cars warning all the black folks t stay off the streets cause theres gonna be trouble. . . ."

"Sam say tha?"

"Thas whut he tol me. N lissen, Pa . . . Ahma git Sam n Pete n Bob n Jack n some mo boys together sos ef anything happens. . . ."

Taylor gripped Jimmy's shoulders.

"Naw, son! Yuh fixin t git us *all* inter trouble now! Yuh cant do nothing like tha! Yuh gotta be careful! If them white folks just *thought* we wuz doin somethin like that theyd crack down on us! Wed hava riot!"

"But we cant let em ride erroun n talk big n we do nothin!"

"Lissen here, son! Yuh do whut Ah tell yuh t do!" He shook Jimmy's shoulders and his voice was husky. "Yuh go tell them boys t do *nothin* till Ah see em, yuh hear me? Yuh young fools fixin t git us *all* murdered!"

"We jus as waal git killed fightin as t git killed doing nothin," said Jimmy sullenly.

"Yuh go n do whut Ah tol yuh, *hear* me? Ah gotta go n see tha mayor. . . ."

"Hes here t see yuh erbout tha demonstration," said Jimmy.

"How yuh know?"

"Cause thas whut everybodys sayin."

"Who yuh hear say tha?"

"Deacon Smiths spreadin the word."

Taylor winced as though struck by a blow and looked at the dust.

"Hes tellin alla deacons n the church membahs tha the mayors here t stop yuh," said Jimmy. "Hes tellin em yuhs mixed up wid the Reds."

"Deacon Smith there now, *too?*"

"Yeah; hes in the basement wida other deacons. Theys waitin t see yuh."

"How long they been there?"

"Bout hafa hour. N Hadley n Greens in the Bible Room, waitin t talk wid yuh, too. . . ."

Fear gripped Taylor and he stammered:

"Ddddid the mmmmayor ssssee em?"

"Naw, ain nobody seen em yit. Ah brought em in thu the back do and tol em t wait fer yuh. Ahm mighty scared wid them Reds waitin fer yuh in the Bible Room and that Chiefa Police waitin fer yuh in the parlor. Ef ol Deacon Smith knowed tha he sho would make a lotta trouble. . . ."

"Where you ma?"

"She upstairs, sewin."

"She know whuts happenin?"

"Naw, Pa."

Taylor stood still, barely breathing.

"Whut yuh gonna do, Pa?" asked Jimmy.

"Yuh go n tell them boys not t do nothin wrong, son. Go on n tell em now! Ah got too much on mah hands now widout yuh boys stirrin up mo trouble!"

"Yessuh."

"Yuh bettah go n do it *now!*"

"Yessuh."

He watched Jimmy hurry down the street. Lawd, Ah hope tha boy don go n git inter trouble. . . .

"Yuh do whut Ah tol yuh, Jimmy!" he yelled.

"Yessuh!" Jimmy hollered back.

He saw Jimmy turn a dusty corner, and go out of sight. Hadley n Greens there in the Bible Room n the Chiefa Police is waitin in the parlor! Ah cant let them white folks see them Reds! N ef Deacon Smith tells on me they'll lynch me. . . . Ah gotta git em out of tha church widout em seein each other. . . . Good Gawd, whut a mess!

NO SOONER had he opened the door of his church than he heard a crescendo of voices. They back awready! Tha committees back! Aw, Ah bet the mayor followed em here. . . . He walked down the hall, turned into the church's waiting room, and saw a roomful of black faces.

"Reveren Taylor! The mayor run us out!"

"He put the police on us!"

The black brothers and sisters ran to Taylor and surrounded him.

"The mayor tol us t git out n don come back no mo!"

A thin black woman swung onto Taylor's arm, crying:

"Whut Ahm gonna do? Ah ain gotta mouthful of bread at home!"

"Sistahs n Brothers, jusa minute," said Taylor. "Firs, tell me whut the mayor said. . . ."

"He say he cant do *nuthin!* N say fer us not t come back t his office no *mo!* N say ef we do hes gonna put us in jail!"

"In *jail?*" asked Taylor.

"Thas whut he said."

"N he tol us not t march, Reveren. He said ef we demonstrated hed put us *all* in jail."

"Who tol em yuh wuz gonna march?" asked Taylor.

"Ah bet it wuz tha ol Deacon Smith," said Sister Harris.

"The Bible says testify whut yuh see n speak whut yuh know," said Sister Davis to Sister Harris.

"Ah knows whut Ahm talkin erbout!" blazed Sister Harris.

"Sistahs n Brothers, les don start no fuss," said Taylor, sighing and dropping his shoulders.

"Whut they tell yuh at the relief station, Reveren Taylor?" asked Sister James.

"They say they cant do nothin," said Taylor.

The thin black woman came and knelt at Taylor's feet, her face in her hands.

"Reveren Taylor, it ain fer me Ahm astin! Its fer mah chillun! Theys hongry! It ain fer me, its fer them! Gawd, have mercy, theys hongry. . . ."

Taylor stepped back, ran his hand into his pocket and pulled out a palmful of loose coins.

"Here, Sistahs n Brothers, split this up between yuh all. Its ever cent Ah got in this worl, so hep me Gawd!"

He laid the coins on a small table. Brother Booker divided them as far as they would go. Then they swarmed around him again.

"Reveren, whut we gonna do?"

"Cant we make the white folks do something fer us?"

"Ahm tireda bein hongry!"

"Reveren, mah babys sick n Ah cant git her no milk!"

"Reveren, whut kin Ah tell mah wife?"

"Lawd knows, Ahm jus erbout sick of this!"

"Whut kin we do, Reveren?"

Taylor looked at them and was ashamed of his own help-lessness and theirs.

"Sistahs n Brothers, les call on the great Gawd who made us n put us in this world. . . ."

He clasped his hands in front of him, closed his eyes, and bowed his head. The room grew still and silent.

"Lawd Gawd Awmighty, Yuh made the sun n the moon n the stars n the earth n the seas n mankind n the beasts of the fields!"

yes jesus

"Yuh made em all, Lawd, n Yuh tol em whut t do!"

yuh made em lawd

"Yuhs strong n powerful n Yo will rules this worl!"

yuh rules it lawd

"Yuh brought the chillun of Israel outta the lan of Egypt!"

yuh sho did

"Yuh made the dry bones rise up outta the valley of death n live!"

yuh made em live lawd

"Yuh saved the Hebrew chillun in the fiery furnace!"

yes jesus

"Yuh stopped the storm n Yuh made the sun stan still!"

yuh stopped it lawd

"Yuh knocked down the walls of Jericho n Yuh kept Jona in the belly of the whale!"

yuh kept im lawd

"Yuh let Yo son Jesus walk on watah n Yuh brought Im back from the dead!"

have mercy jesus

"Yuh made the lame walk!"

yuh did it lawd

"Yuh made the blin see!"

help us now lawd

"Yuh made the deaf hear!"

glory t the mos high

"Lawd, Yuhs a rock in the tima trouble n Yuhs a shelter in the tima storm!"

he is he is

"Lawd, Yuh said Yuhd strike down the wicked men who plagued Yo chillun!"

glory t gawd

"Yuh said Yuhd destroy this ol worl n create a new Heaven n a new Earth!"

wes waitin on yuh jesus

"Lawd, Yuh said call on Yo name n Yuhd answer!"

yuh said it lawd n now wes callin

"Yuh made us n put the breatha life in us!"

yuh did lawd

"Now look down on us, Lawd! Speak t our hearts n let us know what Yo will is! Speak t us like Yuh spoke t Jacob!"

speak lawd n our souls will be clay in yo hans

"Lawd, ack in us n well obey! Try us, Lawd, try us n watch us move t Yo will! Wes helpless at Yo feet, a-waitin fer Yo sign!"

send it lawd

"The white folks say we cant raise nothin on Yo earth! They done put the lans of the worl in their pockets! They done fenced em off n nailed em down! Theys a-tryin t take Yo place, Lawd!"

speak t em lawd

"Yuh put us in this worl n said we could live in it! Yuh said this worl wuz Yo own! Now show us the sign like Yuh showed Saul! Show us the sign n well ack! We ast this in the name of Yo son Jesus who died tha we might live! Amen!"

amen amen

Taylor stopped and opened his eyes. The room was quiet; he could hear the clock ticking softly above his head, and from the rear came the sound of children playing back in the church. The sisters and brothers rose from their knees and began talking in subdued tones.

"But, Reveren, whut kin we *do?*"

"The issues wid Gawd now, Sistahs n Brothers."

"Is we gonna march?"

"Is yuh goin wid us t the mayor?"

"Have faith, Sistahs n Brothers. Gawd takes care of His own."

"But Ahm hongry, Reveren. . . ."

"Now, Sistahs n Brothers, Ah got t go. Ah got business t tend t. . . ."

He pushed ahead of the black hands that clung to his sleeve.

"Reveren Taylor. . . ."

The thin black woman wailed, kneeling:

"Please, Reveren, cant yuh do *somethin.* . . ."

He pushed through the door, closed it, and stood for a moment with his eyes shut and his fingers slowly loosening on the knob, his ears filled with the sound of wailing voices.

How come all this gotta happen at *once?* Folks a-beggin fer bread n the mayor here t see me n them Reds a-waitin in the Bible Room. . . . Ef Deacon Smith knowed that hed ruin me sho! Ah cant let the mayor see them Reds. . . . Now, Gawd! He looked at a door at the far end of the room, then hurried to it and opened it softly.

"May!" he called in a hoarse whisper.

"Hunh?"

"C mere, quick!"

"Whutcha wan, Dan?"

"C mon in the *room,* May!"

She edged through the half-opened door and stood in front of him, wide-eyed.

"Whutcha wan, Dan?"

"Now, lissen. . . ."

"Ain nothin wrong, is it, Dan? Ain nothin happened, is it?"

He grabbed her arm.

"Naw, n don git scared!"

"Ah ain scared!"

"Yuh cant do whut Ah wan yuh t do ef yuhs scared!"

"Ah *ain* scared, Dan!"

"Lissen. . . ."

"Yeah?"

"The mayors here, in the parlor. N the Chiefa Police. . . ."

She stood stock still and seemed not to breathe.

"The *mayor?*"

"Yeah. . . ."

"*Ain* nothin wrong, is it, Dan?"

"There wont be ef yuh lissen n try to do right."

"Be careful, Dan!"

"Yeah," he said, his voice low and husky. "Go in and tell them white folks Ahm sick, hear?"

She stepped back from him and shook her head.

"Gawd *ain* wid yuh when yuh lie, Dan!"

"We *gotta* lie t white folks! Theys on our necks! They *make* us lie t them! Whut kin we do but lie?"

"*Dan!*"

"Lissen t whut Ahm telling yuh, May! Tell the mayor Ahm gittin outta bed t see him. Tell im Ahm dressin, see? Tell im t wait a few minutes."

"Yeah?"

"Then go t the basement n tell Deacon Smith Ahm wid the mayor. Tell im n the other deacons t wait."

"Now?"

"Yeah; but Ah ain thru yit. Yuh know Hadley n Green?"

"Them *Reds?*"

"Yeah. . . ."

"Dan!" said May, her lungs suspiring in one gasp of amazed helplessness.

"May, fer Chrissakes!"

She began to cry.

"Don do nothin wrong, Dan, please! Don't fergit Jimmy! Hes jus a young boy n hes gotta grow up in this town wid these white folks. Don go n do nothin n fix it so he wont have a chance. . . . Me n yuh don mattah, but thinka him."

Taylor swallowed and looked hard at her.

"Dan, please. . . ."

"May, yuh do whut Ah tell yuh t do! Ah know whut Ahm doin. Hadley n Green downstairs, in the Bible Room. Tell em so nobody kin hear yuh, hear?—tell em aftah yuh done tol the others—tell em t come in here. Let em in thru yo room. . . ."

"Naw!"

She tried to get through the door. He ran to her and caught her hand again.

"Yuh do whut Ah tell yuh, May!"

"Ah ain gonna have them Reds in *here* wid tha mayor n Chiefa Police out *there!* Ah *ain!*"

"Go on do whut Ah tell yuh, May!"

"Dan!"

"Go *ahead*, May!"

He pushed her. She went through the door, slowly, looking back at him. When the door was closed he rammed his hands deep into his pants' pockets, turned to the open window, and looked out into the street. It was profoundly quiet, save for the silvery sound of children's voices back of the church. The air was soft, warm, and full of the scent of magnolias and violets. Window panes across the street were blood-red from dying sunlight. A car sped past, lifting a great cloud of yellow-brown dust. He went to the center of the room and stood over a table littered with papers. He cocked his head, listening. He heard a door slam; footsteps echoed and ceased. A big eight-day clock above his head boomed six times; he looked and his eyes strayed up and rested on a gleaming, brass cross. Gawd, hep me now! Jus hep me t go thru wid this! Again he heard a door slam. Lawd, Ah hope May do right now. . . . N Ah hope Jimmy don go n ack a fool. . . . He crossed the floor on tiptoe, opened the door, and peeped into May's room. It was empty. A slender prism of dust-filled sunlight cut across the air. He closed the door, turned, pulled off his coat and threw it across the table. Then he loosened his collar and tie. He went to the window again and leaned with his back against the ledge, watching the door of May's room. He heard a hoarse voice rise and die. Footsteps again sounded and ceased. He frowned, listening. How come its takin May so long? He started when a timid knock came. He hurried to the door and cracked it.

"HELLO, REVEREND TAYLOR!" said Hadley, a white man.

"How yuh, Brother Hadley?"

"N how yuh, Reveren?" asked Green, a black man.

"Ahm fine, Brother Green. C mon in, yuh all."

Hadley and Green edged through the door.

"Say, whuts alla mystery?" asked Green.

"Ssssh! Don't talk so loud," cautioned Taylor. "The mayor n the Chiefa Police is out there."

The Negro and the white man stood stone still.

"Do they know wes here?" asked Green.

"Naw, n don git scared. They done come t see me erbout tha demonstration. . . ."

Hadley and Green looked at each other.

"Pull down tha shade," whispered Green, pointing a shaking, black finger.

Quickly, Hadley moved to one side, out of range of the window. His cheeks flushed pink. Taylor lowered the shade and faced them in the semi-darkness. The eyes of the white man and the black man were upon him steadily.

"Waal?" said Green.

"Ah spose yuh know whuts up," said Taylor.

"Theyre here to scare you," said Hadley.

"Ahm trustin Gawd," sighed Taylor.

"Whut yuh gonna tell em?" asked Green.

"Thas whut Ah wanna see yuh all erbout," said Taylor.

"O.K. Whut kin we do?" asked Green.

Taylor looked around and motioned toward two chairs.
"Set down, Brothers."

"Naw, this is awright," said Green, still standing.

"Come on," said Hadley. "What's on your mind?"

Taylor folded his arms and half sat and half leaned on the edge of the table.

"Yuh all think wes gonna have many folks out in the mawnin fer the demonstration?"

"Whut yuh mean?" asked Green.

"When Ahm talkin wid the mayor and Chiefa Police Ah wanna know how many folks Ahm talkin fer. There ain no use in us havin a demonstration ef ain but a few of us is gonna be out there. The police will try t kill us then. . . ."

"How many folks we can get out tomorrow depends a great deal on you, Reverend," said Hadley.

"Hows that?" asked Taylor.

"If you had let us use your name on those handbills, we could say five thousand easily. . . ."

Taylor turned sharply to Hadley.

"Lissen, Brother, Ah done tol yuh Ah cant do tha! N there ain no use in us talkin erbout it no mo! Ah done told yuh Ah cant let them white folks know Ahm callin folks t demonstrate. Aftah all, Ahma preacher. . . ."

"Its yo duty, Reveren," said Green. "We owes it to our black folks."

"Ahm doin mah duty as Gawd lets me see it," said Taylor.

"All right, Reverend," said Hadley. "Heres what happened: Weve covered the city with fifteen thousand leaflets. Weve contacted every organization we could think of, black and white. In other words, weve done all *we* could. The rest depends on the leaders of each group. If we had their active endorsement, none of us would have to worry about a crowd tomorrow. And if we had a crowd we would not have to worry about the police. If they see the whole town turning out, they'll not start any trouble. Now, youre known. White and black in this town respect you. If you let us send out another leaflet with your name on it calling for. . . ."

Taylor turned from them and drew his hand nervously across his face. Hadley and Green were silent, watching him. Taylor went to the window and pulled back the curtain slightly and peeped out. Without turning he said softly:

"Ah done tol yuh all Ah ain scareda lettin yuh use mah name."

"We don mean *that,*" said Green hastily.

"Ef it wuz jus me who wuz takin the chance," said Taylor, "Ah wouldn't care none. But Gawd knows it ain right fer me to send them po folks out inter the streets in fronta police. Gawd knows, Ah cant do tha!"

"Honest, Reveren," said Green, touching Taylor's arm. "Ah don understan. Yuh done been thu harder things than this befo."

"N Ahll go thu wid em ergin," said Taylor proudly.

"All right!" said Hadley. "You can say the word that can make this thing a success. If you don't and we have no crowd, then youre to blame. . . ."

Taylor's eyes narrowed and when he spoke there was a note of anger in his voice.

"Gawd hep yuh ef yuhs a-tryin t say yuh gonna blame me ef things don go right!"

"Naw, Reveren!" said Green, coming hurriedly forward and spreading his black hands softly upon the air. "Don feel that way! Wes all jus in a jam. We got t do either two things: Call off this demonstration and let the folks stay hongry, er git as many as we kin together n go downtown in the mawnin. Ef we git five thousan down there the police wont bother us. Ef yuh let us send out yo name tellin the black folks. . . ."

"Naw, Brother!" said Taylor emphatically.

"Then the demonstrations going to be smashed," said Hadley. "*You* can stop it! You have the responsibility and the blame!"

Taylor sighed.

"Gawd knows Ah ain t blame. Ahm doin what mah heart tells me t do. . . ."

"Then whats keeping you from working with us?" asked Hadley. "Im a white man and Im here willing to fight for your peoples rights!"

"Ahm wid yuh, Brother!" said Taylor in a voice which carried a deep note of pleading. "Ahm wid yuh no mattah whut yuh *think!* But yuh *cant* use mah name! Ef them white folks knowed Ah wuz callin mah folks in the streets to demonstrate, they wouldn't never gimme a chance t git something fer mah folks ergin. . . ."

"Thats just it, Reverend," said Hadley. "Don't be afraid of their turning you down because your fighting for your people. If they knew youd really fight, theyd dislike you; yes? But you can *make* them give something to *all* of your people, not just to *you*. Dont you see, Taylor, youre standing *between* your people and the white folks. You can make them give something to *all* of them. And the poor, hungry white folks will be with you."

"Ah cant lead mah folks t go ergin them white folks like tha," said Taylor. "Thas *war!*"

Hadley came close to Taylor.

"Reverend, cant you see thats just the way the white folks *want* you to feel? Are you leading your folks just because the white folks *say* you should, or are you leading them because you *want* to? Dont you believe in what youre doing? What kind of leaders are black people to have if the white folks pick them and tell them what to do?"

"Brothers, Ahma Christian, n whut yuhs asting fer is something tha makes blood!" thundered Taylor.

Hadley and Green looked at each other.

"Waal, whut yuh gonna tell the mayor?" asked Green.

Taylor stood in the center of the room with his hands in his pockets, looking down at his feet. His voice came low, as though he were talking to himself, trying to convince himself.

"Ahma tell em mah folks is hongry. Ahma tell em they wanna march. Ahma tell em if they march Ahma march wid em. Ahma tell em they wan bread. . . ."

"Reverend," asked Hadley, "why do you feel that this is so different from all the other times you've gone straight to the white folks and *demanded* things for your people?"

"It is different!" said Taylor.

"You didn't say that when you saved Scott from that *mob!*"

"Tha wuz different, Brother Hadley."

"I dont see it."

Taylor's voice came low.

"Ah feels differently erbout it, Brothers."

"You saved Scotts life. All right, youre saving the lives of your congregation now. Scott was one man, but there are five hundred starving people in your church."

"We ain facin no mob now, Brother Hadley."

"Then what in Gods name are we facin, Reverend? If those police wholl be out there in the morning with their guns and clubs arent a *legal* mob, then what. . . ."

"Its more than a mob, Brother Hadley."

Hadley and Green shook their heads.

"Ah don understand yuh, Reveren," said Green.

"When Ah saved Scott from tha mob, Ah wuz goin ergin *some* of the white folks. But this thing is going ergin em *all!* This is too much like war!"

"You mean youre going against the ones with *money* now!" said Hadley. "Over three thousand of the poor white folks will be with *us*. . . ."

"But, Brother Hadley, the white folks whos got moneys got *everything!* This is jus like civil war!"

"Reverend," said Hadley, "cant you see that if they were not afraid they wouldn't be here asking to *talk* with you? Go in and talk with them, speak to them in the name of five thousand hungry people. Tell the mayor and the Chief of Police that if they dont give the relief back we will demonstrate."

"Ah cant do tha, Brothers. Ah cant let these white folks think Ahm leadin mah folks tha way. Ah tol yuh Brothers when Ah ergreed t work wid yuh Ahd go as fer as Ah could. Waal, Ah done tha. Now, yuh here astin me t threaten this whole town n Ah ain gonna do tha!" said Taylor.

"Yuh astin fer bread, Reveren," said Green.

"Its threatenin, Brothers," said Taylor. "N tha ain Gawds way!"

"So youll let your folks starve before youll stand up and talk to those white folks?" asked Hadley.

"Ahm ackin as Gawd gives me the light to see," said Taylor.

There was silence. Then Hadley laughed, noiselessly.

"Well," he said. "I didn't know you felt this way, Reverend. I thought we could count on you. You know the Party will stand behind you no matter what happens."

"Ahm sorry, Brother Hadley," said Taylor.

"When kin we see yuh t fin out whut the mayor n Chiefa Police say?" asked Green.

Taylor looked at his watch.

"Its a little aftah six now. Make it half-pas six. Thall gimme time t see the Deacon Board."

Green sighed.

"O.K."

"O.K."

Taylor held the door for them. Then he stood in the center of the room and looked miles through the floor. Lawd, Ah hope Ahm doin right. N they think Ahm scared. . . . He flushed hot with shame and anger. He sat in a chair for a moment, then got right up. He drummed his fingers on the corner of the table. Shucks, Ah jus as waal see them white folks now n git it over wid. Ah knowed this wuz comin up! Ah knowed it! He went through May's room, walking slowly, softly, seeing in his mind the picture of the fat, pink face of Mayor Bolton and the lean, red face of Chief of Police Bruden. As he turned into the narrow hall that led to the parlor he heard children yelling in the playground. He went down a stairway, opened a door, and walked through his hushed, dim-lit church. Pale rose light fell slantwise through stained windows and glinted on mahogany pews. He lifted his eyes and saw the figure of Christ on a huge snow-white cross. Gawd, hep me now! Lemme do the right thing! He followed a red carpet to a door that opened into the parlor. He paused and passed his tongue over his dry lips. He could feel his heart beating. Ahll let them do all the talkin. Ahll just tell em mah folks is hongry. Thas all Ah kin do. Slowly, he turned the knob, his lips half parted in dread.

"WHY, HELLO, DAN!"

"Good evenin, Mistah Mayor."

"Howve you been, Dan?"

"Fairly well, wid de hepa Gawd, suh."

Taylor shook hands with a tall, fat white man in a blue serge suit.

"Its been a long time since Ive seen you, Dan."

"Yessuh. It sho has, yo Honah."

"Hows Jimmy?"

"Jus fine, suh."

"Thats a fine boy youve got, Dan."

"Ahm sho glad yuh think so, suh."

"If you raise that boy right he will be a leader of his people some day, Dan."

"Thas the one hope of mah life, suh," said Taylor with deep emotion.

"May was tellin me youre sick," said the mayor.

"Aw, it ain nothin, suh. Jusa summer col, suh."

"I didn't mean to bother you if youre sick, Dan."

"Thas awright, suh. Ahm feelin much bettah now, suh."

"Oh, youll pull through all right; itll take a lot more than a summer cold to kill old war-horses like you and me, eh, Dan?"

The mayor laughed and winked.

"Ahm hopin Gawd spares me a few mo years, suh," said Taylor.

"But at least you look all right now," said the mayor. "Say, Dan, I want you to meet Chief Bruden. This is Dan, Chief, the boy I was telling you about."

"How yuh, Mistah Chief?" asked Taylor.

A black cigar burned red in Bruden's mouth. He shifted his thin body and growled:

"Hello, boy."

"And, Dan, this is Mr. Lowe, head of our fine Industrial Squad."

"How yuh, suh?" asked Taylor.

Lowe nodded with half-closed eyes.

"Sit down, Dan," said the mayor.

"Yessuh."

Taylor sat on the edge of a chair and rested his palms lightly on his knees.

"Maybe our little visit is a surprise, hunh?" asked the mayor.

"Yessuh. It is. But Ahm glad to be of any hep Ah kin, suh."

"Good; I knew youd talk that way. Now, Dan, we want you to help us. Youre a responsible man in this community; that's why we are here."

"Ah tries t do mah duty as Gawd shows it t me, suh."

"That's the spirit, Dan!" The mayor patted Taylor's knee. "Now, Im going to be perfectly frank with you, Dan." The mayor peeled a wrapper from a black cigar. "Here, have one."

"Thank yuh, suh." Taylor put the cigar into his vest pocket. "Ahll smoke it aftah dinner, suh."

There was a silence during which the three white men looked at Taylor.

"Dan," began the mayor, "its not every nigger Id come to and talk this way. Its not every nigger Id trust as Im about to trust you." The mayor looked straight at Taylor. "Im doing this because Ive faith in you. Ive known you for twenty-five years, Dan. During that time I think Ive played pretty fair with you, havent I?"

Taylor swallowed.

"Ahll have t say yuh have, yo Honah."

"Mister Lowe and the Chief here had another plan," said the mayor. "But I wouldn't hear of it. I told them Id work this thing *my* way. I thought *my* way would be much better. After all, Dan, you and I have worked together in the past and I dont see why we cant work together now. Ive backed you up in a lot of things, Dan. Ive backed you even when other white folks said you were wrong. But I believe in doing the right thing. After all, we are human beings, arent we?"

"Yessuh."

"What Ive done for you in the past Im willing to do again. You remember Scott, dont you?"

"Yessuh. Yuhs been a big hep t me n mah folks, suh."

"Well, Dan, my office is always open to you when you want to see me about any of your problems or the problems of your people," said the mayor.

"N Gawd knows Ah sho thanks yuh, suh."

The mayor bit off the tip of his cigar and spat it into a brass spittoon.

"I'm not going to beat about the bush, Dan."

The mayor paused again. There was silence. Taylor felt called upon to say something.

"Yessuh. Ah sho preciates tha, suh."

"You know these Goddam Reds are organizing a demonstration for tomorrow, dont you?" asked the mayor.

Taylor licked his lips before he answered.

"Yessuh. Ah done heard a lotta folks talkin erbout it, suh."

"That's too bad, Dan," said the mayor.

"Folks is talking erbout it everywhere. . . ." began Taylor.

"What *folks?*" interjected Bruden.

"Waal, mos everybody, suh."

Bruden leaned forward and shook his finger in Taylor's face.

"Listen, boy! I want you to get this straight! Reds aint *folks!* Theyre Goddam sonofabitching lousy bastard rats trying to wreck our country, see? Theyre stirring up race hate! Youre old enough to understand that!"

"Hes telling you straight, boy," said Lowe. "And furthermore. . . ."

"Say, whats all this?" demanded the mayor, turning to Lowe and Bruden. "Wait a minute! Whats the big idea of talking to Dan like that? Hes not mixed up in anything like that. Save that kind of talk for bad niggers. . . ."

"The quicker all you niggers get sense enough in your Goddam thick skulls to keep away from them Reds the better off you'll be!" said Bruden, ignoring the mayor.

"Aw, c mon," said the mayor. "Dans all right. Aint that right, Dan?"

Taylor looked down and saw at his feet a sharp jutting angle of sunshine falling obliquely through a window. His neck felt hot. This is the show-down, he thought. Theys tryin t trap me. . . . He cleared his throat and looked up slowly and saw the mayor gazing at him with cold grey eyes. He shifted his body slightly and saw the glint of Chief Bruden's police star; he saw Lowe's red lips twisted in half-smile and half-leer.

"Isnt that right, Dan?" the mayor asked again.

"Yessuh. Whut yuh white folks say is right. N Ah ergrees wid yuh. But Ah ain foolin wid nobody thas tryin t stir up race hate; naw, *suh!* Ah ain never done nothin like that n Ah never will, so hep me Gawd! Now, erbout this demonstration: Yessuh, Ah heard erbout it. Thas all everybodys been talking erbout erroun here fer a week, yo Honah. Waal, suh, Ahll tell yuh. Theys jus hongry. Theys marchin cause they don know whut else t do, n thas the truth from here t Heaven! Mistah Mayor, theys hongry! Jus plain *hongry!* Ah give mah las dime today t a woman wid eight chillun. . . ."

"We know all about that, Dan," said the mayor.

"Everybodys hungry," said Bruden.

"Boy, cant you see we are all in the *same* boat?" asked Lowe.

"Waal. . . ." drawled Taylor.

"Thingsll be straightened out soon, Dan," interjected the mayor soothingly. "We will see that nobody starves."

"Ah beg yo pardon, suh. A man died jus the other day from starvation. . . ."

Taylor's voice died in his throat and he looked at the floor. He knew that he had said too much.

"I reckon that makes you out a liar, don't it?" Bruden asked the mayor.

"Aw, naw, suh!" said Taylor eagerly. "Ah ain disputin nobodys word, suh. Ah jus thought yuh hadnt heard erbout it. . . ."

"We know all about it," said Bruden, turning his head away and looking out of the window, as though he was through with the conversation, as though his mind was made up.

"What do they think theyre going to get by marching?" asked Lowe.

"They think they kin git some bread," said Taylor.

"It wont get em a Goddam crumb!" said Lowe.

There was silence. Taylor looked again at the jutting angle of sunshine and heard the mayor's shoes shifting uneasily on the brown carpet. A match struck; he heard it drop with an angry hiss into the spittoon.

"I dont see why we cant get along, Dan," drawled the mayor.

"Ahm willin t git erlong, Mistah Mayor!" protested Taylor.

"Dan, here we all are, living in good old Dixie. There are twenty-five thousand people in this town. Ten thousand of those people are black, Dan. Theyre your people. Now, its our job to keep order among the whites, and we would like to think of you as being a responsible man to keep order among the blacks. Lets get together, Dan. You know these black people better than we do. We want to feel we can depend on you. Why dont you look at this thing the right way? You know Ill never turn you down if you do the right thing. . . ."

"Mistah Mayor, as Gawds mah judge, Ahm doin right when Ah tell yuh mah folks is hongry. . . ."

"Youre not doing right when you act like a Goddam Red!" said Lowe.

"These niggers around here trust you, Dan," said the mayor. "They'll do what you tell them to do."

"Speak to them," urged Lowe. "Tell them whats right."

"Mistah Mayor, Gawd in Heaven knows mah people is hongry," said Taylor humbly.

The mayor threw his body forward in the chair and rested his hands on his knees.

"Listen, Dan. I know just how you feel. We *all* feel that way. White people are hungry, too. But weve got to be prudent and do this thing right. Dan, youre a leader and youve got great influence over your congregation here." The mayor paused to let the weight of his words sink in. "Dan, I helped you to get that influence by doing your people a lot of favors through *you* when you came into my office a number of times." The mayor looked at Taylor solemnly. "I'm asking you now to use that influence and tell your people to stay *off* the streets tomorrow!"

When Taylor spoke he seemed to be outside of himself, listening to his own words, aghast and fearful.

"Ahm sho thankful as Gawd knows fer all yuh done done fer me n mah people, suh. But mah word don go so fer in times likes these, yo Honah. These folks is lookin t me fer bread n Ah cant give it t em. They hongry n Ah cant tell em where t eat. Theys gonna march no mattah whut Ah say. . . ."

"Youve got influence here, Dan, and you can use it!"

"They wouldnt be marchin ef they wuznt hongry, yo Honah!"

314

"Thats Red talk, nigger!" said Lowe, standing.

"Aw, thats all right, Lowe," said the mayor, placatingly.

"Im not going to sit here and let this Goddam nigger insult me to my face!" said Lowe.

Taylor stood up.

"Ahm sorry, suh!"

"You *will* be sorry when you find a Goddam rope around your neck!" said Lowe.

"Now, now," said the mayor, laying his hand on Lowe's arm. He turned to Taylor. "You dont mean you wont speak to em, do you, Dan?"

"There ain nothin Ah kin say t em, Mistah Mayor. . . ."

"Youre doing the wrong thing, Dan!"

"Ahm lettin God be mah judge, suh!"

"If you dont do the right thing *we* will be your judges!" said Lowe.

"Ahm trustin Gawd, suh."

"Well, Goddammit, you better let Him guide you right!" said Bruden, jumping to his feet.

"But white folks!" pleaded Taylor. "Mah folks cant plant nothin! Its ergin the law! They cant git no work! Whut they gonna do? They don wan no trouble. . . ."

"Youre heading for a plenty right now!" said Bruden.

The mayor spoke and his voice was low and resigned.

"Ive done all I could, Dan. You wouldn't follow my advice, now the rest is up to Mister Lowe and Chief Bruden here."

Bruden's voice came with a shout:

"A niggers a nigger! I was against coming here talking to this nigger like he was a white man in the first place. He needs his teeth kicked down his throat!" Bruden poked the red tip of his cigar at Taylor's face. "Im the Chief of Police of this town, and Im here to see that orders kept! The Chamber of Commerce says therell be no demonstration tomorrow. Therell be three hundred police downtown in the morning to see that thats done. If you send them niggers down there, or if you let these Goddam Reds fool you into it,

Ill not be responsible for whatll happen! Weve never had a riot in this town, but youre plotting one right now when you act like this! And you know wholl get the worst of it!"

"Cant yuh do something, Mistah Mayor? Cant yuh fix it sos we kin git some relief?"

The mayor did not answer; Lowe came close to him.

"We know youve been seeing Hadley and Green! We know whats going on! So watch yourself, nigger!"

"Suh?"

They went out. Taylor stood at the window and saw them get into their car and disappear in a cloud of dust around a corner. He sat down, feeling sweat over all his body. Gawd knows what t do. . . . He brought Lowe n Bruden here t threaten me. . . . N they know erbout Hadley and Green. . . . Somebody tol. . . . He looked up, hearing the soft boom of a clock. Hadley n Greens comin back here at six-thirty. . . . He went down the hall thinking, Lawd, ef Ah only knowed whut t do. . . .

MAY MET HIM in the hall.

"Whut they say, Dan?" she asked with suppressed hysteria.

"Don bother me now, May!"

"There wont be no trouble, will it, Dan?"

"Naw, May! Now, please! Yuh worrin me!"

"Yuhll spoil things fer Jimmy, Dan! Don do nothin wrong! Its fer Jimmy Ahm astin!"

"Itll be awright! Now, lemme go!"

He hurried down the hallway, leaving her crying. Good Gawd! How come she wont leave me erlone. Firs, its Jimmy; then its her. . . . Ef it ain one its the other. . . . He went to the end of the hall, down the steps, turned, and came to the door of the Deacon Room. He heard subdued voices. He knew that the deacons were waiting for him, waiting for some definite word. Shucks, Ahm willin t go thu wid tha

march ef they is. Them white folks cant kill us *all.* . . . He
pushed the door in. The voices ceased. He saw a dense cloud
of tobacco smoke and a circle of black faces. He forced a wan
smile.

"Good evenin, Brothers!" he said.

"How yuh, Reveren?" asked Deacon Bonds.

"Ahm sorry Ahm late," said Taylor.

"Wuz tha the mayor out there?" asked Deacon Williams.

Taylor paused and pulled out his handkerchief.

"Yeah, Brothers, it wuz the mayor. N the Chiefa Police n
tha man Lowe from the Red Squad. . . ."

"RED SQUAD!" shouted Deacon Smith, jumping to his feet
with an outraged look.

"Whut they say, Reveren?" asked Deacon Williams quietly, ignoring Deacon Smith.

Taylor sighed and looked at the floor. For a moment he
loathed them because he knew they were expecting an answer to their questions. They were expecting him to speak
now as he had always spoken, to the point, confidently, and
finally. He had wanted them to do the talking, and now they
were silent, waiting for him to speak. Lawd, Ah hope Ahm
doin right. Ah don wanna lead these folks wrong. . . .

"They know all erbout tha demonstration," he said.

"But whut they *say?*" asked Deacon Bonds.

"Shucks, man! Yuh *know* whut they said!" said Deacon
Smith. "Yuh *know* how them white folks feel erbout this
thing!"

"They don wan us t march," said Taylor. "They said ef we
march theyll put the police on us. . . ."

Deacon Smith leveled his forefinger at Taylor and intoned:
"AH TOL YUH SO!"

"They said therell be a riot," Taylor went on stubbornly.

"Yessuh! Brothers, wes gotta do *right!*" said Deacon Smith,
banging his open palm down on the table. "Ah awways said
wes gotta do *right*, Reveren!"

"Ahm prayin t Gawd t guide us right," said Taylor.

"Yuh sho don ack like it!" said Deacon Smith.

"Let the Reveren finish, will yuh?" asked Deacon Bonds.

"Wes gotta do right!" said Deacon Smith again, sitting down, folding his arms, crossing his legs and turning his face sternly away.

"Whut else they say, Reveren?" asked Deacon Bonds.

Taylor sighed.

"They say wes mixed up with the Reds. . . ."

"N by Gawd we is!" bawled Deacon Smith. "At least *yuh* is! Ah tol yuh t leave them Reds erlone! They don mean *no* body *no* good! When men starts t deny Gawd, nothin good kin come from em!"

"Brother Smith, let the Reveren talk, will yuh?" asked Deacon Williams.

"He ain talkin *sense!*" said Deacon Smith.

"They say therell be three hundred police downtown in the mawnin," said Taylor, ignoring Smith. "They say only Washington kin do something erbout relief, n tha we must wait. . . ."

"N Gawd Awmighty knows thas all we kin do: wait!" said Deacon Smith.

"Fer Chrissakes, Brother Smith, let im talk!" said Deacon Williams. "We all know *yuhs* scared!"

"Ah ain scared! Ah got *sense!* Ah. . . ."

"Yuh sho don ack like it, the way yuh shoot off yo mouth!" said Deacon Williams.

Deacon Smith stood up.

"Yuh cant talk tha way t me!"

"Then keep yo big mouth shut!" said Deacon Williams.

"Whos gonna make me?"

"Brothers, please!" begged Taylor.

"A fool kin see tha the white folks is scared!" said Deacon Williams.

"N jus cause theys *scared*, theyll kill *any*body whuts fool ernuff t go downtown in the mawnin," said Deacon Smith.

"Shucks, Ahm willin t taka chance," said Deacon Hilton.

"Me too!"

"We ain got nothin t lose!"

"Any *fool* kin git his head busted!" said Deacon Smith.

"Brothers, fer the lova Gawd, quit fussin!" said Taylor.

They were silent. Taylor looked at them, letting his eyes rove from face to face.

"Brothers, this is the case," he said finally. "They threatenin us not t march, but they ain saying our folks kin git no relief. Now, Ah figgers ef we had a big crowd downtown in the mawnin they wont bother us. . . ."

"Thas whut *yuh* think," sneered Deacon Smith.

"N ef we don hava big crowd, theyll smash us. Now, its up t us. . . ."

"Reveren, do the *po* white folks say they gonna be *wid* us?" asked Deacon Jones.

"Brother Hadley tol me theys gonna be wid us," said Taylor.

"Tha Hadley is a lie n the trutha Gawd ain in im!" shouted Deacon Smith. "Tha white man is jus tryin t trick yuh, Ahm telling yuh!"

"Waal, we kin never know less we try n see," said Deacon Bonds.

"Yeah, but they ain gonna let yuh try but *once,*" said Deacon Smith.

"Waal, Ah ain got but *one* time t die!" said Deacon Bonds.

"Ah think the white folksll be there," said Taylor. "Theys hongry, too. . . ."

"Yuhll wake up *some* day!" said Deacon Smith.

"Whut yuh gonna do, Reveren?" asked Deacon Williams.

"Do the congregation wanna march?" asked Taylor.

"They say theys *gonna* march!"

"Waal, Ahll march wid em," said Taylor quietly. "They wont march erlone. . . ."

Deacon Smith waved his arms and screamed.

"Yeah, yuhll march! But yuhs scared t let em use yo name! Whut kinda leaders *is* yuh? Ef yuhs gonna ack a fool n be a Red, then how come yuh wont come on out n say so sos we

kin all hear it? Naw, you ain man ernuff t say whut yuh is! Yuh
wanna stan in wid the white folks! Yuh wanna stan in wid the
Reds! Yuh wanna stan in wid the congregation! Yuh wanna
stan in wid the Deacon Board! Yuh wanna stan in wid *ever*
body n yuh stan in wid *no*body!"

"Ahm ackin accordin t mah lights!" said Taylor.

"Waal, they ain lettin yuh see fer!" said Deacon Smith.

"Ef yuh gotta plan bettah than mine, Brother Smith, tell
us erbout it!"

"AH SAY WE OUGHTNT MARCH!"

"Then, whut we gonna do?"

"Wait n see how things come out!"

"Ahm tireda waitin," said Taylor.

"How come yuh didnt send yo name out on them leaflets?"
demanded Deacon Smith. Without waiting for Taylor to answer, he flared: "Ahll tell yuh why yuh didn't! Yuh *scared!*
Yuh didnt wan them white folks t know yuhs mixed up in this
demonstration. Yuh wanted em t think yuh wuz being
pushed erlong by other folks n yuh couldn't help whut wuz
happenin! But, Reveren, as sho as theres a Gawd in Heaven
yuh ain foolin nobody!"

Taylor stood up.

"Brother Smith, Ah knows whut yuhs up t! Yuh tryin t run
me outta mah church, but yuh cant! Gawd Awmighty Himself put me here n Ahm stayin till He says fer me t go! Yuh
been schemin t git me out, but yuh cant do it this way! It ain
right n Gawd knows it ain! Yeah; ef mah folks marches in the
mawnin Ahm marchin wid em!"

"Thas the time, Reveren!"

"We kin show tha ol mayor something!"

"N therell be white folks wid us, too!"

"Ahll go wid the Reveren n the congregation!"

"Ahll go!"

"N me too!"

"Gawd ain wid yuh when yuh ain in the right!" said Deacon Smith.

"Gawd didnt mean fer folks t be hongry!" said Deacon Bonds.

"But He ain wid yuh when yuh stirrin up trouble, makin blood n riots!" said Deacon Smith. "N any man whut sets here n calls himself a leader called by Gawd t preach n leads his folks the wrong way is a fool n the spirita Gawd ain in im!"

"Now, wait a minute there, Brother Smith!" said Taylor. "Yuhs talkin *dangerous!*"

"Ah say any man whut leads his folks inter guns n police. . . ."

"Ain nobody leading us *nowhere!*" said Deacon Bonds.

"We gwine *ourselves!*" said Deacon Williams.

"Ah ain in this!" said Deacon Smith, jumping again to his feet. "Ah ain in this n Ahm gonna do whut Ah kin t hep mah people!"

The room grew quiet.

"Whut yuh mean, Brother Smith?" asked Taylor.

"Ah say Ahm gonna hep mah people!" said Deacon Smith again.

Taylor walked over to him.

"Is yuh gonna tell the white folks on us?"

Deacon Smith did not answer.

"Talk, Brother Smith!" said Taylor. "Tell us whut yuh mean!"

"Ah means whut Ah means!" said Deacon Smith; and he clamped his teeth tight, sat again, crossed his legs, folded his arms and stared at the blank wall.

Taylor swallowed and looked at the floor. Lawd, Ah don know whut to do! Ah wish this wuz over. . . . This niggers gonna tell on us! Hes gonna tell the white folks sos he kin stan in wid em. . . ."

"Brother Smith. . . ." began Taylor.

The door opened and Jimmy stepped into the room.

"Say, Pa!"

"Whut yuh wan, son?"

"Somebodys out front t see yuh. Theys in a car. Theys white folks."

"Scuse me, Brothers," said Taylor. "Ahll be right back."

"Wes gonna set right here till yuh git back," said Deacon Smith.

When outside the door, Taylor turned to Jimmy.

"Who is they, Jimmy? How come they wouldnt come in?"

"Ah dunno, Pa. The car drove up just as Ah wuz comin thu the gate. They white men. They said fer yuh t come right out."

"Awright. N, son, yuh betta go see about yo ma."

"Whuts the mattah?"

"Shes jus upset erbout the demonstration."

"Is they gonna march, Pa?"

"Ah reckon so."

"Is many gonna be out?"

"Ah dunno, son. Ah hope so. Yuh bettah go see erbout yo ma now."

"Yessuh."

"Yuh tell them boys whut Ah tol yuh?"

"Yessuh."

Taylor paused at the front door and peeped out from behind a curtain. In front of his gate was a long black car. Who kin tha be? For a moment he thought the mayor had come back. But his cars grey. . . . He opened the door and walked slowly down the steps. Lawd, maybe we oughtnt go thu wid this demonstration aftah all? We might all be sorry ef somebodys killed in the mawnin. . . . He walked along a flower-bordered path that smelt of violets and magnolias. Dust rested filmily on tree leaves. The sun was almost gone. As he came to the car a white face looked out.

"Yuh Taylor?"

"Yessuh," answered Taylor, smiling.

The rear door of the car opened and the white man stepped to the ground.

"So youre Taylor, hunh?"

"Yessuh," said Taylor again, still smiling, but puzzled. "Kin Ah be of service t yuh, suh?"

Taylor saw it coming, but could do nothing. He remembered afterward that he had wanted to ask, What yuh doin? The blow caught him flush on the point of the jaw, sending him flying backward. His head struck the edge of the runningboard; a flash of red shot before his eyes. He rolled, face downward, into a bed of thick violets. Dazed, he turned his head, trying to speak. He felt a hand grab the back of his collar and jerk him up.

"Get in the car, nigger!"

"Say, whut yuh. . . ."

"Shut up and get in the car, Goddam you!"

A blow came to his right eye. There were three white men now. They lifted him and rammed him down on the floor in the back of the car.

"Say, yuh cant do this!"

"Get your Goddam mouth shut, you bastard!"

A hard palm slapped him straight across his face. He struggled up, protesting.

"You. . . ."

The heel of a shoe came hard into his solar plexus. He doubled up, like a jackknife. His breath left, and he was rigid, half-paralyzed.

"You think you can run this whole Goddam town, don't you? You think a nigger can run over white folks and get away with it?"

He lay still, barely breathing, looking at blurred white faces in the semi-darkness of the roaring car.

THE MOMENT he tried to tell the direction in which the car was moving, he knew he had waited too long. He remembered dimly that they had turned corners at least three times. He lay with closed eyes and wondered what they were going to do with him. She gonna be worried t death, he thought, thinking of May. And then he thought of Jimmy and said to himself, Ah hope he don go n ack a fool now. . . . The numbness which had deadened most of his stomach and chest was leaving. He felt sweat on his back and forehead. The car slowed, turned; then it ran fast again. He knew by the way the rocks crunched beneath the humming rubber tires that they were speeding over gravel. Whut roads this? He could not tell. There were so many gravel roads leading out of town. He tried to recall how long he had lain there half-paralyzed from that kick in the solar plexus. He was confused; it might have been five minutes or it might have been an hour. The car slowed again, turning. He smelt the strong scent of a burning cigarette and heard the toll of a far off church bell. The car stopped; he heard the sound of other cars, gears shifting and motors throbbing. We mus be at some crossroads. But he could not guess which one. He had an impulse to call for help. But there would not be any use in his doing that now. Mabbe they white folks anyhow. He would be better off as he was; even six white men were better than a mob of white men. The car was speeding again, lurching. He smelt dust, clay dust. Then he heard a hard, rasping voice:

"How is he?"

"O.K."

"Keep im quiet!"

"O.K."

He said nothing. He began to wonder how many of them were in the car. Yes, he should have been watching for something like this. They been threatening me fer a long time. Now this is it. The car was gradually slowing with that long slow slowing preceding a final stop. He felt the rubber tires turning over rough ground; his head rocked from side to side, hitting against the lower back of the front seat. Then the car stopped; the motor stopped; for a moment there was complete silence. Then he heard wind sighing in trees. Wes out in the country somewhere. In the woods, he thought.

"O.K.?"

"O.K.!"

He heard a door open.

"C mon, nigger! Get up and watch yourself!"

He pulled up and caught a glimpse of starry sky. As his feet hit the ground his head began to ache. He had lain cramped so long the blood had left his limbs; he took a step, kicking out his legs to restore circulation. His arms were grabbed from behind and he felt the pressure of a kneecap in the center of his spine. He gasped and reeled backward.

"Where you think youre going?"

He rested on his knees, his body full of pain. He heard a car door slam.

"Awright, nigger! Lets go! Straight ahead!"

He got up and twisted his head about to see who had spoken. He saw four blurred white faces and then they were blotted out. He reeled backward again, his head striking the ground. A pain knotted in his temple.

"Get up, nigger! Keep your eyes in front, and walk, God-dammit!"

He pulled up and limped off, his head down. Mabbe they gonna shoot me? His feet and the feet behind him made a soft *cush-cush* in the dew-wet grass and leaves.

"Aw right, nigger!"

He stopped. Slowly he raised his eyes; he saw a tall white man holding a plaited leather whip in his hand, hitting it gently against his trousers' leg.

"You know what this is, nigger?"

He said nothing.

"Wont talk, hunh? Well, this is a nigger-lesson!"

The whip flashed in faint starlight. The blow numbed his lips. He tasted blood.

"You know what this is? Im asking you again, nigger!"

"Nawsuh," he whispered.

"This is a nigger-whip!"

The leather whacked across his shoulders.

"Mistah, Ah ain done nothin!"

"Aw, naw! You aint done nothing! You aint never done a

Goddam thing, have you?" White men were standing close around him now. "All you ever do is play around with Reds, dont you? All you ever do is get crowds of niggers together to threaten white folks, dont you? When we get through with you to-night youll know how to stay in a niggers place! C mon! Get that Goddam vest off!"

He did not move. The whip wrapped itself around his neck, leaving a ring of fire.

"You want me to *beat* it off you?"

He pulled off the vest and held it in his hands.

"C mon! Get that shirt and undershirt off!"

He stripped to his waist and stood trembling. A night wind cooled his sweaty body; he was conscious of his back as he had never been before, conscious of every square inch of black skin there. One of the white men walked off a few paces and stopped.

"Bring im over here!"

"O.K.!"

They guided him with prods and kicks.

"On your knees, nigger!"

He did not move. Again his arms were caught from behind and a kneecap came into the center of his back. Breathless, he dropped, his hands and knees cooling in the wet grass. He lifted his fingers to feel his swelling lips; he felt his wrists being grabbed and carried around the trunk of a tree. He held stiffly and struggled against a rope.

"Let go!"

His arms went limp. He rested his face against a cold tree-trunk. A rope cut into his wrists. They tied his feet together, drawing the rope tight about his ankles. He looked around; they stood watching.

"Well, nigger, what do you know?"

"Nothin, suh."

"Youre a preacher, aint you?"

"Yessuh."

"Well, lets hear you pray some!"

He said nothing. The whip lashed across his bare back, *whick!* He flinched and struggled against the rope that cut his wrists to the bone. The leather thong hummed again, *whick!* and his spine arched inward, like a taut bow.

"Goddam your black soul, pray!"

He twisted his face around, pleading:

"Please, Mistah! Don whip me! Ah ain done nothin. . . ."

Another lash came across his half-turned cheek, *whick!* He jerked around and sheltered his face against the treetrunk. The lash hit his back, *whick!*

"*Hit* that black bastard, Bob!"

"Let me have that whip!"

"Naw, wait a minute!"

He said nothing. He clenched his teeth, his whole body quivering and waiting. A split second after each blow his body would lurch, as though absorbing the shock.

"You going to pray? You want me to beat you till you *cant* pray?"

He said nothing. He was expecting each blow now; he could almost feel them before they came, stinging, burning. Each flick came straight on his back and left a streak of fire, a streak that merged with the last streak, making his whole back a sheet of living flame. He felt his strength ebbing; he could not clench his teeth any more. His mouth hung open.

"Let me have it, Bob?"

"Naw, its my turn!"

There was a pause. Then the blows came again; the pain burned its way into his body, wave upon wave. It seemed that when he held his muscles taut the blows hurt less; but he could not hold taut long. Each blow weakened him; each blow told him that soon he would give out. Warm blood seeped into his trousers, ran down his thighs. He felt he could not stand it any longer; he held his breath, his lungs swelling. Then he sagged, his back a leaping agony of fire; leaping as of itself, as though it were his but he could not control it any longer. The weight of his body rested on his arms; his head dropped to one side.

"Ahhlll ppppray," he sobbed.

"Pray, then! Goddam you, pray!"

He tried to get his breath, tried to form words, hearing trees sighing somewhere. The thong flicked again, *whick!*

"Ain't you going to pray!"

"Yyyyyessuh. . . ."

He struggled to draw enough air into his lungs to make his words sound.

"Ooour Fffather. . . ."

The whip cut hard, *whick!* pouring fire and fire again.

"Have mercy, Lawd!" he screamed.

"Pray, nigger! Pray like you *mean* it!"

". . . wwwhich aaaaart in hheaven . . . hhhallowed bbe Tttthy nname. . . ." The whip struck, *whick!* "Ahm prayin, Mmmmistah!"

"Goddam your black heart, *pray!*"

". . .Tttthine kkkindom ccome . . . Ttthy wwwill bbe ddddone. . . ."

He sobbed, his breath leaving his lungs, going out from him, not wanting to stay to give sound to his words. The whip brought more fire and he could not stand it any longer; his heart seemed about to burst. He screamed, stretched his knees out and twisted his arms till he lay sideways, half on his stomach. The whip came into his stomach, *whick!* He turned over; it came on his back again, *whick!* He stopped struggling and hung limply, his weight suspended on arms he could not feel. Then fire flamed over all his body; he stiffened, glaring upward, wild-eyed.

"Whats the matter, nigger? You hurt?"

"Awright, kill me! Tie me n kill me! Yuh white trash cowards, kill me!"

"Youre tough, aint you? Just wait! Well kill you, you black sonofabitch!"

"Lemme have that whip!"

"C mon, now! Its my turn!"

"Give me that whip, Ellis!"

He was taut, but not feeling the effort to be taut.

"Well git yuh white trash some day! So hep me Gawd, we'll git yuh!"

The whip stopped.

"Say that again, Goddam you!"

The whip lashed, *whick!* but there was no streak of fire now; there was only one sheet of pain stretching all over his body, leaping, jumping, blazing in his flesh.

"Say it!"

He relaxed and closed his eyes. He stretched his legs out, slowly, not listening, not waiting for the whip to fall, *say it whick! say it whick! say it whick!* He groaned. Then he dropped his head and could not feel any more.

MOONLIGHT PAINED his eyeballs and the rustle of tree leaves thundered in his ears. He seemed to have only a head that hurt, a back that blazed, and eyes that ached. In him was a feeling that some power had sucked him deep down into the black earth, had drained all strength from him. He was waiting for that power to go away so he could come back to life, to light. His eyes were half-open, but his lids did not move. He was thirsty; he licked his lips, wanting water. Then the thunder in his ears died, rolling away. He moved his hand and touched his forehead; his arm fell limply in the wet grass and he lay waiting to feel that he wanted to move. As his blood began to flow swiftly again he felt sweat breaking out over his body. It seemed he could hear a tiny, faraway sound whispering over and over like a voice in an empty room: Ah got fever. . . . His back rested on a bed of fire, the imprint of leaves and grass searing him with a scalding persistence. He turned over on his stomach and groaned. Then he jerked up, half-sitting. He was fully conscious now, fighting for his strength, remembering the curses, the prayer and the whip.

The voice whispered again, this time louder: Ah gotta git home.... With fumbling fingers he untied the rope from his ankles and wrists. They didnt kill me, he thought. He stood up and the dark earth swayed and the stars blurred. Lawd, have mercy! He found himself on his knees; he had not known when he had started falling; he just found himself on his knees. Lawd, Ahm weak! He stood up again, more slowly this time, holding onto a tree. He would have to get his shirt; he could not go through the streets with a naked and bleeding back. He put one foot in front of the other with conscious effort, holding his body stiffly. Each slight twist of his shoulders sent a wave of liquid metal over him. In the grass at his feet his shirt was smeared like a white blur. He touched it; it was wet. He held it, instinctively fearing to put it on. When it did touch, his whole back blazed with a pain so intense that it seemed to glow white hot. No, he could not put it on now. Stiffly, he went among the trees, holding the shirt in his hands, looking at the ground.

He stopped at the edge of a dirt road, conscious of the cool steady stars and the fire that smoldered in his back. What roads this? He could not tell. Then he heard a clock striking so faintly that it seemed to be tolling in his own mind. He counted, Wun, Tuh.... Its tuh erclock, he thought. He could not stay here all night; he had to go in one direction or another. He watched the brown dusty road winding away in the darkness, like a twisting ribbon. Then he ducked his head, being seared again with fire and feeling a slight rush of air brush across his face. A small bird wheeled past his eyes and fluttered dizzily in the starlight. He watched it veer and dip, then crash softly into a tree limb. It fell to the ground, flapping tiny wings blindly. Then the bird twittered in fright and sailed straight upward into the starlight, vanishing. He walked northward, not going anywhere in particular, but walked northward because the bird had darted in that direction.

The road curved, turned to gravel, crunching under his

shoes. This mus be the way, he thought. There were fences along the sides of the road now. He went faster, holding his legs stiffly to avoid pulling the muscles in his back. A church steeple loomed in the starlight, slender and faint. Yeah, thas Houstons church. N Ah gotta go thu a white neighborhood, he thought with despair. He saw houses, white, serene and cool in the night. Spose Ah go to Houston? Naw, hes white. *White.* . . . Even tho he preaches the gospel Ah preaches, he might not take me in. . . . He passed a small graveyard surrounded by a high iron picket fence. A *white* graveyard, he thought and snickered bitterly. Lawd God in Heaven, even the dead cant be together! He stopped and held his shirt in his hands. He dreaded trying to put it on, but he had to. Ah cant go thu the streets like this. Gingerly, he draped the shirt over his shoulders; the whole mass of bruised and mangled flesh flamed, glowed white. With a convulsive movement he rammed his arms into the sleeves, thinking that the faster he did it the less pain there would be. The fire raged so he had a wild impulse to run, feeling that he would have no time then to suffer. But he could not run in a white neighborhood. To run would mean to be shot, for a burglar, or anything. Stiff-legged, he went down a road that turned from brown dust to black asphalt. Ahead street lamps glowed in round, rosy hazes.

Far down the shadow-dappled pavement he heard the sound of feet. He walked past a white man, then he listened to the white man's footsteps dying away behind him. He stopped at a corner and held onto a telephone pole. It would be better to keep in the residential district than to go through town. He would be stopped and questioned in town surely. And jailed maybe. Three blocks later on a white boy came up on him so softly and suddenly that he started in panic. After the boy had gone he turned to look; he saw the boy turning, looking at him. He walked on hurriedly. A block later a white woman appeared. When she was some fifty feet away she crossed to the other side of the street. Hate tightened his throat, then he emptied his lungs in a short, silent, bitter

laugh. Ah ain gonna bother yuh, white lady. Ah only wan t
git home. . . .

Like a pillar of fire he went through the white neighborhood. Some days theys gonna burn! Some days theys gonna
burn in Gawd Awmightys fire! How come they make us
suffer so? The worls got too mucha everything! Yit they
bleed us! They fatten on us like leeches! There ain no groun
yuh kin walk on that they don own! N Gawd knows tha ain
right! He made the earth fer us all! He ain tol no lie when
He put us in this worl n said be fruitful n multiply. . . . Fire
fanned his hate; he stopped and looked at the burning stars.
"Gawd, ef yuh gimme the strength Ahll tear this ol buildin
down! Tear it down, Lawd! Tear it down like ol Samson
tore the temple down!" He walked again, mumbling.
"Lawd, tell me whut t do! Speak t me, Lawd!" He caught
his breath; a dark figure came out of the shadows in front of
him. He saw a glint of metal; it was a policeman. He held
erect and walked rapidly. Ahll stop, he thought. He wont
have t ast me t stop. . . . He saw the white face drawing
closer. He stopped and waited.

"Put your hands up, nigger!"

"Yessuh."

He lifted his arms. The policeman patted his hips, his sides.
His back blazed, but he bit his lips and held still.

"Who you work for?"

"Ahma preacher, suh."

"A *preacher?*"

"Yessuh."

"What you doing out here this time of night?"

"Ah wuz visitin a sick man, a janitah, suh, whut comes t
mah church. He works fer Miz Harvey. . . ."

"Who?"

"Miz Harvey, suh."

"Never heard of her, and I've been on this beat for ten
years."

"She lives right back there, suh," he said, half turning and
pointing.

"Well, you look all right. You can go on. But keep out of here at night."

"Yessuh."

He was near his own people now. Across a grassy square he could see the top of the round-house glinting dully in the moonlight. The black asphalt turned to cinders and the houses were low, close together, squatting on the ground as though hiding in fear. He saw his church and relaxed. He came to the steps. Caught hold of a banister and rested a moment.

When inside he went quietly down a hall, mounted the stairs, and came to the door of his room. He groped in the dark and felt the bed. He tried to pull off the shirt. It had stuck. He peeled it. Then he eased onto the bed and lay on his stomach. In the darkness his back seemed to take new fire. He went to the kitchen and wet a cloth with cold water. He lay down again with the cloth spread over him. That helped some. Then he began to shake. He was crying.

THE DOOR CREAKED.

"Tha yuh, Pa?"

"Son?"

"Good Gawd, wes been lookin all over fer yuh! Where yuh been? Mas worried t death!"

"C mon in, son, n close the do."

"Don yuh wanna light?"

"Naw; close the do."

There was a short silence.

"Whuts the mattah, Pa? Yuh sick?"

"Close the do n sit down, son!"

Taylor could hear Jimmy's breathing, then a chair scraping over the floor and the soft rustle of Jimmy's clothes as he sat.

"Whuts the mattah, Pa? Whut happened?"

Taylor stared in the darkness and slowly licked his swollen lips. He wanted to speak, but somehow could not. Then he stiffened, hearing Jimmy rise.

"Set *down*, son!"

"But, Pa. . . ."

Fire seethed not only in Taylor's back, but all over, inside and out. It was the fire of shame. The questions that fell from Jimmy's lips burned as much as the whip had. There rose in him a memory of all the times he had given advice, counsel, and guidance to Jimmy. And he wanted to talk to him now as he had in the past. But his impulses were deadlocked. Then suddenly he heard himself speaking, hoarsely, faintly. His voice was like a whisper rising from his whole body.

"They whipped me, son. . . ."

"Whipped yuh? Who?"

Jimmy ran to the bed and touched him.

"Son, set *down!*"

Taylor's voice was filled with a sort of tense despair. He felt Jimmy's fingers leaving him slowly. There was a silence in which he could hear only his own breath struggling in his throat.

"Yuh mean the *white folks?*"

Taylor buried his face in his pillow and tried to still the heaving in his chest.

"They beat me, son. . . ."

"Ahll git a doctah!"

"Naw!"

"But yuhs hurt!"

"Naw; lock the do! Don let May in here. . . ."

"Goddam them white bastards!"

"Set down, son!"

"Who wuz they, Pa?"

"Yuh cant do nothin, son. Yuhll have t wait. . . ."

"Wes been waitin too long! All we do is wait, *wait!*"

Jimmy's footsteps scuffed across the floor. Taylor sat up.

"Son?"

"Ahma git mah gun n git Pete n Bob n Joe n Sam! Theyll see they cant do this t us!"

Taylor groped in the darkness; he found Jimmy's shoulders.

"C mon son! Ahm awright. . . ."

"Thas the reason why they kill us! We take everything they put on us! We take everthing! *Everthing!*"

"Yuh cant do nothin *erlone,* Jimmy!"

Jimmy's voice was tense, almost hysterical.

"But we kin *make* em know they cant do this t us widout us doin *some*thing! Aw, hell, Pa! Is we gonna be dogs *all* the time?"

"But theyll kill yuh, son!"

"Somebody *has* t die!"

Taylor wanted to tell Jimmy something, but he could not find the words. What he wanted to say boiled in him, but it seemed too big to come out. He flinched from pain, pressing his fingers to his mouth, holding his breath.

"Pa?"

"Yeah, son?"

"Hadley n Green wuz here t see yuh three-fo times."

"Yeah?"

Jimmy said nothing. Taylor twisted around, trying to see his son's face in the darkness.

"Whut they say, son?"

"Aw, hell! It don mattah. . . ."

"Tell me whut they *said!*"

"Ttthey ssaid. . . . Aw, Paw, they didn't know!"

"Whut they *say?*"

"They said yuh had done run out on em. . . ."

"Run *out?*"

"Everbody wuz astin where yuh wuz," said Jimmy. "Nobody knowed. So they tol em yuh run out. N Brother Smith had the Deacon Board t vote yuh outta the church. . . ."

"Vote me *out?*"

"They said they didnt wan yuh fer pastah no mo. It was Smith who made em do it. He tol em yuh had planned a demonstration n lef em holdin the bag. He fussed n stormed at em. They thought they wuz doin right. . . ."

Taylor lay on his bed of fire in the darkness and cried. He felt Jimmy's fingers again on his face.

"Its awright, Pa. Well git erlong somehow. . . ."

"Seems like Gawds don lef me! Ahd die fer mah people ef Ah only knowed how. . . ."

"Pa. . . ."

"How come Ah cant never do nothin? All mah life Ah done tried n cant do nothin! *Nothin!*"

"Its awright, Pa!"

"Ah done lived all mah life on mah knees, a-beggin n a-pleadin wid the white folks. N all they gimme wuz crumbs! All they did wuz kick me! N then they come wida gun n ast me t give mah own soul! N ef Ah so much as talk lika man they try t kill me. . . ."

He buried his face in the pillow, trying to sink himself into something so deeply that he could never feel again. He heard Jimmy turning the key in the lock.

"Son!"

Again he ran to Jimmy and held him.

"*Don* do tha, son!"

"Thingsll awways be like this less we *fight!*"

"Set down, son! Yo po ol pas a-*beggin* yuh t set down!"

He pulled Jimmy back to the bed. But even then it did not seem he could speak as he wanted to. He felt what he wanted to say, but it was elusive and hard to formulate.

"Son. . . ."

"Ah ain gonna live this way, Pa!"

He groped for Jimmy's shoulders in the darkness and squeezed them till the joints of his fingers cracked. And when words came they seemed to be tearing themselves from him, as though they were being pushed upward like hot lava out of a mountain from deep down.

"Don be a fool, son! Don thow yo life erway! We cant do nothin erlone."

"But theys gonna treat us this way as long as we *let* em!"

He had to make Jimmy understand; for it seemed that in making him understand, in telling him, he, too, would understand.

"We gotta git wid the *people,* son. Too long we done

tried t do this thing our way n when we failed we wanted
t turn out n pay-off the white folks. Then they kill us up
like flies. Its the *people*, son! Wes too much erlone this
way! Wes los when wes erlone! Wes gonna be wid our
folks. . . ."

"But theys killin us!"

"N theyll keep on killin us less we learn how t fight! Son,
its the people we mus gid wid us! Wes empty n weak this way!
The reason we cant do nothin is cause wes so much erlone. . . ."

"Them Reds wuz right," said Jimmy.

"Ah dunno," said Taylor. "But let nothin come tween yuh
n *yo* people. Even the Reds cant do nothin ef yuh lose yo
people. . . ." Fire burned him as he talked, and he talked as
though trying to escape it. "Membah whut Ah tol yuh prayer
wuz, son?"

There was silence, then Jimmy answered slowly:

"Yuh mean lettin Gawd be so real in yo life tha everthing
yuh do is cause of Im?"

"Yeah, but its different now, son. Its the *people!* Theys the
ones whut mus be real t us! Gawds wid the people! N the
peoples gotta be real as Gawd t us! We cant hep ourselves er
the people when wes erlone. Ah been wrong erbout a lotta
things Ah tol yuh, son. Ah tol yuh them things cause Ah
thought they wuz right. Ah told yuh t work hard n climb t
the top. Ah told yuh folks would lissen t yuh then. But they
wont, son! All the will, all the strength, all the power, all the
numbahs is in the people! Yuh cant live by yoself! When they
beat me tonight, they beat *me*. . . . There wuznt nothin Ah
could do but lay there n hate n pray n cry. . . . Ah couldnt
feel mah people, Ah couldnt *see* mah people, Ah couldnt
hear mah people. . . . All Ah could feel wuz the whip cuttin
mah blood out. . . ."

In the darkness he imagined he could see Jimmy's face as
he had seen it a thousand times, looking eagerly, his eyes
staring before him, fashioning his words into images, into life.
He hoped Jimmy was doing that now.

"Ahll awways hate them bastards! Ahll *aw*ways hate em!"

"Theres other ways, son."

"Yuhs sick, Pa. . . ."

"Wes all sick, son. Wes gotta think erbout the people, night n day, think erbout em so hard tha our po selves is fergotten. . . . Whut they suffer is whut Ah suffered las night when they whipped me. Wes gotta keep the people wid us."

Jimmy was silent. A soft knock came at the door.

"DAN!"

"Thas Ma," said Jimmy.

Taylor heard Jimmy rise to his feet; he gripped Jimmy's hands.

"Please, Pa! Let her come in n hep yuh!"

"Naw."

"Dan!"

Jimmy broke from him; he heard the key turn in the lock. The door opened.

"Dan! Fer Gawds sake, whuts the mattah?"

Jimmy switched on the light. Taylor lay blinking at May's anxious face. He felt shame again, knowing that he should not feel it, but feeling it anyway. He turned over and buried his face in his hands.

"Dan!"

She ran and knelt at the side of the bed.

"They tried t kill im, Ma! They beat im!" said Jimmy.

"Ah knowed them white folks wuz gonna do something like this! Ah knowed it," sobbed May.

Taylor sat up.

"Yuh be still! Lay down!" said May.

She pushed him back onto the bed.

"Cant yuh do something fer im, Ma? Hes sufferin tha way."

Taylor heard May leave the room and come back.

"Hol still, Dan. This ain gonna hurt yuh. . . ."

He felt warm water laving him, then something cool that

smelled of oil. He heard Jimmy moving to and fro, getting things for May. When his back was dressed he felt the bed had somehow changed. He wondered at the strange peace that seeped into his mind and body there in the room with May and Jimmy, with the white folks far off in the darkness.

"Feel bettah, Dan?"

"Ahm awright."

"Yuh hongry?"

"Naw."

He wanted to talk to Jimmy again, to tell him about the black people. But he could not think of words that would say what he wanted to say. He would tell it somehow later on. He began to toss, moving jerkily, more now from restlessness of mind than from the dying fire still lingering in his body.

SUDDENLY the doorbell pealed. Taylor turned and saw May and Jimmy looking at each other.

"Somebody at the do," said Jimmy in a tense voice.

"Yuh reckon they white folks?" asked May.

"Yuh bettah go down, Jimmy," said Taylor.

"Ef its any white folks tell em Dans out," said May.

Jimmy's footsteps died away on the stairs. A door slammed. There were faint sounds of voices. Footsteps echoed, came on the stairs, grew loud. Taylor knew that more than one person was coming up. He lifted himself and sat on the edge of the bed.

"Dan, yuh cant git up! Yuhll make yoself sick!"

He ignored her. The door opened and Jimmy ran in.

"Its Brother Bonds, Pa!"

Bonds stood in the doorway with his head wrapped in blood-stained bandages. His face twitched and his eyes stared at something beyond the walls of the room, as though his attention had been riveted once and for always upon one fixed spot.

"Whut happened, Brother?" asked Taylor.

Bonds stared, dazed, with hunched and beaten shoulders. Then he sank to the floor, sobbing softly:

"They beat me! They beat mah chillun! They beat mah wife! They beat us all cause Ah tol em t git outta mah house! Lawd, how long Yuh gonna let em treat us this way? How long Yuh gonna let em make us suffer?"

May sobbed. Jimmy ran out of the room. Taylor caught him on the stairs.

"Don be a fool, boy! Yuh c mon back here, *now!*"

Jimmy flopped on the edge of a chair and mumbled to himself. The room was quiet save for the rustle of tree leaves that drifted in from the outside and the sound of Bonds sobbing on the floor. As Taylor stood his own suffering was drowned in a sense of widening horror. There was in his mind a vivid picture of all the little dingy huts where black men and women were crouched, afraid to stir out of doors. Bonds stopped crying and looked at Taylor; again that sense of shame spread over Taylor, inside and out. It stirred him to speech.

"Who else they beat, Brother?"

"Seem like everbody, Reveren! Them two Commoonists got beat something terrible n they put em in jail. N Ah heard they kilt one black man whut tried t fight back. They ketched everbody they kin on the streets n lettin em have it. They ridin up n down in cars. . . ."

Jimmy cursed. The doorbell pealed again.

"Git me a shirt, May!"

"Dan, yuh ain able t do nothin!"

The doorbell pealed again, then again. Taylor started toward the dresser; but May got there before he did and gave him a shirt.

"Dan, be careful!"

"C mon downstairs, Brother Bonds. N yuh, too, Jimmy," said Taylor.

THE CHURCH'S waiting room was full. Black men and women sat and stood, saying nothing, waiting. Arms were in slings; necks were wrapped in white cloth; legs were bound in blood-stained rags.

"LOOK AT WHUT YUH DONE DONE!" a voice bawled.

It was Deacon Smith. Taylor's eyes went from face to face; he knew them all. Every Sunday they sat in the pews of his church, praying, singing, and trusting the God he gave them. The mute eyes and silent lips pinned him to a fiery spot of loneliness. He wanted to protest that loneliness, wanted to break it down; but he did not know how. No parables sprang to his lips now to give form and meaning to his words; alone and naked, he stood ashamed. Jimmy came through the door and placed his hand on his shoulder.

"Its daylight, Pa. The folks is gatherin in the playground! Theys waiten fer yuh. . . ."

Taylor went into the yard with the crowd at his heels. It was broad daylight and the sun shone. The men in their overalls and the women with children stood about him on all sides, silent. A fat black woman elbowed her way in and faced him.

"Waal, Reveren, we done got beat up. Now, is we gonna march?"

"Yuh wanna march?" asked Taylor.

"It don make no difference wid me," she said. "Them white folks cant do no mo than theys already done."

The crowd chimed in.

"N Gawd knows they cant!"

"Ahll go ef the nex one goes!"

"Ah gotta die sometime, so Ah just as waal die now!"

"They cant kill us but once!"

"Ahm tired anyhow! Ah don care!"

"The white folks says theys gonna meet us at the park!"

Taylor turned to Jimmy.

"Son, git yo boys together n tell em t roun up everbody!"

"Yessuh!"

May was pulling at his sleeve.

"Dan, yuh *cant* do this. . . ."

Deacon Smith pushed his way in and faced him.

"Yuhll never set foot in a church ergin ef yuh lead them po black folks downtown t be killed!"

The crowd surged.

"Ain nobody leadin us nowhere!"

"We goin ourselves!"

"Is we gonna march, Reveren?"

"Yeah; soon as the crowd gits together," said Taylor.

"Ain nobody t blame but yuh ef yuh carry em t their *death!*" warned Deacon Smith.

"How come yuh don shut yo old big mouth n let the Reveren talk?" asked the fat woman.

"Sistah, Ah got as much right t speak as yuh!"

"Waal, don speak to me, yuh hear!"

"Somebody has t say something when ain *nobody* got no sense!"

"Man, don yuh tell me Ah ain got no sense!"

"Yuh sho don ack like it!"

"Ah got as much sense as yuh got!"

"How come yuh don use it?"

The fat sister slapped Deacon Smith straight across his face. Taylor ran between them and pried them apart. The crowd surged and screamed.

"Ef he touches Sistah Henry ergin Ahll kill im!"

"He ain got no bisness talkin tha way t a woman!"

Taylor dragged the fat woman toward the gate. The crowd followed, yelling. He stopped and faced them. They circled around, tightly, asking questions. May had hold of his sleeve. Jimmy came to him.

"Pa, theys comin!"

Taylor turned and walked across the yard with the crowd following. He took two planks and laid them upon the ends of two saw-horses and made a solid platform. He climbed up and stood in the quiet sunshine. He did not know exactly what it was he wanted to say, but whatever it was he would say it when they were quiet. He felt neither fear nor joy, just an humble confidence in himself, as though he were standing before his mirror in his room. Then he was conscious that they were quiet; he took one swift look over their heads, heads that stretched away to the street and beyond, a solid block of black, silent faces; then he looked down, not to the dust, but just a slight lowering of eyes, as though he were no longer looking at them, but at something within himself.

"Sistahs n Brothers, they tell me the Deacon Boards done voted me outta the church. Ef thas awright wid yuh, its awright wid me. The white folks says Ahma bad nigger n they don wanna have nothin else t do wid me. N thas awright, too. But theres one thing Ah wanna say. Ah knows how yuh feel erbout bein hongry. N how yuh feel is no different from how Ah feel. Yuh been waitin a week fer me t say whut yuh ought t do. Yuh been wonderin how come Ah didnt tell yuh whut yuh oughta do. Waal. . . ."

He paused and looked over the silent crowd; then again his eyes, his gaze, went inward.

"Sistahs n Brothers, the reason Ah didnt say nothin is cause Ah didnt know *whut* t say. N the only reason Ahm speakin now is cause Ah *do* know. Ah know whut t do. . . ."

He paused again, swallowing. The same feeling which had gripped him so hard last night when he had been talking to Jimmy seized him. He opened his mouth to continue; his lips moved several times before words came; and when they did come they fell with a light and hoarse whisper.

"Sistahs n Brothers, las night the white folks took me out t the woods. They took me out cause Ah tol em yuh wuz hongry. They ast me t tell yuh not t march, n Ah tol em Ah wouldnt. Then they beat me. They tied me t a tree n beat me till Ah couldnt feel no mo. They beat me cause Ah wouldnt tell yuh not t ast fer bread. They said yuhd blieve everthing Ah said. All the time they wuz hepin me, all the time they been givin me favors, they wuz doin it sos *they* could tell *me* to tell *yuh* how t ack! Sistahs n Brothers, as Gawds mah judge, Ah thought Ah wuz doin right when Ah did that. Ah thought Ah wuz doin right when Ah told yuh t do the things they said. N cause Ah wouldnt do it this time, they tied me t a tree n beat me till mah blood run. . . ."

Mist covered his eyes. He heard the crowd murmuring; but he did not care if they were murmuring for or against him; he wanted to finish, to say what he had been trying so hard to say for many long hours.

"Sistahs n Brothers, they whipped me n made me take the name of *Gawd* in vain! They made me say mah prayers n beat me n laughed! They beat me till Ah couldnt membah nothin! All last night Ah wuz lying stretched out on the ground wid mah back burnin. . . . All this mawning before day Ah wuz limpin thu white folks streets. Sistahs n Brothers, Ah *know* now! Ah done seen the *sign!* Wes gotta git together. Ah know whut yo life is! Ah done felt it! Its *fire!* Its like the fire that burned me las night! Its sufferin! Its hell! Ah cant bear this fire erlone! Ah know now whut t do! Wes gotta git close t one ernother! Gawds done spoke! Gawds done sent His sign. Now its fer us t ack. . . ."

The crowd started yelling:

"Well go ef yuh go!"

"Wes ready!"

"The white folks says theyll meet us at the park!"

The fat black woman started singing:

> *So the sign of the fire by night*
> *N the sign of the cloud by day*
> *A-hoverin oer*
> *Jus befo*
> *As we journey on our way. . . .*

Taylor got down. He moved with the crowd slowly toward the street. May went with him, looking, wondering, saying nothing. Jimmy was at his side. They sang as they marched.

More joined along the way. When they reached the park that separated the white district from the black, the poor whites were waiting. Taylor trembled when he saw them join, swelling the mass that moved toward the town. He looked ahead and saw black and white marching; he looked behind and saw black and white marching. And still they sang:

"So the sign of the fire by night. . . ."

They turned into the street that led to town.

"N the sign of the cloud by day. . . ."

Taylor saw blue-coated policemen standing along the curb.

"A-hoverin oer. . . ."

Taylor felt himself moving between the silent lines of blue-coated white men, moving with a sea of placards and banners, moving under the sun like a pregnant cloud. He said to himself, They ain gonna bother us! They bettah *not* bother us. . . .

"Jus befo. . . ."

Across a valley, in front of him, he could see the buildings of the town sprawled on a hill.

"As we journey on our way. . . ."

They were tramping on pavement now. And the blue-coated men stood still and silent. Taylor saw Deacon Smith standing on the curb, and Smith's face merged with the faces of the others, meaningless, lost. Ahead was the City Hall, white and clean in the sunshine. The autos stopped at the street corners while the crowd passed; and as they entered the downtown section people massed quietly on the sidewalks. Then the crowd began to slow, barely moving. Taylor looked ahead and wondered what was about to happen; he wondered without fear; as though whatever would or could happen could not hurt this many-limbed, many-legged, many-handed crowd that was he. He felt May clinging to his sleeve. Jimmy was peering ahead. A policeman came running up to him.

"You Taylor?"

"Yussuh," he said, quietly, his gaze straight and steady.

"The mayors down front; he wants to see you!"

"Tell im Ahm back here," said Taylor.

"But he wants to see the leader up front!"

"Tell im Ahm back here," said Taylor again.

The man hesitated, then left; they waited, quiet, still. Then the crowd parted. Taylor saw Mayor Bolton hurrying toward him, his face beet-red.

"Dan, tell your people not to make any trouble! We dont want any trouble, Dan. . . ."

"There ain gonna be no trouble, yo Honah!"

"Well, tell them they can get food if they go back home, peacefully. . . ."

"Yuh tell em, yo Honah!"

They looked at each other for a moment. Then the mayor turned and walked back. Taylor saw him mount the rear seat of an auto and lift his trembling hands high above the crowd, asking for silence, his face a pasty white.

A baptism of clean joy swept over Taylor. He kept his eyes on the sea of black and white faces. The song swelled louder and vibrated through him. This is the way! he thought. Gawd ain no lie! He ain no lie! His eyes grew wet with tears, blurring his vision: the sky trembled; the buildings wavered as if about to topple; and the earth shook. . . . He mumbled out loud, exultingly:

"Freedom belongs t the strong!"

Lawd Today

Lawd Today *represents Wright's first attempt at a full-size
novel; he began writing it in 1932 and completed it in 1937.
Wright conceived the book as an Afro-American counterpart
to Joyce's* Ulysses, *depicting in a varied though generally
good-humored mood, one day in the life of Jake Jackson, one
of the middle-class Negroes who thrived in the richer areas
of the Chicago South Side, between Stoney Island and 63rd
Street. These were people who dreamed of becoming doctors
and lawyers but, caught in the grip of racial pressures and
economic exploitation, lured by all the enticements of a con-
sumer society, they never even managed to complete their
education before practicing what Wright called the "three
A's": Automobile, Alimony and Abortion."*

*The influence of Joyce, but also of such naturalists as James
T. Farrell and John Dos Passos, is felt in Wright's experimen-
tal prose, but his has a unique quality that makes his hero-
victim—as human and as likable as he is—at times, irritat-
ing, narrow-minded and prejudiced. Dos Passos had tried to
objectify his novels by superimposing concrete material
upon the narrative and through the movie-like techniques of
his "Newsreel" and "Camera Eye" sections. Wright resorts to
the same process, constantly bringing in Jake's immediate*

Lawd Today *was originally published by Walker & Company in 1963. This
selection is chapters 1–3 of "Part I: Commonplace" and chapters 1–3 of
"Part III: Rat's Alley" of the original work.*

surrounding *(what the radio blares forth, what he can read in the headlines, or a pamphlet, the movie stills he looks at), but whereas Dos Passos used that technique as a film director might use a realistic backdrop, Wright employs it to define Jake in space and history—that is, within the racial prison. The irony is that the radio series on the Civil War commemorating Lincoln's birthday simply does not concern Jake and his pals. They have been excluded from American history and they have found shelter in daydreams or wishful thinking.*

Similarly, in order to further define Jake's inner tensions, Wright breaks the narration by means of interior monologue to allow his protagonist to confront his secret self. This tends to interiorize the psychological conflict generated by fear and it emphasizes the mental castration. Conversely, Wright also relies on a free-flowing, warm, often rollicking humor. His characters talk and dream and play the dozens (bandying of insults between teenage Blacks) in the best tradition of Black folklore. The result is a lively, impressionistic picture of ghetto life treated in a largely (though ambiguous) comic perspective. It is the kind of life that Native Son *(1940) will explore as a tragedy.*

It is interesting to note that Lawd Today *was published posthumously in 1963. It was rejected earlier by scores of publishers who thought it too loosely structured and immature. Yet after Wright's death this story seemed to be a missing part of Wright's early development as a novelist and worthy of publication.*

COMMONPLACE

> . . . a vast Sargasso Sea—a prodigious welter of uncon-
> scious life, swept by groundswells of half-conscious emo-
> tion. . . .
>
> Van Wyck Brooks' *America's Coming-of-Age*

Ladies and Gentlemen, Jack Bassett speaking! Station WGN, Tribune Square, Chicago. At the next tonebeat the time will be exactly eight o'clock, Central Standard Time . . . ting! . . . courtesy the Neverstop Watch Company, Ladies and Gentlemen!

Look out of your window! What do you see flapping so proudly and sedately at every corner and over every building entrance? Doesn't it make your heart skip a beat to see Old Glory floating there so beautifully in the morning breeze?

My Dear Friends, our flag is flying high today in honor of one of our greatest Americans, a man who saved his country and bestowed the blessings of liberty and freedom upon millions of his fellowmen!

This is February twelfth, Abraham Lincoln's Birthday!

At this time Professor Weatherspoon, Head of the Department of History at the University of Chicago, will tell you of Lincoln's background and his glorious career. Professor Weatherspoon! Ummmmmmmpph! . . . Uuummmmmmmmmmphmmm! . . . Good morning, everybody!

NO MATTER HOW HARD he squinted his eyes and craned his neck, he could not see the top of the steps. But somebody was calling and he had to go up. He hollered, *Yeah, I'm coming right up, in just a minute!* And then he started. It was hard work, climbing steps like these. He panted and the calves of his legs ached. He stopped and looked to see if he could tell where the steps ended, but there were just steps and steps and steps. *Shucks, they needn't be in such a helluva hurry,* he thought as he stretched his legs and covered three and four steps at a time. Then, suddenly, the steps seemed funny, like a great big round barrel rolling or a long log spinning in water, and he was on top treading for all he was worth and that voice was still calling. He stopped again, disgusted. *Hell, there just ain't no end to these steps! I'm just wasting time! Ain't moving a peg! And that old sonofabitch up there sounds just like my boss, too!*

Jake stirred and burrowed his head deeper into a pillow. He sighed, swallowed, pulled his knees up, and turned his face from the sun glare.

The steps blazed and shivered in a mist of bright gold, as if about to vanish. Then they grew real and solid. He was still running, thinking: *That guy's still calling. What in hell can he be wanting?* He hollered again, *Keep your shirt on, for Chrissakes! I'm coming!* He was flying up steps now, mounting whole blocks of steps, miles and miles of steps, but even at that the end was not in sight. *What to hell? There's a joke here somewhere! Damn tooting!* He stopped, sighed, wiped sweat from his forehead, and looked to see how many steps he had covered. He was right where he had started! He shook his head, mumbling to himself, *Jeeesus, all that running for nothing . . . Yeah, there's a trick in this.* But that guy, that guy who had a voice like his boss, was still calling.

Jake turned and lay on his stomach. His head rested in the crook of his right elbow. His left arm clung close to his side, dingy palm upcurled. He smacked his lips softly, as though over a dainty and dissolving morsel.

The steps stretched endlessly up. He was taking them five at a time now, not even pausing for breath. A deep sweet gladness suffused his limbs. He would get there soon if he kept this up. All steps ended somewhere. He yelled, *I'm coming! I'm coming!* Then the voice boomed so loud in his ears he stopped and tried to make out what it was saying.

Jake struggled out of sleep and propped himself upon an elbow. A pair of piggish eyes blinked at sunlight. Low growls escaped his half-parted lips and his hands fumbled comically for the runaway sheet. He swallowed several times and his

Adam's apple jumped up and down from his chin to his collarbone, like a toy monkey on a string. His eyes smarted, watering. He saw the bed and the dresser and the carpet and the walls melting and shifting and merging into a blur. His loins felt heavy and exhausted. He closed his eyes and his mind groped, thinking, *What was I dreaming?* He remembered being on the very brink of something, on the verge of a deep joy. *Now what was I dreaming?* He tried to think, but a wide gap yawned in his mind. And that guy was still calling.

. . . Garrison, forerunner of Lincoln, was a man whose soul was aflame with a holy cause. Going against the advice of his friends and the warnings of his enemies, he declared himself outspokenly against slavery and oppression. . . .

Gawddamn! That old radio woke me up! A vague sense of rows and rows of steps came again. *Now what was I dreaming?* It seemed very, very important that he should remember. He screwed up his eyes, but the dream steps were drowned in a vast blackness, like a slow movie fadeout. He had been going somewhere in a great big hurry; he had been thirsting, longing for something. But each time he had got almost to it, each time it was almost his, somebody had called.

. . . I am in earnest—I will not equivocate—I will not excuse—I will not retreat a single inch—and I will be heard. . . .

Jake's mouth twitched. He flung one black leg from under the sheet and groaned. The air of the room was close. Heat was melting tiny cakes of grease in his nappy hair. He raised his hand and scratched at a thin stream of slickness oozing down the ebony nape of his neck. His face wrinkled, he opened his mouth and bawled:
"Lil!"
"Hunh?"
"Shut that door!"
"Hunh?"
"Shut that Gawddamn door, I said!"

He heard the door slam. *That bitch! How come she leave that door open and wake me up?* He settled down again and the mood of his dream came back. He imagined his loins straining against a warm, nude body. He breathed softly as the muscles of his diaphragm grew taut. A hot, melting ball glowed in his solar plexus. His head drooped and his lips touched the starched pillowcase. He doubled his legs, bringing his knees to the pit of his stomach. He felt the warm body pressing close to him, covering him, heating his blood. *Milkman! Milkman!* He jumped. *Gawddamn!* It was no use; he could not sleep anymore. Through a six-inch opening in the window came the harsh throb of an auto motor. He sat up, his eyes meeting a glare of sunshine pouring slantwise through voile curtains. *Gawd, is it morning already?* He wagged his head and tried to swallow a nasty taste. He made a wry face and tried again. *Arrrrrk! Naw.* He simply could not swallow it. He eased down again, his head striking a sharp edge. He fumbled with his hand and brought before his eyes a small, yellow booklet. UNITY, he read. A MAGAZINE DEVOTED TO CHRISTIAN HEALING. He saw the picture of a haloed, bearded man draped in white folds; the man's hand was resting upon the blond curls of a blue-eyed girl. Beneath the picture ran a caption: EVERY HOUR OF THE DAY AND NIGHT JESUS FLOWS ALL THROUGH ME. *What makes Lil keep all this trash in bed?* He hurled the book across the room, hearing the leaves flutter with a dry sound.

He stood up, dazed somewhat from sleep. He licked his lips and rubbed his eyes with the backs of his hands. His mouth gaped, revealing two rows of gleaming gold. It gaped wide. Wider. Wider still. Then it closed slowly, emitting a hippopotamic grunt, *Yyaaarph!* His eyes watered sympathetically as he stood rigid with his head tilted backward. *Jeeesus, I feel rotten.* He drew a long breath; something itched deep in his nose. Then it came:

"Ker . . . ker . . . kerchoossneeeeze!"

He bent double. When he straightened he wiped his nose

and eyes on the sleeves of his red-gold pyjamas, and groaned: "Aw, hell. . . ."

He was thirsty and his mouth tasted salty. He licked his lips and swallowed again to get rid of that disgusting taste. Adding to his sluggish confusion was a sickening hunger. His stomach felt like a vacuum with a black rat gnawing around inside of it. He got a cigarette from his pack and struck a match. His fingers trembled so the flame flickered out. *My nerves is just all shot,* he thought. When the cigarette was lit he screwed up his eyes and scratched himself, slowly, along the ribs, deep in the groin, around the navel, and between the thighs. He wanted a little more sleep, just a little more. But he knew it was useless. *How come Lil leave that door open? How come she turn that radio on so early?* He flushed hot with anger, but the smell of boiling coffee and sizzling bacon cooled him. He sighed, looking aimlessly around the room, at the curtains, at the sunshine, at the blooming red flowers in the carpet. His attention centered on his scheme rack, a little honeycomblike wooden case before which were piled hundreds and hundreds of tiny white cards. *Lawd, I ain't fooled with that scheme in almost a month now. And I got to go up and pass a test on it in about two weeks.* Merely to think of it made his head feel heavy. He had to learn that scheme, learn where each card went, and when it went where it went, and on what train. *Let's see now. Six o'clock sweat. Chicago and Evans. 15. Number 2. Except on Sundays. That's for Paris, Illinois. Then at nine-thirty comes Chicago and Evans. 9. Number 2. Let's see now. That's except Saturdays. Then comes ten forty-five. Yeah, that's Danville and Cairo. 131. No. 1. That goes by way of. . . .* He frowned, screwing up his eyes and biting his lips. *Where do that Danville and Carbondale go?* He could not remember. And he had nine hundred little white cards like that to commit to memory. Well, he would try to study a little after breakfast. After he had eaten a good meal his mind would be fresh and keen.

As in a dream he ambled to the bathroom, his fat black feet spreading like cobra heads upon the carpet. He turned the cold water faucet in the washbowl and looked around for a glass. *That bitch! How come she can't never do nothing right? You can never find a thing you want when she's around!* Stooping, he cupped his fingers under the stream and gulped huge swallows of water overflowing the brim of his palms. *Yeah, I feel lots better now.* He stood up, fronting the mirror. The reflection showed a face round as a full moon and dark as a starless midnight. In an oily expanse of blackness were set two cunning eyes under which hung flabby pouches. A broad nose squatted fat and soft, its two holes gaping militantly frontward like the barrels of a shotgun. Lips were full, moist, and drooped loosely, trembling when he walked. A soft roll of fat seeped out of his neck, buttressing his chin. Shaggy sideburns frizzled each temple.

He ran his fingers through his hair, scratching an itchy scalp. He brought them away sticky and greasy. Thrusting out his jaw, he touched bristles on his chin. He needed a hair cut and a shave. Badly. *Shucks, how come you got to waste a hour getting your hair cut? How come you got to shave every day?* He took down his mug and shaving brush and turned on the hot water. Wisps of vapor warmed his chest and face. *Christ, that feels good!* The smell of coffee and sizzling bacon became stronger. Slowly, he was waking up; even his mind began to work a little.

He cocked his head, poising his whitely lathered brush an inch from his chin. He heard Lil talking to somebody in the kitchen. He bent lower, listening. *What in hell can she find to talk about all the time? I certainly would like to know. And bawling her out don't seem to do a bit of good, neither. Yeah, she's going to keep on with her foolishness till I teach her a damn good lesson one of these days. And furthermore, it ain't right for a decent woman to stand talking common that way to strangers. And she knows that!* Jake sat the mug down, hurried to the bathroom door, and listened with his ear to the keyhole. *Still talking! And laughing, too! What to hell? What she think this is, a picnic?* He slammed down the brush and pushed through the door.

He entered the kitchen just as Lil threw back her head, laughing. Her shoulders were shaking. But when she saw Jake she sobered. The milkman hastily picked up his rack.

"Good morning," said the milkman.

Jake did not answer. He came and stood in the middle of the floor, his legs wide apart.

"You up already, Jake?" Lil asked in a strained voice.

Jake shook his head, his mouth twisting into a crooked smile. "Naw, I'm still asleep."

Lil fumbled for a dishtowel and began to polish an already glittering spot on the stove. The milkman groped for the doorknob.

"Well, I reckon I'll be getting along," he said.

"Be sure and bring me an extra pint of cream tomorrow," said Lil.

"O.K.," said the milkman, and was gone.

Jake slouched heavily into a chair and frowned at the floor. Lil went to the icebox and got a carton of eggs. She bit her lip and kept her shoulders stiff, as though expecting a blow.

"Lil?" His voice held a familiar, ominous portent.

She lowered her head an inch and placed a skillet on the stove. As she lit the gas her face was placid, as though she had not heard. Sometimes that forestalled him, pretending like that.

"Lil!" Anger was creeping into his voice.

"I hears you, Jake." She spoke placatingly.

"Act like it then!"

She broke an egg into the skillet. Jake's toes gripped the linoleum as though even they were angry with her.

"Woman, I'm still talking to you!"

She sprinkled salt over the egg.

"What's wrong with you?"

"Nothing."

"Don't you hear me talking?"

"Yeah, I hears you, Jake."

"Why in hell don't you act like it?"

She broke a second egg. A part of the white caught on the edge of the skillet and hardened slowly. Jake rose from his chair.

"Is you deaf?"

"Naw, I ain't deaf. I hears you real plain."

"I just wanted to know," he said. "On account of if you was, I can fix you so you can hear real good from now on."

His face was six inches from hers.

"What in hell can you see in a milkman's mug to make you want to keep talking to him all day—that's what I want to know!"

Lil cleared her throat, bent lower over the skillet, and fiddled the eggs with a long-handled fork.

"Now, listen, woman, I'm talking to you!"

"Nothing," she answered. "I don't see nothing."

"How come you keep talking to him?"

Business of turning the first egg over. Jake gripped her shoulder, pulling her from the stove.

"Ain't you going to talk to me?"

"Please, Jake, for Chrissake, let's don't start all that again!"

"Start what? What in hell you mean? Is you crazy! You's the one what's starting! Ain't I told you about that milkman before, a dozen times if one?"

Tenderly, Lil flipped the second egg over with a wide paddle. Jake gripped her arm, digging long nails into her flesh.

"I'm talking to you, bitch!"

"Yes, Jake."

"Ain't I told you about that milkman before?"

"Yes, Jake."

"How come you keep talking to him?"

Lil turned and faced him meekly. Her shoulders slumped as if she were placing all evidence before him for an impartial judgment, as if she were throwing herself upon his mercy, his ultimate sense of fairness.

"What you want me to do, Jake? Act like I'm wild? Can't I say good morning to folks when they say good morning to me? Honest to Gawd, I said no more to that milkman than I do to Mrs. Thomas. . . ."

"I ain't no fool! I heard you talking to that milkman ten minutes on end! I reckon he can't hear good, hunh? I reckon it takes ten minutes to tell him to bring you a bottle of cream, hunh? Woman, don't you try to play me cheap!"

"I ain't playing you cheap."

"You turned that radio on so I wouldn't hear what you was telling him!"

"Lawd, Jake. . . ."

"Now just say you didn't!"

She gaped at him.

"I ain't blind! I can see what's going on before my eyes! You can't put a damn thing over on me, and ain't no use you trying. And I reckon that sweet laugh you gave him was part of the order, too, hunh?" He swayed his body forward, his face leering.

Lil sighed.

"I sure wish you wasn't so foolish, Jake."

He shoved her from the stove again.

"Don't you call me a fool!"

"I didn't call you a fool!"

"Watch out how you talk to me!"

"I wish you could look at things sort of straight."

"I can look straight enough to see what you doing!"

Lil turned on him. As she spoke her whole body shook as though she had lost control of her nerves. She seemed impelled by an imperious, inner need.

"Just 'cause you so loose you think everybody's loose! If you was half as fair with me as I is with you, we wouldn't never fuss. But it's just like a person who's cheating to think another one is. . . ." She stopped abruptly, choking. "And you know . . . you know . . . you know I ain't in no condition to dddo wwwhat yyyou thinking. . . . You . . ." The muscles in her throat grew tight with resentment and she could not go on.

"Aw, cut the sob stuff! It don't work with me! You ain't as sick as you always trying to make out! You can always do everything you want to do but *that!*"

"You ought to be 'shamed!"

"Aw, I'm on to you! You just done made up your mind that you ain't going to be no good to me, that's all. But don't you think you putting that much over on me!" He measured a distance of half an inch on his thumb and forefinger. "I know what you up to! You just one more no good woman, that's all!"

"If I is, you the cause of it! You the cause of it! You the cause of it!" she repeated monotonously.

"Shut up!"

"You the cause. . . ."

"I said shut up!"

The words died in her throat.

"You ain't no good and you ain't never been no good! You been that way every since I married you! And don't think it's just lately I noticed it, neither! Even before you started going to that Gawddamn doctor you was no good!"

Lil clutched convulsively at her apron. Her fork tinkled to the floor. She picked it up and faced him again, her eyes swollen now with tears. She panted her words, her eyes wide.

"Naw, I ain't no good! And I thank my Gawd in Heaven I'll never be no good to you no more! And I hopes to Christ I'll never be! I ain't no good and I thank Gawd now! I'm sick! Yeah, I'm sick! And you the cause of it. So when you think of wanting any of me just remember you the cause of it! You tricked me! You knows you did! You knowed I didn't know what was happening to me when you fooled me into going to that old quack doctor. . . . Now you black and evil enough to try to take it all out on me. . . . Maybe I'll never be well again. . . . I wished I had gone on and had that baby than bbbe aaall mmmessed up this way. . . ."

Her knees sagged. She was crying hard now. Jake watched her closely with eyes that glittered.

"You ain't no good and you ain't never been no good!"

She turned her face to the window to cheat him of the satisfaction of her tears. Eggs were burning and the kitchen was filling with smoke.

"Tend to your cooking, you slut! I reckon you think I ought to be happy standing here watching my money burning up on a skillet!"

"I can't do nothing when yyyou kkkeep on bbobothering me!"

"Shut up and cook!"

She dried her eyes, and, coughing because of the smoke, dumped the charred eggs into a garbage pail, and washed the skillet.

"You can do everything you want to do but tend to your own business!" he told her with deep gravity.

He was quiet because he had won; she was quiet because she had lost. But neither was quit of the other. He knew that she would not take the last word. And she felt that he was not yet satisfied with what he had done. Silently, both searched for words that would wound. Seconds passed. Lil found such words first.

"Jake," she began quietly, "you better make a payment to the doctor. I had to go to see him yestiddy and the bill was almost five hundred dollars. He ain't been paid a thing in almost a month now, and it's getting long past due."

He turned away, waving a scornful palm.

"Tell him I ain't got no money."

"You get paid day after tomorrow."

"That's none of your Gawddamn business!"

"Well, you just as well pay him now. He says I got to have a operation, and the bill'll be twice as big."

"Got to have *what?*"

"A operation."

"Operation?"

"I got to be operated on in a month."

"When he tell you that?"

"Yestiddy, when I saw him."

"Operated on for what?"

"He says I got a tumor."

"Tumor?"

"Yeah, a tumor!"

Jake looked at her as though he had never seen her before.

"What in hell you doing going getting a tumor?"

"I done run off too many times fooling with you! That's how come I got it!"

"That's a Gawddamn lie!"

"Well, the doctor says so!"

"That's just your little red wagon, then!"

"He says it'll cost five hundred dollars, and that's just *your* little red wagon!"

"Yeah," Jake said through clenched teeth. "I can just see myself giving that damn quack five hundred dollars for you to get rid of a tumor. What you think I is, the United States' Mint? And you got the nerve to tell me I'm the cause of it! How about all the other niggers you been running around with?"

"There ain't been nobody but you!"

"Tell that quack he can get my money when hell freezes over!"

"If you don't pay 'im he can get your job!"

Jake's eyes went red. She had touched his sore spot—his government job. Her complaint on him at the Post Office would throw him out of work. Twice before she had complained, and one more time would just about put an end to him.

"You mighty damn eager to pay that quack. You ain't no good to me but you's a plenty damn good to him. You been going to that sonofabitch a long time, almost seven years. I can't make out what in hell he's doing to keep treating you all this time. . . ."

"Whatever he's doing's all your fault and you got to pay for it!"

"I done ask you for the last time to shut up!"

He stiffened. His jaws clamped vicelike. He wanted to slap her, slap her a blow that would make her hold her mouth forever. But he could not do that without being egged on more. He had reached that point where deep in him he longed for her to goad him just a little more, just a bit more. He wanted ever so badly to slap her, but he wanted to feel impelled. He trembled. His eyes wandered nervously about the kitchen, seeking for a clue, for a point of departure. Suddenly, he felt the emptiness of his stomach and remembered his hunger.

"Quit your Gawddamn jawing and put something to eat on my table!"

Lil looked at him quietly.

"You ain't washed. You ain't ready to eat yet."

Something tightened in him. All the hate of his marriage welled up. Lil seemed to have gone far beyond the power of his words to cut and wound.

"If you don't like the way I'm running this show, why in hell don't you get out?"

Lil poured cream into a pitcher.

"I'm staying 'cause this is my home, and you going to support me! Don't think you going to get out of it, neither, not long as you working. . . ."

Nails bit into palms. If he could only think of something to say to her that would make her so mad she would get up and leave, something so hot and hard that she would never want to forgive him, never want to see him again—something that would get rid of her once and for always.

"I can't see how come any slut wants to be hanging around a man who don't want her, I just can't see. . . ."

"I knows you can't see, but I'm staying! I knows you don't want me, but you going to support me!"

He rammed his hands into the pockets of his pyjamas, and leaned against the window casing.

"And suppose I don't support you?"

"Then I'll go down to that Post Office and tell 'em!"

"The day you go down to that Post Office and snitch on me again, that's the day you going to be sorry!"

"And the day you stop paying these bills that's the day you going to be sorry!"

He came to her side.

"I done took about enough off of you!"

"You ain't through taking yet!"

"Shut up, you lowbellied slut!"

"If I'm a slut now I was one when you married me!"

"I didn't want you in the first place!"

"You had a funny way of showing it!"

"If you hadn't lied and said you was big, I wouldn't've never married you, neither."

"You went around with your tongue lapping out to get me," said Lil, placing knives and forks upon the table.

"Don't cross talk me, woman!"

"You did!"

"Listen, pack your duds and get going! I don't want you!"

"Make me!"

"I don't want you, hear me!"

"And I don't want you, neither! All I want from you is support, and I'm going to get it or get your job!"

He leaned over her, his eyes fastened on her bare neck, his hands hanging limply at his sides.

"You can't talk this way to me!"

"Then don't talk to me!"

A hot sense of elation bubbled in him. He felt the muscles of his back stiffening. Just a few more words from her, just a few more, and, by God, he would slap her into the middle of next Christmas. His right hand itched. His voice dropped to a low growl.

"I'm asking you for the last time to shut up!"

Lil knew she was risking danger, but she could not resist.

"Make me!"

She dodged, but too late. Jake's open palm caught her

square on her cheek, sounding like a pistol shot. She spun around from the force of the blow, falling weakly against the wall, screaming.

"Don't you hit me no more! Don't you hit me no more!"

He was at her side, his raised palm open and threatening.

"I said shut up!"

She ducked and let out a sharp scream. He jerked her from the wall. She stumbled into the middle of the floor, barricading her face behind arms and elbows.

"I ask you to shut up!"

As she screamed again, he brushed her arms aside and slapped her a quick onetwo with the front and back of his palm on both sides of her face. She sank to her knees, her bosom too full to utter a sound.

"Ain't you going to shut up!"

He stood over her, his legs wide apart, his hands dug deep into his pockets, looking at her heaving bosom.

"Get up!"

"I'm going to fix you," she sobbed. "So help me Gawd, I'm going to fix you. . . ."

"I said get up!"

He kicked her in her side with his foot.

"This is the last time you going to do this to me!"

"I told you to get up! You act like you want some more!"

He bent over to slap again. Quickly she dragged along the floor out of his reach, and pulled to her feet, turning her face from him.

"You want some more?"

"Naw, Jake. . . ."

He caught her left wrist in his right hand.

"Tell me what you going to do about it?"

"Jake, please. . . ."

"Tell me what you going to do about it?" he asked again, twisting her arm slowly up her back.

"Turn me loose!"

He gave her arm a six-inch twist. Pain made her suck her

breath in sharply. She fell to her knees.

"You breaking my arm!"

"Tell me what you going to do about it?"

"Nothing," she breathed. "Nothing."

He shoved her from him.

"Put something to eat on my table before I give you some more!"

Sniffing and blinded by tears, she fumbled for the handle of the coffee pot.

HE LUMBERED BACK to the bathroom, massaging his tingling palms and mumbling to himself. He had slapped Lil so hard his fingers felt cold. But deep in him he knew he had not done what he wanted; he had not solved anything. *This bitch is ruining me,* he thought as he stared at the white lather drying on his shaving brush. She was taking every ounce of joy out of his life. She had piled up a big doctor's bill, a bill so big that it seemed he could never pay it. Then she had gone like a fool and burned up his eggs, eggs that cost cold, hard cash. *And on top of that she goes and gets herself a Gawddamn tumor!* He slammed the brush into the bowl and turned on the hot water. Each week his bills were mounting; each week he was falling further behind. He gritted his teeth. *That bitch!*

About him sunshine poured through green curtains, splashed the white bathtub, glinted on the metal faucets and shivered in little ghostly patches on the tile floor. He softened his brush and looked miles deep into the white tiles, thinking: *If Lil goes and haves that operation it'll put me almost a thousand dollars in debt to that doctor. And that ain't counting all the other bills I owe, neither. And if I don't pay 'em they'll kick me off my job. . . .* A wave of self-pity swept through him. *What to hell? What in the world can a man do? I'm just like a slave. . . .* He owed so many debts he did not know which debt to pay first. And a thousand dollar doctor bill would just about fix him for good. If he went to a loan bank and borrowed a thousand dollars, how long would it take him to pay it back? *Let's see now,* he thought, moving his lips silently. *If I pay back two and a half on each payday, that'll make five dollars a month. Let's see now. Five dollars a month? Twelve months in a year. Five times twelve is . . . is. . . . Let's see now. Five times two is ten. Write your naught and carry your one. Five times one is five, and one to carry makes six. Yeah, sixty dollars. Sixty dollars a year.* Now how many years would it take him to pay that off? In his imagination he pictured the numeral one and annexed three naughts. He then drew two long white lines and placed the figure sixty to the left. *Now let's see. Six into ten goes how many times? That's right! One! And six from ten leaves four. All right, go on and bring down the naught, making it forty. And six into forty goes. . . . Let's see now.* He screwed up his eyes as he had done long years ago when standing at the blackboard in grammar school. *Six into forty goes. . . . Four times six is twenty-four. And five times six is thirty. And six times six is thirty-six. Yeah, six times. And there's just a little left over. But that don't matter much. The main thing is that it'll take sixteen years. . . . Sixteen years! Good Gawd!* Then there were other bills: the furniture bill and the rent bill and the gas bill and the light bill and the bill at the Boston Store and the insurance bill and the milk bill. His eyes grew misty with tears, tears of hatred for Lil and tears of pity for himself. *My life is just all shot to hell. I wouldn't be in all this mess if it wasn't for her. She ain't no good no way I can figger it!*

He was broke. There was but one way out; he would have to go to somebody, like Jones, maybe, and borrow enough to tide him over till the fifteenth of the month. But even if he borrowed he would not pay the doctor today. *I'll be Gawd-damned if I pay that quack today! Naw, naw, not today!* He had already promised Al and Bob and Slim he would stand the treats tonight. He could not get out of that so easily. It was his turn, and what kind of a sport would he be if he held them up? *They'll call me cheap. Aw, to hell with that quack! He'll just have to wait, that's all! Ain't no sense in a man working himself to death just to pay a quack doctor bill. And if Lil gets smart and tries any of them sly tricks of hers.* . . . He swallowed.

He whipped the brush around in the mug, thinking, *And what to hell! She oughtn't be so damned worried, nohow. Ain't she always reading Unity books? Ain't she always talking about how she trusts Gawd? Yeah, she ought to ask Gawd to get rid of that tumor for her.* His face softened. Out of the soil of his anger an idea bloomed. *The very next time she tells me about that damned tumor I'll tell her to let Unity take care of it. Let them bastards send up a silent prayer! Give her a dose of her own sweet medicine!* He smiled, his wounded vanity soothed.

His temper subsided and he turned to the mirror. *Can't I put off shaving 'til tomorrow? My face don't look so bad, do it?* He touched the stiff bristles, reflectively. *Naw, I can't go round all day with my face looking like this.* He caught more hot water and lathered his brush. The bristles rustled with a dry sound as he mopped his chin. Whitened, he opened the medicine cabinet and searched the shelves. *Where's my razor?* The last time he had used it he had left it in here, right behind the iodine. He pushed back cold cream jars and blue-green bath salts. No razor. *That bitch!*

"Lil!"

"Hunh?"

"Where in Gawd's name you hide my razor?"

"Razor?"

"Yeah, razor! Is your ears stopped up?"

Lil came to the bathroom door with a salt shaker in one hand and a dishtowel in the other. Her eyes avoided him.

"Come on in here, woman, and find my razor! Can't you see I'm *waiting!*"

"Just a minute. . . ."

"Where you put my razor?"

"I seen it somewhere. . . ."

"*Put,* you mean. How come you hide it, anyhow?"

"I didn't hide. . . ."

"Why can't you leave my things where they belong?"

Lil jammed the salt shaker into her apron pocket and went into the bedroom. Jake ambled after, scowling.

"How come you looking in here?"

"I'm trying to remember where I put it. . . ."

"Remember?" he growled. "Remember? Yeah, like you remember burning eggs under your nose."

"Jake, give me a second. . . ."

"Give you hell! Get my razor!"

Absent-mindedly, she banged drawers, pulled up a dresser scarf, and glanced under a pillow. Jake came to her side.

"What you looking under that pillow for?"

"Honest to Jesus, Jake, I'm trying to think. . . ."

He grabbed her arm.

"Who was here yestiddy after I was gone?"

Her shoulders slumped. Jake placed one hand firmly about her throat.

"You want me to open your mouth to see if you got a tongue?"

"Naw, Jake."

"What in hell make you want to hide my razor?"

She tried to answer, but he tightened his fingers.

"Can't you talk, you dumb bitch!"

"Jake, nnnobody wwwas hhhere. . . ."

"You lying!"

"I cccross my hhheart and sssswear. . . ."

He pushed her to the wall.

"Find my razor before I choke you into a black spasm!"

Meekly, she searched. Finally, both to her surprise and Jake's she found the razor under a shallow dish upon the dresser. He snatched it from her.

"Jake, don't you remember you left it in here yestiddy?"

He remembered, but the mere act of remembering made him angrier.

"Did I ask you anything?"

"Naw, but you. . . ."

"Then hold your old big mouth till I speak to you!"

Lifting the razor to the light, he examined it. Unchipped. He squinted his eyes, but he could not even see a tiny hair. If he could only find just one little nick! But not one! He could scarcely keep the irritation out of his voice.

"Get back in the kitchen and keep your hands off of my things, hear me? If you don't I'm going to fix you good one of these mornings!"

He stropped the razor, shaved, nicked himself, cursed, and jabbed the wound with a styptic pencil. He inspected the tiny scratch minutely, wondering if it would disfigure his face in any way. *Yeah, that bitch! She's always making me nervous. I wouldn't've cut myself if it hadn't been for her damn dumbness!*

But when he was in the tub his anger ebbed. The warm water laved his loins. He stretched out, closed his eyes, and let his body soak. He kicked his legs, revelling in the feel of suds. On drifting wisps of vapor his mind winged away. Deep in the tile walls he saw the dim outlines of a soft, brown body. His eyelids drooped. The water lapped at his diaphragm and his flesh swooned in oozy eddies. A sweet lump rose in his stomach and traveled upwards, filling his throat. He lifted the washrag and squeezed it slowly, making the water trickle against his skin. His lips sagged and he sighed. The woman's body hovered nearer, growing in solidity. Uneasily, in spite of himself, he stirred; the delicious feeling petered out. He shook his head and studied the shiny soap bubbles, thinking, *Jeeesus.* He sang:

> *"I woke up too soon*
> *The spell was broken*
> *I woke up too soon*
> *Ending a dream*
>
> *You were so beautiful*
> *So wonderful*

And so divine
There was such tenderness in your caress
You were almost mine. . . ."

As he soaped his armpits and groin:

"You took away my soldiers when you took away your
love
You said it was a plaything I wasn't worthy of
You packed away my soldiers on a shelf 'way up above
And I'm just little boy blue. . . .

"You took away my candy when you took away your kiss
I never thought to lose a thing would make me feel like
this
But now I know you took away the thing I'll always miss
And I'm just little boy blue. . . ."

He dried himself, pulled on his BVD's, socks, and washed
his hands in a stream of sunshine. He felt good, but the
bathtub mood still lingered.

"Got me doing things, things I never thought I'd do-oo-oo
Got me doing things, some are silly, some are new-oo-oo
Got me saying things, things I never said before-o-o
Got me saying things like you're the one I adore-o-o. . . ."

He next tackled the big job of the morning. His hair had
to be combed, combed flat so that not a ripple, not a crinkle,
not a crease must show. Going to the mirror, he surveyed the
unruly strands with the apprehensive air of a veteran field
marshal inspecting the fortifications and wire-entanglements
of an alien army. He wore his hair in the style of Negro bangs.
His nappy forelocks reared fanwise in a wooly black flare
which had to be bullied into a billiard ball smoothness.

Years of dealing with this foe had taught him many devices
of strategy. The first barrage was with water, and plenty of
it. Going to the washbowl, he dampened his hair till rivulets

streamed down his neck. Then, seizing his comb like a Colt
.45, he tried to force an opening through enemy lines. The
battle waxed furious. The comb suffered heavy losses, and fell
back slowly. One by one teeth snapped until they littered
bathmat and washbowl. Mangled and broken things they lay
there, brave soldiers fallen in action, many of them clutched
in the death grip of enemy hairs. After three minutes of
attack the strands abandoned their trenches and retreated
disorderly.

Jake now brought forth the most powerful weapon at his
command. This deadly contraption was a pink jar of hair
pomade labeled, LAY 'EM LOW. Its chief ingredient was a
stout beeswax, a substance as fatal to insurgent kinks as was
mustard gas in Flanders. He rammed his forefinger deep into
the jar and pulled forth on a nail a dab of yellow stickiness
the size of a walnut. He smeared it vigorously between his
palms, and delivered a sudden broadside. Not a man fell.
Only with the impact of a second assault did a few waver or
weaken. Tightening his lips and spreading his fingers, he
launched drive upon drive till the brave fellows broke at the
knees. Then he pinned them tight, pummelled them into a
foul and gluey morass.

He was breathing hard. He resorted to the comb again. A
hot skirmish on the left and right flanks had each warweary
strand clinging to his scalp like troops in shell holes under
bombardment. The enemy was conquered! Jake peered into
the mirror. His head was a solid mass of black slickness. He
smiled, thinking with satisfaction *If a fly'd light on that he'd
slip up and break his neck.* . . .

He went into the bedroom and looked through the pockets
of his trousers for a stocking cap. This ingenious implement
of exploitation, this standing army which a conquering nation leaves to guard a conquered one, is made from the top
of a woman's stocking. It is elastic, about four inches long,
tied securely at the top, and when stretched tightly over the
cranium resembles the gleaming skin of a huge onion. He

was in a hurry, for, failing to get his hair under this peace treaty immediately, it would soon flounce back into a thousand triumphant kinks. He searched in vain. After a few minutes he stood in the middle of the room, empty-handed, angry-eyed.

"Lil!"

No answer.

"Liiiil!"

No answer.

"Woman, you hear me calling!"

Still no answer. His voice swelled throughout the flat like the roar of a lion.

"Liiiiiiiiiiiiiiiil!"

"Just a minute, Jake."

She came leisurely to the door.

"Where was you?"

"On the back porch."

"You don't belong there."

"I. . . ."

"How come you didn't answer when I called?"

"I didn't hear you. . . ."

"Running your old fat mouth like always, hunh?"

She hung her head.

"Who was you talking to this time?"

"Mrs. Thomas."

"What in hell can you find to talk about all the time?"

She swallowed and sighed.

"Tell me what you want, Jake. I'm cooking breakfast."

"Well, just you wait awhile now. If you got time enough to gab with that Thomas bitch then you got time enough to wait till I tell you what I want." He continued to smooth his hair down with the palms of his hands.

Lil closed her eyes and leaned weakly against the bed-post.

"Where's my stocking cap?"

"Stocking cap?"

"Yeah, stocking cap! Stocking cap! Stocking cap! Can't you never understand nothing?"

"I don't know, Jake. I ain't had it. I don't need no cap like that nohow." Complacently she patted her own smooth and kinkless hair.

"What you trying to signify?"

He advanced a step.

"I ain't trying to signify nothing," she said quickly.

"Well don't, if you knows what's good for you! I done told you I wants a stocking cap!"

"But I ain't got nothing but my new stockings. You done ruined all my stockings already, tearing 'em up for caps. And how you lose so many caps, anyhow?"

"What's that got to do with it? I said I wants a cap!"

"But I ain't *got* none, Jake!"

"Get one, then!"

"I told you I ain't got nothing but my *new* stockings!"

"Ain't you going to get me a cap?"

"I ain't. . . ."

"I'll get one!"

He brushed her aside and headed for her dresser.

"Jake, please! Not my *new* stockings!"

"GET ME A STOCKING CAP!"

She scurried for the clothes closet.

He stood waiting, thinking: *She better not fool with me no more today.* . . .

She returned with an old hose.

"Here, Jake. You better take good care of this, 'cause if you lose it I ain't got no more."

"Thought you said you didn't have none?"

She averted her eyes and left the room. Tugging, he pulled the cap down over his hair. An hour of pressure would dry the water and grease. His hair would remain in place all day. Going to the mirror, he struck a pose and smiled. Again he sang:

"I think of you with every breath I take
And every breath becomes a sigh
Not a sigh of despair
But a sigh that I care for you. . . ."

JAKE STOOD before the ten suits hanging in his closet and tried to make up his mind. His fingers strayed from one to the other, feeling the texture of the goods. He did not want to wear the black, nor the blue, nor the brown. They were all right, but he just did not want to wear them. He was not in the mood. He shook his head at a grey tweed. It was much too light in color and weight for winter wear. And so was the tan. He passed over three more because they were double-breasted. *Shucks, everybody's wearing double-breasted suits these days.* His choice finally narrowed down to a light green one-button sack and a winereddish ensemble with pleated trousers. He liked the winereddish one because it was so roomy and made him look fifteen or twenty pounds heavier, like a big time football player. *But shucks, I done wore that old suit so much lately.* He fingered the green; he pictured himself swinging along the street in the sunshine. He imagined eyes following him. *Yeah, I'll wear that green.* After he had slid into the trousers, he stood looking down at the keen creases, smiling with critical approval.

"Sharp as a tack," he said.

And because he was wearing the green suit, he decided on low-cut, brown suede shoes with high Cuban heels and toes that tapered to a point. He tied the shoestrings in a neat, tight bow. Spotlessly white spats capped the bargain. Next, he put on a soft-collared lavender shirt which contrasted pleasingly with his broad, red, elastic suspenders. Then he tried a black tie, a green tie, a brown tie, and a red tie. In the end he selected a wide yellow one studded with tiny blue halfmoons. He added a delicate finishing touch by inserting a huge imitation ruby that burned like a smear of fresh blood. Squaring his shoulders, he buttoned coat and vest and adjusted with sensitive fingers the purple embroidered orange handkerchief that peeped out of his breast pocket. He sprayed each of his coat lapels with violet-scented perfume, then pivoted on his heels in the middle of the rug and brought himself to a sudden halt in front of the dresser mirror.

"Like a Maltese kitten," he said.

Well, I reckon I'll go in and eat some now, eat a nice, big, hot breakfast. Then I'll study my scheme some. Yeah, I got to study that scheme. I can't keep on putting it off and putting it off all the time. Then I'll walk out awhile. Hunt up some of the old gang, maybe. . . .

Breakfast was laid on the kitchen table. He sat down opposite Lil, who was reading a copy of *Unity*, with her face cupped mournfully in her hands. Jake stared at her, and then at the turnedback page that faced him. Across the top of it he saw a wide spread of yellow, Egyptian wings, under which ran a slogan: A PAGE OF SUNSHINE FOR EVERY DAY. Her interest in the book irked him. *Every time she pokes her head into them damn books I can't hardly talk to her.* He groped for something to say, something that would rouse her out of her smug complacency. *By Gawd, she sets there just like I didn't slap her a few seconds ago!* He picked up the sugar bowl.

"Well?"

Lil lifted her eyes momentarily.

"Hunh?"

"Ain't you eating?"

"Naw."

"What's griping you?"

"Nothing."

"How come you ain't eating?"

"I just ain't hungry."

"Well, I *is!* And you ain't hurting me a damn bit if you don't *never* eat!"

He sweetened his coffee and sucked a long sip.

"Where my paper?"

Lil fetched the morning's paper from the porch. Rearing back in the chair, he opened it and read the headline aloud.

ROOSEVELT STRIKES AT MONEY CHANGERS
WILL DRIVE THEM FROM THE TEMPLE, HE SAYS

"Hunh," Jake grunted as he laid the paper aside and took up a slice of toast. "That's what *he* says! And what he says is just so much hot air. Nobody'll ever tell these rich American men what to do. Naw siree! Not so long as Gawd's sun shines. Cold, hard cash runs this country, always did and always will. You can put that in your hat and bet your bottom dollar on it. And what to hell! Who is these old Democrats, anyhow? I'll tell you what they is! They's crazy troublemakers! They ain't got no money. And what in hell can a man do without money? Tell me that! Nothing! And empty words don't mean a damn thing, neither. Say, who's going to tell old man Morgan and old man Rockefeller and old man Ford what to do? Who? WHO?" Jake stabbed the air with his fork. "Why them men owns and runs the country! And furthermore, these old Democrats is always starting wars. Old Wilson started one, and now they want to put another Democrat in office to start another one. Everybody knows these old Democrats is hotheaded, so why put 'em in office? People's crazy! Crazy with the heat! They don't know white from black! Shucks, old Hoover was doing all right, only nobody couldn't see it, that's all. . . . I'm going to stick with the Republicans. Old Abe Lincoln is the ship and all else is the sea. . . ." Now, who said that? . . .

He frowned, screwing up his eyes. He crammed a piece of toast in his mouth, chewed, and flushed it down with a gulp of coffee. Lil went to the sink and took a tall, dark bottle from a shelf. Jake watched her pour a tablespoon level full.

"What's that you drinking?"

"Medicine," she answered.

"What kind is it?"

"Mrs. Lydia E. Pinkham's Vegetable Compound."

"What you taking it for?"

"My nerves."

"Aw, that stuff ain't doing you no good. You just throwing my money away. . . ."

"I'm sick, Jake."

"You always sick."

She swallowed the medicine.

"I got to take something," she sighed.

Jake jerked his lips, took a mouthful of egg and bacon, and turned to the paper again. *I'm going to stop her from throwing my money away one of these days. . . .*

GERMANY DEMANDS ARMS EQUALITY
VOWS TO BOLT LEAGUE IF DENIED

"See! There she goes! What did I tell you? They's loose again! I always did say they should've wiped them monkeys off the map while they was at it. Them sonsofbitches is sure one slick and trickery lot—I'm here to tell you. I remembers way back during the War when old Reverend Harmond— he's dead now, poor fellow—said that them guys was closer to savages than anybody. And, by Gawd, he sure knowed what he was talking about, too! Yeah, you better watch them German Devils; they's a ornery and lousy lot as sure as you born. You know one thing? They say them German guys got some kind of a poison gas over there that's so strong and powerful that all they got to do is just skeet some of it in the air and when you smell it you'll curl up and die like a chinch! Just think of that! You know, they say them German soljers took them little Beljum babies—little, innocent, newborn babies, mind you, now—raped 'em and stuck 'em with bayonets to telegram posts. How can people do things like that? And shucks, if they happen to come across a French woman, no matter how old she was, that was just too bad. Every soljer in the German army would pile her, and when they got through there wasn't nothing left. Just think now: one soljer after another getting on one poor little woman, and she just laying there and can't do nothing. And ain't no policemen around to bother you. . . ." Jake paused, wagged his head, and gazed deep into the checkered tablecloth. "A soljer gets a chance to do a lot of things. . . ."

He poised a piece of egg on the tip of his fork and squinted at another headline.

G-MEN SPREAD NET FOR GANGSTERS

"Now what's wrong with them Government? What they want to bother them poor guys for? They ain't doing nothing but robbing a few banks. Aw, I know what's wrong with 'em. They's just jealous because they's not splitting their dough with them, that's all. They don't want them gangsters to make so much money. Why, them gangsters is sports, *real* sports. . . . The papers say they ain't never snitched on none of their pals. I was reading just the other day where one of them guys was laying in the hospital dying and the cops was trying to get him to tell who shot 'im and he wouldn't talk, wouldn't say a word. He just looked up at 'em and smiled! By Gawd, it takes guts to die like that. And all the time they's alive they walk around knowing that at any time somebody might shoot 'em down. Jeeesus, it takes nerve to be a gangster! But they have a plenty of fun. Always got a flock of gals hanging on their arms. Dress swell in sporty clothes. Drive them long, sleek automobiles. And got money to throw away. . . . They don't live long, but I bet they sure have a hell of a sweet time while they do live. Better time than a lot of us who work hard every day for a measly living."

He broke a piece of toast and spread it with strawberry jam. As he chewed he watched Lil's eyes following the printed lines of her *Unity. That woman's going to read herself blind!* Again he searched for something to say that would rouse her to a sharp sense of his presence.

"I think anybody that don't like gangsters is crazy!" he said loudly.

"Hunh?"

"The government is out after gangsters," said Jake, tapping the paper with his knife.

"Gangsters?"

"Yeah, gangsters, deaf woman!"

Lil stared. Jake laid down his knife, cocked his head, and looked at her with infinite compassion.

"Woman, what makes you so dumb? Don't you never try using your brains sometimes? Don't you never think of nothing that's serious?"

"I don't know, Jake."

"How come you don't know?"

"I wasn't listening to you reading."

"You could learn something if you didn't keep that empty head of yours stuck into them Gawddamn *Unity* books all the time."

Lil's eyes widened.

"Jake, this is Gawd's word!"

"Gawd's hooey! It's a gyp game, that's all!"

"You blaspheming Gawd!"

"So what?"

"Don't you know that Gawd can slap you dead right where you is?"

"Aw, woman, don't be dumb!" he said, glaring as though she had threatened him. "This is the last time you're going to read that stuff in my house, get me? Don't send no more of my money off for that damn trash, you hear?"

Lil swallowed. Jake turned disdainfully to the paper.

HITLER CALLS ON WORLD TO SMASH JEWS

"Now, that's something for everybody to think about. It shows that people's waking up. That's what's wrong with this country, too many Jews, Dagos, Hunkies, and Mexicans. We colored people would be much better off if they had kept them rascals out. Naw, the American white man went to sleep; he didn't have sense enough to let us black people have a break. He had to let them Jews and all in. Now they got the country sewed up; every store you see is run by a Jew, and the foreigners. And they don't think about nobody but themselves. They ought to send 'em all back where they came from. That's what I say."

Jake paused and drained his cup.

"You want some more coffee?"

"Yeah, fill it up."

He stirred his cup and read again.

EINSTEIN SAYS SPACE BENDS

"Humph! Now this is what I call crazy! Yes, siree, just plumb crazy! This guy takes the prize. What in hell do he know about space bending? How in hell can he see space bending when he can't even *see* space? I'm asking you? You know one thing, these old newspapers sure tries hard to fool folks. See, now, a dumb guy would fall for all this kind of stuff. See how folks get their minds made up for 'em? You got to watch sharp and do your own thinking in this old world if you don't want to be fooled. Now, if you ask me, this guy Einstein's just fooling everybody, just saying things to get his name in the papers. Shucks, I could do that. And suppose space do bend, what to hell then? . . . I bet my soul he's a Jew."

Jake turned the page.

COMMUNISTS RIOT IN STREETS OF NEW YORK

"Gawddamn! Wonder how come the police let them guys go on like that? Now them guys, them Commoonists and Bolshehicks, is the craziest guys going! They don't know what they want. They done come 'way over here and wants to tell us how to run *our* country when their *own* country ain't run right. Can you beat that for the nerve of a brass monkey? I'm asking you? Why don't they stay in their own country if they don't like the good old USA? That's what I want to know! And they go around fooling folks, telling 'em they going to divide up everything. And some folks ain't got no better sense than to believe it, neither. Just weak-minded, that's all! Now look here, if I got two suits and another guy ain't got none, they want to take one of mine and let *him* have it! A fool can see that that's wrong! And how are they going to do all this? With bombs and dynamite! What can be wrong with some folks' brains? I wonder! And over in Roosia where they in power, folks is starving to death. And now they want to get us in the same fix. What's wrong with folks when they act like that? If they get in power and tell you to do something and you don't do it, then they lines you up against a wall and shoots you down! That's no lie, I was reading it just the other day in the *Tribune. . . .*"

"But, Jake!"

"Hunh?"

"Folks is starving over here, too."

"Aw, you talk like a fool!"

"The papers said so."

"Nobody but lazy folks can starve in this country!"

"But they can't get no work."

"They don't want no work!"

"And they burned a colored man alive the other day."

"Who?"

"The white people in this country."

"Shut up! You don't know what you talking about!"

"Well, they *did!*"

"How you know?"

"It was in the papers."

"Aw, that was down South, anyhow."

"But the South's a part of this country."

Jake stopped chewing and glared at her.

"Woman, is you a *Red?*"

Lil blinked. Jake turned back to the paper.

HOODLUMS ABDUCT MILLIONAIRE'S SON

"Well, what you know about that? You see, it just goes to show that rich folks has their troubles just the same as us. After all, it ain't no difference. I'm telling you, Old Man Trouble don't mind nobody. You'd think them folks with all their millions and millions of dollars would be safe and sound from everything. But they ain't, not by a long shot. When you get right down at the bottom of things and start thinking real hard about 'em you begin to see that that's the funny thing about life. When you boil it all low you'll see that everybody gets a equal break in the end. . . ." He looked out of the window, dreamily. "Well, I guess all of us got to get a certain amount of worry in this old world, no matter what. Look like things just works that way, somehow or other. The good Lawd's done got it all figgered out in His own good fashion. It's got to be that way so there can be some justice in this world, I reckon. . . ." His voice trailed off uncertainly.

He drained his cup of coffee, lit a cigarette, leaned his elbows on the table, and sighed. The coffee warmed his blood; he could feel his heart pumping pleasantly. Each time he inhaled the huge breaths of smoke it seemed as though he were going to fall asleep. His head lolled; a lazy thought crawled slowly through his brain. *Lawd, how good it feels after you done eat a good meal.* His eyelids drooped. *Wouldn't it be good now if I could go back to bed and sleep some? Yeah, but that would start Lil's old big mouth again. And I don't want to hear her no more today.* Not that he cared two straws about what Lil would say, but he just did not feel like arguing on a full stomach. It would be much better to go out somewhere, get some fresh air, and loaf around till worktime. Maybe he would walk over to the poolhall and hear what the old gang was saying. Or maybe he would drop over to Bob's place and play a game or two of bridge. *And I got to get a haircut.* No, he must not forget to get his haircut; he could not be around the sweet girls tonight with hair bristling like cockle burrs on his neck. *Yeah, I'll walk out awhile.* He sighed, his legs feeling deliciously heavy.

"Jake," Lil called humbly from across the table.

He held still, pretending he had not heard. *That bitch is going to ask me for something.* He knew it; he could feel it in his bones.

"Jake," she called again, this time a little louder.

"Hunh?"

"What you want me to fix for dinner?"

"Nothing."

"I got to fix something. So tell me what you want."

"I said *nothing.*"

"Ain't you going to be home for dinner?"

"Naw."

"But I ain't got no money, Jake."

"I told you I wasn't going to be home for dinner."

"I got to have some money. I got to eat, even if you ain't here."

"I ain't got no money!"

"But everything's out! I got to get something."

"What in hell do you do with so much money?"

"I spends it right here in the house for something to eat."

"I give you *two* dollars the other day."

"But that's all gone!"

"Aw, you just throw money away."

"I made two dollars last for three days!"

"Go to the store and ask the man to let you have something on credit."

"The bill up there's so *big.*"

"Ask 'im anyhow!"

"He told me to ask you when you going to pay 'im."

"Tell 'im I'll pay 'im soon."

"We owe so much I'm 'shamed to go there."

"Woman, if you 'shamed to go and ask a man for something to eat, you just stay hungry, see?"

"Jake, please, leave me some money."

"Go to another store and get some groceries."

"I can't!"

"How come? You lame?"

"We owe 'em all bills. They won't let me have nothing."

"Listen, for the last time, I ain't got no money! NOW QUIT TALKING TO ME!"

Jake waddled into the living room and slouched across a soft chair; his legs dangled over the sides and his head nestled in the hollow of a pillow. *Gawd, I feel lazy. . . . And that ain't no lie. . . . A good cup of coffee sure makes you feel good.* It made his body languid and made his mind work rapidly. *Jeeesus, if I could only feel this way all the time. . . .*

Dreamily, he looked out the window. The day was dazzlingly bright. That portion of the sky he could see was marvelously blue. Tons of golden sunshine splashed the streets and houses. How queer the drab bricks looked when lit by the light of the sun! The upstretching branches of the trees seemed to be pleading for spring rain. How oddly beautiful it was to be February! A lost spring day set like a jewel amongst the dreary winter ones! *Yeah, it's almost warm enough to go without a winter coat.*

He yawned and scratched his thigh, thinking: *I ought to go in and study my scheme some now. Right now would be a good time to put in some hard work.* But he did not move. His body relaxed; he could feel his toes tingling pleasantly. He gazed drowsily at the keen creases in his trousers, thinking *I don't feel like studying now. Maybe I'll wait till morning. That'll be better. . . .*

A sweet looseness seeped into Jake's bones. He closed his eyes and his blood sogged slowly through his veins like warm milk. He could feel a faint tinge of the sun's warmth even through the windowpane. He pushed his fingers down into his trousers, between his belt and the flat of his stomach. His lips became moist and sagged. His groin felt hot; an uneasy feeling, elusive and light as a feather, played over the surface of his stomach. The muscles of his thighs stretched taut and his mind became hazy. Out of a mist loomed the face of a woman, of *the* woman. The face was brown, winsome, and delicately oval-shaped. Eyelids drooped with languorous passion. Wet lips hovered closer and closer. He could almost see the velvety sheen of her skin. His head swam; his skin glowed as though it were near a soft flame. He doubled his legs as a fugitive feeling of delight burned in his diaphragm. He stirred restlessly, and his shoulders twitched as though he were a child nestling deeper into a mother's bosom. A tiny trickle of saliva drooled out of the corner of his mouth; a look of suspense came into his face. . . .

"Jaaake!"

He jerked, frowned, and wiped his mouth with the back of his hand.

"Hell," he breathed.

He closed his eyes and curled himself again, seeking to recapture the lost mood.

"Jaaaaaaake!"

His face contorted savagely.

"What in *hell* you want?"

"You looked in the mailbox yet?"

"Hell, naw! And quit bothering me!"

Again he lowered his head, trying to resuscitate the mood. He was very still, very quiet, but, alas, the mood would not come. *Gawddamit to hell! A man just can't get no rest or peace around Lil.*

He screwed up his eyes, stretched his arms above his head, and yawned.

"Aaaaaaaaahhheellll," he whispered in a breath that seemed to escape involuntarily.

He put on a light grey top coat with huge buttons of liquid pearl and a black hat with a tiny red feather peeping timidly in the back. Grabbing his mahogany-handled cane, he went slowly down the steps, his mind lost in a warm fog.

RATS' ALLEY

But at my back in a cold blast I hear
The rattle of the bones, and chuckle
spread from ear to ear.
—T. S. Eliot's *Wasteland*

. . . A shot, a scream, a cloud of smoke—all in a split second of time. The bullet entered the left side of President Lincoln's head, passed through the brain, and stopped just short of the left eye. He was rushed to a room opposite Ford's Theatre, and there he lingered among tender friends until morning. At twenty-two minutes past seven o'clock he died. As he breathed his last, Secretary Stanton said:

"Now, he belongs to the ages. . . ."

WHEN THEY WERE least expecting it, when their minds had strayed on a daydreaming pilgrimage, the gong for quitting time boomed throughout the Mailing Division.

"TWELVE-THIRTY CLERKS CHECKOUT!"

As though they were dead men suddenly come to life, they dropped the mail and ran to the timecard racks; then, holding to banisters, they galloped down the winding steel stairs three steps at a time and pushed their way into the smelly washroom.

"Make it snappy!" called Jake, rubbing white lather about his neck.

"Cccome on, fffor Cchrissake!" coughed Slim. "I wwwant to wwwash!"

"Move over!" said Al.

"Youall wait for me!" Bob yelled, running for the commodes.

As they received their hats, coats, and canes their faces

assumed expressions of healthy interest. Legs and arms
which had moved listlessly swung with buoyant energy;
voices which had been low monotones rose in relieved
shouts.

"Let's go!" called Jake, jamming his arms awkardly into his
coat.

"Coming!"

They filed out upon the front steps and stood huddled amid
swirling snowflakes with their coat collars turned up. Heavy
spouts of vapor rolled from their lips and lingered a moment
in the cold air, then vanished. About them the muffled thunder of traffic crashed in a falling shroud of white. The headlights of autos swerved around corners and glared momentarily.

"Well where do we go from here?" asked Al.

"How about some cigars?" asked Jake.

"Sure thing."

A few minutes later they were standing in a doorway,
puffing cigars and looking at the passing traffic with a superb
detachment. They were almost satisfied now, but not quite.
Each felt that something was lacking, and that lack hungered
over and above ordinary hunger; they could feel it in their
stomachs, in their legs, even in the tips of their fingers. Jake
rolled his cigar from one corner of his mouth to the other.

"Say, how about some likker?"

"Now you talking!"

With a halfpint flask sagging in each of his coat pockets,
Jake stood again in a doorway.

"It's near eleven bells," said Al.

"Let's get going."

"I want to buy a paper first," said Slim. "Here, boy!"

"Wheeeee!" Al whistled through his teeth for a roving taxi.

Brakes screamed; a car swerved to the curb; a door swung
open, and the four of them piled in.

"Forty-five fifty-eight Calumet!" Jake called.

"O.K."

As the car lumbered southward over snow-covered streets, Jake nestled into a corner and felt the flasks pressing against his sides.

"How about a little nip?"

Jake, Al, and Slim drank.

"Aw, come on, Bob. One shot won't hurt you."

"Naw."

"Aw, man, take a drink."

Bob sat tensely on the edge of the seat. His lips moved several times, but he said nothing. Jake pushed the bottle into his hands; he held it, his lips parted in fascination and indecision.

"Don't be a wet blanket!"

Bob tilted the flask and drank.

"It sure can't kill me," he said, blowing to cool the fiery burn.

"You don't live but once," said Al.

Slim pulled out the newspaper and squinted at the headline.

"What's the news?" asked Jake, closing his eyes.

"They say Japan's done grabbed *all* Manchooria."

"Yeah?"

"And they say a hundred million Chinks in China's done gone Red."

"Now them Chinks is funny folks," said Bob.

"Yeah, they eat with sticks."

"They eat rats, too."

"And rotten eggs."

"A Chink'll do *any*thing."

"They say they killing up more Jews in Germany," read Slim.

"*Some*body always killing them Jews!"

"You know, I saw in the papers where they plotting to rule the whole world."

"Yeah, they got all the gold hid away now."

"Them rookies is *slick.*"

"And they done lynched another nigger down South," said Slim.

"Yeah?" asked Jake, turning slightly.

"They burnt 'im alive," said Slim.

"Well, Gawddammit, they ought to lynch 'em if they ain't got no better senses to stay down there."

"I wouldn't live in a place like that," said Al.

"That's how come I left," said Bob.

"They say old Roosia's done gone and got a army of eighteen million men," said Slim.

"Aw, them Reds can't fight," said Al.

"And here's the picture of a guy who can play the violin with his toes," said Slim.

"With his *toes?*"

"Let's see it!"

"Gee, that's going some!"

"Say, I seen a guy shoot pool blindfolded once."

"I seen a guy play a guitar standing on his *head.*"

"Some folks can do almost anything."

"It's a natural born gift."

Slim threw the paper aside and they rode awhile in silence. Jake thought of the one hundred dollars on his hip and sang:

"Yellow taxis, yellow money, yellow women. . . ."

They chuckled and puffed languidly. Now and then they took the black weeds out of their mouths and eyed the glowing tips.

"Damn good smoke."

"You bet."

"Draws well."

"Yeah."

The taxi swung to a snowbanked curb.

"Well, here we is, boys!" Jake announced. The snow had slackened a bit. As Jake paid the bill Slim led the way into the vestibule.

"Looks like a swell joint."

388

"Hope they got some red-hot mamas up there."

"Don't worry about that."

In answer to Slim's three pressures of the bell the door buzzed. Midway up the steps they could hear the sound of muffled music and the rhythm of pounding feet. At the top of the landing they were met by a buxom, brown-skinned woman.

"Hello, Rose!" called Jake.

"Glory be! If it ain't my four Aggravating Papas!" said Rose, flinging her arms wide.

"And you don't know how aggravating," said Jake as he caught her around the waist.

"Look like you's ready for business tonight," said Rose.

"You'll be surprised," said Slim, slapping her fleshy buttocks.

Rose shook her finger at them playfully.

"Come on, now! Be a good boy for mama! I'm mighty proud you brought your pals along, Jake. We can have some good times here. . . . Now, youall just come right in and take off your coats and hats and hang 'em in the closet and make yourselves at home. What you don't see, ask for it. And when you gets hungry step back in the diningroom and eat some of the best chitterlings you ever tasted. Ain't no need for youall to be a bit bashful around here. Just throw your troubles away. . . ."

They pushed into a big room jammed with dancers. Shouts, laughter, and snatches of song swung through the smoky air. A threepiece jazz band—a cornet, a drum, and a piano—made raucous music in a corner. There were gamblers, pimps, petty thieves, dope peddlers, smallfry politicians, grafters, racketeers of various shades, athletes, high school and college students in search of "life," and hordes of sexeager youngsters. The women were white, ivory, yellow, light brown, medium brown, solid brown, dark brown, near black, and black. They wore red, yellow, brown, blue, purple, and black gowns with V shapes reaching down almost to their waists. Their bosoms were high and bulging, and they danced with an obvious exaggeration of motion.

With the stump of his cigar clamped in his teeth, Jake stood just inside the door and looked over the crowd. He watched the women's bodies swing and a warm glow spread from his stomach to his chest. A deep sense of ease and freedom pervaded him; he stood with his legs wide apart and with his thumbs hooked in the armholes of his vest. *This don't look like a bad crowd.* He knew some of them from other times. There was Blue Juice, a pimp who boasted that he controlled more women than any single Negro on the South Side. There was Ben Kitty, known far and wide for his skill at billiards. And there was a tall, slender, brown-skinned man called One Barrel; it was reputed that he was so stingy he breathed only out of one barrel of his nose. *Naw, this ain't bad at all.* Jake smiled and listened to voices call to and fro.

"Have a sip, Daddy!"

"Come on and let's get lowdown!"

"I don't care! I don't care!"

"Whip that piano, Bopeep!"

"Aw, dance that thing!"

"Lawd! Lawd!"

Bob tugged at Jake's sleeve.

"Say, Jake?"

"Yeah?"

"Slip me something. I'm going to shoot some craps in the backroom."

"Sure," said Jake, laughing and slipping a five dollar bill into Bob's hand. "You just out of luck, Bob."

"Call me when youall's ready to eat."

"O.K."

Slim grabbed a stocky, mulatto girl and started dancing. Al was talking to a thin black girl.

"Say, partner?"

Jake turned and faced a short, skinny, black man with bloodshot eyes.

"Want some weeds?"

"Naw."

"Only two bits."

"Naw."

"Aw, come on."

"Naw, I tell you!"

Jake walked off. He did not want to smoke any Marijuana cigarettes. *Likker's good enough for me.* He saw some of the younger men and women huddled in corners sucking hungrily at cigarettes. They inhaled deeply, held the smoke in their lungs as long as they could, and beat their chests to absorb the essence of the smoke. *That's a sissy's way to get high.*

Jake lolled, his eyes roving somberly. He was trying to pick out a woman. Finally, he went to a yellow one who was walking alone to and fro in front of a window at the far end of the room. She was of medium height with broad hips and she welcomed him with a wide, wet smile. He walked her to the center of the floor and they swung into a dance.

"Where you been all my life?" he asked, tightening his arm.

"Where you been all *my* life?" she countered, nestling close.

Back and across the room they swayed like trees bending in strong winds. Feet went thrumpthrump, thrumpthrump, thrumpthrump. . . .

"Shake that thing!" somebody yelled.

"What's your name?" Jake asked his girl.

"Blanche, Sweet Papa. What might be yours?"

"Just Jake," he said, swinging her through a narrow opening between the dancers.

"You works in the Post Office, Sweet?"

"Sure thing, Baby."

"Look like you and me's going to hit it off O.K.," she said, throwing the naked part of her arm about his neck.

"I knows we is," he said.

"Sweet Papa," she breathed into his ear.

"How long you been in this joint?" he asked.

"About a week."

"Like it?"

"I don't mind."

"How's tricks."

"Slow."

"Don't look like a babe like you ought to have no trouble."

"Honey, these niggers ain't got no money."

"I got money."

"You look like it."

"Been in Chi long?"

"About a week, I told you."

"Oh, so you started right in here."

"Yeah, but I'm looking for a steady daddy."

"String along with me, Babe."

She laughed. They stood still in a tight knot of dancers and moved only their hips and knees. Jake looked at the yellow sweep of her bosom. *She ain't bad.* The music sank low, sobbing the *St. Louis Blues;* he felt Blanche rolling her stomach to him, softly. Their eyes met and his lips parted.

"Say?" he asked.

"What's the matter, Papa?"

"Who learned you that?"

"You'd be surprised."

Jake laughed and whirled her over the floor. *Naw, she ain't bad at all.*

"I'm hungry."

"Plenty of grub in the back."

"What you say, let's eat?"

"Just's you say, Papa."

Jake gathered his party and led them through two rear rooms and into a little curtained nook. Rose hovered above them.

"I had this table all saved just 'specially for youall," she said. "I thought youall'd want it sort of privatelike."

"You knows your stuff, Rose," said Jake.

"Nothing different," she answered.

"This is a mellow joint," said Al.

"How come you ain't got a gal?" Rose asked Bob.

"Oh, I'm laying off for awhile," Bob mumbled.

"He's teething," said Jake.

They laughed. Bob rolled his eyes, took out his flask, and swallowed a deep drink. Rose placed her hand tenderly on the back of his neck.

"Listen," she said. "When you gets well come and see me and I'll fix it so's you won't never have to teethe no more."

"I'll be around," said Bob.

"Now, youall get ready to eat a heap tonight," coaxed Rose, polishing the top of the table with her dishtowel.

"What you got that's good?" asked Jake.

"Well, I got some chitterlings, turnip greens cooked with smoked ribs, Spanish rice, slaw, spaghetti, egg cornbread, pigtails, barbecue, beer, and whiskey," sang Rose.

Al sucked back loose saliva.

"Hush your mouth!"

"Folks, order anything you want!" said Jake, with a sweeping wave of his hand.

"I wants some chitterlings," said Blanche.

"I wants some of that barbecue," said Slim's girl.

"Make it four chitterlings and four barbecues and beer and slaw all around," bawled Jake. "The stuff's on me tonight!"

"Coming up!" sang Rose.

"Have some cigarettes," said Jake.

They lit up and blew smoke into one another's faces. The men appraised the girls' lips, throats, shoulders, and bosoms. The girls sighed and looked wistfully at their plates.

"It's been a long time since we's been around with any Post Office dudes," sighed Blanche.

"Well, you got a good chance to make up for lost time tonight," said Jake.

There was a short silence during which each man edged his chair closer to the table.

The girls' eyes assumed lights of coy innocence and the men's jaws assumed lines of aggressiveness.

"Youall sure ought to see our rooms upstairs," suggested Blanche.

"Yeah?"

"We got the cutest beds. . . ."

"You know who we is?" asked Slim.

"Who?"

"We's the official bed inspectors," he said.

They laughed. The lights were lowered just enough to give the room a dreamlike air. The naked flesh of the women's arms gleamed satinly under the soft sheens of the floor lamp. Rose brought two long platters of steaming food.

"Go to it, folks! This ain't no dicty joint and you can eat till you bust!"

Rose went from glass to glass and poured foaming beer.

"I'm going to turn on the radio so's youall can have some music," she said as she left. "And if you want anything, just call."

"O.K."

A crashing chord of martial music rose and died away; a voice spoke.

. . . At Antietam McClellan and Lee clashed in a sanguinary struggle in which the blood of twenty-two thousand men stained the soil. . . .

"What in hell is *that?*"

"Aw," drawled Bob, nodding sleepily. "That's that Civil War. . . ."

"Slide the salt down this way!"

"Give me that cornbread!"

"Hand me that sauce!"

"Llllet mmmme ssse. . . . Let me see that sssssslaw," coughed Slim.

The hot, greasy food was washed down by huge draughts of cold beer.

"More beer here, Rose!" Jake bawled.

"Coming, Mister Post Office Man!" she sang, sidling up to get the empty bottles.

They ate, ramming knives deep into their mouths.

"Pheeeeeeeeeeeeew!" exclaimed Al's girl. "I ain't going to eat no more. I'm scared of getting too fat."

"Too *fat?*"

"Yeah."

Al raised his eyes and looked intently at her fleshy bosom.

"Don't let a little thing like that worry you none, Sweetheart," he said eagerly through a mouthful of chitterlings whose grease oozed from the corners of his lips. "The fatter the berry the sweeter the juice!"

"Why, you naaaaaaasty maaaaaaan!" she said, widening her eyes in mock shame.

The girls dropped their knives and forks and covered their mouths with their hands to smother giggles. Jake, Al, and Bob, and Slim leaned back in chairs, opened their mouths as wide as their jaws would permit, clapped their hands protectingly over their swollen stomachs, and gave vent to a roar of merriment that drowned out the radio. When their guffaws had simmered down to mere sniffles, Jake asked Al:

"How you know about how much juice in a fat berry?"

"Oh, I know, all right," said Al, wiping the crumbs and grease from his lips with the back of his hand.

"Talk like you done had some business with fat berries," said Blanche.

"I ain't missed it," said Al.

They laughed again.

"If that's the case, you gals better eat a heap," said Slim.

"Oh, I reckon we got juice enough," said Blanche.

"You *sure?*" asked Jake.

"We *ought* to know," said Blanche.

"Who told you?" asked Jake.

"Ain't nobody never kicked on us none," said Blanche.

"That's fair enough," said Al, waving his fork. "If ain't nobody else kicked, then we can't kick."

"If our customers ain't satisfied, they tell us. If they is they tell others," said Blanche.

The four men bent low over their plates as their mouths flew open again. The girls clapped them heartily on their backs to increase their ribaldry.

Now Sherman's troops were sweeping a belt many miles wide with the zest of men out for a holiday. They were robbing it of every edible thing. They burnt mills. They tore up railroads and piled the rails in blazing heaps and twisted them while still hot around the trunks of forest trees. . . .

"How's we doing!"

"Hey, hey!"

"Youall's O.K.," said Slim.

"You got my vote," said Al.

"Say, Rose! More chitterlings and barbacue here!" called Jake.

When they had sopped their plates and drained the last of the beer, they leaned back in their chairs, sighing and suppressing belches. The beer and hot food made them sleepy. Blanche yawned.

"Shucks, I feel like a snake what's done swallowed a chicken," she mumbled.

The men tried to smile, but could not; they were full and listless.

"Let's dance, folks," said Jake in a dead tone.

"O.K. with me," sighed Al.

No one moved. The music in the front room was now going so loud that they heard it even through the partitions. Feet went thrumpthrump, thrumpthrump, thrumpthrump. . . . The house seemed to rock in a vast darkness. The monotonous rhythm was like a thousand fingers tapping the taut skin of a kettle drum in the midst of a deep forest. At intervals the muffled cry of the cornet rose up and died away like the midnight wail of a lovesick tomcat. The piano moaned like a woman in labor.

"Aw, I want to dance," said Al's girl.

"Me too," said Slim's girl.

"O.K.," said Al.

No one moved. Jake yawned and belched.

"Rose!" he called.

"Coming!"

"How about some likker!"

"Sure thing!"

It was not until they had had four rounds of whiskey that they felt like moving.

"This stuff's really good," said Jake.

. . . With malice toward none, with charity for all, with firmness in the right as God gives us to see the right, let us finish the work we are in. . . .

"Come on! Let's finish the bottle!"

"Yeah, let's drink!"

Bob swayed forward, slobbering.

"Yeeeeeeah, what to hell!"

WHEN THE BOTTLE was empty, Jake reached for his pocketbook, placed it upon the table, and exposed to view a thick wad of green bills. Blanche peeped into it and exclaimed:

"Lawd, man! You sure well-heeled!"

He smiled at her.

"What's the matter, Honey?" He turned to Rose. "What I owe you, Sweetmeat?"

"Just twelve fifty," she said diffidently.

Jake gave her three five dollar bills.

"Keep the change, Toots!"

"That's what I love about a sport!" sang Rose.

He led his party back to the front room. Stimulated by alcohol, they glided on to the floor in answer to the call of the music. Their limp bodies swayed bonelessly to every tug of the rhythm. The air was heavy and damp. They tightened their arms as the music grew personal, selfish, sexual. Their eyes became vague and dreamy. Stomach rubbed stomach. Sweat beaded on black temples. Nostrils gleamed. Thick lips grew wet and sagged, trembling when bodies were swung. Now and then a slight moan was heard; it was as though someone had become so charged with emotion that he could contain it no longer. The pounding piano, the incessant shuffling of feet, and the sobbing cornet invoked a spirit of emotional surrender so intense that its driving force manifested itself in the hard, drawn lines of their faces. Feet went thrumpthrump, thrumpthrump, thrumpthrump. . . . Rose pushed her way into the center of the room and yelled:

"Is everybody happy?"

"In Heaven with my feets hanging out!"

"We's got the world in a jug. . . ."

". . . and the stopper in our hands!"

Rose filled her lungs and yelled again:

"I SAY, IS EVERYBODY HAPPY?"

"Yeah, Lawd!"

"WELL, GIVE 'EM SOME MUSIC AND LET 'EM DANCE THE TIME DOWN!"

The band beat out *Tiger Rag*. As Jake danced his head was tilted backward. The expression upon his face was peculiar, paradoxical; it was relaxed and flabby, yet somehow eager and watchful. There was in it a sort of childish trustfulness. The music caroled its promise of an unattainable satisfaction and lured him to a land whose boundaries receded with each step he took. When the music slowed he felt tired, but when it went faster, he went faster. Each time it reached a high pitch of intensity he verged on the limits of physical feeling, as though beyond this was nothing but sleep, death; but when it sank, quavering, sighing, disillusioned, his muscles slackened, hungering for more. The room became so crowded he could hardly move. Bopeep played *Is It True*

What They Say About Dixie?, and he slid over the floor, shifting from foot to foot. With each twist of his shoulders he felt the yielding softness of Blanche's body; he placed the open palm of his right hand in the center of her back and pressed her closer to him; he straightened till he felt her touching him at almost every point; then he pranced and swayed in one spot in a tight knot of dancers, his lips hanging loose. Blanche's breath came warm on the side of his neck and he heard her whisper:

"That's murder, Papa."

"I want to be electrocuted," he said.

"Oh, play it, Mister Piano Man, play it!" a young, black girl yelled, breaking suddenly from her partner and dancing alone in the center of the room, flinging her legs and arms in all directions. The rest paused, formed a circle about her and began to clap their hands, each clap falling midway between the beats of the music and creating a sharp and imperious syncopation. The girl's eyes rolled wildly; her head bobbed back and forth and she flung her limbs heavily as though she were drugged with warm wine. She advanced with the palms of her hands holding hard to her thighs and retreated with the tips of her fingers pressed deep into the soft flesh of her stomach. The dance became slower and slower till nothing moved but the muscles in her hips. Finally she gaped her mouth like a fish out of water and sank to her knees, moaning:

"Lawd . . . Lawd. . . ."

"Do it, gal!"

"Show 'em you ain't scared!"

"Come on, Papa," Blanche urged. "Let's get in close where we can see."

"O.K., Baby."

He caught her around the waist and rammed his way into the crowd. All about him he felt the pressure of eager bodies. Blanche lunged suddenly and her arms clung to his neck for support. He held her on her feet.

"What's the matter?"

Blanche turned and sneered:

"Watch where you going, nigger!"

Jake whirled, ready for fight. A tall, black man bowed and grinned.

" 'Scuse me," he said meekly.

"How come you can't look where you walking?" Jake growled, starting forward.

Blanche pulled him back.

"Aw, Daddy, forget 'im. He ain't nobody."

Jake's jaws clamped tight and his eyes followed the man till he disappeared through a rear door. He felt good tonight; he felt like hitting somebody. *What he doing trying to run over me?*

Another girl had come into the center of the ring and was dancing to the tune of *Sister Kate*. Her hair flew about her head, sometimes screening her face. Her thin body whirled like a spinning top; her dress rose and floated at the level of her hips, revealing the smooth, cool brown of her legs.

"Dance that thing, gal!" croaked a man who was so drunk he looked cross-eyed.

Another girl came in. Bopeep played *Handy Man*. With her feet still, she swayed her hips and crooned:

"He hauls my ashes
He strokes my fiddle
Threads my needle
Creams my wheat
Lawd, he's a damn good man to have around. . . ."

"Do it, Sadie, do it!"

Jake felt giddy; he clapped his hands, closed his eyes, threw back his head, and yelled:

"DO IT A LONG OLD TIME!"

A stout, black woman waddled into the center of the ring and called to Bopeep:

"Play my piece!"

She sang in a cracked, nasal alto, uttering one line while she walled her eyes to the left, and uttering another line while she walled her eyes to the right.

> *"Two old maids in a folding bed*
> *One turned to the other, and said:*
> *'Yes, we have no bananas, Delight,*
> *We have no bananas tonight. . . .' "*

Jake bent double with laughter.

> *"Two old maids in a folding bed*
> *One turned to the other and said:*
> *'Darling, you are growing old;*
> *There're silver threads among your gold. . . .' "*

Jake hugged Blanche and screamed. When the song ended she danced. Her flaccid buttocks and bosom shivered like fluid. Her eyes were closed, her face lifted ceilingward, her lips tightly compressed. She seemed absorbed in an intense feeling burning in her stomach and she clawed her fingers hungrily in the air.

"Pick them cherries, gal! Pick 'em!"

Abruptly, the dance changed; her legs leaped into the air; her body ran riot with a goal of its own. The muscles of her stomach rose and fell insatiably. The music whirled faster and she whirled faster. She seemed to have lost all conscious control, seemed possessed by the impelling excitement of her nervous system. The climax came when she clasped her knees together in a steellike clamp and wrapped her arms tightly about her heaving bosom. She trembled from head to feet, her face distorted in orgiastic agony.

A thin black woman grabbed her boy friend and bit his ear till blood came.

"Lawd, today!"

Jake pulled Blanche into a corner. His eyes burned red and he bit his lips.

"Say, how about it?" he asked tensely, huskily.

"About what?"

"What you going to charge?"

He held her arm in a nervous grip.

"Quit! You hurting my arm!"

"Aw, come on."

She disengaged herself and cooed:

"What you talking about, Honey?"

"I want you. Ain't that plain? Now, what you going to charge me?"

Blanche smiled and walked off as though she had not heard. He followed, like a little dog.

"Aw, come on!"

"Not much," she said, looking off.

"But *how* much?"

"I'll charge you what it's worth."

"What's it worth?"

"Well. . . ."

"Well, *what?*"

She walked off again. Jake tugged her sleeve. She turned and looked at him intently.

"How much you got, Big Boy?"

"What's that got to do with it?"

She rounded her lips and spoke coolly:

"Ten dollars."

"Jeeesus," said Jake. "What you think I is?"

"Take it or leave it, Big Boy. If you don't want to do business, I'm moving on. . . ."

"Wait a minute."

He frowned, dropped his cigarette, crushed it with his heel, and blew out a lungful of smoke. *Ten bucks is a lot of money. But, shucks. . . .*

"Where can we go?"

"Upstairs."

"O.K.," he said. "What about my pals, two more?"

"Stay here. I'll see if I can't make it ten apiece."

Impatiently, he waited in a corner with his hands jammed

into his pockets. He saw Blanche talking with Blue Juice at
the far end of the room. Blue Juice was looking at him, and
the shadow of a doubt flitted across his roused senses. He lit
another cigarette, still watching Blanche. *What.... What she
talking to him....* He looked away. A relaxation was settling
in his nerves. *I'm going to buy some more likker,* he thought
as he clinked the coins in his pocket. Blanche came back
smiling.

"It's O.K.," she said.

"Come on," said Jake. "Let's see Rose. I want some
likker."

When in the back room he took the bottle from Rose and
reached for his pocketbook. It was not in his hip pocket. He
felt the others, then sat the bottle down and went through
each pocket, his lips hanging open.

"Where's my money?" he mumbled.

"Is you done lost something, Sugar?" Blanche asked.

"I can't find my money."

He searched his pockets again, took a step backward and
looked from Blanche to Rose.

"Somebody done got my money," he said incredulously.

"Maybe you dropped it somewhere," suggested Rose.

Jake headed for the rear room where they had eaten. Rose
and Blanche followed, looking at each other. He jerked back
the chairs, looked under the table. It was not there. He stood
silently and stared at the floor.

"Is you done lost it, Honey?" asked Blanche, tearful with
distress.

Jake looked at her and his mind cleared slowly. *I done been
tricked!* But by whom? How? Then he remembered the tall,
black Negro who had bumped into him. He remembered
Blanche clinging to his neck, diverting his attention from the
man.

"Did that black nigger what bumped into me take my
money?"

"What you talking about, Sweetheart?"

"You know what I'm talking about!"

"I swear I don't!"

"That nigger what bumped into me when we was watching 'em dancing!"

"What nigger?" pleaded Blanche.

"That sonofabitch!"

Jake whirled and elbowed his way through the crowd. Rose and Blanche trailed. He stood in the center of the front room and stared at the dancers. The man was nowhere around. He turned to Blanche.

"Where's the nigger?" he growled.

"You mean the man I cussed at?"

"You know Gawddamn well what I mean!"

"Honey, that man been gone from here."

"Where he gone?"

"How I know?"

"What kind of a looking man was he?" asked Rose, tenderly placing her hand on his sleeve. Jake opened his mouth to answer, but no words came. He felt like a fool. He wanted to grab something and smash it. Grab just anything and smash it to death. He knew it was useless to try to get his money now, and knowing filled him with rage. *These lowlife bastards! I ain't going to let 'em play me cheap and get away with it! Ain't no man alive going to play me for a sucker!* The room grew misty and he looked at Blanche, at her yellow throat, at her red lips, at her wide, dark eyes.

"I don't want no trouble," he drawled.

"Oh, Lawd!" moaned Rose, wringing her hands. "Mister Jake, we ain't got your money."

Jake felt people crowding around him and he gave a hard shove with his elbow.

"Don't crowd me now," he said huskily. " 'Cause I might hurt somebody."

They backed away and left him standing in an empty circle. He could not take his eyes off Blanche's yellow face. His muscles were flexing slowly.

"I'm asking you for the last time to tell me who got my money," he said.

"That man's gone, Honey," whined Blanche.

He grabbed her arm.

"Where he go!"

"Turn me loose! You crazy!"

Jake raised his palm.

"You know who got my money!"

"Don't you hit me!" she screamed.

Jake grabbed for her and felt a hard hand on his shoulder. He was spun around.

"Don't you touch that woman!"

He looked into the black face of Blue Juice.

"Hunh?" Jake asked.

"I don't chew my tobacco but once," spat Blue Juice.

He saw Ben Kitty and One Barrel standing ready for him, their legs wide apart, their hands thrust deep into their pockets. His neck flushed hot as fire. He had been robbed and these men were here to see that he did not bother Blanche who had helped to rob him. He swallowed and something seemed to turn upsidedown in his stomach. *They got my money. These bastards!*

"Where's the nigger that bumped into me?"

"Go find 'im!" said Blue Juice.

"I'd like to make you tell where he is!" Jake said to Blanche.

"Do it," said Blue Juice. "Do it and get your gutstring cut loose."

Jake saw Bob, Al, and Slim edge into the crowd.

"What's the matter, Jake?"

"Somebody bothering you?"

"Say, what's this?"

"These bastards done rolled me," said Jake, emboldened by the presence of his friends.

"You calling me a bastard?" asked Blue Juice, stepping closer.

The crowd closed in and Jake felt himself being pushed

against a wall. The music had stopped and he could hear his blood beating in his temples. His breath came fast and short.

"The nigger who took my dough's a bastard!" he said stubbornly.

"Did I take your dough?" asked Blue Juice.

Jake did not answer.

"Just say I did and I'll make you think you's a cat trying to cover up mess on a tin roof!"

"Who got your money, Jake?" asked Al.

"This woman here knows who got it," said Jake.

"She don't know," said Blue Juice.

"What you taking up for her, for?" asked Jake.

" 'Cause I'm man enough to," said Blue Juice.

"It ain't no skin off your nose if I make that bitch tell!"

"Don't you call her a bitch!"

"I *did!*" said Jake with hot pride.

He saw the blow coming and tried to duck, but tried too late. It caught him low on the neck; a pain shot through his chest; the room tilted and he fell flat on his face. He heard screams, heard Al and Slim calling. He scrambled to his feet and reached for Blue Juice. Something hit him at the base of the skull and the world went red, then grey. He was on the floor, in a world of grey pain, hearing screams and pounding feet. His whole life flowed hotly into his eyes, his stomach, his hands. *I'll kill 'im! I'll kill 'im!* He rolled over and tried to get up; he was still on his knees when something cold touched his temple, like cold metal it was, and it touched lightly, like a feather. He felt himself pitching forward, felt his fingers clawing weakly at the ridges in the wooden floor, and then suddenly the world went black. . . .

JAKE JAKE JAKE. His head sagged from side to side. *Jake Jake Jake.* He heard someone calling. *Hunh? Hunh?* He was trying to answer, trying to see where he was, wondering what made everything so awfully cold. A hard pain throbbed in his

temples and at the base of his skull. A white and black world
wavered before his eyes, then slowly righted itself, grew real,
solid, freezing. His strength came gradually and his feet
slipped on ice as he tried to stand.

"Jake! Jake!"

"Yeeeeeah," he drawled.

"How you feel? You O.K.?"

"Yeah."

He raised his eyes and saw Slim bending over and cough-
ing out great white plumes of vapor. Bob was lurching near
a fence, moaning. He understood now. They were in an alley.
The snow had stopped and the sky had cleared to a hazy blue.
An icy wind ached his face and burned the tips of his ears.
He wanted to sink into the ground and sleep forever.

"Come on," said Al. "Let's go somewhere and get warm."

They struggled to the street and stumbled into a beer
tavern. Jake flopped limply into a chair, propped his elbows
on a table, held his head in his hands, and closed his eyes.
Gawddamn everything!

"If I had a gun I'd go back up there and blow that whore's
brains out," he groaned.

"Aw, forget her. Them guys'd kill you," said Al.

"That's a nest of rattlesnakes," said Slim.

"Every nigger in that joint had a gun or a knife or a blackjack."

"I kept feeling that whore was tricking me," Jake mumbled.

Bob lay with his head cradled in his arms.

"Wake up, Bob!" said Al.

"What's the matter with 'im?" asked Jake.

"He's almost out. His dose and that whiskey just about fixed
'im."

Jake sorted out some coins.

"Here, get a halfpint," he said, giving the money to Al.

The three of them drank. They tried to awaken Bob, but
he would not move.

"Somebody'll have to lug 'im home," sighed Jake.

"Slim and me'll take 'im," said Al. "We live his way."

"Lawd, but what happened? The last thing I remember I was trying to get a piece of that Blue Juice."

"They ganged you."

"Them guys is in a syndicate."

"We had to battle like wildcats to get you out of there alive."

"Old Ben Kitty was on you like white on rice."

"The whole mob of 'em was trying to do you in."

"It was old One Barrel what socked you behind the head, then I grabbed 'im."

"And old Blue Juice hit you in the temple with brass knuckles."

"Yeah," said Jake. "I thought the whole building had done fell on me. They hurt youall?"

"Naw, they backed up a little when they saw we'd fight."

"But boy, if it hadn't been for Rose pleading and screaming they was planning on using guns."

"And that Blanche dame did a quick fadeout."

"I saw her with a knife a foot long."

"That bitch!" said Jake.

"Where in Gawd's name you find that place?" asked Slim.

"Some bird down at the *Nook* told me to go there."

"He sure sent you into a mess of trouble."

"Some guy wanted to call the Law and Rose almost scratched his eyes out."

"I'm sure glad didn't no Law come."

"Yeah, they'd've been hard on us at the job about getting in jail."

"It would've been the end of me," sighed Jake.

Al clenched his fist and let it fall disgustedly.

"Just when we had them dames all lined up, this had to happen!"

"Jeeesus, look at me!" Jake demanded, almost indignantly. "Every red cent of that hundred dollars is gone. I'm right where I started!"

"Aw, hell! Ain't no use in thinking bout it."

"Naw, you'll go nuts then."
They drank again.
"My head feels big's a barrel."
"What time you got?"
"Three-thirty."
"Jeeesus!"
"Is it that late?"
"Yep."
"Let's get going."
"Yeah, we got to work tomorrow."
But they did not move. Above their heads an old clock ticked away the time. Jake blew his nose, pulled the stopper out of the bottle, drank and passed it around.
"Come on, let's get some sleep."
Al and Slim lifted Bob. Jake walked alone, rocking a little and pushing his flask into his hip pocket. He caught his breath as he went through the door; the wind was keen and painful.
"It's cold!"
"It must be below zero!"
As they huddled in the doorway, Bob lurched toward the ground. Al caught him.
"Try to stand up, Bob! You ain't no baby!"
They lit cigarettes behind turned up coat collars.
"I sure would've been in a tough spot if it hadn't been for youall," sighed Jake.
"We got to watch out sharp next time."
"Yeah, we got to be careful."
Jake yawned.
"I'm sleepy."
"Me too."
"Let's get out of this cold."
They stepped gingerly to the sidewalk.
"Well," sighed Al. "I'll do you like the farmer did the potato."
"Plant you now and dig you later."
Slim laughed without opening his mouth.

"Aw, we had a good time, anyway."

"Oh, yeah."

"Sure."

Slim shifted restlessly from foot to foot and looked around.

"Say, how about another drink?" he asked abruptly.

"Sure," said Jake.

They drank again and licked their lips. Bob began to whimper.

"It's coming down on 'im again," said Al.

Bob broke from Al and crawled on his hands and knees in the snow. When Al tried to lift him, he fought him off and beat his fists against the air.

"He's wet," said Al.

"Pick 'im up," said Jake. "Don't let 'im wallow in that snow."

Bob bent his head to his knees and screamed; his scream was as sharp as the cold wind. When his breath was gone he lifted his face with teeth clenched and bared.

"Come on, Bob," said Slim, tugging at his shoulder.

"Nigger, you'll freeze to death like that," admonished Al.

"Here," said Jake. "Make 'im drink."

"Hold 'im up! He can't stand!"

"Here, Bob, drink! It'll make you feel better!"

"Hell, he won't drink."

"But, shucks, we got to make 'im drink. How you going to lug 'im home with him moaning and screaming like that?"

Al and Slim lifted Bob, and Jake forced whiskey down his throat.

"Drink, man! You'll catch pneumonia fooling around like this."

The whiskey drooled down Bob's lips and chin.

"Take 'im home," said Jake.

Al and Slim moved forward heavily, supporting Bob between them.

"Well, so long."

"So long."

Jake heard Slim's wracking cough, heard Al's heavy voice
pleading with Bob, heard their footsteps crunching in the
snow, dying away. He watched them bend against the icy
wind as they turned a corner.

He was alone in the deserted street with a deep sense of
desolation. He could hardly hold his eyes open. His head
throbbed and a loud ringing filled his ears. He pulled his hat
low over his face, felt the flask in his hip pocket, patted it, and
sneezed. *Hell,* he sighed and wiped his nose with the back
of his hand. Whiskey burned like a ball of fire in his solar
plexus and braced him against the wind. Each step he took
called for concentration and effort. He coughed and a string
of phlegm swung from his lips. He bent over and shook; it still
swung. He caught the string between his fingers and flung it
to the snow. He stumbled blindly as the full force of the
alcohol swept over him. Holding to a lamppost, he took out
his money and counted it, piece by piece. He had exactly
eighty-five cents. *One hundred dollars gone in one night!*
And I got to pay Doc. Gawddamn that whore! He straightened, smiled, and yelled to the top of his voice:

"BUT WHEN I WAS FLYING I WAS A FLYING FOOL!"

He tried to put his money back into his pocket and
dropped the nickels and dimes into the soft snow. He
scratched with his fingers, but could not find a penny. He spat
and lurched on. *Shucks, there's more money where that came*
from. His mind cleared a bit and he found himself standing
on a dark corner. A streetcar clanked by. He looked up,
startled. Then he simpered and waved his hand at the car's
disappearing tail light. A cold, swift wind lifted his hat and
carried it into darkness. He clutched wildly. Stumbled.

"That sonofaBITCH!"

He was a block from home now. Just as he was about to step
into the street a black limousine shot past and set his coat and
tie awry. He wagged his head. *Got to be careful. Can't get*
run over. Naw, naw, not by a long shot. He took another
drink and things began to whirl. Streetlamps swelled to the

size of dull moons, rising and falling when he lowered and lifted his eyes. The snow-covered pavement developed tall hillocks and deep valleys. Hard lines curved sinuously and curves assumed the rigidity of angles. Another streetcar flew by, its screech gritting painfully into his raw nerves. He stopped and shouted:

"WHEN YOU GET TO WHERE YOU GOING TELL 'EM ABOUT ME!"

After what seemed hours of confusion he found himself hugging tightly at a steel telephone pole, opposite his home. A dim light burned in his window. *Yeah, she's up there! I'm going up and pay her off tonight! By Gawd, I'll teach her who's boss, who wears the pants. . . .* When in the vestibule it took him five minutes to find his keys and open the door. He paused several times on the stairs and shook his head to clear away the mists. He listened in front of his flat, but could not hear a sound. The key finally found the hole and he pushed the door in softly. He stood a moment, as though frozen, looking, not breathing. On the edge of a circle of light cast by the floor lamp Lil knelt at the side of the bed, her face lying on the quilt, turned toward him. She was asleep. *Ain't this a bitch! Gone to sleep on her knees, praying. . . . So help me Gawd, I'm going to give her something to pray for!* He slipped off his coat and hat and dropped them to the floor. The room was like a dim, warm dream, and his head seemed far away from his body, whirling. He stuck a cigarette in the corner of his mouth and lit it, then brought out the half-filled flask, still watching Lil sleeping on her knees. He drained the bottle and waited. His flesh began to tingle; a hot flame spread out from his stomach and engulfed him. The room swayed. His lips flexed and he hurled the empty bottle with a swift motion square into the dresser mirror. There was a crash and splintering glass showered the floor. Lil awoke with a violent start and straightened in fright. She screamed and backed into a corner while still on her knees. Jake lurched toward her.

"That wake you up?"

"Jake!"

"Yeeeah, this is Jake. Ain't you glad to see me?"

"You drunk," she breathed.

"How you think I'd be?"

"Please, Jake! You drunk, go to bed!"

"Like hell I will! I'm going to learn you something tonight!"

She was sitting on her knees with her legs doubled under her. He looked at the brown sweep of her calves, brown that dissolved and merged with the warm air of the room.

"Get up!"

"Hush," she whispered. "Folks can hear you."

"GAWDDAMMIT, I WANT 'EM TO HEAR!"

She started to cry.

"You thought you was going to make me lose my job, didn't you? Well, you didn't! I still got it and I'm going to keep it even if I have to split your head wide open!" He was standing over her, his face wet with sweat, his eyes red. "Next time you snitch on me I'm going to send you to the crazyhouse, you hear? The white folks said you was crazy, and you is! You hear me, YOU CRAZY!"

"You'll wake everybody up, Jake. You drunk. . . ."

"GAWDDAMN RIGHT I'M DRUNK! I want the world to know I'm drunk! I don't care what they think! They don't feed me! And I want 'em to know you's a lousy, crazy bitch!"

"Gawd have mercy on you, Jake."

"I don't want nobody to have no mercy on me!"

"You don't never stay home and when you do come in you come in drunk."

"What I want to stay home for? To look at *you?* Like hell!"

"While you out having a good time with your money, I'm here sick and hungry."

"That's your hard luck!"

"You got your friends to drink and talk with and I ain't got nothing."

"You don't need nothing."

"Jake, don't you never think of nobody but yourself?"

"Gawd made me like I is, and I'm going to stay that way!"

"You making my life full of misery."

"Look at me! I'm laughing, ain't I?"

"You kill everything you touch."

"If you don't shut your big mouth I *will* kill you!"

He caught the wall to steady himself. His cigarette fell from his lips and hot sparks showered his hands. A hammer of pain beat at the base of his skull. Fumes of darkness circled around him: he was straining with all his might to keep from falling. He kept telling himself, *I got to show her. I got to show this bitch something!* He grabbed the window shade and gave it a twist that sent it to the top of the ceiling, flapping. *I'll show her!* He turned to the dresser and reached three times for a toy glass elephant; finally he caught it in his fist. The room whirled and Lil's brown legs whirled with it, crowding his eyes. He threw the elephant into the window-pane; glass splintered and icy wind rushed in.

"Jake! Jake!"

He threw a bowl. A brush. A glass puppy. He reached for something else; the room tilted and he pulled off the dresser scarf, emptying the things on the floor with a loud clatter. There was a heavy deafness in his ears and he had to shout in order to hear himself.

"LET 'EM HEAR! LET 'EM HEAR!"

He tried to get to her and stumbled over a chair. She rose, crouching, her mouth open, her eyes wide. With numbed fingers he clutched a handful of her gown on each shoulder and jerked.

"Don't beat me! Don't beat me, Jake!"

He grabbed for her throat and she gave a lunge; he went backwards and pulled her with him. She got up and started for the door. While still on his knees he caught the hem of her gown and held her. He stumbled to his feet and rammed her against a wall.

"You hit me, didn't you?"

"Naw, Jake!"

He ripped her gown half open. She sucked her breath in sharply, lunged again and threw him against the bed. When she struggled for the door this time he caught her wrist and swung her around.

"I'm going to see how sick you is!"

She tried to wrench herself free.

"Where you think you going?"

"Naw, naw," she spoke in a breath softer than a whisper with her eyes fixed in horror upon his face. He attempted to drag her to the middle of the floor and she sank to her knees. He tried to lift her and she bit his hand. Blood leaped to his head and he knocked her into the floor lamp, sending it sprawling. The room darkened save for the cold light of the sky.

"You bitch!" he breathed in a voice half curse and half sob.

He bent and slapped her across her eyes and she screamed. He bent to slap her again but she eluded him and crawled over the bed. Her cheeks were bleeding. He looked at her, his breath coming slowly and heavily through his open mouth, drying his lips. The room was freezing cold; in the semidarkness he saw her breath turning white as it struck the icy wind. *I'm going to fix you!* When he went toward her she stooped quickly and came up with a jagged edge of window-pane clutched in her fist. Her voice was high, hysterical, in one breath, on a dead level.

"Naw. . . . Naw. . . ."

His jaw sagged. He swallowed, wanting another drink.

"Put that glass down!"

He lunged for her arm and missed.

"JAKE!"

When he grabbed for her again she brought the piece of glass down across his head. A hot anger made him hold his breath.

"I'm going to kill you!"

She backed to the wall, holding the piece of glass above her head. He leapt, trying to grasp her wrists; she struck him again. He staggered, growled, and tried to catch her hand. When she hit him this time he flopped weakly on the bed; he felt something warm oozing down his left cheek. A black whirlpool was sucking him under. He looked dully at the busted window, at the shards of glass glinting fitfully on the floor. He dabbed at his scalp with the edge of a sheet and fumbled at his shirt with sticky fingers, leaving red prints. He rubbed his eyes and face clumsily with cold fists and a convulsion of nervous misery made him sigh out a plaintive whimper. His face twitched. He belched. He shuddered from the chill that was seeping into the marrow of his bones as darkness roared in his brain.

Lil dropped the piece of glass; its edges were stained from cuts in her hand. She stood over Jake a moment and watched his drunken sleep. Then she pulled down the shade, wrapped herself in a coat and sank to the floor. She pressed a wad of her gown hard into the cuts in her palm to stem the flow of blood and rested her head on her knees.

"Lawd, I wish I was dead," she sobbed softly.

Outside an icy wind swept around the corner of the building, whining and moaning like an idiot in a deep black pit.

Native Son

Although Wright had sketched out the story in Chicago before he left for New York, Native Son was written, essentially, in a few months in 1938–39. He based Bigger Thomas, the protagonist, on several rebellious Black youngsters he had met at different times in his career. When the Robert Nixon case (a black youngster was accused of killing a white woman) broke out in Chicago during the writing of the novel, he was delighted to use—as Theodore Dreiser had done in An American Tragedy with the Chester Gillette/ Grace Brown case—a number of actual details and most of the press coverage. His article "How Bigger Was Born," written in the spring of 1940, is an attempt to retrace this genesis, but above all it serves as a justification for Wright's ideological perspectives, which made him consider the Bigger Thomases in the United States as potential revolutionaries and reactionaries at the same time. When the novel appeared, Wright was promptly branded as a radical, a Communist and a Black extremist by a number of critics, such as Burton Rascoe and David Cohn, but—and this is less widely known —the publication of Native Son also endangered for a time Wright's good standing in Communist circles, where many thought the picture of Negro life was not militant enough in the perspective of the class struggle.

Native Son was originally published by Harper & Brothers in 1940. This selection is "Book One: Fear" of the original work.

The novel was an immediate success. The first book by a Black American to become a Book-of-the-Month-Club selection, it catapulted Wright into fame before being adapted for the Broadway stage the following year.

Ever since its publication, commentary on Native Son *has reflected the fundamental reactions of America to its minorities and to its own history. This is because Wright fathomed in it the horror and hatred created by racial and economic oppression to a degree rarely surpassed. At the end of "How Bigger Was Born" Wright says:*

We do have in the Negro the embodiment of a past, tragic enough to appease the spiritual hunger of even a James and we have in the oppression of the Negro a shadow athwart our national life dense and heavy enough to satisfy even the gloomy broodings of a Hawthorne. And if Poe were alive, he would not have to invent horror; horror would invent him.

More important still, beyond his preoccupation to make the reader live with the protagonist and immediately share Bigger's essential humanity, Wright strikes a decisive blow at the core of race relations in America by having his Black rebel break the supreme taboo in taking a white woman as his victim. He also raises the question of revolutionary consciousness in violence when Bigger says to his somewhat baffled lawyer: "What I killed for must've been good! . . . It must've been good! . . . When a man kills, it's for something . . . I didn't know I was really alive in this world until I felt things hard enough to kill for 'em." Wright's message has never been forgotten. His frank depiction of the Black situation made it impossible to repeat the old, pious lies about race relations in America, and it literally liberated the next generation of Afro-American writers.

FEAR

Brrrrrrriiiiiiiiiiiiiiiiiiinng!

An alarm clock clanged in the dark and silent room. A bed spring creaked. A woman's voice sang out impatiently:

"Bigger, shut that thing off!"

A surly grunt sounded above the tinny ring of metal. Naked feet swished dryly across the planks in the wooden floor and the clang ceased abruptly.

"Turn on the light, Bigger."

"Awright," came a sleepy mumble.

Light flooded the room and revealed a black boy standing in a narrow space between two iron beds, rubbing his eyes with the backs of his hands. From a bed to his right the woman spoke again:

"Buddy, get up from there! I got a big washing on my hands today and I want you-all out of here."

Another black boy rolled from bed and stood up. The woman also rose and stood in her nightgown.

"Turn your heads so I can dress," she said.

The two boys averted their eyes and gazed into a far corner of the room. The woman rushed out of her nightgown and put on a pair of step-ins. She turned to the bed from which she had risen and called:

"Vera! Get up from there!"

"What time is it, Ma?" asked a muffled, adolescent voice from beneath a quilt.

"Get up from there, I say!"

"O.K., Ma."

A brown-skinned girl in a cotton gown got up and stretched her arms above her head and yawned. Sleepily, she sat on a chair and fumbled with her stockings. The two boys kept their faces averted while their mother and sister put on enough clothes to keep them from feeling ashamed; and the mother and sister did the same while the boys dressed. Abruptly, they all paused, holding their clothes in their hands, their attention caught by a light tapping in the thinly plastered walls of the room. They forgot their conspiracy against shame and their eyes strayed apprehensively over the floor.

"There he is again, Bigger!" the woman screamed, and the tiny one-room apartment galvanized into violent action. A chair toppled as the woman, half-dressed and in her stocking feet, scrambled breathlessly upon the bed. Her two sons, barefoot, stood tense and motionless, their eyes searching anxiously under the bed and chairs. The girl ran into a corner, half-stooped and gathered the hem of her slip into both of her hands and held it tightly over her knees.

"Oh! Oh!" she wailed.

"There he goes!"

The woman pointed a shaking finger. Her eyes were round with fascinated horror.

"Where?"

"I don't see 'im!"

"Bigger, he's behind the trunk!" the girl whimpered.

"Vera!" the woman screamed. "Get up here on the bed! Don't let that thing *bite* you!"

Frantically, Vera climbed upon the bed and the woman caught hold of her. With their arms entwined about each other, the black mother and the brown daughter gazed open-mouthed at the trunk in the corner.

Bigger looked round the room wildly, then darted to a curtain and swept it aside and grabbed two heavy iron skillets from a wall above a gas stove. He whirled and called softly to his brother, his eyes glued to the trunk.

"Buddy!"

"Yeah?"

"Here; take this skillet."

"O.K."

"Now, get over by the door!"

"O.K."

Buddy crouched by the door and held the iron skillet by
its handle, his arm flexed and poised. Save for the quick, deep
breathing of the four people, the room was quiet. Bigger
crept on tiptoe toward the trunk with the skillet clutched
stiffly in his hand, his eyes dancing and watching every inch
of the wooden floor in front of him. He paused and, without
moving an eye or muscle, called:

"Buddy!"

"Hunh?"

"Put that box in front of the hole so he can't get out!"

"O.K."

Buddy ran to a wooden box and shoved it quickly in front
of a gaping hole in the molding and then backed again to the
door, holding the skillet ready. Bigger eased to the trunk and
peered behind it cautiously. He saw nothing. Carefully, he
stuck out his bare foot and pushed the trunk a few inches.

"There he is!" the mother screamed again.

A huge black rat squealed and leaped at Bigger's trouser-
leg and snagged it in his teeth, hanging on.

"Goddamn!" Bigger whispered fiercely, whirling and kicking out his leg with all the strength of his body. The force of
his movement shook the rat loose and it sailed through the
air and struck a wall. Instantly, it rolled over and leaped
again. Bigger dodged and the rat landed against a table leg.
With clenched teeth, Bigger held the skillet; he was afraid to
hurl it, fearing that he might miss. The rat squeaked and
turned and ran in a narrow circle, looking for a place to hide;
it leaped again past Bigger and scurried on dry rasping feet
to one side of the box and then to the other, searching for the
hole. Then it turned and reared upon its hind legs.

"Hit 'im, Bigger!" Buddy shouted.

"Kill 'im!" the woman screamed.

The rat's belly pulsed with fear. Bigger advanced a step
and the rat emitted a long thin song of defiance, its black
beady eyes glittering, its tiny forefeet pawing the air rest-

lessly. Bigger swung the skillet; it skidded over the floor, missing the rat, and clattered to a stop against a wall.

"Goddamn!"

The rat leaped. Bigger sprang to one side. The rat stopped under a chair and let out a furious screak. Bigger moved slowly backward toward the door.

"Gimme that skillet, Buddy," he asked quietly, not taking his eyes from the rat.

Buddy extended his hand. Bigger caught the skillet and lifted it high in the air. The rat scuttled across the floor and stopped again at the box and searched quickly for the hole; then it reared once more and bared long yellow fangs, piping shrilly, belly quivering.

Bigger aimed and let the skillet fly with a heavy grunt. There was a shattering of wood as the box caved in. The woman screamed and hid her face in her hands. Bigger tiptoed forward and peered.

"I got 'im," he muttered, his clenched teeth bared in a smile. "By God, I got 'im."

He kicked the splintered box out of the way and the flat black body of the rat lay exposed, its two long yellow tusks showing distinctly. Bigger took a shoe and pounded the rat's head, crushing it, cursing hysterically:

"You sonofa*bitch!*"

The woman on the bed sank to her knees and buried her face in the quilts and sobbed:

"Lord, Lord, have mercy. . . ."

"Aw, Mama," Vera whimpered, bending to her. "Don't cry. It's dead now."

The two brothers stood over the dead rat and spoke in tones of awed admiration.

"Gee, but he's a big bastard."

"That sonofabitch could cut your throat."

"He's over a foot long."

"How in hell do they get so big?"

"Eating garbage and anything else they can get."

"Look, Bigger, there's a three-inch rip in your pant-leg."

"Yeah; he was after me, all right."

"Please, Bigger, take 'im out," Vera begged.

"Aw, don't be so scary," Buddy said.

The woman on the bed continued to sob. Bigger took a piece of newspaper and gingerly lifted the rat by its tail and held it out at arm's length.

"Bigger, take 'im out," Vera begged again.

Bigger laughed and approached the bed with the dangling rat, swinging it to and fro like a pendulum, enjoying his sister's fear.

"Bigger!" Vera gasped convulsively; she screamed and swayed and closed her eyes and fell headlong across her mother and rolled limply from the bed to the floor.

"Bigger, for God's sake!" the mother sobbed, rising and bending over Vera. "Don't do that! Throw that rat out!"

He laid the rat down and started to dress.

"Bigger, help me lift Vera to the bed," the mother said.

He paused and turned round.

"What's the matter?" he asked, feigning ignorance.

"Do what I asked you, will you, boy?"

He went to the bed and helped his mother lift Vera. Vera's eyes were closed. He turned away and finished dressing. He wrapped the rat in a newspaper and went out of the door and down the stairs and put it into a garbage can at the corner of an alley. When he returned to the room his mother was still bent over Vera, placing a wet towel upon her head. She straightened and faced him, her cheeks and eyes wet with tears and her lips tight with anger.

"Boy, sometimes I wonder what makes you act like you do."

"What I do now?" he demanded belligerently.

"Sometimes you act the biggest fool I ever saw."

"What you talking about?"

"You scared your sister with that rat and she *fainted!* Ain't you got no sense at *all?*"

"Aw, I didn't know she was that scary."

"Buddy!" the mother called.

"Yessum."

"Take a newspaper and spread it over that spot."

"Yessum."

Buddy opened out a newspaper and covered the smear of blood on the floor where the rat had been crushed. Bigger went to the window and stood looking out abstractedly into the street. His mother glared at his back.

"Bigger, sometimes I wonder why I birthed you," she said bitterly.

Bigger looked at her and turned away.

"Maybe you oughtn't've. Maybe you ought to left me where I was."

"You shut your sassy mouth!"

"Aw, for chrissakes!" Bigger said, lighting a cigarette.

"Buddy, pick up them skillets and put 'em in the sink," the mother said.

"Yessum."

Bigger walked across the floor and sat on the bed. His mother's eyes followed him.

"We wouldn't have to live in this garbage dump if you had any manhood in you," she said.

"Aw, don't start that again."

"How you feel, Vera?" the mother asked.

Vera raised her head and looked about the room as though expecting to see another rat.

"Oh, Mama!"

"You poor thing!"

"I couldn't help it. Bigger scared me."

"Did you hurt yourself?"

"I bumped my head."

"Here; take it easy. You'll be all right."

"How come Bigger acts that way?" Vera asked, crying again.

"He's just crazy," the mother said. "Just plain dumb black crazy."

"I'll be late for my sewing class at the Y.W.C.A.," Vera said.

"Here; stretch out on the bed. You'll feel better in a little while," the mother said.

She left Vera on the bed and turned a pair of cold eyes upon Bigger.

"Suppose you wake up some morning and find your sister dead? What would you think then?" she asked. "Suppose those rats cut our veins at night when we sleep? Naw! Nothing like that ever bothers you! All you care about is your own pleasure! Even when the relief offers you a job you won't take it till they threaten to cut off your food and starve you! Bigger, honest, you the most no-countest man I ever seen in all my life!"

"You done told me that a thousand times," he said, not looking round.

"Well, I'm telling you agin! And mark my word, some of these days you going to set down and *cry*. Some of these days you going to wish you had made something out of yourself, instead of just a tramp. But it'll be too late then."

"Stop prophesying about me," he said.

"I prophesy much as I please! And if you don't like it, you can get out. We can get along without you. We can live in one room just like we living now, even with you gone," she said.

"Aw, for chrissakes!" he said, his voice filled with nervous irritation.

"You'll regret how you living some day," she went on. "If you don't stop running with that gang of yours and do right you'll end up where you never thought you would. You think I don't know what you boys is doing, but I do. And the gallows is at the end of the road you traveling, boy. Just remember that." She turned and looked at Buddy. "Throw that box outside, Buddy."

"Yessum."

There was silence. Buddy took the box out. The mother went behind the curtain to the gas stove. Vera sat up in bed and swung her feet to the floor.

"Lay back down, Vera," the mother said.

"I feel all right now, Ma. I got to go to my sewing class."

"Well, if you feel like it, set the table," the mother said, going behind the curtain again. "Lord, I get so tired of this I don't know what to do," her voice floated plaintively from behind the curtain. "All I ever do is try to make a home for you children and you don't care."

"Aw, Ma," Vera protested. "Don't say that."

"Vera, sometimes I just want to lay down and quit."

"Ma, please don't say that."

"I can't last many more years, living like this."

"I'll be old enough to work soon, Ma."

"I reckon I'll be dead then. I reckon God'll call me home."

Vera went behind the curtain and Bigger heard her trying to comfort his mother. He shut their voices out of his mind. He hated his family because he knew that they were suffering and that he was powerless to help them. He knew that the moment he allowed himself to feel to its fullness how they lived, the shame and misery of their lives, he would be swept out of himself with fear and despair. So he held toward them an attitude of iron reserve; he lived with them, but behind a wall, a curtain. And toward himself he was even more exacting. He knew that the moment he allowed what his life meant to enter fully into his consciousness, he would either kill himself or someone else. So he denied himself and acted tough.

He got up and crushed his cigarette upon the window sill. Vera came into the room and placed knives and forks upon the table.

"Get ready to eat, you-all," the mother called.

He sat at the table. The odor of frying bacon and boiling coffee drifted to him from behind the curtain. His mother's voice floated to him in song.

> *Life is like a mountain railroad*
> *With an engineer that's brave*

We must make the run successful
From the cradle to the grave. . . .

The song irked him and he was glad when she stopped and came into the room with a pot of coffee and a plate of crinkled bacon. Vera brought the bread in and they sat down. His mother closed her eyes and lowered her head and mumbled,

"Lord, we thank Thee for the food You done placed before us for the nourishment of our bodies. Amen." She lifted her eyes and without changing her tone of voice, said, "You going to have to learn to get up earlier than this, Bigger, to hold a job."

He did not answer or look up.

"You want me to pour you some coffee?" Vera asked.

"Yeah."

"You going to take the job, ain't you, Bigger?" his mother asked.

He laid down his fork and stared at her.

"I told you last night I was going to take it. How many times you want to ask me?"

"Well, don't bite her head off," Vera said. "She only asked you a question."

"Pass the bread and stop being smart."

"You know you have to see Mr. Dalton at five-thirty," his mother said.

"You done said that ten times."

"I don't want you to forget, son."

"And you know how you can forget," Vera said.

"Aw, lay off Bigger," Buddy said. "He told you he was going to take the job."

"Don't tell 'em nothing," Bigger said.

"You shut your mouth, Buddy, or get up from this table," the mother said. "I'm not going to take any stinking sass from you. One fool in the family's enough."

"Lay off, Ma," Buddy said.

"Bigger's setting here like he ain't glad to get a job," she said.

"What you want me to do? Shout?" Bigger asked.

"Oh, Bigger!" his sister said.

"I wish you'd keep your big mouth out of this!" he told his sister.

"If you get that job," his mother said in a low, kind tone of voice, busy slicing a loaf of bread, "I can fix up a nice place for you children. You could be comfortable and not have to live like pigs."

"Bigger ain't decent enough to think of nothing like that," Vera said.

"God, I wish you-all would let me eat," Bigger said.

His mother talked on as though she had not heard him and he stopped listening.

"Ma's talking to you, Bigger," Vera said.

"So *what?*"

"Don't be that way, Bigger!"

He laid down his fork and his strong black fingers gripped the edge of the table; there was silence save for the tinkling of his brother's fork against a plate. He kept staring at his sister till her eyes fell.

"I wish you'd let me eat," he said again.

As he ate he felt that they were thinking of the job he was to get that evening and it made him angry; he felt that they had tricked him into a cheap surrender.

"I need some carfare," he said.

"Here's all I got," his mother said, pushing a quarter to the side of his plate.

He put the quarter in his pocket and drained his cup of coffee in one long swallow. He got his coat and cap and went to the door.

"You know, Bigger," his mother said, "if you don't take that job the relief'll cut us off. We won't have any food."

"I told you I'd take it!" he shouted and slammed the door.

He went down the steps into the vestibule and stood looking out into the street through the plate glass of the front door. Now and then a street car rattled past over steel tracks. He was sick of his life at home. Day in and day out there was nothing but shouts and bickering. But what could he do? Each time he asked himself that question his mind hit a blank wall and he stopped thinking. Across the street directly in front of him, he saw a truck pull to a stop at the curb and two white men in overalls got out with pails and brushes. Yes, he could take the job at Dalton's and be miserable, or he could refuse it and starve. It maddened him to think that he did not have a wider choice of action. Well, he could not stand here all day like this. What was he to do with himself? He tried to decide if he wanted to buy a ten-cent magazine, or go to a movie, or go to the poolroom and talk with the gang, or just loaf around. With his hands deep in his pockets, another cigarette slanting across his chin, he brooded and watched the men at work across the street. They were pasting a huge colored poster to a signboard. The poster showed a white face.

"That's Buckley!" He spoke softly to himself. "He's running for State's Attorney again." The men were slapping the poster with wet brushes. He looked at the round florid face and wagged his head. "I bet that sonofabitch rakes off a million bucks in graft a year. Boy, if I was in his shoes for just one day I'd *never* have to worry again."

When the men were through they gathered up their pails and brushes and got into the truck and drove off. He looked at the poster: the white face was fleshy but stern; one hand was uplifted and its index finger pointed straight out into the street at each passer-by. The poster showed one of those faces that looked straight at you when you looked at it and all the while you were walking and turning your head to look at it it kept looking unblinkingly back at you until you got so far from it you had to take your eyes away, and then it stopped, like a movie blackout. Above the top of the poster were tall red letters: IF YOU BREAK THE LAW, YOU CAN'T WIN!

He snuffed his cigarette and laughed silently. "You crook," he mumbled, shaking his head. "You let whoever pays *you* off win!" He opened the door and met the morning air. He went along the sidewalk with his head down, fingering the quarter in his pocket. He stopped and searched all of his pockets; in his vest pocket he found a lone copper cent. That made a total of twenty-six cents, fourteen cents of which would have to be saved for carfare to Mr. Dalton's; that is, if he decided to take the job. In order to buy a magazine and go to the movies he would have to have at least twenty cents more. "Goddammit, I'm always broke!" he mumbled.

He stood on the corner in the sunshine, watching cars and people pass. He needed more money; if he did not get more than he had now he would not know what to do with himself for the rest of the day. He wanted to see a movie; his senses hungered for it. In a movie he could dream without effort; all he had to do was lean back in a seat and keep his eyes open.

He thought of Gus and G.H. and Jack. Should he go to the poolroom and talk with them? But there was no use in his going unless they were ready to do what they had been long planning to do. If they could, it would mean some sure and quick money. From three o'clock to four o'clock in the afternoon there was no policeman on duty in the block where Blum's Delicatessen was and it would be safe. One of them could hold a gun on Blum and keep him from yelling; one could watch the front door; one could watch the back; and one could get the money from the box under the counter. Then all four of them could lock Blum in the store and run out through the back and duck down the alley and meet an hour later, either at Doc's poolroom or at the South Side Boy's Club, and split the money.

Holding up Blum ought not take more than two minutes, at the most. And it would be their last job. But it would be the toughest one that they had ever pulled. All the other times they had raided newsstands, fruit stands, and apartments. And, too, they had never held up a white man before. They had always robbed Negroes. They felt that it was much easier and safer to rob their own people, for they knew that white policemen never really searched diligently for Negroes who committed crimes against other Negroes. For months they had talked of robbing Blum's, but had not been able to bring themselves to do it. They had the feeling that the robbing of Blum's would be a violation of ultimate taboo; it would be a trespassing into territory where the full wrath of an alien white world would be turned loose upon them; in short, it would be a symbolic challenge of the white world's rule over them; a challenge which they yearned to make, but were afraid to. Yes; if they could rob Blum's, it would be a real hold-up, in more senses than one. In comparison, all of their other jobs had been play.

"Good-bye, Bigger."

He looked up and saw Vera passing with a sewing kit dangling from her arm. She paused at the corner and came back to him.

"Now, what you want?"

"Bigger, please. . . . You're getting a good job now. Why don't you stay away from Jack and Gus and G.H. and keep out of trouble?"

"You keep your big mouth out of my business!"

"But, Bigger!"

"Go on to school, will you!"

She turned abruptly and walked on. He knew that his mother had been talking to Vera and Buddy about him, telling them that if he got into any more trouble he would be sent to prison and not just to the reform school, where they sent him last time. He did not mind what his mother said to Buddy about him. Buddy was all right. Tough, plenty. But Vera was a sappy girl; she did not have any more sense than to believe everything she was told.

He walked toward the poolroom. When he got to the door he saw Gus half a block away, coming toward him. He stopped and waited. It was Gus who had first thought of robbing Blum's.

"Hi, Bigger!"

"What you saying, Gus?"

"Nothing. Seen G.H. or Jack yet?"

"Naw. You?"

"Naw. Say, got a cigarette?"

"Yeah."

Bigger took out his pack and gave Gus a cigarette; he lit his and held the match for Gus. They leaned their backs against the red-brick wall of a building, smoking, their cigarettes slanting white across their black chins. To the east Bigger saw the sun burning a dazzling yellow. In the sky above him a few big white clouds drifted. He puffed silently, relaxed, his mind pleasantly vacant of purpose. Every slight movement in the street evoked a casual curiosity in him. Automatically, his eyes followed each car as it whirred over the smooth black asphalt. A woman came by and he watched the gentle sway of her body until she disappeared into a doorway. He sighed, scratched his chin and mumbled,

"Kinda warm today."

"Yeah," Gus said.

"You get more heat from this sun than from them old radiators at home."

"Yeah; them old white landlords sure don't give much heat."

"And they always knocking at your door for money."

"I'll be glad when summer comes."

"Me too," Bigger said.

He stretched his arms above his head and yawned; his eyes moistened. The sharp precision of the world of steel and stone dissolved into blurred waves. He blinked and the world grew hard again, mechanical, distinct. A weaving motion in the sky made him turn his eyes upward; he saw a slender streak of billowing white blooming against the deep blue. A plane was writing high up in the air.

"Look!" Bigger said.

"What?"

"That plane writing up there," Bigger said, pointing.

"Oh!"

They squinted at a tiny ribbon of unfolding vapor that spelled out the word: USE ... The plane was so far away that at times the strong glare of the sun blanked it from sight.

"You can hardly see it," Gus said.

"Looks like a little bird," Bigger breathed with childlike wonder.

"Them white boys sure can fly," Gus said.

"Yeah," Bigger said, wistfully. "They get a chance to do everything."

Noiselessly, the tiny plane looped and veered, vanishing and appearing, leaving behind it a long trail of white plumage, like coils of fluffy paste being squeezed from a tube; a plume-coil that grew and swelled and slowly began to fade into the air at the edges. The plane wrote another word: SPEED ...

"How high you reckon he is?" Bigger asked.

"I don't know. Maybe a hundred miles; maybe a thousand."

"I could fly one of them things if I had a chance," Bigger mumbled reflectively, as though talking to himself.

Gus pulled down the corners of his lips, stepped out from the wall, squared his shoulders, doffed his cap, bowed low and spoke with mock deference:

"Yessuh."

"You go to hell," Bigger said, smiling.

"Yessuh," Gus said again.

"I *could* fly a plane if I had a chance," Bigger said.

"If you wasn't black and if you had some money and if they'd let you go to that aviation school, you *could* fly a plane," Gus said.

For a moment Bigger contemplated all the "ifs" that Gus had mentioned. Then both boys broke into hard laughter, looking at each other through squinted eyes. When their laughter subsided, Bigger said in a voice that was half-question and half-statement:

"It's funny how the white folks treat us, ain't it?"

"It better be funny," Gus said.

"Maybe they right in not wanting us to fly," Bigger said. " 'Cause if I took a plane up I'd take a couple of bombs along and drop 'em as sure as hell. . . ."

They laughed again, still looking upward. The plane sailed and dipped and spread another word against the sky: GASO-LINE. . . .

"Use Speed Gasoline," Bigger mused, rolling the words slowly from his lips. "God, I'd like to fly up there in that sky."

"God'll let you fly when He gives you your wings up in heaven," Gus said.

They laughed again, reclining against the wall, smoking, the lids of their eyes drooped softly against the sun. Cars whizzed past on rubber tires. Bigger's face was metallically black in the strong sunlight. There was in his eyes a pensive, brooding amusement, as of a man who had been long confronted and tantalized by a riddle whose answer seemed always just on the verge of escaping him, but prodding him irresistibly on to seek its solution. The silence irked Bigger; he was anxious to do something to evade looking so squarely at this problem.

"Let's play 'white,' " Bigger said, referring to a game of play-acting in which he and his friends imitated the ways and manners of white folks.

"I don't feel like it," Gus said.

"General!" Bigger pronounced in a sonorous tone, looking at Gus expectantly.

"Aw, hell! I don't want to play," Gus whined.

"You'll be court-martialed," Bigger said, snapping out his words with military precision.

"Nigger, you nuts!" Gus laughed.

"General!" Bigger tried again, determinedly.

Gus looked wearily at Bigger, then straightened, saluted and answered:

"Yessuh."

"Send your men over the river at dawn and attack the

enemy's left flank," Bigger ordered.

"Yessuh."

"Send the Fifth, Sixth, and Seventh Regiments," Bigger said, frowning. "And attack with tanks, gas, planes, and infantry."

"Yessuh!" Gus said again, saluting and clicking his heels.

For a moment they were silent, facing each other, their shoulders thrown back, their lips compressed to hold down the mounting impulse to laugh. Then they guffawed, partly at themselves and partly at the vast white world that sprawled and towered in the sun before them.

"Say, what's a 'left flank'?" Gus asked.

"I don't know," Bigger said. "I heard it in the movies."

They laughed again. After a bit they relaxed and leaned against the wall, smoking. Bigger saw Gus cup his left hand to his ear, as though holding a telephone receiver; and cup his right hand to his mouth, as though talking into a transmitter.

"Hello," Gus said.

"Hello," Bigger said. "Who's this?"

"This is Mr. J. P. Morgan speaking," Gus said.

"Yessuh, Mr. Morgan," Bigger said; his eyes filled with mock adulation and respect.

"I want you to sell twenty thousand shares of U. S. Steel in the market this morning," Gus said.

"At what price, suh?" Bigger asked.

"Aw, just dump 'em at any price," Gus said with casual irritation. "We're holding too much."

"Yessuh," Bigger said.

"And call me at my club at two this afternoon and tell me if the President telephoned," Gus said.

"Yessuh, Mr. Morgan," Bigger said.

Both of them made gestures signifying that they were hanging up telephone receivers; then they bent double, laughing.

"I bet that's *just* the way they talk," Gus said.

"I wouldn't be surprised," Bigger said.

They were silent again. Presently, Bigger cupped his hand to his mouth and spoke through an imaginary telephone transmitter.

"Hello."

"Hello," Gus answered. "Who's this?"

"This is the President of the United States speaking," Bigger said.

"Oh, yessuh, Mr. President," Gus said.

"I'm calling a cabinet meeting this afternoon at four o'clock and you, as Secretary of State, *must* be there."

"Well, now, Mr. President," Gus said, "I'm pretty busy. They raising sand over there in Germany and I got to send 'em a note. . . ."

"But this is important," Bigger said.

"What you going to take up at this cabinet meeting?" Gus asked.

"Well, you see, the niggers is raising sand all over the country," Bigger said, struggling to keep back his laughter. "We've got to do something with these black folks. . . ."

"Oh, if it's about the niggers, I'll be right there, Mr. President," Gus said.

They hung up imaginary receivers and leaned against the wall and laughed. A street car rattled by. Bigger sighed and swore.

"Goddammit!"

"What's the matter?"

"They don't let us do *nothing*."

"Who?"

"The *white* folks."

"You talk like you just now finding that out," Gus said.

"Naw. But I just can't get used to it," Bigger said. "I swear to God I can't. I know I oughtn't think about it, but I can't help it. Every time I think about it I feel like somebody's poking a red-hot iron down my throat. Goddammit, look! We live here and they live there. We black and they white. They got things and we ain't. They do things and we can't. It's just like living in jail. Half the time I feel like I'm on the outside of the world peeping in through a knot-hole in the fence. . . ."

"Aw, ain't no use feeling that way about it. It don't help none," Gus said.

"You know one thing?" Bigger said.

"What?"

"Sometimes I feel like something awful's going to happen to me," Bigger spoke with a tinge of bitter pride in his voice.

"What you mean?" Gus asked, looking at him quickly. There was fear in Gus's eyes.

"I don't know. I just feel that way. Every time I get to thinking about me being black and they being white, me being here and they being there, I feel like something awful's going to happen to me. . . ."

"Aw, for chrissakes! There ain't nothing you can do about it. How come you want to worry yourself? You black and they make the laws. . . ."

"Why they make us live in one corner of the city? Why don't they let us fly planes and run ships. . . ."

Gus hunched Bigger with his elbow and mumbled good-naturedly, "Aw, nigger, quit thinking about it. You'll go nuts."

The plane was gone from the sky and the white plumes of floating smoke were thinly spread, vanishing. Because he was restless and had time on his hands, Bigger yawned again and hoisted his arms high above his head.

"Nothing ever happens," he complained.

"What you want to happen?"

"Anything," Bigger said with a wide sweep of his dingy palm, a sweep that included all the possible activities of the world.

Then their eyes were riveted; a slate-colored pigeon swooped down to the middle of the steel car tracks and began strutting to and fro with ruffled feathers, its fat neck

bobbing with regal pride. A street car rumbled forward and
the pigeon rose swiftly through the air on wings stretched so
taut and sheer that Bigger could see the gold of the sun
through their translucent tips. He tilted his head and
watched the slate-colored bird flap and wheel out of sight
over the edge of a high roof.

"Now, if I could only do that," Bigger said.

Gus laughed.

"Nigger, you nuts."

"I reckon we the only things in this city that can't go where
we want to go and do what we want to do."

"Don't think about it," Gus said.

"I can't help it."

"That's why you feeling like something awful's going to
happen to you," Gus said. "You think too much."

"What in hell can a man do?" Bigger asked, turning to Gus.

"Get drunk and sleep it off."

"I can't. I'm broke."

Bigger crushed his cigarette and took out another one and
offered the package to Gus. They continued smoking. A huge
truck swept past, lifting scraps of white paper into the sunshine; the bits settled down slowly.

"Gus?"

"Hunh?"

"You know where the white folks live?"

"Yeah," Gus said, pointing eastward. "Over across the
'line'; over there on Cottage Grove Avenue."

"Naw; they don't," Bigger said.

"What you mean?" Gus asked, puzzled. "Then, where do
they live?"

Bigger doubled his fist and struck his solar plexus.

"Right down here in my stomach," he said.

Gus looked at Bigger searchingly, then away, as though
ashamed.

"Yeah; I know what you mean," he whispered.

"Every time I think of 'em, I *feel* 'em," Bigger said.

"Yeah; and in your chest and throat, too," Gus said.

"It's like fire."

"And sometimes you can't hardly breathe. . . ."

Bigger's eyes were wide and placid, gazing into space.

"That's when I feel like something awful's going to happen to me. . . ." Bigger paused, narrowed his eyes. "Naw; it ain't like something going to happen to me. It's . . . It's like I was going to do something I can't help. . . ."

"Yeah!" Gus said with uneasy eagerness. His eyes were full of a look compounded of fear and admiration for Bigger. "Yeah; I know what you mean. It's like you going to fall and don't know where you going to land. . . ."

Gus's voice trailed off. The sun slid behind a big white cloud and the street was plunged in cool shadow; quickly the sun edged forth again and it was bright and warm once more. A long sleek black car, its fenders glinting like glass in the sun, shot past them at high speed and turned a corner a few blocks away. Bigger pursed his lips and sang:

"Zoooooooooom!"

"They got everything," Gus said.

"They own the world," Bigger said.

"Aw, what the hell," Gus said. "Let's go in the poolroom."

"O.K."

They walked toward the door of the poolroom.

"Say, you taking that job you told us about?" Gus asked.

"I don't know."

"You talk like you don't want it."

"Oh, hell, yes! I want the job," Bigger said.

They looked at each other and laughed. They went inside. The poolroom was empty, save for a fat, black man who held a half-smoked, unlit cigar in his mouth and leaned on the front counter. To the rear burned a single green-shaded bulb.

"Hi, Doc," Bigger said.

"You boys kinda early this morning," Doc said.

"Jack or G.H. around yet?" Bigger asked.

"Naw," Doc said.

"Let's shoot a game," Gus said.

"I'm broke," Bigger said.

"I got some money."

"Switch on the light. The balls are racked," Doc said.

Bigger turned on the light. They lagged for first shot. Bigger won. They started playing. Bigger's shots were poor; he was thinking of Blum's, fascinated with the idea of the robbery, and a little afraid of it.

"Remember what we talked about so much?" Bigger asked in a flat, neutral tone.

"Naw."

"Old Blum."

"Oh," Gus said. "We ain't talked about that for a month. How come you think of it all of a sudden?"

"Let's clean the place out."

"I don't know."

"It was your plan from the start," Bigger said.

Gus straightened and stared at Bigger, then at Doc who was looking out of the front window.

"You going to tell Doc? Can't you never learn to talk low?"

"Aw, I was just asking you, do you want to try it?"

"Naw."

"How come? You scared 'cause he's a white man?"

"Naw. But Blum keeps a gun. Suppose he beats us to it?"

"Aw, you scared; that's all. He's a white man and you scared."

"The hell I'm scared," Gus, hurt and stung, defended himself.

Bigger went to Gus and placed an arm about his shoulders.

"Listen, you won't have to go in. You just stand at the door and keep watch, see? Me and Jack and G.H.'ll go in. If anybody comes along, you whistle and we'll go out the back way. That's all."

The front door opened; they stopped talking and turned their heads.

"Here comes Jack and G.H. now," Bigger said.

Jack and G.H. walked to the rear of the poolroom.

"What you guys doing?" Jack asked.

"Shooting a game. Wanna play?" Bigger asked.

"You asking 'em to play and I'm paying for the game," Gus said.

They all laughed and Bigger laughed with them but stopped quickly. He felt that the joke was on him and he took a seat alongside the wall and propped his feet upon the rungs of a chair, as though he had not heard. Gus and G.H. kept on laughing.

"You niggers is crazy," Bigger said. "You laugh like monkeys and you ain't got nerve enough to do nothing but talk."

"What you mean?" G.H. asked.

"I got a haul all figured out," Bigger said.

"What haul?"

"Old Blum's."

There was silence. Jack lit a cigarette. Gus looked away, avoiding the conversation.

"If old Blum was a black man, you-all would be itching to go. 'Cause he's white, everybody's scared."

"I ain't scared," Jack said. "I'm with you."

"You say you got it all figured out?" G.H. asked.

Bigger took a deep breath and looked from face to face. It seemed to him that he should not have to explain.

"Look, it'll be easy. There ain't nothing to be scared of. Between three and four ain't nobody in the store but the old man. The cop is way down at the other end of the block. One of us'll stay outside and watch. Three of us'll go in, see? One of us'll throw a gun on old Blum; one of us'll make for the cash box under the counter; one of us'll make for the back door and have it open so we can make a quick get-away down the back alley. . . . That's all. It won't take three minutes."

"I thought we said we wasn't never going to use a gun," G.H. said. "And we ain't bothered no white folks before."

"Can't you see? This is something *big*," Bigger said.

He waited for more objections. When none were forth-coming, he talked again.

"We can do it, if you niggers ain't scared."

Save for the sound of Doc's whistling up front, there was silence. Bigger watched Jack closely; he knew that the situa-tion was one in which Jack's word would be decisive. Bigger was afraid of Gus, because he knew that Gus would not hold out if Jack said yes. Gus stood at the table, toying with a cue stick, his eyes straying lazily over the billiard balls scattered about the table in the array of an unfinished game. Bigger rose and sent the balls whirling with a sweep of his hand, then looked straight at Gus as the gleaming balls kissed and rebounded from the rubber cushions, zig-zagging across the table's green cloth. Even though Bigger had asked Gus to be with him in the robbery, the fear that Gus would really go made the muscles of Bigger's stomach tighten; he was hot all over. He felt as if he wanted to sneeze and could not; only it was more nervous than wanting to sneeze. He grew hotter, tighter; his nerves were taut and his teeth were on edge. He felt that something would soon snap within him.

"Goddammit! Say something, somebody!"

"I'm in," Jack said again.

"I'll go if the rest goes," G.H. said.

Gus stood without speaking and Bigger felt a curious sensa-tion—half-sensual, half-thoughtful. He was divided and pulled against himself. He had handled things just right so far; all but Gus had consented. The way things stood now there were three against Gus, and that was just as he had wanted it to be. Bigger was afraid of robbing a white man and he knew that Gus was afraid, too. Blum's store was small and Blum was alone, but Bigger could not think of robbing him without being flanked by his three pals. But even with his pals he was afraid. He had argued all of his pals but one into consenting to the robbery, and toward the lone man who held out he felt a hot hate and fear; he had transferred his fear of the whites to Gus. He hated Gus because he knew that

Gus was afraid, as even he was; and he feared Gus because
he felt that Gus would consent and then he would be compelled to go through with the robbery. Like a man about to
shoot himself and dreading to shoot and yet knowing that he
has to shoot and feeling it all at once and powerfully, he
watched Gus and waited for him to say yes. But Gus did not
speak. Bigger's teeth clamped so tight that his jaws ached. He
edged toward Gus, not looking at Gus, but feeling the presence of Gus over all his body, through him, in and out of him,
and hating himself and Gus because he felt it. Then he could
not stand it any longer. The hysterical tensity of his nerves
urged him to speak, to free himself. He faced Gus, his eyes
red with anger and fear, his fists clenched and held stiffly to
his sides.

"You black sonofabitch," he said in a voice that did not
vary in tone. "You scared 'cause he's a white man."

"Don't cuss me, Bigger," Gus said quietly.

"I *am* cussing you!"

"You don't have to cuss me," Gus said.

"Then why don't you use that black tongue of yours?"
Bigger asked. "Why don't you say what you going to do?"

"I don't have to use my tongue unless I *want* to!"

"You bastard! You scared bastard!"

"You ain't my boss," Gus said.

"You yellow!" Bigger said. "You scared to rob a white
man."

"Aw, Bigger. Don't say that," G.H. said. "Leave 'im alone."

"He's yellow," Bigger said. "He won't go with us."

"I didn't say I wouldn't go," Gus said.

"Then, for chrissakes, say what you going to do," Bigger
said.

Gus leaned on his cue stick and gazed at Bigger and Bigger's stomach tightened as though he were expecting a blow
and were getting ready for it. His fists clenched harder. In a
split second he felt how his fist and arm and body would feel
if he hit Gus squarely in the mouth, drawing blood; Gus

would fall and he would walk out and the whole thing would be over and the robbery would not take place. And his thinking and feeling in this way made the choking tightness rising from the pit of his stomach to his throat slacken a little.

"You see, Bigger," began Gus in a tone that was a compromise between kindness and pride. "You see, Bigger, you the cause of all the trouble we ever have. It's your hot temper. Now, how come you want to cuss me? Ain't I got a right to make up my mind? Naw; that ain't your way. You start cussing. You say I'm scared. It's *you* who's scared. You scared I'm going to say yes and you'll have to go through with the job. . . ."

"Say that again! Say that again and I'll take one of these balls and sink it in your goddamn mouth," Bigger said, his pride wounded to the quick.

"Aw, for chrissakes," Jack said.

"You *see* how he is," Gus said.

"Why don't you say what you going to do?" Bigger demanded.

"Aw, I'm going with you-all," Gus said in a nervous tone that sought to hide itself; a tone that hurried on to other things. "I'm going, but Bigger don't have to act like that. He don't have to cuss me."

"Why didn't you say that at first?" Bigger asked; his anger amounted almost to frenzy. "You make a man want to sock you!"

". . . I'll help on the haul," Gus continued, as though Bigger had not spoken. "I'll help just like I always help. But I'll be goddamn if I'm taking orders from *you*, Bigger! You just a scared coward! You calling me scared so nobody'll see how scared *you* is!"

Bigger leaped at him, but Jack ran between them. G.H. caught Gus's arm and led him aside.

"Who's asking you to take orders?" Bigger said. "I never want to give orders to a piss-sop like you!"

"You boys cut out that racket back there!" Doc called.

They stood silently about the pool table. Bigger's eyes followed Gus as Gus put his cue stick in the rack and brushed chalk dust from his trousers and walked a little distance away. Bigger's stomach burned and a hazy black cloud hovered a moment before his eyes, and left. Mixed images of violence ran like sand through his mind, dry and fast, vanishing. He could stab Gus with his knife; he could slap him; he could kick him; he could trip him up and send him sprawling on his face. He could do a lot of things to Gus for making him feel this way.

"Come on, G.H.," Gus said.

"Where we going?"

"Let's walk."

"O.K."

"What we gonna do?" Jack asked. "Meet here at three?"

"Sure," Bigger said. "Didn't we just decide?"

"I'll be here," Gus said, with his back turned.

When Gus and G.H. had gone Bigger sat down and felt cold sweat on his skin. It was planned now and he would have to go through with it. His teeth gritted and the last image he had seen of Gus going through the door lingered in his mind. He could have taken one of the cue sticks and gripped it hard and swung it at the back of Gus's head, feeling the impact of the hard wood cracking against the bottom of the skull. The tight feeling was still in him and he knew that it would remain until they were actually doing the job, until they were in the store taking the money.

"You and Gus sure don't get along none," Jack said, shaking his head.

Bigger turned and looked at Jack; he had forgotten that Jack was still there.

"Aw, that yellow black bastard," Bigger said.

"He's all right," Jack said.

"He's scared," Bigger said. "To make him ready for a job, you have to make him scared two ways. You have to make him more scared of what'll happen to him if he don't do the job than of what'll happen to him if he pulls the job."

"If we going to Blum's today, we oughtn't fuss like this," Jack said. "We got a job on our hands, a real job."

"Sure. Sure, I know," Bigger said.

Bigger felt an urgent need to hide his growing and deepening feeling of hysteria; he had to get rid of it or else he would succumb to it. He longed for a stimulus powerful enough to focus his attention and drain off his energies. He wanted to run. Or listen to some swing music. Or laugh or joke. Or read a *Real Detective Story Magazine.* Or go to a movie. Or visit Bessie. All that morning he had lurked behind his curtain of indifference and looked at things, snapping and glaring at whatever had tried to make him come out into the open. But now he was out; the thought of the job at Blum's and the tilt he had had with Gus had snared him into things and his self-trust was gone. Confidence could only come again now through action so violent that it would make him forget. These were the rhythms of his life: indifference and violence; periods of abstract brooding and periods of intense desire; moments of silence and moments of anger—like water ebbing and flowing from the tug of a far-away, invisible force. Being this way was a need of his as deep as eating. He was like a strange plant blooming in the day and wilting at night; but the sun that made it bloom and the cold darkness that made it wilt were never seen. It was his own sun and darkness, a private and personal sun and darkness. He was bitterly proud of his swiftly changing moods and boasted when he had to suffer the results of them. It was the way he was, he would say; he could not help it, he would say, and his head would wag. And it was his sullen stare and the violent action that followed that made Gus and Jack and G.H. hate and fear him as much as he hated and feared himself.

"Where you want to go?" Jack asked. "I'm tired of setting."

"Let's walk," Bigger said.

They went to the front door. Bigger paused and looked

round the poolroom with a wild and exasperated expression, his lips tightening with resolution.

"Goin'?" Doc asked, not moving his head.

"Yeah," Bigger said.

"See you later," Jack said.

They walked along the street in the morning sunshine. They waited leisurely at corners for cars to pass; it was not that they feared cars, but they had plenty of time. They reached South Parkway smoking freshly lit cigarettes.

"I'd like to see a movie," Bigger said.

"*Trader Horn's* running again at the Regal. They're bringing a lot of old pictures back."

"How much is it?"

"Twenty cents."

"O.K. Let's see it."

Bigger strode silently beside Jack for six blocks. It was noon when they reached Forty-seventh Street and South Parkway. The Regal was just opening. Bigger lingered in the lobby and looked at the colored posters while Jack bought the tickets. Two features were advertised: one, *The Gay Woman,* was pictured on the posters in images of white men and white women lolling on beaches, swimming, and dancing in night clubs; the other, *Trader Horn,* was shown on the posters in terms of black men and black women dancing against a wild background of barbaric jungle. Bigger looked up and saw Jack standing at his side.

"Come on. Let's go in," Jack said.

"O.K."

He followed Jack into the darkened movie. The shadows were soothing to his eyes after the glare of the sun. The picture had not started and he slouched far down in a seat and listened to a pipe organ shudder in waves of nostalgic tone, like a voice humming hauntingly within him. He moved restlessly, looking round as though expecting to see someone sneaking up on him. The organ sang forth full, then dropped almost to silence.

"You reckon we'll do all right at Blum's?" he asked in a drawling voice tinged with uneasiness.

"Aw, sure," Jack said; but his voice, too, was uneasy.

"You know, I'd just as soon go to jail as take that damn relief job," Bigger said.

"Don't say that. Everything'll be all right."

"You reckon it will?"

"Sure."

"I don't give a damn."

"Let's think about how we'll do it, not about how we'll get caught."

"Scared?"

"Naw. You?"

"Hell, naw!"

They were silent, listening to the organ. It sounded for a long moment on a trembling note, then died away. Then it stole forth again in whispering tones that could scarcely be heard.

"We better take our guns along this time," Bigger said.

"O.K. But we gotta be careful. We don't wanna kill nobody."

"Yeah. But I'll feel safer with a gun this time."

"Gee, I wished it was three o'clock now. I wished it was over."

"Me too."

The organ sighed into silence and the screen flashed with the rhythm of moving shadows. There was a short newsreel which Bigger watched without much interest. Then came *The Gay Woman* in which, amid scenes of cocktail drinking, dancing, golfing, swimming, and spinning roulette wheels, a rich young white woman kept clandestine appointments with her lover while her millionaire husband was busy in the offices of a vast paper mill. Several times Bigger nudged Jack in the ribs with his elbow as the giddy young woman duped her husband and kept from him the knowledge of what she was doing.

"She sure got her old man fooled," Bigger said.

"Looks like it. He's so busy making money he don't know what's going on," Jack said. "Them rich chicks'll do anything."

"Yeah. And she's a hot looking number, all right," Bigger said. "Say, maybe I'll be working for folks like that if I take that relief job. Maybe I'll be driving 'em around. . . ."

"Sure," Jack said. "Man, you ought to take that job. You don't know what you might run into. My ma used to work for rich white folks and you ought to hear the tales she used to tell. . . ."

"What she say?" Bigger asked eagerly.

"Ah, man, them rich white women'll go to bed with anybody, from a poodle on up. Shucks, they even have their chauffeurs. Say, if you run into anything on that new job that's too much for you to handle, let me know. . . ."

They laughed. The play ran on and Bigger saw a night club floor thronged with whirling couples and heard a swing band playing music. The rich young woman was dancing and laughing with her lover.

"I'd like to be invited to a place like that just to find out what it feels like," Bigger mused.

"Man, if them folks saw you they'd run," Jack said. "They'd think a gorilla broke loose from the zoo and put on a tuxedo."

They bent over low in their seats and giggled without restraint. When Bigger sat up again he saw the picture flashing on. A tall waiter was serving two slender glasses of drinks to the rich young woman and her lover.

"I bet their mattresses is stuffed with paper dollars," Bigger said.

"Man, them folks don't even have to turn over in their sleep," Jack said. "A butler stands by their beds at night, and when he hears 'em sigh, he gently rolls 'em over. . . ."

They laughed again, then fell silent abruptly. The music accompanying the picture dropped to a low, rumbling note and the rich young woman turned and looked toward the front door of the night club from which a chorus of shouts and screams was heard.

"I bet it's her husband," Jack said.

"Yeah," Bigger said.

Bigger saw a sweating, wild-eyed young man fight his way past a group of waiters and whirling dancers.

"He looks like a crazy man," Jack said.

"What you reckon he wants?" Bigger asked, as though he himself was outraged at the sight of the frenzied intruder.

"Damn if I know," Jack muttered preoccupiedly.

Bigger watched the wild young man elude the waiters and run in the direction of the rich woman's table. The music of the swing band stopped and men and women scurried frantically into corners and doorways. There were shouts: *Stop 'im! Grab 'im!* The wild man halted a few feet from the rich woman and reached inside of his coat and drew forth a black object. There were more screams: *He's got a bomb! Stop 'im!* Bigger saw the woman's lover leap to the center of the floor, fling his hands high into the air and catch the bomb just as the wild man threw it. As the rich woman fainted, her lover hurled the bomb out of a window, shattering a pane. Bigger saw a white flash light up the night outside as the bomb exploded deafeningly. Then he was looking at the wild man who was now pinned to the floor by a dozen hands. He heard a woman scream: *He's a Communist!*

"Say, Jack?"

"Hunh?"

"What's a Communist?"

"A Communist is a red, ain't he?"

"Yeah; but what's a red?"

"Damn if I know. It's a race of folks who live in Russia, ain't it?"

"They must be wild."

"Looks like it. That guy was trying to kill somebody."

The scenes showed the wild man weeping on his knees and cursing through his tears. *I wanted to kill 'em,* he sobbed.

Bigger now understood that the wild bomb-thrower was a Communist who had mistaken the rich woman's lover for her husband and had tried to kill him.

"Reds must don't like rich folks," Jack said.

"They sure must don't," Bigger said. "Every time you hear about one, he's trying to kill somebody or tear things up."

The picture continued and showed the rich young woman in a fit of remorse, telling her lover that she thanked him for saving her life, but that what had happened had taught her that her husband needed her. *Suppose it had been he?* she whimpered.

"She's going back to her old man," Bigger said.

"Oh, yeah," Jack said. "They got to kiss in the end."

Bigger saw the rich young woman rush home to her millionaire husband. There were long embraces and kisses as the rich woman and the rich man vowed never to leave each other and to forgive each other.

"You reckon folks really act like that?" Bigger asked, full of the sense of a life he had never seen.

"Sure, man. They rich," Jack said.

"I wonder if this guy I'm going to work for is a rich man like that?" Bigger asked.

"Maybe so," Jack said.

"Shucks. I got a great mind to take that job," Bigger said.

"Sure. You don't know what you might see."

They laughed. Bigger turned his eyes to the screen, but he did not look. He was filled with a sense of excitement about his new job. Was what he had heard about rich white people really true? Was he going to work for people like you saw in the movies? If he were, then he'd see a lot of things from the inside; he'd get the dope, the low-down. He looked at *Trader Horn* unfold and saw pictures of naked black men and women whirling in wild dances and heard drums beating and then gradually the African scene changed and was replaced by images in his own mind of white men and women dressed in black and white clothes, laughing, talking, drinking and dancing. Those were smart people: they knew how to get hold of money, millions of it. Maybe if he were working for them something would happen and he would get some of it. He would see just how they did it. Sure, it was all a game and white people knew how to play it. And rich white people were not so hard on Negroes: it was the poor whites who hated Negroes. They hated Negroes because they didn't have their share of the money. His mother had always told him that rich white people liked Negroes better than they did poor whites. He felt that if he were a poor white and did not get his share of the money, then he would deserve to be kicked. Poor white people were stupid. It was the rich white people who were smart and knew how to treat people. He remembered hearing somebody tell a story of a Negro chauffeur who had married a rich white girl and the girl's family had shipped the couple out of the country and had supplied them with money.

Yes, his going to work for the Daltons was something big. Maybe Mr. Dalton was a millionaire. Maybe he had a daughter who was a hot kind of girl; maybe she spent lots of money; maybe she'd like to come to the South Side and see the sights sometimes. Or maybe she had a secret sweetheart and only he would know about it because he would have to drive her around; maybe she would give him money not to tell.

He was a fool for wanting to rob Blum's just when he was about to get a good job. Why hadn't he thought of that before? Why take a fool's chance when other things, big things, could happen? If something slipped up this afternoon he would be out of a job and in jail, maybe. And he wasn't so hot about robbing Blum's, anyway. He frowned in the darkened movie, hearing the roll of tom-toms and the screams of black men and women dancing free and wild, men and women who were adjusted to their soil and at home in their world, secure from fear and hysteria.

"Come on, Bigger," Jack said. "We gotta go."

"Hunh?"

"It's twenty to three."

He rose and walked down the dark aisle over the soft, invisible carpet. He had seen practically nothing of the picture, but he did not care. As he walked into the lobby his insides tightened again with the thought of Gus and Blum's.

"Swell, wasn't it?"

"Yeah; it was a killer," Bigger said.

He walked alongside Jack briskly until they came to Thirty-ninth Street.

"We better get our guns," Bigger said.

"Yeah."

"We got about fifteen minutes."

"O.K."

"So long."

He walked home with a mounting feeling of fear. When he reached his doorway, he hesitated about going up. He didn't want to rob Blum's; he was scared. But he had to go through with it now. Noiselessly, he went up the steps and inserted his key in the lock; the door swung in silently and he heard his mother singing behind the curtain.

> Lord, I want to be a Christian,
> In my heart, in my heart,
> Lord, I want to be a Christian,
> In my heart, in my heart. . . .

He tiptoed into the room and lifted the top mattress of his bed and pulled forth the gun and slipped it inside of his shirt. Just as he was about to open the door his mother paused in her singing.

"That you, Bigger?"

He stepped quickly into the outer hallway and slammed the door and bounded headlong down the stairs. He went to the vestibule and swung through the door into the street, feeling that ball of hot tightness growing larger and heavier in his stomach and chest. He opened his mouth to breathe.

He headed for Doc's and came to the door and looked inside. Jack and G.H. were shooting pool at a rear table. Gus was not there. He felt a slight lessening of nervous tension and swallowed. He looked up and down the street; very few people were out and the cop was not in sight. A clock in a window across the street told him that it was twelve minutes to three. Well, this was it; he had to go in. He lifted his left hand and wiped sweat from his forehead in a long slow gesture. He hesitated a moment longer at the door, then went in, walking with firm steps to the rear table. He did not speak to Jack or G.H., nor they to him. He lit a cigarette with shaking fingers and watched the spinning billiard balls roll and gleam and clack over the green stretch of cloth, dropping into holes after bounding to and fro from the rubber cushions. He felt impelled to say something to ease the swelling in his chest. Hurriedly, he flicked his cigarette into a spittoon and, with twin eddies of blue smoke jutting from his black nostrils, shouted hoarsely,

"Jack, I betcha two bits you can't make it!"

Jack did not answer; the ball shot straight across the table and vanished into a side pocket.

"You would've lost," Jack said.

"Too late now," Bigger said. "You wouldn't bet, so *you* lost."

He spoke without looking. His entire body hungered for keen sensation, something exciting and violent to relieve the tautness. It was now ten minutes to three and Gus had not come. If Gus stayed away much longer, it would be too late. And Gus knew that. If they were going to do anything, it certainly ought to be done before folks started coming into the streets to buy their food for supper, and while the cop was down at the other end of the block.

"That bastard!" Bigger said. "I knew it!"

"Oh, he'll be along," Jack said.

"Sometimes I'd like to cut his yellow heart out," Bigger said, fingering the knife in his pocket.

"Maybe he's hanging around some meat," G.H. said.

"He's just scared," Bigger said. "Scared to rob a white man."

The billiard balls clacked. Jack chalked his cue stick and the metallic noise made Bigger grit his teeth until they ached. He didn't like that noise; it made him feel like cutting something with his knife.

"If he makes us miss this job, I'll fix 'im, so help me," Bigger said. "He oughtn't be late. Every time somebody's late, things go wrong. Look at the big guys. You don't ever hear of them being late, do you? Naw! They work like clocks!"

"Ain't none of us got more guts'n Gus," G.H. said. "He's been with us every time."

"Aw, shut your trap," Bigger said.

"There you go again, Bigger," G.H. said. "Gus was just talking about how you act this morning. You get too nervous when something's coming off. . . ."

"Don't tell me I'm nervous," Bigger said.

"If we don't do it today, we can do it tomorrow," Jack said.

"Tomorrow's Sunday, fool!"

"Bigger, for chrissakes! Don't holler!" Jack said tensely.

Bigger looked at Jack hard and long, then turned away with a grimace.

"Don't tell the world what we're trying to do," Jack whispered in a mollifying tone.

Bigger walked to the front of the store and stood looking out of the plate glass window. Then, suddenly, he felt sick. He saw Gus coming along the street. And his muscles stiffened. He was going to do something to Gus; just what, he did not know. As Gus neared he heard him whistling: "The Mer-ry-Go-Round Broke Down. . . ." The door swung in.

"Hi, Bigger," Gus said.

Bigger did not answer. Gus passed him and started toward the rear tables. Bigger whirled and kicked him hard. Gus flopped on his face with a single movement of his body. With a look that showed that he was looking at Gus on the floor and at Jack and G.H. at the rear table and at Doc—looking at them all at once in a kind of smiling, roving, turning-slowly glance—Bigger laughed, softly at first, then harder, louder, hysterically; feeling something like hot water bubbling inside of him and trying to come out. Gus got up and stood, quiet, his mouth open and his eyes dead-black with hate.

"Take it easy, boys," Doc said, looking up from behind his counter, and then bending over again.

"What you kick me for?" Gus asked.

"'Cause I wanted to," Bigger said.

Gus looked at Bigger with lowered eyes. G.H. and Jack leaned on their cue sticks and watched silently.

"I'm going to fix you one of these days," Gus threatened.

"Say that again," Bigger said.

Doc laughed, straightening and looking at Bigger.

"Lay off the boy, Bigger."

Gus turned and walked toward the rear tables. Bigger, with an amazing bound, grabbed him in the back of his collar.

"I asked you to say that again!"

"Quit, Bigger!" Gus spluttered, choking, sinking to his knees.

"Don't tell me to quit!"

The muscles of his body gave a tightening lunge and he saw his fist come down on the side of Gus's head; he had struck him really before he was conscious of doing so.

"Don't hurt 'im," Jack said.

"I'll kill 'im," Bigger said through shut teeth, tightening his hold on Gus's collar, choking him harder.

"T-turn m-m-m-me l-loose." Gus gurgled, struggling.

"Make me!" Bigger said, drawing his fingers tighter.

Gus was very still, resting on his knees. Then, like a taut bow finding release, he sprang to his feet, shaking loose from Bigger and turning to get away. Bigger staggered back against the wall, breathless for a moment. Bigger's hand moved so swiftly that nobody saw it; a gleaming blade flashed. He made a long step, as graceful as an animal leaping, threw out his left foot and tripped Gus to the floor. Gus turned over to rise, but Bigger was on top of him, with the knife open and ready.

"Get up! Get up and I'll slice your tonsils!"

Gus lay still.

"That's all right, Bigger," Gus said in surrender. "Lemme up."

"You trying to make a fool out of me, ain't you?"

"Naw," Gus said, his lips scarcely moving.

"You goddamn right you ain't." Bigger said.

His face softened a bit and the hard glint in his bloodshot eyes died. But he still knelt with the open knife. Then he stood.

"Get up!" he said.

"Please, Bigger!"

"You want me to slice you?"

He stooped again and placed the knife at Gus's throat. Gus did not move and his large black eyes looked pleadingly. Bigger was not satisfied: he felt his muscles tightening again.

"Get up! I ain't going to ask you no more!"

Slowly, Gus stood. Bigger held the open blade an inch from Gus's lips.

"Lick it," Bigger said, his body tingling with elation.

Gus's eyes filled with tears.

"Lick it, I said! You think I'm playing?"

Gus looked round the room without moving his head, just rolling his eyes in a mute appeal for help. But no one moved. Bigger's left fist was slowly lifting to strike. Gus's lips moved toward the knife; he stuck out his tongue and touched the blade. Gus's lips quivered and tears streamed down his cheeks.

"Hahahaha!" Doc laughed.

"Aw, leave 'im alone," Jack called.

Bigger watched Gus with lips twisted in a crooked smile.

"Say, Bigger, ain't you scared 'im enough?" Doc asked.

Bigger did not answer. His eyes gleamed hard again, pregnant with another idea.

"Put your hands up, way up!" he said.

Gus swallowed and stretched his hands high along the wall.

"Leave 'im alone, Bigger," G.H. called weakly.

"I'm doing this," Bigger said.

He put the tip of the blade into Gus's shirt and then made an arc with his arm, as though cutting a circle.

"How would you like me to cut your belly button out?"

Gus did not answer. Sweat trickled down his temples. His lips hung wide, loose.

"Shut them liver lips of yours!"

Gus did not move a muscle. Bigger pushed the knife harder into Gus's stomach.

"Bigger!" Gus said in a tense whisper.

"Shut your mouth!"

Gus shut his mouth. Doc laughed. Jack and G.H. laughed. Then Bigger stepped back and looked at Gus with a smile.

"You clown," he said. "Put your hands down and set on that chair." He watched Gus sit. "That ought to teach you not to be late next time, see?"

"We ain't late, Bigger. We still got time. . . ."

"Shut up! It *is* late!" Bigger insisted commandingly.

Bigger turned aside; then, hearing a sharp scrape on the floor, stiffened. Gus sprang from the chair and grabbed a billiard ball from the table and threw it with a half-sob and half-curse. Bigger flung his hands upward to shield his face and the impact of the ball struck his wrist. He had shut his eyes when he had glimpsed the ball sailing through the air toward him and when he opened his eyes Gus was flying through the rear door and at the same time he heard the ball hit the floor and roll away. A hard pain throbbed in his hand. He sprang forward, cursing.

"You sonofabitch!"

He slipped on a cue stick lying in the middle of the floor and tumbled forward.

"That's enough now, Bigger," Doc said, laughing.

Jack and G.H. also laughed. Bigger rose and faced them, holding his hurt hand. His eyes were red and he stared with speechless hate.

"Just keep laughing," he said.

"Behave yourself, boy," Doc said.

"Just keep laughing," Bigger said again, taking out his knife.

"Watch what you're doing now," Doc cautioned.

"Aw, Bigger," Jack said, backing away toward the rear door.

"You done spoiled things now," G.H. said. "I reckon that was what you wanted. . . ."

"You go to hell!" Bigger shouted, drowning out G.H.'s voice.

Doc bent down behind the counter and when he stood up he had something in his hand which he did not show. He stood there laughing. White spittle showed at the corners of Bigger's lips. He walked to the billiard table, his eyes on Doc. Then he began to cut the green cloth on the table with long sweeping strokes of his arm. He never took his eyes from Doc's face.

"Why, you sonofabitch!" Doc said. "I ought to shoot you, so help me God! Get out, before I call a cop!"

Bigger walked slowly past Doc, looking at him, not hurrying, and holding the open knife in his hand. He paused in the doorway and looked back. Jack and G.H. were gone.

"Get out of here!" Doc said, showing a gun.

"Don't you like it?" Bigger asked.

"Get out before I shoot you!" Doc said. "And don't you ever set your black feet inside here again!"

Doc was angry and Bigger was afraid. He shut the knife and slipped it in his pocket and swung through the door to the street. He blinked his eyes from the bright sunshine; his nerves were so taut that he had difficulty in breathing. Halfway down the block he passed Blum's store; he looked out of the corners of his eyes through the plate glass window and saw that Blum was alone and the store was empty of customers. Yes; they would have had time to rob the store; in fact, they still had time. He had lied to Gus and G.H. and Jack. He walked on; there was not a policeman in sight. Yes; they could have robbed the store and could have gotten away. He hoped the fight he had had with Gus covered up what he was trying to hide. At least the fight made him feel the equal of them. And he felt the equal of Doc, too; had he not slashed his table and dared him to use his gun?

He had an overwhelming desire to be alone; he walked to the middle of the next block and turned into an alley. He began to laugh, softly, tensely; he stopped still in his tracks and felt something warm roll down his cheek and he brushed it away. "Jesus," he breathed. "I laughed so hard I cried." Carefully, he dried his face on his coat sleeve, then stood for two whole minutes staring at the shadow of a telephone pole on the alley pavement. Suddenly he straightened and walked on with a single expulsion of breath. "What the hell!" He stumbled violently over a tiny crack in the pavement. "Goddamn!" he said. When he reached the end of the alley, he turned into a street, walking slowly in the sunshine, his hands jammed deep into his pockets, his head down, depressed.

He went home and sat in a chair by the window, looking out dreamily.

"That you, Bigger?" his mother called from behind the curtain.

"Yeah," he said.

"What you run in here and run out for, a little while ago?"

"Nothing."

"Don't you go and get into no trouble, now, boy."

"Aw, Ma! Leave me alone."

He listened awhile to her rubbing clothes on the metal washboard, then he gazed abstractedly into the street, thinking of how he had felt when he fought Gus in Doc's poolroom. He was relieved and glad that in an hour he was going to see about that job at the Dalton place. He was disgusted with the gang; he knew that what had happened today put an end to his being with them in any more jobs. Like a man staring regretfully but hopelessly at the stump of a cut-off arm or leg, he knew that the fear of robbing a white man had had hold of him when he started that fight with Gus; but he knew it in a way that kept it from coming to his mind in the form of a hard and sharp idea. His confused emotions had made him feel instinctively that it would be better to fight Gus and spoil the plan of the robbery than to confront a white man with a gun. But he kept this knowledge of his fear thrust firmly down in him; his courage to live depended upon how successfully his fear was hidden from his consciousness. He had fought Gus because Gus was late; that was the reason his emotions accepted and he did not try to justify himself in his own eyes, or in the eyes of the gang. He did not think enough of them to feel that he had to; he did not consider himself as being responsible to them for what he did, even though they had been involved as deeply as he in the planned robbery. He felt that same way toward everyone. As long as he could remember, he had never been responsible to anyone. The moment a situation became so that it exacted something of him, he rebelled. That was the way he lived; he passed his days trying to defeat or gratify powerful impulses in a world he feared.

Outside his window he saw the sun dying over the rooftops in the western sky and watched the first shade of dusk fall. Now and then a street car ran past. The rusty radiator hissed at the far end of the room. All day long it had been springlike; but now dark clouds were slowly swallowing the sun. All at once the street lamps came on and the sky was black and close to the house-tops.

Inside his shirt he felt the cold metal of the gun resting against his naked skin; he ought to put it back between the mattresses. No! He would keep it. He would take it with him to the Dalton place. He felt that he would be safer if he took it. He was not planning to use it and there was nothing in particular that he was afraid of, but there was in him an uneasiness and distrust that made him feel that he ought to have it along. He was going among white people, so he would take his knife and his gun; it would make him feel that he was the equal of them, give him a sense of completeness. Then he thought of a good reason why he should take it; in order to get to the Dalton place, he had to go through a white neighborhood. He had not heard of any Negroes being molested recently, but he felt that it was always possible.

Far away a clock boomed five times. He sighed and got up and yawned and stretched his arms high above his head to loosen the muscles of his body. He got his overcoat, for it was growing cold outdoors; then got his cap. He tiptoed to the door, wanting to slip out without his mother hearing him. Just as he was about to open it, she called,

"Bigger!"

He stopped and frowned.

"Yeah, Ma."

"You going to see about that job?"

"Yeah."

"Ain't you going to eat?"

"I ain't got time now."

She came to the door, wiping her soapy hands upon an apron.

"Here; take this quarter and buy you something."

"O.K."

"And be careful, son."

He went out and walked south to Forty-sixth Street, then eastward. Well, he would see in a few moments if the Daltons for whom he was to work were like the people he had seen and heard in the movie. But while walking through this quiet and spacious white neighborhood, he did not feel the pull and mystery of the thing as strongly as he had in the movie. The houses he passed were huge; lights glowed softly in win-

dows. The streets were empty, save for an occasional car that
zoomed past on swift rubber tires. This was a cold and distant
world; a world of white secrets carefully guarded. He could
feel a pride, a certainty, and a confidence in these streets and
houses. He came to Drexel Boulevard and began to look for
4605. When he came to it, he stopped and stood before a
high, black, iron picket fence, feeling constricted inside. All
he had felt in the movie was gone; only fear and emptiness
filled him now.

Would they expect him to come in the front way or back?
It was queer that he had not thought of that. Goddamn! He
walked the length of the picket fence in front of the house,
seeking for a walk leading to the rear. But there was none.
Other than the front gate, there was only a driveway, the
entrance to which was securely locked. Suppose a policeman
saw him wandering in a white neighborhood like this? It
would be thought that he was trying to rob or rape somebody. He grew angry. Why had he come to take this goddamn job? He could have stayed among his own people and
escaped feeling this fear and hate. This was not his world; he
had been foolish in thinking that he would have liked it. He
stood in the middle of the sidewalk with his jaws clamped
tight; he wanted to strike something with his fists. Well
. . . Goddamn! There was nothing to do but go in the front
way. If he were doing wrong, they could not kill him, at least;
all they could do was to tell him that he could not get the job.

Timidly, he lifted the latch on the gate and walked to the
steps. He paused, waiting for someone to challenge him.
Nothing happened. Maybe nobody was home? He went to
the door and saw a dim light burning in a shaded niche above
a doorbell. He pushed it and was startled to hear a soft gong
sound within. Maybe he had pushed it too hard? Aw, what
the hell! He had to do better than this; he relaxed his taut
muscles and stood at ease, waiting. The doorknob turned.
The door opened. He saw a white face. It was a woman.

"Hello!"

"Yessum," he said.

"You want to see somebody?"

"Er . . . Er . . . I want to see Mr. Dalton."

"Are you the Thomas boy?"

"Yessum."

"Come in."

He edged through the door slowly, then stopped halfway. The woman was so close to him that he could see a tiny mole at the corner of her mouth. He held his breath. It seemed that there was not room enough for him to pass without actually touching her.

"Come on in," the woman said.

"Yessum," he whispered.

He squeezed through and stood uncertainly in a softly lighted hallway.

"Follow me," she said.

With cap in hand and shoulders sloped, he followed, walking over a rug so soft and deep that it seemed he was going to fall at each step he took. He went into a dimly lit room.

"Take a seat," she said. "I'll tell Mr. Dalton that you're here and he'll be out in a moment."

"Yessum."

He sat and looked up at the woman; she was staring at him and he looked away in confusion. He was glad when she left. That old bastard! What's so damn funny about me? I'm just like she is. . . . He felt that the position in which he was sitting was too awkward and found that he was on the very edge of the chair. He rose slightly to sit farther back; but when he sat he sank down so suddenly and deeply that he thought the chair had collapsed under him. He bounded halfway up, in fear; then, realizing what had happened, he sank distrustfully down again. He looked round the room; it was lit by dim lights glowing from a hidden source. He tried to find them by roving his eyes, but could not. He had not expected anything like this; he had not thought that this world would be so utterly different from his own that it would intimidate him. On the smooth walls were several paintings whose nature he tried to make out, but failed. He would have liked to examine them, but dared not. Then he listened; a faint sound of piano music floated to him from somewhere. He was sitting in a white home; dim lights burned round him; strange objects challenged him; and he was feeling angry and uncomfortable.

"All right. Come this way."

He started at the sound of a man's voice.

"Suh?"

"Come this way."

Misjudging how far back he was sitting in the chair, his first attempt to rise failed and he slipped back, resting on his side. Grabbing the arms of the chair, he pulled himself upright and found a tall, lean, white-haired man holding a piece of paper in his hand. The man was gazing at him with an amused smile that made him conscious of every square inch of skin on his black body.

"Thomas?" the man asked. "Bigger Thomas?"

"Yessuh," he whispered; not speaking, really, but hearing his words issue involuntarily from his lips, as of a force of their own.

"Come this way."

"Yessuh."

He followed the man out of the room and down a hall. The man stopped abruptly. Bigger paused, bewildered; then he saw coming slowly toward him a tall, thin, white woman, walking silently, her hands lifted delicately in the air and touching the walls to either side of her. Bigger stepped back to let her pass. Her face and hair were completely white; she seemed to him like a ghost. The man took her arm gently and held her for a moment. Bigger saw that she was old and her gray eyes looked stony.

"Are you all right?" the man asked.

"Yes," she answered.

"Where's Peggy?"

"She's preparing dinner. I'm quite all right, Henry."

"You shouldn't be alone this way. When is Mrs. Patterson coming back?" the man asked.

"She'll be back Monday. But Mary's here. I'm all right; don't worry about me. Is someone with you?"

"Oh, yes. This is the boy the relief sent."

"The relief people were very anxious for you to work for us," the woman said; she did not move her body or face as she talked, but she spoke in a tone of voice that indicated that she was speaking to Bigger. "I hope you'll like it here."

"Yessum," Bigger whispered faintly, wondering as he did so if he ought to say anything at all.

"How far did you go in school?"

"To the eighth grade, mam."

"Don't you think it would be a wise procedure to inject him into his new environment at once, so he could get the feel of things?" the woman asked, addressing herself by the tone of her voice to the man now.

"Well, tomorrow'll be time enough," the man said hesitantly.

"I think it's important emotionally that he feels free to trust his environment," the woman said. "Using the analysis contained in the case record the relief sent us, I think we should evoke an immediate feeling of confidence . . ."

"But that's too abrupt," the man said.

Bigger listened, blinking and bewildered. The long strange words they used made no sense to him; it was another language. He felt from the tone of their voices that they were having a difference of opinion about him, but he could not determine what it was about. It made him uneasy, tense, as though there were influences and presences about him which he could feel but not see. He felt strangely blind.

"Well, let's try it," the woman said.

"Oh, all right. We'll see. We'll see," the man said.

The man let go of the woman and she walked on slowly, the long white fingers of her hands just barely touching the walls. Behind the woman, following at the hem of her dress, was a big white cat, pacing without sound. She's blind! Bigger thought in amazement.

"Come on; this way," the man said.

"Yessuh."

He wondered if the man had seen him staring at the woman. He would have to be careful here. There were so many strange things. He followed the man into a room.

"Sit down."

"Yessuh," he said, sitting.

"That was Mrs. Dalton," the man said. "She's blind."

"Yessuh."

"She has a very deep interest in colored people."

"Yessuh," Bigger whispered. He was conscious of the effort to breathe; he licked his lips and fumbled nervously with his cap.

"Well, I'm Mr. Dalton."

"Yessuh."

"Do you think you'd like driving a car?"

"Oh, yessuh."

"Did you bring the paper?"

"Suh?"

"Didn't the relief give you a note to me?"

"Oh, yessuh!"

He had completely forgotten about the paper. He stood to reach into his vest pocket and, in doing so, dropped his cap. For a moment his impulses were deadlocked; he did not know if he should pick up his cap and then find the paper, or find the paper and then pick up his cap. He decided to pick up his cap.

"Put your cap here," said Mr. Dalton, indicating a place on his desk.

"Yessuh."

Then he was stone-still; the white cat bounded past him and leaped upon the desk; it sat looking at him with large placid eyes and mewed plaintively.

"What's the matter, Kate?" Mr. Dalton asked, stroking the cat's fur and smiling. Mr. Dalton turned back to Bigger. "Did you find it?"

"Nawsuh. But I got it here, somewhere."

He hated himself at that moment. Why was he acting and feeling this way? He wanted to wave his hand and blot out the white man who was making him feel like this. If not that, he wanted to blot himself out. He had not raised his eyes to the level of Mr. Dalton's face once since he had been in the house. He stood with his knees slightly bent, his lips partly open, his shoulders stooped; and his eyes held a look that went only to the surface of things. There was an organic conviction in him that this was the way white folks wanted him to be when in their presence; none had ever told him that in so many words, but their manner had made him feel that they did. He laid the cap down, noticing that Mr. Dalton was watching him closely. Maybe he was not acting right? Goddamn! Clumsily, he searched for the paper. He could not find it at first and he felt called upon to say something for taking so long.

"I had it right here in my vest pocket," he mumbled.

"Take your time."

"Oh, here it is."

He drew the paper forth. It was crumpled and soiled. Nervously, he straightened it out and handed it to Mr. Dalton, holding it by its very tip end.

"All right, now," said Mr. Dalton. "Let's see what you've got here. You live at 3721 Indiana Avenue?"

"Yessuh."

Mr. Dalton paused, frowned, and looked up at the ceiling.

"What kind of a building is that over there?"

"You mean where I live, suh?"

"Yes."

"Oh, it's just an old building."

"Where do you pay rent?"

"Down on Thirty-first Street."

"To the South Side Real Estate Company?"

"Yessuh."

Bigger wondered what all these questions could mean; he had heard that Mr. Dalton owned the South Side Real Estate Company, but he was not sure.

"How much rent do you pay?"

"Eight dollars a week."

"For how many rooms?"

"We just got one, suh."

"I see. . . . Now, Bigger, tell me, how old are you?"

"I'm twenty, suh."

"Married?"

"Nawsuh."

"Sit down. You needn't stand. And I won't be long."

"Yessuh."

He sat. The white cat still contemplated him with large, moist eyes.

"Now, you have a mother, a brother, and a sister?"

"Yessuh."

"There are four of you?"

"Yessuh, there's four of us," he stammered, trying to show that he was not as stupid as he might appear. He felt a need to speak more, for he felt that maybe Mr. Dalton expected it. And he suddenly remembered the many times his mother had told him not to look at the floor when talking with white folks or asking for a job. He lifted his eyes and saw Mr. Dalton watching him closely. He dropped his eyes again.

"They call you Bigger?"

"Yessuh."

"Now, Bigger, I'd like to talk with you a little. . . ."

Yes, goddammit! He knew what was coming. He would be asked about that time he had been accused of stealing auto tires and had been sent to the reform school. He felt guilty, condemned. He should not have come here.

"The relief people said some funny things about you. I'd like to talk to you about them. Now, you needn't feel ashamed with me," said Mr. Dalton, smiling. "I was a boy myself once and I think I know how things are. So just be yourself. . . ." Mr. Dalton pulled out a package of cigarettes. "Here; have one."

"Nawsuh; thank you, suh."

"You don't smoke?"

"Yessuh. But I just don't want one now."

"Now, Bigger, the relief people said you were a very good worker when you were interested in what you were doing. Is that true?"

"Well, I do my work, suh."

"But they said you were always in trouble. How do you explain that?"

"I don't know, suh."

"Why did they send you to the reform school?"

His eyes glared at the floor.

"They said I was stealing!" he blurted defensively. "But I wasn't."

"Are you sure?"

"Yessuh."

"Well, how did you get mixed up in it?"

"I was with some boys and the police picked us up."

Mr. Dalton said nothing. Bigger heard a clock ticking somewhere behind him and he had a foolish impulse to look at it. But he restrained himself.

"Well, Bigger, how do you feel about it now?"

"Suh? 'Bout what?"

"If you had a job, would you steal now?"

"Oh, nawsuh. I don't steal."

"Well," said Mr. Dalton, "they say you can drive a car and I'm going to give you a job."

He said nothing.

"You think you can handle it?"

"Oh, yessuh."

"The pay calls for $20 a week, but I'm going to give you $25. The extra $5 is for yourself, for you to spend as you like.

You will get the clothes you need and your meals. You're to sleep in the back room, above the kitchen. You can give the $20 to your mother to keep your brother and sister in school. How does that sound?"

"It sounds all right. Yessuh."

"I think we'll get along."

"Yessuh."

"I don't think we'll have any trouble."

"Nawsuh."

"Now, Bigger," said Mr. Dalton, "since that's settled, let's see what you'll have to do every day. I leave every morning for my office at nine. It's a twenty-minute drive. You are to be back at ten and take Miss Dalton to school. At twelve, you call for Miss Dalton at the University. From then until night you are more or less free. If either Miss Dalton or I go out at night, of course, you do the driving. You work every day, but we don't get up till noon on Sundays. So you will have Sunday mornings to yourself, unless something unexpected happens. You get one full day off every two weeks."

"Yessuh."

"You think you can handle that?"

"Oh, yessuh."

"And any time you're bothered about anything, come and see me. Let's talk it over."

"Yessuh."

"Oh, Father!" a girl's voice sang out.

"Yes, Mary," said Mr. Dalton.

Bigger turned and saw a white girl walk into the room. She was very slender.

"Oh, I didn't know you were busy."

"That's all right, Mary. What is it?"

Bigger saw that the girl was looking at him.

"Is this the new chauffeur, Father?"

"What do you want, Mary?"

"Will you get the tickets for the Thursday concert?"

"At Orchestra Hall?"

"Yes."

"Yes. I'll get them."

"Is this the new chauffeur?"

"Yes," said Mr. Dalton. "This is Bigger Thomas."

"Hello, Bigger," the girl said.

Bigger swallowed. He looked at Mr. Dalton, then felt that he should not have looked.

"Good evening, mam."

The girl came close to him and stopped just opposite his chair.

"Bigger, do you belong to a union?" she asked.

"Now, Mary!" said Mr. Dalton, frowning.

"Well, Father, he should," the girl said, turning to him, then back to Bigger. "Do you?"

"Mary. . . ." said Mr. Dalton.

"I'm just asking him a question, Father!"

Bigger hesitated. He hated the girl then. Why did she have to do this when he was trying to get a job?

"No'm," he mumbled, his head down and his eyes glowering.

"And why not?" the girl asked.

Bigger heard Mr. Dalton mumble something. He wished Mr. Dalton would speak and end this thing. He looked up and saw Mr. Dalton staring at the girl. She's making me lose my job! he thought. Goddamn! He knew nothing about unions, except that they were considered bad. And what did she mean by talking to him this way in front of Mr. Dalton, who, surely, didn't like unions?

"We can settle about the union later, Mary," said Mr. Dalton.

"But you wouldn't mind belonging to a union, would you?" the girl asked.

"I don't know, mam," Bigger said.

"Now, Mary, you can see that the boy is new," said Mr. Dalton. "Leave him alone."

The girl turned and poked out a red tongue at him.

"All right, Mr. Capitalist!" She turned again to Bigger. "Isn't he a capitalist, Bigger?"

Bigger looked at the floor and did not answer. He did not know what a capitalist was.

The girl started to leave, but stopped.

"Oh, Father, if he hasn't anything else to do, let him drive me to my lecture at the University tonight."

"I'm talking to him now, Mary. He'll be through in a moment."

The girl picked up the cat and walked from the room. There was a short interval of silence. Bigger wished the girl had not said anything about unions. Maybe he would not be hired now. Or, if hired, maybe he would be fired soon if she kept acting like that. He had never seen anyone like her before. She was not a bit the way he had imagined she would be.

"Oh, Mary!" Mr. Dalton called.

"Yes, Father," Bigger heard her answer from the hallway.

Mr. Dalton rose and left the room. He sat still, listening. Once or twice he thought he heard the girl laugh, but he was not sure. The best thing he could do was to leave that crazy girl alone. He had heard about unions; in his mind unions and Communists were linked. He relaxed a little, then stiffened when he heard Mr. Dalton walk back into the room. Wordlessly, the white man sat behind the desk and picked up the paper and looked at it in a long silence. Bigger watched him with lowered eyes; he knew that Mr. Dalton was thinking of something other than that paper, In his heart he cursed the crazy girl. Maybe Mr. Dalton was deciding not to hire him. Goddamn! Maybe he would not get the extra five dollars a week now. *Goddamn that woman!* She spoiled everything! Maybe Mr. Dalton would feel that he could not trust him.

"Oh, Bigger," said Mr. Dalton.

"Yessuh."

"I want you to know why I'm hiring you."

"Yessuh."

"You see, Bigger, I'm a supporter of the National Association for the Advancement of Colored People. Did you ever hear of that organization?"

"Nawsuh."

"Well, it doesn't matter," said Mr. Dalton. "Have you had your dinner?"

"Nawsuh."

"Well, I think you'll do."

Mr. Dalton pushed a button. There was silence. The woman who had answered the front door came in.

"Yes, Mr. Dalton."

"Peggy, this is Bigger. He's going to drive for us. Give him something to eat, and show him where he's to sleep and where the car is."

"Yes, Mr. Dalton."

"And, Bigger, at eight-thirty, drive Miss Dalton out to the University and wait for her," said Mr. Dalton.

"Yessuh."

"That's all now."

"Yessuh."

"Come with me," Peggy said.

Bigger rose and got his cap and followed the woman through the house to the kitchen. The air was full of the scent of food cooking and pots bubbled on the stove.

"Sit here," Peggy said, clearing a place for him at a white-topped table. He sat and rested his cap on his knees. He felt a little better now that he was out of the front part of the house, but still not quite comfortable.

"Dinner isn't quite ready yet," Peggy said. "You like bacon and eggs?"

"Yessum."

"Coffee?"

"Yessum."

He sat looking at the white walls of the kitchen and heard the woman stir about behind him.

"Did Mr. Dalton tell you about the furnace?"

"No'm."

"Well, he must have forgotten it. You're supposed to attend to that, too. I'll show you where it is before you go."

"You mean I got to keep the fire going, mam?"

"Yes. But it's easy. Did you ever fire before?"

"No'm."

"You can learn. There's nothing to it."

"Yessum."

Peggy seemed kind enough, but maybe she was being kind in order to shove her part of the work on him. Well, he would wait and see. If she got nasty, he would talk to Mr. Dalton about her. He smelt the odor of frying bacon and realized that he was very hungry. He had forgotten to buy a sandwich with the quarter his mother had given him, and he had not eaten since morning. Peggy placed a plate, knife, fork, spoon, sugar, cream, and bread before him; then she dished up the bacon and eggs.

"You can get more if you want it."

The food was good. This was not going to be a bad job. The only thing bad so far was that crazy girl. He chewed his bacon and eggs while some remote part of his mind considered in amazement how different this rich girl was from the one he had seen in the movies. The woman he had watched on the screen had not seemed dangerous and his mind had been able to do with her as it liked, but this rich girl walked over everything, put herself in the way and, what was strange beyond understanding, talked and acted so simply and directly that she confounded him. He had quite forgotten that Peggy was in the kitchen and when his plate was empty he took a soft piece of bread and began to sop it clean, carrying the bread to his mouth in huge chunks.

"You want some more?"

He stopped chewing and laid the bread aside. He had not wanted to let her see him do that; he did that only at home.

"No'm," he said. "I got a plenty."

"You reckon you'll like it here?" Peggy asked.

"Yessum. I hope so."

"This is a swell place," Peggy said. "About as good as you'll find anywhere. The last colored man who worked for us stayed ten years."

Bigger wondered why she said "us." She must stand in with the old man and old woman pretty good, he thought.

"Ten years?" he said.

"Yes; ten years. His name was Green. He was a good man, too."

"How come he to leave?"

"Oh, he was smart, that Green was. He took a job with the government. Mrs. Dalton made him go to night school. Mrs. Dalton's always trying to help somebody."

Yes; Bigger knew that. But he was not going to any night school. He looked at Peggy; she was bent over the sink, washing dishes. Her words had challenged him and he felt he had to say something.

"Yessum, he was smart," he said. "And ten years is a long time."

"Oh, it wasn't so long," Peggy said. "I've been here twenty years myself. I always was one for sticking to a job. I always say when you get a good place, then stick there. A rolling stone gathers no moss, and it's true."

Bigger said nothing.

"Everything's simple and nice around here," Peggy said. "They've got millions, but they live like human beings. They don't put on airs and strut. Mrs. Dalton believes that people should be that way."

"Yessum."

"They're Christian people and believe in everybody working hard, and living a clean life. Some people think we ought to have more servants than we do, but we get along. It's just like one big family."

"Yessum."

"Mr. Dalton's a fine man," Peggy said.

"Oh, yessum. He is."

"You know, he does a lot for your people."

"My people?" asked Bigger, puzzled.

"Yes, the colored people. He gave over five million dollars to colored schools."

"Oh!"

"But Mrs. Dalton's the one who's really nice. If it wasn't for her, he would not be doing what he does. She made him rich. She had millions when he married her. Of course, he made a lot of money himself afterwards out of real estate. But most of the money's hers. She's blind, poor thing. She lost her sight ten years ago. Did you see her yet?"

"Yessum."

"Was she alone?"

"Yessum."

"Poor thing! Mrs. Patterson, who takes care of her, is away for the week-end and she's all alone. Isn't it too bad, about her?"

"Oh, yessum," he said, trying to get into his voice some of the pity for Mrs. Dalton that he thought Peggy expected him to feel.

"It's really more than a job you've got here," Peggy went on. "It's just like home. I'm always telling Mrs. Dalton that this is the only home I'll ever know. I wasn't in this country but two years before I started working here. . . ."

"Oh," said Bigger, looking at her.

"I'm Irish, you know," she said. "My folks in the old country feel about England like the colored folks feel about this country. So I know something about colored people. Oh, these are fine people, fine as silk. Even the girl. Did you meet her yet?"

"Yessum."

"Tonight?"

"Yessum."

Peggy turned and looked at him sharply.

"She's a sweet thing, she is," she said. "I've known her since she was two years old. To me she's still a baby and will always be one. But she's kind of wild, she is. Always in hot water. Keeps her folks worried to death, she does. She runs around with a wild and crazy bunch of reds. . . ."

"Reds!" Bigger exclaimed.

"Yes. But she don't mean nothing by it," Peggy said. "Like her mother and father, she feels sorry for people and she thinks the reds'll do something for 'em. The Lord only knows where she got her wild ways, but she's got 'em. If you stay around here, you'll get to know her. But don't you pay no attention to her red friends. They just keep up a lot of fuss."

Bigger wanted to ask her to tell him more about the girl, but thought that he had better not do that now.

"If you're through, I'll show you the furnace and the car, and where your room is," she said and turned the fire low under the pots on the stove.

"Yessum."

He rose and followed her out of the kitchen, down a narrow stairway at the end of which was the basement. It was dark: Bigger heard a sharp click and the light came on.

"This way. . . . What did you say your name was?"

"Bigger, mam."

"What?"

"Bigger."

He smelt the scent of coal and ashes and heard the fire roaring. He saw a red bed of embers glowing in the furnace.

"This is the furnace," she said.

"Yessum."

"Every morning you'll find the garbage here; you burn it and put the bucket on the dumb-waiter."

"Yessum."

"You never have to use a shovel for coal. It's a self-feeder. Look, see?"

Peggy pulled a lever and there came a loud rattle of fine lumps of coal sliding down a metal chute. Bigger stooped and saw, through the cracks of the furnace, the coal spreading out fanwise over the red bed of fire.

"That's fine," he mumbled in admiration.

"And you don't have to worry about water, either. It fills itself."

Bigger liked that; it was easy; it would be fun, almost.

"Your biggest trouble will be taking out the ashes and sweeping. And keep track of how the coal runs; when it's low, tell me or Mr. Dalton and we'll order some more."

"Yessum. I can handle it."

"Now, to get to your room all you have to do is go up these back stairs. Come on."

He followed up a stretch of stairs. She opened a door and switched on a light and Bigger saw a large room whose walls were covered with pictures of girls' faces and prize fighters.

"This was Green's room. He was always one for pictures. But he kept things neat and nice. It's plenty warm here. Oh, yes; before I forget. Here are the keys to the room and the garage and the car. Now, I'll show you the garage. You have to get to it from the outside."

He followed her down the steps and outside into the driveway. It was much warmer.

"Looks like snow," Peggy said.

"Yessum."

"This is the garage," she said, unlocking and pushing open a door which, as it swung in, made lights come on automatically. "You always bring the car out and wait at the side door for the folks. Let's see. You say you're driving Miss Dalton tonight?"

"Yessum."

"Well, she leaves at eight-thirty. So you're free until then. You can look over your room if you want to."

"Yessum. I reckon I will."

Bigger went behind Peggy down the stairs and back into the basement. She went to the kitchen and he went to his room. He stood in the middle of the floor, looking at the walls. There were pictures of Jack Johnson, Joe Louis, Jack Dempsey, and Henry Armstrong; there were others of Ginger Rogers, Jean Harlow, and Janet Gaynor. The room was large and had two radiators. He felt the bed; it was soft. Gee! He would bring Bessie here some night. Not right at once; he would wait until he had learned the ropes of the place. A room all to himself! He could bring a pint of liquor up here and drink it in peace. He would not have to slip around any more. He would not have to sleep with Buddy and stand Buddy's kicking all night long. He lit a cigarette and stretched himself full length upon the bed. Ohhhh. . . . This was not going to be bad at all. He looked at his dollar watch; it was seven. In a little while he would go down and examine the car. And he would buy himself another watch, too. A dollar watch was not good enough for a job like this; he would buy a gold one. There were a lot of new things he could get. Oh, boy! This would be an easy life. Everything was all right, except that girl. She worried him. She might cause him to lose his job if she kept talking about unions. She was a funny girl, all right. Never in his life had he met anyone like her. She puzzled him. She was rich, but she didn't act like she was rich. She acted like . . . Well, he didn't know exactly what she did act like. In all of the white women he had met, mostly on jobs and at relief stations, there was always a certain coldness and reserve; they stood their distance and spoke to him from afar. But this girl waded right in and hit him between the eyes with her words and ways. Aw, hell! What good was there in thinking about her like this? Maybe she was all right. Maybe he would just have to get used to her; that was all. I bet she spends a plenty of dough, he thought. And the old man had given five million dollars to colored people. If a man could give five million dollars away, the millions must be as common to him as nickels. He rose up and sat on the edge of the bed.

What make of car was he to drive? He had not thought to look when Peggy had opened the garage door. He hoped it would be a Packard, or a Lincoln, or a Rolls Royce. Boy! Would he drive! Just wait! Of course, he would be careful when he was driving Miss or Mr. Dalton. But when he was alone he would burn up the pavement; he would make those tires smoke!

He licked his lips; he was thirsty. He looked at his watch; it was ten past eight. He would go to the kitchen and get a drink of water and then drive the car out of the garage. He went down the steps, through the basement to the stairs leading to the kitchen door. Though he did not know it, he walked on tiptoe. He eased the door open and peeped in. What he saw made him suck his breath in; Mrs. Dalton in flowing white clothes was standing stonestill in the middle of the kitchen floor. There was silence, save for the slow ticking of a large clock on a white wall. For a moment he did not know if he should go in or go back down the steps; his thirst was gone. Mrs. Dalton's face was held in an attitude of intense listening and her hands were hanging loosely at her sides. To Bigger her face seemed to be capable of hearing in every pore of the skin and listening always to some low voice speaking. Sitting quietly on the floor beside her was the white cat, its large black eyes fastened upon him. It made him uneasy just to look at her and that white cat; he was about to close the door and tiptoe softly back down the stairs when she spoke.

"Are you the new boy?"

"Yessum."

"Did you want something?"

"I didn't mean to disturb you, mam. I—I . . . I just wanted a drink of water."

"Well, come on in. I think you'll find a glass somewhere."

He went to the sink, watching her as he walked, feeling that she could see him even though he knew that she was blind. His skin tingled. He took a glass from a narrow shelf and filled it from a faucet. As he drank he stole a glance at her over the rim of the glass. Her face was still, tilted, waiting. It reminded him of a dead man's face he had once seen. Then he realized that Mrs. Dalton had turned and listened to the sound of his feet as he had walked. She knows exactly where I'm standing, he thought.

"You like your room?" she asked; and as she spoke he realized that she had been standing there waiting to hear the sound of his glass as it clinked on the sink.

"Oh, yessum."

"I hope you're a careful driver."

"Oh, yessum. I'll be careful."

"Did you ever drive before?"

"Yessum. But it was a grocery truck."

He had the feeling that talking to a blind person was like talking to someone whom he himself could scarcely see.

"How far did you say you went in school, Bigger?"

"To the eighth grade, mam."

"Did you ever think of going back?"

"Well, I gotta work now, mam.

"Suppose you had the chance to go back?"

"Well, I don't know, mam."

"The last man who worked here went to night school and got an education."

"Yessum."

"What would you want to be if you had an education?"

"I don't know, mam."

"Did you ever think about it?"

"No'm."

"You would rather work?"

"I reckon I would, mam."

"Well, we'll talk about that some other time. I think you'd better get the car for Miss Dalton now."

"Yessum."

He left her standing in the middle of the kitchen floor, exactly as he had found her. He did not know just how to take her; she made him feel that she would judge all he did harshly but kindly. He had a feeling toward her that was akin to that which he held toward his mother. The difference in his feelings toward Mrs. Dalton and his mother was that he felt that his mother wanted him to do the things *she* wanted him to do, and he felt that Mrs. Dalton wanted him to do the things she felt that *he* should have wanted to do. But he did not want to go to night school. Night school was all right; but he had other plans. Well, he didn't know just what they were right now, but he was working them out.

The night air had grown warmer. A wind had risen. He lit a cigarette and unlocked the garage; the door swung in and again he was surprised and pleased to see the lights spring on automatically. These people's got everything, he mused. He examined the car; it was a dark blue Buick, with steel spoke wheels and of a new make. He stepped back from it and looked it over; then he opened the door and looked at the dashboard. He was a little disappointed that the car was not so expensive as he had hoped, but what it lacked in price was more than made up for in color and style. "It's all right," he said half-aloud. He got in and backed it into the driveway and turned it round and pulled it up to the side door.

"Is that you, Bigger?"

The girl stood on the steps.

"Yessum."

He got out and held the rear door open for her.

"Thank you."

He touched his cap and wondered if it were the right thing to do.

"Is it that university-school out there on the Midway, mam?"

Through the rear mirror above him he saw her hesitate before answering.

"Yes; that's the one."

He pulled the car into the street and headed south, driving about thirty-five miles an hour. He handled the car expertly, picking up speed at the beginning of each block and slowing slightly as he approached each street intersection.

"You drive well," she said.

"Yessum," he said proudly.

He watched her through the rear mirror as he drove; she was kind of pretty, but very little. She looked like a doll in a show window: black eyes, white face, red lips. And she was not acting at all now as she had acted when he first saw her. In fact, she had a remote look in her eyes. He stopped the car at Forty-seventh Street for a red light; he did not have to stop again until he reached Fifty-first Street where a long line of cars formed in front of him and a long line in back. He held the steering wheel lightly, waiting for the line to move forward. He had a keen sense of power when driving; the feel of a car added something to him. He loved to press his foot against a pedal and sail along, watching others stand still, seeing the asphalt road unwind under him. The lights flashed from red to green and he nosed the car forward.

"Bigger!"

"Yessum."

"Turn at this corner and pull up on a side street."

"Here, mam?"

"Yes; here."

Now, what on earth did this mean? He pulled the car off Cottage Grove Avenue and drew to a curb. He turned to look at her and was startled to see that she was sitting on the sheer edge of the back seat, her face some six inches from his.

"I scare you?" she asked softly, smiling.

"Oh, no'm," he mumbled, bewildered.

He watched her through the mirror. Her tiny white hands dangled over the back of the front seat and her eyes looked out vacantly.

"I don't know how to say what I'm going to say," she said.

He said nothing. There was a long silence. What in all hell did this girl want? A street car rumbled by. Behind him, reflected in the rear mirror, he saw the traffic lights flash from green to red, and back again. Well, whatever she was going to say, he wished she would say it and get it over. This girl was strange. She did the unexpected every minute. He waited for her to speak. She took her hands from the back of the front seat and fumbled in her purse.

"Gotta match?"

"Yessum."

He dug a match from his vest pocket.

"Strike it," she said.

He blinked. He struck the match and held the flame for her. She smoked awhile in silence.

"You're not a tattletale, are you?" she asked with a smile.

He opened his mouth to reply, but no words came. What she had asked and the tone of voice in which she had asked it made him feel that he ought to have answered in some way; but what?

"I'm not going to the University," she said at last. "But you can forget that. I want you to drive me to the Loop. But if anyone should ask you, then I went to the University, see, Bigger?"

"Yessum, it's all right with me," he mumbled.

"I think I can trust you."

"Yessum."

"After all, I'm on your side."

Now, what did *that* mean? She was on *his* side. What side was he on? Did she mean that she liked colored people? Well, he had heard that about her whole family. Was she really crazy? How much did her folks know of how she acted? But if she were really crazy, why did Mr. Dalton let him drive her out?

"I'm going to meet a friend of mine who's also a friend of yours," she said.

"Friend of mine!" he could not help exclaiming.

"Oh, you don't know him yet," she said, laughing.

"Oh."

"Go to the Outer Drive and then to 16 Lake Street."

"Yessum."

Maybe she was talking about the reds? *That* was it! But none of his friends were reds. What was all this? If Mr. Dalton should ask him if he had taken her to the University, he would have to say yes and depend upon her to back him up. But suppose Mr. Dalton had someone watching, someone who would tell where he had really taken her? He had heard that many rich people had detectives working for them. If only he knew what this was all about he would feel much better. And she had said that she was going to meet someone who was a friend of his. He didn't want to meet any Communists. They didn't have any money. He felt that it was all right for a man to go to jail for robbery, but to go to jail for fooling around with reds was bunk. Well, he would drive her; that was what he had been hired for. But he was going to watch his step in this business. The only thing he hoped was that she would not make him lose his job. He pulled the car off the Outer Drive at Seventh Street, drove north on Michigan Boulevard to Lake Street, then headed west for two blocks, looking for number 16.

"It's right here, Bigger."

"Yessum."

He pulled to a stop in front of a dark building.

"Wait," she said, getting out of the car.

He saw her smiling broadly at him, almost laughing. He felt that she knew every feeling and thought he had at that moment and he turned his head away in confusion. Goddamn that woman!

"I won't be long," she said.

She started off, then turned back.

"Take it easy, Bigger. You'll understand it better bye and bye."

"Yessum," he said, trying to smile; but couldn't.

"Isn't there a song like that, a song your people sing?"

"Like what, mam?"

"We'll understand it better bye and bye?"

"Oh, yessum."

She was an odd girl, all right. He felt something in her over and above the fear she inspired in him. She responded to him as if he were human, as if he lived in the same world as she.

And he had never felt that before in a white person. But why? Was this some kind of game? The guarded feeling of freedom he had while listening to her was tangled with the hard fact that she was white and rich, a part of the world of people who told him what he could and could not do.

He looked at the building into which she had gone; it was old and unpainted; there were no lights in the windows or doorway. Maybe she was meeting her sweetheart? If that was all, then things would straighten out. But if she had gone to meet those Communists? And what were Communists like, anyway? Was *she* one? What made people Communists? He remembered seeing many cartoons of Communists in newspapers and always they had flaming torches in their hands and wore beards and were trying to commit murder or set things on fire. People who acted that way were crazy. All he could recall having heard about Communists was associated in his mind with darkness, old houses, people speaking in whispers, and trade unions on strike. And this was something like it.

He stiffened; the door into which she had gone opened. She came out, followed by a young white man. They walked to the car; but, instead of getting into the back seat, they came to the side of the car and stood, facing him.

"Oh, Bigger, this is Jan. And Jan, this is Bigger Thomas."

Jan smiled broadly, then extended an open palm toward him. Bigger's entire body tightened with suspense and dread.

"How are you, Bigger?"

Bigger's right hand gripped the steering wheel and he wondered if he ought to shake hands with this white man.

"I'm fine," he mumbled.

Jan's hand was still extended. Bigger's right hand raised itself about three inches, then stopped in mid-air.

"Come on and shake," Jan said.

Bigger extended a limp palm, his mouth open in astonishment. He felt Jan's fingers tighten about his own. He tried to pull his hand away, ever so gently, but Jan held on, firmly, smiling.

"We may as well get to know each other," Jan said. "I'm a friend of Mary's."

"Yessuh," he mumbled.

"First of all," Jan continued, putting his foot upon the running-board, "don't say *sir* to me. I'll call you Bigger and you'll call me Jan. That's the way it'll be between us. How's that?"

Bigger did not answer. Mary was smiling. Jan still gripped his hand and Bigger held his head at an oblique angle, so that he could, by merely shifting his eyes, look at Jan and then out into the street whenever he did not wish to meet Jan's gaze. He heard Mary laughing softly.

"It's all right, Bigger," she said. "Jan *means* it."

He flushed warm with anger. Goddam her soul to hell! Was she laughing at him? Were they making fun of him? What was it that they wanted? Why didn't they leave him alone? He was not bothering them. Yes, anything could happen with people like these. His entire mind and body were painfully concentrated into a single sharp point of attention. He was trying desperately to understand. He felt foolish sitting behind the steering wheel like this and letting a white man hold his hand. What would people passing along the street think? He was very conscious of his black skin and there was in him a prodding conviction that Jan and men like him had made it so that he would be conscious of that black skin. Did not white people despise a black skin? Then why was Jan doing this? Why was Mary standing there so eagerly, with shining eyes? What could they get out of this? Maybe they did not despise him? But they made him feel his black skin by just standing there looking at him, one holding his hand and the other smiling. He felt he had no physical existence at all right then; he was something he hated, the badge of shame which he knew was attached to a black skin. It was a shadowy region, a No Man's Land, the ground that separated the white world from the black that he stood upon. He felt naked, transparent; he felt that this white man, having helped to put him down, having helped to deform him, held him up now to look at him and be amused. At that moment he felt toward Mary and Jan a dumb, cold, and inarticulate hate.

"Let me drive awhile," Jan said, letting go of his hand and opening the door.

Bigger looked at Mary. She came forward and touched his arm.

"It's all right, Bigger," she said.

He turned in the seat to get out, but Jan stopped him.

"No; stay in and move over."

He slid over and Jan took his place at the wheel. He was still feeling his hand strangely; it seemed that the pressure of Jan's fingers had left an indelible imprint. Mary was getting into the front seat, too.

"Move over, Bigger," she said.

He moved closer to Jan. Mary pushed herself in, wedging tightly between him and the outer door of the car. There were white people to either side of him; he was sitting between two vast white looming walls. Never in his life had he been so close to a white woman. He smelt the odor of her hair and felt the soft pressure of her thigh against his own. Jan headed the car back to the Outer Drive, weaving in and out of the line of traffic. Soon they were speeding along the lake front, past a huge flat sheet of dully gleaming water. The sky was heavy with snow clouds and the wind was blowing strong.

"Isn't it glorious tonight?" she asked.

"God, yes!" Jan said.

Bigger listened to the tone of their voices, to their strange accents, to the exuberant phrases that flowed so freely from their lips.

"That sky!"

"And that water!"

"It's so beautiful it makes you ache just to look at it," said Mary.

"This is a beautiful world, Bigger," Jan said, turning to him. "Look at that skyline!"

Bigger looked without turning his head; he just rolled his eyes. Stretching to one side of him was a vast sweep of tall buildings flecked with tiny squares of yellow light.

"We'll own all that some day, Bigger," Jan said with a wave of his hand. "After the revolution it'll be ours. But we'll have to fight for it. What a world to win, Bigger! And when that day comes, things'll be different. There'll be no white and no black; there'll be no rich and no poor."

Bigger said nothing. The car whirred along.

"We seem strange to you, don't we, Bigger?" Mary asked.

"Oh, no'm," he breathed softly, knowing that she did not believe him, but finding it impossible to answer her in any other way.

His arms and legs were aching from being cramped into so small a space, but he dared not move. He knew that they would not have cared if he had made himself more comfortable, but his moving would have called attention to himself and his black body. And he did not want that. These people made him feel things he did not want to feel. If he were white, if he were like them, it would have been different. But he was black. So he sat still, his arms and legs aching.

"Say, Bigger," asked Jan, "where can we get a good meal on the South Side?"

"Well," Bigger said, reflectively.

"We want to go to a *real* place," Mary said, turning to him gaily.

"You want to go to a night club?" Bigger asked in a tone that indicated that he was simply mentioning names and not recommending places to go.

"No; we want to eat."

"Look, Bigger. We want one of those places where colored

people eat, not one of those show places."

What *did* these people want? When he answered his voice was neutral and toneless.

"Well, there's Ernie's Kitchen Shack. . . ."

"That sounds good!"

"Let's go there, Jan," Mary said.

"O.K.," Jan said. "Where is it?"

"It's at Forty-seventh Street and Indiana," Bigger told them.

Jan swung the car off the Outer Drive at Thirty-first Street and drove westward to Indiana Avenue. Bigger wanted Jan to drive faster, so that they could reach Ernie's Kitchen Shack in the shortest possible time. That would allow him a chance to sit in the car and stretch out his cramped and aching legs while they ate. Jan turned onto Indiana Avenue and headed south. Bigger wondered what Jack and Gus and G. H. would say if they saw him sitting between two white people in a car like this. They would tease him about such a thing as long as they could remember it. He felt Mary turn in her seat. She placed her hand on his arm.

"You know, Bigger, I've long wanted to go into those houses," she said, pointing to the tall, dark apartment buildings looming to either side of them, "and just *see* how your people live. You know what I mean? I've been to England, France and Mexico, but I don't know how people live ten blocks from me. We know so *little* about each other. I just want to *see*. I want to *know* these people. Never in my life have I been inside of a Negro home. Yet they *must* live like we live. They're *human*. . . . There are twelve million of them. . . . They live in our country. . . . In the same city with us. . . ." her voice trailed off wistfully.

There was silence. The car sped through the Black Belt, past tall buildings holding black life. Bigger knew that they were thinking of his life and the life of his people. Suddenly he wanted to seize some heavy object in his hand and grip it with all the strength in his body and in some strange way rise up and stand in naked space above the speeding car and with one final blow blot it out—with himself and them in it. His heart was beating fast and he struggled to control his breath. This thing was getting the better of him; he felt that he should not give way to his feelings like this. But he could not help it. Why didn't they leave him alone? What had he done to them? What good could they get out of sitting here making him feel so miserable?

"Tell me where it is, Bigger," Jan said.

"Yessuh."

Bigger looked out and saw that they were at Forty-sixth Street.

"It's at the end of the next block, suh."

"Can I park along here somewhere?"

"Oh; yessuh."

"Bigger, *please!* Don't say *sir* to me. . . . I don't *like* it. You're a man just like I am; I'm no better than you. Maybe other white men like it. But I don't. Look, Bigger. . . ."

"Yes. . . ." Bigger paused, swallowed, and looked down at his black hands. "O.K.," he mumbled, hoping that they did not hear the choke in his voice.

"You see, Bigger. . . ." Jan began.

Mary reached her hand round back of Bigger and touched Jan's shoulder.

"Let's get out," she said hurriedly.

Jan pulled the car to the curb and opened the door and stepped out. Bigger slipped behind the steering wheel again, glad to have room at last for his arms and legs. Mary got out of the other door. Now, he could get some rest. So intensely taken up was he with his own immediate sensations that he did not look up until he felt something strange in the long silence. When he did look he saw, in a split second of time, Mary turn her eyes away from his face. She was looking at Jan and Jan was looking at her. There was no mistaking the meaning of the look in their eyes. To Bigger it was plainly a bewildered and questioning look, a look that asked: What on earth is wrong with him? Bigger's teeth clamped tight and he stared straight before him.

"Aren't you coming with us, Bigger?" Mary asked in a sweet tone that made him want to leap at her.

The people in Ernie's Kitchen Shack knew him and he did not want them to see him with these white people. He knew that if he went in they would ask one another: *Who're them white folks Bigger's hanging around with?*

"I—I . . . I don't want to go in. . . ." he whispered breathlessly.

"Aren't you hungry?" Jan asked.

"Naw; I ain't hungry."

Jan and Mary came close to the car.

"Come and sit with us anyhow," Jan said.

"I . . . I . . ." Bigger stammered.

"It'll be all right," Mary said.

"I can stay here. Somebody has to watch the car," he said.

"Oh, to hell with the car!" Mary said. "Come on in."

"I don't want to eat," Bigger said stubbornly.

"Well," Jan sighed. "If that's the way you feel about it, we won't go in."

Bigger felt trapped. Oh, goddamn! He saw in a flash that he could have made all of this very easy if he had simply acted from the beginning as if they were doing nothing unusual. But he did not understand them; he distrusted them, really hated them. He was puzzled as to why they were treating him this way. But, after all, this was his job and it was just as painful to sit here and let them stare at him as it was to go in.

"O.K.," he mumbled angrily.

He got out and slammed the door. Mary came close to him and caught his arm. He stared at her in a long silence; it was the first time he had ever looked directly at her, and he was able to do so only because he was angry.

"Bigger," she said, "you don't have to come in unless you really want to. Please, don't think . . . Oh, Bigger . . . We're not trying to make you feel badly. . . ."

Her voice stopped. In the dim light of the street lamp Bigger saw her eyes cloud and her lips tremble. She swayed against the car. He stepped backward, as though she were contaminated with an invisible contagion. Jan slipped his arm about her waist, supporting her. Bigger heard her sob softly. Good God! He had a wild impulse to turn around and walk away. He felt ensnared in a tangle of deep shadows, shadows as black as the night that stretched above his head. The way he had acted had made her cry, and yet the way she had acted had made him feel that he had to act as he had toward her. In his relations with her he felt that he was riding a seesaw; never were they on a common level; either he or she was up in the air. Mary dried her eyes and Jan whispered something to her. Bigger wondered what he could say to his mother, or the relief, or Mr. Dalton, if he left them. They would be sure to ask why he had walked off his job, and he would not be able to tell.

"I'm all right, now, Jan," he heard Mary say. "I'm sorry. I'm just a fool, I suppose. . . . I acted a ninny." She lifted her eyes to Bigger. "Don't mind me, Bigger. I'm just silly, I guess. . . ."

He said nothing.

"Come on, Bigger," Jan said in a voice that sought to cover up everything. "Let's eat."

Jan caught his arm and tried to pull him forward, but Bigger hung back. Jan and Mary walked toward the entrance of the café and Bigger followed, confused and resentful. Jan went to a small table near a wall.

"Sit down, Bigger."

Bigger sat. Jan and Mary sat in front of him.

"You like fried chicken?" Jan asked.

"Yessuh," he whispered.

He scratched his head. How on earth could he learn not to say *yessuh* and *yessum* to white people in one night when he had been saying it all his life long? He looked before him in such a way that his eyes would not meet theirs. The waitress came and Jan ordered three beers and three portions of fried chicken.

"Hi, Bigger!"

He turned and saw Jack waving at him, but staring at Jan and Mary. He waved a stiff palm in return. Goddamn! Jack walked away hurriedly. Cautiously, Bigger looked round; the waitresses and several people at other tables were staring at him. They all knew him and he knew that they were wondering as he would have wondered if he had been in their places. Mary touched his arm.

"Have you ever been here before, Bigger?"

He groped for neutral words, words that would convey information but not indicate any shade of his own feelings.

"A few times."

"It's very nice," Mary said.

Somebody put a nickel in an automatic phonograph and they listened to the music. Then Bigger felt a hand grab his shoulder.

"Hi, Bigger! Where you been?"

He looked up and saw Bessie laughing in his face.

"Hi," he said gruffly.

"Oh, 'scuse me. I didn't know you had company," she said, walking away with her eyes upon Jan and Mary.

"Tell her to come over, Bigger," Mary said.

Bessie had gone to a far table and was sitting with another girl.

"She's over there now," Bigger said.

The waitress brought the beer and chicken.

"This is simply grand!" Mary exclaimed.

"You got something there," Jan said, looking at Bigger. "Did I say that right, Bigger?"

Bigger hesitated.

"That's the way they say it," he spoke flatly.

Jan and Mary were eating. Bigger picked up a piece of chicken and bit it. When he tried to chew he found his mouth dry. It seemed that the very organic functions of his body had

altered; and when he realized why, when he understood the
cause, he could not chew the food. After two or three bites,
he stopped and sipped his beer.

"Eat your chicken," Mary said. "It's good!"

"I ain't hungry," he mumbled.

"Want some more beer?" Jan asked after a long silence.

Maybe if he got a little drunk it would help him.

"I don't mind," he said.

Jan ordered another round.

"Do they keep anything stronger than beer here?" Jan
asked.

"They got anything you want," Bigger said.

Jan ordered a fifth of rum and poured a round. Bigger felt
the liquor warming him. After a second drink Jan began to
talk.

"Where were you born, Bigger?"

"In the South."

"Whereabouts?"

"Mississippi."

"How far did you go in school?"

"To the eighth grade."

"Why did you stop?"

"No money."

"Did you go to school in the North or South?"

"Mostly in the South. I went two years up here."

"How long have you been in Chicago?"

"Oh, about five years."

"You like it here?"

"It'll do."

"You live with your people?"

"My mother, brother, and sister."

"Where's your father?"

"Dead."

"How long ago was that?"

"He got killed in a riot when I was a kid—in the
South."

There was silence. The rum was helping Bigger.

"And what was done about it?" Jan asked.

"Nothing, far as I know."

"How do you feel about it?"

"I don't know."

"Listen, Bigger, that's what we want to *stop*. That's what we Communists are fighting. We want to stop people from treating others that way. I'm a member of the Party. Mary sympathizes. Don't you think if we got together we could stop things like that?"

"I don't know," Bigger said; he was feeling the rum rising to his head. "There's a lot of white people in the world."

"You've read about the Scottsboro boys?"

"I heard about 'em."

"Don't you think we did a good job in helping to keep 'em from killing those boys?"

"It was all right."

"You know, Bigger," said Mary, "we'd like to be friends of yours."

He said nothing. He drained his glass and Jan poured another round. He was getting drunk enough to look straight at them now. Mary was smiling at him.

"You'll get used to us," she said.

Jan stoppered the bottle of rum.

"We'd better go," he said.

"Yes," Mary said. "Oh, Bigger, I'm going to Detroit at nine in the morning and I want you to take my small trunk down to the station. Tell Father and he'll let you make up your time. You better come for the trunk at eight-thirty."

"I'll take it down."

Jan paid the bill and they went back to the car. Bigger got behind the steering wheel. He was feeling good. Jan and Mary got into the back seat. As Bigger drove he saw her resting in Jan's arms.

"Drive around in the park awhile, will you, Bigger?"

"O.K."

He turned into Washington Park and pulled the car slowly round and round the long gradual curves. Now and then he watched Jan kiss Mary in the reflection of the rear mirror above his head.

"You got a girl, Bigger?" Mary asked.

"I got a girl," he said.

"I'd like to meet her some time."

He did not answer. Mary's eyes stared dreamily before her, as if she were planning future things to do. Then she turned to Jan and laid her hand tenderly upon his arm.

"How was the demonstration?"

"Pretty good. But the cops arrested three comrades."

"Who were they?"

"A Y. C. L.-er and two Negro women. Oh, by the way, Mary. We need money for bail badly."

"How much?"

"Three thousand."

"I'll mail you a check."

"Swell."

"Did you work hard today?"

"Yeah. I was at a meeting until three this morning. Max and I've been trying to raise bail money all day today."

"Max is a darling, isn't he?"

"He's one of the best lawyers we've got."

Bigger listened; he knew that they were talking communism and he tried to understand. But he couldn't.

"Jan."

"Yes, honey."

"I'm coming out of school this spring and I'm going to join the Party."

"*Gee*, you're a brick!"

"But I'll have to be careful."

"Say, how's about your working with me, in the office?"

"No, I want to work among Negroes. That's where people are needed. It seems as though they've been pushed out of everything."

"That's true."

"When I see what they've done to those people, it makes me *so* mad. . . ."

"Yes; it's awful."

"And I feel so helpless and useless. I want to *do* something."

"I knew all along you'd come through."

"Say, Jan, do you know many Negroes? I want to meet some."

"I don't know any very well. But you'll meet them when you're in the Party."

"They have so much *emo*tion! What a people! If we could ever get them going. . . ."

"We can't have a revolution without 'em," Jan said. "They've got to be organized. They've got spirit. They'll give the Party something it needs."

"And their songs—the spirituals! Aren't they marvelous?" Bigger saw her turn to him. "Say, Bigger, can you sing?"

"I can't sing," he said.

"Aw, Bigger," she said, pouting. She tilted her head, closed her eyes and opened her mouth.

> *"Swing low, sweet chariot,*
> *Coming fer to carry me home. . . ."*

Jan joined in and Bigger smiled derisively. Hell, that ain't the tune, he thought.

"Come on, Bigger, and help us sing it," Jan said.

"I can't sing," he said again.

They were silent. The car purred along. Then he heard Jan speaking in low tones.

"Where's the bottle?"

"Right here."

"I want a sip."

"I'll take one, too, honey."

"Going heavy tonight, ain't you?"

"About as heavy as you."

They laughed. Bigger drove in silence. He heard the faint, musical gurgle of liquor.

"Jan!"

"What?"

"That was a *big* sip!"

"Here; you get even."

Through the rear mirror he saw her tilt the bottle and drink.

"Maybe Bigger wants another one, Jan. Ask him."

"Oh, say, Bigger! Here; take a swig!"

He slowed the car and reached back for the bottle; he tilted it twice, taking two huge swallows.

"Woooow!" Mary laughed.

"You took a *swig*, all right," Jan said.

Bigger wiped his mouth with the back of his hand and continued driving slowly through the dark park. Now and then he heard the half-empty bottle of rum gurgling. They getting plastered, he thought, feeling the effect of the rum creeping outward to his fingers and upward to his lips. Presently, he heard Mary giggle. Hell, she's plastered already! The car rolled slowly round and round the sloping curves. The rum's soft heat was spreading fanwise out from his stomach, engulfing his whole body. He was not driving; he was simply sitting and floating along smoothly through darkness. His hands rested lightly on the steering wheel and his body slouched lazily down in the seat. He looked at the mirror; they were drinking again. They plastered, all right, he thought. He pulled the car softly round the curves, looking at the road before him one second and up at the mirror the next. He heard Jan whispering; then he heard them both sigh. His lips were numb. I'm almost drunk, he thought. His sense of the city and park fell away; he was floating in the car and Jan and Mary were in back, kissing. A long time passed.

"It's one o'clock, honey," Mary said. "I better go in."

"O.K. But let's drive a little more. It's great here."

"Father says I'm a bad girl."

"I'm sorry, darling."

"I'll call you in the morning before I go."

"Sure. What time?"

"About eight-thirty."

"Gee, but I hate to see you go to Detroit."

"I hate to go too. But I got to. You see, honey, I got to make up for being bad with you down in Florida. I got to do what Mother and Father say for awhile."

"I hate to see you go just the same."

"I'll be back in a couple of days."

"A couple of days is a long time."

"You're silly, but you're sweet," she said, laughing and kissing him.

"You better drive on, Bigger," Jan called.

Bigger drove out of the park onto Cottage Grove Avenue and headed north. The city streets were empty and quiet and dark and the tires of the car hummed over the asphalt. When he reached Forty-sixth Street, a block from the Dalton home, he heard a street car rumbling faintly behind him, far down the avenue.

"Here comes my car," Jan said, turning to peer through the rear window.

"Oh, gee, honey!" Mary said. "You've got such a long way to go. If I had the time, I'd ride you home. But I've been out so late as it is that Mama's going to be suspicious."

"Don't worry. I'll be all right."

"Oh, say! Let Bigger drive you home."

"Nonsense! Why should he drive me all that distance this time of morning?"

"Then you'd better take this car, honey."

"No. I'll see you home first."

"But, honey, the cars run only every half hour when it's late like this," Mary said. "You'll get ill, waiting out here in the cold. Look, you take this car. I'll get home all right. It's only a block. . . ."

"Are you sure you'll be all right?"

"Of course. I'm in sight of home now. There; see. . . ."

Through the rear mirror Bigger saw her pointing to the Dalton home.

"O.K.," Jan said. "You'd better stop here and let me off, Bigger."

He stopped the car. Bigger heard them speak in whispers.

"Good-bye, Jan."

"Good-bye, honey."

"I'll call you tomorrow?"

"Sure."

Jan stood at the front door of the car and held out his palm. Bigger shook timidly.

"It's been great meeting you, Bigger," Jan said.

"O.K.," Bigger mumbled.

"I'm damn glad I know you. Look. Have another drink."

Bigger took a big swallow.

"You better give me one, too, Jan. It'll make me sleep," Mary said.

"You're sure you haven't had enough?"

"Aw, come on, honey."

She got out of the car and stood on the curb. Jan gave her the bottle and she tilted it.

"Whoa!" Jan said.

"What's the matter?"

"I don't want you to pass out."

"I can hold it."

Jan tilted the bottle and emptied it, then laid it in the gutter. He fumbled clumsily in his pockets for something. He swayed; he was drunk.

"You lose something, honey?" Mary lisped; she, too, was drunk.

"Naw; I got some stuff here I want Bigger to read. Listen, Bigger, I got some pamphlets here. I want you to read 'em, see?"

Bigger held out his hand and received a small batch of booklets.

"O.K."

"I really want you to read 'em, now. We'll have a talk 'bout 'em in a coupla days. . . ." His speech was thick.

"I'll read 'em," Bigger said, stifling a yawn and stuffing the booklets into his pocket.

"I'll see that he reads 'em," Mary said.

Jan kissed her again. Bigger heard the Loop-bound car rumbling forward.

"Well, good-bye," he said.

"Goo'-bye, honey," Mary said. "I'm gonna ride up front with Bigger."

She got into the front seat. The street car clanged to a stop. Jan swung onto it and it started north. Bigger drove toward Drexel Boulevard. Mary slumped down in the seat and sighed. Her legs sprawled wide apart. The car rolled along. Bigger's head was spinning.

"You're very nice, Bigger," she said.

He looked at her. Her face was pasty white. Her eyes were glassy. She was very drunk.

"I don't know," he said.

"My! But you say the *fun*niest things," she giggled.

"Maybe," he said.

She leaned her head on his shoulder.

"You don't mind, do you?"

"I don't mind."

"You know, for *three* hours you haven't said *yes* or *no.*"

She doubled up with laughter. He tightened with hate. Again she was looking inside of him and he did not like it. She sat up and dabbed at her eyes with a handkerchief. He kept his eyes straight in front of him and swung the car into the driveway and brought it to a stop. He got out and opened the door. She did not move. Her eyes were closed.

"We're here," he said.

She tried to get up and slipped back into the seat.

"Aw, shucks!"

She's drunk, *really* drunk, Bigger thought. She stretched out her hand.

"Here; gimme a lift. I'm wobbly. . . ."

She was resting on the small of her back and her dress was pulled up so far that he could see where her stockings ended on her thighs. He stood looking at her for a moment; she raised her eyes and looked at him. She laughed.

"Help me, Bigger. I'm stuck."

He helped her and his hands felt the softness of her body as she stepped to the ground. Her dark eyes looked at him feverishly from deep sockets. Her hair was in his face, filling him with its scent. He gritted his teeth, feeling a little dizzy.

"Where's my hat? I dropped it shomewhere. . . ."

She swayed as she spoke and he tightened his arms about her, holding her up. He looked around; her hat was lying on the running board.

"Here it is," he said.

As he picked it up he wondered what a white man would think seeing him here with her like this. Suppose old man Dalton saw him now? Apprehensively, he looked up at the big house. It was dark and silent.

"Well," Mary sighed. "I suppose I better go to bed. . . ."

He turned her loose, but had to catch her again to keep her off the pavement. He led her to the steps.

"Can you make it?"

She looked at him as though she had been challenged.

"Sure. Turn me loose. . . ."

He took his arm from her and she mounted the steps firmly and then stumbled loudly on the wooden porch. Bigger made a move toward her, but stopped, his hands outstretched, frozen with fear. Good God, she'll wake up everybody! She was half-bent over, resting on one knee and one hand, looking back at him in amused astonishment. That girl's crazy! She pulled up and walked slowly back down the steps, holding onto the railing. She swayed before him, smiling.

"I sure am drunk. . . ."

He watched her with a mingled feeling of helplessness, admiration, and hate. If her father saw him here with her now, his job would be over. But she was beautiful, slender, with an air that made him feel that she did not hate him with the hate of other white people. But, for all of that, she was white and he hated her. She closed her eyes slowly, then opened them; she was trying desperately to take hold of herself. Since she was not able to get to her room alone, ought he to call Mr. Dalton or Peggy? Naw. . . . That would betray her. And, too, in spite of his hate for her, he was excited standing here watching her like this. Her eyes closed again and she swayed toward him. He caught her.

"I'd better help you," he said.

"Let's go the back way, Bigger. I'll stumble sure as hell . . . and wake up everybody . . . if we go up the front. . . ."

Her feet dragged on the concrete as he led her to the basement. He switched on the light, supporting her with his free hand.

"I didn't know I was sho drunk," she mumbled.

He led her slowly up the narrow stairs to the kitchen door, his hand circling her waist and the tips of his fingers feeling the soft swelling of her breasts. Each second she was leaning more heavily against him.

"Try to stand up," he whispered fiercely as they reached the kitchen door.

He was thinking that perhaps Mrs. Dalton was standing in flowing white and staring with stony blind eyes in the middle of the floor, as she had been when he had come for the glass of water. He eased the door back and looked. The kitchen was empty and dark, save for a faint blue hazy light that seeped through a window from the winter sky.

"Come on."

She pulled heavily on him, her arm about his neck. He pushed the door in and took a step inside and stopped, waiting, listening. He felt her hair brush his lips. His skin glowed

warm and his muscles flexed; he looked at her face in the dim
light, his senses drunk with the odor of her hair and skin. He
stood for a moment, then whispered in excitement and fear:

"Come on; you got to get to your room."

He led her out of the kitchen into the hallway; he had to
walk her a step at a time. The hall was empty and dark; slowly
he half-walked and half-dragged her to the back stairs. Again
he hated her; he shook her.

"Come on; wake up!"

She did not move or open her eyes; finally she mumbled
something and swayed limply. His fingers felt the soft curves
of her body and he was still, looking at her, enveloped in a
sense of physical elation. This little bitch! he thought. Her
face was touching his. He turned her round and began to
mount the steps, one by one. He heard a slight creaking and
stopped. He looked, straining his eyes in the gloom. But there
was no one. When he got to the top of the steps she was
completely limp and was still trying to mumble something.
Goddamn! He could move her only by lifting her bodily. He
caught her in his arms and carried her down the hall, then
paused. Which was her door? Goddamn!

"Where's your room?" he whispered.

She did not answer. Was she completely out? He could not
leave her here; if he took his hands from her she would sink
to the floor and lie there all night. He shook her hard, speaking as loudly as he dared.

"Where's your room?"

Momentarily, she roused herself and looked at him with
blank eyes.

"Where's your room?" he asked again.

She rolled her eyes toward a door. He got her as far as the
door and stopped. Was this really her room? Was she too
drunk to know? Suppose he opened the door to Mr. and Mrs.
Dalton's room? Well, all they could do was fire him. It wasn't
his fault that she was drunk. He felt strange, possessed, or as
if he were acting upon a stage in front of a crowd of people.

Carefully, he freed one hand and turned the knob of the
door. He waited; nothing happened. He pushed the door in
quietly; the room was dark and silent. He felt along the wall
with his fingers for the electric switch and could not find it.
He stood, holding her in his arms, fearful, in doubt. His eyes
were growing used to the darkness and a little light seeped
into the room from the winter sky through a window. At the
far end of the room he made out the shadowy form of a white
bed. He lifted her and brought her into the room and closed
the door softly.

"Here; wake up, now."

He tried to stand her on her feet and found her weak as
jelly. He held her in his arms again, listening in the darkness.
His senses reeled from the scent of her hair and skin. She was
much smaller than Bessie, his girl, but much softer. Her face
was buried in his shoulder; his arms tightened about her. Her
face turned slowly and he held his face still, waiting for her
face to come round, in front of his. Then her head leaned
backward, slowly, gently; it was as though she had given up.
Her lips, faintly moist in the hazy blue light, were parted and
he saw the furtive glints of her white teeth. Her eyes were
closed. He stared at her dim face, the forehead capped with
curly black hair. He eased his hand, the fingers spread wide,
up the center of her back and her face came toward him and
her lips touched his, like something he had imagined. He
stood her on her feet and she swayed against him.

He lifted her and laid her on the bed. Something urged
him to leave at once, but he leaned over her, excited, looking
at her face in the dim light, not wanting to take his hands
from her breasts. She tossed and mumbled sleepily. He tightened his fingers on her breasts, kissing her again, feeling her
move toward him. He was aware only of her body now; his
lips trembled. Then he stiffened. The door behind him had
creaked.

He turned and a hysterical terror seized him, as though he
were falling from a great height in a dream. A white blur was

standing by the door, silent, ghostlike. It filled his eyes and gripped his body. It was Mrs. Dalton. He wanted to knock her out of his way and bolt from the room.

"Mary!" she spoke softly, questioningly.

Bigger held his breath. Mary mumbled again; he bent over her, his fists clenched in fear. He knew that Mrs. Dalton could not see him; but he knew that if Mary spoke she would come to the side of the bed and discover him, touch him. He waited tensely, afraid to move for fear of bumping into something in the dark and betraying his presence.

"Mary!"

He felt Mary trying to rise and quickly he pushed her head back to the pillow.

"She must be asleep," Mrs. Dalton mumbled.

He wanted to move from the bed, but was afraid he would stumble over something and Mrs. Dalton would hear him, would know that someone besides Mary was in the room. Frenzy dominated him. He held his hand over her mouth and his head was cocked at an angle that enabled him to see Mary and Mrs. Dalton by merely shifting his eyes. Mary mumbled and tried to rise again. Frantically, he caught a corner of the pillow and brought it to her lips. He had to stop her from mumbling, or he would be caught. Mrs. Dalton was moving slowly toward him and he grew tight and full, as though about to explode. Mary's fingernails tore at his hands and he caught the pillow and covered her entire face with it, firmly. Mary's body surged upward and he pushed downward upon the pillow with all of his weight, determined that she must not move or make any sound that would betray him. His eyes were filled with the white blur moving toward him in the shadows of the room. Again Mary's body heaved and he held the pillow in a grip that took all of his strength. For a long time he felt the sharp pain of her fingernails biting into his wrists. The white blur was still.

"Mary? Is that you?"

He clenched his teeth and held his breath, intimidated to

the core by the awesome white blur floating toward him. His muscles flexed taut as steel and he pressed the pillow, feeling the bed give slowly, evenly, but silently. Then suddenly her fingernails did not bite into his wrists. Mary's fingers loosened. He did not feel her surging and heaving against him. Her body was still.

"Mary! Is that *you?*"

He could see Mrs. Dalton plainly now. As he took his hands from the pillow he heard a long slow sigh go up from the bed into the air of the darkened room, a sigh which afterwards, when he remembered it, seemed final, irrevocable.

"Mary! Are you ill?"

He stood up. With each of her movements toward the bed his body made a movement to match hers, away from her, his feet not lifting themselves from the floor, but sliding softly and silently over the smooth deep rug, his muscles flexed so taut they ached. Mrs. Dalton now stood over the bed. Her hands reached out and touched Mary.

"Mary! Are you asleep? I heard you moving about. . . ."

Mrs. Dalton straightened suddenly and took a quick step back.

"You're dead drunk! You *stink* with whiskey!"

She stood silently in the hazy blue light, then she knelt at the side of the bed. Bigger heard her whispering. She's praying, he thought in amazement and the words echoed in his mind as though someone had spoken them aloud. Finally, Mrs. Dalton stood up and her face tilted to that upward angle at which she always held it. He waited, his teeth clamped, his fists clenched. She moved slowly toward the door; he could scarcely see her now. The door creaked; then silence.

He relaxed and sank to the floor, his breath going in a long gasp. He was weak and wet with sweat. He stayed crouched and bent, hearing the sound of his breathing filling the darkness. Gradually, the intensity of his sensations subsided and he was aware of the room. He felt that he had been in the grip of a weird spell and was now free. The fingertips of his right hand were pressed deeply into the soft fibers of the rug and his whole body vibrated from the wild pounding of his heart. He had to get out of the room, and quickly. Suppose that had been *Mr.* Dalton? His escape had been narrow enough, as it was.

He stood and listened. Mrs. Dalton might be out there in the hallway. How could he get out of the room? He all but shuddered with the intensity of his loathing for this house and all it had made him feel since he had first come into it. He reached his hand behind him and touched the wall; he was glad to have something solid at his back. He looked at the shadowy bed and remembered Mary as some person he had not seen in a long time. She was still there. Had he hurt her? He went to the bed and stood over her; her face lay sideways on the pillow. His hand moved toward her, but stopped in mid-air. He blinked his eyes and stared at Mary's face; it was darker than when he had first bent over her. Her mouth was open and her eyes bulged glassily. Her bosom, her bosom, her—her bosom was not moving! He could not hear her breath coming and going now as he had when he had first brought her into the room! He bent and moved her head with his hand and found that she was relaxed and limp. He snatched his hand away. Thought and feeling were balked in him; there was something he was trying to tell himself desperately, but could not. Then, convulsively, he sucked his breath in and huge words formed slowly, ringing in his ears: *She's dead. . . .*

The reality of the room fell from him; the vast city of white people that sprawled outside took its place. She was dead and he had killed her. He was a murderer, a Negro murderer, a black murderer. He had killed a white woman. He had to get away from here. Mrs. Dalton had been in the room while he was there, but she had not known it. But, *had* she? No! Yes! Maybe she had gone for help? No. If she had known she would have screamed. She didn't know. He had to slip out of the house. Yes. He could go home to bed and tomorrow he could tell them that he had driven Mary home and had left her at the side door.

In the darkness his fear made live in him an element which he reckoned with as "them." He had to construct a case for "them." But, *Jan!* Oh . . . Jan would give him away. When it was found that she was dead Jan would say that he had left them together in the car at Forty-sixth Street and Cottage Grove Avenue. But he would tell them that that was not true. And, after all, was not Jan a *red?* Was not his word as good as Jan's? He would say that Jan had come home with them. No one must know that he was the last person who had been with her.

Fingerprints! He had read about them in magazines. His fingerprints would give him away, surely! They could prove that he had been inside of her room! But suppose he told them that he had come to get the trunk? That was it! The *trunk!* His fingerprints had a right to be there. He looked round and saw her trunk on the other side of the bed, open, the top standing up. He could take the trunk to the basement and put the car into the garage and then go home. *No!* There was a better way. He would not put the car into the garage! He would say that Jan had come to the house and he had left Jan outside in the car. But there was still a *better way!* Make them think that Jan did it. Reds'd do anything. Didn't the papers say so? He would tell them that he had brought Jan and Mary home in the car and Mary had asked him to go with her to her room to get the trunk—and Jan was *with* them! —and he had got the trunk and had taken it to the basement and when he had gone he had left Mary and Jan—who had come back down—sitting in the car, kissing. . . . *That's it!*

He heard a clock ticking and searched for it with his eyes; it was at the head of Mary's bed, its white dial glowing in the blue darkness. It was five minutes past three. Jan had left them at Forty-sixth Street and Cottage Grove. *Jan didn't leave at Forty-sixth Street; he rode with us. . . .*

He went to the trunk and eased the top down and dragged

it over the rug to the middle of the floor. He lifted the top and felt inside; it was half-empty.

Then he was still, barely breathing, filled with another idea. Hadn't Mr. Dalton said that they did not get up early on Sunday mornings? Hadn't Mary said that she was going to Detroit? If Mary were missing when they got up, would they not think that she had already gone to Detroit? He . . . *Yes!* He could, he could put her *in* the trunk! She was small. Yes; put her in the trunk. She had said that she would be gone for three days. For three days, then, maybe no one would know. He would have three days of time. She was a crazy girl anyhow. She was always running around with reds, wasn't she? Anything could happen to her. People would think that she was up to some of her crazy ways when they missed her. Yes, reds'd do anything. Didn't the papers say so?

He went to the bed; he would have to lift her into the trunk. He did not want to touch her, but he knew he had to. He bent over. His hands were outstretched, trembling in mid-air. He had to touch her and lift her and put her in the trunk. He tried to move his hands and could not. It was as though he expected her to scream when he touched her. Goddamn! It all seemed foolish! He wanted to laugh. It was unreal. Like a nightmare. He had to lift a dead woman and was afraid. He felt that he had been dreaming of something like this for a long time, and then, suddenly, it was true. He heard the clock ticking. Time was passing. It would soon be morning. He had to act. He could not stand here all night like this; he might go to the electric chair. He shuddered and something cold crawled over his skin. Goddamn!

He pushed his hand gently under her body and lifted it. He stood with her in his arms; she was limp. He took her to the trunk and involuntarily jerked his head round and saw a white blur standing at the door and his body was instantly wrapped in a sheet of blazing terror and a hard ache seized his head and then the white blur went away. *I thought that was her.* . . . His heart pounded.

He stood with her body in his arms in the silent room and cold facts battered him like waves sweeping in from the sea: she was dead; she was white; she was a woman; he had killed her; he was black; he might be caught; he did not want to be caught; if he were they would kill him.

He stooped to put her in the trunk. Could he get her in? He looked again toward the door, expecting to see the white blur; but nothing was there. He turned her on her side in his arms; he was breathing hard and his body trembled. He eased her down, listening to the soft rustle of her clothes. He pushed her head into a corner, but her legs were too long and would not go in.

He thought he heard a noise and straightened; it seemed to him that his breathing was as loud as wind in a storm. He listened and heard nothing. He had to get her legs in! Bend her legs at the knees, he thought. Yes, almost. A little more . . . He bent them some more. Sweat dripped from his chin onto his hands. He doubled her knees and pushed her completely into the trunk. That much was done. He eased the top down and fumbled in the darkness for the latch and heard it click loudly.

He stood up and caught hold of one of the handles of the trunk and pulled. The trunk would not move. He was weak and his hands were slippery with sweat. He gritted his teeth and caught the trunk with both hands and pulled it to the door. He opened the door and looked into the hall: it was empty and silent. He stood the trunk on end and carried his right hand over his left shoulder and stooped and caught the strap and lifted the trunk to his back. Now, he would have to stand up. He strained; the muscles of his shoulders and legs quivered with effort. He rose, swaying, biting his lips.

Putting one foot carefully before the other, he went down the hall, down the stairs, then through another hall to the kitchen and paused. His back ached and the strap cut into his palm like fire. The trunk seemed to weigh a ton. He expected the white blur to step before him at any moment and hold out its hand and touch the trunk and demand to know what was in it. He wanted to put the trunk down and rest; but he was afraid that he would not be able to lift it again. He walked across the kitchen floor, down the steps, leaving the kitchen door open behind him. He stood in the darkened basement with the trunk upon his back and listened to the roaring draft of the furnace and saw the coals burning red through the cracks. He stooped, waiting to hear the bottom of the trunk touch the concrete floor. He bent more and rested on one knee. Goddamn! His hand, seared with fire, slipped from the strap and the trunk hit the floor with a loud clatter. He bent forward and squeezed his right hand in his left to still the fiery pain.

He stared at the furnace. He trembled with another idea. He—he could, he—he could put her, he could put her *in* the furnace. He would *burn* her! That was the safest thing of all to do. He went to the furnace and opened the door. A huge red bed of coals blazed and quivered with molten fury.

He opened the trunk. She was as he had put her: her head buried in one corner and her knees bent and doubled toward her stomach. He would have to lift her again. He stooped and caught her shoulders and lifted her in his arms. He went to the door of the furnace and paused. The fire seethed. Ought he to put her in head or feet first? Because he was tired and scared, and because her feet were nearer, he pushed her in feet first. The heat blasted his hands.

He had all but her shoulders in. He looked into the furnace; her clothes were ablaze and smoke was filling the interior so that he could scarcely see. The draft roared upward, droning in his ears. He gripped her shoulders and pushed hard, but the body would not go any farther. He tried again, but her head still remained out. Now. . . . Goddamn! He wanted to strike something with his fist. What could he do? He stepped back and looked.

A noise made him whirl; two green burning pools—pools of accusation and guilt—stared at him from a white blur that sat perched upon the edge of the trunk. His mouth opened in a silent scream and his body became hotly paralyzed. It was the white cat and its round green eyes gazed past him at the white face hanging limply from the fiery furnace door. *God!* He closed his mouth and swallowed. Should he catch the cat and kill it and put it in the furnace, too? He made a move. The cat stood up; its white fur bristled; its back arched. He tried to grab it and it bounded past him with a long wail of fear and scampered up the steps and through the door and out of sight. Oh! He had left the kitchen door open. *That* was it. He closed the door and stood again before the furnace, thinking, Cats can't talk. . . .

He got his knife from his pocket and opened it and stood by the furnace, looking at Mary's white throat. Could he do it? He had to. Would there be blood? Oh, Lord! He looked round with a haunted and pleading look in his eyes. He saw a pile of old newspapers stacked carefully in a corner. He got a thick wad of them and held them under the head. He touched the sharp blade to the throat, just touched it, as if expecting the knife to cut the white flesh of itself, as if he did not have to put pressure behind it. Wistfully, he gazed at the edge of the blade resting on the white skin; the gleaming metal reflected the tremulous fury of the coals. Yes; he *had* to. Gently, he sawed the blade into the flesh and struck a bone. He gritted his teeth and cut harder. As yet there was no blood anywhere but on the knife. But the bone made it difficult. Sweat crawled down his back. Then blood crept outward in widening circles of pink on the newspapers, spreading quickly now. He whacked at the bone with the knife. The head hung limply on the newspapers, the curly black hair dragging about in blood. He whacked harder, but the head would not come off.

He paused, hysterical. He wanted to run from the basement and go as far as possible from the sight of this bloody throat. But he could not. He must not. He *had* to burn this girl. With eyes glazed, with nerves tingling with excitement, he looked about the basement. He saw a hatchet. *Yes!* That would do it. He spread a neat layer of newspapers beneath the head, so that the blood would not drip on the floor. He got the hatchet, held the head at a slanting angle with his left hand and, after pausing in an attitude of prayer, sent the blade of the hatchet into the bone of the throat with all the strength of his body. The head rolled off.

He was not crying, but his lips were trembling and his chest was heaving. He wanted to lie down upon the floor and sleep off the horror of this thing. But he had to get out of here. Quickly, he wrapped the head in the newspapers and used the wad to push the bloody trunk of the body deeper into the furnace. Then he shoved the head in. The hatchet went next.

Would there be coal enough to burn the body? No one would come down here before ten o'clock in the morning, maybe. He looked at his watch. It was four o'clock. He got another piece of paper and wiped his knife with it. He put the paper into the furnace and the knife into his pocket. He pulled the lever and coal rattled against the sides of the tin chute and he saw the whole furnace blaze and the draft roared still louder. When the body was covered with coal, he pushed the lever back. Now!

Then, abruptly, he stepped back from the furnace and looked at it, his mouth open. Hell! Folks'd *smell* it! There would be an odor and someone would look in the furnace. Aimlessly, his eyes searched the basement. There! That ought to do it! He saw the smutty blades of an electric exhaust fan high up in the wall of the basement, back of the furnace. He found the switch and threw it. There was a quick whir, then a hum. Things would be all right now; the exhaust fan would suck the air out of the basement and there would be no scent.

He shut the trunk and pushed it into a corner. In the morning he would take it to the station. He looked around to see if he had left anything that would betray him; he saw nothing.

He went out of the back door; a few fine flakes of snow

were floating down. It had grown colder. The car was still in the driveway. Yes; he would leave it there.

Jan and Mary were sitting in the car, kissing. They said, Good night, Bigger. . . . And he said, Good night. . . . And he touched his hand to his cap. . . .

As he passed the car he saw the door was still open. Mary's purse was on the floor. He took it and closed the door. Naw! Leave it open; he opened it and went on down the driveway.

The streets were empty and silent. The wind chilled his wet body. He tucked the purse under his arm and walked. What would happen now? Ought he to run away? He stopped at a street corner and looked into the purse. There was a thick roll of bills; tens and twenties. . . . Good! He would wait until morning to decide what to do. He was tired and sleepy.

He hurried home and ran up the steps and went on tiptoe into the room. His mother and brother and sister breathed regularly in sleep. He began to undress, thinking, *I'll tell 'em I left her with Jan in the car after I took the trunk down in the basement. In the morning I'll take the trunk to the station, like she told me. . . .*

He felt something heavy sagging in his shirt; it was the gun. He took it out; it was warm and wet. He shoved it under the pillow. *They can't say I did it. If they do, they can't prove it.*

He eased the covers of the bed back and slipped beneath them and stretched out beside Buddy; in five minutes he was sound asleep.

The Man Who Lived Underground

The first draft of "The Man Who Lived Underground," a short novel based on a prisoner's story from True Detective *magazine, was written in 1942. This version began with a rather naturalistic description of the life of a black servant. However, when the story was published in 1945 in* Cross Section, *Wright had discarded his original opening in favor of the description of an anonymous man creeping into a sewer. This new beginning enabled Wright's surrealistic and symbolical treatment of the existentialist themes of flight, fear, guilt and freedom to take on a larger, more universal quality. An early attempt at "writing fiction beyond the categories of white and black," this story combines the same themes employed in* Native Son *with a meditation on the metaphysical situation of Man placed by chance beyond the norms and barriers of good and evil, a situation which Wright treats in greater detail in* The Outsider. *Esthetically, "The Man Who Lived Underground" is certainly the most perfect of Wright's short works because of a fine blending of powerful narrative and constant use of the close-up technique with a rich allegorical and symbolic treatment. It can be read as a parable of the human quest for meaning, which leads to the discovery of the individual's responsibility and*

"The Man Who Lived Underground" originally appeared in *Cross Section* magazine in 1945 and was later published in *Eight Men*, World Publishing Co., in 1961.

relationship to his fellow men. Its implications on the artistic level are also evident in Fred Daniels' central act of gratuitous creation, performed in rebellion against the world of money, exchange and consumption. In more ways than one, the man who lived underground is a contemporary Everyman, as well as an avatar of the oppressed Black.

I'VE GOT TO HIDE, he told himself. His chest heaved as he waited, crouching in a dark corner of the vestibule. He was tired of running and dodging. Either he had to find a place to hide, or he had to surrender. A police car swished by through the rain, its siren rising sharply. They're looking for me all over . . . He crept to the door and squinted through the fogged plate glass. He stiffened as the siren rose and died in the distance. Yes, he had to hide, but where? He gritted his teeth. Then a sudden movement in the street caught his attention. A throng of tiny columns of water snaked into the air from the perforations of a manhole cover. The columns stopped abruptly, as though the perforations had become clogged; a gray spout of sewer water jutted up from underground and lifted the circular metal cover, juggled it for a moment, then let it fall with a clang.

He hatched a tentative plan: he would wait until the siren sounded far off, then he would go out. He smoked and waited, tense. At last the siren gave him his signal; it wailed, dying, going away from him. He stepped to the sidewalk, then paused and looked curiously at the open manhole, half expecting the cover to leap up again. He went to the center of the street and stooped and peered into the hole, but could see nothing. Water rustled in the black depths.

He started with terror; the siren sounded so near that he had the idea that he had been dreaming and had awakened to find the car upon him. He dropped instinctively to his knees and his hands grasped the rim of the manhole. The

siren seemed to hoot directly above him and with a wild gasp
of exertion he snatched the cover far enough off to admit his
body. He swung his legs over the opening and lowered himself into watery darkness. He hung for an eternal moment to
the rim by his finger tips, then he felt rough metal prongs and
at once he knew that sewer workmen used these ridges to
lower themselves into manholes. Fist over fist, he let his body
sink until he could feel no more prongs. He swayed in dank
space; the siren seemed to howl at the very rim of the manhole. He dropped and was washed violently into an ocean of
warm, leaping water. His head was battered against a wall
and he wondered if this were death. Frenziedly his fingers
clawed and sank into a crevice. He steadied himself and
measured the strength of the current with his own muscular
tension. He stood slowly in water that dashed past his knees
with fearful velocity.

He heard a prolonged scream of brakes and the siren broke
off. Oh, God! They had found him! Looming above his head
in the rain a white face hovered over the hole. "How did this
damn thing get off?" he heard a policeman ask. He saw the
steel cover move slowly until the hole looked like a quarter
moon turned black. "Give me a hand here," someone called.
The cover clanged into place, muffling the sights and sounds
of the upper world. Knee-deep in the pulsing current, he
breathed with aching chest, filling his lungs with the hot
stench of yeasty rot.

From the perforations of the manhole cover, delicate
lances of hazy violet sifted down and wove a mottled pattern
upon the surface of the streaking current. His lips parted as
a car swept past along the wet pavement overhead, its heavy
rumble soon dying out, like the hum of a plane speeding
through a dense cloud. He had never thought that cars could
sound like that; everything seemed strange and unreal under
here. He stood in darkness for a long time, knee-deep in
rustling water, musing.

The odor of rot had become so general that he no longer

smelled it. He got his cigarettes, but discovered that his matches were wet. He searched and found a dry folder in the
pocket of his shirt and managed to strike one; it flared
weirdly in the wet gloom, glowing greenishly, turning red,
orange, then yellow. He lit a crumpled cigarette; then, by the
flickering light of the match, he looked for support so that he
would not have to keep his muscles flexed against the pouring water. His pupils narrowed and he saw to either side of
him two steaming walls that rose and curved inward some six
feet above his head to form a dripping, mouse-colored dome.
The bottom of the sewer was a sloping V-trough. To the left,
the sewer vanished in ashen fog. To the right was a steep
down-curve into which water plunged.

He saw now that had he not regained his feet in time, he
would have been swept to death, or had he entered any other
manhole he would have probably drowned. Above the rush
of the current he heard sharper juttings of water; tiny
streams were spewing into the sewer from smaller conduits.
The match died; he struck another and saw a mass of debris
sweep past him and clog the throat of the down-curve. At
once the water began rising rapidly. Could he climb out
before he drowned? A long hiss sounded and the debris was
sucked from sight; the current lowered. He understood now
what had made the water toss the manhole cover; the down-
curve had become temporarily obstructed and the perforations had become clogged.

He was in danger; he might slide into a down-curve; he
might wander with a lighted match into a pocket of gas and
blow himself up; or he might contract some horrible disease
. . . Though he wanted to leave, an irrational impulse held
him rooted. To the left, the convex ceiling swooped to a
height of less than five feet. With cigarette slanting from
pursed lips, he waded with taut muscles, his feet sloshing
over the slimy bottom, his shoes sinking into spongy slop, the
slate-colored water cracking in creamy foam against his
knees. Pressing his flat left palm against the lowered ceiling,

he struck another match and saw a metal pole nestling in a niche of the wall. Yes, some sewer workman had left it. He reached for it, then jerked his head away as a whisper of scurrying life whisked past and was still. He held the match close and saw a huge rat, wet with slime, blinking beady eyes and baring tiny fangs. The light blinded the rat and the frizzled head moved aimlessly. He grabbed the pole and let it fly against the rat's soft body; there was shrill piping and the grizzly body splashed into the dun-colored water and was snatched out of sight, spinning in the scuttling stream.

He swallowed and pushed on, following the curve of the misty cavern, sounding the water with the pole. By the faint light of another manhole cover he saw, amid loose wet brick, a hole with walls of damp earth leading into blackness. Gingerly he poked the pole into it; it was hollow and went beyond the length of the pole. He shoved the pole before him, hoisted himself upward, got to his hands and knees, and crawled. After a few yards he paused, struck to wonderment by the silence; it seemed that he had traveled a million miles away from the world. As he inched forward again he could sense the bottom of the dirt tunnel becoming dry and lowering slightly. Slowly he rose and to his astonishment he stood erect. He could not hear the rustling of the water now and he felt confoundingly alone, yet lured by the darkness and silence.

He crept a long way, then stopped, curious, afraid. He put his right foot forward and it dangled in space; he drew back in fear. He thrust the pole outward and it swung in emptiness. He trembled, imagining the earth crumbling and burying him alive. He scratched a match and saw that the dirt floor sheered away steeply and widened into a sort of cave some five feet below him. An old sewer, he muttered. He cocked his head, hearing a feathery cadence which he could not identify. The match ceased to burn.

Using the pole as a kind of ladder, he slid down and stood in darkness. The air was a little fresher and he could still hear vague noises. Where was he? He felt suddenly that someone was standing near him and he turned sharply, but there was only darkness. He poked cautiously and felt a brick wall; he followed it and the strange sounds grew louder. He ought to get out of here. This was crazy. He could not remain here for any length of time; there was no food and no place to sleep. But the faint sounds tantalized him; they were strange but familiar. Was it a motor? A baby crying? Music? A siren? He groped on, and the sounds came so clearly that he could feel the pitch and timbre of human voices. Yes, singing! That was it! He listened with open mouth. It was a church service. Enchanted, he groped toward the waves of melody.

> *Jesus, take me to your home above*
> *And fold me in the bosom of Thy love . . .*

The singing was on the other side of a brick wall. Excited, he wanted to watch the service without being seen. Whose church was it? He knew most of the churches in this area above ground, but the singing sounded too strange and detached for him to guess. He looked to the left, to the right, down to the black dirt, then upward and was startled to see a bright sliver of light slicing the darkness like the blade of a razor. He struck one of his two remaining matches and saw rusty pipes running along an old concrete ceiling. Photographically he located the exact position of the pipes in his mind. The match flame sank and he sprang upward; his hands clutched a pipe. He swung his legs and tossed his body onto the bed of pipes and they creaked, swaying up and down; he thought that the tier was about to crash, but nothing happened. He edged to the crevice and saw a segment of black men and women, dressed in white robes, singing, holding tattered songbooks in their black palms. His first impulse was to laugh, but he checked himself.

What was he doing? He was crushed with a sense of guilt. Would God strike him dead for that? The singing swept on and he shook his head, disagreeing in spite of himself. They oughtn't to do that, he thought. But he could think of no reason *why* they should not do it. Just singing with the air of the sewer blowing in on them . . . He felt that he was gazing upon something abysmally obscene, yet he could not bring himself to leave.

After a long time he grew numb and dropped to the dirt. Pain throbbed in his legs and a deeper pain, induced by the sight of those black people groveling and begging for something they could never get, churned in him. A vague conviction made him feel that those people should stand unrepentant and yield no quarter in singing and praying, yet *he* had run away from the police, had pleaded with them to believe in *his* innocence. He shook his head, bewildered.

How long had he been down here? He did not know. This was a new kind of living for him; the intensity of feelings he had experienced when looking at the church people sing made him certain that he had been down here a long time, but his mind told him that the time must have been short. In this darkness the only notion he had of time was when a match flared and measured time by its fleeting light. He groped back through the hole toward the sewer and the waves of song subsided and finally he could not hear them at all. He came to where the earth hole ended and he heard the noise of the current and time lived again for him, measuring the moments by the wash of water.

The rain must have slackened, for the flow of water had lessened and came only to his ankles. Ought he to go up into the streets and take his chances on hiding somewhere else? But they would surely catch him. The mere thought of dodging and running again from the police made him tense. No, he would stay and plot how to elude them. But what could he do down here? He walked forward into the sewer and came to another manhole cover; he stood beneath it, debating. Fine pencils of gold spilled suddenly from the little circles in the manhole cover and trembled on the surface of the current. Yes, street lamps . . . It must be night . . .

He went forward for about a quarter of an hour, wading aimlessly, poking the pole carefully before him. Then he stopped, his eyes fixed and intent. What's that? A strangely familiar image attracted and repelled him. Lit by the yellow stems from another manhole cover was a tiny nude body of a baby snagged by debris and half-submerged in water. Thinking that the baby was alive, he moved impulsively to save it, but his roused feelings told him that it was dead, cold, nothing, the same nothingness he had felt while watching the men and women singing in the church. Water blossomed about the tiny legs, the tiny arms, the tiny head, and rushed onward. The eyes were closed, as though in sleep; the fists were clenched, as though in protest; and the mouth gaped black in a soundless cry.

He straightened and drew in his breath, feeling that he had been staring for all eternity at the ripples of veined water skimming impersonally over the shriveled limbs. He felt as condemned as when the policemen had accused him. Involuntarily he lifted his hand to brush the vision away, but his arm fell listlessly to his side. Then he acted; he closed his eyes and reached forward slowly with the soggy shoe of his right foot and shoved the dead baby from where it had been lodged. He kept his eyes closed, seeing the little body twisting in the current as it floated from sight. He opened his eyes, shivered, placed his knuckles in the sockets, hearing the water speed in the somber shadows.

He tramped on, sensing at times a sudden quickening in the current as he passed some conduit whose waters were swelling the stream that slid by his feet. A few minutes later he was standing under another manhole cover, listening to the faint rumble of noises above ground. Streetcars and trucks, he mused. He looked down and saw a stagnant pool of gray-green sludge; at intervals a balloon pocket rose from the scum, glistening a bluish-purple, and burst. Then another. He turned, shook his head, and tramped back to the dirt cave by the church, his lips quivering.

Back in the cave, he sat and leaned his back against a dirt wall. His body was trembling slightly. Finally his senses quieted and he slept. When he awakened he felt stiff and cold. He had to leave this foul place, but leaving meant facing those policemen who had wrongly accused him. No, he could not go back aboveground. He remembered the beating they had given him and how he had signed his name to a confession, a confession which he had not even read. He had been too tired when they had shouted at him, demanding that he sign his name; he had signed it to end his pain.

He stood and groped about in the darkness. The church singing had stopped. How long had he slept? He did not know. But he felt refreshed and hungry. He doubled his fist nervously, realizing that he could not make a decision. As he walked about he stumbled over an old rusty iron pipe. He picked it up and felt a jagged edge. Yes, there was a brick wall and he could dig into it. What would he find? Smiling, he groped to the brick wall, sat, and began digging idly into damp cement. I can't make any noise, he cautioned himself. As time passed he grew thirsty, but there was no water. He had to kill time or go aboveground. The cement came out of the wall easily; he extracted four bricks and felt a soft draft blowing into his face. He stopped, afraid. What was beyond? He waited a long time and nothing happened; then he began digging again, soundlessly, slowly; he enlarged the hole and crawled through into a dark room and collided with another wall. He felt his way to the right; the wall ended and his fingers toyed in space, like the antennae of an insect.

He fumbled on and his feet struck something hollow, like wood. What's this? He felt with his fingers. Steps . . . He stooped and pulled off his shoes and mounted the stairs and saw a yellow chink of light shining and heard a low voice speaking. He placed his eye to a keyhole and saw the nude waxen figure of a man stretched out upon a white table. The voice, low-pitched and vibrant, mumbled indistinguishable words, neither rising nor falling. He craned his neck and squinted to see the man who was talking, but he could not locate him. Above the naked figure was suspended a huge glass container filled with a blood-red liquid from which a white rubber tube dangled. He crouched closer to the door and saw the tip end of a black object lined with pink satin. A coffin, he breathed. This is an undertaker's establishment. . . . A fine-spun lace of ice covered his body and he shuddered. A throaty chuckle sounded in the depths of the yellow room.

He turned to leave. Three steps down it occurred to him that a light switch should be nearby; he felt along the wall, found an electric button, pressed it, and a blinding glare smote his pupils so hard that he was sightless, defenseless. His pupils contracted and he wrinkled his nostrils at a peculiar odor. At once he knew that he had been dimly aware of this odor in the darkness, but the light had brought it sharply to his attention. Some kind of stuff they used to embalm, he thought. He went down the steps and saw piles of lumber, coffins, and a long workbench. In one corner was a tool chest. Yes, he could use tools, could tunnel through walls with them. He lifted the lid of the chest and saw nails, a hammer, a crowbar, a screwdriver, a light bulb, and a long length of electric wire. Good! He would lug these back to his cave.

He was about to hoist the chest to his shoulders when he discovered a door behind the furnace. Where did it lead? He tried to open it and found it securely bolted. Using the crowbar so as to make no sound, he pried the door open; it swung on creaking hinges, outward. Fresh air came to his face and he caught the faint roar of faraway sound. Easy now, he told himself. He widened the door and a lump of coal rattled toward him. A coalbin . . . Evidently the door led into another basement. The roaring noise was louder now, but he could not identify it. Where was he? He groped slowly over the coal pile, then ranged in darkness over a gritty floor. The roaring noise seemed to come from above him, then below. His fingers followed a wall until he touched a wooden ridge. A door, he breathed.

The noise died to a low pitch; he felt his skin prickle. It seemed that he was playing a game with an unseen person whose intelligence outstripped his. He put his ear to the flat surface of the door. Yes, voices . . . Was this a prize fight stadium? The sound of the voices came near and sharp, but he could not tell if they were joyous or despairing. He twisted the knob until he heard a soft click and felt the springy weight of the door swinging toward him. He was afraid to open it, yet captured by curiosity and wonder. He jerked the door wide and saw on the far side of the basement a furnace glowing red. Ten feet away was still another door, half ajar. He crossed and peered through the door into an empty, high-ceilinged corridor that terminated in a dark complex of shadow. The belling voices rolled about him and his eagerness mounted. He stepped into the corridor and the voices swelled louder. He crept on and came to a narrow stairway leading circularly upward; there was no question but that he was going to ascend those stairs.

Mounting the spiraled staircase, he heard the voices roll in a steady wave, then leap to crescendo, only to die away, but always remaining audible. Ahead of him glowed red letters: E—X—I—T. At the top of the steps he paused in front of a black curtain that fluttered uncertainly. He parted the folds and looked into a convex depth that gleamed with clusters of shimmering lights. Sprawling below him was a stretch of human faces, tilted upward, chanting, whistling, screaming, laughing. Dangling before the faces, high upon a screen of silver, were jerking shadows. A movie, he said with slow laughter breaking from his lips.

He stood in a box in the reserved section of a movie house and the impulse he had had to tell the people in the church to stop their singing seized him. These people were laughing at their lives, he thought with amazement. They were shouting and yelling at the animated shadows of themselves. His compassion fired his imagination and he stepped out of the box, walked out upon thin air, walked on down to the audience; and, hovering in the air just above them, he stretched out his hand to touch them . . . His tension snapped and he found himself back in the box, looking down into the sea of faces. No; it could not be done; he could not awaken them. He sighed. Yes, these people were children, sleeping in their living, awake in their dying.

He turned away, parted the black curtain, and looked out. He saw no one. He started down the white stone steps and when he reached the bottom he saw a man in trim blue uniform coming toward him. So used had he become to being underground that he thought that he could walk past the man, as though he were a ghost. But the man stopped. And he stopped.

"Looking for the men's room, sir?" the man asked, and, without waiting for an answer, he turned and pointed. "This way, sir. The first door to your right."

He watched the man turn and walk up the steps and go out of sight. Then he laughed. What a funny fellow! He went back to the basement and stood in the red darkness, watching the glowing embers in the furnace. He went to the sink and turned the faucet and the water flowed in a smooth silent stream that looked like a spout of blood. He brushed the mad image from his mind and began to wash his hands leisurely, looking about for the usual bar of soap. He found one and rubbed it in his palms until a rich lather bloomed in his cupped fingers, like a scarlet sponge. He scrubbed and rinsed his hands meticulously, then hunted for a towel; there was none. He shut off the water, pulled off his shirt, dried his hands on it; when he put it on again he was grateful for the cool dampness that came to his skin.

Yes, he was thirsty; he turned on the faucet again, bowled his fingers and when the water bubbled over the brim of his cupped palms, he drank in long, slow swallows. His bladder grew tight; he shut off the water, faced the wall, bent his head, and watched a red stream strike the floor. His nostrils wrinkled against acrid wisps of vapor; though he had tramped in the waters of the sewer, he stepped back from the wall so that his shoes, wet with sewer slime, would not touch his urine.

He heard footsteps and crawled quickly into the coalbin. Lumps rattled noisily. The footsteps came into the basement and stopped. Who was it? Had someone heard him and come down to investigate? He waited, crouching, sweating. For a long time there was silence, then he heard the clang of metal and a brighter glow lit the room. Somebody's tending the furnace, he thought. Footsteps came closer and he stiffened. Looming before him was a white face lined with coal dust, the face of an old man with watery blue eyes. Highlights spotted his gaunt cheekbones, and he held a huge shovel. There was a screechy scrape of metal against stone, and the old man lifted a shovelful of coal and went from sight.

The room dimmed momentarily, then a yellow glare came as coal flared at the furnace door. Six times the old man came to the bin and went to the furnace with shovels of coal, but not once did he lift his eyes. Finally he dropped the shovel, mopped his face with a dirty handkerchief, and sighed: "Wheeew!" He turned slowly and trudged out of the basement, his footsteps dying away.

He stood, and lumps of coal clattered down the pile. He stepped from the bin and was startled to see the shadowy outline of an electric bulb hanging above his head. Why had not the old man turned it on? Oh, yes . . . He understood. The old man had worked here for so long that he had no need for light; he had learned a way of seeing in his dark world, like those sightless worms that inch along underground by a sense of touch.

His eyes fell upon a lunch pail and he was afraid to hope that it was full. He picked it up; it was heavy. He opened it. *Sandwiches!* He looked guiltily around; he was alone. He searched farther and found a folder of matches and a half-empty tin of tobacco; he put them eagerly into his pocket and clicked off the light. With the lunch pail under his arm, he went through the door, groped over the pile of coal, and stood again in the lighted basement of the undertaking establishment. I've got to get those tools, he told himself. And turn off that light. He tiptoed back up the steps and switched off the light; the invisible voice still droned on behind the door. He crept down and, seeing with his fingers, opened the lunch pail and tore off a piece of paper bag and brought out the tin and spilled grains of tobacco into the makeshift concave. He rolled it and wet it with spittle, then inserted one end into his mouth and lit it: he sucked smoke that bit his lungs. The nicotine reached his brain, went out along his arms to his finger tips, down to his stomach, and over all the tired nerves of his body.

He carted the tools to the hole he had made in the wall. Would the noise of the falling chest betray him? But he would have to take a chance; he had to have those tools. He lifted the chest and shoved it; it hit the dirt on the other side of the wall with a loud clatter. He waited, listening; nothing happened. Head first, he slithered through and stood in the cave. He grinned, filled with a cunning idea. Yes, he would now go back into the basement of the undertaking establishment and crouch behind the coal pile and dig another hole. Sure! Fumbling, he opened the tool chest and extracted a crowbar, a screwdriver, and a hammer; he fastened them securely about his person.

With another lumpish cigarette in his flexed lips, he crawled back through the hole and over the coal pile and sat, facing the brick wall. He jabbed with the crowbar and the cement sheered away; quicker than he thought, a brick came loose. He worked an hour; the other bricks did not come easily. He sighed, weak from effort. I ought to rest a little, he thought. I'm hungry. He felt his way back to the cave and stumbled along the wall till he came to the tool chest. He sat upon it, opened the lunch pail, and took out two thick sandwiches. He smelled them. Pork chops . . . His mouth watered. He closed his eyes and devoured a sandwich, savoring the smooth rye bread and juicy meat. He ate rapidly, gulping

down lumpy mouthfuls that made him long for water. He ate
the other sandwich and found an apple and gobbled that up
too, sucking the core till the last trace of flavor was drained from it. Then, like a dog, he ground the meat bones with
his teeth, enjoying the salty, tangy marrow. He finished
and stretched out full length on the ground and went to
sleep. . . .

. . . His body was washed by cold water that gradually
turned warm and he was buoyed upon a stream and swept
out to sea where waves rolled gently and suddenly he found
himself walking upon the water how strange and delightful
to walk upon the water and he came upon a nude woman
holding a nude baby in her arms and the woman was sinking
into the water holding the baby above her head and screaming *help* and he ran over the water to the woman and he
reached her just before she went down and he took the baby
from her hands and stood watching the breaking bubbles
where the woman sank and he called *lady* and still no answer
yes dive down there and rescue that woman but he could not
take this baby with him and he stooped and laid the baby
tenderly upon the surface of the water expecting it to sink
but it floated and he leaped into the water and held his
breath and strained his eyes to see through the gloomy volume of water but there was no woman and he opened his
mouth and called *lady* and the water bubbled and his chest
ached and his arms were tired but he could not see the
woman and he called again *lady lady* and his feet touched
sand at the bottom of the sea and his chest felt as though it
would burst and he bent his knees and propelled himself
upward and water rushed past him and his head bobbed out
and he breathed deeply and looked around where was the
baby the baby was gone and he rushed over the water looking for the baby calling *where is it* and the empty sky and sea
threw back his voice *where is it* and he began to doubt that
he could stand upon the water and then he was sinking and
as he struggled the water rushed him downward spinning

dizzily and he opened his mouth to call for help and water surged into his lungs and he choked . . .

He groaned and leaped erect in the dark, his eyes wide. The images of terror that thronged his brain would not let him sleep. He rose, made sure that the tools were hitched to his belt, and groped his way to the coal pile and found the rectangular gap from which he had taken the bricks. He took out the crowbar and hacked. Then dread paralyzed him. How long had he slept? Was it day or night now? He had to be careful. Someone might hear him if it were day. He hewed softly for hours at the cement, working silently. Faintly quivering in the air above him was the dim sound of yelling voices. Crazy people, he muttered. They're still there in that movie . . .

Having rested, he found the digging much easier. He soon had a dozen bricks out. His spirits rose. He took out another brick and his fingers fluttered in space. Good! What lay ahead of him? Another basement? He made the hole larger, climbed through, walked over an uneven floor and felt a metal surface. He lighted a match and saw that he was standing behind a furnace in a basement; before him, on the far side of the room, was a door. He crossed and opened it; it was full of odds and ends. Daylight spilled from a window above his head.

Then he was aware of a soft, continuous tapping. What was it? A clock? No, it was louder than a clock and more irregular. He placed an old empty box beneath the window, stood upon it, and looked into an areaway. He eased the window up and crawled through; the sound of the tapping came clearly now. He glanced about; he was alone. Then he looked upward at a series of window ledges. The tapping identified itself. That's a typewriter, he said to himself. It seemed to be coming from just above. He grasped the ridges of a rain pipe and lifted himself upward; through a half-inch opening of window he saw a doorknob about three feet away. No, it was not a doorknob; it was a small circular disk made of stainless steel with many fine markings upon it. He held his breath; an eerie white hand, seemingly detached from its arm, touched the metal knob and whirled it, first to the left, then to the right. It's a safe! . . . Suddenly he could see the dial no more; a huge metal door swung slowly toward him and he was looking into a safe filled with green wads of paper money, rows of coins wrapped in brown paper, and glass jars and boxes of various sizes. His heart quickened. Good Lord! The white hand went in and out of the safe, taking wads of bills and cylinders of coins. The hand vanished and he heard the muffled click of the big door as it closed. Only the steel dial was visible now. The typewriter still tapped in his ears, but he could not see it. He blinked, wondering if what he had seen was real. There was more money in that safe than he had seen in all his life.

As he clung to the rain pipe, a daring idea came to him and he pulled the screwdriver from his belt. If the white hand twirled that dial again, he would be able to see how far to left and right it spun and he would have the combination! His blood tingled. I can scratch the numbers right here, he thought. Holding the pipe with one hand, he made the sharp edge of the screwdriver bite into the brick wall. Yes, he could do it. Now, he was set. Now, he had a reason for staying here in the underground. He waited for a long time, but the white hand did not return. Goddamn! Had he been more alert, he could have counted the twirls and he would have had the combination. He got down and stood in the areaway, sunk in reflection.

How could he get into that room? He climbed back into the basement and saw wooden steps leading upward. Was that the room where the safe stood? Fearing that the dial was now being twirled, he clambered through the window, hoisted himself up the rain pipe, and peered; he saw only the naked gleam of the steel dial. He got down and doubled his fists. Well, he would explore the basement. He returned to the basement room and mounted the steps to the door and squinted through the keyhole; all was dark, but the tapping was still somewhere near, still faint and directionless. He pushed the door in; along one wall of a room was a table piled with radios and electrical equipment. A radio shop, he muttered.

Well, he could rig up a radio in his cave. He found a sack, slid the radio into it, and slung it across his back. Closing the door, he went down the steps and stood again in the basement, disappointed. He had not solved the problem of the steel dial and he was irked. He set the radio on the floor and again hoisted himself through the window and up the rain pipe and squinted; the metal door was swinging shut. Goddamn! He's worked the combination again. If I had been patient, I'd have had it! How could he get into that room? He *had* to get into it. He could jimmy the window, but it would be much better if he could get in without any traces. To the right of him, he calculated, should be the basement of the building that held the safe; therefore, if he dug a hole right *here*, he ought to reach his goal.

He began a quiet scraping; it was hard work, for the bricks were not damp. He eventually got one out and lowered it softly to the floor. He had to be careful; perhaps people were beyond this wall. He extracted a second layer of brick and found still another. He gritted his teeth, ready to quit. I'll dig one more, he resolved. When the next brick came out he felt air blowing into his face. He waited to be challenged, but nothing happened.

He enlarged the hole and pulled himself through and stood in quiet darkness. He scratched a match to flame and saw steps; he mounted and peered through a keyhole: Darkness . . . He strained to hear the typewriter, but there was only silence. Maybe the office had closed? He twisted the knob and swung the door in; a frigid blast made him shiver. In the shadows before him were halves and quarters of hogs and lambs and steers hanging from metal hooks on the low ceiling, red meat encased in folds of cold white fat. Fronting him was frost-coated glass from behind which came indistinguishable sounds. The odor of fresh raw meat sickened him and he backed away. A meat market, he whispered.

He ducked his head, suddenly blinded by light. He narrowed his eyes; the red-white rows of meat were drenched in yellow glare. A man wearing a crimson-spotted jacket came in and took down a bloody meat cleaver. He eased the door to, holding it ajar just enough to watch the man, hoping that the darkness in which he stood would keep him from being seen. The man took down a hunk of steer and placed it upon a bloody wooden block and bent forward and whacked with the cleaver. The man's face was hard, square, grim; a jet of mustache smudged his upper lip and a glistening cowlick of hair fell over his left eye. Each time he lifted the cleaver and brought it down upon the meat, he let out a short, deep-chested grunt. After he had cut the meat, he wiped blood off the wooden block with a sticky wad of gunny sack and hung the cleaver upon a hook. His face was proud as he placed the chunk of meat in the crook of his elbow and left.

The door slammed and the light went off; once more he stood in shadow. His tension ebbed. From behind the frosted glass he heard the man's voice: "Forty-eight cents a pound, ma'am." He shuddered, feeling that there was something he had to do. But what? He stared fixedly at the cleaver, then he sneezed and was terrified for fear that the man had heard him. But the door did not open. He took down the cleaver and examined the sharp edge smeared with cold blood. Behind the ice-coated glass a cash register rang with a vibrating, musical tinkle.

Absent-mindedly holding the meat cleaver, he rubbed the glass with his thumb and cleared a spot that enabled him to see into the front of the store. The shop was empty, save for the man who was now putting on his hat and coat. Beyond the front window a wan sun shone in the streets; people passed and now and then a fragment of laughter or the whir of a speeding auto came to him. He peered closer and saw on the right counter of the shop a mosquito netting covering pears, grapes, lemons, oranges, bananas, peaches, and plums. His stomach contracted.

The man clicked out the light and he gritted his teeth, muttering, Don't lock the icebox door . . . The man went through the door of the shop and locked it from the outside. Thank God! Now, he would eat some more! He waited, trembling. The sun died and its rays lingered on in the sky, turning the streets to dusk. He opened the door and stepped inside the shop. In reverse letters across the front window was: NICK'S FRUITS AND MEATS. He laughed, picked up a soft ripe yellow pear and bit into it; juice squirted; his mouth ached as his saliva glands reacted to the acid of the fruit. He ate three pears, gobbled six bananas, and made away with several oranges, taking a bit out of their tops and holding them to his lips and squeezing them as he hungrily sucked the juice.

He found a faucet, turned it on, laid the cleaver aside, pursed his lips under the stream until his stomach felt about to burst. He straightened and belched, feeling satisfied for the first time since he had been underground. He sat upon the floor, rolled and lit a cigarette, his bloodshot eyes squinting against the film of drifting smoke. He watched a patch of sky turn red, then purple; night fell and he lit another cigarette, brooding. Some part of him was trying to remember the world he had left, and another part of him did not want to remember it. Sprawling before him in his mind was his wife, Mrs. Wooten for whom he worked, the three policemen who had picked him up . . . He possessed them now more completely than he had ever possessed them when he had lived above ground. How this had come about he could not say, but he had no desire to go back to them. He laughed, crushed the cigarette, and stood up.

He went to the front door and gazed out. Emotionally he hovered between the world aboveground and the world underground. He longed to go out, but sober judgment urged him to remain here. Then impulsively he pried the lock loose with one swift twist of the crowbar; the door swung outward. Through the twilight he saw a white man and a white woman coming toward him. He held himself tense, waiting for them to pass; but they came directly to the door and confronted him.

"I want to buy a pound of grapes," the woman said.

Terrified, he stepped back into the store. The white man stood to one side and the woman entered.

"Give me a pound of dark ones," the woman said.

The white man came slowly forward, blinking his eyes.

"Where's Nick?" the man asked.

"Were you just closing?" the woman asked.

"Yes, ma'am," he mumbled. For a second he did not breathe, then he mumbled again: "Yes, ma'am."

"I'm sorry," the woman said.

The street lamps came on, lighting the store somewhat. Ought he run? But that would raise an alarm. He moved slowly, dreamily, to a counter and lifted up a bunch of grapes and showed them to the woman.

"Fine," the woman said. "But isn't that more than a pound?"

He did not answer. The man was staring at him intently.

"Put them in a bag for me," the woman said, fumbling with her purse.

"Yes, ma'am."

He saw a pile of paper bags under a narrow ledge; he opened one and put the grapes in.

"Thanks," the woman said, taking the bag and placing a dime in his dark palm.

"Where's Nick?" the man asked again. "At supper?"

"Sir? Yes, sir," he breathed.

They left the store and he stood trembling in the doorway. When they were out of sight, he burst out laughing and crying. A trolley car rolled noisily past and he controlled himself quickly. He flung the dime to the pavement with a gesture of contempt and stepped into the warm night air. A few shy stars trembled above him. The look of things was beautiful, yet he felt a lurking threat. He went to an unattended newsstand and looked at a stack of papers. He saw a headline: HUNT NEGRO FOR MURDER.

He felt that someone had slipped up on him from behind and was stripping off his clothes; he looked about wildly, went quickly back into the store, picked up the meat cleaver where he had left it near the sink, then made his way through the icebox to the basement. He stood for a long time, breathing heavily. They know I didn't do anything, he muttered. But how could he prove it? He had signed a confession. Though innocent, he felt guilty, condemned. He struck a match and held it near the steel blade, fascinated and repelled by the dried blotches of blood. Then his fingers gripped the handle of the cleaver with all the strength of his body, he wanted to fling the cleaver from him, but he could not. The match flame wavered and fled; he struggled through the hole and put the cleaver in the sack with the radio. He was determined to keep it, for what purpose he did not know.

He was about to leave when he remembered the safe. Where was it? He wanted to give up, but felt that he ought to make one more try. Opposite the last hole he had dug, he tunneled again, plying the crowbar. Once he was so exhausted that he lay on the concrete floor and panted. Finally he made another hole. He wriggled through and his nostrils filled with the fresh smell of coal. He struck a match; yes, the usual steps led upward. He tiptoed to a door and eased it open. A fair-haired white girl stood in front of a steel cabinet, her blue eyes wide upon him. She turned chalky and gave a high-pitched scream. He bounded down the steps and raced to his hole and clambered through, replacing the bricks with nervous haste. He paused, hearing loud voices.

"What's the matter, Alice?"

"A man . . ."

"What man? Where?"

"A man was at that door . . ."

"Oh, nonsense!"

"He was looking at me through the door!"

"Aw, you're dreaming."

"I *did* see a man!"

The girl was crying now.

"There's nobody here."

Another man's voice sounded.

"What is it, Bob?"

"Alice says she saw a man in here, in that door!"

"Let's take a look."

He waited, poised for flight. Footsteps descended the stairs.

"There's nobody down here."

"The window's locked."

"And there's no door."

"You ought to fire that dame."

"Oh, I don't know. Women are that way."

"She's too hysterical."

The men laughed. Footsteps sounded again on the stairs. A door slammed. He sighed, relieved that he had escaped. But he had not done what he had set out to do; his glimpse of the room had been too brief to determine if the safe was there. He had to know. Boldly he groped through the hole once more; he reached the steps and pulled off his shoes and tip-toed up and peered through the keyhole. His head accidentally touched the door and it swung silently in a fraction of an inch; he saw the girl bent over the cabinet, her back to him. Beyond her was the safe. He crept back down the steps, thinking exultingly: I found it!

Now he had to get the combination. Even if the window in the areaway was locked and bolted, he could gain entrance when the office closed. He scoured through the holes he had dug and stood again in the basement where he had left the radio and the cleaver. Again he crawled out of the window and lifted himself up the rain pipe and peered. The steel dial showed lonely and bright, reflecting the yellow glow of an unseen light. Resigned to a long wait, he sat and leaned against the wall. From far off came the faint sounds of life aboveground; once he looked with a baffled expression at the dark sky. Frequently he rose and climbed the pipe to see the white hand spin the dial, but nothing happened. He bit his lip with impatience. It was not the money that was luring him, but the mere fact that he could get it with impunity. Was the hand now twirling the dial? He rose and looked, but the white hand was not in sight.

Perhaps it would be better to watch continuously? Yes; he clung to the pipe and watched the dial until his eyes thickened with tears. Exhausted, he stood again in the areaway. He heard a door being shut and he clawed up the pipe and looked. He jerked tense as a vague figure passed in front of him. He stared unblinkingly, hugging the pipe with one hand and holding the screwdriver with the other, ready to etch the combination upon the wall. His ears caught: *Dong . . . Dong . . . Dong . . . Dong . . . Dong . . . Dong . . . Dong . . .* Seven o'clock, he whispered. Maybe they were closing now? What kind of a store would be open as late as this? he wondered. Did anyone live in the rear? Was there a night watchman? Perhaps the safe was *already* locked for the night! Goddamn! While he had been eating in that shop, they had locked up everything . . . Then, just as he was about to give up, the white hand touched the dial and turned it once to the right and stopped at six. With quivering fingers, he etched 1—R—6 upon the brick wall with the tip of the screwdriver. The hand twirled the dial twice to the left and stopped at two, and he engraved 2—L—2 upon the wall. The dial was spun four times to the right and stopped at six again; he wrote 4—R—6. The dial rotated three times to the left and was centered straight up and down; he wrote 3—L—0. The door swung open and again he saw the piles of green money and the rows of wrapped coins. I got it, he said grimly.

Then he was stone still, astonished. There were two hands now. A right hand lifted a wad of green bills and deftly slipped it up the sleeve of a left arm. The hands trembled; again the right hand slipped a packet of bills up the left sleeve. He's stealing, he said to himself. He grew indignant, as if the money belonged to him. Though *he* had planned to steal the money, he despised and pitied the man. He felt that his stealing the money and the man's stealing were two entirely different things. He wanted to steal the money merely for the sensation involved in getting it, and he had no intention whatever of spending a penny of it; but he knew that the man who was now stealing it was going to spend it, perhaps for pleasure. The huge steel door closed with a soft click.

Though angry, he was somewhat satisfied. The office would close soon. I'll clean the place out, he mused. He imagined the entire office staff cringing with fear; the police would question everyone for a crime they had not committed, just as they had questioned him. And they would have no idea of how the money had been stolen until they discovered the holes he had tunneled in the walls of the basements. He lowered himself and laughed mischievously, with the abandoned glee of an adolescent.

He flattened himself against the wall as the window above him closed with rasping sound. He looked; somebody was bolting the window securely with a metal screen. That won't help you, he snickered to himself. He clung to the rain pipe until the yellow light in the office went out. He went back into the basement, picked up the sack containing the radio and cleaver, and crawled through the two holes he had dug and groped his way into the basement of the building that held the safe. He moved in slow motion, breathing softly. Be careful now, he told himself. There might be a night watchman . . . In his memory was the combination written in bold white characters as upon a blackboard. Eel-like he squeezed through the last hole and crept up the steps and put his hand on the knob and pushed the door in about three inches. Then his courage ebbed; his imagination wove dangers for him.

Perhaps the night watchman was waiting in there, ready to shoot. He dangled his cap on a forefinger and poked it past the jamb of the door. If anyone fired, they would hit his cap; but nothing happened. He widened the door, holding the crowbar high above his head, ready to beat off an assailant. He stood like that for five minutes; the rumble of a streetcar brought him to himself. He entered the room. Moonlight floated in from a side window. He confronted the safe, then checked himself. Better take a look around first . . . He stepped about and found a closed door. Was the night watchman in there? He opened it and saw a washbowl, a faucet, and a commode. To the left was still another door that opened into a huge dark room that seemed empty; on the far side of that room he made out the shadow of still another door. Nobody's here, he told himself.

He turned back to the safe and fingered the dial; it spun with ease. He laughed and twirled it just for fun. Get to work, he told himself. He turned the dial to the figures he saw on the blackboard of his memory; it was so easy that he felt that the safe had not been locked at all. The heavy door eased loose and he caught hold of the handle and pulled hard, but the door swung open with a slow momentum of its own. Breathless, he gaped at wads of green bills, rows of wrapped coins, curious glass jars full of white pellets, and many oblong green metal boxes. He glanced guiltily over his shoulder; it seemed impossible that someone should not call to him to stop.

They'll be surprised in the morning, he thought. He opened the top of the sack and lifted a wad of compactly tied bills; the money was crisp and new. He admired the smooth, cleancut edges. The fellows in Washington sure know how to make this stuff, he mused. He rubbed the money with his fingers, as though expecting it to reveal hidden qualities. He lifted the wad to his nose and smelled the fresh odor of ink. Just like any other paper, he mumbled. He dropped the wad into the sack and picked up another. Holding the bag, he thought and laughed.

There was in him no sense of possessiveness; he was intrigued with the form and color of the money, with the manifold reactions which he knew that men above-ground held toward it. The sack was one-third full when it occurred to him to examine the denominations of the bills; without realizing it, he had put many wads of one-dollar bills into the sack. Aw, nuts, he said in disgust. Take the big ones . . . He dumped the one-dollar bills onto the floor and swept all the hundred-dollar bills he could find into the sack, then he raked in rolls of coins with crooked fingers.

He walked to a desk upon which sat a typewriter, the same machine which the blond girl had used. He was fascinated by it; never in his life had he used one of them. It was a queer instrument of business, something beyond the rim of his life. Whenever he had been in an office where a girl was typing, he had almost always spoken in whispers. Remembering vaguely what he had seen others do, he inserted a sheet of paper into the machine; it went in lopsided and he did not know how to straighten it. Spelling in a soft diffident voice, he pecked out his name on the keys: *freddaniels.* He looked at it and laughed. He would learn to type correctly one of these days.

Yes, he would take the typewriter too. He lifted the machine and placed it atop the bulk of money in the sack. He did not feel that he was stealing, for the cleaver, the radio, the money, and the typewriter were all on the same level of value, all meant the same thing to him. They were the serious toys of the men who lived in the dead world of sunshine and rain he had left, the world that had condemned him, branded him guilty.

But what kind of a place is this? he wondered. What was in that dark room to his rear? He felt for his matches and found that he had only one left. He leaned the sack against the safe and groped forward into the room, encountering smooth, metallic objects that felt like machines. Baffled, he touched a wall and tried vainly to locate an electric switch. Well, he *had* to strike his last match. He knelt and struck it, cupping the flame near the floor with his palms. The place seemed to be a factory, with benches and tables. There were bulbs with green shades spaced about the tables; he turned on a light and twisted it low so that the glare was limited. He saw a half-filled packet of cigarettes and appropriated it. There were stools at the benches and he concluded that men worked here at some trade. He wandered and found a few half-used folders of matches. If only he could find more cigarettes! But there were none.

But what kind of a place was this? On a bench he saw a pad of paper captioned: PEER'S—MANUFACTURING JEWELERS. His lips formed an "O," then he snapped off the light and ran back to the safe and lifted one of the glass jars and stared at the tiny white pellets. Gingerly he picked up one and found that it was wrapped in tissue paper. He peeled the paper and saw a glittering stone that looked like glass, glinting white and blue sparks. Diamonds, he breathed.

Roughly he tore the paper from the pellets and soon his palm quivered with precious fire. Trembling, he took all four glass jars from the safe and put them into the sack. He grabbed one of the metal boxes, shook it, and heard a tinny rattle. He pried off the lid with the screwdriver. Rings! Hundreds of them . . . Were they worth anything? He scooped up a handful and jets of fire shot fitfully from the stones. These are diamonds too, he said. He pried open another box. Watches! A chorus of soft, metallic ticking filled his ears. For a moment he could not move, then he dumped all the boxes into the sack.

He shut the safe door, then stood looking around, anxious not to overlook anything. Oh! He had seen a door in the room where the machines were. What was in there? More valuables? He re-entered the room, crossed the floor, and stood undecided before the door. He finally caught hold of the knob and pushed the door in; the room beyond was dark. He advanced cautiously inside and ran his fingers along the wall for the usual switch, then he was stark still. *Something had moved in the room!* What was it? Ought he to creep out, taking the rings and diamonds and money? Why risk what he already had? He waited and the ensuing silence gave him confidence to explore further. Dare he strike a match? Would not a match flame make him a good target? He tensed again as he heard a faint sigh; he was now convinced that there was something alive near him, something that lived and breathed. On tiptoe he felt slowly along the wall, hoping that he would not collide with anything. Luck was with him; he found the light switch.

No; don't turn the light on . . . Then suddenly he realized that he did not know in what direction the door was. Goddamn! He had to turn the light on or strike a match. He fingered the switch for a long time, then thought of an idea. He knelt upon the floor, reached his arm up to the switch and flicked the button, hoping that if anyone shot, the bullet would go above his head. The moment the light came on he narrowed his eyes to see quickly. He sucked in his breath and his body gave a violent twitch and was still. In front of him, so close that it made him want to bound up and scream, was a human face.

He was afraid to move lest he touch the man. If the man had opened his eyes at that moment, there was no telling what he might have done. The man—long and rawboned— was stretched out on his back upon a little cot, sleeping in his clothes, his head cushioned by a dirty pillow; his face, clouded by a dark stubble of beard, looked straight up to the ceiling. The man sighed, and he grew tense to defend himself; the man mumbled and turned his face away from the light. I've got to turn off that light, he thought. Just as he was about to rise, he saw a gun and cartridge belt on the floor at the man's side. Yes, he would take the gun and cartridge belt, not to use them, but just to keep them, as one takes a memento from a country fair. He picked them up and was about to click off the light when his eyes fell upon a photograph perched upon a chair near the man's head; it was the picture of a woman, smiling, shown against a background of open fields; at the woman's side were two young children, a boy and a girl. He smiled indulgently; he could send a bullet into that man's brain and time would be over for him . . .

He clicked off the light and crept silently back into the room where the safe stood; he fastened the cartridge belt about him and adjusted the holster at his right hip. He strutted about the room on tiptoe, lolling his head nonchalantly, then paused, abruptly pulled the gun, and pointed it with grim face toward an imaginary foe. "Boom!" he whispered fiercely. Then he bent forward with silent laughter. That's just like they do it in the movies, he said.

He contemplated his loot for a long time, then got a towel from the washroom and tied the sack securely. When he looked up he was momentarily frightened by his shadow looming on the wall before him. He lifted the sack, dragged it down the basement steps, lugged it across the basement, gasping for breath. After he had struggled through the hole, he clumsily replaced the bricks, then tussled with the sack until he got it to the cave. He stood in the dark, wet with sweat, brooding about the diamonds, the rings, the watches, the money; he remembered the singing in the church, the people yelling in the movie, the dead baby, the nude man stretched out upon the white table . . . He saw these items hovering before his eyes and felt that some dim meaning linked them together, that some magical relationship made them kin. He stared with vacant eyes, convinced that all of these images, with their tongueless reality, were striving to tell him something . . .

Later, seeing with his fingers, he untied the sack and set each item neatly upon the dirt floor. Exploring, he took the bulb, the socket, and the wire out of the tool chest; he was elated to find a double socket at one end of the wire. He crammed the stuff into his pockets and hoisted himself upon the rusty pipes and squinted into the church; it was dim and empty. Somewhere in this wall were live electric wires; but where? He lowered himself, groped and tapped the wall with the butt of the screwdriver, listening vainly for hollow sounds. I'll just take a chance and dig, he said.

For an hour he tried to dislodge a brick, and when he struck a match, he found that he had dug a depth of only an inch! No use in digging here, he sighed. By the flickering light of a match, he looked upward, then lowered his eyes, only to glance up again, startled. Directly above his head, beyond the pipes, was a wealth of electric wiring. I'll be damned, he snickered.

He got an old dull knife from the chest and, seeing again with his fingers, separated the two strands of wire and cut away the insulation. Twice he received a slight shock. He scraped the wiring clean and managed to join the two twin ends, then screwed in the bulb. The sudden illumination blinded him and he shut his lids to kill the pain in his eyeballs. I've got that much done, he thought jubilantly.

He placed the bulb on the dirt floor and the light cast a blatant glare on the bleak clay walls. Next he plugged one end of the wire that dangled from the radio into the light socket and bent down and switched on the button; almost at once there was the harsh sound of static, but no words or music. Why won't it work? he wondered. Had he damaged the mechanism in any way? Maybe it needed grounding? Yes . . . He rummaged in the tool chest and found another length of wire, fastened it to the ground of the radio, and then tied the opposite end to a pipe. Rising and growing distinct, a slow strain of music entranced him with its measured sound. He sat upon the chest, deliriously happy.

Later he searched again in the chest and found a half-gallon can of glue; he opened it and smelled a sharp odor. Then he recalled that he had not even looked at the money. He took a wad of green bills and weighed it in his palm, then broke the seal and held one of the bills up to the light and studied it closely. *The United States of America will pay to the bearer on demand one hundred dollars,* he read in slow speech; then: *This note is legal tender for all debts, public and private.* . . . He broke into a musing laugh, feeling that he was reading of the doings of people who lived on some far-off planet. He turned the bill over and saw on the other side of it a delicately beautiful building gleaming with paint and set amidst green grass. He had no desire whatever to count the money; it was what it stood for—the various currents of life swirling aboveground—that captivated him. Next he opened the rolls of coins and let them slide from their paper wrappings to the ground; the bright, new gleaming pennies and nickels and dimes piled high at his feet, a glowing mound of shimmering copper and silver. He sifted them through his fingers, listening to their tinkle as they struck the conical heap.

Oh, yes! He had forgotten. He would now write his name on the typewriter. He inserted a piece of paper and poised his fingers to write. But what was his name? He stared, trying to remember. He stood and glared about the dirt cave, his name on the tip of his lips. But it would not come to him. Why was he here? Yes, he had been running away from the police. But why? His mind was blank. He bit his lips and sat again, feeling a vague terror. But why worry? He laughed, then pecked slowly: *itwasalonghotday.* He was determined to type the sentence without making any mistakes. How did one make capital letters? He experimented and luckily discovered how to lock the machine for capital letters and then shift it back to lower case. Next he discovered how to make spaces, then he wrote neatly and correctly: *It was a long hot day.* Just why he selected that sentence he did not know; it was merely the ritual of performing the thing that appealed to him. He took the sheet out of the machine and looked around with stiff neck and hard eyes and spoke to an imaginary person:

"Yes, I'll have the contracts ready tomorrow."

He laughed. That's just the way they talk, he said. He grew weary of the game and pushed the machine aside. His eyes fell upon the can of glue, and a mischievous idea bloomed in him, filling him with nervous eagerness. He leaped up and opened the can of glue, then broke the seals on all the wads of money. I'm going to have some wallpaper, he said with a luxurious, physical laugh that made him bend at the knees. He took the towel with which he had tied the sack and balled it into a swab and dipped it into the can of glue and dabbed glue onto the wall; then he pasted one green bill by the side of another. He stepped back and cocked his head. Jesus! That's funny . . . He slapped his thighs and guffawed. He had triumphed over the world aboveground! He was free! If only people could see this! He wanted to run from this cave and yell his discovery to the world.

He swabbed all the dirt walls of the cave and pasted them with green bills; when he had finished the walls blazed with a yellow-green fire. Yes, this room would be his hide-out; between him and the world that had branded him guilty would stand this mocking symbol. He had not stolen the money; he had simply picked it up, just as a man would pick up firewood in a forest. And that was how the world aboveground now seemed to him, a wild forest filled with death.

The walls of money finally palled on him and he looked about for new interests to feed his emotions. The cleaver! He drove a nail into the wall and hung the bloody cleaver upon it. Still another idea welled up. He pried open the metal boxes and lined them side by side on the dirt floor. He grinned at the gold and fire. From one box he lifted up a fistful of ticking gold watches and dangled them by their gleaming chains. He stared with an idle smile, then began to wind them up; he did not attempt to set them at any given hour, for there was no time for him now. He took a fistful of nails and drove them into the papered walls and hung the watches upon them, letting them swing down by their glittering chains, trembling and ticking busily against the back-drop of green with the lemon sheen of the electric light shining upon the metal watch casings, converting the golden disks into blobs of liquid yellow. Hardly had he hung up the last watch than the idea extended itself; he took more nails from the chest and drove them into the green paper and took the boxes of rings and went from nail to nail and hung up the golden bands. The blue and white sparks from the stones filled the cave with brittle laughter, as though enjoying his hilarious secret. People certainly can do some funny things, he said to himself.

He sat upon the tool chest, alternately laughing and shaking his head soberly. Hours later he became conscious of the gun sagging at his hip and he pulled it from the holster. He had seen men fire guns in movies, but somehow his life had never led him into contact with firearms. A desire to feel the sensation others felt in firing came over him. But someone might hear . . . Well, what if they did? They would not know where the shot had come from. Not in their wildest notions would they think that it had come from under the streets! He tightened his fingers on the trigger; there was a deafening report and it seemed that the entire underground had caved in upon his eardrums; and in the same instant there flashed an orange-blue spurt of flame that died quickly but lingered on as a vivid after-image. He smelled the acrid stench of burnt powder filling his lungs and he dropped the gun abruptly.

The intensity of his feelings died and he hung the gun and cartridge belt upon the wall. Next he lifted the jars of diamonds and turned them bottom upward, dumping the white pellets upon the ground. One by one he picked them up and peeled the tissue paper from them and piled them in a neat heap. He wiped his sweaty hands on his trousers, lit a cigarette, and commenced playing another game. He imagined that he was a rich man who lived aboveground in the obscene sunshine and he was strolling through a park of a summer morning, smiling, nodding to his neighbors, sucking an after-breakfast cigar. Many times he crossed the floor of the cave, avoiding the diamonds with his feet, yet subtly gauging his footsteps so that his shoes, wet with sewer slime, would strike the diamonds at some undetermined moment. After twenty minutes of sauntering, his right foot smashed into the heap and diamonds lay scattered in all directions, glinting with a million tiny chuckles of icy laughter. Oh, shucks, he mumbled in mock regret, intrigued by the damage he had wrought. He continued walking, ignoring the brittle fire. He felt that he had a glorious victory locked in his heart.

He stooped and flung the diamonds more evenly over the floor and they showered rich sparks, collaborating with him. He went over the floor and trampled the stones just deeply enough for them to be faintly visible, as though they were set deliberately in the prongs of a thousand rings. A ghostly light bathed the cave. He sat on the chest and frowned. Maybe anything's right, he mumbled. Yes, if the world as men had made it was right, then anything else was right, any act a man took to satisfy himself, murder, theft, torture.

He straightened with a start. What was happening to him? He was drawn to these crazy thoughts, yet they made him feel vaguely guilty. He would stretch out upon the ground, then get up; he would want to crawl again through the holes he had dug, but would restrain himself; he would think of going again up into the streets, but fear would hold him still. He stood in the middle of the cave, surrounded by green walls and a laughing floor, trembling. He was going to do something, but what? Yes, he was afraid of himself, afraid of doing some nameless thing.

To control himself, he turned on the radio. A melancholy piece of music rose. Brooding over the diamonds on the floor was like looking up into a sky full of restless stars; then the illusion turned into its opposite: he was high up in the air looking down at the twinkling lights of a sprawling city. The music ended and a man recited news events. In the same attitude in which he had contemplated the city, so now, as he heard the cultivated tone, he looked down upon land and sea as men fought, as cities were razed, as planes scattered death upon open towns, as long lines of trenches wavered and broke. He heard the names of generals and the names of mountains and the names of countries and the names and numbers of divisions that were in action on different battle fronts. He saw black smoke billowing from the stacks of warships as they neared each other over wastes of water and he heard their huge guns thunder as red-hot shells screamed across the surface of night seas. He saw hundreds of planes wheeling and droning in the sky and heard the clatter of machine guns as they fought each other and he saw planes falling in plumes of smoke and blaze of fire. He saw steel tanks rumbling across fields of ripe wheat to meet other tanks and there was a loud clang of steel as numberless tanks collided. He saw troops with fixed bayonets charging in waves against other troops who held fixed bayonets and men groaned as steel ripped into their bodies and they went down to die . . . The voice of the radio faded and he was staring at the diamonds on the floor at his feet.

He shut off the radio, fighting an irrational compulsion to act. He walked aimlessly about the cave, touching the walls with his finger tips. Suddenly he stood still. *What was the matter with him?* Yes, he knew . . . It was these walls; these crazy walls were filling him with a wild urge to climb out into the dark sunshine aboveground. Quickly he doused the light to banish the shouting walls, then sat again upon the tool chest. Yes, he was trapped. His muscles were flexed taut and sweat ran down his face. He knew now that he could not stay here and he could not go out. He lit a cigarette with shaking fingers; the match flame revealed the green-papered walls with militant distinctness; the purple on the gun barrel glinted like a threat; the meat cleaver brooded with its eloquent splotches of blood; the mound of silver and copper smoldered angrily; the diamonds winked at him from the floor; and the gold watches ticked and trembled, crowning time the king of consciousness, defining the limits of living ... The match blaze died and he bolted from where he stood and collided brutally with the nails upon the walls. The spell was broken. He shuddered, feeling that, in spite of his fear, sooner or later he would go up into that dead sunshine and somehow say something to somebody about all this.

He sat again upon the tool chest. Fatigue weighed upon his forehead and eyes. Minutes passed and he relaxed. He dozed, but his imagination was alert. He saw himself rising, wading again in the sweeping water of the sewer; he came to a manhole and climbed out and was amazed to discover that he had hoisted himself into a room filled with armed policemen who were watching him intently. He jumped awake in the dark; he had not moved. He sighed, closed his eyes, and slept again; this time his imagination designed a scheme of protection for him. His dreaming made him feel that he was standing in a room watching over his own nude body lying stiff and cold upon a white table. At the far end of the room he saw a crowd of people huddled in a corner, afraid of his body. Though lying dead upon the table, he was standing in some mysterious way at his side, warding off the people, guarding his body, and laughing to himself as he observed the situation. They're scared of me, he thought.

He awakened with a start, leaped to his feet, and stood in the center of the black cave. It was a full minute before he moved again. He hovered between sleeping and waking, unprotected, a prey of wild fears. He could neither see nor hear. One part of him was asleep; his blood coursed slowly and his flesh was numb. On the other hand he was roused to a strange, high pitch of tension. He lifted his fingers to his face, as though about to weep. Gradually his hands lowered and he struck a match, looking about, expecting to see a door through which he could walk to safety; but there was no door, only the green walls and the moving floor. The match flame died and it was dark again.

Five minutes later he was still standing when the thought came to him that he had been asleep. Yes . . . But he was not yet fully awake; he was still queerly blind and dead. How long had he slept? Where was he? Then suddenly he recalled the green-papered walls of the cave and in the same instant he heard loud singing coming from the church beyond the wall. Yes, they woke me up, he muttered. He hoisted himself and lay atop the bed of pipes and brought his face to the narrow slit. Men and women stood here and there between pews. A song ended and a young black girl tossed back her head and closed her eyes and broke plaintively into another hymn:

> Glad, glad, glad, oh, so glad
> I got Jesus in my soul . . .

Those few words were all she sang, but what her words did not say, her emotions said as she repeated the lines, varying the mood and tempo, making her tone express meanings which her conscious mind did not know. Another woman melted her voice with the girl's, and then an old man's voice merged with that of the two women. Soon the entire congregation was singing:

> Glad, glad, glad, oh, so glad
> I got Jesus in my soul . . .

They're wrong, he whispered in the lyric darkness. He felt that their search for a happiness they could never find made them feel that they had committed some dreadful offense which they could not remember or understand. He was now in possession of the feeling that had gripped him when he had first come into the underground. It came to him in a series of questions: Why was this sense of guilt so seemingly innate, so easy to come by, to think, to feel, so verily physical? It seemed that when one felt this guilt one was retracing in one's feelings a faint pattern designed long before; it seemed that one was always trying to remember a gigantic shock that had left a haunting impression upon one's body which one could not forget or shake off, but which had been forgotten by the conscious mind, creating in one's life a state of eternal anxiety.

He had to tear himself away from this; he got down from the pipes. His nerves were so taut that he seemed to feel his brain pushing through his skull. He felt that he had to do something, but he could not figure out what it was. Yet he knew that if he stood here until he made up his mind, he would never move. He crawled through the hole he had made in the brick wall and the exertion afforded him respite from tension. When he entered the basement of the radio store, he stopped in fear, hearing loud voices.

"Come on, boy! Tell us what you did with the radio!"

"Mister, I didn't steal the radio! I swear!"

He heard a dull thumping sound and he imagined a boy being struck violently.

"Please, mister!"

"Did you take it to a pawn shop?"

"No, sir! I didn't steal the radio! I got a radio at home," the boy's voice pleaded hysterically. "Go to my home and look!"

There came to his ears the sound of another blow. It was so funny that he had to clap his hand over his mouth to keep from laughing out loud. They're beating some poor boy, he whispered to himself, shaking his head. He felt a sort of distant pity for the boy and wondered if he ought to bring back the radio and leave it in the basement. No. Perhaps it was a good thing that they were beating the boy; perhaps the beating would bring to the boy's attention, for the first time in his life, the secret of his existence, the guilt that he could never get rid of.

Smiling, he scampered over a coal pile and stood again in the basement of the building where he had stolen the money and jewelry. He lifted himself into the areaway, climbed the rain pipe, and squinted through a two-inch opening of window. The guilty familiarity of what he saw made his muscles tighten. Framed before him in a bright tableau of daylight was the night watchman sitting upon the edge of a chair, stripped to the waist, his head sagging forward, his eyes red and puffy. The watchman's face and shoulders were stippled with red and black welts. Back of the watchman stood the safe, the steel door wide open, showing the empty vault. Yes, they think he did it, he mused.

Footsteps sounded in the room and a man in a blue suit passed in front of him, then another, then still another. Policemen, he breathed. Yes, they were trying to make the watchman confess, just as they had once made him confess to a crime he had not done. He stared into the room, trying to recall something. Oh . . . Those were the same policemen who had beaten him, had made him sign that paper when he had been too tired and sick to care. Now, they were doing the same thing to the watchman. His heart pounded as he saw one of the policemen shake a finger into the watchman's face.

"Why don't you admit it's an inside job, Thompson?" the policeman said.

"I've told you all I know," the watchman mumbled through swollen lips.

"But nobody was here but you!" the policeman shouted.

"I was sleeping," the watchman said. "It was wrong, but I was sleeping all that night!"

"Stop telling us that lie!"

"It's the truth!"

"When did you get the combination?"

"I don't know how to open the safe," the watchman said.

He clung to the rain pipe, tense; he wanted to laugh, but he controlled himself. He felt a great sense of power; yes, he could go back to the cave, rip the money off the walls, pick up the diamonds and rings, and bring them here and write a note, telling them where to look for their foolish toys. No . . . What good would that do? It was not worth the effort. The watchman was guilty; although he was not guilty of the crime of which he had been accused, he was guilty, had always been guilty. The only thing that worried him was that the man who had been really stealing was not being accused. But he consoled himself: they'll catch him sometime during his life.

He saw one of the policemen slap the watchman across the mouth.

"Come clean, you bastard!"

"I've told you all I know," the watchman mumbled like a child.

One of the police went to the rear of the watchman's chair and jerked it from under him; the watchman pitched forward upon his face.

"Get up!" a policeman said.

Trembling, the watchman pulled himself up and sat limply again in the chair.

"Now, are you going to talk?"

"I've told you all I know," the watchman gasped.

"Where did you hide the stuff?"

"I didn't take it!"

"Thompson, your brains are in your feet," one of the policemen said. "We're going to string you up and get them back into your skull."

He watched the policemen clamp handcuffs on the watchman's wrists and ankles; then they lifted the watchman and swung him upside-down and hoisted his feet to the edge of a door. The watchman hung, head down, his eyes bulging. They're crazy, he whispered to himself as he clung to the ridges of the pipe.

"You going to talk?" a policeman shouted into the watchman's ear.

He heard the watchman groan.

"We'll let you hang there till you talk, see?"

He saw the watchman close his eyes.

"Let's take 'im down. He passed out," a policeman said.

He grinned as he watched them take the body down and

dump it carelessly upon the floor. The policeman took off the handcuffs.

"Let 'im come to. Let's get a smoke," a policeman said.

The three policeman left the scope of his vision. A door slammed. He had an impulse to yell to the watchman that he could escape through the hole in the basement and live with him in the cave. But he wouldn't understand, he told himself. After a moment he saw the watchman rise and stand, swaying from weakness. He stumbled across the room to a desk, opened a drawer, and took out a gun. He's going to kill himself, he thought, intent, eager, detached, yearning to see the end of the man's actions. As the watchman stared vaguely about he lifted the gun to his temple; he stood like that for some minutes, biting his lips until a line of blood etched its way down a corner of his chin. No, he oughtn't do that, he said to himself in a mood of pity.

"Don't!" he half whispered and half yelled.

The watchman looked wildly about; he had heard him. But it did not help; there was a loud report and the watchman's head jerked violently and he fell like a log and lay prone, the gun clattering over the floor.

The three policemen came running into the room with drawn guns. One of the policemen knelt and rolled the watchman's body over and stared at a ragged, scarlet hole in the temple.

"Our hunch was right," the kneeling policeman said. "He was guilty, all right."

"Well, this ends the case," another policeman said.

"He knew he was licked," the third one said with grim satisfaction.

He eased down the rain pipe, crawled back through the holes he had made, and went back into his cave. A fever burned in his bones. He had to act, yet he was afraid. His eyes stared in the darkness as though propped open by invisible hands, as though they had become lidless. His muscles were rigid and he stood for what seemed to him a thousand years.

When he moved again his actions were informed with precision, his muscular system reinforced from a reservoir of energy. He crawled through the hole of earth, dropped into the gray sewer current, and sloshed ahead. When his right foot went forward at a street intersection, he fell backward and shot down into water. In a spasm of terror his right hand grabbed the concrete ledge of a down-curve and he felt the streaking water tugging violently at his body. The current reached his neck and for a moment he was still. He knew that if he moved clumsily he would be sucked under. He held onto the ledge with both hands and slowly pulled himself up. He sighed, standing once more in the sweeping water, thankful that he had missed death.

He waded on through sludge, moving with care, until he came to a web of light sifting down from a manhole cover. He saw steel hooks running up the side of the sewer wall; he caught hold and lifted himself and put his shoulder to the cover and moved it an inch. A crash of sound came to him as he looked into a hot glare of sunshine through which blurred shapes moved. Fear scalded him and he dropped back into the pallid current and stood paralyzed in the shadows. A heavy car rumbled past overhead, jarring the pavement, warning him to stay in his world of dark light, knocking the cover back into place with an imperious clang.

He did not know how much fear he felt, for fear claimed him completely; yet it was not a fear of the police or of people, but a cold dread at the thought of the actions he knew he would perform if he went out into that cruel sunshine. His mind said no; his body said yes; and his mind could not understand his feelings. A low whine broke from him and he was in the act of uncoiling. He climbed upward and heard the faint honking of auto horns. Like a frantic cat clutching a rag, he clung to the steel prongs and heaved his shoulder against the cover and pushed it off halfway. For a split second his eyes were drowned in the terror of yellow light and he was in a deeper darkness than he had ever known in the underground.

Partly out of the hole, he blinked, regaining enough sight to make out meaningful forms. An odd thing was happening: No one was rushing forward to challenge him. He had imagined the moment of his emergence as a desperate tussle with men who wanted to cart him off to be killed; instead, life froze about him as the traffic stopped. He pushed the cover aside, stood, swaying in a world so fragile that he expected it to collapse and drop him into some deep void. But nobody seemed to pay him heed. The cars were now swerving to shun him and the gaping hole.

"Why in hell don't you put up a red light, dummy?" a raucous voice yelled.

He understood; they thought that he was a sewer workman. He walked toward the sidewalk, weaving unsteadily through the moving traffic.

"Look where you're going, nigger!"

"That's right! Stay there and get killed!"

"You blind, you bastard?"

"Go home and sleep your drunk off!"

A policeman stood at the curb, looking in the opposite direction. When he passed the policeman, he feared that he would be grabbed, but nothing happened. Where was he? Was this real? He wanted to look about to get his bearings, but felt that something awful would happen to him if he did. He wandered into a spacious doorway of a store that sold men's clothing and saw his reflection in a long mirror: his cheekbones protruded from a hairy black face; his greasy cap was perched askew upon his head and his eyes were red and glassy. His shirt and trousers were caked with mud and hung loosely. His hands were gummed with a black stickiness. He threw back his head and laughed so loudly that passers-by stopped and stared.

He ambled on down the sidewalk, not having the merest notion of where he was going. Yet, sleeping within him, was the drive to go somewhere and say something to somebody. Half an hour later his ears caught the sound of spirited singing.

> *The Lamb, the Lamb, the Lamb*
> *I hear thy voice a-calling*
> *The Lamb, the Lamb, the Lamb*
> *I feel thy grace a-falling*

A church! He exclaimed. He broke into a run and came to brick steps leading downward to a subbasement. This is it! The church into which he had peered. Yes, he was going in and tell them. What? He did not know; but, once face to face with them, he would think of what to say. Must be Sunday, he mused. He ran down the steps and jerked the door open; the church was crowded and a deluge of song swept over him.

> *The Lamb, the Lamb, the Lamb*
> *Tell me again your story*
> *The Lamb, the Lamb, the Lamb*
> *Flood my soul with your glory*

He stared at the singing faces with a trembling smile.

"Say!" he shouted.

Many turned to look at him, but the song rolled on. His arm was jerked violently.

"I'm sorry, Brother, but you can't do that in here," a man said.

"But, mister!"

"You can't act rowdy in God's house," the man said.

"He's filthy," another man said.

"But I want to tell 'em," he said loudly.

"He stinks," someone muttered.

The song had stopped, but at once another one began.

> *Oh, wondrous sight upon the cross*
> *Vision sweet and divine*

Oh, wondrous sight upon the cross
Full of such love sublime

He attempted to twist away, but other hands grabbed him and rushed him into the doorway.

"Let me alone!" he screamed, struggling.

"Get out!"

"He's drunk," somebody said. "He ought to be ashamed!"

"He acts crazy!"

He felt that he was failing and he grew frantic.

"But, mister, let me tell—"

"Get away from this door, or I'll call the police!"

He stared, his trembling smile fading in a sense of wonderment.

"The police," he repeated vacantly.

"Now, get!"

He was pushed toward the brick steps and the door banged shut. The waves of song came.

Oh, wondrous sight, wondrous sight
Lift my heavy heart above
Oh, wondrous sight, wondrous sight
Fill my weary soul with love

He was smiling again now. Yes, the police . . . That was it! Why had he not thought of it before? The idea had been deep down in him, and only now did it assume supreme importance. He looked up and saw a street sign: COURT STREET— HARTSDALE AVENUE. He turned and walked northward, his mind filled with the image of the police station. Yes, that was where they had beaten him, accused him, and had made him sign a confession of his guilt. He would go there and clear up everything, make a statement. What statement? He did not know. He was the statement, and since it was all so clear to him, surely he would be able to make it clear to others.

He came to the corner of Hartsdale Avenue and turned westward. Yeah, there's the station . . . A policeman came down the steps and walked past him without a glance. He mounted the stone steps and went through the door, paused; he was in a hallway where several policemen were standing, talking, smoking. One turned to him.

"What do you want, boy?"

He looked at the policeman and laughed.

"What in hell are you laughing about?" the policeman asked.

He stopped laughing and stared. His whole being was full of what he wanted to say to them, but he could not say it.

"Are you looking for the Desk Sergeant?"

"Yes, sir," he said quickly; then: "Oh, no, sir."

"Well, make up your mind, now."

Four policemen grouped themselves around him.

"I'm looking for the men," he said.

"What men?"

Peculiarly, at that moment he could not remember the names of the policemen; he recalled their beating him, the confession he had signed, and how he had run away from them. He saw the cave next to the church, the money on the walls, the guns, the rings, the cleaver, the watches, and the diamonds on the floor.

"They brought me here," he began.

"When?"

His mind flew back over the blur of the time lived in the underground blackness. He had no idea of how much time had elapsed, but the intensity of what had happened to him told him that it could not have transpired in a short space of time, yet his mind told him that time must have been brief.

"It was a long time ago." He spoke like a child relating a dimly remembered dream. "It was a long time," he repeated, following the promptings of his emotions. "They beat me . . . I was scared . . . I ran away."

A policeman raised a finger to his temple and made a derisive circle.

"Nuts," the policeman said.

"Do you know what place this is, boy?"

"Yes, sir. The police station," he answered sturdily, almost proudly.

"Well, who do you want to see?"

"The men," he said again, feeling that surely they knew the men. "You know the men," he said in a hurt tone.

"What's your name?"

He opened his lips to answer and no words came. He had forgotten. But what did it matter if he had? It was not important.

"Where do you live?"

Where did he live? It had been so long ago since he had lived up here in this strange world that he felt it was foolish even to try to remember. Then for a moment the old mood that had dominated him in the underground surged back. He leaned forward and spoke eagerly.

"They said I killed the woman."

"What woman?" a policeman asked.

"And I signed a paper that said I was guilty," he went on, ignoring their questions. "Then I ran off . . ."

"Did you run off from an institution?"

"No, sir," he said, blinking and shaking his head. "I came from under the ground. I pushed off the manhole cover and climbed out . . ."

"All right, now," a policeman said, placing an arm about his shoulder. "We'll send you to the psycho and you'll be taken care of."

"Maybe he's a Fifth Columnist!" a policeman shouted.

There was laughter and, despite his anxiety, he joined in. But the laughter lasted so long that it irked him.

"I got to find those men," he protested mildly.

"Say, boy, what have you been drinking?"

"Water," he said. "I got some water in a basement."

"Were the men you ran away from dressed in white, boy?"

"No, sir," he said brightly. "They were men like you."

An elderly policeman caught hold of his arm.

"Try and think hard. Where did they pick you up?"

He knitted his brows in an effort to remember, but he was blank inside. The policeman stood before him demanding logical answers and he could no longer think with his mind; he thought with his feelings and no words came.

"I was guilty," he said. "Oh, no, sir. I wasn't then, I mean, mister!"

"Aw, talk sense. Now, where did they pick you up?"

He felt challenged and his mind began reconstructing events in reverse; his feelings ranged back over the long hours and he saw the cave, the sewer, the bloody room where it was said that a woman had been killed.

"Oh, yes, sir," he said, smiling. "I was coming from Mrs. Wooten's."

"Who is she?"

"I work for her."

"Where does she live?"

"Next door to Mrs. Peabody, the woman who was killed."

The policeman were very quiet now, looking at him intently.

"What do you know about Mrs. Peabody's death, boy?"

"Nothing, sir. But they said I killed her. But it doesn't make any difference. I'm guilty!"

"What are you talking about, boy?"

His smile faded and he was possessed with memories of the underground; he saw the cave next to the church and his lips moved to speak. But how could he say it? The distance between what he felt and what these men meant was vast. Something told him, as he stood there looking into their faces, that he would never be able to tell them, that they would never believe him even if he told them.

"All the people I saw was guilty," he began slowly.

"Aw, nuts," a policeman muttered.

"Say," another policeman said, "that Peabody woman was killed over on Winewood. That's Number Ten's beat."

"Where's Number Ten?" a policeman asked.

"Upstairs in the swing room," someone answered.

"Take this boy up, Sam," a policeman ordered.

"O.K. Come along, boy."

An elderly policeman caught hold of his arm and led him up a flight of wooden stairs, down a long hall, and to a door.

"Squad Ten!" the policeman called through the door.

"What?" a gruff voice answered.

"Someone to see you!"

"About what?"

The old policeman pushed the door in and then shoved him into the room.

He stared, his lips open, his heart barely beating. Before him were the three policemen who had picked him up and had beaten him to extract the confession. They were seated about a small table, playing cards. The air was blue with smoke and sunshine poured through a high window, lighting up fantastic smoke shapes. He saw one of the policemen look up; the policeman's face was tired and a cigarette drooped limply from one corner of his mouth and both of his fat, puffy eyes were squinting and his hands gripped his cards.

"Lawson!" the man exclaimed.

The moment the man's name sounded he remembered the names of all of them: Lawson, Murphy, and Johnson. How simple it was. He waited, smiling, wondering how they would react when they knew that he had come back.

"Looking for me?" the man who had been called Lawson mumbled, sorting his cards. "For what?"

So far only Murphy, the red-headed one, had recognized him.

"Don't you-all remember me?" he blurted, running to the table.

All three of the policemen were looking at him now. Lawson, who seemed the leader, jumped to his feet.

"Where in hell have you been?"

"Do you know 'im, Lawson?" the old policeman asked.

"Huh?" Lawson frowned. "Oh, yes. I'll handle 'im." The

old policeman left the room and Lawson crossed to the door and turned the key in the lock. "Come here, boy," he ordered in a cold tone.

He did not move; he looked from face to face. Yes, he would tell them about his cave.

"He looks batty to me," Johnson said, the one who had not spoken before.

"Why in hell did you come back here?" Lawson said.

"I—I just didn't want to run away no more," he said. "I'm all right, now." He paused; the men's attitude puzzled him.

"You've been hiding, huh?" Lawson asked in a tone that denoted that he had not heard his previous words. "You told us you were sick, and when we left you in the room, you jumped out of the window and ran away."

Panic filled him. Yes, they were indifferent to what he would say! They were waiting for him to speak and they would laugh at him. He had to rescue himself from this bog; he had to force the reality of himself upon them.

"Mister, I took a sackful of money and pasted it on the walls . . ." he began.

"I'll be damned," Lawson said.

"Listen," said Murphy, "let me tell you something for your own good. We don't want you, see? You're free, free as air. Now go home and forget it. It was all a mistake. We caught the guy who did the Peabody job. He wasn't colored at all. He was an Eyetalian."

"Shut up!" Lawson yelled. "Have you no sense!"

"But I want to tell 'im," Murphy said.

"We can't let this crazy fool go," Lawson exploded. "He acts nuts, but this may be a stunt . . ."

"I was down in the basement," he began in a childlike tone, as though repeating a lesson learned by heart; "and I went into a movie . . ." His voice failed. He was getting ahead of his story. First, he ought to tell them about the singing in the church, but what words could he use? He looked at them appealingly. "I went into a shop and took a sackful of money and diamonds and watches and rings . . . I didn't steal 'em, I'll give 'em all back. I just took 'em to play with . . ." He paused, stunned by their disbelieving eyes.

Lawson lit a cigarette and looked at him coldly.

"What did you do with the money?" he asked in a quiet, waiting voice.

"I pasted the hundred-dollar bills on the walls."

"What walls?" Lawson asked.

"The walls of the dirt room," he said, smiling, "the room next to the church. I hung up the rings and the watches and I stamped the diamonds into the dirt . . ." He saw that they were not understanding what he was saying. He grew frantic to make them believe, his voice tumbled on eagerly. "I saw a dead baby and a dead man . . ."

"Aw, you're nuts," Lawson snarled, shoving him into a chair.

"But, mister . . ."

"Johnson, where's the paper he signed?" Lawson asked.

"What paper?"

"The confession, fool!"

Johnson pulled out his billfold and extracted a crumpled piece of paper.

"Yes, sir, mister," he said, stretching forth his hand. "That's the paper I signed . . ."

Lawson slapped him and he would have toppled had his chair not struck a wall behind him. Lawson scratched a match and held the paper over the flame; the confession burned down to Lawson's fingertips.

He stared, thunderstruck; the sun of the underground was fleeting and the terrible darkness of the day stood before him. They did not believe him, but he *had* to make them believe him!

"But, mister . . ."

"It's going to be all right, boy," Lawson said with a quiet, soothing laugh. "I've burned your confession, see? You didn't sign anything." Lawson came close to him with the black ashes cupped in his palm. "You don't remember a thing about this, do you?"

"Don't you-all be scared of me," he pleaded, sensing their uneasiness. "I'll sign another paper, if you want me to. I'll show you the cave."

"What's your game, boy?" Lawson asked suddenly.

"What are you trying to find out?" Johnson asked.

"Who sent you here?" Murphy demanded.

"Nobody sent me, mister," he said. "I just want to show you the room . . ."

"Aw, he's plumb bats," Murphy said. "Let's ship 'im to the psycho."

"No," Lawson said. "He's playing a game and I wish to God I knew what it was."

There flashed through his mind a definite way to make them believe him; he rose from the chair with nervous excitement.

"Mister, I saw the night watchman blow his brains out because you accused him of stealing," he told them. "But he didn't steal the money and diamonds. I took 'em."

Tigerishly Lawson grabbed his collar and lifted him bodily. *"Who told you about that?"*

"Don't get excited, Lawson," Johnson said. "He read about it in the papers."

Lawson flung him away.

"He couldn't have," Lawson said, pulling papers from his pocket. "I haven't turned in the reports yet."

"Then how *did* he find out?" Murphy asked.

"Let's get out of here," Lawson said with quick resolution. "Listen, boy, we're going to take you to a nice, quiet place, see?"

"Yes, sir," he said. "And I'll show you the underground."

"Goddamn," Lawson muttered, fastening the gun at his hip. He narrowed his eyes at Johnson and Murphy. "Listen," he spoke just above a whisper, "say nothing about this, you hear?"

"O.K.," Johnson said.

"Sure," Murphy said.

Lawson unlocked the door and Johnson and Murphy led him down the stairs. The hallway was crowded with policemen.

"What have you got there, Lawson?"

"What did he do, Lawson?"

"He's psycho, ain't he, Lawson?"

Lawson did not answer; Johnson and Murphy led him to the car parked at the curb, pushed him into the back seat. Lawson got behind the steering wheel and the car rolled forward.

"What's up, Lawson?" Murphy asked.

"Listen," Lawson began slowly, "we tell the papers that he spilled about the Peabody job, then he escapes. The Wop is caught and we tell the papers that we steered them wrong to trap the real guy, see? Now this dope shows up and acts nuts. If we let him go, he'll squeal that we framed him, see?"

"I'm all right, mister," he said, feeling Murphy's and Johnson's arm locked rigidly into his. "I'm guilty . . . I'll show you everything in the underground. I laughed and laughed . . ."

"Shut that fool up!" Lawson ordered.

Johnson tapped him across the head with a blackjack and he fell back against the seat cushion, dazed.

"Yes, sir," he mumbled. "I'm all right."

The car sped along Hartsdale Avenue, then swung onto Pine Street and rolled to State Street, then turned south. It slowed to a stop, turned in the middle of a block, and headed north again.

"You're going around in circles, Lawson," Murphy said.

Lawson did not answer; he was hunched over the steering wheel. Finally he pulled the car to a stop at a curb.

"Say, boy, tell us the truth," Lawson asked quietly. "Where did you hide?"

"I didn't hide, mister."

The three policemen were staring at him now; he felt that

for the first time they were willing to understand him.

"Then what happened?"

"Mister, when I looked through all of those holes and saw how people were living, I loved 'em . . ."

"Cut out that crazy talk!" Lawson snapped. "Who sent you back here?"

"Nobody, mister."

"Maybe he's talking straight," Johnson ventured.

"All right," Lawson said. "Nobody hid you. Now, tell us *where* you hid."

"I went underground . . ."

"What goddamn underground do you keep talking about?"

"I just went . . ." He paused and looked into the street, then pointed to a manhole cover. "I went down in there and stayed."

"In the *sewer?*"

"Yes, sir."

The policemen burst into a sudden laugh and ended quickly. Lawson swung the car around and drove to Woodside Avenue; he brought the car to a stop in front of a tall apartment building.

"What're we going to do, Lawson?" Murphy asked.

"I'm taking him up to my place," Lawson said. "We've got to wait until night. There's nothing we can do now."

They took him out of the car and led him into a vestibule.

"Take the steps," Lawson muttered.

They led him up four flights of stairs and into the living room of a small apartment. Johnson and Murphy let go of his arms and he stood uncertainly in the middle of the room.

"Now, listen, boy," Lawson began, "forget those wild lies you've been telling us. Where did you hide?"

"I just went underground, like I told you."

The room rocked with laughter. Lawson went to a cabinet and got a bottle of whiskey; he placed glasses for Johnson and Murphy. The three of them drank.

He felt that he could not explain himself to them. He tried to muster all the sprawling images that floated in him; the images stood out sharply in his mind, but he could not make them have the meaning for others that they had for him. He felt so helpless that he began to cry.

"He's nuts, all right," Johnson said. "All nuts cry like that."

Murphy crossed the room and slapped him.

"Stop that raving!"

A sense of excitement flooded him; he ran to Murphy and grabbed his arm.

"Let me show you the cave," he said. "Come on, and you'll see!"

Before he knew it a sharp blow had clipped him on the chin; darkness covered his eyes. He dimly felt himself being lifted and laid out on the sofa. He heard low voices and struggled to rise, but hard hands held him down. His brain was clearing now. He pulled to a sitting posture and stared with glazed eyes. It had grown dark. How long had he been out?

"Say, boy," Lawson said soothingly, "will you show us the underground?"

His eyes shone and his heart swelled with gratitude. Lawson believed him! He rose, glad; he grabbed Lawson's arm, making the policeman spill whiskey from the glass to his shirt.

"Take it easy, goddammit," Lawson said.

"Yes, sir."

"O.K. We'll take you down. But you'd better be telling us the truth, you hear?"

He clapped his hands in wild joy.

"I'll show you everything!"

He had triumphed at last! He would now do what he had felt was compelling him all along. At last he would be free of his burden.

"Take 'im down," Lawson ordered.

They led him down to the vestibule; when he reached the sidewalk he saw that it was night and a fine rain was falling.

"It's just like when I went down," he told them.

"What?" Lawson asked.

"The rain," he said, sweeping his arm in a wide arc. "It was raining when I went down. The rain made the water rise and lift the cover off."

"Cut it out," Lawson snapped.

They did not believe him now, but they would. A mood of high selflessness throbbed in him. He could barely contain his rising spirits. They would see what he had seen; they would feel what he had felt. He would lead them through all the holes he had dug and . . . He wanted to make a hymn, prance about in physical ecstasy, throw his arm about the policemen in fellowship.

"Get into the car," Lawson ordered.

He climbed in and Johnson and Murphy sat at either side of him; Lawson slid behind the steering wheel and started the motor.

"Now, tell us where to go," Lawson said.

"It's right around the corner from where the lady was killed," he said.

The car rolled slowly and he closed his eyes, remembering the song he had heard in the church, the song that had wrought him to such a high pitch of terror and pity. He sang softly, lolling his head:

> *Glad, glad, glad, oh, so glad*
> *I got Jesus in my soul . . .*

"Mister," he said, stopping his song, "you ought to see how funny the rings look on the wall." He giggled. "I fired a pistol, too. Just once, to see how it felt."

"What do you suppose he's suffering from?" Johnson asked.

"Delusions of grandeur, maybe," Murphy said.

"Maybe it's because he lives in a white man's world," Lawson said.

"Say, boy, what did you eat down there?" Murphy asked, prodding Johnson anticipatorily with his elbow.

"Pears, oranges, bananas, and pork chops," he said.

The car filled with laughter.

"You didn't eat any watermelon?" Lawson asked, smiling.

"No, sir," he answered calmly. "I didn't see any."

The three policemen roared harder and louder.

"Boy, you're sure some case," Murphy said, shaking his head in wonder.

The car pulled to a curb.

"All right, boy," Lawson said. "Tell us where to go."

He peered through the rain and saw where he had gone down. The streets, save for a few dim lamps glowing softly through the rain, were dark and empty.

"Right there, mister," he said, pointing.

"Come on; let's take a look," Lawson said.

"Well, suppose he did hide down there," Johnson said, "what is that supposed to prove?"

"I don't believe he hid down there," Murphy said.

"It won't hurt to look," Lawson said. "Leave things to me."

Lawson got out of the car and looked up and down the street.

He was eager to show them the cave now. If he could show them what he had seen, then they would feel what he had felt and they in turn would show it to others and those others would feel as they had felt, and soon everybody would be governed by the same impulse of pity.

"Take 'im out," Lawson ordered.

Johnson and Murphy opened the door and pushed him out; he stood trembling in the rain, smiling. Again Lawson looked up and down the street; no one was in sight. The rain came down hard, slanting like black wires across the wind-swept air.

"All right," Lawson said. "Show us."

He walked to the center of the street, stopped and inserted a finger in one of the tiny holes of the cover and tugged, but he was too weak to budge it.

"Did you really go down in there, boy?" Lawson asked; there was a doubt in his voice.

"Yes, sir. Just a minute. I'll show you."

"Help 'im get that damn thing off," Lawson said.

Johnson stepped forward and lifted the cover; it clanged against the wet pavement. The hole gaped round and black.

"I went down in there," he announced with pride.

Lawson gazed at him for a long time without speaking, then he reached his right hand to his holster and drew his gun.

"Mister, I got a gun just like that down there," he said, laughing and looking into Lawson's face, "I fired it once then hung it on the wall. I'll show you."

"Show us how you went down," Lawson said quietly.

"I'll go down first, mister, and then you-all can come after me, hear?" he spoke like a little boy playing a game.

"Sure, sure," Lawson said soothingly. "Go ahead. We'll come."

He looked brightly at the policemen; he was bursting with happiness. He bent down and placed his hands on the rim of the hole and sat on the edge, his feet dangling into watery darkness. He heard the familiar drone of the gray current. He lowered his body and hung for a moment by his fingers, then he went downward on the steel prongs, hand over hand, until he reached the last rung. He dropped and his feet hit the water and he felt the stiff current trying to suck him away. He balanced himself quickly and looked back upward at the policemen.

"Come on, you-all!" he yelled, casting his voice above the rustling at his feet.

The vague forms that towered above him in the rain did not move. He laughed, feeling that they doubted him. But, once they saw the things he had done, they would never doubt again.

"Come on! The cave isn't far!" he yelled. "But be careful when your feet hit the water, because the current's pretty rough down here!"

Lawson still held the gun. Murphy and Johnson looked at Lawson quizzically.

"What are we going to do, Lawson?" Murphy asked.

"We are not going to follow that crazy nigger down into that sewer, are we?" Johnson asked.

"Come on, you-all!" he begged in a shout.

He saw Lawson raise the gun and point it directly at him. Lawson's face twitched, as though he were hesitating. Then there was a thunderous report and a streak of fire ripped through his chest. He was hurled into the water, flat on his back. He looked in amazement at the blurred white faces looming above him. They shot me, he said to himself. The water flowed past him, blossoming in foam about his arms, his legs, and his head. His jaw sagged and his mouth gaped soundless. A vast pain gripped his head and gradually squeezed out consciousness. As from a great distance he heard hollow voices.

"What did you shoot him for, Lawson?"

"I had to."

"Why?"

"You've got to shoot his kind. They'd wreck things."

As though in a deep dream, he heard a metallic clank; they had replaced the manhole cover, shutting out forever the sound of wind and rain. From overhead came the muffled roar of a powerful motor and the swish of a speeding car. He felt the strong tide pushing him slowly into the middle of the sewer, turning him about. For a split second there hovered before his eyes the glittering cave, the shouting walls, and the laughing floor . . . Then his mouth was full of thick, bitter water. The current spun him around. He sighed and closed his eyes, a whirling object rushing alone in the darkness, veering, tossing, lost in the heart of the earth.

The Outsider

Wright moved to Paris after the publication of Black Boy *in
1945. The following years were the period in his life during
which he found it urgently necessary to search for a new
faith in order to replace the set of Marxist assumptions that
had more or less guided his earlier writing.*

By the time he published The Outsider, *in 1953, that uneasy search was ending. He saw the novel as:*

> *The first literary effort of mine projected out of a heart
> preoccupied with no ideological burden save that of rend-
> ering an account of reality as it strikes my sensibilities and
> imagination. . . . My hero could have been of any race.
> . . . I have tried to render my sense of our contemporary
> living as I see it and feel it. All I ask the reader is that he
> peruse these pages with a heart as honest and humble as
> I had when writing them.*

*This pregnant and important novel, which presents ideo-
logical choices and poses existential problems along the lines
of a rather melodramatic, detective-story narrative, was certainly not accepted at the time for what it was—the first
really existentialist American novel. "The Man Who Lived
Underground", written in 1942, and the development it
represented in Wright's evolution had gone generally unno-*

The Outsider was originally published by Harper & Brothers in 1953. This
selection is from the chapters "Dread," "Descent," "Despair," and "Decision" of the original work.

ticed. And many of the more perceptive critics who saw that the race element was only secondary in The Outsider *failed to recognize its philosophical originality and the relevance of the problems it posed to modern society. Not to speak of his European audience, it is significant that the readers who apparently derived most from Wright's teachings in the novel were the younger black intellectuals who shared the distrust of mass society which Wright had projected in somewhat extreme symbolic terms. Beyond the discussion of self-identity and political ideology,* The Outsider *explores on a philosophical level the problem of rebellion that* Native Son *had posed in psychological and social terms in the context of ghetto life. Trying to give answers along Nietzschean lines, advocating man's total freedom and his ability to be "his own little God," Cross Damon, the protagonist, is led to horror and despondency after a series of dramatic murders. As a condemnation of totalitarianism, the novel consists of much more than the settling of political accounts. It provides, in fact, Wright's final considerations on the question of man's relation to man in modern society. It is certainly easier today than it was in 1953 to perceive Damon's "sense of being alienated" as the emergence of what contemporary thinkers call "counter-culture" or "cultural revolution" rather than political revolution.*

*   *The Outsider *has often been called a splendid failure. It suffers from a number of aesthetic flaws, the major of which may be a preponderance of philosophical exchanges over narrative and action. We have selected the episodes dealing with Cross Damon's life in Chicago in Book One, and the accidental way he is allowed to break out of the trap of his circumstances; then, in Book Three, the climactic scene of violence in which he is led to slay both Herndon, a Fascist, and Blount, a Communist leader. Also in that section we*

have his conflict with Communist Hilton and his second
confrontation with District Attorney Ely Houston. Finally in
Book Five, are the scenes relating to Damon's despair after
the suicide of the woman he loved, Eva Blount, his exposure
by Houston, and his death at the hands of the Communists.

DATING FROM THIS PERIOD, a wave of self-loathing began to
engulf Cross. Until now he had managed to keep up his
classes at the University, but he lost heart for study and
dropped out of school. Each time he realized how much he
had lost control of his life, his self-hatred swelled. He knew
himself too well to blame Gladys and he was scrupulous
enough to let her know it, which baffled and tortured her all
the more. She longed for some simple definition of their
troubles that she could grasp. She thought that she was losing
her physical appeal for him and she went, without telling him
—and submitted to an extraordinarily expensive operation to
have her breasts lifted! That more than anything else had
depressed Cross, filled him with a compassion mingled with
disgust. He had been so stunned by it that he could never
discuss it with her.

One afternoon in a bar, dawdling over a drink, he recalled
how shocked Gladys had been when she had come home
from the hospital with Junior and had found him in bed with
the girl. That fantastic happening had now become accepted
as an "accident." Well, why couldn't another "accident" happen? One so fatal and unique that it would make her remember the last one as a guide by which to interpret it! He was
far from planning anything overtly criminal; it was a complicated psychological attack whose consequences would clarify
Gladys' feelings about him. But what on earth could that
"accident" be? It would have to be so decisive that she would
tell him to go and never come back. He would support her
and the children, of course. He sipped his drink idly, turning

his wish carefully over in his mind. Then his self-hate, his aversion for Gladys, his perpetual toying with his own feelings resulted in a sudden, confoundingly luminous idea. He had it! By God, this was it! It would flow from him as naturally as it would be embraced by her, and it was simple. Could he carry it out? It would take cool nerve, insight, timing, and ruthless execution. What decided him was a cynical question: "If I fail, I'll be no worse off than I am now, will I?"

He always finished his night shift in the Post Office at four o'clock in the morning; then, with his cronies, he went to The Salty Dog, a bar around the corner from his house, for what they jokingly called a "daycap," since they slept during the day. At five o'clock he went home for breakfast, which Gladys prepared in the kitchen in her kimono. Afterward he went directly to bed. But on *that* morning, he would not stop for his "daycap"; he would go back for his drink *after* he had done it. Such timing would make his actions seem more normal. Furthermore, his going back to have a drink with the boys would give him an alibi, in case he needed one. Above all, the children should be sound asleep when he did it; he did not want to disturb them in any way.

He decided upon a Friday morning to carry his plan into action. After he left work he detached himself unobtrusively from his friends and went directly home, arriving shortly after four o'clock. Gladys had just gone into the kitchen and was putting a pot of coffee on the gas stove. He walked in and advanced wordlessly upon her, his eyes fastened on her face.

"Oh, good morning, Cross," she said, glancing at the electric clock on the wall. "You're early, aren't you?"

He stood directly in front of her, his eyes unblinking and his face a blank mask.

"What's the matter?" she asked, backing away a step.

He reached forward and gave her a slap with his open palm, not hard, but stinging and with enough force to send her stumbling backward into a corner.

"Cross!" her voice was not loud, but charged with shock.

Then for a moment she was still as stone, staring at him, her lips parted, her hands lifted to shield her face. She lay against the wall, her open kimono showing her full breasts. The sound that came from her now coincided with her recognition of danger.

"No, no, no . . ." She spoke in low, clipped words, the inflection of her voice rising.

As he advanced toward her again, her mouth opened slowly and her chest heaved as she drew in her breath to scream. He roughly seized both of her hands in his left hand and slapped her once more, then stood leering down at her with a twisted face.

"Oh, God!" she screamed. "Don't kill me, Cross!"

As if pulled by cables of steel, he whirled and walked from the kitchen and out of the front door, hearing Gladys sobbing. He had not uttered a single syllable and the whole assault had taken no more than a minute. When he reached the door of the bar, he stood a moment to collect himself. He saw his pals sitting in the rear; he eased himself toward them and sat down.

"Where did you go, Crossy?" big, fat Joe asked carelessly.

"I was making a phone call," he said, lighting a cigarette and controlling his hand to keep it from trembling.

They began arguing politics. He spoke with composure, glancing now and then at the clock on the wall, wondering what was happening at home. He was pleased that the children had not heard him. Would she call the police? He doubted it; she would wait and talk to him first. Would she tell the children? He did not think so. Would she go to see his mother? Maybe. Her mind must be in a turmoil. . . . At five-thirty, he said casually: "Well, guys, I've got to cut out and get some shut-eye."

He rose and waved good-by. Now was the test. If his abrupt, physical attack upon Gladys provoked an immediate storm of reaction, then it would go badly for him; but if she was frantically trying to find some explanation for it, then all might go well. The main strategy was not to let her settle upon any one reason for it, to keep her judgment torturingly uncertain. Everything depended upon how much pretended incredulity he could show, how much simulated surprise he could convincingly sustain. As he turned into the walk leading to the house, he had a bad moment; a surging impulse made him want to turn about and dodge it all. He shook it off, entered the front door, walked down the hallway and went into the bathroom. That had always been his routine and he adhered to it now. As he washed he whistled a tune, not steadily, but in snatches, not like a man intentionally trying to create an impression of carefreeness, but like a man with nothing serious on his mind. There was not a sound of movement in the house. Where was Gladys? Had she funked and fled? No; she would not leave the children. . . . He emerged from the bathroom and went into the kitchen; he knew that she was not there, but he had to act as though he expected to find her frying his bacon and eggs. On the gas stove a blue flame glowed under the coffeepot and the scent of burning metal assailed his nostrils. He went to the stove and saw that the coffee had evaporated from the pot and that the metal around the bottom gleamed bright red. He shut off the gas and looked over his shoulder. That meant that Gladys had quit the kitchen the moment he had left the house. That's normal. . . .

"Gladys!" he called out quietly, questioningly.

There was no answer. He made for the bedroom, calling again: "Gladys!"

Silence. He opened the bedroom door and asked into the semigloom: "Gladys, aren't you up yet?"

Silence. He hesitated a second, then switched on the wall light. Gladys was huddled on the bed, her eyes black with fear. She was so immobile that at first he thought that maybe she was dead, had died of shock. But, no; he could see her chest slowly rising and falling.

"What's the matter?" he asked softly.

She did not answer. Tears rolled down her cheeks and her fingers writhed.

"Didn't you know you left the coffeepot on the fire? All the water boiled out and it was red hot. . . ."

She did not move.

"What's the matter? Are you ill?" he asked.

He walked toward her and she lunged violently backward, falling from the bed to the floor, leaving one of her bedroom slippers on the quilt. He stopped, blinked his eyes in simulated bewilderment. He advanced upon her again and Gladys shook her head wildly.

"No, no, no . . . Don't hit me, Cross! *Don't* . . . *!*" she whimpered convulsively, barricading her face and head with her elbows.

He stared at her, his mouth drooping open in mock amazement. "What's the matter with you?"

"Cross," she sobbed. "I never thought you'd *hit* me."

He stepped away from her imperceptibly, as though stunned. "*Hit* you? What in the world are you talking about?"

He went to her and she shrank, burrowing herself against the wall. He caught hold of her shoulder and she lifted her eyes and stared at him and he returned her stare with make-believe astonishment until her eyes fell.

"What's the matter, Gladys! You're shaking! Here, let me put you to bed. I'll call a doctor. . . ."

He was still holding on to her shoulder and felt a slight lessening of tension in her muscles. Trembling, she allowed him to lead her to the bed and push her gently upon it. She looked at him with eyes filled with shock.

"Lie down and keep still," he said hurriedly, feigning deep anxiety. "I'll have the doctor here in a minute. If you felt like that, why didn't you phone me at the Post Office?"

Delicately he pulled the cover over her, went to the telephone at the bedside, picked it up, dialed the first letter and then glanced at her.

"No, no, no . . . No, Cross," she begged; her eyes were pools of bewilderment. She breathed uncertainly. Her gaze fell and her fingers fluttered.

"Now, listen, you'd better have the doctor take a look at you," he said, pitching his voice to a tone of half command and half entreaty.

She began to sob again, burying her face in the pillow. He sat on the edge of the bed and patted her shoulder.

"Take it easy. Have you any pains? What's happened? Where are the children?"

She stared at him again, unable to believe the evidence of her senses. Her head rocked on its neck. Her mouth trembled and she had to move her lips several times before she could speak.

"Why did you do it?" she whimpered. Then she spoke fully, almost rising to a point of objectivity. "Do you hate me that much?"

"Do *what?*" He asked, replacing the receiver upon the hook of the transmitter. *"Hate* you? What *are* you talking about?"

"Oh, God!" she cried. "You *know* what you did?"

Fear filled him for a second. She was in her crisis now; would she veer against him or would she still float in indecision?

"You're dreaming!" he shot at her. "Do you know what you are saying?"

"You hit me. . . . You beat me. . . . What *for?*" she asked insistently.

"Beat you?" he echoed, as though he had to repeat the word to believe in its reality. His face was the living personification of stupefied surprise. "You are out of your mind. Now, look here, be calm. Tell me what happened."

She looked distractedly about the room like a rat searching for a hole. She was a tiny child hearing a grownup tell a tale that it did not believe, but it dared not challenge that tale because it had no way of successfully disputing it, feeling that its reasoning was not acceptable.

"Cross, you came into the kitchen and knocked me down," she explained in a low voice.

"You're crazy!" He stood and pretended to look suspiciously about the room. "Who's been here?"

"You!"

"Good Lord, you're wild!" He shook his head. "I *just* left the bar; I went there directly from work and had a drink, like always. . . . Look, get hold of yourself." He aped bewilderment. "Have you been drinking?"

"Oh, Cross!"

"Listen, if you don't stop I'll call the doctor. You've got the children to look after." He copied tones of responsibility.

She stared at him, dumbfounded. Slowly, she shook her head. *Yes!* The idea was working in her mind. It was coming off much easier than he had thought. But he had to be firm and not retreat from his position.

"When do you think I hit you, Gladys?"

"I *didn't* imagine it," she whimpered.

It was working; she was beginning to wonder if what had happened had not been wiped from his memory. Silence followed. The restoration of normality must depend upon *his* initiative; what had so mysteriously occurred must seem to have been swallowed up in his mind as though it had never transpired; he must not in any way grant it one whit of objective reality.

"Look, kid," he began kindly. "I know we aren't the loving couple one reads about in books. But you mustn't let our troubles break you down. There's no sense in brooding till you start imagining things. You need a rest. . . ."

She clutched his arm. "Cross, don't you *remember* what you did?"

"Gladys, really, I hate to say it, but you're *off!*"

"I'm sane, Cross," she said, unable to restrain her tears.

She collected her senses; she was no longer physically afraid; she was fearful of something more menacingly dark than a slap.

"I don't know what's happened to you," he played his role.

"Cross, you *remember* you hit me," she moaned.

"I *didn't!*" His face grew hard. "You're mixed up. . . . Tell me, *who's* been here?"

"Nobody," she breathed.

"Who else saw me come in here?"

"Nobody," she whispered, her eyes widening with understanding.

"Look, Junior's coming," he spoke in a low, rapid voice. "Brace up. . . . You'll upset him."

"Is it possible?" she asked herself in a despairing whisper.

She pulled herself unsteadily from the bed to the dresser and began arranging her hair with palsied hands. He could see her watching his reflection in the mirror; he had to be careful. She had forgotten her bedroom slipper on the quilt; he got it and held it out to her.

"Here; you better put it on," he said in a neutral voice.

She obeyed him with movements charged with suppressed fear. But when he looked at her she glanced quickly away.

Junior, four years of age, came running in in his pajamas. "I'm hungry," he sang, lifting an earnest, brown face to his father.

Cross swept the boy up in his arms and fondled him. Watching Cross out of the corners of her eyes, Gladys went hesitantly from the room to prepare breakfast. Cross burrowed his head playfully into Junior's stomach and the boy giggled. He was now certain that he could handle it. This was the beginning, the setup; next time would be the payoff.

During the following week, under the cover of anxious solicitude, Cross craftily urged Gladys to see a doctor and she politely refused. A few days later she timidly begged *him* to see a doctor, telling him that she was certain that what had happened was a recurrence of what he had done with the girl. In a tone of play-acting shock, looking her levelly in the eyes, he scoffed at her interpretation and assured her that he was absolutely sane. He now made it a rigorous rule never to refer to the "accident"; all mention of it had to come from her. And, as time went on, she found it more and more difficult to bring it up; but he knew that the thought of it was continually hovering in the back of her mind.

One day, touching his cheek gently as she spoke—hoping by the gesture to negate any hint that she thought him insane —she expressed concern that he might harm the children "while in one of your spells." He patted her shoulder and said soothingly: "Don't worry, darling. Everything's all right." She beseeched him to cut his drinking, his smoking, to sleep more. She strove to keep more order in the house, chiding the children lovingly not to "make noise and get on poor papa's nerves."

He chose Easter Sunday morning for his next attack. He knew that nothing would be further from Gladys' mind then, for her attention would be involved in coloring Easter eggs and arranging new clothes for the children's Easter outing. He worked the night of Easter Eve and went straight home and found Gladys alone in the kitchen; she whirled with fear as he came in, for she knew that he was early as on that other fateful morning. Again he walked slowly toward her, wordlessly, his facial expression simulating dementia.

"No, no, no . . . !"

He slapped her resoundingly and she went down like a log.

"Junior!" she yelled. "Somebody help me!"

He stopped and slapped her once more, his face contorted in an imitation of rage; then he turned and rushed out, hurried to the bar and joined Joe, Pink and Booker, who had not missed him this time. He sat coolly talking and drinking with them, but his mind was trying to picture what was happening at home. At a little past five he went back, let himself in with his key, and headed as usual to the bathroom to wash up. He lathered his hands and whistled softly. Suddenly he was still, hearing muffled footsteps moving haltingly along the hallway. What's she doing . . .? Then all was quiet. He dried his face and hands and when he emerged he did not have to look for Gladys, for there she was at the door, confronting him with his gun, pointing it straight at his heart.

"Cross," she said heavily, struggling to manage her greeting, "I can't bear with you another minute. Pack your things and get out, *now!* You're crazy. You're a danger to yourself and everyone else!"

He saw such fear in her face that he was afraid that she would lose control of herself and pull the trigger.

"My God," his voice rang with sincerity. "Take it *easy. . . .*"

His nervousness made Gladys step quickly away from him and wave the gun threateningly.

"If you come near me, I'll shoot!" she cried. "And I'll go free, because you're crazy!"

Her arm trembled and she reached toward him, the gun barrel coming within inches of his right temple.

"Gladys," he breathed, leaning weakly against a wall. "I can't get my clothes unless you let me pass."

"You're sick, Cross," she pronounced in neutral, distant tones.

Realizing that she was blocking his path, she stepped cautiously to one side. He went into the bedroom and began to pack. She waited in the doorway, still nervously clutching the gun.

"Gladys," he started to protest.

"Get out!" she ordered in a frenzy.

He packed a suitcase and stood looking at her out of the corners of his eyes. "I'll come back for the rest of my stuff later—"

"You let me know and I'll *send* your things," she said. "Don't ever set foot in this house without first telling me, you hear! If you do, it'll be dangerous for you."

"I'll phone you," he mumbled.

She held open the front door, still brandishing the gun in her shaking hand. He walked over the threshold, sweating, fearing that he would stumble.

"See a doctor, Cross," she said, slamming the door.

On the sidewalk he paused and saw her peering at him from behind one of the lace window curtains in the living room, still grasping the gun. He resolved to buy another gun; he felt naked without one. Walking away, he felt good.

Cross roused himself on the jolting trolley, wiped a clear spot on the sweaty windowpane and saw that he had ridden past Gladys' place. Good God . . . He rushed to the front of the car and when it slowed he swung off. As he neared the house his steps faltered. He was doubtful that Gladys would help him, but his predicament was so bad he had to try, whatever the outcome. He mounted the steps and paused; his instincts warned him away from this Gladys whom he had made hate him too well. But he had to see her. He pushed the button of the doorbell and almost in the moment of his pushing it, the door flung open and Gladys stood before him, grim, erect. Out of a tightly organized face two deep-set eyes regarded him with composed hate.

"Hello, Gladys," he mumbled.

"I've been waiting for you," she said with placid irony. "I watched you creep up the walk like a doomed man. Are you scared of your home now?"

"I want to talk to you about something important," he told her.

A twisted smile played on Gladys' rouged lips. "I suppose it's about Miss Dorothy Powers, hunh?"

Anger flashed through him. No; he had to be calm.

"That's it, Gladys," he admitted, forcing a smile.

She stepped to one side and he moved gingerly into the hallway, feeling for the first time intimidated by Gladys. He glanced about apprehensively, his body screaming for a drink to brace him for this ordeal.

"Where're the kids?" he asked to fill the gaping silence.

"I knew you were coming," she announced, "so I sent them to a friend's house this afternoon."

He walked into the living room and sat. Gladys followed

and stood at the other end of the room and regarded him with hostile eyes. He could feel that she was clamoring for an emotional scene. Well, he'd refuse her the satisfaction. He'd be polite, bantering, if possible.

"A young lady visited you this morning, I think," he said, trying to rid his voice of anxiety.

"You mean that bitch you sent—!"

"Gladys, I didn't send anybody here," he cut in quickly.

"Cross, for God's sake, why do you insist on being such a crawling coward? You *sent* her here—"

"I didn't, I tell you!"

"You're lying!"

"Gladys, I know how you feel about me—"

"You ought to," she spat at him. "Do you think you can walk over me? Well, you won't, ever! You sent that little whore here to beg me . . ."

He tried to stop listening. It was going worse than he thought. Well, if she wanted to blast Dot, let her. The main thing was the question of divorce.

"There is one thing, by God," she roared, "that you are going to do! You are going to *respect* me. You can't send a filthy, stinking little tart like that to talk to me. You can be sure I gave your bitch a hot welcome, and she won't forget it, not soon!" Gladys groped for words, her mouth open. "And while I'm on it, let me settle one more question. You'll *not* get a divorce. For a rotten slut like her, *never!* That's the way I feel and I'm not ashamed of it! If you can be dirty, then so can I! Keep on living with her, but if she asks you to make her respectable, tell her you can't! Take your Dorothy and sleep with her and let her give you a litter of bastards. That's all she's fit for, and you, too, it seems! Is that clear?"

Her hysterical tirade made him ashamed for her. The satisfaction she was deriving from it was obscene.

"Look, I'm not going to argue with your feelings." He clutched at words to stem the tide. "Let's arrange something. I'm supporting you and the children—"

"And by the living hell, you'll keep on!"

"Okay. I agree. But your welfare depends on my job—"

He jerked as she burst into a gale of cynical laughter. "So, you've been to the Post Office?" she asked. "They put the fear of God into you, hunh? That's why you came crawling to me. . . ."

Cross froze. Had she already told the postal officials about the possibility of his being convicted of rape? He had come to bargain with her, but if she had already talked, the game was all but lost.

"What are you talking about?" he asked quietly.

"Cross, are you stupid?" There was a mocking pity in her tone. "I must protect myself. . . . That little whore of yours wasn't gone from here an hour before my lawyer and I were at the Post Office—"

"Why?"

He knew why she had gone, but he wanted to know how far she had gone. Maybe his job was already lost!

Gladys spoke quietly, as though she were a schoolteacher explaining a complicated problem to a dullard. She came to within a few feet of Cross and sat.

"Cross, you really cannot expect me to think of you and your troubles," she said. "You're intelligent and you know what you're doing. I had to act in my own defense. I went straight to the Postmaster and told him that your Miss Powers was about to charge you with rape—"

"Did she tell you that?" Cross asked, feeling that his chair was whirling him round.

"Of course she did," Gladys informed him with a smile. "Do you think she's informing you of her moves against you? The Postmaster knows, of course, that you cannot marry the girl. . . . And if you are convicted, you're ruined. Now, the Postal Inspector has your case, see?"

Cross had no will to stop her; he knew that she was summing up his situation accurately.

"Cross, don't be naïve," she continued. "There's nothing

that Miss Powers can do but charge you, unless she's willing to live with you and bear your child. . . . And I doubt if she loves you that much." She paused, lit a cigarette, eyeing Cross the while. "Now, there are some rather disagreeable things I must say to you.

"Number One: You're signing this house over to me at once. Number Two: You're signing over the car to me. Number Three: You're going to the Post Office tonight and borrow eight hundred dollars from the Postal Union on your salary. I've already made the arrangements with the Postal Inspector. He's okayed it. I want that money to clear the titles of both the house and the car." She stood, lifted her hand to bar his words. "I know you want to say no," she said. "But you can't. Cross, understand this: so far as I'm concerned, you're *through!* I'm squeezing you like a lemon. If you don't do what I'm asking, in the morning I shall keep an appointment with Miss Powers. She, *I,* and her lawyer will go to the Forty-ninth Street Police Station and I will help her bring charges against you. I'm not justifying my actions. I'm not apologizing, see? I'm just telling you. That's how things stand between us, Cross."

He was willing to sign over everything, but he did not want to borrow the money; it would mean debts for two years to come. And he could use that money to try to bribe Dot. . . .

"They may not let me have the money," he said.

"Mr. Dumb," she said scornfully, "if the Postal Union thought you were going to be indicted for rape, they wouldn't let you have the money, because you wouldn't have a job. I let them think the girl would abort the child, that you'd pay her off. . . . I made sure with the Postmaster that your job was safe, and the Postal Union has been told that it's all right. . . ."

"But the girl can *still* charge me," Cross protested without strength. "What game's this you're playing?"

"*My* game," Gladys said.

"The eight hundred dollars," he was pleading now, "could keep the girl and I could make payments to you—"

"I don't give a damn about that girl," she snapped. "What happens between you and her is your business!"

Gladys was using Dot to drag money from him and at the same time betraying Dot. Cross wanted to close his eyes and sleep this nightmare away.

"If you get eight hundred dollars, you won't help the girl?"

"Hell, no! Why should I? Let that bitch rot!"

He was properly trapped. There was nothing more to say. This was a cold and vindictive Gladys created by him. He rose and moved toward the door.

"What's your answer?" she asked.

"Okay. I'll get the money. I'll phone you tonight."

"Oh, there's one other thing," she said, opening the door for him. "Is your life insurance paid up?"

"Hunh?" His voice sounded far away. "Yes; yes . . ."

"Have you changed the beneficiary?" she asked.

"No; why should I?"

"I just wanted to know," she said.

He felt as though he were already dead and was listening to her speak about him. He went out and did not glance back. He was not aware of trampling through the deep snow. About him were sounds that had no meaning. When he came fully to himself, his feet were like two icy stumps. I must have fever. . . . He paused and stared around him. He was tired. Oh, God, I got to get that money for Gladys. . . . He looked about for a taxi. Oh, there's the El. . . . He ran for the entrance, stumbled up the steps, fished a dime from his pocket, and rushed to the platform just as a Loopbound train slid to a stop. He found a seat, fell into it, and sat hunched over, brooding.

Seeing Gladys had compounded his problems. If he did what she wanted, he was lost; and if he didn't, he was lost. Yet, because he could not make up his mind to ditch it all, he had to follow her demands.

Before reaching Roosevelt Road the El dipped underground. Cross rose, swaying with the speed of the train, and
traversed each coach until he came to the first car, whose
front window looked out upon a dim stretch of tunnel. He
leaned his forehead against the glass and stared at the rushing ribbons of steel rails whose glinting surfaces vanished
beneath his feet.

At his station, he got off and went toward the Post Office,
a mass of steel and stone with yellow windows glowing. The
night air was still; it had begun to grow a little warmer. It's
going to snow again, he thought idly. Yes, he'd see about the
loan right now, but he'd not work tonight. He hungered for
sleep. He flashed his badge to the guard at the door and went
inside. Where's that Postal Union office? Yes; there on the
right. . . . He pushed open the door and saw Finch, the Union
secretary, sitting quietly, his hat on, chewing an unlighted
cigar and holding a deck of soiled playing cards in his hands.
Cross approached Finch's desk and for a moment they stared
at each other. He suddenly hated Finch's whiteness, not ra-
cially, but just because Finch was white and safe and calm
and he was not.

"Damon, huh?"

"Yes."

"I was waiting for you," Finch said. "Sit down."

Cross obeyed. He did not want to look at Finch; he knew
the man knew his troubles and it made him ashamed; instead, he stared stupidly at the pudgy, soft fingers as they
shuffled the cards.

"You look like an accident going somewhere to happen,"
Finch commented.

"I'm under the weather," Cross confessed. "I want to
renew that eight-hundred-dollar loan I had last year—"

"Oh, yes." Finch looked up. "Your wife's been in."

White fingers took the cigar from thin lips and a brown
stream of tobacco juice spewed into a spittoon. Finch replaced the cigar, chewed it, and settled it carefully again in
his jaw.

"You colored boys get into a lot of trouble on the South Side." Finch gave a superior smile. "You must have a hot time out there every day, huh?"

Cross stiffened. Letting Finch call it racial behavior was a kind of compound interest he had to pay on his loan.

"Is the loan possible?" Cross asked.

"The Postmaster said it's all right," Finch said, finally stacking the cards and flinging them to one side, as though ridding himself of something unpleasant. "Half of my time's spent taking care of you colored boys. . . . What goes on on the South Side?"

Cross cleared his throat to control himself. "I don't know," he mumbled. "I'm offering my house as security—"

"I'm ahead of you, Damon," Finch said. "On the strength of your wife's plea, I've had the papers all drawn up. Boy, you've got a good wife. You ought to take care of her—"

"I do," Cross mumbled.

"If you did, you wouldn't be in this mess," Finch said. He pushed the contract toward Cross. "Here, sign. . . ."

Cross signed clumsily, his nervousness letting a blob of ink smear across the page. He fumbled with a blotter to soak it up.

"Let me do that," Finch said, taking the blotter from Cross. "Looks like a chicken with dirty feet ran over this contract." He handed Cross a carbon copy of the contract, then opened a drawer and pulled out a sheaf of vouchers. "How do you want this? A check or cash?"

"Cash. I'd like the money tonight."

"Why not? It's your money."

Finch initialed a voucher for cash and flipped it at Cross.

"Okay. Get going," Finch said, yanking his thumb toward the door.

Cross stood and wanted to spit at the man. He edged forward and opened the door.

"Shut the door when you go out," Finch called, picking up his deck of cards and beginning to shuffle them again.

"Yes; of course," Cross said.

He pulled the door softly shut and sighed. Well, that was done. Then he stiffened. One of the Assistant Postmasters was bearing down upon him, his gray eyes intent on Cross's face.

"Damon, just a moment!"

"Yes, sir," Cross answered, waiting.

The Assistant Postmaster pointed a forefinger at Cross. "Damon, don't ever come to this Post Office again on an errand like this. If it hadn't been for your wife, I wouldn't touch this stink with a ten-foot pole. Look, you had one loan and paid it. Do the same with this. We're here to handle the mails, not emotional dramas. Now, this eight hundred ought to settle your little business, huh?"

"Yes, sir," he lied; it would only settle the claims of Gladys, but it would not help him with Dot. "Let me explain, sir. . . ."

"Don't tell me about it. I don't want to know."

"I'd like the night off, sir," Cross said. "I'll take it out of my vacation days."

"And what other service can I render you?" the Assistant Postmaster asked with mockery.

"I'm ill," Cross said peevishly.

"You look it," the Assistant Postmaster said. "Okay. Take it. But I know a guy called Damon who's going to find the Post Office a hard line to walk from here on out."

Cross bit his lip, and went down to the cashier's office of the Postal Union and presented his voucher.

"Cash, eh?" the teller asked, smiling. "What're you going to do with all that money? Buy the Tribune Tower?"

Cross pretended that he had not heard. He pushed the pile of fifty-dollar bills into his wallet, sought a telephone booth and dialed Gladys.

"I got the money," he told her.

"I want it first thing in the morning," she said flatly.

"I'll bring it by at noon."

"All right."

He made for the exit, showed his badge to the guard and stepped into the street. It was snowing again; fat, white flakes drifted lazily down from a night sky. An El train rattled past overhead. He sighed, feeling relieved. He had to be careful and not let a pickpocket rob him of the money. He put his badge and the duplicate copy of the loan contract into the pocket of his overcoat and stuffed his wallet into his shirt, next to his skin. His job now was to head off Dot.

Diving into a subway, he paid his fare and, two minutes later, when a train roared up, walked into the first coach and sank into a seat, closing his eyes. The train pulled into motion; he opened his eyes and noticed another Negro, shabbily dressed, about his own color and build, sitting across the aisle from him. The movement of the coach rocked some of the tension out of him, but not enough to let him relax. He went to the front window and stood looking at the twin ribbons of steel rails sliding under the train.

A moment later, when the train was streaking through the underground, darkness suddenly gouged his eyes and a clap of thunder hit his ears. He was spinning through space, his body smashing against steel; then he was aware of being lifted and brutally catapulted through darkness. Screams of men and women rent the black air.

Afterward Cross remembered that when the lights had gone out he had involuntarily blinked his eyes, feeling that the cause of the sudden darkness was some fault in the functioning of his pupils. About him were sounds of ripping metal and then something thumped against his head, knocking him out. How long he was unconscious, he did not know. When he came to he realized that his body was in an almost upright position, jammed between what seemed like two walls of steel. The right side of his skull was gripped by pain and something wet and warm trickled down the side of his face. His left leg was being wrenched and his right leg was pinioned, crushed to numbness in what seemed like a vise. He groaned. The words: *It's a subway wreck!* shaped themselves in his consciousness.

Abruptly the thunder ceased and the only sounds he heard were screams. In the blackness that walled before his eyes, Cross was afraid to move. *How badly am I hurt? Is it over?* He became aware that he was holding his head tucked down to dodge another attack of annihilation. Lifting his eyes he saw far ahead of him a jutting spray of blue electric sparks showering down from somewhere. He had to get out of this, now, NOW . . . Gingerly, he groped with his fingers and what he touched made him project images of what his fingers felt and he screamed. He imagined he saw the profile of a human face drenched in blood. He snatched his hand away and wiped it dry upon his coat.

He breathed softly, listening: a viscous liquid was slowly falling drop by drop somewhere near him: the whimper of a woman seemed to be issuing from a half-conscious body: a quiet coughing seemed to be trying to dislodge something thick and wet from a sticky throat: an incessant grunt grew fainter and fainter until it was heard no more. . . .

He was calm now, thinking. His lighter must be in his left pants pocket. Twisting, he reached for it, felt it with the ends of his fingers. Yes! Purpose gripped him and, squeezing the tips of his fingers together, he caught hold of the lighter and slowly pulled it out. He pushed the lever and a bluish flame shed feeble light amid a welter of tangled forms. Lines zig-zagged and solids floated in shadows, vanishing into meaninglessness; images dissolved into other images and his mind was full of a sense of shifting significances.

He saw that the seats of the train were above his head; the coach had turned over, twisted within the tube of the underground, and he was standing on the shattered lights of the ceiling. Seats had ripped from the floor and had fallen to the ceiling where he stood.

Cross shut his eyes and bit his lips, his ears assailed by screams. He had to get out of here! He bent lower and

looked; a white face with unblinking eyes was wedged at the
level of his knees and beneath that face he could make out
a dark pool of fluid that reflected the flickering flame of his
lighter. He moved the flame over shards of glinting glass and
saw again that window and the shower of blue electric sparks
still sprinkling down. . . . Yes; he had to get to that window.
. . . But his legs . . . He had to get them free. . . . He bent and
looked closer; his right leg was gripped between the steel
wall of the coach and a seat that had tumbled from the floor
to the ceiling. He pushed at the seat and it would not budge.
Again he shoved his weight at the seat. Why didn't it move?
He stooped lower with the light and saw that the seat that
jammed his leg to the wall was anchored in place by the
man's head, which, in turn, was rammed by another seat. The
man's face was fronting Cross.

Cross lifted the pressure of his finger from the lever and
the flame went out. He thought: That man's head is keeping
this seat from moving. . . . Could he get that head out of his
way? He pressed the lever again and looked. He could just
reach the man's head with his right hand. Yes; he had to
shove it out of the way. He held the lighter in his left hand,
shut his eyes, and felt the palm of his right hand touching the
yielding flesh of the man's face, expecting to hear a protest.
. . . He opened his eyes; no breath seemed to be coming from
the nostrils or mouth. Cross shuddered. If the man was dead,
then any action he took to free himself was right. . . . He held
his fingers to the man's parted lips and could feel no stir of
air. For a few seconds he watched the man's chest and could
detect no movement. The man's dead. . . . But how could he
get that head out of his way? Again he pushed his right hand
with all of his strength against the face and it budged only a
fraction of an inch. Goddamn . . . He panted with despair,
regarding the man's head as an obstacle; it was no longer
flesh and blood, but a rock, a chunk of wood to be whacked
at until it was gone. . . .

He searched vainly in the moving shadows for something

to hold in his hand, still hearing the sounds of screams. He felt in his overcoat pocket; the gun was there. Yes . . . He pulled it out. Could he beat down that foolishly staring face belonging to that head pushing against the seat wedging his leg to the wall? He shut his eyes and lifted the gun by the barrel and brought down the butt, and, even though his eyes were closed, he could see the gun butt crashing into the defenseless face. . . . Sweat broke out on his forehead and rivulets of water oozed from his armpits.

He opened his eyes; the bloody face had sunk only a few inches; the nostrils, teeth, chin, and eyes were pulped. Cross sucked in his breath; a few more blows would dislodge it. He shut his eyes and hammered again and suddenly he heard a splashing thud and he knew that the head had given way, for his blows were now falling on air. . . . He looked; the mangled face was on the floor; most of the flesh had been ripped away. He had done it; he could move his leg.

Now, he had to free his other leg. Peering with the lighter, he saw that his left leg was hooked under a fallen seat. With his right leg free, he hoisted himself up and saw that he would get loose if he could use his left leg as a ramrod to shove at the seat. Pricked by splinters of glass, he hauled himself upward and perched on the back of an overturned seat and, with his left foot, he gave a wild kick against the seat. It did not move. Bracing himself, he settled his heel against the back of the seat, eased his overcoat—which was hindering his movements—down a little from his shoulders, shut his eyes and pushed against the seat. It fell away. Both of his legs were free. An awful stench filled his nostrils.

He looked toward the gutted window; the blue electric sparks were still falling. From somewhere came a banging of metal against metal, like an urgent warning. That window was the way out. He crept forward over the ceiling of the overturned coach, past twisted and bloody forms, crunching shattered electric bulbs under his feet, feeling his shoes slopping through sticky liquid. He moved on tiptoe, as though afraid of waking the sleeping dead. He reached the window and saw that a young woman's body had been crushed almost flat just beneath it. The girl was dead, but, if he was to get through that window, he had the choice of standing upon her crushed body or remaining where he was. He stepped upon the body, feeling his shoes sinking into the lifeless flesh and seeing blood bubbling from the woman's mouth as his weight bore down on her breast. He reached for the window, avoiding the jagged edges of glass. Outside the blue electric sparks rained down, emitting a ghostly light. He did not need his lighter now. He crawled through and lowered his feet to the ground. He had to be careful and not step upon any live wires or the third rail. . . . His feet sought for gravel.

He stood for a moment, collecting himself. His head throbbed. When he moved his right leg it pained him. His body was clammy and trembling. For a moment he felt as though he would lose consciousness, but he remained on his feet. Screams, more distant now, came to his ears. He moved forward in the bluish gloom. Yes, ahead of him were amber lights! He pushed on and could hear distant voices and they were not the voices of the wounded. He had been lucky. I'd better let a doctor look at me. . . . He now realized how fantastically fortunate he had been; had he remained in his seat, he would have been crushed to death. . . .

He picked his way catlike over wooden trestles and then stopped. His overcoat . . .? Oh, God, he had left it somewhere back in that death-filled darkness, but he could not recall how it had gotten away from him. The gun was still in his pants' pocket. With stiff and sweaty fingers he lit a cigarette and walked on. From above ground he caught the faint wail of sirens and ahead of him he saw dim traces of light in the circular tunnel. Later he made out blurred, white uniforms and he knew that they were doctors and nurses.

He trudged past overturned coaches whose windows were gutted of glass. He could see doctors and nurses quite clearly now. He heard someone yell: "Here comes another one! He seems all right!"

They had seen him and were running to meet him. A doctor and a nurse caught hold of his arms.

"Are you all right?" the doctor asked.

"I guess so," he answered out of a daze.

"You are lucky," the nurse said.

"Get 'im to an ambulance," the doctor told the nurse. "I want to take a look back here."

The doctor hurried off into the tunnel of darkness, spotting his way with a flashlight.

"Can you walk all right?" the nurse asked him.

"Yeah."

"Does anything hurt you?"

"My leg, my right leg . . ."

"Come along, if you can manage," she said. "They'll see about it. . . . What happened?"

"I don't know."

She led him toward a group of doctors and nurses clustered on the subway station platform. He saw policemen pouring upon the underground tracks and heard someone shout: "Tell 'em the current's cut off!"

Cross felt hands lifting him onto the platform, and now another nurse had hold of his arm. About him was a babble of voices. He began to revive, feeling a little more like himself.

"I'm all right now," he told the nurse.

"But you must go to the hospital and be examined," the nurse told him. "Come. The ambulance is waiting."

She led him through a throng of policemen to the sidewalk where masses of excited people clogged the streets. The nurse tried to guide him through the crowd but they were brought to a standstill. A policeman saw them and tried to clear a path for them.

"That's one of 'em," Cross heard someone say. "But he doesn't seem hurt."

Cross could see the ambulances now; there were internes with stretchers rushing toward the subway station.

"You can get through now," the policeman said.

"Look," Cross told the nurse. "I'll go and get into an ambulance. I'm all right. Go back and help the others."

"Are you sure you're all right?" the nurse asked.

"Absolutely," Cross assured her.

She let go of him and he was alone. He started in the direction of the ambulances. The crowd ignored him. He looked down at his clothes; save for the blood on his shoes, he was all right. His overcoat had protected him somewhat. He paused. Why in hell should he go to a hospital? He was not wounded, only bruised. What he wanted more than medicine was a good, stiff drink of whisky. Were the doctors and nurses watching him? He looked around; they were not. . . . And the policeman had disappeared. The hell with it. . . . He crossed the street and peered at his dim reflection in the plate-glass window of a clothing store. His eyes were muddy and his face was caked with dirt and dried blood. He mopped at his cheek with his coat sleeve, rubbing it clean. Otherwise, he looked quite normal. Some whisky would fix him up, he told himself, and went in search of a drink.

A fine snow was falling, hanging in the air like a delicate veil. He limped down Roosevelt Road and found a second-rate bar that had sawdust on the floor and an odor of stale bread and beer. He was glad of the warmth that caressed his face; he had been too preoccupied to notice that he was half-frozen. But what happened to his overcoat? He ordered a double whisky and thought back over the underground accident. Then he remembered that he must have lost it when he had climbed on that overturned seat to free his leg. That was it; he'd had to pull his arms out of the coat and had been in such a frenzy he'd forgotten to put it on again. Well, he would buy another one. An overcoat was nothing in such a holocaust. He fingered the lump on the right side of his head; it was sore, but not serious. A man sure needs luck, he told himself.

The bar was filled with foreign-born workingmen who didn't seem to notice his disheveled clothing. Over his head a loudspeaker blared. He was leaning on his elbow when he heard the radio commentator announce:

We interrupt this program to bring you a special news bulletin. One half hour ago, a southbound subway train crashed headlong into another southbound train that had come to a standstill about six hundred yards from the Roosevelt Road subway station. The cause of the accident is being investigated. Access to the wrecked trains is difficult because debris has blocked the underground tubes and rescuers are having to cut their way through thick steel beams with acetylene torches. Although it is too early to give any details, it is feared that the loss of life has been heavy. In the immediate area all subway traffic has been suspended. Doctors and nurses have been rushed to the scene of the disaster. Keep tuned to this station for further details.

Cross smiled. How quick they were! Then suddenly he started so violently that the white man drinking next to him drew back in astonishment. *That money!* He shoved his hand into his shirt. . . . *It was there!* Thank God . . . He leaned weakly against the bar. If he had lost the eight hundred dollars, the only thing left for him would have been to jump into the Chicago River.

He paid his bill and hobbled back into the street where snow was still sifting down. Tomorrow at noon he had to see Gladys. And he'd go home now and wash up and then see Dot. . . . He was hungry; yes, he'd first go to a South Side restaurant and have a decent meal. But he would not take a subway. Hell, no . . . He'd treat himself to something better this time. At a corner he limped into a taxi and called out: "Forty-seventh and South Park."

He leaned back and wondered why his life had been spared. Or had it been? To say that he had been "spared" implied that some God was watching over him, and he did not believe that. It was simply the way the dice had rolled. He stretched out his right leg, testing it; the flesh was still sore to the touch, but he could keep on his feet. Funny, that morning he had been ready to blow his brains out, but when his body had been tossed about in that darkness, he had wanted to live.

His postal badge! The loan papers! They too were in the pocket of his overcoat. He'd have to report their being lost the first thing in the morning to the postal officials. . . . The taxi swerved to a curb at Forty-seventh and South Park. He paid the driver, limped out, walked through tumbling snowflakes and entered Dug's, a small restaurant that served the kind of food he liked. He went into the men's room, washed himself and then examined his face in the mirror. Not bad . . . He looked as though he had been on a two-day drunk, that was all. He grinned, re-entered the restaurant, which was almost empty, and ordered a steak, fried potatoes, coffee, and ice cream. He took a sip of water, listening to the radio that was going near the front window.

. . . This is John Harlan speaking. I'm broadcasting from the scene of the subway wreck at Roosevelt Road. It is snowing here and the visibility is rather bad. I have my microphone with me on the El platform and I'm able to see directly down to the subway entrance where doctors, nurses, attendants, and policemen are working frantically to bring the wounded from the underground. The scene is being illuminated by huge spotlights attached to telephone poles. Beyond the subway entrance, stretching far into the street and blocking the traffic, is a crowd of more than five thousand people standing silently in the falling snow. They have been here for almost an hour waiting for news of friends or relatives believed to have been passengers on the ill-fated subway trains that collided with a heavy loss of life more than an hour ago. . . .

I see the internes bringing out another victim. A body is on the stretcher. It's the body of a woman, it seems; yes, I can see her long brown hair. . . . Wait a minute. I'll see if I can get the police to identify her for us.

So engrossed was Cross in listening that he did not see the waitress when she placed his food before him. They're acting like it's a baseball game, he thought with astonishment. He was glad now that he had walked so unceremoniously away from the accident. He surely would not have wanted anybody to blare out his name over the airways as a victim. He shrugged his shoulders. They'll give us a commercial soon, he thought. The radio commentator resumed:

The name of the last accident victim is Mrs. Maybelle Broadman of 68 Green Street, Ravenswood Park. She is being taken directly to the Michael Reese Hospital. . . .

Ladies and gentlemen, I see the internes coming out with another stretcher. I can't tell yet if the victim is a man or a woman, for the stretcher is completely covered. It's a man. . . . I can tell by the blood-stained overcoat which is draped over the foot of the stretcher. . . . That is the forty-fourth victim taken so far from the wreckage of underground trains. Just a minute; I'll try to get the identity of the last victim who was brought out. . . .

In spite of himself, his interest was captured by the description of the happenings at the scene of the accident. As he waited for more news, he chewed and swallowed a mouthful of steak and lifted his cup of coffee to his lips.

Ladies and gentlemen, while we are endeavoring to establish the identity of the last man taken from the scene of the subway accident at Roosevelt Road, I'm going to ask one of the eyewitnesses, who was a passenger on the subway train, to say a few words about what he saw and felt when the disaster occurred. I have here at my side Mr. Glenn Williams, a salesman of 136 Rush Street, who escaped with but a few minor bruises. Mr. Williams, could you tell us what happened? Where were you on the train . . .?

WELL, I WAS IN A COACH TOWARD THE MIDDLE OF THE TRAIN. EVERYTHING SEEMED TO BE GOING ALL RIGHT. I WAS READING THE EVENING PAPER, THE TRAIN WAS FULL. I WAS SEATED. I GUESS WE WERE ABOUT A MINUTE FROM THE ROOSEVELT ROAD STATION, WHERE I WAS TO GET OFF, WHEN A GREAT CRASH CAME AND ALL

THE LIGHTS WENT OFF. I FELT MYSELF BEING KNOCKED OFF MY
SEAT. . . .

I must interrupt you, Mr. Williams. I'm sorry. Ladies and gentlemen, the police have just informed me of the identity of the last victim taken from the subway crash at Roosevelt Road. His name is Cross Damon, a twenty-six-year-old postal clerk who lived at 244 East 57th Street on the South Side. Mr. Damon's body was crushed and mangled beyond recognition or hope of direct identification. His identity has been established, however, by his overcoat, private papers, and his Post Office badge. . . . His body is being taken directly to the Cook County Morgue. Relatives must address all inquiries there. . . .
Now, Mr. Williams, will you kindly . . .?

Cross was still holding the cup of coffee in his right hand, his fingers tense upon the handle. He stared, stupefied. *What?* He half stood, then sat down again. Good God! He . . . *dead!* He had a wild impulse to laugh. The damn fools! They were really crazy! Well, it was his overcoat that had led them wrong. . . . Yes, that was it. He ought to phone them right now! He looked around the restaurant; except for himself, the place was now empty of customers. That tall, black girl who had been eating in the corner had gone. . . . Dug, the proprietor, who knew him, was not there. The waitress was a new one and he did not know her and she did not know him. He saw her watching him curiously. She must think I'm loony, he thought.

"Is there anything wrong, sir?"

He did not answer. This was rich! *He was dead!* He had to tell this to the gang at The Salty Dog, right now! Old Doc Huggins would die laughing. . . .

"Is the food all right, sir?"

"Hunh? Oh, yes. Look, what do I owe you?"

"Aren't you going to eat?"

"No, I've forgotten something. I got to go at once. . . ."

"Well, sir. It's one seventy-five. You see, even if you don't eat, they had to prepare it. We can't serve that food to any-body else, sir, you know. So you'll have to pay. . . ."

"That's all right. Here," he said, tossing her two one-dollar bills.

He hurried out into the spinning snow and headed for The Salty Dog. This was the damnedest thing! It was even more freakish than his having escaped alive from the subway acci-dent itself. When he reached the corner, he halted abruptly. He was stunned and shaken by the power of an idea that took his breath away and left him standing open-mouthed like an idiot amid the crazy flakes.

He was dead. . . . All right . . . Okay . . . Why the hell *not?* Why should he refute it? Why should he deny it? He, of all the people on earth, had a million reasons for being dead and staying dead! An intuitive sense of freedom flashed through his mind. Was there a slight chance here of his being able to start all over again? To live a new life? It would solve every problem he had if the world and all the people who knew him could think of him as dead. . . . He felt dizzy as he tried to encompass the totality of the idea that had come so sud-denly and unsought into his mind, for its implications ramified in so many directions that he could not grasp them all at once. Was it possible that he could somehow make this false account of his death become real? Could he pull off a thing like that? What did one do in a case like this? These questions made him feel that the world about him held countless dangers; he suddenly felt like a criminal, and he was grateful for the nervous flakes of snow which screened his face from the eyes of passers-by. Oh, God. . . . He had to sit down somewhere alone and think this thing out; it was too new, too odd, too complicated. How could he let them go on believing he was dead? But suppose later they found out that the body that they had dragged from the wreckage was not his? What then? Well, could he not hide away for a few days until they made up their minds? If they buried that body as the body of Cross Damon, then he was dead, really, legally, morally dead. Had any of his friends seen him since he had come up out of the subway? No, not one. And no one had known him at the subway station. No doubt that doctor and those nurses had already, in their excitement, forgotten that they had ever seen him. He was certain that no one he knew had seen him in that dingy bar on Roosevelt Road. And if he was really serious about this, then he ought not to go into The Salty Dog. What wild luck! And Dug had not been in! And that waitress was new and could not have known him from Adam . . .!

Then, if he was to do this thing, no one who knew him must see him now. . . . From this moment on he had to vanish. . . . Hide . . . Now! And his mother must not see him. . . . And Dot must not see him. . . . Gladys must be led to believe that he was dead. . . . His sons . . .? Good God . . . Doing this meant leaving them forever! Did he want to do that? He had to make up his mind. . . . Well, they were not close to him as it was; so leaving them was merely making final and formal what had already happened. And how was Gladys to live? Ah, she'd get his insurance money, ten thousand dollars! His cheeks felt hot. Gladys would be taken care of. And no doubt his old mother would now swallow her pride and go and live with Gladys. And the stern logic of Dot's position would force her to have the child aborted. . . . He trembled, looking about him in the snow-scattered street, his eyes smoldering with excitement. A keen sensation of vitality invaded every cell of his body and a slow, strange smile stole across his lips. It was as though he was living out a daring dream. If, after hiding away for a few days, they discovered that that body was not his, why, he could always come forth and say that the accident had wounded him in such a way that he had temporarily lost his memory. That would be his alibi. . . . And weren't such claims being made every day? He had often read of cases of amnesia. . . . It might work. Why not? It was surely worth trying. What had he to lose? His job. It was already compromised by Dot's possible accusations against him. And only tonight he had signed an obligation to pay a debt that would take him two years to discharge. . . . And if he were dead, all of that would be at an end.

All right; what next? He could not plot or plan this by talking it over with anybody. He would have to sit down alone and figure this thing out carefully. And he had to keep shy of those sections of the city where he might meet people who knew him. Where could he go? Yes, down around Twenty-second Street, the area of the bums and whores and sporting houses. . . . And he had eight hundred dollars in cash in his shirt next to his skin! Holy Moses! It all made *sense!* This eight hundred dollars would be his stake until he could launch himself anew somewhere else. . . . It all fitted. . . . He would be a damn fool if he didn't try it. All of his life he had been hankering after his personal freedom, and now freedom was knocking at his door, begging him to come in. He shivered in the cold. Yes, he had to go to his room and get his clothes. . . . But, no . . . Someone would surely see him. He could not take that chance. Funny, it was hard to think straight about this. He had to break right now the chains of habit that bound him to the present. And that was not easy. Each act of his consciousness sought to drag him back to what he wanted to flee.

He had to act, NOW! Each second he stood here like this made it more dangerous for him to do what he wanted. Yet he remained standing as though some power over which he had no control held him rooted. His judgment told him to move on, and yet he stood. Already he felt like the hunted. Waves of realization rolled through him: he had to break with everything he had ever known and create a new life. Could he do it? If he could conceive of it, he should be able to do it. This thing suited his personality, his leanings. Yes, take a taxi to Twenty-second Street. . . . No, the driver might remember him; the South Side was a small place. The subway . . .? No, he might meet another postal clerk. He would walk over to State Street and take a trolley northward to

Twenty-second Street. He was not likely to meet anybody in that direction.

At last he moved through the shaking flakes of snow. If it did not work, he could explain it all away. But, by God, it *had* to work. It was up to him to *make* it work. He was walking fast, caught up in a sense of drama, trying to work out a new destiny.

He recalled now the other Negro passenger on the train who had sat across the aisle opposite him; the man had been about his own general build, size, and color. What had happened was simple; they had mistaken that man's body for his own! The body had been so disfigured that direct identification had been impossible, and, when they had found his overcoat with his postal badge and the contract papers in the pocket, they had leaped to the conclusion that it was the body of Cross Damon. Would anyone demand that that body be subjected to further examination to determine if it was really his? The insurance company? But why would they do that unless somebody put the idea in their heads? Would Gladys? Hell, no . . . She would be content to get the ten thousand dollars of insurance money and probably some more money from the subway company. Dot? She wouldn't know what to do. His mother? Poor Mama . . . She'll just think that God has finally paid me off, he mused.

He seethed with impatience; he was both scared and glad, yearning to find shelter before meeting anyone he knew. Anxiety now drove a sharp sense of distance between him and his environment. Already the world around him seemed to be withdrawing, and he could feel in his heart a certain pathos about it. There was no racial tone to his reactions; he was just a man, *any* man who had had an opportunity to flee and had seized upon it. He was afraid of his surroundings and he knew that his surroundings did not know that he was afraid. In a way, he was a criminal, not so much because of what he was doing, but because of what he was feeling. It was for much more than merely criminal reasons that he was fleeing to escape his identity, his old hateful consciousness. There was a kind of innocence that made him want to shape for himself the kind of life he felt he wanted, but he knew that that innocence was deeply forbidden. In a debate with himself that went on without words, he asked himself if one had the right to such an attitude. Well, he would see. . . .

He took a northbound trolley on State Street and pushed his way apprehensively into the packed crowd and stood swaying. Was there anything in his manner that would attract attention? Could others tell that he was nervous, trying to hide a secret? How could one act normally when one was *trying* to act normally? He caught hold of a strap and, his shoulders jostling others, rocked with the motion of the trolley.

He began to see that this project of deception he had taken upon himself back there in the winging snow of the street was much bigger than he had realized. It was a supreme challenge that went straight to the very heart of life. What was he to do with himself? For years he had been longing for his own way to live and act, and now that it was almost his, all he could feel was an uncomfortable sense of looseness. What puzzled him most was that he could not think of concrete things to do. He was going to a cheap hotel in order to hide for a few days, but beyond that he had no ideas, no plans. He would have to imagine this thing out, dream it out, invent it, like a writer constructing a tale, he told himself grimly as he watched the blurred street lamps flash past the trolley's frosted window.

As he neared Twenty-second Street, he edged forward through the crowd, keeping his head down to conceal his face. He swung off and shivered from the penetrating dampness that bit into his bones. He was still limping, thinking: I got to find a hotel now. . . . But . . . Who was he? His name? Age? Occupation? He slowed his feet. It was not easy to break with one's life. It was not difficult to see that one was always much, much more than what one thought one was.

His past? What was his past if he wanted to become another person? His past had come to him without his asking and almost without his knowing; at some moment in the welter of his spent days he had just simply awakened to the fact that he had a past, and that was all. Now, his past would have to be a deliberately constructed thing. And how did one go about that? If he went into a hotel they would ask him his name and he would not be able to say that he was Cross Damon, postal clerk. . . . He stood still in the flood of falling snow. Question upon question bombarded him. Could he imagine a past that would fit in with his present personality? Was there more than one way in which one could account for oneself? His mind came to a standstill. If he could not figure out anything about the past, then maybe it was the future that must determine what and who he was to be. . . . The whole hastily conceived project all but crumpled. Maybe this dream of a new life was too mad? But I ought to be able to do this, he told himself. He liked the nature of this dare; there was in it something that appealed to him deeply. Others took their lives for granted; he, he would have to mold his with a conscious aim. Why not? Was he not free to do so? That all men were free was the fondest and deepest conviction of his life. And his acting upon this wild plan would be but an expression of his perfect freedom. He would do with himself what he would, what he liked.

He did not have to decide every detail tonight; just enough had to be fabricated in order to get a hotel room without rousing too much suspicion. Later, he would go into it more thoroughly, casting about for who he was or what he wanted to be.

He went into an ill-lighted tavern that reeked of disinfectant and sat in a rear booth and listened to the radio pour forth jazz music that linked itself with his sense of homelessness. The strains of blue and sensual notes were akin to him not only by virtue of their having been created by black men, but because they had come out of the hearts of men who had been rejected and yet who still lived and shared the lives of their rejectors. Those notes possessed the frightened ecstasy of the unrepentant and sent his feelings tumbling in a mood of joyful abandonment. The tavern was filled with a mixture of white and black sporting people and no one turned to look at him. He ordered a beer and sat hunched over it, wondering who he would be for the next four or five days until he left for, say, New York. To begin his new life he would relive something he knew well, something that would not tax too greatly his inventive powers. He would be a Negro who had just come up fresh from the Deep South looking for work. His name? Well . . . Charles . . . Charles what? Webb . . . Yes, that was good enough for the time being. Charles Webb . . . Yes, he had just got in from Memphis; he had had a hard time with whites down there and he was damn glad of being in the North. What had he done in Memphis? He had been a porter in a drugstore. . . . He repressed a smile. *He loved this!*

When he went out he bought a stack of newspapers to keep track of developments in the subway accident. He searched for a hotel, the cheaper and more disreputable the better. If there was the slightest doubt about his being dead, he would come forth with a story to square it all; but if all sailed smoothly, he was free.

He came finally to an eight-story hotel with tattered window shades and bare light bulbs burning in the lobby. The hotels in this district were so questionable that they rarely drew a color line. Next door was a liquor store in which he bought a bottle of whisky. He entered the hotel and a short, fat white woman studied him appraisingly from behind a counter.

"I'm looking for a room," he said. "A single."

"For how long?"

"Maybe a week."

"You got any luggage?"

"No'm. Not with me."

"Then you have to pay in advance, you know."

"Oh, yes'm. I can do that. How much is it?"

"One-fifty a night. I'll put you on the top floor. But no noise in the room, see?"

"I don't make any noise," he told her.

"They all say that," she commented, sliding him a sheet of paper. "Here; fill that out."

He answered the questions, identifying himself as Charles Webb from Memphis. When he returned the form to her, she pointed to the bottle he had under his arm.

"Look," she said. "I don't care what you do in your room, but I don't want any trouble, see? Some people get drunk and hurt others."

"Lady, I never really hurt anybody in my life but myself," he told her before he realized what he was saying.

The woman looked at him sharply; she opened her mouth to reply, but thought better of it. He knew that that had been a foolish thing to say; it was completely out of character. He had to be careful.

"Come on," the woman said, leading him down a narrow hallway to a skinny Negro with a small, black face who stood in a tiny elevator and eyed Cross sullenly.

"Take this man up to room eighty-nine, Buck. Here's the key," the woman ordered.

"Yes'm," Buck sang.

He rode up with Buck, who weighed him with his eyes. Cross knew that a bundle of newspapers and a bottle of whisky were not the normal accouterments of a Negro migrant from Memphis. He would have to do better than this. Five minutes later he was settled in his garishly papered room. The white lip of a stained sink jutted out. The floor was bare and dirty. He lay across the lumpy bed and sighed. His limbs ached from fatigue. The hard light of the bare electric bulb swinging from the ceiling stung his eyes; he doubled a piece of newspaper and tied it about the bulb to reduce the glare. He opened the bottle and took a deep swig.

Undoubtedly Gladys had now heard that he was dead.

How was she taking it? He was perversely curious to know if she was sorry. And, good God, his poor old mother! She had always predicted that he would end up badly, but he had presented her with a morally clean way of dying, a way that would induce even in his enemies a feeling of forgiving compassion. And Dot . . . ? She would find out through the newspapers or over the radio. He could almost hear Myrtle telling Dot that she had the worst luck of any girl in the whole round world. . . . He was foolishly toying with the idea of trying to disguise his voice and calling Dot on the telephone when he fell asleep . . .

Late the next morning, Cross awakened with a pale winter sun falling full into his eyes. He lay without moving, staring dully. Was this his room? Around him was a low murmur of voices and the subdued music of radios coming from other rooms. His body felt weak and he could not quickly orient himself. He swung his feet to the floor, kicking over the whisky bottle. For a moment he watched the bubbling liquid flow; then he righted the bottle, corked it, and the action helped to bring back to his mind the events of last night. He had quit, run off; *he was dead.*

He yearned for just one more glimpse of his mother, his three sons; he hungered for just one last embrace with Dot. . . . But this was crazy. Either he went through with this thing or he did not; it was all or nothing. He was being brought gradually to a comprehension of the force of habit in his and others' lives. He had to break with others and, in breaking with them, he would break with himself. He must sever all ties of memory and sentimentality, blot out, above all, the insidious tug of longing. Only the future must loom before him so magnetically that it could condition his present and give him those hours and days out of which he could build a new past. Yes, it would help him greatly if he went to New York; other faces and circumstances would be a better setting out of which to forge himself anew. But first he had to make sure that he was dead. . . .

He washed himself and mulled over his situation. When a man had been born and bred with other men, had shared and participated in their traditions, he was not required of himself to conceive the total meaning or direction of his life; broad, basic definitions of his existence were already contained implicitly in the general scope of other men's hopes and fears; and, by living and acting with them—a living and acting he will have commenced long before he could have been able to give his real consent—he will have assumed the responsibility for promises and pledges made for him and in his name by others. Now, depending only upon his lonely will, he saw that to map out his life entirely upon his own assumptions was a task that terrified him just to think of it, for he knew that he first had to know what he thought life was, had to know consciously all the multitude of assumptions which other men took for granted, and he did not know them and he knew that he did not know them. The question summed itself up: What's a man? He had unknowingly set himself a project of no less magnitude than contained in that awful question.

He looked through the newspapers, finding only more extended accounts of what he had heard last night on the radio. For the latest news he would have to buy today's papers. Yes; and the Negro weekly papers would be upon the newsstands in the Black Belt neighborhoods tonight or in the morning. They would tell the tale; they would carry detailed stories of all Negroes who had been involved in the accident.

He spent the morning shopping for an overcoat and other necessities in a poor West Side working-class district where he was certain he wouldn't encounter any of his acquaintances. He was frugal, for he didn't know what the coming days would bring. How would he spend his time? Yes; he would lay in a pile of good books. . . . No. What the hell was he thinking of? Books? What he had before him was of far more interest than any book he would ever buy; it was out of realities such as this that books were made. He was full of excitement as he realized that eventually he would not only have to think and feel this out, but he would have to act and live it out.

The relationship of his consciousness to the world had become subtly altered in a way that nagged him uneasily because he could not define it. His break with the routine of his days disturbed the tone and pitch of reality. His repudiation of his ties was as though his feelings had been water and those watery feelings had been projected by his desires out upon the surface of the world, like water upon pavements and roofs after a spring rain; and his loyalty to that world, like the sun, had brightened that world and made it glitter with meaning; and now, since last night, since he had broken all of the promises and pledges he had ever made, the water of meaning had begun to drain off the world, had begun to dry up and leave the look of things changed; and now he was seeing an alien and unjustifiable world completely different from him. It was no longer *his* world; it was just *a* world. . . .

He bought a tiny radio and went back to his hotel room. He was so spent from yesterday's exertions that he slept again. In the late afternoon there was a soft tapping upon his door and he awakened in terror. Who was it? Had somebody tracked him down? Ought he answer? He tiptoed to the door in his stockinged feet and stopped and peered through the keyhole. It was a woman; he could see the falling folds of a polka-dot dress. The landlady? The knock came again and he saw a tiny patch of white skin as the woman's hand fell to her side. She was white. . . .

He made sure that his gun was handy, then scampered back to bed and called out sleepily: "Who is it?"

"May I speak to you a moment?"

It was a woman's voice. He hesitated, opened the door, and saw a young white girl of about eighteen standing before him.

"Gotta match?" she asked, lifting a cigarette to her mouth and keeping her eyes boldly on his face.

He caught on; she was selling herself. But was she safe? Was she stooling for the police?

"Sure," he said, taking out his lighter and holding the flame for her.

"You're new here," she said.

"Yeah," he said. "I got in last night."

"So I heard," she smiled.

"Seems like news travels pretty fast around here."

"Pretty fast for those who wanna find out things," she said.

She had black, curly hair, bluish-gray-green deep-set eyes, was about five feet two in height, and seemed to weigh around a hundred and five or six pounds. Her breasts were ample, her legs large but shapely; her lips were full but over-rouged and she reeked of too much cheap perfume.

"Having fun in the city, Big Boy?" She arched her eyebrows as she spoke, then looked past him into the interior of his room.

Ought he bother with her? He wanted to, but his situation was too delicate for him to get mixed up with this fetching little tart. Yet he was suddenly hungry for her; she was woman as body of woman. . . .

"I don't know anybody around here yet," he said.

"Are you stingy with that fire water?" she asked, nodding toward his whisky bottle sitting on the night table.

"Naw," he laughed, making up his mind.

She entered slowly, glancing at him out of the corner of her eyes as she went past; he followed the movements of her body as she walked to the center of the room and sat, crossing her legs and tossing back her hair and letting her breasts take a more prominent place on her body. He closed the door and placed the bottle between them.

"What do they call you?" he asked, pouring her a drink.

"Jenny," she said. "You?"

"Charlie, just Good-Time Charlie," he said, laughing.

He saw her looking appraisingly about the room. "Traveling light, huh?"

"Just passing through," he said. "Heading west."

She sipped her drink, then rose and turned on his radio; dance music came and she stood moving rhythmically. He rose and made dance movements with her, holding her close to him, seeing in his mind the sloping curves of her body.

"Want to spend the afternoon with me?" he asked.

"Why not?"

"Look, baby, seeing this isn't the Gold Coast, what do you want?"

"I got to pay my rent," she said flatly.

"The hell with that," he told her. "How much do you want? That's all I asked you."

"I want five," she said at last.

"I'll give you three," he countered.

"I said five, you piker—"

"I said three, and you can take it or leave it; I don't want to argue with you."

"Okay," she said, shrugging.

"Let's drink some more."

"Suits me."

When the dance music stopped she turned off the radio, pulled down the window shade, and rolled back the covers of the bed. Wordlessly, she began to undress and he wondered what she was thinking of. Clad in nylon panties, she came to him and held out her hand. Her breasts were firm and the nipples were pink.

"I'll take it now, baby," she said.

"But why *now*?" he demanded.

"Listen, I'm selling; you're buying. Pay now or nothing doing," she said. "I know how men feel when they get through."

Cross laughed; he liked her brassy manner. Nobody taught her that; sense of that order was derived only through experience. He handed her three one-dollar bills which she put into the pocket of her dress, looking at him solemnly as she did so. She pulled off her panties and climbed into bed and lay staring vacantly.

"They could paint this damn place," she said matter-of-factly.

"What?" he asked, surprised, looking vaguely around the room.

"They could paint that ceiling sometime," she repeated.

Cross studied her, then laughed. "Yes; I guess they could," he admitted.

"You're not from Memphis," she said suddenly.

He whirled and glared at her, a sense of hot danger leaping into his throat. Did she know something or was she merely guessing? Was he that bad an actor? If he thought that she was spying on him, he would have grabbed the whisky bottle and whacked her across the head with it and knocked her cold and run. . . . Naw, she's just fishing, he told himself. But I got to be careful. . . . He was so shaken by sudden dread that he didn't want to get into bed with her.

"How do you know?" he asked.

"You don't talk like it," she said, puffing at her cigarette.

He relaxed. It was true that his accent was not completely of the Deep South. He drew upon the bottle to stifle his anxiety and when he took her in his arms he did not recall the fear that had scalded him. She responded so mechanically and wearily that only sheer physical hunger kept him with her. The edge gone from his desire, he lay looking at her and wondering how a woman so young could have achieved so ravaged a sense of life. His loneliness was rekindled and he lit a cigarette and grumbled: "You could have at least tried a little."

"You're not from Memphis," she said with finality.

"You're dodging the point," he reminded her with anger in his voice. "I said that you could at least pretend when you're in bed."

"You think it's important?" She looked cynically at him. "What do you want for three dollars?"

"You agreed to the price," he said brusquely.

"Hell, that's nothing," she said casually, squinting her eyes against the smoke of her cigarette. "I might've done it for nothing. Why didn't you ask me?"

She was fishing around to know him and he did not want it. He washed and dressed while she still lolled in the nude on his bed, her eyes thoughtful. He should not act now with these girls as he used to; things were changed with him and he had to change too. And she was taking her own goddamn time about leaving. Resentment rose in him as he realized that he had made less impression on her physical feelings than if he had spat into the roaring waters of Niagara Falls. . . .

"Haven't you got something to do?" he asked her.

"I can take a hint," she said pleasantly, rolling off the bed and getting into her panties.

"Be seeing you," she said after she had dressed.

"Not if I see you first."

"You'll be glad to see me if you're in a certain mood," she said; she touched him under the chin with her finger and left.

He lay on the bed, feeling spiteful toward even the scent of her perfume that lingered on in the room. He rose, opened the window wide, let in a blast of freezing air, and peered over the ledge of the sill, his sight plunging downward eight floors to the street where tiny men and women moved like little black beetles in the white snow. I wouldn't like to fall down there, he thought aimlessly and turned back into the room, closing the window.

He went down for lunch and got the afternoon newspapers. The final list of the dead was over one hundred, making the accident the worst in Chicago's history. The mayor had appointed a committee to launch an investigation, for the cause of the tragedy was still obscure. The *Herald-Examiner* carried two full pages of photographs of some of the dead and Cross was pricked by a sense of the bizarre when he saw his own face staring back at him. He knew at once that Gladys had given that photograph to the newspapers, for she alone possessed the batch of old snaps from which it had been taken. By God, she really believes it, he thought with wry glee.

Then anxiousness seized him. If Jenny saw that photograph, wouldn't she recognize him? He studied the photograph again; it showed him wearing football togs, sporting a mustache, and his face was much thinner and younger. . . . No; Jenny wouldn't recognize him from that. . . .

Early that evening the snow stopped falling and Chicago lay white and silent under huge drifts that made the streets almost impassable. Cross was glad, for it kept down the number of pedestrians and lessened his chances of being seen by anyone he knew. Near midnight he went to Thirty-fifth Street and bought a batch of Negro weeklies and rushed back to his room, not daring to open them on the street or in the trolley. There, on the front pages, were big photographs of himself. His funeral had been set for Monday afternoon at 3 P.M. at the Church of the Good Shepherd. He laughed out loud. It was working like a charm! He wondered vaguely, while downing a drink, just how badly mangled his body was supposed to have been. Then he saw the answer; an odd item in the Chicago *Defender* reported:

Subway officials stated that the body of Cross Damon had been so completely mangled that his remains had to be scooped up and wrapped in heavy cellophane before they could be placed in a coffin.

He giggled so long that tears came into his eyes.

A little after two o'clock that morning, when the snow-drenched streets were almost empty, he took a trolley to Gladys' neighborhood. He was afraid to loiter, for many people knew him by sight. From a distance of half a block he observed his home: lights were blazing in every window. She's got plenty to do these days, he said to himself, repressing a desire to howl with laughter. But as the image of his three sons rose before him, he sobered. He was never to see them again, except like this, from a distance. His eyes misted.

They were his future self, and he had given up that future for a restricted but more intense future. . . .

He went next to Thirty-seventh and Indiana Avenue and crept into a snow-choked alleyway in back of Dot's apartment building and figured out where her window would be. Yes, it was there, on the third floor. . . . A light burned behind the shade. Was Dot really sorry? Had she wept over him? Or had her weeping been over her own state of unexpected abandonment? The light in her window went out suddenly and he wondered if she was going to bed. He hurried around to the street, watching like a cat for passers-by, and secreted himself in a dark doorway opposite the entrance of the building in which she lived. After a short time he saw Dot and Myrtle come out, moving slowly through the snow and darkness with their heads and shoulders bent as under a weight of bewildered sorrow. He noticed that Myrtle was carrying a suitcase. Yes, Dot was no doubt on her way to see a doctor about the abortion. Only that could account for their having a suitcase with them. He couldn't have arranged things so neatly if he had tried dying for real!

The next morning was Sunday and it was clear and cold, with a sharp, freezing wind sweeping in over the city from Lake Michigan. He felt driven to haunt the neighborhood of his mother. How was she taking his death? Her lonely plight saddened him more than anything else. She lived in a neighborhood where no one knew him and he waited in a bar near a window to get a glimpse of her as she left for church. His overcoat was turned up about his chin and his hat was pulled low over his eyes. He smoked, toyed with a glass of beer, keeping his eyes hard upon the entrance of her house. True enough, at a quarter to eleven she came out, dressed in black, her face hidden by a veil, and picked her way gingerly over the deep snow toward her church some two blocks away. Cross felt hot tears stinging his cheeks for the first time since his childhood. He longed to run to her, fall on his knees in the snow and clasp her to him, begging forgiveness. His poor, sad, baffled old Mama . . . But if he went to her, she would collapse in the snow and might well die of the shock.

His worry that something might go wrong with his burial was what kept Cross awake the whole of the Sunday night before his funeral. Had there been no inquiries about the Negro's body that they had mistaken for his own? Who had that man been? Would his family come forward at the last moment and ask questions? Maybe his wife would claim the body. In fact, anybody's raising a question would endanger his whole plan. But perhaps no one had known that the Negro had been on the train. As he recalled now the man had seemed rather shabbily dressed. Perhaps the man's wife, if he had had a wife, thought that he had run off? Cross chided himself for worrying. In the minds of whites, what's one Negro more or less? If the rites went off without someone's raising a question, then he would consider the whole thing settled.

Monday morning was bright and cold; the temperature dipped to ten below zero. Gusts of wind swept in from Lake Michigan, setting up swirling eddies of powdered snow in the quiet streets. Cross stood moodily at his window and stared out at the frozen world, occupied with the question of how he was to spy on his burial. The Chicago *World* had reported that his body had been laid out at the Jefferson Resting Home and that "his postal colleagues and a host of friends" had sent numerous floral wreaths; his death had been referred to as a "great loss to the South Side community." He felt that if he could get a sneaking glimpse of Gladys and the funeral procession, he would feel certain in judging how soundly his death had been accepted. Spying upon the church was easy; he had, late one night, rented a top-floor room in the building opposite the church, identifying himself to the old black landlady as John Clark, a student visiting Chicago as a tourist for a week. He had already made two visits to the room, bowing respectfully to the landlady, and had observed the church at leisure.

A little after ten that morning, just after he had returned from breakfast, Jenny came to see him and her manner was so friendly that one would have thought she had known him for years. Cross was decidedly in no mood for her company, fearing that she might ask him where he was going when he was ready to leave to spy on his last rites.

"I got the blues today," he growled at her.

"Maybe I can cheer you up," she said, seating herself even though he hadn't asked her to. There was something in her manner that warned him to be on guard. She had a mouthful of chewing gum.

"Nothing to drink this morning?" she asked.

"Empty pocket, empty bottle," he lied.

"What kind of work did you do in Memphis?" she asked.

"Why in hell do you want to know that?" he demanded.

"Just curious, that's all," she answered innocently, chewing vigorously. "Something tells me you got some money."

"Yeah; I opened the safe with a bar of soap and got a million bucks," he joshed her. "Now tell me, are you working for the police?"

She paled. Her jaws stopped moving. Then she said: "Well, I never . . . !"

"Then why in hell do you keep on questioning me?"

"You *are* scared of something!" she exclaimed.

She had trapped him so neatly that he wanted to slap her. Yet he knew that it was he who had betrayed his fear and made her suspicious of him. He decided that she was honest; but honest or not, he could not use her. Her present attitude might be buttressed by good faith, but she was tough and if she found out that he had something to conceal, she might blackmail him.

"Look—Why don't you tell Jenny about your troubles? Maybe we can team up together," she said seriously.

"Forget it, Jenny. You'll save yourself time."

"You're in no mood for talking today," she said, rising. "See you when you're feeling better."

She let herself out of the room and he sat brooding. Maybe he ought to play safe and move? Was Jenny stooling for the police? But he had no criminal record and even if the police should question him, there was nothing they could pin on him. He had only a day to wait; he would remain where he was. Later, after the descent of the catastrophe, he wondered why he had not acted upon his sense of foreboding and moved. . . .

It was nearing two o'clock when Cross, filled with trepidation, took a trolley to the South Side. He found himself being irresistibly drawn to Gladys' home and, rashly, he boarded an El that passed in sight of the house and rode back and forth, snatching a quick glimpse of the front door each time the train sped past. He would ride a station past the house in one direction, get off, traverse the footbridge, and ride past the house again in the other direction to the station beyond it, get off again and return. It was not until nearly two-thirty that he saw any signs of life; the front door opened and Gladys and his mother—both dressed in deep black—came out on the sidewalk and stood in the snow. Junior, Peter, and Robert followed, being led by a distant cousin of Gladys. Excited, Cross got off the train, concealed himself behind a billboard on the El platform, and saw a man garbed formally in black go up to Gladys, his mother, and the children, and tip his hat to them. No doubt the undertaker, Cross thought. His eyes lingered on his mother and his sons and, as they left, a light seemed to go out of the winter sky. He would never see them again. . . .

His heart bubbled with hot panic when a voice sounded in his ear: "Do you know 'em?"

He spun and looked into the face of a young Negro dressed in the uniform of the El company. He had never seen the man before.

"No," he answered, relaxing.

"That's the family of a guy who was killed in the subway accident last week," the man spoke in a detached voice. "I reckon they must be going to the funeral."

"Oh," Cross said, keeping his face averted. "I read about that."

"Man, that guy wasn't nothing but meatballs and spaghetti when the subway got through with 'im," the man went on.

An El train rolled to a stop and Cross hurried into it; he had seen and heard enough. He rushed to his rented room and sat at a window overlooking the church entrance. Fifteen minutes later the hearse arrived. There's Tom . . .! Tom was his old friend from the Post Office and he was one of the pallbearers. And there was Frank. . . . And Pinkie . . . And Booker . . . And Joe Thomas . . . He could not make out the others, for their faces were turned. He watched them lift the black coffin and march slowly into the church. The undertaker's assistants followed, carrying many wreaths of flowers inside. He saw the undertaker lead Gladys, his mother, and his three sons into the church. He opened the window a crack and caught an echo of a melancholy hymn. . . . The service was so long that he wondered what the preacher could have found to say about him. He was certain, however, of one thing: whatever was being said had no relationship at all to him, his life, or the feelings he was supposed to have had.

An hour later the church doors opened and the crowd began to file out, first Gladys, then his mother; finally his three sons came, led by the preacher and the undertaker. Again he saw them sliding the black coffin into the hearse. Soon a long procession of black cars pulled off through the snow. It was over. He had witnessed a scene about which he could never in his life talk with anybody. And he *did* hanker to talk about it. When men shared normal experiences, they could talk about them without fear, but he had to hug this secret to his heart.

The procession had gone and the church doors had shut. He had to go back to his hotel and prepare to catch a train for New York. But he did not move. He was empty, face to face with a sense of dread more intense than anything he had ever felt before. He was alone. He was not only without friends, their hopes, their fears, and loves to buoy him up, but he was a man tossed back upon himself when that self meant only a hope of hope. The church across the street was still there, but somehow it had changed into a strange pile of white, lonely stone, as bleak and denuded of meaning as he was. And the snowy street, like the church, assumed a dumb, lifeless aspect. He lit a cigarette and sat on the edge of the bed and stared about the room. His movements were mechanical. The dingy walls seemed to loom over against him, asking wordlessly questions that he could not answer. Nothing made meaning; his life seemed to have turned into a static dream whose frozen images would remain unchanged throughout eternity.

HE WAS ENTERING the building when the door of the apartment of Langley Herndon opened. Cross saw a white face watching him from behind thick spectacles. He shut the door to the street, taking his time, then turned and started up the stairs.

"Hey, *you!* Wait a minute!"

It was the voice of a man who was used to issuing orders. Cross paused, turned his head, and registered a look of make-believe surprise.

"What do you want here?" the man asked, coming up to him.

"What do you mean?" Cross countered. "I'm going up to my room."

"Your *room?* Are you *living* here?" Herndon demanded.

"Of course. And who are you? Why are you asking me all this?"

"I just happen to own this goddamn building, that's all," Herndon said with rough irony. "I say who can and who can't live here!"

"But I'm not going into *your* apartment," he pretended to misunderstand. "I live upstairs—"

"I don't give a good goddamn *where* you live!" Herndon snapped. "You can't stay in this building—"

"Now, wait a minute! I've signed a lease with Mr. Blount—"

"You can't talk to me that way!"

Herndon advanced and Cross doubled his fist.

"Watch out! You're old and I don't want to hurt you!" He saw Herndon pause and blink his eyes. "If you want to talk to me, all right. But don't touch me, see?"

Herndon was short, gray, flabby, with a wide mouth. His eyes were inflamed and teary at the corners. His hair was black and slicked flat to the crown of a large, partly bald skull. He was violently agitated and seemed not to know what move to make. His face grew brick red.

"How long have you been in this building?" Herndon asked finally.

"For almost a week," Cross lied.

Herndon looked him over, his eyes traveling from Cross's necktie to his shoes.

"Say, come in here," Herndon said suddenly. "I want to talk to you."

Cross thought, he's going to try to scare me in another way now. . . . He stepped into a nicely furnished room which had a large desk. A wood fire burned in the grate and shadows danced along the walls. Herndon studied Cross for some seconds.

"Listen," he began in a tone of voice that indicated that he was stooping to give advice to someone who he doubted had sense enough to profit by it. "You are being misled. For thirty years I've had a strict policy about renting, and nobody's going to make me change it. This lease you're talking about —it's nothing. Forget it. The quicker, the better for you. I'm going to see Blount tonight and give 'im hell. Get me straight. I don't give a good goddamn about what happens to you, see? I could crush you, if I wanted to. Now, go upstairs and pack your stuff and get the hell out of there! You're black and you don't belong here and you goddamn well know it."

"Thanks," Cross said in a low, clear voice. "I'm staying here as long as Mr. Blount says I can. It's your move."

"So, you're a Communist, hey?"

"No, I'm not."

"Oh, yes, you are, and you think you're being smart," Herndon's voice was rising. "I can take care of your kind. You Reds think you—"

"I told you that I'm not a Communist; I'm *anti*-Communist!" Cross said sternly.

"I don't give a good goddamn *what* kind of a Communist you are!" Herndon shouted.

"I didn't think you did," Cross said quietly. "That's why I insisted on telling you. I'm black and that's what's riling you. But I will not move from here."

Herndon, his lips quivering, yanked open a drawer of the desk.

"Be careful, man," Cross warned him, ramming his hand into his coat pocket. "I'm armed. If you pull out a gun, I'll shoot you!" Cross was bent forward, his entire body tense, his eyes not blinking.

Herndon slammed the drawer shut and came to the side of his desk.

"Get out of here, you black sonofabitch!" he shouted, his body trembling with rage. "Get out of this house! Get out of this building! Get out of my sight! If I see you again, I'll kill you, you hear?"

Cross did not move; he stood towering over Herndon, whose mouth held flecks of foam at the corners.

"I'm going, but I never turn my back on a man who's yelling at me," he said slowly.

Herndon's lips moved soundlessly. Cross kept his eyes on Herndon and walked backward to the door, still clutching his gun. With his left hand he groped for the knob, turned it, and pulled the door open.

"Mr. Herndon, whenever you're in my presence, be careful," Cross said. "You've threatened me and I won't forget it."

He went through the door and shut it. Things would happen fast now. He smiled as he went upstairs. The encounter with Herndon had given him a lift, had almost made the last shred of dreaminess leave him. This thing'll be decided to-night one way or the other, he told himself as he entered the apartment.

Eva returned an hour later. He had to be careful in her presence; he must not let her feel that he had spied on her intimate life.

"Oh, Lionel!" she called.

He went into the hallway and saw Eva still wearing her coat; her cheeks were red and excitement was in her eyes.

"Yes?"

"Herndon says he wants to see Gil as soon as he comes in," Eva said breathlessly. "What happened? Did you have a run-in with 'im?"

"We had it," Cross said.

"Did it get rough?"

"He wanted to pull a gun, but I told him I had one, too."

"Oh, Lord—" She leaned weakly against the wall. "Poor Lionel . . ."

Her eyes were full of pity, and Cross knew that she felt that he too was a victim of the Party, that the Party was using him for bait. I'm tougher than you think, he said to himself.

"It's nothing," he said. "I like his kind."

"Oh, dear! Where's Gil?" She was trembling.

"Now, Eva, don't worry," Cross tried to soothe her. "Nothing's going to happen for the moment, anyway. His next move will be to try to scare Gil, and I don't think Gil scares easily."

"Don't you want a drink or something?" she asked, looking at him as though she expected to see him collapse.

"I never refuse a drink," he said.

She brought out a bottle of cognac.

"I brought this from France last summer, thinking I might need it sometime," she said. "And now's the time."

Cross looked at her and smiled. Bless her; she's feeling

good because she feels that she's of some use to me. . . .

"Look," he said, pushing the glass she had filled to her. "I think you need this more than I do."

She drank from the glass and poured one for him.

"What do you think will happen, Lionel?" she asked in a whisper. "That Herndon's capable of anything—Oh, God, Lionel, do you think it's *worth* it?"

Cross could see that she was on the verge of telling him to ditch the Party, to get out, to save himself. At that moment he heard Gil's key turning in the lock of the door and a pall of anxiety came over Eva's face. Cross could see Gil hanging up his coat in the hallway. As Gil entered, Eva turned as though to speak to Cross, but checked herself.

"Hello, everybody," Gil said placidly.

"Tired, Gil?" Eva asked; she was trying to act natural.

"Not especially," he said, shrugging. He drew his wallet from his coat pocket and extracted a paper from it, saying: "Here's the permit for your gun, Lionel. The Party had a lawyer pull some strings. . . . But be careful, guy."

"Thanks," Cross said. "I might really need the permit. I met Herndon today."

"Really? And how was it?"

"Rugged."

Eva rushed forward and caught hold of the lapels of Gil's coat. "You mustn't let Lionel get into this," she said hysterically. "Herndon said he wanted to see you the moment you came in. . . . And he's already threatened Lionel with a gun—"

"Let Lionel tell me what happened," Gil said, gently pushing Eva to one side, struggling to master his annoyance.

"Well," Cross began, "I was returning from—"

"Just a moment," Gil said. He took out his pipe and began to fill it with tobacco; then he paused and looked intently at Eva. Eva stared; she seemed on the verge of speaking, but controlled herself.

"I must see about dinner," she mumbled, flushing red. She

left the room and Gil lit his pipe, sucked at it.

"I'm listening," he said.

Cross related what had happened, leaving out nothing. Gil made no comment; he rose and stood at a window looking out, smoking silently. Then he turned, sat at his desk and began writing. Eva came on tiptoe to the door, peered in apprehensively, then left. Cross lit a cigarette and waited. I'll make him guess at what I'm feeling just as I have to guess at what he's feeling, he told himself.

The doorbell pealed. Gil paused in his writing, lifted his hand from the page, then began writing again. Eva came to the door, her eyes round with fear.

"Gil," she called timidly.

"Yes," Gil answered, but not turning or looking at her.

"Maybe it's Herndon—Shall I answer?" she asked in a whisper.

"You're always to answer the door," he said calmly.

As though seeking support, Eva looked at Cross.

"If it's Herndon, do be careful," she said.

"Eva!" Gil barked at her.

"I'll answer it," Cross said.

"No, Lionel. Eva will answer the door," Gil said in slow, heavy accents of authority.

Cross wanted to rise and take the man by the throat. Why does he act like that? Then he tried to dismiss it from his mind. After all, I'm no angel, it's really none of my business. . . . He was now sorry that he had read Eva's diary; his knowing her as he did made it impossible for him to regard her with detachment. Eva lingered a moment longer at the door, then vanished.

"Oh!" Eva's frightened voice came from the hallway a moment later.

"I'm sorry, Eva—Did I scare you? Is Gil home? I got to see 'im quick—It's awfully important—"

"Come in, Bob—But what's the matter? You look sick— Did you have some trouble downstairs?"

"Trouble? Yes. But not downstairs . . . What do you mean? Is Gil here?"

"He's in the living room," Eva said.

Gil had stopped writing, his pen poised over the sheet of paper. His eyes hardened as Bob, his face twitching, his eyes bloodshot and staring, appeared in the doorway.

"Hey, Lane," Bob called to Cross; there was no heartiness in his voice.

Gil whirled in his seat and demanded: "What do you want here, Bob?"

Bob acted as if he had not heard; he sank weakly into a chair. He looked at Gil and forced a sick grin that faded quickly and his face went lifeless, his eyes staring at the floor in a kind of stupor. A large drop of mucus formed at the tip of his flat, brown nose, hovered there for a second, then dropped to his upper lip. He licked at it, unaware that he did so.

"Gil," he begged, "you've got to help me."

Eva stood in the doorway. Cross sat watching. Gil was looking at Bob with half-turned body. Bob turned to Cross.

"Lane, you got to talk to 'im for me—"

"Bob!" Gil shouted, his tone full of warning. "Lane has nothing to do with this, and you damn well know it! What are you trying to do? Disturb his faith in the Party? You've said enough already to be brought up on serious charges!"

"I just want to talk to 'im—"

"You're trying to influence Lane!" Gil shouted again, leaping to his feet. "You're organizing against the Party right *here* in my presence!"

"No, no, Gil—"

"You're trying to turn Lane against the Party right under my eyes."

"Oh, God, no!"

"You are guilty right now of ideological factionalism!"

"What's that?" Bob asked incredulously.

"You are trying to get Lane to support your ideas," Gil accused.

Bob sighed; he had come to plead innocent to one crime and now he found himself accused of still another crime. Cross felt certain that Gil did not want him to witness this.

"I'll go to my room," he offered.

"No; stay right here," Gil ordered.

And Cross suddenly realized that Gil wanted him to see what was happening. Gil's chastisement of Bob could either be a warning or an object lesson. How efficient this is, Cross marveled. Not a single word or gesture is wasted. By observing this, Cross, too, could learn how to break and ravage the spirits of others, or he could see what would happen to him if he disobeyed. Eva remained in the doorway, her eyes fixed upon Bob's face. Gil was looking at her with eyes full of warning, but she wasn't aware of his gaze. Then, the moment she saw it, she blushed and hurriedly left the room.

"Now, what's the matter with you, Bob?" Gil asked at last.

Bob had not taken off his hat or his coat. Dirty snow melted on his shoes and tiny rings of water were forming on the carpet. Bob spoke in a broken whimper: "The Party voted to expel me, Gil—"

"I know that," Gil said calmly.

"But Gil, I don't wanna leave the Party— You got to help me— My life's in the Party— The Party's all I got in the world —I made a mistake—"

"Tell that to the Party," Gil said, turning and sitting again at his desk.

"Oh, please, Gil— You don't understand— I don't even want to say it, man— You *know* my problem—I'm British— Only the *Party* knows it!" Bob rose and went to the back of Gil and whispered despairingly: "Listen, an hour ago the Immigration men came to my flat, see? Lucky, I didn't go to the door—Sarah went. She told 'em in a loud voice that I was out—I heard 'em talking to Sarah and I slipped down the back stairs—I came here, to *you,* Gil— You're my friend—

Gil, for God's sake, don't let 'em do this; don't let the Party do this to me—"

"How do you know it was the Party?" Gil asked.

"But *only* the Party knew!"

"But how do you *know* the Party did it?" Gil demanded.

"Listen, I once heard Hilton threaten another West Indian Negro like me— He said he could drop an unsigned note to the Immigration folks if he didn't behave—"

"But have you any *proof* that the Party told the Government?" Gil demanded.

Bob shook his head; his eyes were blank and empty. Cross saw the point; if Bob had no proof, what harm could Bob's accusation do?

"Naw; I ain't got no proof. . . ."

Gil rose and stood over Bob.

"Are you accusing the Party of playing the role of stool pigeon?" he thundered.

Bob winced as though he had been slapped.

"No!"

"Then what in hell *are* you saying?"

"Gil, listen to me. Ten years ago I had to run off from Trinidad to keep the British from putting me in jail for Party activity— If I go back, they'll snatch me off the boat and take me straight to jail for *ten* years— Ten years in jail in the tropics is death—I mean *death,* man—don't you understand?"

"I understand," Gil said, nodding his head. "But that doesn't explain why you fought the Party."

"I didn't know I was *fighting* the Party. . . . I don't want to fight the Party. . . ."

"You took a position *against* the Party. . . . That's counter-revolution. And for counter-revolutionists the Party has no mercy," Gil told him.

"Gil, you got to tell 'em to give me another chance. . . . The Party can *hide* me. . . . Let me go to Mexico, anywhere—"

"Who are you to defy the Party?"

"I ain't nobody, *nothing.* . . ." Bob slid from his chair and lay prone on the floor. "This is *too* much, Gil—Please, please, don't let 'em do this to me. I was wrong. I confess. And I'll do anything you say, Gil! You're on the Central Committee and they'll listen to you. I been to headquarters and they won't even talk to me—"

Cross was stunned. He wanted to rise and place his foot on Bob's neck and cut off the flow of whining words. Gil watched Bob with calm, placid eyes and Cross wondered how many men and women Gil had seen in that prostrate position of penitent surrender that he could stare at Bob with so aloof and yet engrossed a passion.

"Did you meet anybody when you came up here?" Gil asked suddenly.

Bob blinked his eyes bewilderedly. "Meet anybody? No; I didn't see anybody. . . . Gil, *please!*"

"All right, Bob. You can go now."

Bob sat up; his hand went to his mouth in dismay.

"Where?"

"I don't care *where* you go—"

"But they'll get me, Gil! Look, I'll give my *life* to the Party!"

"The Party doesn't want your life." Gil smiled.

Cross closed his eyes. He hated Bob for his weakness. No wonder Gil wouldn't give in! The more merciless Gil was the more Bob would yield. Eva came to the door, her eyes avoiding Bob. Cross could see her legs trembling.

"Gil, dinner's ready."

"Go ahead and eat, Lionel. I'll join you later," Gil said.

Cross rose and went out of the room, his eyes avoiding Bob, who sobbed on the floor. He had no appetite, but he sat at the table and Eva served him. As he chewed his food, he heard Gil's voice rising in accusation, then Bob's voice falling in meek pleas. Then came a pause during which Bob coughed loudly. Finally there was a sound of footsteps in the hallway. Gil was saying something to Bob at the door, then the door closed. Cross looked at Eva; her eyes were full of fear, and her hand shook slightly as she ate. Gil came briskly to the table, sat, keeping his eyes in front of him. He volunteered no information and acted as though he knew no one would dare ask for any.

"God, I'm hungry," Gil said pleasantly and reached for the platter of roast beef.

After he had served himself generously, Gil turned to Cross and asked: "Say, did you see who won the chess tournament in Moscow? I was too busy to buy a paper."

"No, I don't know who won," Cross said, slightly nonplused.

"Do you play chess?" Gil asked.

"No."

"You ought to learn. It's wonderful for relaxation," Gil advised him.

As dinner proceeded in silence, Cross was aware that a feeling of tranquillity had descended upon him. In his mind Gil had receded far off until he had become a tiny, little luminous figure upon which all of his attention was focused. It was as if he were squinting his eye along the barrel of a rifle toward some distant and elusive target and at long last the center of the target had come within the hairline of the sight.

After he had drained his cup of coffee, Gil chuckled softly and asked: "What time is it?" He looked at his wrist watch. "Hummm . . . Ten past nine— I'd better get down and see Herr Herndon."

"Do you want me to come with you?" Cross asked.

"Why?" Gil asked, lifting his brows in surprise.

Cross said nothing. Eva sat stiffly, staring with protesting eyes into her empty coffee cup. Then she lifted her eyes to Gil and Cross saw the light of protest die. God, she's scared, Cross thought. If she's that afraid of him, how she must hate him!

Gil stood and went into the hallway, then out the door. Eva rose suddenly, as though she had to drown her anxieties in activity, and began clearing the dishes from the table.

"I'll help you," Cross said, taking a stack of plates and starting for the kitchen.

"No, Lionel—"

"Why not?" he said.

"You don't have to, you know," she said.

"I want to," he said. He wanted to be near her.

Then they both were still. They heard loud voices coming from downstairs. Cross could distinguish Gil's voice, then Herndon's. They were at it strongly. The dishes slid from Eva's hands to the table with a clatter; then she clutched the back of the chair till her knuckles showed white.

"Do you think I ought to go down?" he asked Eva.

She shook her head.

"No. If he said no, then don't. He'd be awfully angry, and when he's angry he doesn't speak for weeks—" She caught herself; she had said more than she had intended. "Lionel, really, don't bother with the dishes. Do what you like. . . ." Irritation was in her voice.

He knew that he was making her more nervous; she didn't want him to see her state of mind.

"Okay."

He went to his room and the voices were clearer; he put his ear to the floor and heard shouts full of hot anger, but no words were distinguishable. He lay on his bed, then jerked upright; he heard a sharp snapping like wood breaking, then a dull thump, and all was silent. The door of his room flew open and Eva stood there, clasping her hands in front of her, staring at him with eyes filled with terror. "What was that?"

Cross went to her; she clutched his hands tightly.

"Don't you think I ought to go down?" he asked.

"Yes," she agreed impulsively. Then her body flinched and she shut her eyes in desperation. "No; no; he'd be angry. He'd think that you thought he couldn't handle it—" Tears leaped into her eyes and she turned from him. "If he gets

hurt, he'll wonder why we didn't do something. He'll think
I did it on purpose—"

"On *purpose?*" he asked.

Yes; she was fighting against a wish for something to happen to Gil; she was longing for someone to put him out of her
life. . . .

A hoarse scream came from downstairs.

"I'm going down," Cross said suddenly.

"Yes, Lionel," Eva breathed; she was pale, trembling.

He went quickly into the hallway. He realized as he went
down the steps that he was acting more as a kind of proxy for
Eva's feelings than his own. *I* really don't care, he thought.
When he reached the landing of the first floor, he paused,
listening to the sound of grunts, scuffling feet, and the thud
of blows. He crept on tiptoe to the door. . . . Was it locked?
He turned the knob; the door swung in and Cross looked at
the two men grappling with each other. Gil lashed out with
his right fist, bashing Herndon on the ear and sending him
reeling backward. Herndon collided with a table and when
he turned Cross could see that he had the fire poker in his
right hand. Cross looked quickly at Gil and saw that his face
was covered with bloody streaks where the fire poker had
ripped into his flesh.

Both men were oblivious of Cross, who stood in the doorway with a bitter smile on his face. Cross could barely contain
himself as he watched the battle. Which man did he hate
more? Many times during the past hours he had wished both
of them dead and now he was watching them batter each
other's brains out. . . .

He spun round at the sound of footsteps behind him on the
stairs. Eva was descending with wild eyes, her hair flying
behind her. He grabbed her shoulders and held her, wanting
to keep her out of the room. Eva twisted loose and ran to the
doorway. Cross followed and stood behind her. Eva grabbed
hold of both jambs of the door and screamed as she saw Gil
sinking to the floor under the blows of Herndon's fire poker.

Herndon turned and stared at Eva, still clutching the poker in his right hand. He had the look of a man struggling to awaken from a dream. Then Cross saw the muscles of Herndon's face twitch as he advanced menacingly toward them.

"Get out, or I'll kill you both!" Herndon growled.

Eva screamed again, backed violently into Cross, then turned and ran up the stairs. Before Cross could move, Herndon was upon him and he ducked in time to save his head from a blow from the poker, which caught him on his right shoulder, leaving a searing line of fire in his flesh. He leaped aside and watched Herndon stumble toward the rear of the hall. Cross felt for his gun, then decided to run—not through fear of Herndon but because he hoped Herndon would re-enter the room and battle again with Gil. . . . He took the stairs four at a time, then, halfway up, he heard another scuffling lunge behind him; he glanced back. Gil had rushed out of the room and had grabbed Herndon; the two men now wrestled for possession of the fire poker, rolling, clawing, going from Cross's sight as they fell through the doorway back into the room. Cross caressed his bruised shoulder and looked upward; the door of Gil's apartment was open and he heard Eva's frantic voice.

"Don't you understand? I want the police! For God's sake—" Cross entered the hallway. Eva thrust the telephone into his hands.

"Lionel, here; call the police. . . . I can't make the operator understand anything."

"Okay," he breathed.

"Are you hurt?"

"Not much . . ."

He picked up the telephone, jiggled the hook, then paused, turning his head as another burst of sound came from downstairs. Eva sprang through the doorway, heading downstairs.

"Eva!" He left the phone and ran after her, catching her

on the landing and dragging her back into the apartment.

"No, no," he told her. "You can't go down there. . . . *You* call the police—"

"I don't know what to do," she cried.

"I'll go down and help Gil," he said.

Eva stared at him helplessly. He thrust the telephone into her hands and ran from the room, stumbling down the stairs. In the lower hallway, he stood, hearing the sound of the fight. He debated: yes; he *had* to help Gil. . . . What would Gil say if he didn't? His failure to help would be something he could never explain. . . .

Again he stood in the doorway of Herndon's apartment. Herndon was rushing at Gil, the poker raised to strike. Gil backed off, his hands lifted to protect his face and head. Herndon crashed the poker into Gil's hands, which seemed to wilt under the blow. The poker flew from Herndon's fingers and clattered to the floor. Gil snatched it up quickly and charged into Herndon, his face livid with fury, he whacked Herndon's head and face and Cross heard the tinkling of glass shards as Herndon's spectacles broke and showered from his eyes.

Cross watched, disdainful, detached. He saw a broken table leg lying near the fireplace; one of them had no doubt crashed into the table and the heavy oaken leg had snapped in two near the top. Teeth bared, Gil lifted the poker again to smash Herndon; but, as his arm was about to descend, the tip of the poker caught in the glass chandelier swinging from the ceiling. There was a musical storm of falling crystal and the ceiling light went out, leaving the room lit only by the leaping shadows of the fire. The force that Gil had put behind that swooping blow now carried him headlong to the floor, the poker bounding free.

Catlike, Herndon was on it and before Gil could rise Herndon was covering him with deadly blows.

Suddenly Cross knew what he wanted to do. He was acting before he knew it. He reached down and seized hold of the heavy oaken leg of the table and lifted it high in the air, feeling the solid weight of the wood in his hand, and then he sent it flying squarely into the bloody forehead of Herndon. The impact of the blow sent a tremor along the muscles of his arm. Herndon fell like an ox and lay still. He had crushed the man's skull. Tense, he stood looking down at Herndon, waiting to see if he would move again. He was concentrated, aware of nothing but Herndon's still, bloody form. Then he was startled; he whirled to see Gil struggling heavily to his feet, blood streaming from his face and neck, clotting his eyes. Cross stared for a moment. He was not through. The imperious feeling that had impelled him to action was not fulfilled. His eyes were unblinkingly on Gil's face. Yes, this other insect had to be crushed, blotted out of existence. . . .

His fingers gradually tightened about the oaken table leg; his arm lifted slowly into the air. Gil was dabbing clumsily with his handkerchief at the blood on his neck and cheeks. Cross let go with the table leg, smashing it into the left side of Gil's head. Gil trembled for a split second, then fell headlong toward the fireplace, where flames danced and cast wild red shadows over the walls. Cross's hand sank slowly to his side, the table leg resting lightly on the floor, its edges stained with blood. There was silence save for the slow ticking of an ornate clock on the desk.

He filled his lungs and sighed deeply. For perhaps a minute he did not move; his senses gradually assumed a tone of anxiety and he stared more intently at the two bloody forms stretched grotesquely on the smeared rug. Then he sucked in his breath and whirled toward the door. Oh, God, it was still open! Had anyone seen him? He rushed to it and closed it; then turned back to the room and the two inert forms. Were they dead? He touched Herndon's shoulder; the man was still; the wide, thin lips hung open; blood oozed from one corner of the mouth. Cross hesitated a second, then lifted the table leg and chopped again into the skull. The body rolled over from the force of the blow.

Cross now turned to Gil, whose head lay near the fire. He caught hold of one of Gil's legs and yanked the body from the fireplace into the center of the room where he could get a better chance to deliver another blow at the head. Again he lifted the table leg and whacked at Gil and he knew that Gil would never move again.

The universe seemed to be rushing at him with all its totality. He was anchored once again in life, in the flow of things; the world glowed with an intensity so sharp it made his body ache. He had had no plan when he had dealt those blows of death, but now he feared for himself, felt the need for a plan of defense. He knew exactly what he had done; he had done it deliberately, even though he had not planned it. His mind hadn't been blank when he had done it, and he resolved that he would never claim it had been.

He took one last quick look about the room. One of the drawers of Herndon's desk was open and Cross could see the butt of Herndon's gun half pulled out. He could almost reconstruct what had happened between the two men. Gil had no doubt grabbed Herndon just as Herndon had been about to seize the gun. And after that they had fought so desperately that neither of them had had a chance to get the gun, or they had forgotten it. . . .

The plan sprang full and ripe in his imagination, his body, his senses; he took out his handkerchief and quickly wiped the table leg which he held in his hand, making sure that no trace of his fingerprints would remain. He went to Herndon, holding the table leg with the handkerchief so that his hand would not touch it, and forced the fingers of Herndon's right hand about it several times so that the man's prints would be found. . . . He was breathing heavily. The winking shadows of the fire flicked warningly through the room. Still holding the leg with the handkerchief, he went to Gil and closed Gil's loose fingers about it. He took the fire poker, wiped it clean and inserted it in the fingers of Herndon's right hand. . . . No; he changed his mind; he'd let the fire poker rest a few inches from Herndon's hand. That was more natural. . . . He looked swiftly around to make sure that he was leaving no marks of his having been in the room. He had to hurry. . . . The door? Fingerprints on the knob . . .? No; he would not bother about them. After all, if he had made things *too* clean, the police would get suspicious. . . . And he had been down here talking to Herndon earlier this afternoon. . . . Sure . . . His prints had a right to be on the door. Go up to Eva. . . . What would he tell her? There would be questions from the police, from Party leaders, from Eva, from everybody. . . . The newspapers . . . ? What would they say? Well, he was just a Negro roomer who had gone down at the suggestion of Mrs. Blount to see what was happening and had seen them fighting. . . .

He opened the door; the downstairs hallway was empty. He caught hold of the door handle and was about to shut it when an idea came to him. Suppose someone came to see Herndon and found both Herndon and Gil dead? Ah, yes; it was better to push the tiny lever on the lock and let the door lock itself. The door would be locked when the police and the Party leaders arrived. That was the trick. They would have to knock down the door. *And he, on his second trip down, had not been able to see what was happening; he had only heard sounds.* . . . He adjusted the lock and pulled the door to, hearing it catch. He tried the handle; it was locked. Now, what motive on earth could he have had in killing the two of them? Let them figure that out. . . .

He started up the stairs, then paused and looked down at himself. Was there any blood on him? He looked at his hands, his coat, his shoes. He could see nothing. Oh, yes; his handkerchief; it was bloody from where he had wiped the fingerprints from the fire poker and the table leg. . . . He would have to burn it. Yes; he'd put it into the kitchen incinerator the first chance he got. And, to be absolutely sure, he would ditch the clothes he was wearing. The police had scientific ways of examining particles and arriving at damaging conclusions. He stood in front of Gil's apartment door and composed himself. Yes; he had to act hurriedly and frantically now. He grabbed hold of the door knob and rattled it brutally. It was locked.

"Eva!" he yelled.

"Is that you, Lionel? Is Gil with you?"

"It's me; Lionel! Open the door quick!"

He heard the night-chain rattling; she had locked herself in. She opened the door and backed fearfully away from him.

"Did you call the police?" he asked her.

"No. I called Jack Hilton; he's calling the police— What happened?"

He searched her face; her eyes were bleak and frightened. Would she be glad that Gil was dead? Didn't she want him dead so that she could be free?

"The door down there is locked and I can't hear a thing," he told her. "Gil's still in there. . . ."

"Oh, God," she whimpered.

He longed to know what was going on in her mind. Was she hoping that Gil was dead? And was she feeling guilty because she was hoping it? If so, then she'd act violently now; she'd try to ease her burden of guilt.

"The door's locked?" she repeated in a quiet voice.

"Yes."

"I'm terrified. . . . Lionel, call Jack Hilton again and tell him — He thinks maybe Gil's all right now—"

Her voice died in her throat and she had spun around and was out of the door before Cross could grab her. He debated: he had a wound on his shoulder to prove that he had tried to help Gil and maybe it would be a good thing for Eva to see that the door was locked. Then Eva, panting and whimpering, came rushing in again.

"He's there!" she gasped. "He's coming up here. . . ."

"Who?"

"Herndon—I saw 'im on the stairs— He has his gun—"

Was she crazy? Herndon was dead. Eva ran past him into her bedroom. Cross approached the door and looked out; he heard footsteps mounting the stairs to the floor above him. Ah, Eva had thought she had seen Herndon, but she had mistaken another man for Herndon. . . . He shut the door and put on the night-chain. Yes; that was something that could be used in his favor. Eva had thought that she had seen Herndon coming up the stairs! *That meant that her testimony would indicate that Herndon was still living after he had come up to the apartment for the second time. . . . That could mean that Gil and Herndon killed each other!* By God, *that* was the plan! He would stick to that story. . . .

"Eva!" he called to her. "Give me Hilton's phone number!"

When she did not answer, he went to her. She was lying on the floor of her bedroom; she had fainted. He lifted her to her bed, got a wet towel from the bathroom and patted her face with it. Her eyelids fluttered.

"Give me Hilton's phone number," he insisted.

"My purse," she murmured.

He got her purse and she gave him an address book and whispered: "Find the number there, under H. . . ."

Cross found the number, then walked slowly toward the telephone. His mind clearly grasped the entire situation and every muscle of his body was relaxed. Now, I'd like to see them figure that out, he told himself with a grim smile. I killed two little gods. . . . He paused, frowning. But they would have killed me too if they had found me like that. . . . Yet he could not get it straight. Just a moment ago it had all seemed so simple. But now it was knotted and complicated. There was in him no regret for what he had done; no, none at all. But how *could* he have done it? He too had acted like a little god. He had stood amidst those red and flickering shadows, tense and consumed with cold rage, and had judged them and had found them guilty of insulting his sense of life and had carried out a sentence of death upon them. As Hilton and Gil had acted toward Bob, so had he acted toward Gil and Herndon; he had assumed the role of policeman, judge, supreme court, and executioner—all in one swift and terrible moment. But, if he resented their being little gods, how could he do the same? His self-assurance ebbed, his pride waned under the impact of his own reflections. Oh, Christ, their disease had reached out and claimed him too. He had been subverted by the contagion of the lawless; he had been defeated by that which he had sought to destroy. He sank listlessly into the chair by the side of the telephone. Yet, no matter what happened, he had to call Hilton; he had to phone that little god . . . ! He was limp. What was the matter with him? He was, yes, he was trapped in the coils of his own actions. He had acted, had shattered the dream that surrounded him, and now the world, including himself in it, had turned mockingly into a concrete, waking nightmare from which he could see no way of escaping. He had become what he had tried to destroy, had taken on the guise of the monster he had slain. Held to a point of attention more by the logic of events than by his own reasoning, charged with a sense of meaninglessness, he bent toward the telephone and dialed. . . .

THE DOORBELL RANG. Eva broke from him, smiled, kissed him and ran to the door. It was Sarah, grim, gaunt of face, her eyes dark and full of anger.

"Is Hilton here?" she asked without ceremony.

"No; he's gone," Eva told her.

Cross went to Sarah.

"What's the matter? Where's Bob?" Cross asked her.

"I want to see Hilton," Sarah said, ignoring his question. "I'm going to kill him—"

"Oh, darling," Eva cried. "What's wrong?"

Sarah doubled her fists and lifted them toward the ceiling in a rage of bitter hate.

"The Party told on Bob— The Immigration men caught

him this morning when he came to the apartment for his clothes— Bob's dead— He can't live out those years in that prison in Trinidad— And I'm going to pay off whoever did it— Bob said that Hilton threatened to do it, and only Hilton and the Party knew about Bob's being illegally in the country. . . ."

She sank into a chair and sobbed.

"But how could that be possible?" Eva demanded, turning to Cross.

Cross was witnessing the birth of a new Eva. He knew that when she had been with Gil, she would never have been able openly to question or challenge a Party decision. And now she was demanding answers.

"It's all my fault," Sarah wept. "I pushed him to disobey the decision. . . . He did what I asked and now they got 'im. . . . He was screaming when they took him away." She clenched her teeth. "How they fooled 'im. Last night he phoned me and said that Gil had told him that everything would be fixed. He was to go to Mexico—"

"Sarah." Cross took hold of her shoulder. "I have something to tell you. Gil is dead. He was killed last night."

Sarah stared. "What did you say?"

"Gil's dead. He was killed last night—he was in an argument with his landlord downstairs. . . ."

Sarah rose and stood as though she herself had been condemned. Then impulsively she put her arms about Eva.

"God have mercy," she cried.

Cross watched the two women, both of whom had lost their husbands. One man had died suddenly; the other would die slowly over the years behind the bars of a prison on a hot island.

"I could kill whoever did that to Bob," Eva said.

Cross's lips parted. That was what he had been wanting to do to Hilton, *kill* him; but he had fought down the notion. Now Eva was planting it again in his mind. No, no; he would not kill again. Then what did one do when confronted with the Hiltons of this world? Let them trample freely over whom they liked? Never . . . But then what? To kill Hilton was a way of redeeming what Hilton had done to Bob. But it was also a way of making Hilton's acts right somehow. To kill him was a way, really, of exonerating him, of justifying him. Yet, what other course was there? To make an appeal to the heart of a man like Hilton was out of the question, for he was beyond sentiment. This was a problem only men akin to Hilton and Gil could really see and understand, for they alone knew how far cut off from life one was when one assumed the godlike role. Was there no turning back? Once the tie had snapped, was it forever? Cross knew that the only difference between him and Hilton was that his demonism was not buttressed by ideas, a goal. So why should he care? But he did. And he hated Hilton as one can only hate something which is a part of one's own heart.

"Lionel, can't we do something?" Eva asked, oblivious of the gravity of her question. "Let's start *now!* Let's redeem ourselves and help Bob some way."

"But what can we do? Bob's gone now—" Cross explained gently.

"It's too late to help Bob," Sarah said. "They've got 'im."

"This has got to stop," Eva cried. "Isn't there some way, Lionel? There must be. . . . Men like that should be *killed!*"

She embraced Sarah again and the two women wept for the men they had lost.

"Sarah, tell me, what Party plans did Bob hurt when he continued to organize?" Cross asked her.

"They were planning to launch a campaign for peace, and if Bob's union had been known as Red—and it was bound to be if Bob had kept on—everybody would have balked at signing any peace appeals. That's all. . . . Bob got in their way and they kicked him to death." Sarah's eyes narrowed. "The police give you the third degree but the Party gave Bob the fourth degree. . . ."

"This must not *be,*" Eva said in tones of horror.

Cross wandered restlessly back into the living room. He searched in his pockets and found Hilton's card, then stood staring, holding his wallet in his hand. Yes; if he went to see Hilton, it would be better to leave his money behind. God only knows what might happen. . . . He secreted his wad of greenbacks in his suitcase and again stood brooding. Suddenly he moved with purpose; he strode into the hallway and put on his overcoat.

"I'm going down for a bit," he told Eva. He studied Sarah for a moment. "Sarah, why don't you stay with Eva awhile?"

"Sure. I hate being by myself in that empty flat now. . . ."

When Cross went down into the snowy street, his gun was nestling close to his hip as he walked. He reached the corner, paused, staring thoughtfully. He should go back and remain with Eva. He was safe there, safe from himself. To mull over Hilton's crimes would unhinge his impulses and make him want to act in that wild, crazy fashion again. But he kept on walking until he saw the dark red brick bulk of the Edward Hotel where Hilton lived. Was he in? And what would he say to Hilton when he found him? He did not know. Yet he had an irrational compulsion to see Hilton. . . . He entered the hotel lobby and walked to the desk.

"Is Mr. John Hilton in?" he asked the clerk on duty.

"Mr. Hilton, Mr. Hilton—" The clerk turned and studied the board on which hung the keys to the rooms. "Room 342 . . . I'm sorry, sir. But he's out."

"Do you know when he'll be back?"

"I'm sorry. I don't know. He left no message."

"Thank you."

Cross went out into the streets again, walking at random. It was afternoon and he had not eaten. The day was gray, sunless; the air was damp, cold. He passed men and women whose faces expressed the intensity of their personal concerns. His eyes drifted distractedly over drugstore windows, the façades of stone and brick houses, the long green buses pulling through icy streets, and now and then idly up at some tall apartment-hotel building. He longed suddenly to be near Eva; but that, too, was a dubious thing. Why not flee now and start afresh? But he had done that once and it had led to nothing, to the nowhere in which he now lived. Running off was no solution, for he would simply take his problems with him. In any new place he would be worse off, for Eva wouldn't be there.

He entered a drugstore and ate a ham sandwich and drank a cup of hot coffee, neither of which he tasted. Had he gotten himself into such an emotional state that nothing meant anything any more, or had *too* much meaning now entered his life, more meaning than he could handle? On the streets again he came to a tavern and went in and drank a glass of beer. He saw a pinball machine in a corner; he dropped a coin into the slot, thumped the tiny shining balls with a lever and watched them veer and jump and bounce amid the flickering lights; he heard the excited clatter of machinery as the scores flashed in yellow numbers on a glass screen in front of him and there was a girl in a scanty red bathing suit who danced and leaped and romped on a gleaming, curving sandy beach under tall palm trees. . . . He played twice and did not win. What the hell was he doing? Was he so lost that he had to resort to this for distraction? Disgust drove him at last out into the streets again.

Hilton lay like a coiled threat deep in his mind. He had condemned Bob to ten years of suffering and Cross was now trying to find some way of getting at him. . . . His anger kept rising. Only the presence of Eva could make him try to forget himself. Yes, he would make of that girl his life's project, his life's aim; he would take her hand and lead her and, in leading her, he would be leading himself out of despair toward some kind of hope. . . . Suppose Hilton tried to take Eva from him; Hilton had the authority of the Party and could make endless trouble. . . . He had to have it out with that man, *now*—

He turned and made his way back to the Edward Hotel and entered. But why ask for Hilton, he told himself. Just go up and knock on the door of his room. Sure. . . . He crossed the lobby and stood in front of the elevator, waiting. Naw; walk up. . . . He turned and saw that no one was observing him and he took the stairs to the right. Yes; Room 342 would be on the third floor. . . . When he reached the third-floor corridor, he looked for the number. He came to the door of Hilton's room and paused; the door stood open and he could hear the whirr of a vacuum cleaner. He stepped to one side and waited. Was Hilton married? Or living with some girl? Strangely, he'd never considered that Hilton might not be alone. . . . He peered into the doorway for an instant and saw the white uniform and the bare, dark brown arm of a Negro maid. Then he stiffened as he heard footsteps and he walked quickly away, looking over his shoulder. The Negro maid came out with a pile of dirty linen over her arm and headed down the hallway, leaving the door open. She was no doubt going to dump the soiled linen into some receptacle. Cross thought quickly; there might be a bare chance of hiding in the room. . . . The maid went out of sight and he ducked through the door and looked about frantically. Yes; the clothes closet. He opened it, slid in, and crouched in a corner, smelling the sweet-sour odor of stale sweat. He pulled the door shut. Footsteps sounded again and he heard the maid humming a spiritual. Then the low whine of the vacuum cleaner came to his ears, and when it stopped there was the musical flow of water in the bathroom. More footsteps, silence. Had she gone? He heard the door slam and all was quiet. A moment later he emerged and looked about; the room was empty. A grayish light seeped in through half-closed Venetian blinds. He lookd in the bathroom to make sure that he was alone, then turned to the top of the dresser and studied the comb, brush, and tube of shaving soap. He began pulling out dresser drawers. Clothing, pamphlets, a scrapbook, a flashlight . . .

His breath caught in his throat. *What!* Good God in Heaven! What was this? That *Hilton!* What a tricky bastard . . . On top of a pair of pajamas lay the balled and bloody handkerchief which he thought he had burnt by dropping it into the incinerator! The crumpled handkerchief showed burnt spots where it had lain on a pile of hot ashes; in fact, one corner was charred black. . . . He stood without moving a muscle, unable to believe what his eyes saw so plainly. So Hilton had known all along! But why hadn't he said anything? Why had Hilton defended him so ardently before the police?

Then he understood. . . . Hilton was saving this handkerchief as his trump card; he was trying to *own* him morally. . . . Hilton had seen him drop that handkerchief into the incinerator and had pretended that he had noticed nothing; and when he had gone back to his room, Hilton had gone downstairs and had gotten it . . . had bribed the cop at the door, perhaps. . . . Or he had gone down to the basement this morning on leaving the apartment and had raked it out of the ashes. The fact was: Hilton had *proof* of his guilt! Eva had been in his room last night and maybe Hilton had eavesdropped at his door . . . ? Of course! That was the meaning of that last crack that Hilton had made just before he had left the apartment. Hilton had asked him to look after Eva and when he had said that he would do so, Hilton had said, "I *know* you will."

Gingerly, he stuffed the handkerchief into his pocket, then paused. No; it was not safe to put the handkerchief in his pocket like that. He withdrew the spotted handkerchief and then pulled out his clean, freshly laundered one. He wrapped the spotted handkerchief in the clean one; if he happened to pull out his handkerchief, he wouldn't run the risk of dangling the bloody one carelessly in the face of some stranger.

He rummaged further in the dresser drawers. A gun! A .32 and fully loaded . . . He took it and broke it and emptied the bullets into his palm and pocketed them. Now he was ready to face Hilton. Where was he? Had he gone to the headquarters of the Communist Party? If he had, why hadn't he taken the handkerchief with him? Or did he have some other idea in mind? Anyway, it seemed that Hilton had not acted against him yet. Well, he'd had his chance; he wouldn't act, not *now*. What a fool he'd been! These Communists were so tricky that it was hard to cope with them. When Hilton came, he would have to be on his guard each second, for the man was dangerous. How calm he had acted this morning! A disciplined man, cold, precise, farseeing, ruthless. Hilton was after power and keeping his mouth shut about Cross's guilt was but one more step in getting hold of a bright young man whose life he would own and whose talents would serve him in his struggle for power. . . .

Cross saw a little radio on the night table at the bedside. He looked at his wrist watch; it was nearing five o'clock. Where was Hilton? Had he gone to the police? No; if he had, he certainly would have taken the handkerchief with him as evidence. . . . He sat in a chair near the bed and turned on the radio, softly, and listened to the low, surging beat of jazz music. He kept his hand in his pocket on his gun and waited. . . .

Half an hour later he jerked alert. A key turned with a click in the lock of the door. Cross quickly twirled the knob on the radio, leaving the radio still turned on, going in a soft hum. His hand was on his gun and the gun was jammed deep in his overcoat pocket. The door swung in and Hilton, with a toothpick slanting downward from one corner of his thin lips, came into the room and stopped short, blinking his eyes at the sight of Cross. Hilton's body twitched as from an electric shock; then he rushed to the dresser and yanked open the drawer that had held his .32. . . . He's quick, Cross thought. He smiled at Hilton, stepped past him and shut the door to the corridor. Hilton was pawing frantically in the dresser drawer, then he was still for a second. He spun around and faced Cross, his eyes bulging, his hands empty and trembling.

"I've got your gun, Hilton," Cross told him matter-of-factly.

Cross pulled out the .32 with his left hand and at the same time he drew his .38 with his right.

"Say," Hilton began in a whisper. "What's wrong?"

"Are you asking me?" Cross mocked him.

Hilton's face was gray, his eyes like flat discs of metal. He moved nervously, backing away from Cross one moment and advancing the next, his mouth working spasmodically.

"If you shout, Hilton, I'll just have to shoot you," Cross told him, gravely. "Have some sense. I'm in danger, and I won't hesitate to shoot, see? I was a fool to underestimate you once, but I won't do it twice."

Cross could almost see the rapid calculations spinning around in Hilton's brain. He had backed off to a wall now.

"What do you want, Lane?" he asked.

"Why didn't you tell me you knew what I'd done?" Cross asked.

"What you'd done?" Hilton pretended amazement. "What are you talking about?"

"Quit stalling, Hilton," Cross said. "Look, I found the handkerchief. . . . You got it out of the incinerator—"

"Oh," Hilton said, turning pale.

"You knew what I'd done. Why didn't you tell the cops?"

"Because I was glad that you'd done it," Hilton said promptly, simply. "It solved a multitude of problems for me. Gil stood between me and one of the most important assignments on the Central Committee. Gil is gone and I've already got the job. I've wanted Eva for a long time; you freed her. . . . Gil's death was like a gift dropped from the sky."

Cross recalled how Hilton had spoken of Gil last night. . . . But he hadn't thought that much hate and cupidity had been behind those casual words!

"And when did you know I'd done it?"

"Your coolness made me suspect you right off," Hilton said without a trace of emotion. "I'm not so stupid a white man that I can't tell the difference between fear and self-possession in a Negro. You were self-possessed. The cops thought you were just another scared darky. Okay, Lane. You got the handkerchief. Let's make a deal. Let's be reasonable. You wanted Eva. Well, you got her. . . . Okay. Take off and let's call it quits—"

"So you think it was to get Eva that I did it?"

"Hell, yes. She's nuts about you and you're in love with her," Hilton said.

"It wasn't because of Eva," Cross told him.

"Then what was it?"

"You'll never know."

"Another revolutionary group?"

"No."

"You're with the police, then?"

"Hell, no."

"Then why did you do it?"

Cross laughed. Just as every man, perhaps, has his price, so every man, it seems, has a limit to his intelligence. Hilton knew that Cross was sincere and it bewildered him.

"I'll trade with you," Hilton urged him. "I don't know what your angle is, but shooting's not going to help anybody. . . ."

"It's not that easy," Cross told him. "You and your crowd are smart. I trust *nobody* now."

Hilton's voice came in a low, urgent stream of words, all precise and straight to the point.

"I won't tell anybody, the Party or the police," he swore. "Look, I just left Party headquarters. I'm taking Gil's place, in addition to my other assignment. So everything's settled. I wanted to get my hands on a quick boy like you, but you got away. Okay. No hard feelings. You go your way and I'll go mine. To hell with Gil. I don't care. I know you'll never speak of it, and God knows I won't. After all, I helped you with the D.A., didn't I? I kept making a racket about how Herndon was the murderer, didn't I? And Eva worships you. . . . You got what you want, huh? Things went your way."

"What about Bob?"

"Bob?" Hilton blinked. "What the hell do you care?" His

eyes were round with surprise. "Was he your brother or something?"

"No. You sent Bob to Trinidad, to his death—"

"So what? There are a million Bob Hunters. What do they mean? They don't count. . . ."

Cross smiled bitterly. How those quiet words riled him! He had to deal with this man in a way that would make him feel what he felt.

"Sit down, Hilton."

Hilton hesitated; he did not know what was coming; his eyes darted.

"Make no mistake, Hilton," Cross warned him. "I'd kill you in a minute. If you've got any tricks in mind, forget 'em."

"I've no tricks, Lane. I want to live. . . ."

"So did Bob," Cross said. "Now, sit down. . . . In that chair there, where I can see you."

Hilton sat down and Cross sat on the edge of the bed and held his gun on Hilton.

"I want to know some things, Hilton," he began.

"Let's be reasonable," Hilton said. "Let's not be foolish about this. There's no sense in being drastic. . . ."

The man had begun to plead for his life.

"How is it that you care so much for your life and nothing for Bob's?" Cross demanded.

"And what in hell do *you* care for life?" Hilton asked.

Cross smiled bitterly. It was a fair question.

"Who do you think *you* are to kill as *you* did?" Hilton demanded. "Herndon's no loss. But Gil was helping you, wasn't he? He took you into his home, trusted you, didn't he? And I shielded you from the cops, didn't I? What are you kicking about, Lane? Let's call it quits."

"No," Cross said thoughtfully. "There's something here I want to understand. . . . I'm caught in these compulsions, just like you are. But, Hilton, I'm reluctantly in it. I don't like it. I want to get out of it."

"But killing me isn't going to get you out of it," Hilton

reminded him eagerly. "The only way out is to *stop.*"

"I won't stop; I can't stop as long as men like you keep playing your dirty games," Cross said; and there was a genuine despair in his voice. "I won't ever feel free as long as you exist, even if you aren't hunting me down. You and men like you are my enemies. Bob Hunters will go on being shipped to their deaths as long as you live. . . . And don't give me this goddamn argument about your helping me. You help others when it *suits* you, and when it doesn't, you *don't!*"

"That's the law of life," Hilton stated simply.

"It isn't," Cross contradicted him in a frenzy that made Hilton's face turn still whiter. "Maybe you're trying to *make* it into a law—"

"It's what I've found, Lane; and it's what you'll find too."

"I don't believe it," Cross said, knowing what Hilton had said was true. "And even if it's true now, we can change it. We can make it different; it *must* be different. . . ."

"Why?" Hilton asked mockingly.

"Because—because—"

"You're looking for paradise on earth," Hilton told him, managing a soft smile. "You're confused, Lane. You're seeking for something that doesn't exist. You want to redeem life on this earth with so-called meaning—But what you see before your eyes is all there is. Get all that idealistic rot out of your head, boy—"

"I'm *not* idealistic," Cross insisted.

"You are!" Hilton swore. "You're an inverted idealist. You're groping for some over-all concept to tie all life together. There is none, Lane." Hilton was struggling to master his fear; he was trying to get at Cross's feelings, trying to make him feel that he was his older brother, that they shared basically the same views of life, and that Cross should accept his guidance. "Living in this world, Lane, is what we make it, and we make what there is of it. Beyond that there's nothing, nothing at all. . . . To think that there's something is foolish; to act as if there is something is mad. . . . Now, let's do business like rational men. Let's make a deal. You do what you want to do, and I'll do what I want. We'll leave each other alone. I don't give a *damn* what you do. . . ."

But Cross was not moved. He still held the gun on Hilton, smiling a little, appreciating Hilton's tactics. Then he shook his head; he could not accept what he had heard. Somewhere there was an anchorage to be found. The logic of Hilton reduced all actions of life to a kind of trading in death. And that was not his sense of it; he had killed, but not to exalt that. He had been trying to find a way out, to test himself, to see, to know; but not killing just to live. . . .

"You don't feel that there is any real justification for anything, hunh, Hilton?"

"No! I am here, alive, real. That's all the justification there is and will ever be, Lane," Hilton spoke earnestly. "Let's start from that. I let you live and you let me live. . . ."

"Why should I, if there's no justification? And suppose we break our contract?"

"Then one of us dies, that's all. What the hell is there so important about men dying? Tell me. We're not like the goddamn bourgeois, Lane. We don't make deals in shoes, cotton, iron, and wool. We make deals in human lives. Those are the good deals, the important deals, the history-making deals when they are made in a big way. Sweep your illusions aside, Lane. Get down to what is left, and that is: life, life; bare, naked, unjustifiable life; just life existing there and for no reason and no end. The end and the reason are for us to say, to project. That's all. My wanting to live even in this reasonless way is the only check and guarantee you have that I'll keep my promise."

"That's not *enough!*" Cross shouted.

"You're a romantic fool!" Hilton shouted in turn. "You're a kid! An idiot! You're just going about spilling blood for no reason at all, looking for what doesn't exist!"

"And what do *you* kill for?" Cross asked tauntingly.

"Practical reasons."

"And Bob was betrayed to death for practical reasons?"

"Yes. For practical reasons."

"But they were such trivial practical reasons," Cross protested, remembering the agony on Bob's face. "Couldn't there be—?"

"A pretense? Why? Look at it simply, Lane. Why fool yourself? You know and understand too much to go about looking for rainbows. Let's trade. I've no proof against you. If anything ever happens to you, I'll help you; I'll remember and will stand by you. After all, Lane, no matter what plan I had in mind, I wasn't going to kill you—"

"That's just it!" Cross burst out. "I might forgive you if you had been going to kill me. But, no; you were going to make me a slave. I would never have been able to draw a free breath as long as I lived if you had had your way. I'd have suffered, night and day. You would have dominated my consciousness. No, no, Hilton, there's more here than you say. Goddammit, there *is!* If not, then why all this meaningless suffering? If you had killed me, that would have been a simple act. Killing Bob might have been in a way merciful. He wasn't happy. But to make him suffer ten long years! Hell, *no!* You say life is just life, a simple act of accidental possession in the hands of him who happens to have it. But what's *suffering?* That rests in the senses. . . . You might argue that you could snatch a life, blot out a consciousness and get away with it because you're strong and free enough to do it; but why turn a consciousness into a flame of suffering and let it lie, squirming . . . ? No!" Cross's eyes were unblinking, seeing not Hilton sitting there staring at him, but Eva's diary, those pages telling of deception, of shame, of fear; and, too, he was remembering his own agonies in Chicago. He rose from the bed and looked wildly about the room.

"No, Lane," Hilton was saying. "What are you going to do?"

Yes, he would turn up the radio, good and loud; it would help drown out the pistol shot. He turned the knob up and a leaping flood of jazz music filled the room. Hilton rose slowly, sensing that Cross was preparing to act. Cross kept the gun on him, then he saw the bed. Yes, make him get down there on the mattress, and the sound of the shot would not be heard.

"Lane, Lane, you're crazy!" Hilton was saying, his head shaking.

"Take it easy, Hilton," Cross told him.

"You can't get away with it, Lane!" Hilton begged. "They'll hear the shot—somebody will know—they'll catch you. Listen, you want money? I got a few thousand—I'll give you anything—but *don't* do this. . . ."

Cross was possessed. He was crouching a little and his finger was conscious of the trigger. No, not yet; load the .32 and use it. . . . That was better. . . . He backed off from Hilton, pulled out the .32, and, aiming his own gun with his right hand, he awkwardly took one bullet from his pocket, wiped it clean of his fingerprints and slipped it into a chamber of Hilton's gun, his eyes hard on Hilton's face. His fingers fumbled as he worked.

Trusting, hoping for luck, Hilton rushed at him and Cross met the attack with a sharp blow from the butt of his gun across Hilton's forehead. The man slumped to the floor, still conscious, his eyes filmed with fear.

"No, Lane; no, no!"

Hilton was weeping now, suffering. Cross knew that he had to do it quickly or he could not do it at all. He grabbed Hilton by the collar, and yanked him toward the bed. He was surprised at how light the man was. Hilton, in his fear, offered little resistance, as though he thought that being pliable might make Cross compassionate enough to spare his life.

"No, no, no . . . for God's sake, Lane, don't kill me!"

He put his gun in his pocket and held the .32 in his right hand. He kicked Hilton and muttered: "Get on the bed!"

He had to act quickly, or this man's wild face would make

him stop. Hilton, with glazed eyes, scrambled obediently upon the bed.

"Lane, Lane, listen—*please!*" he sobbed.

Cross grabbed Hilton's head and, pulling one corner of the mattress up, he forced it over Hilton's head. Quick, quick, or he could not do it. Hilton's fingers were now clawing at his hand. Cross placed the .32 at Hilton's temple and squeezed the trigger; there was a click. Oh, God, five of the chambers were empty; only one chamber was filled. Hilton's mouth was moving, but terror robbed him of speech. Cross squeezed the trigger again and another empty click sounded, then again and then there was a spurt of blue flame and a gaping hole showed in Hilton's temple. Cross became aware of the dancing waves of jazz music that swirled around the room. He saw the black powder burns circling the bloody bullet hole in Hilton's temple.

He dropped the corner of the mattress and lowered the volume of the radio. Hilton's hands still moved; a labored breathing went in and out of the thin lips; there was a groan and the form on the bed was quiet. Cross strained, listening. There were no sounds in the corridor. He had to get out of here. . . . The .32 . . . Yes . . . He wiped it clean of fingerprints on the sheet of the bed and tossed it beside Hilton's hand. He paused, then forced the gun into Hilton's fingers.

He looked about. His fingerprints—Suddenly he did not want to try to save himself. What was the use? But he had to. He took a dirty shirt of Hilton's and wiped wherever he thought he had touched. He had to go, had to get out of this room. He was more concerned with getting away from the sight of that grotesquely gray face with its gaping mouth than with saving himself. He went to the door, opened it slowly and looked into the corridor. He saw the retreating back of a man. He waited until the man had turned a corner, then he went out of the room, drawing the door to, and walked toward the elevator. He seemed to be floating along without effort; he was never able to remember afterward making any

attempt to run or hide. But when he got to the elevator, he
pushed a button and then seemed to realize that he mustn't
be seen by the elevator boy. The shadow of the car heaved
into view through the glass door of the elevator and he
ducked away. He saw a flight of steps leading down; he took
them, running, then slowed and walked on down to the
lobby. Act natural, he told himself. He walked across the
lobby, passing one or two people who glanced casually at
him. He came to the newsstand and stopped.

"A *Daily News*," he said.

He paid for the paper and, as he turned to walk to the door,
a way to establish a partial alibi for himself came to him.
. . . Ought he try it? Why not? Holding the paper before his
eyes and pretending to scan the headlines, he glanced
quickly about. No one seemed to be aware of him. Yes, he
would do it.

He went casually to the desk and asked the clerk: "Is Mr.
Hilton in?"

"Oh, yes; I think he's in now, sir," the clerk replied; he
evidently remembered that Cross had asked for Hilton before. Turning, he examined the board holding the keys, then
spoke to a brunette girl who sat facing a switchboard. "Will
you ring Mr. Hilton, please . . . ? Room 342."

"Okay," the girl said.

"Whom shall we tell him is calling?" the clerk asked.

"Lionel Lane."

"Tell him Mr. Lane is calling," the clerk told the girl.

Cross watched the girl plug in on Room 342 and jiggle a
tiny lever. A young woman with a suitcase came to the desk
and Cross stepped to one side and listened as she inquired for
a room. . . .

"There's no answer from Mr. Hilton," the girl at the
switchboard told the clerk.

"But I saw him go up a few minutes ago," the clerk said.

"I'll try again," the girl said.

"Did you have an appointment with him?"

"Well, yes. He asked me to come and see him as soon as possible. No time was specified," Cross explained.

"She's ringing him again," the clerk said, giving the woman with the suitcase the hotel register to sign.

Cross sat down. He hoped that his present actions would indicate in any future inquiry that he had not been upstairs. Would a murderer act as calm and polite as he was acting now?

"There's no response at all from Mr. Hilton's room," Cross heard the girl say.

"I'm sorry, sir," the clerk said, "but we don't seem to be able to locate Mr. Hilton."

"That's all right," Cross said, rising.

"Would you like to leave a message?"

"All right," Cross said.

On a pad of paper supplied by the clerk, Cross wrote:

Dear Hilton: I was by to see you twice this afternoon. I'll try again tomorrow morning. Everything's fine. Hope you got some sleep after that session last night.

LANE

P.S. Don't worry about anything. Eva's doing wonderfully well. P.P.S. Since you're so busy, why don't you phone me instead and let's fix a time?

He folded the note and handed it to the clerk, who pushed it into the letter slot, numbered 342, of the keyboard behind him.

"Thank you," Cross said.

"You're welcome, sir."

It was not until Cross had gone out into the cold streets that the full reaction to what he had done began to set in. He trembled as he walked. Had he acted normal enough? Wasn't it in favor of his innocence that he had asked for Jack Hilton *twice?* As his mind grasped more fully the folly of his having killed Hilton, a sense of nauseous depression seized him. He had killed Jack Hilton for many reasons: to redeem Bob's betrayal, for the sake of Sarah's indignation, for Eva's deceived heart; but mainly it had been to rid himself of that sense of outrage that Hilton's attitude had evoked in him, Hilton's assumption that he could have made a slave of him. He was deeper now than ever in the consequences flowing from his compulsive acts. He would be caught. . . . Surely they would come at him now. To be found on the fringes of *two* crimes would certainly make the police think something was wrong. . . . All right, so what? He was already lost anyway. . . .

But was it as bad as all that? Didn't he have an ironical array of invisible allies on his side? Wouldn't the police have a rather difficult job proving his guilt in terms of motives? What motives could they impute to him? The police would first have to prove that he had killed Gil and Herndon before they could get near his motive for having killed Hilton. . . . Lacking concrete evidence, the police would have to fall back on psychological motives. And in that realm he was certain that even Houston, that old outlaw who had trapped himself with the law, that outsider who was privy to the secrets of the moon's dark side, would find it well-nigh impossible to bring himself to the point of believing him guilty. . . . Even if Houston should actually believe him guilty, would he dare express his theories about it publicly? Houston had a passion for toying with daring ideas, but juggling with possibilities and saying definitely that a man committed a particular crime because of those possibilities were two wholly different things. And especially when the crime stemmed from such a ghostly set of reasons. . . .

He turned off Eighth Street and walked toward home. As he neared Herndon's apartment building he became aware that a police car was pulling slowly into Charles Street at the opposite end of the block. He panicked. Did they know already? He had to act natural, keep his wits about him. A confrontation regarding the death of Hilton would be far more serious than the questions he had answered about Gil and Herndon.

Yes, the occupants of the police car had evidently spotted

him, for the car slowed and he arrived at the entrance to Herndon's building at the same time that the car did. He paid no attention to the car and turned to mount the steps of the stoop. The door of the car flew open and a cop leaped to the sidewalk, ran, grabbed his arm, and spun him around.

"Just a minute!"

Cross gaped at the cop a moment in simulated surprise.

"What's the matter? What do you want?"

"We want to talk to you!"

Two more policemen came running from the car and the three of them surrounded him in the growing darkness. Several people paused and stared. One of the cops barked roughly:

"Get going. This is none of your business!"

The passers-by moved reluctantly on.

"What do you want?" Cross asked.

"You're Lionel Lane?"

"That's right."

"You'd better come with us."

"I'll come willingly, but why?"

"You'll know soon enough."

He allowed himself to be led, looking in alarm from one face to the other. He would pretend to be stunned; he would not talk. As they pushed him into the car, he glanced up at the lighted windows of Eva's apartment and wondered if she knew. He was sitting jammed between the policemen when the car jerked into motion and the siren rose to a wail as the car picked up speed. Then his breath was knocked out of him as the cops seized him from both left and right and patted his pockets. They found his gun and snatched it.

"Ah, a Colt .38 . . . so you carry a gun, hunh?"

"Of course . . ."

"What the hell do you mean, 'Of course'? "

The cop broke the gun and extracted the bullets.

"I've a permit to carry a gun," he told them.

There was a moment's silence. Cross took his wallet from

his inside coat pocket and tendered the permit.

"Jesus! It was issued yesterday," a cop exclaimed.

"Has the gun been fired?"

"Doesn't look or smell like it. . . ."

Three minutes later the siren died and the car pulled to a screeching stop and the doors were yanked open. Cross was pushed out and hustled into the interior of a police station and made to sit facing a tough, wide-mouthed, gray-haired policeman who sat behind a desk. A plaque on the desk identified the man as Captain Ross.

"We picked him up in front of where he lives," a cop reported to the captain. "We grabbed him about two minutes after we got the call. He had this. . . ." The cop put Cross's gun on the desk. "Here's his permit."

The captain quickly examined the gun, then eyed Cross intently. He rose and stood over Cross.

"Frisk him," the captain ordered.

One policeman held him while another swiftly emptied his pockets and piled his package of cigarettes, his ring of keys, his wallet, his lighter, his loose coins, and his folded newspaper upon the desk. He had a moment of wild panic when the policeman pulled the balled handkerchief from his pocket. . . . But the policeman handled it gingerly, as though he was afraid of germs.

"Okay," the captain said. "Take your stuff. What do you do for a living?"

"I'm a student."

"Where?"

"Well, I haven't enrolled yet—"

"Where were you going when the officer met you?"

"Home. I was in front of the house where I live."

"Why do you carry a gun?"

"My life has been threatened."

"By whom?"

"My landlord, who was—"

"When was this?"

"Yesterday. You see—"

"Have you used this gun recently?"

"No. I haven't fired the gun in over five years."

"Do you know John Hilton?"

"Of course. I just left his hotel—"

"You had an appointment with him?"

"That's right. But why are you asking me all this—?"

"We'll do the questioning. Now, what was the purpose of your visit to Mr. Hilton?"

"He invited me to see him."

"What did you say to him?"

The police had not mentioned that Hilton was dead, and Cross knew that they were trying to trap him into some inadvertent admission that he knew that Hilton was dead or that he had recently seen him.

"Nothing. He wasn't in."

"But you *saw* him?"

"No, I didn't."

"Did you have a quarrel with him?"

"No. I've never quarreled with him."

"You were good friends?"

"I wouldn't quite say that."

"Why?"

"I just met the man two nights ago—"

"And when you saw him just a few minutes ago—"

"I haven't seen Mr. Hilton since ten o'clock this morning."

"Did he give you an appointment to see him another time?"

"What do you mean?"

"I mean, when you left him this afternoon, when did he tell you that you could see him?"

"But I didn't *see* him this afternoon, I tell you."

"What did he want to see you about?"

"Well," Cross allowed himself to relax a little. "He wanted to talk politics. . . . Look, you know as well as I that Hilton's a Communist. But I thought it was legal to talk to him."

The captain sat down and pulled from the desk drawer the

note which he had given to the clerk in the hotel.

"Did you write this?"

Cross acted astonished as he examined the note.

"Yes. I wrote this this afternoon, about forty-five minutes ago; or maybe half an hour. . . . But how did you get this? I left it for Mr. Hilton. . . ."

"Did you push it under the door of his room?"

"No. I left it at the desk. But where did you get it?"

"We found it," the captain said vaguely.

"Then Hilton must have dropped it out of his pocket, or something like that. Or maybe the hotel clerk dropped it, lost it. . . . But I could swear I left it at the desk with the clerk." Cross allowed himself to be confused, bewildered. He looked nonplused from one face to another. The policemen were puzzled. "What's this all about? What do you want with me? Did Mr. Hilton say something to you?"

"Mr. Hilton had an accident—"

"Oh," Cross said in surprise. "Not serious, I hope—An automobile accident?"

"You tried to see Hilton earlier today?" the captain asked, ignoring the question.

"Yes."

"And he wasn't in?"

"That's right."

"Did you see Hilton at any time today?"

"Yes. It was this morning when he left the apartment where I live. But what's this all about? What has that got to do with his being hurt? If you told me what you wanted, maybe I could help you," Cross said.

"When did you see Hilton *after* he left you this morning?" the captain continued to ignore his request for more information. "You saw him?"

"No."

"Did Hilton ever threaten you?"

"No; why should he? Look, let me explain. . . . Hilton came last night—"

"We're doing the questioning. You just answer!" the captain reminded him. "Do you know anyone who'd want to harm Hilton?"

Cross gaped and let his eyes assume a roundness of understanding. This was the closest the captain had come to saying that some *person* had hurt Hilton. Should he try to confuse them by telling them about Bob and Sarah? Bob and Sarah had real, ordinary motives for wanting to kill Hilton and both of them had airtight alibis. . . . So what harm would it do to tell of the row that Bob had had with Gil and Hilton? It would give their literal minds something to chew upon for a few minutes.

"Well, look now . . . let me think—"

"Don't think! Talk! Tell what you know. This is serious."

"Well, it's kind of complicated and I'm rather a stranger to all of them, you see. These people, you know, are Communists, all of them. They had a hot argument the other night about Party matters. . . ."

"What people and where was the argument?"

"Bob Hunter and Hilton—It was at Bob's place—"

"Go on; get to the point!"

His eyes roved from face to face. Yes, they were eager to hear the story. Bob was on Ellis Island and had the best of all possible alibis. And no doubt Sarah could prove that she had been with Eva at the time that Hilton was killed. He told them the tale of Bob's illegal entry into the country, of how Hilton had—according to Bob's way of explaining it—threatened to have him deported to Trinidad, if he did not obey the Party. . . .

"You see, according to Bob, Hilton was going to tip off the Immigration authorities and have him picked up," Cross said.

"Where's this Bob Hunter now?" the captain demanded.

"He was at Ellis Island the last I heard," Cross said. "They picked him up for deportation."

The faces of the policemen showed keen disappointment.

"And his wife, Sarah? Where's she now?"

"At my house, maybe. That is, if she's not gone to her own home by now—"

"Where does she live?"

He gave them the information. He was sure that Sarah could readily account for herself.

"Lane, did you go up to Hilton's room?" the captain asked suddenly, softly.

"No; I told you he wasn't in."

"Did you ever fire a .32?"

"No. I own a .38. You see my gun—"

"Aren't you associated with Hilton in some way?"

"No. Why do you ask?"

"You could have walked up the stairs, you know," the captain suggested.

"What stairs?" Cross asked.

"The hotel stairs. Didn't you walk up to Hilton's room?"

"Good God, no! I told you I didn't *see* Hilton!"

There was silence. The captain turned to his desk and wrote something hurriedly upon a pad, tore off the sheet and handed it to a policeman.

"Check at Ellis Island about this Bob Hunter. Make sure he's still there and hasn't been out. . . . And send out a radio call for this Sarah, his wife—"

"Say!" Cross exclaimed. "Look, here—" He pretended to be overcome with contrition. "I didn't mean to get Sarah in trouble. . . . She's all upset about her husband. I'm sure that she hasn't done anything to anybody. She'll hate me for making people think that she's done something. . . ."

"We'll take good care and keep what you've told us strictly confidential, Mr. Lane," the captain said. "Now, let me tell you that Hilton was found dead a few minutes ago in his hotel room. . . ."

Cross lifted his head with a jerk and stared at the captain.

"Dead?" he echoed.

"Yeah."

He kept his eyes intently upon the captain's face, then took a deep breath; he looked disbelievingly around the room at the faces and leaned weakly forward and rested his hands on the edge of the captain's desk, as though for support.

"God," he sighed. "And I was trying to see him all afternoon."

"You did not go to his room?"

"Of course not. He wasn't in. . . ." He paused. "God, he might've been dead when I was asking for him."

"That's possible," the captain said.

"And only last night his friend, Mr. Blount, was killed—What's happening—?"

"Blount? Gilbert Blount?" the captain asked.

"Yes. That was Hilton's friend. I'm living in Mr. Blount's apartment. I just spoke to the District Attorney this morning about all of that—"

The policemen were astonished. He knew that their minds were wandering far from him now.

"Get the District Attorney's office on the telephone," the captain ordered. "We'll see what this is all about."

"Yes, sir," a policeman answered and left the room.

Cross sat and waited.

"How deep are you in this Communist business?" the captain asked.

Cross relaxed a bit; their minds were now working normally, leading them into paths where they could find nothing against him.

"I'm not in it at all," he answered. "I don't belong to any political organizations."

"How long have you known Blount?"

"Two days."

"How did you come to meet him?"

"At Bob Hunter's place."

"How did you meet Bob Hunter?"

"On a train."

"And Hilton? How long have you known him?"

"Two days. I met them both the same night."

"Did you ever hear anybody threaten either of them?"

"No."

"Did Bob Hunter or his wife ever threaten them?"

"They had a hot argument, but nobody threatened anybody."

"By the way, let me see your draft card."

Cross handed him his draft card; the captain examined it, copied down some information and gave it back to him.

"Where were you born?"

"In Newark, New Jersey."

"Where did you go to school?"

"In Newark."

The captain's manner made Cross feel that he had given up any hope of linking him with the killing of Hilton.

"Now, Lane, account for your movements during the afternoon."

Cross sighed, looked at the ceiling, then at the faces around him. He laughed and said:

"You'll have to let me think a minute—"

"Take your time," the captain said.

He told them of his movements in complete detail, leaving out only the half hour he had been in Hilton's room. He was deliberately shrewd enough to get the sequence of his actions twisted, and several times he had to interrupt himself and reorder the chronology of events. He told them of his visit to the drugstore, the bar, of his two visits to the hotel, the newspaper he had bought. He told of waiting in the lobby while the girl at the switchboard tried to ring Hilton. When he was pressed to give a conception of how much time he had spent in each place, he grew vague in a helpless sort of way and would not commit himself. Instead he tried to recall in concrete detail all the many tiny things he had done or seen. He even told them of his playing the pinball machine and he extended the number of times he had tried to win. . . .

"We'll check on all of this," the captain told him. "Lane,

you can go now. But don't change your address. And say nothing about this to anyone."

"Just as you say, Captain. And if I can help you in any way, I'd be glad to do so. I didn't know Hilton very well, but I'd do what I could—"

The telephone rang and the captain picked up the receiver and listened.

"Okay," he said, hanging up. "Lane, I'm afraid that you'll have to stick around. The D.A.'s coming over."

"You mean Mr. Houston?"

"Yes."

"Sure. He's a swell guy. I've got a date to have dinner with him Sunday evening. . . ."

The policemen looked at one another.

He sat alone in an anteroom waiting for the arrival of Houston. What would the old hunchback think now? Even if he *thought* him guilty, what could he do? Would Houston want to hold him for investigation? But wouldn't he need real evidence to do that? Houston could, of course, put him in the Tombs and then carry on his investigation. But would he? Wouldn't he be thrown off and think that these two crimes were of a political nature? That some Communist had become disgruntled and had killed Gil and had to kill Herndon to silence him? And that maybe the same disgruntled Communist had had to kill Hilton to silence him also? While he waited, one of the cops came to him and gave him his gun and the permit.

"The D.A.'s on his way over," the cop said.

"Thanks," Cross said, pocketing his gun.

Cross saw Houston arrive; a policeman escorted him into the captain's office. They're giving me a going-over in there, Cross thought. Half an hour later Cross was taken into the captain's office to confront Houston. They were alone. Houston was grim, tense. He moved lightly and nervously about the room, more stooped and humped than ever, throwing a darting glance at Cross from time to time. Finally he stopped in front of Cross and said: "You seem to be getting to know the police pretty well."

"Looks like it, doesn't it?" Cross said.

"Is there anything you want to add to what you've told the captain?" Houston asked.

"No; not that I can think of."

"You were *not* in Hilton's room today?"

"Absolutely not."

"And you are *not* in the Party?" Houston asked.

"No. I'm not a member of the Party and I never have been."

"Had they asked you to join?"

"Of course."

"And what did you say?"

"I stalled. I talked with them about general subjects—"

"And you did *not* see Hilton?"

"I did not."

"When did you last see him?"

"When he left Blount's apartment this morning."

"Were you in communication with him by phone or in any other way since then?"

"No. There'd be no reason for me to be."

Houston paused and brought his fist down on the edge of the captain's desk.

"I wonder what these damned totalitarians are killing each other about!"

"That would be hard to tell," Cross said softly.

"Lane, you know something about how men's minds work. Now, do you think that what we were discussing this morning could have any relation or bearing on these killings?"

Cross felt dread enter him. Houston was again sniffing around on that highly dangerous ground.

"I don't know, Mr. Houston," he said. "It's all fantastic."

"And nothing like it *could* happen." Houston spoke as though he was protesting against something in his own mind. "It's these Communists. . . . They're involved in something.

Maybe Blount and Hilton were mixed up in spying. . . ."

"And Herndon?" Cross felt compelled to ask.

"Goddammit, it doesn't make sense," Houston spluttered, planting himself in front of Cross. "There *must* be a *third* man involved in this."

"It's beginning to appear like it," Cross said, looking Houston straight in the eyes.

Again Houston was wading in his direction. But could Houston permit himself to accept what he was undoubtedly thinking? Could he bring himself to admit that he was standing and looking at a man who acknowledged no laws? Didn't the very thought create a dizzy kind of guilt? He saw the hunchback blink his eyes and shake his head. . . . Yes; he's backing off from it; he's scared. . . .

"There's absolutely nothing concrete to go on in all of this," Houston said, as though he was talking to Cross directly for the first time. "I have to keep fighting myself to reject the one and only theory that could tie all of this together. . . ."

"What theory is that?"

Cross held his body so tense that he feared that Houston would notice it.

"Could there be a man in whose mind and consciousness all the hopes and inhibitions of the last two thousand years have died? A man whose consciousness has not been conditioned by our culture? A man speaking our language, dressing and behaving as we do, and yet living on a completely different plane? A man who would be the return of ancient man, pre-Christian man? Do you know what I mean?"

Cross felt his body grow hot. His judgment told him to keep quiet, to pretend ignorance; but his emotions clamored to enter this discussion, to tell what he knew. He drew his breath, pushed his personal feelings aside, and when he spoke he was discussing himself in terms that were displaced and projected:

"He's a man living in our modern industrial cities, but he is devoid of all the moral influences of Christianity. He has all the unique advantages of being privy to our knowledge, but he has either rejected it or has somehow escaped its influence. That he's an atheist goes without saying, but he'd be something more than an atheist. He'd be something like a pagan, but a pagan who feels no need to worship. . . . And, by the nature of things, such a man sooner or later is bound to appear. Modern man sleeps in the myths of the Greeks and the Jews. Those myths are now dying in his head and in his heart. They can no longer serve him. When they are really gone, those myths, *man* returns. Ancient man . . . And what's there to guide him? Nothing at all but his own desires, which would be his only values."

Cross confessed his crime as much as he dared. Houston stood looking moodily out of a dingy window.

"I don't believe it," Houston muttered at last. "It's the Communists. They know something of this. I'm sure of that." But there was no conviction in his voice. He turned to Cross and spoke without looking at him. "All right, Lane. That's all."

"I'll be seeing you Sunday night at Frank's, huh?"

"What?" Houston asked; he seemed preoccupied. "Oh, yes. Of course. And keep away from those Communists, boy."

"I shall."

Houston's eyes still avoided him. He was rigid a moment, then he turned and strode out of the captain's office, leaving the door ajar. Cross watched his humped back disappear down a dim corridor. He didn't dare. . . . The hunchback had looked right at it and had turned his face away! The captain entered.

"That's all, Lane."

"Good evening, sir."

He went out into the street. Yes, he was going to Eva. . . . Out of the corner of his eye he was vaguely conscious of a man leaning against the wall of a building and reading a newspaper. I wonder if they are trailing me . . . ? He'd see.

He was spent; he needed a drink. He headed toward Sixth Avenue, saw a bar; he paused and looked over his shoulder. Yes; the man was following him. . . . He went into the bar and had a whisky. God, how could he get out of this? He wanted to rise and yell for help. Would it not be better to see Houston and tell him that he had gotten in too deep, that he was afraid of himself? His head felt hot; his fingers were trembling. He yearned for the sight of Eva. If only he could talk to some- body! To wander always alone was too much. . . . Once again he had killed and he feared that this time he would be caught. Maybe I *want* to be caught, he told himself. Is that it? He didn't care. . . . He had done what he wanted to do, hadn't he? Then why worry. . . . He paid for his drink and went out into the streets again. The man with the newspaper fell in slowly behind him. He had to see Eva, yet he feared seeing her. He knew that he had to tell her everything now; he *had* to tell. . . .

THROUGH THE CLOSED DOOR of his room came the faint tinkling of the front doorbell. He stood still, waiting, wonder- ing. Was it Menti again with his everlasting Hank? He placed his ear to the door panel and listened.

"Is Lane, or Damon, in?"

It was Houston's voice. Had he dug up any new evidence against him? Was he coming finally to arrest him?

Sarah's voice sounded cold and clipped: "He's in his room. There . . ."

Footsteps echoed down the hallway and died in front of his door. Cross sank onto the bed. He would let Houston take the initiative. Eva was dead and there was no fight in him. A series of sharp knocks sounded on the door.

"Come in," he called.

The door swung open and there was Houston and behind him loomed a tall, blue-coated officer. Under Houston's arm was a package wrapped in brown paper. Houston turned to the officer and said: "Wait down the hall."

"Yes, sir."

The officer left and Houston came in and closed the door softly behind him. He approached Cross, smiling vaguely. Houston had a relaxed, confident air and Cross felt that his time had come. He *knows* now. . . . All right; if this was the end, then he didn't care. . . . Houston looked around, found a chair, dragged it to the bed and eased his deformed body onto it, some two feet from Cross. Cross felt sweat breaking out over his chest and he cursed himself for being unable to control his physical reactions. Well, why didn't the hunchback sonofabitch speak? Why did he sit there with that goddamn gloating smirk on his face? He longed for his gun; if he had it in his hands he would shoot the hell out of that little triumphant god even if he burned for it. . . . All right; he had lost, but Houston would see that he could take his defeat without flinching.

"Damon, I've solved it. You're guilty. You killed Blount, Herndon, and Hilton. . . ."

Houston's voice rang with finality. Cross waited. Slowly Houston unwrapped the brown package and there lay the set of thin angular notebooks: the diaries of Eva. . . .

"You're a lucky, blundering fool," Houston spat at him. "The only witness I could have put in the box against you was Eva Blount, and she's dead. If she hadn't leaped from that window, you'd be on your way to the electric chair. . . . If she had lived, she would have told me what you told her, and what you *told* her made her kill herself. I've found out that much, Damon." Houston rubbed his hands nervously across his eyes. "Goddammit, I was your unwitting accomplice for seventy-two hours! I just couldn't bring myself to admit what I knew in my heart to be true! And no doubt you were banking on just that. What made that girl kill herself was what made me unable to admit that you were guilty. I wonder if you planned it like that? No; I don't think you did. It was too perfect to be planned. You depended upon the human heart rejecting a

horror of that magnitude and you were almost right, almost successful. . . ."

"How did you get those diaries?" Cross asked him. "From
the Party?"

"No. An officer took them from this room when you and
the others were in the police station," Houston said. "I've
read them and I understand it *all* now."

"Did she mention me in there?" he asked, feeling that he
had to know at once.

"Only a little, toward the end— What she said didn't matter. It was what she *was* that mattered," Houston told him.
"She said that she loved you, but that was all."

Houston carelessly tossed the notebooks on the bed, at
Cross's side. Cross was surprised, wondering why Houston
was returning the books to him.

"It was all very simple when at last I'd found the key,"
Houston began in a slow, measured tone. "And the key was
this deceived woman, Eva Blount. . . . Look, Damon, I'm an
honest man; I'm not going to brag or lie to you. Right off I
want to confess that I was haywire in the beginning. That
damned Communist Party pushed me off on the wrong
track. That paranoiac Blimin was at my office day and night,
demanding action, yelling that you had killed Blount and
Herndon because of Eva. . . . The Party claimed at first that
you were a Trotskyite; then they swore that you were a
government spy. In the end they screamed that you saw an
opportunity to kill Blount and take his wife and you took it.
. . . Funny, isn't it, how they misread things? Every man
interprets the world in the light of his habits and desires. The
Party shouted at me: 'He sold out to get the girl!' Their own
slogans blinded them. They argued that you had to kill Herndon because Herndon had seen you kill Blount; further, they
claimed that Hilton had found out somehow and that you
then had to kill him. Despite the fact that they could not offer
any evidence in support of this, I, at first, felt that it did sound
rather plausible. But deep down I was worried; it was *too* pat;

it didn't suit your character, didn't fit what you told me that morning on the train. Remember? 'Man's nothing in particular. . . .'

"What a baffling chase you gave us! In the first place, you seemed so innocent, *too* innocent; we made only the most perfunctory investigations. . . . When we began to feel that you *must* know something, we checked your draft card and found a fire had destroyed the records! I wonder if you could have had anything to do with that? You won't answer? All right; it isn't important. . . . Then, for twenty-four hours, we made no new moves against you. But Hilton's death told us that we were up against something sinister. We decided to track down every lead, no matter how trivial. . . .

"It was not until we, almost as an afterthought, tried to verify your birth certificate that we began to think of you seriously as a possible murderer. What a joke that certificate was! In Newark the clerks in the Bureau of Vital Statistics remembered you, but we thought that we were surely on the wrong track when we heard their description of you. You're a good actor. You should have been on the stage. . . . When we were certain that you were Lionel Lane and that Lionel Lane was dead, we were back where we started from. We decided that you had assumed this man's name, and we swung then toward thinking that you were in some Communist opposition group. But that fizzled. No political group in America had ever heard of you. . . .

"Then we began checking your fingerprints and we ran into another stone wall. For the second time we discovered that you were dead. Cross Damon, Negro postal clerk of Chicago: *dead* . . . killed in a subway accident. The FBI flew to Chicago to make sure. They reported to me that you were no more. They even exhumed the other Negro's body, but that didn't tell us anything. Then the police started checking with the Missing Persons Bureau. We found that a man of your height and description had been reported missing the day after you were *supposed* to have been killed. Who was this man? He cleaned and dressed chickens in a meat market. . . .

"Finally we had to rely on comparing descriptions of you that we got from Chicago with what we could observe of you here in New York, then we knew that we had the right man. We knew you were Cross Damon, no matter how many dead men you were hiding behind.

"But was it possible that Cross Damon was doing all of this killing? But why? That was the most baffling aspect of all. You'll never know how I struggled against accepting your guilt. *I didn't want to believe it.* After having isolated you, identified you, we faced a riddle. Nothing in your entire background had touched politics. Then I had a brainstorm. I wired Chicago to send me a list of the titles of the books you'd left behind in your room and when they wired back a long list I was delighted. . . . That was the first real clue. Your Nietzsche, your Hegel, your Jaspers, your Heidegger, your Husserl, your Kierkegaard, and your Dostoevski were the clues. . . . I said to myself that we were dealing with a man who had wallowed in guilty thought. But the more I pondered this thing, the sorrier I felt for you. I began to feel as though I'd killed Blount, Herndon, and Hilton myself.

"And when I read those diaries and saw into the deceived heart of this Eva, I knew damn well that you didn't kill to get her. She was hysterically waiting for some man to ask her to run off from that impossible Blount and his Party. . . . I visited her studio and looked at those projections of nonobjective horror she had painted; then I read her diaries and I knew you'd love her, understand her; she was a sensitive artist and represented in her life and work a quality of suffering that would move a heart like yours. In spirit, Eva was your sister. Both of you were abandoned, fearful, without a form or discipline for living; and, therefore, you were both a prey to compulsions. In the face of life, she shrank, but you advanced. But here, attack or retreat is a form of fear. No; you didn't kill to get her; you didn't have to. You'd want to lead her, remake her, save her, and at bottom you'd be wanting, in doing this, to save yourself. . . . And she was ripe to respond on the same basis; she wanted to *help* you. . . .

"Damon, last night you said something that hurt me. When I had the cops pick you up and bring you to my office, when I was putting the heat on you, you told me—well, you implied that I was a kind of monster for confronting you with your wife and children. No, Damon, I'm not that kind of a man. If I were a sadist, I could have had you locked up in the Tombs days ago for investigation, but I didn't." Houston smiled ironically. "I wouldn't deliberately torture anything or anybody on this earth. But, of course, I do so live that I find myself in situations where people are suffering. After all, why did I become District Attorney? But, hell, that's another story.

"No; I wasn't torturing you last night. I was trying to identify you; I had to be absolutely certain that you were Cross Damon, postal clerk of Chicago, supposedly dead, married, and so on. But there was another thing I wanted to know. I had to see how you would react when I told you of your mother's death, how you would react when you saw your sons. . . . I'm a District Attorney, Damon; I was tracking down emotional clues; I was doing my police work . . .

"You were so inhuman that I wouldn't have believed it unless I'd seen it. Many sociologists say that the American Negro hasn't had time to become completely adjusted to our mores, that the life of the family of the Western world hasn't had time to sink in. But with you, you're adjusted and more. You've grown up and gone beyond our rituals. I knew you were beyond organized religion, but I didn't suspect that you were already beyond the family. Last night you stood there in my office and committed the greatest and last crime of all. You didn't bat your eye when I told you that your mother was dead. It hurt you, yes; I could see it, but you rode it out. Boy, you killed your mother long, long ago. . . . You must have known your mother well, understood her both emotionally and intellectually; and when one can see and weigh one's mother like that, well, she's dead to one. . . . And when you saw those three fine sons of yours! They tugged at your heart and memory and you were wildly angry and ashamed; but you rode out that too; you overcame it. And I said to myself: 'This man *could* have killed Blount, Herndon, and Hilton. Only *he* could have done it. He has the emotional capacity —or *lack* of it!—to do it.'

"Then I sat down and thought. After all, Damon, as I told you, I'm close enough to you, being a hunchback, being an outsider, to know how some of your feelings and thought processes *must* go. In a sense, I'm your brother. . . . We men are not complete strangers on this earth. The world changes, but men are always the same. And especially the various basic types of men—and you are an ancient, fundamental type—run the same.

"When I first talked to you in the Blount apartment, how you must have laughed at me! I walked all around you and couldn't see you! And then Hilton started his crazy, class-conscious pressure. Strange, the Communists had access to this insight as well as I and they didn't want to see. . . ."

Cross was still. Yes; he was caught. But where was the *proof?* Eva couldn't witness against him. Had Houston, then, some hidden evidence? If this was the best that Houston could do, why, he would simply walk into court and keep his damned mouth shut and let him see if he could convict him.

"Damon, you're an atheist," Houston resumed, "and that is the heart of this matter. You know what convinced me that you were guilty? No; I didn't find any clues you'd left behind. . . . It was in a realm far afield that I found conclusive proof. Where?" Houston lifted his arm toward the window. "Right out there in those teeming streets. . . . Damon, you act individually just as modern man lives in the mass each day.

"You see, hopeful men seize upon every tiny incident and read the dreams of their hearts into them. Each hour of the day men are asking: 'Do you think we'll have peace? Don't you think what General So-and-So said means we'll have war? Don't you think that the White House pronouncement means that prices will be lower?' Or maybe he observes that his neighbor is reading a radical book and comes to the conclusion that he is a spy and ought to be killed? And, Damon, that was the way you were living. The only difference was that your compulsions were negative, had no direction. . . .

"In the old days we were concerned with mobs, with thousands of men running amuck in the streets. The mob has conquered completely. When the mob has grown so vast that you cannot see it, then it is everywhere. Today the compulsive acts of the lynching mobs have become enthroned in each individual heart. Every man now acts as a criminal, a policeman, a judge, and an executioner. . . .

"But to come back to this individual mob-you who is called Cross Damon. What an atheist you are! You know, real atheists are rare, really. A genuine atheist is a real Christian turned upside down; God descends from the sky and takes up abode, so to speak, behind the fleshy bars of his heart! Men argue about not believing in God and the mere act of doing so makes them believers. It is only when they don't feel the need to deny Him that they really don't believe in Him." Houston rose in his excitement and paced the floor, as though he had forgotten the existence of Cross. *"You went all the way!* You have drawn all the conclusions and deductions that could be drawn from the atheistic position and you have inherited the feelings that only real atheists can have. At first I didn't believe it, but when you stared so unfeelingly at your sons, when you laughed when your poor wife could not summon enough strength to identify you, I knew that you were beyond the pale of all the *little* feelings, the *humble* feelings, the *human* feelings. . . . *I knew that you could do anything!* Not in a towering rage, not to save falling mankind, not to establish social justice, not for glory. . . . But just because you happen to feel like that one day.

"You are a free man. Ideas don't knock you off your feet, make you dizzy, make you fall down and serve others. You always suspect that ideas are in the service of other people. . . . Oh, I *know* you, boy!"

Cross hovered over a vast void. Was this man making fun of him or was he sympathizing with him? What he had feared most had come; there was nothing he could hide from Houston. He kept his eyes on the floor, afraid to look up at Houston's passion-inflamed face.

"You felt that you were right, but not in the sense that you had to insist upon it. No! Does one explain when he says he wants three teaspoons of sugar in his coffee instead of two? You don't have to justify that, do you? You had risen—or sunk!—to that attitude toward the lives of those about you. . . .

"But, Damon, you made one fatal mistake. You saw through all the ideologies, pretenses, frauds, but you did not see through *yourself.* How magnificently you tossed away this God who plagues and helps man so much! But you did not and could not toss out of your heart that part of you from which the God notion had come. And what part of a man is that? It is desire. . . . Don't you know it? Why didn't you just live a quiet life like all other men? That's the correct way of being godless. Why be restless? Why let desire plague you? Why not conquer it too?"

Houston was questioning Cross in a kind manner, as a brother would question him.

"Desire? Why does man desire? It's crazy, for it's almost certain that he'll never get what he desires. . . . Isn't desire a kind of warning in man to let him know that he is limited? A danger signal of man to himself? Desire is the mad thing, the irrational thing. Damon, you peeled off layer after layer of illusion and make-believe and stripped yourself down to just simply naked desire and you thought that you had gotten hold of the core of reality. And, in a sense, you had. But what does one *do* with desire? Man desires ultimately to be a god.

Man desires *everything*. . . . Why not? Desire is a restless, floating demon. . . . Desire tries to seize itself and never can. . . . It's an illusion, but the most solid one! Desire is what snared you, my boy. You felt that what obstructed desire could be killed; what annoyed, could be gotten rid of. . . .

"Only a man feeling like that could have gone down into that room and seen those two men fighting it out, and then killed *both* of them! Not taking sides . . . Not preferring the lesser evil . . . Just a sweeping and supreme gesture of disdain and disgust for both of them! And only a man akin to them could have hated them that much, and you know it, Damon! You slew them just because they offended you. It was just like taking a cinder out of your eye because it stings a bit. . . ."

Houston paused in front of Cross and chuckled. Cross looked at him and said to himself: That must have been how I looked when Sarah saw me laughing at her! Sarah had leaped to her feet and had tried to beat him with her doubled fists, had shouted and cursed him; but he could not afford to act that way with Houston. Pride held him still. To show resentment would give the game away. No; he would sit and take it all.

"How you must have felt in that awful room! I wish you'd tell me. Did you calculate every movement? Or did you act without knowing it? Did you realize what you were doing, or did you invent the idea of it afterward? How did those two men look to you? And which one did you kill first? I'll bet a million dollars that, even though you're a free man, you killed Herndon first, eh? You're a Negro and you know what fascism means to you and your people. Even a man like you cannot be as indifferent as he would like. . . . Your feet, Damon, I'll bet, were of earthy clay and you killed Herndon first. . . . Won't you tell me? No? All right . . . I won't press you; these are unimportat details. . . .

"Of course, I don't believe that Eva Blount saw Herndon on those stairs. I can't *prove* that she didn't, but I don't believe it. She was wrought up; she wished Blount out of her life, wanted him dead. She imagined she saw Herndon. And I'll bet you seized upon her fantasy and tried to fool us all with it. . . .

"I know that Blount wouldn't have touched you. He thought he had snared you into his ideological spiderweb and that you were his slave, his moral slave, the slave who believes in the ideas that are given to him. . . . But, if you killed Blount first, Herndon would have killed you the next instant, wouldn't he? I'm right, hunh? And you must certainly have gotten a rich, deep satisfaction out of killing that nigger-hater, Herndon. And Blount's face must have been a study in amazement when you suddenly turned on him. . . .

"Then you wiped off all the fingerprints; there were none of yours in the room except on the door. And they had a right to be there, for you had been in the room talking to Herndon that afternoon, hadn't you?

"All right . . . Now comes a gap that I can't fill—I don't know how Hilton found out that you had killed the two of them. . . . Did you tell him? No; you don't want to answer? All right. You can tell me. . . . No; you must not. Then I'd be bound by my oath of office and I'd have to use it against you. . . . Get the point, Damon?

"But I don't think you told Hilton anything. You're much too clever for that. Anyhow, he found out some way. These Communists eat and breathe suspicion. He had his eyes on you from the beginning, according to the Party, but not for any reason, just in general. And he caught you in your little godly game. . . .

"You went to see him. You must have known that he knew. I must admit that I'm a bit foggy about this part of it. He had asked you to come and talk to him about joining the Party. But I can't believe that you went there for that. *That* might have been your excuse. But that was not your purpose. After all, Damon, I'm only human. I can't know all. I'm not a god and do not claim to be one, or want to be one. I curb my desires, you see?

"But, if I know the Hilton type, and I do to some extent, I'd expect a deal to be made. Damon, why wasn't there a deal, an understanding arrived at between you and Hilton? Maybe the reality of this beautiful Eva had begun to enter the picture to some extent then? Maybe you two just hated each other naturally because you were so much alike? You little gods who traffic in human life, who buy and sell the souls of men, why couldn't you have made a trade?

"Maybe you couldn't trust each other, huh? That's the big trouble with gods when they get together. Gods cannot share power; each god must have all the power or he's no god. For what's a god if he has a rival? Look at Hitler and Stalin. . . . Boy, if they could have been reasonable, they could have divided this whole earth up between them. But, no; each felt that he and he alone had to have the whole earth. So they chewed each other up. When gods fall out, little worms can live. . . .

"But joking aside . . . You killed Hilton with his own gun and you didn't leave a clue. How did you get into the hotel? You were at the hotel desk early that afternoon, but no one remembers seeing you there after that, either entering or leaving. Of course, they have a liberal policy at the Edward Hotel and Negroes leaving or entering wouldn't be the occasion for anybody's noticing, would they? And sometimes I suppose all things work together for the loves and desires of little gods?"

Cross felt dead. How could this man lay open his life with such decisive strokes? With such mocking cynicism? God-damn him to hell!

"Now, these diaries . . . this girl deceived by the Party . . . this naïve child made the mistake of thinking that she had found in you something clean, pure, something her heart had dreamed of. In *you*, of all the men on earth! She looked upon you and your people as her brothers and sisters in suffering. . . . What irony! Hurt, deceived, she projected her desires on you. Afraid of deception, she embraced a fount of deception!

Full of timid, feminine desire, she flings her arms about a furnace of desire and is consumed in it. . . . Then you, in your desert of loneliness, must have told her what you had done. She'd fought the Party for you, told them on her life that you were an innocent man. . . . And, in a sense, she was right; you were innocent of what the Party was charging. But, for a reason I do not know, you told her and she leaped. . . . That's how I figure it. What you told her was too much for her. You made her feel that she could no longer trust any person on this earth. She leaped from that window to escape the kind of a world you showed her! You *drove* her out of life. What you told her was the crowning horror of all the horrors! The apex of deception. . . . And you *had* to tell her; you wanted her help. But did you tell her that Gil had not done anything to you? Did you tell her that you killed Gil for *nothing?* Did you, could you go that far? I wonder. . . .

"Damon, those diaries told me that you were guilty, and that girl's leaping from that window was proof of it. Will you admit it? No? Your silence is a confession! Your inability to challenge me is proof! I'm waiting. . . . *Speak!* Tell me I'm wrong. . . . You *can't!*"

Houston turned, opened the door of the room and went out. Cross lay watching the door swing a little to and fro on a squeaky hinge. Well, Houston was going to get the cops and they were going to take him to the station now. . . . This was the end. But what evidence did Houston have? What facts to buttress all of this? So far he had cited nothing but psychological facts. Come to think of it, they were not even psychological facts. They were feelings, lightning-like intuitions which only a man who had lived long on that lower (or was it a higher?) level of life could know. He heard Houston's footsteps coming back. He braced himself.

Houston entered the room with a glass of water in his right hand. He stood looking at Cross a solemn moment, then he lifted the glass to his lips and drained it thirstily, his humped body resembling that of a huge, waiting spider.

"I was thirsty," Houston confessed in the voice of a man who had satisfied a physical need. He sighed. "I haven't spoken so much since I was facing a jury a month ago."

Cross could bear it no longer; his lips trembled.

"Get it over with! If you think you'll drag one word from me, you're crazy!" he shouted.

"Now," Houston spoke in a soothing tone, "don't spoil it all. You were playing your role so well. . . ."

"You're gloating over me! Okay, start your damned wheels turning!"

"Hold on. I'm not through yet," Houston said, with a feeling of deep relish in his voice. "You'll be punished, but not in the way you think. Ah, I know. . . . You have visions of lashes, third-degree sessions, blinding spotlights in your eyes, questions popping at you for hours on end. You may even think of mobs, for all I know. And all of this because the cops want you to confess. But, Damon, you've confessed already. . . ."

Hot tension leaped in Cross. Had he overlooked something silly that would send him to the chair? Had he left some foolish thing undone that would make him look like an adolescent boy stealing apples from a neighbor's orchard?

"Confession?" he stammered. "What do you mean?"

Houston threw back his head and laughed. "You confessed to *me*, just to *me*, to *me* alone. See? I've no concrete evidence to use in court against you."

Was the man crazy? What was he getting at?

"Listen, Damon, you made your own law," Houston pronounced. "And, by God, I, for one, am going to let you live by it. I'm pretty certain you're finished with this killing phase. . . . So, I'm going to let you go. See? Yes; just go! *You're free!* Just like that." Houston snapped his fingers in Cross's face. "I'm going to let you keep this in your heart until the end of your days! Sleep with it, eat with it, brood over it, make love with it. . . . You are going to punish yourself, see? You are your own law, so you'll be your own judge. . . . I wouldn't *help* you by taking you to jail. I've very little concrete evidence to haul you into court on anyhow; it's likely I couldn't convict you. And I won't give you the satisfaction of sitting in a court of law with those tight lips of yours and gloating at me or any jury while we tried to prove the impossible. What the hell could a jury of housewives make out of a guy like you? I won't give you the chance to make that kind of a fool out of me, Damon. I'm much too smart for that.

"These killings will be marked unsolved. And, in a sense, they are. Even now I cannot say why you killed in a rational manner, in a manner that would persuade others . . . I haven't told anyone of what I've found out about you." Houston tapped his head. "It's all right here. And it'll stay there. You're trembling. . . . Oh, yes; I understand now. You thought that I was going to get the cop to arrest you when I went out for that glass of water. You're sweating. Boy, you'll sweat tears of terror, night and day. That's the lot of a little god. Didn't you know that gods were lonely? When you eat, a part of you will stand back, shy and embarrassed. When you make love, a part of you will turn away in shame. From now on, there will be a dead hand holding life back from you. . . . Will you find your way back? I doubt it. To whom could you tell your story, Damon? Who will listen? A psychoanalyst? You have no respect for them, and what the hell could they do for you? They'd be frightened of you; they'd rush out of their consulting rooms, their hair standing on end, screaming with terror. No; they are not for you, my boy. It's between *you* and *you*, you and yourself."

Houston stood looking down with musing eyes at Cross. And Cross felt sweat running down his face; it was on his chest, seeping down his arms. Even his legs were wet. Suddenly he wanted to beg this man not to leave him. He could not believe that it was like this that it was to end. . . . But he could make no move.

"That's all," Houston said. "Whatever nameless powers that be, may they have something like mercy on your tormented soul."

He turned and strode out of the room. Cross could hear him speaking in low tones to Sarah; then he heard the echo of his footsteps along the hallway, the front door open and close. He was alone. He felt like screaming for Houston to come back, to talk to him, to tell him what to do. But he clamped his teeth and held still. I'm alone, he said to himself. He felt dizzy. Terror wrapped him around in a sheet of flame and his body wept tears. . . . The prop had gone; Houston had gone; the world against which he had pitched his rebellion had pitied him, almost forgiven him. . . . The thing he had been fighting had turned its face from him as though he was no longer worthy of having an opponent and this rejection was a judgment so inhuman that he could not bear to think of it.

He had broken all of his promises to the world and the people in it, but he had never reckoned on that world turning on him and breaking its promise to him too! He was not to be punished! Men would not give meaning to what he had done! Society would not even look at it, recognize it! That was not fair, wasn't right, just. . . . The ludicrous nature of his protest came to him and he smiled wryly at his own self-deception. Always back deep in his mind, he had counted on their railing at him, storming, cursing, condemning. Instead, nothing, silence, the silence that roars like an indifferent cataract, the silence that reaches like a casual clap of thunder to the end of space and time. . . .

He had to talk to somebody! But to whom? No; he had to keep this crime choked in his throat. He, like others, had to pretend that nothing like this could ever happen; he had to collaborate and help keep the secret. He had to go forward into the future and pretend that the world was as tradition said it was. . . .

His head dropped senselessly to the bed cover and he drifted off into that state of bleak relaxation that comes after an exhausting strain. He was not sleeping, not fully awake; he was existing, with an alien world looming implacably over

696

and against him. But all of his compulsions were gone, leaving him empty of even desire. . . .

He did not stir from his room until late the next morning, and when he did emerge, it was to go into the kitchen with Eva's diary. Since Houston had laid his self-hate and his self-love so mockingly naked, he felt that he no longer had any right to keep the diary and he was resolved to burn it. He opened one of the notebooks and tore out a sheet; just before touching the page to the flame of his lighter, he let his eyes stray listlessly over the lines, reading:

MARCH 3rd

Last night was in Harlem and had dinner with Bob and Sarah Hunter. A tall, sensitive young Negro, Lionel Lane, was there; he was tense and seemed to be seeking for something in life. He struck me as one who would leave no stone unturned to find his destiny. Gil was taken with him and asked him to come and live with us awhile. Will he too be "used" as I have been? How can I warn him? I dreamed of him after going to bed—I thought he asked me to come and see him and I was afraid because he lived in Harlem— Then I became so ashamed of my fear that I decided to go anyhow. I dreamed that when I got to Harlem there was, for some reason, a huge crowd of people waiting to see me and I felt quite embarrassed and lost. I was trembling, fearing to be asked to explain why I was in Harlem. Lionel came and rescued me; he was so magnificently himself, so self-assured among his own people who loved and respected him. The moment he arrived the crowd changed its attitude toward me. Then he took my arm and led me down the street; he was smiling as we passed in front of the masses of strange people. A wave of happiness flooded me and I fainted. Is not all virtue with the oppressed who are not corrupted? I must find some way of saving this boy from the muck in which my life has become bogged. But how can I do it?

MARCH 4th

Lionel is now in the apartment and I'm filled with a sense of dread. I'd planned to remain in all day, but since he is here, I've decided to go out. I'll go to a concert in the afternoon. That is as good an excuse as any to get away. But I must try to save him from his own naïveté. He is so quiet, trusting, sensitive. What is he thinking all the time? I see him sitting and brooding and his eyes hold the most self-absorbed look I've ever seen in a human being. God, he must be suffering. Is he mulling over the past wrongs done to him and his people? I wish I could help someone like that.

Cross crumpled the sheet, held it to the flame, and watched it burn. Once he turned his head sharply, feeling that Eva was standing near, watching him. . . . Slowly he burned the pages, dropped the charred remains in the sink, ran water over them and flushed them down the drain. When he finished he lifted his eyes and looked out the window.

Bright sunshine was flooding the world with warm, yellow light and he became aware of the soft, faint sounds of water dripping. Yes, a thaw had set in. The ice was melting; the snow was dissolving and flowing from the roofs. . . .

He heard the front door of the apartment open and close; a moment later Sarah came into the kitchen. She had been out into the streets and was still wearing her overcoat.

"I knew you were tired and I didn't want to awaken you," she began without ceremony. "But now you are up and I can talk to you."

"Yes, Sarah. What is it?"

"I want you to move." She did not look at him as she spoke.

"Of course. What do I owe you for our staying here?"

"Nothing." Her voice was bitter.

"I can pay my way." He wanted to help her, but he did not know how.

"I don't want your money," she said. "I'm starting a new life. . . . I went to confession this morning." Her voice was metallic, cold.

"I'm glad for you," Cross said. He was suddenly resentful of the fact that Sarah had failed to see that he, of his own accord, was about to move. "Is your telling me to move so bluntly your first act of Christian charity?"

Sarah's eyes hardened.

"This is *my* apartment—" she began.

"I don't dispute that," Cross told her. "But I thought religion would make you a little kind. . . . I'm all packed to go. I've enough money to take care of myself for a bit. . . . And for that, I'm damned lucky. I'm glad that I'm not at your mercy. . . ."

"I don't want to argue with you—"

"You won't. I'll get out in five minutes."

There was no communication between them. Couldn't they part as friends who had a little sympathy for each other? Cross looked at her and knew at once that there was no way. Sarah desired too much. Only a great promise could lift her up and help her to live again. Promises . . . ? Could he ever make promises again? And he could not promise anything to Sarah; she had already received from her church a promise covering the whole of her life on this earth and the life to come. . . . He turned from her, entered his room, picked up his suitcase, and went into the hall. Sarah stood in the kitchen doorway, looking at him.

"Good-by, Sarah."

She didn't answer; he saw her face reflect a struggle. He started toward her and she burst into tears, whirled, turned into the kitchen and slammed the door. He pivoted on his heels and walked on down the hall, opened the door and went out.

The streets were wet under the glare of a bright sun. He paused on the stoop; he had no notion where he was going. He heard water gurgling in the gutters, running toward the conduits of the sewers. He walked toward Seventh Avenue, thinking: Was it possible that all he had learned in the last few weeks would remain locked forever in his heart? Would he ever be able to say anything about it? And Eva . . . ?

He became aware of someone following him and he turned. It was Menti, and behind Menti was the sullen, inexpressive Hank, whose hands were jammed as always in his overcoat pockets, his eyes staring hard at Cross from beneath the brim of a dirty hat.

Cross stopped and waited for Menti to catch up with him. "Are you following me, Menti?"

"Where are you going?" Menti asked, grinning.

"I don't know. Tell the Party that I said I didn't know."

"Leaving town?"

"I don't know."

"How can one get in touch with you?"

"You can't."

"You won't have an address?"

"Maybe not."

"Well, I'll be seeing you," Menti said. "Don't forget the Party."

"How could I ever forget the Party?"

Menti grinned and turned away. Cross kept on to the end of the block. He was moving again among people. But how could he ever make a bridge from him to them? To live with them again would mean making promises, commitments. But he had strayed so far that little commitments were now of no avail. He would have to start all over again. And it was impossible to do that *alone.* . . .

He checked his suitcase and went into a movie and sat looking at the gliding shadows on the screen without understanding their import. Two hours later he came out and had lunch. Once again he stood on the sidewalk, will-less, aimless. Then he was agitated. There was Menti down at the far end of the block, and Hank was behind him. They were watching him. Goddamn them . . .

He came to Lenox Avenue and headed downtown. He saw another movie house. He looked over his shoulder; Menti and Hank were moving toward him. . . . Quickly he paid his admission and ducked into the sheltering darkness, looking now and then to see if Menti or his man was near. . . . He could not find them.

When he emerged three hours later, stiff and thirsty, Menti and Hank were not to be seen. Had he ditched them? Maybe . . . Dusk was falling on Harlem. Neon lights gleamed in the deepening mists. He went into a bar and sat in the rear, facing the door, keeping watch. He downed several whiskies which he could not feel or taste. What was he going to do? Find another room or leave town . . . ?

Once more on the sidewalk, he looked for Menti. Suddenly he longed for the shelter of a well-lighted place, something like a huge hotel lobby with throngs of people and hard, glaring electric bulbs shedding clarity and safety upon everything. . . . He found himself facing Central Park. He paused at a street corner till the red traffic light turned green, then he crossed and walked alongside Central Park, heading downtown.

He glanced over his shoulder, feeling that he was being followed; but there was no one to be seen on the night streets behind him. An occasional car whizzed past, its headlights illuminating the foggy night about him for a moment, then leaving him alone in the dark once more. Ahead he saw a young couple coming toward him, engrossed in each other. . . . A sense of Eva flashed through him and he knew that the bleakness he was now feeling came from the desire he had had of having her with him. . . . This homelessness would not have been so difficult to bear if he had not based his hopes on being with her.

Again he paused and glanced over his shoulder. Yes; there were two dark forms lurking in the shadows about a block away. Menti and Hank were after him. . . . And he was in a bad spot here next to Central Park. He was in danger; he looked around him in panic. He had to hide somewhere, quickly. . . . If he could dodge them tonight, he would leave the city first thing tomorrow morning. . . . A taxi? But there was none in sight. If only he had the shelter of the home of a friend in which to hide. . . . There's a taxi. . . .

"Taxi!" he bellowed.

The taxi slowed and pulled to a curb half a block away alongside the park. He broke into a wild run, waving his hand to assure the driver that he was coming. He ran with the park flanking him. He was lucky, after all. . . .

A second later he heard a snapping sound, like a twig being broken, and then a faint footfall; there was a shower of something like loose gravel and in the same instant he felt tearing through his chest a searing streak of fire; a loud, sharp report smote his ears, and his body jerked. The next moment he was sprawled flat on his back, staring toward a sky he could not see. Pain ripped at his chest. He had been shot. He heard footsteps running. The Party . . . Then his inner world began to turn as dark as that world around him. He heard vague voices.

"You hurt, Mister?"

He felt someone tugging at his arm and pain rose from his chest in one huge red wave and engulfed him.

When Cross opened his eyes again he was aware of a dim light in a partially darkened room. He was cold and tired. As some measure of consciousness returned, he struggled to lift himself upon his elbow, but he felt an alien hand softly restraining him.

"You must be still."

It was the voice of a woman. He struggled to focus his eyes and mumbled: "What happened?"

"You're hurt. Lie still."

The nurse was a foggy blur of white. Yes, he was in a hospital and then he felt again that awful ball of fire in his chest and he was aware that he was straining to breathe. He tried to lift his right hand, but it was too, too heavy. They got me, he thought. He felt no wonder, hate, or surprise. He had been going to the taxi and they had shot him. . . . A fit of uncontrollable coughing seized him and shadows closed in again.

A long time later, his eyes fluttered weakly open and he saw daylight. The dim figure of a nurse in white leaned over him and beyond her he was vaguely conscious of other people whose presence seemed remote and unimportant.

"Damon," a familiar voice came into his ear. "Can you hear me?"

He heard the question, but it seemed foolish to try to answer. He attempted again to focus his eyes, but could not.

"Damon, this is Houston, the District Attorney. Can you talk a little?"

A fleeting smile passed through him, making his lips twitch slightly. Houston! His pal! The old hunchback! The wise old scared outlaw who had found a way of embracing his fear so that he could live and act without being too scared! He longed to see Houston; once more he sought to focus his eyes, but the face looming over him remained a blob of pink.

"Who shot you, Damon? Did you see him?"

How foolish and unessential it was to ask that now! What did it matter?

"Was it the Party? Can you hear me? Was it the Party folks who shot you?" The voice was insistent.

Yes; he'd try to answer; he struggled to move his tongue and shape his lips and he whispered: "I don't know. I think so. . . ."

"Don't try to talk too much, Damon. Just listen and answer briefly. Save your strength. . . . Did the Party find out you had killed Gil and Hilton?"

"No," he whispered.

"Then why do you think they shot you?"

"They guessed. . . ."

"You didn't confess, didn't tell 'em?"

"No."

"Did they have any proof? How did they know?"

"They didn't know. . . . They didn't understand me. . . . And they shoot what they don't understand. . . ."

"Listen, if you can give me anything to go on, I'll prosecute them."

Cross sighed. His lips were dry, burning. What silliness was Houston talking? He had been living by a law and that law had turned on him. That was all.

"Forget it," he whispered.

"But if you know anything—"

"Skip it."

Pain seized him again and he felt someone holding his arm; they were injecting a sedative into him to quiet the pain.

"Damon, this is Houston still. . . . Look, is there anything you want to tell me? These killings, were there more of them?"

Oh, God, that poor clown of a Joe Thomas!

"Yes . . ."

"Where?"

"One other man . . . in Chicago. His name was Joe Thomas. . . . I killed him in a hotel room to keep him from . . . betraying me. . . ."

"Is that all?"

"That's all. . . . Isn't that . . . enough?"

He felt suddenly sleepy and he had to fight against it. He had nestling blackly deep in him a knowledge of his pending end that made him know he had but a short time to say anything.

"Damon, can you hear me?"

"Yes," he managed to whisper.

Houston's voice seemed to be closer now and the tone had changed; it was the voice of a brother asking an urgent, confidential question.

"Damon, listen to me, just listen and think about what I'm asking and then try to answer. This is Houston still talking to you. . . . Damon, you were an outsider. You know what I mean. You lived apart. . . . Damon, tell me, why did you choose to live that way?"

The damned old curious outlaw! He never forgot anything. He was still on his trail. . . . Still hunting him down. . . . Sure; he'd tell 'im. . . .

"I wanted to be free . . . to feel what I was worth . . . what living meant to me. . . . I loved life too . . . much. . . ."

"And what did you find?"

"Nothing . . ." He lay very still and summoned all of his strength. "The search can't be done alone." He let his voice issue from a dry throat in which he felt death lurking. "Never alone. . . . Alone a man is nothing. . . . Man is a promise that he must never break. . . ."

"Is there anything, Damon, you want me to tell anybody?"

His mind reeled at the question. There was so much and yet it was so little. . . .

"I wish I had some way to give the meaning of my life to others. . . . To make a bridge from man to man . . . Starting from scratch every time is . . . is no good. Tell them not to come down this road. . . . Men hate themselves and it makes them hate others. . . . We must find some way of being good to ourselves. . . . Man is all we've got. . . . I wish I could ask men to meet themselves. . . . We're different from what we seem. . . . Maybe worse, maybe better . . . But certainly different . . . We're strangers to ourselves." He was silent for a moment, then he continued, whispering: "Don't think I'm so odd and strange. . . . I'm not. . . . I'm legion. . . . I've lived alone, but I'm everywhere. . . . Man is returning to the earth. . . . For a long time he has been sleeping, wrapped in a dream. . . . He is awakening now, awakening from his dream and finding himself in a waking nightmare. . . . The myth men are going. . . . The real men, the last men are coming. . . . Somebody must prepare the way for them . . . Tell the world what they are like. . . . We are here already, if others but had the courage to see us. . . ."

He felt a weak impulse to laugh. His strength was flowing rapidly from him. His eyes would not focus. The world that was visible was a gray, translucent screen that had begun to shimmer and waver. He closed his eyes and struggled with his tongue and lips to try to shape words.

"Do you understand what I mean, Damon?" Houston asked softly. "I'm talking about *you*, your life. How was it with *you*, Damon?"

His eyes stared bleakly. His effort was supreme; his lips parted; his tongue moved; he cursed that damned ball of seething fire that raged in his chest and managed to get his reluctant breath past it to make words:

"It . . . it was . . . horrible. . . ."

There was a short silence, then Houston's voice came again: "What do you mean? What was horrible?"

The effort to keep his heavy eyes open was too much and it was not worth trying. He stopped fighting and let his lids droop and darkness soothed him for a moment; once more he struggled grimly to control his lips and tongue, to still that exploding ball of fire that leaped white-hot in his chest; then he said in a soft, falling, dying whisper:

"All of it. . . ."

"But why? *Why?* Try and tell me. . . ."

"Because in my heart . . . I'm . . . I felt . . . I'm *innocent.* . . . That's what made the horror. . . ."

He felt his dull head falling helplessly to one side. Huge black shadows were descending softly down upon him. He took a chest full of air and sighed. . . .

He was dead.

Savage Holiday

Written in 1953 and published as a paperback the following year, Savage Holiday was completely ignored by the
critics and, until recently, has been generally dismissed as a
potboiler. This heavily psychoanalytical novel was, however,
quite dear to the heart of its author. Wright even considered
it at one time as part of a magnum opus dealing with the
evolution of consciousness and with the relationship between the individual's instinct for self-satisfaction and the
frustration brought about by social imperatives.

Savage Holiday was largely inspired by the case of Clinton
Brewer, a Black murderer whom Wright helped get paroled
in 1943, as well as by Dr. Fredric Wertham's Dark Legend.
This short novel is the dramatic story of a white man who
accidentally brings about a boy's death and later stabs the
boy's mother to punish his own (dead) mother by proxy for
her possible sexual promiscuity during his childhood. Aptly
named Gene Fowler kills because of "a guilty dream which
he had wanted to disown and forget but which he had had
to reenact in order to make its memory and reality clear to
him," Wright explains in the conclusion of the story.

The most gripping episode is not the butchering of Mabel
Blake by Fowler but, rather, Fowler's being locked out by
chance, naked on his doorstep. His fears and imaginings are
typical of his puritanical and bourgeois upbringing. They

Savage Holiday was originally published by Avon Books in 1954.

also reflect the wider existential predicament of any man trapped by chance—or should we say by fate?

HE PULLED FROM BED and lifted his six feet to full height; he yawned and rubbed his eyes with the backs of his hands. He stripped off his pajamas and loomed naked, his chest covered with a matting of black hair, his genitals all but obscured by a dark forest, his legs rendered spiderlike by their hirsute coating. Tufts of black hair protruded even from under his arms. Nude, Erskine looked anything but pious or Christian. He pulled on his robe and lumbered into the kitchen and filled the coffee pot, lit the flame of the gas stove, listening to Tony's shouting:

"Bang! Bang! Bang! You're dead!"

He sighed. If only he could take that child to Sunday School! As twigs are bent, so grow the trees . . . Twice he'd shyly asked Mrs. Blake's permission to take Tony to Sunday School and she'd consented, but each Sunday morning when he'd been ready to go, she'd been sleeping and Tony had not been properly dressed. Too much nightclubbing, too much whiskey, and God knows what else . . . His nose wrinkled in disgust as he doffed his robe and entered the bathroom. He adjusted the hot and cold water faucets until the twin streams ran tepid. He was about to take off his wrist watch preparatory to stepping under the shower when his doorbell shrilled.

"Who is it?" he called, turning and standing in the bathroom door, his right hand lifted to reach for his robe.

"Paper boy!" an adolescent voice called. "Wanna collect this morning, please!"

"Oh, yes. Just a moment," he answered.

He'd promised to pay that boy this morning but, gosh, he'd forgot to get change. Still nude, he crossed the room and put his mouth to the door panel and called out:

"Say, will next week be all right? Really, I've no change; I'm sorry . . . Or do you want to take down a twenty-dollar bill and get some—?"

"See you next week, Mister!" the boy called to him. "You owe me two-twenty; that right?"

"That's right," he told the boy.

He heard the thud of his thick Sunday paper hit the carpeted floor of the hallway outside and then the muffled sound of swift feet rushing toward the elevator; he caught the clank of the elevator door opening and closing . . . Yes; he'd have to remember and pay that paper boy next Sunday; it wasn't right to keep a kid like that waiting for his money . . . He might have need of it . . .

Then he heard his coffee pot boil over in the kitchen. Golly! He'd made that flame too high! Still nude, he sprinted into the kitchen and lowered the gas fire. The redolence of coffee roused his hunger; he opened the refrigerator and hauled out the eggs, the butter, the bacon, a jar of strawberry jam, and a tin of chilled fruit juice. Padding on bare feet, he visualized the plate of succulent food he'd have.

About to reenter the bathroom, he paused. Better get my paper . . . Two weeks ago his Sunday paper had been stolen. Secreting his naked body, he cracked the door and peered to left and right in the sunlit hallway. Nobody's there . . . Half of the bulk of his Sunday paper lay near his toes, but the other half, evidently having slid, was scattered at the foot of the stairway. Feeling a draft of air on the skin of his unclothed body, he stooped and gathered the wad of papers at his feet, his left hand holding open the door behind him. Why did that boy fling his paper about like this? Mad maybe because I didn't pay 'im . . .

He pushed the door back into his room and waited to see if it would remain open. He saw it swinging to, towards him, slowly. He'd have to open the door wide, all the way back to the wall; and, in that way, he'd have time enough to grab the other section of the paper and get back to his door before it closed. Pushing his door all the way back until it collided with the wall of the room, he watched it; it was still. He sprang nudely forward in the brightly-lighted hallway and, with a sweep of his right hand, scooped up the second half of his paper, pivoted on his bare heels, and was about to rush forward to reenter his apartment when the door began to veer slowly to, towards him. With his left hand outstretched, he dashed toward the door and reached the sill just as the door, pushed by a strong current of air, slammed shut with a thunderous metallic bang in his face. He blinked, quickly seized hold of the doorknob with his right hand and rattled it firmly. The door did not budge; it was locked!

He frowned, staring, a look of mute protest in his eyes. He became dismayingly conscious of his nudity; a sense of hot panic flooded him; he felt as though a huge x-ray eye was glaring into his very soul; and in the same instant he felt that he had shrunk in size, had become something small, shameful . . . With flexed lips he rattled the knob of the door brutally; the door still held. He knew that his door was locked, but he felt, irrationally, that it would just *have* to open and admit him before anyone saw him here nude in the hallway . . . Then his lips parted in comprehension as he remembered that only last month he had had the lock on the door changed, had installed a new system of steel bolts. There had been a series of robberies in the building and he had taken that precaution to protect himself. Now, even if he hurled his whole weight of two hundred pounds against it, that door would stand fast . . .

"Oh, God," he breathed.

Again he clutched the knob of his door and shook it with fury, looking with dread over his shoulder as he did so, fearing that someone might come into the hallway. The door remained secure, solid, burglarproof. He glanced down at his hairy legs, his frizzled chest; save for the clumsy hunk of the Sunday edition of the *New York Times*, he was nude, frightfully nude.

Erskine's moral conditioning leaped to the fore, lava-like; there flashed into his mind an image of Mrs. Blake who lived in the apartment next to his, the door that was but six inches from his right hand; also there rose up before his shocked eyes the prim face of Miss Brownell, a faded, graying spinster of forty-odd, who lived just across the hall from him; and he saw, as though staring up into the stern face of a judge in a courtroom, the gray, respectable faces of Mr. and Mrs. Fenley—Fenley of the Chase National Bank!—who lived in the apartment which was just to the left of the elevator. Good God! He was superintendent of the Mount Ararat Sunday School; he was a consulting advisor to the Longevity Life Insurance Company; he had a bank balance of over forty thousand dollars in cash; he had more than one hundred thousand dollars in solid securities, including government bonds; he was a member of Rotary; a thirty-second degree Mason; and here he was standing nude, with a foolish expression on his face, before the locked door of his apartment on a Sunday morning . . .

A fine film of sweat broke out over the skin of his face. Again he grasped the doorknob and strained at it, hoping that his sheer passion for modesty would somehow twist those cold bolts of steel; but the door held and he knew that steel was steel and would not bend. There was no doubt about it; he was locked out, locked out naked in the hallway and at any second one of his neighbors' doors would open and someone would walk out and find him . . . They'd scream, maybe, if they were women. Good God, what could he do? His face was wet with sweat now.

He tensed as the faint sound of the elevator door opening downstairs came to him, echoing hollowly up the elevator shaft. Somebody was coming up! Maybe to this floor! He glared about in the sun-flooded hallway, searching for nooks and crannies in which to hide, clutching awkwardly his bundle of Sunday papers. His hairy body, as he glanced down at

it, seemed huge and repulsive, like that of a giant; but, when
he looked off, his body felt puny, shriveled, like that of a
dwarf. And the hallway in which he stood was white, smooth,
modern; it held no Gothic recesses, no Victorian curves, no
Byzantine incrustations in, or behind which, he could hide.

The elevator was coming up . . . He felt that he was in the
spell of a dream; he wanted to shake his head, blink his eyes
and rid himself of this nightmare. But he remained hairy,
nude, trembling in the morning sun. If that was Miss Brownell coming up, she might scream; she'd surely complain,
maybe to the police . . . He felt dizzy and his vision blurred.
The muted hum of the rising elevator came nearer. Where
could he hide himself? He prayed that whoever was coming
up in the elevator was not getting off at this floor. Flattening
his back against the cold, wooden panels of his door, pressing
the bunch of newspapers tightly against his middle, he closed
his eyes, reverting for a moment to the primitive feelings
that children have—reasoning that if he shut his eyes he
would not be seen. The muscles of his legs quivered and
sweat broke out in the matted hair of his chest. He heard the
elevator pass his floor and keep on rising . . . Thank God!

He relaxed, swallowed; then, gritting his teeth till they
ached, he whirled and rattled his doorknob again, knowing
that the door would not open, but rattling the knob because
he *had* to do *something* . . . Whom could he call for help? But
if he called out, somebody was sure to open a door and he
could not control who it would be . . . God . . . He felt like
vomiting and, on top of it all, through the locked and bolted
door, he heard his coffee pot boiling over again.

He stiffened, hearing the telephone ring in Miss Brownell's
apartment. *What could he do?* The sound of a distant door
opening and closing came to him, then he heard the far-off
music of a radio. It was getting late; the morning was passing;
each second brought discovery closer. Despair made him feel
weak as he heard the elevator descending and a minute later
he heard the elevator door opening and closing downstairs.

Then the soft, low whine of the elevator wafted up; it was climbing towards him once more . . . Lord . . . Once more he stood with his back glued to the panels of the door, shielding himself with the newspapers, his body as still as a tree, sweat dripping from his chin. The drone of the elevator came nearer; it reached the tenth floor and passed, going upward again. He sighed.

He had to do something, but what? He wanted to run, but fought off the urge, fearing that any move he made would worsen his predicament. Hell, he breathed, giving vent to a curse for the first time in many long years.

Oh, he had an idea! Yes; that's what he'd do . . . If he got into the elevator and rode down to the first floor, he could conceal himself in the elevator and call to Westerman, the building superintendent. Yes, that was his only chance . . . What a foolish, wild, idiotic thing to do—trapping one's self naked in a building in broad daylight! Get hold of that superintendent; that was the thing . . . The superintendent had a passkey for every apartment in the building.

He crept on the tips of his toes to the elevator, holding the Sunday newspaper in front of him, feeling that perhaps even the inert metal of the elevator machinery would scorn his nakedness and refuse to obey. But, when he did push the button, the elevator responded and he could hear the dull purr of the electric motor and could see, through the dim square of glass set high in the elevator door, the wobbly steel cables lifting the cage of the elevator upwards, towards him. He kept his eyes on the shut doors of other apartments. God, if only he could get hold of that superintendent . . .

The elevator finally arrived. He squinted through the door's dark rectangle of glass; it was empty . . . He yanked open the door and stepped inside, feeling lost and foolish to be entering an elevator naked like this. He had the sensation of being transparent; he felt vaguely that he had had this same experience somewhere and at some time before in his life. He pushed the button for the first floor and his body shook from the sudden descent of the elevator. God, if he had only five minutes of grace before anyone showed up!

He looked at his watch; it was only eight o'clock, yet he felt that he'd been dodging naked like this for hours . . . Down; down; down; the elevator moved so slowly that he felt that it would take an eternity to get to the bottom. When he looked at the newspapers that he was crushing against his body, he saw that they showed dark and gray where his sweat, dripping from his chin, was dampening them.

The elevator stopped with a soft bounce at the first floor; he peeped through the cloudy square of glass and saw two laughing young girls, seemingly in their late teens, about to open the door. He sprang and grabbed the door with his right hand and, hugging the newspapers with his left elbow, reached with his left hand, not daring to breathe, and pushed the button for the tenth floor. At once the elevator started up again and he let his breath expire through parted lips. Yes; he'd have to get out of this elevator; it was too dangerous . . .

But how could he get back into his apartment? The elevator buzzer rang in his ears and he shivered; somebody was ringing for the elevator . . . ! He kept his teeth clamped and something seemed to be jumping in his stomach, like a nerve cut loose from his ganglion, writhing. He brushed rivulets of water from his forehead, bit his lips, waited, counting the floors: seventh, eighth, ninth, tenth . . . The elevator halted; he reached forward to open the door, but paused and stared through the murky block of glass to see if the hallway was empty. Then, just as he was about to open the door, the elevator started again, going *downward!*

He searched frantically for the red emergency button, found it, jammed it fumblingly with the forefinger of his right hand; the elevator stopped. He wanted to scream and bring this spell of unreality to an end; but this unreality was real; he was experiencing this . . . Now, the button for the tenth floor. He reached out to push it, but, before his finger touched it, the elvator was climbing *upward!* A chorus of buzzings was now sounding in his ears; many people were calling for the elevator . . . For a moment he stood paralyzed, realizing that now a backlog of tenants was waiting on several floors, all trying to get possession of the elevator.

He had to stop the elevator, but his overanxiousness warped his judgment and made him lose time. It seemed that he had to look longer than ordinarily to find the right button to push. Again he leaped upon the red emergency button and hit it and the elevator jolted to a halt. His eyes darted and found the button for the tenth floor; he extended his hand to push it, and, before he could touch it, the elevator moved, going *down* once more.

He groaned. A desire to do nothing to save himself shot through him. But he couldn't act like that . . . Again he pounced on the red emergency button and rammed it with his finger, but his hand was trembling so that when he tried to punch the button for the tenth floor, he pushed, by mistake, the one for the fifteenth floor. Damn! Obediently, the elevator was lifting upward. Once more he shoved the red button; the elevator stopped dead, shaking him. He was now between the eleventh and twelfth floors. And, before he could touch the button for the tenth floor, the elevator dropped downward, taking his naked body—dripping as though he were in a Turkish bath—to the first floor where those two young girls were undoubtedly still waiting . . .

Stupidly, he stared at the rows of buttons. Once again he broke the elevator's descent by pressing the red button again and quickly indented the button for the tenth floor, and the elevator went into action *too* quickly, so quickly that he was not certain if *he* or someone *else* had pressed the button, if *he* or someone *else* had put the elevator into action. In suspense he watched the floors pass. He couldn't stand it; he had to know *who* had set the elevator into motion . . . He stopped the machinery again and, with a dart of his finger that was like the lick of a serpent's tongue, he flicked the button for the tenth floor; the elevator sank, even and smooth in its glide. The elevator stopped at the tenth floor, *his* floor.

His knees were bent with tension. Then he sucked in his breath. Through the dingy plate of glass he saw Miss Brownell standing there, her hand stretched out to enter the elevator. A growl rose in his throat and he flung himself against the door. *What could he do?*

Yes; he had to get to the eleventh floor where the hallway was empty, and leave the elevator! And he'd hide on the stairway until Miss Brownell had gone. He pushed the button for the eleventh floor and the elevator lifted upward and he knew that it was *he* who commanded the elevator to move this time. There was now a loud banging on the elevator doors . . .

"What's the matter?"

"Send that elevator down!" a man's voice boomed.

"Wait, will you?" Erskine screamed, his body shaking with rage, shame, despair, and a sickness which he could not name.

The elevator came to a standstill at the eleventh floor and, through the cloudy square of glass, he saw his way clear. He opened the door and stepped out, feeling that he was escaping an enormous throng of encircling, hostile people armed with long, sharp knives, intent upon chopping off his arms, his legs, his genitals, his head . . . Squeezing the wet wad of newspapers close to his drenched skin, he crept down the stairway, leaving dark tracks of water each time his naked feet touched the purplish carpet. His body was so hot that the warm air of the hallway seemed, by contrast, cold. The sunlit hall was quiet save for muffled sounds of radios coming from surrounding apartments.

He heard the elevator going down. Hugging the cold, marble wall, he descended. There . . . He could see a tip of Miss Brownell's wide hat and a stretch of her white dress as she waited for the elevator. He clung to the wall and tried to master his breathing. Finally he saw Miss Brownell's white hand reach for the handle of the elevator door; the door opened; she stepped inside; now, at last, the hallway on his floor was free . . . So long had he waited for this respite that he now, quite foolishly, felt that he had almost solved his problem. He ran to the door of his apartment and, knowing that it was locked, rattled the knob once again, hearing the elevator settling downstairs on the first floor. He heard the door opening and closing; then the sound of the elevator moving into motion again floated to him.

His eyes glistened and he stared about crazily. *What could he do?* Then his lips opened in surprise. YES, THERE WAS HIS BATHROOM WINDOW WHICH WAS KEPT OPEN ALWAYS A FEW INCHES AND HE COULD MAYBE CLIMB INTO IT FROM THE BALCONY THAT WAS JUST BENEATH THAT WINDOW . . . Maybe he could get into his apartment that way . . . ? He'd be publicly exposed on the balcony for a few seconds, but that was better than this terror . . . It was worth trying. He should have thought of it earlier. Now, maybe he had a chance, if only that door leading to the balcony was unlocked.

He sketched out his plan of action, visualizing each move, listening with dread to the drone of the machinery as it lifted the elevator . . . *God, it was stopping at this floor . . . !*

Springing into action, he dropped the newspapers, bolted down the hallway and veered for the door as fast as his naked feet could skim across the carpet. In one vicious, sweeping movement, he seized hold of the knob of the door and yanked violently at it and felt it opening in his wet hand. He was fronting a brightly lighted balcony and his eyes were staring straight into the full morning sun and he was blinded for a moment. His momentum now carried him out upon the balcony and he was turning his naked body in the direction of the window of his bathroom even before he saw where he was going.

His right leg encountered some strange object and he went tumbling forward on his face, his long, hairy arms flaying the air rapaciously, like the paws of a huge beast clutching for something to devour, to rend to pieces . . . He steadied himself partially by clawing at the brick wall and then he saw, in one swift, sweeping glance, little Tony's tricycle over which he had tripped and fallen and also there flashed before his stunned eyes a quick image of Manhattan's far-flung skyline in a white burst of vision and also, like a crashing blow against his skull, Tony, his little white face registering shock, staring at him, clad in a cowboy's outfit, standing atop his electric hobbyhorse near the edge of the balcony, his slight, frail body outlined, like an image cut from a colored cardboard, against a blue immensity of horizon . . .

The physical force that had carried him through the doorway now propelled him towards little Tony who was holding a toy pistol gripped in his right hand . . . Erskine checked himself in his blind rush; his naked foot slipped on the concrete and he fell against the top railing encircling the balcony, feeling it shake, sway, and wobble as his two hundred pounds struck it. He was lying now with one of his shoulders resting against the railing . . . Tony, poised atop the electric hobby-horse, opened his mouth to scream and then, slowly —it seemed to Erskine's imagination when he thought of it afterwards that the child had been floating in air—little Tony fell backwards and uttered one word:

"Naaaaaw . . . !"

The child went backwards, toward the void yawning beyond the edge of the balcony, his left hand lashing out, clutching for something to grab hold of, to hold onto, and his right hand still gripping the toy pistol. Erskine sensed that Tony was trying to seize hold of the top iron railing that encircled the balcony; and, as he struggled to say something, to yell a warning, to move, he saw little Tony fall onto the top iron railing and for a split second the child was poised there. The electric hobbyhorse had also fallen against the iron railing which still trembled under Erskine's shoulder. In the glare of golden sun the tableau was frozen for a moment, with Tony staring at Erskine with eyes of horror. Erskine's hand reached hesitantly towards Tony and Tony's little body convulsed with panic. Erskine's hand dropped; he felt that Tony feared him . . . Tony! he screamed without words and wanted to take hold of the child's leg, but he was afraid to move. Then, impulsively, he stretched out his arms toward Tony and Tony's little left hand groped flutteringly for the top iron railing; he actually saw Tony's tiny fingers close over the iron railing and then the railing began to sag and bend under the combined weight of Erskine's body, Tony's body, and the electric hobbyhorse; the railing gave way . . . Erskine saw a brick come loose from the wall and Tony went from sight, plunging downward, the fingers of his left hand loosening about the iron railing and finally leaving it; Tony was gone downward, down ten floors to the street below . . .

"Tony," Erskine sang out in a low moan.

Then he was still, nude, dripping wet, not breathing, his senses refusing to acknowledge what had happened all too clearly before his eyes. Tony had fallen off the balcony! No; no . . . ! *He'd be killed . . . !* He forgot that he was naked and stood staring at the loosened iron railing, his hands lifted in midair, the fingers curved and turned inward toward his hirsute body that gleamed wetly in the brilliant sunlight. Then he moved slowly and hesitantly toward the iron railing which now dangled loose and protruded over the side of the balcony. He wanted to look down there, but the mere thought made him dizzy . . . Mechanically, he glanced at his bathroom window. He was straining his ears, waiting to hear some sound—a sound that he thought would surely stop the beating of his heart. Then he heard it; there came a distant, definite, soft, crushing yet pulpy: *PLOP!*

A spasm went through his body; he covered his face with his hands; he knew that Tony's body had at last hit the black pavement far below; it seemed that he had been standing here naked on this balcony in the hot morning's sun waiting for an eternity to hear that awful sound, a sound that would reverberate down all the long corridors of his years in this world, a sound that would follow him, like a taunting echo, even unto his grave . . .

Big Black Good Man

In 1960, the year he died, Wright gathered for publication in one volume a number of short stories that had appeared in magazines and anthologies. Some, such as "The Man Who Was Almost a Man," had been written in the thirties. Others, like "The Man Who Killed a Shadow," in the mid-forties. Only a few of them were recent ones: "Man of All Work," "Man, God Ain't Like That" (both written originally as radio plays, hence the exclusive use of dialogue in them), and "Big Black Good Man," published in November 1957 in Esquire Magazine. *Although one may think of Stephen Crane's "The Blue Hotel" when reading "Big Black Good Man," Wright did not build his story upon a fictional reminiscence but rather upon a real episode about which he learned while making a lecture tour in Scandinavia. Actually, he started to jot down the story during his return train trip from Copenhagen to Paris and completed it in a few days.*

In this story, as well as in his "Man of All Work" and "Man, God Ain't Like That," there comes to the fore a quality in Wright's fiction that had hitherto remained somewhat concealed since the writing of Lawd Today—*the comic touch. The humor verges on bitter satire in "Man, God Ain't Like That," a story of the devastation wreaked by white missionaries upon Africans and the resulting violence, and*

"Big Black Good Man" originally appeared in *Esquire*, Vol. 50, November 1957.

it remains on the parodic, tongue-in-cheeck level in the true-to-life plot of "Man of All Works." In contrast, the comedy in "Big Black Good Man" comes through clearly in places, such as the confrontation between the Danish hotel keeper and the black American sailor. As the fears and prejudices of the former are exposed and explored through a clever reversal of color symbolism and stereotypes, the essence of blackness seems to emerge as potentially threatening but eventually well-meaning and deeply human.

THROUGH THE OPEN WINDOW Olaf Jenson could smell the sea and hear the occasional foghorn of a freighter; outside, rain pelted down through an August night, drumming softly upon the pavements of Copenhagen, inducing drowsiness, bringing dreamy memory, relaxing the tired muscles of his work-wracked body. He sat slumped in a swivel chair with his legs outstretched and his feet propped atop an edge of his desk. An inch of white ash tipped the end of his brown cigar and now and then he inserted the end of the stogie into his mouth and drew gently upon it, letting wisps of blue smoke eddy from the corners of his wide, thin lips. The watery gray irises behind the thick lenses of his eyeglasses gave him a look of abstraction, of absentmindedness, of an almost genial idiocy. He sighed, reached for his half-empty bottle of beer, and drained it into his glass and downed it with a long slow gulp, then licked his lips. Replacing the cigar, he slapped his right palm against his thigh and said half aloud:

"Well, I'll be sixty tomorrow. I'm not rich, but I'm not poor either . . . Really, I can't complain. Got good health. Traveled all over the world and had my share of the girls when I was young . . . And my Karen's a good wife. I own my home. Got no debts. And I love digging in my garden in the spring . . . Grew the biggest carrots of anybody last year. Ain't saved much money, but what the hell . . . Money ain't everything.

Got a good job. Night portering ain't too bad." He shook his head and yawned. "Karen and I could of had some children, though. Would of been good company . . . 'Specially for Karen. And I could of taught 'em languages . . . English, French, German, Danish, Dutch, Swedish, Norwegian, and Spanish . . ." He took the cigar out of his mouth and eyed the white ash critically. "Hell of a lot of good language learning did me . . . Never got anything out of it. But those ten years in New York were fun . . . Maybe I could of got rich if I'd stayed in America . . . Maybe. But I'm satisfied. You can't have everything."

Behind him the office door opened and a young man, a medical student occupying room number nine, entered.

"Good evening," the student said.

"Good evening," Olaf said, turning.

The student went to the keyboard and took hold of the round, brown knob that anchored his key.

"Rain, rain, rain," the student said.

"That's Denmark for you," Olaf smiled at him.

"This dampness keeps me clogged up like a drainpipe," the student complained.

"That's Denmark for you," Olaf repeated with a smile.

"Good night," the student said.

"Good night, son," Olaf sighed, watching the door close.

Well, my tenants are my children, Olaf told himself. Almost all of his children were in their rooms now . . . Only seventy-two and forty-four were missing . . . Seventy-two might've gone to Sweden . . . And forty-four was maybe staying at his girl's place tonight, like he sometimes did . . . He studied the pear-shaped blobs of hard rubber, reddish brown like ripe fruit, that hung from the keyboard, then glanced at his watch. Only room thirty, eighty-one, and one hundred and one were empty . . . And it was almost midnight. In a few moments he could take a nap. Nobody hardly ever came looking for accommodations after midnight, unless a stray freighter came in, bringing thirsty, women-hungry sailors. Olaf chuckled softly. Why in hell was I ever a sailor? The whole time I was at sea I was thinking and dreaming about women. Then why didn't I stay on land where women could be had? Hunh? Sailors are crazy . . .

But he liked sailors. They reminded him of his youth, and there was something so direct, simple, and childlike about them. They always said straight out what they wanted, and what they wanted was almost always women and whisky . . . "Well, there's no harm in that . . . Nothing could be more natural," Olaf sighed, looking thirstily at his empty beer bottle. No; he'd not drink any more tonight; he'd had enough; he'd go to sleep . . .

He was bending forward and loosening his shoelaces when he heard the office door crack open. He lifted his eyes, then sucked in his breath. He did not straighten; he just stared up and around at the huge black thing that filled the doorway. His reflexes refused to function; it was not fear; it was just simple astonishment. He was staring at the biggest, strangest, and blackest man he'd ever seen in all his life.

"Good evening," the black giant said in a voice that filled the small office. "Say, you got a room?"

Olaf sat up slowly, not to answer but to look at this brooding black vision; it towered darkly some six and a half feet into the air, almost touching the ceiling, and its skin was so black that it had a bluish tint. And the sheer bulk of the man! . . . His chest bulged like a barrel; his rocklike and humped shoulders hinted of mountain ridges; the stomach ballooned like a threatening stone; and the legs were like telephone poles . . . The big black cloud of a man now lumbered into the office, bending to get its buffalolike head under the door frame, then advanced slowly upon Olaf, like a stormy sky descending.

"You got a room?" the big black man asked again in a resounding voice.

Olaf now noticed that the ebony giant was well dressed,

carried a wonderful new suitcase, and wore black shoes that
gleamed despite the raindrops that peppered their toes.

"You're American?" Olaf asked him.

"Yeah, man; sure," the black giant answered.

"Sailor?"

"Yeah. American Continental Lines."

Olaf had not answered the black man's question. It was not
that the hotel did not admit men of color; Olaf took in all
comers—blacks, yellows, whites, and browns . . . To Olaf,
men were men, and, in his day, he'd worked and eaten and
slept and fought with all kinds of men. But this particular
black man . . . Well, he didn't seem human. Too big, too black,
too loud, too direct, and probably too violent to boot . . . Olaf's
five feet seven inches scarcely reached the black giant's
shoulder and his frail body weighed less, perhaps, than one
of the man's gigantic legs . . . There was something about the
man's intense blackness and ungainly bigness that frightened
and insulted Olaf; he felt as though this man had come here
expressly to remind him how puny, how tiny, and how weak
and how white he was. Olaf knew, while registering his reactions, that he was being irrational and foolish; yet, for the first
time in his life, he was emotionally determined to refuse a
man a room solely on the basis of the man's size and color
. . . Olaf's lips parted as he groped for the right words in
which to couch his refusal, but the black giant bent forward
and boomed:

"I asked you if you got a room. I got to put up somewhere
tonight, man."

"Yes, we got a room," Olaf murmured.

And at once he was ashamed and confused. Sheer fear had
made him yield. And he seethed against himself for his involuntary weakness. Well, he'd look over his book and pretend that he'd made a mistake; he'd tell this hunk of blackness that there was really no free room in the hotel, and that
he was so sorry . . . Then, just as he took out the hotel register
to make believe that he was poring over it, a thick roll of

American bank notes, crisp and green, was thrust under his nose.

"Keep this for me, will you?" the black giant commanded. "Cause I'm gonna get drunk tonight and I don't wanna lose it."

Olaf stared at the roll; it was huge, in denominations of fifties and hundreds. Olaf's eyes widened.

"How much is there?" he asked.

"Two thousand six hundred," the giant said. "Just put it into an envelope and write 'Jim' on it and lock it in your safe, hunh?"

The black mass of man had spoken in a manner that indicated that it was taking it for granted that Olaf would obey. Olaf was licked. Resentment clogged the pores of his wrinkled white skin. His hands trembled as he picked up the money. No; he couldn't refuse this man . . . The impulse to deny him was strong, but each time he was about to act upon it something thwarted him, made him shy off. He clutched about desperately for an idea. Oh yes, he could say that if he planned to stay for only one night, then he could not have the room, for it was against the policy of the hotel to rent rooms for only one night . . .

"How long are you staying? Just tonight?" Olaf asked.

"Naw. I'll be here for five or six days, I reckon," the giant answered offhandedly.

"You take room number thirty," Olaf heard himself saying. "It's forty kroner a day."

"That's all right with me," the giant said.

With slow, stiff movements, Olaf put the money in the safe and then turned and stared helplessly up into the living, breathing blackness looming above him. Suddenly he became conscious of the outstretched palm of the black giant; he was silently demanding the key to the room. His eyes downcast, Olaf surrendered the key, marveling at the black man's tremendous hands . . . He could kill me with one blow, Olaf told himself in fear.

Feeling himself beaten, Olaf reached for the suitcase, but the black hand of the giant whisked it out of his grasp.

"That's too heavy for you, big boy; I'll take it," the giant said.

Olaf let him, He thinks I'm nothing . . . He led the way down the corridor, sensing the giant's lumbering presence behind him. Olaf opened the door of number thirty and stood politely to one side, allowing the black giant to enter. At once the room seemed like a doll's house, so dwarfed and filled and tiny it was with a great living blackness . . . Flinging his suitcase upon a chair, the giant turned. The two men looked directly at each other now. Olaf saw that the giant's eyes were tiny and red, buried, it seemed, in muscle and fat. Black cheeks spread, flat and broad, topping the wide and flaring nostrils. The mouth was the biggest that Olaf had ever seen on a human face; the lips were thick, pursed, parted, showing snow-white teeth. The black neck was like a bull's . . . The giant advanced upon Olaf and stood over him.

"I want a bottle of whisky and a woman," he said. "Can you fix me up?"

"Yes," Olaf whispered, wild with anger and insult.

But what was he angry about? He'd had requests like this every night from all sorts of men and he was used to fulfilling them; he was a night porter in a cheap, water-front Copenhagen hotel that catered to sailors and students. Yes, men needed women, but this man, Olaf felt, ought to have a special sort of woman. He felt a deep and strange reluctance to phone any of the women whom he habitually sent to men. Yet he had promised. Could he lie and say that none was available? No. That sounded too fishy. The black giant sat upon the bed, staring straight before him. Olaf moved about quickly, pulling down the window shades, taking the pink coverlet off the bed, nudging the giant with his elbow to make him move as he did so . . . That's the way to treat 'im . . . Show 'im I ain't scared of 'im . . . But he was still seeking for an excuse to refuse. And he could think of nothing. He felt hypnotized, mentally immobilized. He stood hesitantly at the door.

"You send the whisky and the woman quick, pal?" the black giant asked, rousing himself from a brooding stare.

"Yes," Olaf grunted, shutting the door.

Goddamn, Olaf sighed. He sat in his office at his desk before the phone. Why did *he* have to come here? . . . I'm not prejudiced . . . No, not at all . . . But . . . He couldn't think any more. God oughtn't make men as big and black as that . . . But what the hell was he worrying about? He'd sent women of all races to men of all colors . . . So why not a woman to the black giant? Oh, only if the man were small, brown, and intelligent-looking . . . Olaf felt trapped.

With a reflex movement of his hand, he picked up the phone and dialed Lena. She was big and strong and always cut him in for fifteen per cent instead of the usual ten per cent. Lena had four small children to feed and clothe. Lena was willing; she was, she said, coming over right now. She didn't give a good goddamn about how big and black the man was . . .

"Why you ask me that?" Lena wanted to know over the phone. "You never asked that before . . ."

"But this one is *big*," Olaf found himself saying.

"He's just a man," Lena told him, her voice singing stridently, laughingly over the wire. "You just leave that to me. You don't have to do anything. *I'll* handle 'im."

Lena had a key to the hotel door downstairs, but tonight Olaf stayed awake. He wanted to see her. Why? He didn't know. He stretched out on the sofa in his office, but sleep was far from him. When Lena arrived, he told her again how big and black the man was.

"You told me that over the phone," Lena reminded him.

Olaf said nothing. Lena flounced off on her errand of mercy. Olaf shut the office door, then opened it and left it ajar. But why? He didn't know. He lay upon the sofa and stared at the ceiling. He glanced at his watch; it was almost two o'clock . . . She's staying in there a long time . . . Ah, God, but he could do with a drink . . . Why was he so damned worked up and nervous about a nigger and a white whore? . . . He'd never been so upset in all his life. Before he knew it, he had drifted off to sleep. Then he heard the office door swinging creakingly open on its rusty hinges. Lena stood in it, grim and businesslike, her face scrubbed free of powder and rouge. Olaf scrambled to his feet, adjusting his eyeglasses, blinking.

"How was it?" he asked her in a confidential whisper.

Lena's eyes blazed.

"What the hell's that to you?" she snapped. "There's your cut," she said, flinging him his money, tossing it upon the covers of the sofa. "You're sure nosy tonight. You wanna take over my work?"

Olaf's pasty cheeks burned red.

"You go to hell," he said, slamming the door.

"I'll meet you there!" Lena's shouting voice reached him dimly.

He was being a fool; there was no doubt about it. But, try as he might, he could not shake off a primitive hate for that black mountain of energy, of muscle, of bone; he envied the easy manner in which it moved with such a creeping and powerful motion; he winced at the booming and commanding voice that came to him when the tiny little eyes were not even looking at him; he shivered at the sight of those vast and clawlike hands that seemed always to hint of death . . .

Olaf kept his counsel. He never spoke to Karen about the sordid doings at the hotel. Such things were not for women like Karen. He knew instinctively that Karen would have been amazed had he told her that he was worried sick about a nigger and a blonde whore . . . No; he couldn't talk to anybody about it, not even the hard-bitten old bitch who owned the hotel. She was concerned only about money; she didn't give a damn about how big and how black a client was as long as he paid his room rent.

Next evening, when Olaf arrived for duty, there was no sight or sound of the black giant. A little later after one o'clock in the morning he appeared, left his key, and went out wordlessly. A few moments past two the giant returned, took his key from the board, and paused.

"I want that Lena again tonight. And another bottle of whisky," he said boomingly.

"I'll call her and see if she's in," Olaf said.

"Do that," the black giant said and was gone.

He thinks he's God, Olaf fumed. He picked up the phone and ordered Lena and a bottle of whisky, and there was a taste of ashes in his mouth. On the third night came the same request: Lena and whisky. When the black giant appeared on the fifth night, Olaf was about to make a sarcastic remark to the effect that maybe he ought to marry Lena, but he checked it in time . . . After all, he could kill me with one hand, he told himself.

Olaf was nervous and angry with himself for being nervous. Other black sailors came and asked for girls and Olaf sent them, but with none of the fear and loathing that he sent Lena and a bottle of whisky to the giant . . . All right, the black giant's stay was almost up. He'd said that he was staying for five or six nights; tomorrow night was the sixth night and that ought to be the end of this nameless terror.

On the sixth night Olaf sat in his swivel chair with his bottle of beer and waited, his teeth on edge, his fingers drumming the desk. But what the hell am I fretting for? . . . The hell with 'im . . . Olaf sat and dozed. Occasionally he'd awaken and listen to the foghorns of freighters sounding as ships came and went in the misty Copenhagen harbor. He was half asleep when he felt a rough hand on his shoulder. He blinked his eyes open. The giant, black and vast and powerful, all but blotted out his vision.

"What I owe you, man?" the giant demanded. "And I want my money"

"Sure," Olaf said, relieved, but filled as always with fear of this living wall of black flesh.

With fumbling hands, he made out the bill and received payment, then gave the giant his roll of money, laying it on the desk so as not to let his hands touch the flesh of the black mountain. Well, his ordeal was over. It was past two o'clock in the morning. Olaf even managed a wry smile and muttered a guttural "Thanks" for the generous tip that the giant tossed him.

Then a strange tension entered the office. The office door was shut and Olaf was alone with the black mass of power, yearning for it to leave. But the black mass of power stood still, immobile, looking down at Olaf. And Olaf could not, for the life of him, guess at what was transpiring in that mysterious black mind. The two of them simply stared at each other for a full two minutes, the giant's tiny little beady eyes blinking slowly as they seemed to measure and search Olaf's face. Olaf's vision dimmed for a second as terror seized him and he could feel a flush of heat overspread his body. Then Olaf sucked in his breath as the devil of blackness commanded:

"Stand up!"

Olaf was paralyzed. Sweat broke on his face. His worst premonitions about this black beast were coming true. This evil blackness was about to attack him, maybe kill him . . . Slowly Olaf shook his head, his terror permitting him to breathe:

"What're you talking about?"

"Stand up, I say!" the black giant bellowed.

As though hypnotized, Olaf tried to rise; then he felt the black paw of the beast helping him roughly to his feet.

They stood an inch apart. Olaf's pasty-white features were glued to the giant's swollen black face. The ebony ensemble of eyes and nose and mouth and cheeks looked down at Olaf, silently; then, with a slow and deliberate movement of his gorillalike arms, he lifted his mammoth hands to Olaf's throat. Olaf had long known and felt that this dreadful moment was coming; he felt trapped in a nightmare. He could not move. He wanted to scream, but could find no words. His lips refused to open; his tongue felt icy and inert. Then he knew that his end had come when the giant's black fingers slowly, softly encircled his throat while a horrible grin of delight broke out on the sooty face . . . Olaf lost control of the reflexes of his body and he felt a hot stickiness flooding his underwear . . . He stared without breathing, gazing into the grinning blackness of the face that was bent over him, feeling the black fingers caressing his throat and waiting to feel the sharp, stinging ache and pain of the bones in his neck being snapped, crushed . . . He knew all along that I hated 'im . . . Yes, and now he's going to kill me for it, Olaf told himself with despair.

The black fingers still circled Olaf's neck, not closing, but gently massaging it, as it were, moving to and fro, while the obscene face grinned into his. Olaf could feel the giant's warm breath blowing on his eyelashes and he felt like a chicken about to have its neck wrung and its body tossed to flip and flap dyingly in the dust of the barnyard . . . Then suddenly the black giant withdrew his fingers from Olaf's neck and stepped back a pace, still grinning. Olaf sighed, trembling, his body seeming to shrink; he waited. Shame sheeted him for the hot wetness that was in his trousers. Oh, God, he's teasing me . . . He's showing me how easily he can kill me . . . He swallowed, waiting, his eyes stones of gray.

The giant's barrel-like chest gave forth a low, rumbling chuckle of delight.

"You laugh?" Olaf asked whimperingly.

"Sure I laugh," the giant shouted.

"Please don't hurt me," Olaf managed to say.

"I wouldn't hurt you, boy," the giant said in a tone of mockery. "So long."

And he was gone. Olaf fell limply into the swivel chair and fought off losing consciousness. Then he wept. He was showing me how easily he could kill me . . . He made me shake with terror and then laughed and left . . . Slowly, Olaf recovered, stood, then gave vent to a string of curses:

"Goddamn 'im! My gun's right there in the desk drawer; I should of shot 'im. Jesus, I hope the ship he's on sinks . . . I hope he drowns and the sharks eat 'im . . ."

Later, he thought of going to the police, but sheer shame kept him back; and, anyway, the giant was probably on board his ship by now. And he had to get home and clean himself. Oh, Lord, what could he tell Karen? Yes, he would say that his stomach had been upset . . . He'd change clothes and return to work. He phoned the hotel owner that he was ill and wanted an hour off; the old bitch said that she was coming right over and that poor Olaf could have the evening off.

Olaf went home and lied to Karen. Then he lay awake the rest of the night dreaming of revenge. He saw that freighter on which the giant was sailing; he saw it springing a dangerous leak and saw a torrent of sea water flooding, gushing into all the compartments of the ship until it found the bunk in which the black giant slept. Ah, yes, the foamy, surging waters would surprise that sleeping black bastard of a giant and he would drown, gasping and choking like a trapped rat, his tiny eyes bulging until they glittered red, the bitter water of the sea pounding his lungs until they ached and finally burst . . . The ship would sink slowly to the bottom of the cold, black, silent depths of the sea and a shark, a *white* one, would glide aimlessly about the shut portholes until it found an open one and it would slither inside and nose about until it found that swollen, rotting, stinking carcass of the black beast and it would then begin to nibble at the decomposing mass of tarlike flesh, eating the bones clean . . . Olaf always pictured the giant's bones as being jet black and shining.

Once or twice, during these fantasies of cannibalistic revenge, Olaf felt a little guilty about all the many innocent people, women and children, all white and blonde, who would have to go down into watery graves in order that that white shark could devour the evil giant's black flesh . . . But, despite feelings of remorse, the fantasy lived persistently on, and when Olaf found himself alone, it would crowd and cloud his mind to the exclusion of all else, affording him the only revenge he knew. To make me suffer just for the pleasure of it, he fumed. Just to show me how strong he was . . . Olaf learned how to hate, and got pleasure out of it.

Summer fled on wings of rain. Autumn flooded Denmark with color. Winter made rain and snow fall on Copenhagen. Finally spring came, bringing violets and roses. Olaf kept to his job. For many months he feared the return of the black giant. But when a year had passed and the giant had not put in an appearance, Olaf allowed his revenge fantasy to peter out, indulging in it only when recalling the shame that the black monster had made him feel.

Then one rainy August night, a year later, Olaf sat drowsing at his desk, his bottle of beer before him, tilting back in his swivel chair, his feet resting atop a corner of his desk, his mind mulling over the more pleasant aspects of his life. The office door cracked open. Olaf glanced boredly up and around. His heart jumped and skipped a beat. The black nightmare of terror and shame that he had hoped that he had lost forever was again upon him . . . Resplendently dressed, suitcase in hand, the black looming mountain filled the doorway. Olaf's thin lips parted and a silent moan, half a curse, escaped them.

"Hi," the black giant boomed from the doorway.

Olaf could not reply. But a sudden resolve swept him: this time he would even the score. If this black beast came within so much as three feet of him, he would snatch his gun out of the drawer and shoot him dead, so help him God . . .

"No rooms tonight," Olaf heard himself announcing in a determined voice.

The black giant grinned; it was the same infernal grimace of delight and triumph that he had had when his damnable black fingers had been around his throat . . .

"Don't want no room tonight," the giant announced.

"Then what are you doing here?" Olaf asked in a loud but tremulous voice.

The giant swept toward Olaf and stood over him; and Olaf could not move, despite his oath to kill him . . .

"What do you want then?" Olaf demanded once more, ashamed that he could not lift his voice above a whisper.

The giant still grinned, then tossed what seemed the same suitcase upon Olaf's sofa and bent over it; he zippered it open with a sweep of his clawlike hand and rummaged in it, drawing forth a flat, gleaming white object done up in glowing cellophane. Olaf watched with lowered lids, wondering what trick was now being played on him. Then, before he could defend himself, the giant had whirled and again long, black, snakelike fingers were encircling Olaf's throat . . . Olaf stiffened, his right hand clawing blindly for the drawer where the gun was kept. But the giant was quick.

"Wait," he bellowed, pushing Olaf back from the desk.

The giant turned quickly to the sofa and, still holding his fingers in a wide circle that seemed a noose for Olaf's neck, he inserted the rounded fingers into the top of the flat, gleaming object. Olaf had the drawer open and his sweaty fingers were now touching his gun, but something made him freeze. The flat, gleaming object was a shirt and the black giant's circled fingers were fitting themselves into its neck . . .

"A perfect fit!" the giant shouted.

Olaf stared, trying to understand. His fingers loosened about the gun. A mixture of a laugh and a curse struggled in him. He watched the giant plunge his hands into the suitcase and pull out other flat, gleaming shirts.

"One, two, three, four, five, six," the black giant intoned, his voice crisp and businesslike. "Six nylon shirts. And they're all yours. One shirt for each time Lena came . . . See, Daddy-O?"

The black, cupped hands, filled with billowing nylon whiteness, were extended under Olaf's nose. Olaf eased his damp fingers from his gun and pushed the drawer closed, staring at the shirts and then at the black giant's grinning face.

"Don't you like 'em?" the giant asked.

Olaf began to laugh hysterically, then suddenly he was crying, his eyes so flooded with tears that the pile of dazzling nylon looked like snow in the dead of winter. Was this true? Could he believe it? Maybe this too was a trick? But, no. There were six shirts, all nylon, and the black giant had had Lena six nights.

"What's the matter with you, Daddy-O?" the giant asked. "You blowing your top? Laughing and crying . . ."

Olaf swallowed, dabbed his withered fists at his dimmed eyes; then he realized that he had his glasses on. He took them off and dried his eyes and sat up. He sighed, the tension and shame and fear and haunting dread of his fantasy went from him, and he leaned limply back in his chair . . .

"Try one on," the giant ordered.

Olaf fumbled with the buttons of his shirt, let down his suspenders, and pulled the shirt off. He donned a gleaming nylon one and the giant began buttoning it for him.

"Perfect, Daddy-O," the giant said.

His spectacled face framed in sparkling nylon, Olaf sat with trembling lips. So he'd not been trying to kill me after all.

"You want Lena, don't you?" he asked the giant in a soft whisper. "But I don't know where she is. She never came back here after you left—"

"I know where Lena is," the giant told him. "We been writing to each other. I'm going to her house. And, Daddy-O, I'm late." The giant zippered the suitcase shut and stood a moment gazing down at Olaf, his tiny little red eyes blinking slowly. Then Olaf realized that there was a compassion in that stare that he had never seen before.

"And I thought you wanted to kill me," Olaf told him. "I was scared of you . . ."

"Me? Kill you?" the giant blinked. "When?"

"That night when you put your fingers about my throat—"

"What?" the giant asked, then roared with laughter. "Daddy-O, you're a funny little man. I wouldn't hurt you. I like you. You a *good* man. You helped me."

Olaf smiled, clutching the pile of nylon shirts in his arms.

"You're a good man too," Olaf murmured. Then loudly: "You're a big black good man."

"Daddy-O, you're crazy," the giant said.

He swept his suitcase from the sofa, spun on his heel, and was at the door in one stride.

"Thanks!" Olaf cried after him.

The black giant paused, turned his vast black head, and flashed a grin.

"Daddy-O, drop dead," he said and was gone.

The Long Dream

Written in Paris in the mid-fifties and published in 1958,
The Long Dream *is the first volume of a trilogy depicting the
gradual liberation of a Black American from the ways of
thinking imposed upon him by racial oppression. Its mild
critical success can largely be explained by the fact that the
story took place during the preceding decade. Many Americans felt that Wright had been away from his native land for
too long; several reviewers spoke of his having lost his roots
and his sense of the changing realities in his mother country.
Some critics even used aesthetic considerations as a guise to
reproach him with being un-American in his stubborn self-
exile in Europe. Yet, if he had not progressed, Wright had
retained much of his power as a storyteller. Tyree Tucker
undoubtedly stands as the best example of a Black father in
all of Wright's fiction. In many respects he represents the
father Wright himself would have liked to have had.*

*The novel treats the youth and coming of age of a middle-
class Negro, Rex "Fishbelly" Tucker, in a small Mississippi
city. It retraces Fishbelly's initiation to life, sex, money and
power, to the racial situation and its dangerous games. Together with the economic, social and racial implications of
class and caste in the Deep South, Wright wanted to show—
he declares in a contemporary interview granted to a French
magazine—that:*

The Long Dream was originally published by Doubleday & Company, Inc.
in 1958. This selection is chapters 23–32 of the original work.

the absorption of the values of the dominant group by a black child can take the most fantastic forms. Fish is a plant forced to develop under abnormal conditions of growth, especially as concerns his relationship to the white woman. This complex is impressed upon him by his environment: the school, his conversations with his playmates, the street, his family, etc. He reads newspapers displaying sexy white females; he looks at billboards where the huge bosoms of movie-stars are advertised; in Negro bars, white pin-ups stare at him from the walls, next to the everpresent, enticing Coca-Cola blonde. He is forced to dream of white women and to suppress his dreams deep into his innermost being. . . . The white woman is valued, overvalued by a culture which depicts her as a highly desirable, a sexually desirable, object which, of course, the Negro can only approach under the penalty of death. . . . Since sex and money are the only realities in the world he is born in, Fish naturally becomes a man by securing money and sexual satisfaction.

Rather than the early sections of the novel, whose development somewhat retraces that of Black Boy, *we have selected the traumatic episodes of a dance-hall fire, Tyree's confrontation with the police chief and his subsequent murder, and Fishbelly's own difficulties with the white power structure, all of which reflect the irrational character of race relations in the South.*

HE BOUGHT THE JALOPY, some new clothes, and, on the afternoon of the Fourth of July, he called for Gladys.

"Baby, we dancing at the Grove tonight," he told her. "Zeke and Tony's joining the Army and we pitching a boogie-woogie."

"Fish, I thought you'd throwed me over," Gladys chided him.

"I been working night and day. I got a lot to tell you," he hinted at disclosures. "I'm making a new deal all around. . . . Let's start with me." He turned as though he were modeling clothes. "You like my new suit?"

"It's a cool killer, Fish." She fingered the cloth's texture. "Real tweed, ain't it?"

"English stuff," he bragged. "No white man in town's got any better. Outside is a jalopy and it's all mine."

"Gee, Fish. Let's take a spin," she suggested eagerly.

"That's just what I was going to say," he told her. "Today we celebrate. I been having it tough—"

"I ain't seen you but four times this month—"

"I'm going to make it up to you, honey," he consoled her, leading her to the jalopy. "It ain't no Rolls-Royce, but it'll take us places and bring us back."

His attention banished the slight roundedness from her shoulders and kindled an elusive sparkle in the depths of her brooding eyes. She climbed into the car and shook her tumbling brown hair out of her face and looked at the world with a new confidence.

"I ain't dressed for no Fourth of July," she said, tugging critically at her skimpy skirt.

"I'm gitting you some new things," he said as they pulled off. "Where to?"

"Straight through the center of town," she called in childlike glee.

"Right," he assented.

Black boys tossed firecrackers into dusty streets and detonations sounded under the car wheels. He loved her tawny skin, the tilt of her head; when she was out of the smoky dimness of the Grove, her body showed lithe and her face had a proud profile. They rolled swiftly through the Black Belt, hearing explosions, and entered the well-swept, tree-shaded streets of the white area.

"It's nice here," Gladys said.

"Yeah. They keep it clean. We got ten thousand folks and the whites got fifteen thousand; we all pay the same taxes, but they don't keep our streets clean like this," he told her. "They got four times as much space to live in as we got. We live in a hole; they live in the open. . . ."

She was silent. He braked the car for a red light in front of a drugstore before which loitered a group of teen-age, blue-jeaned white boys. Fishbelly saw their unsmiling, baffled eyes staring at Gladys, then they nudged one another with their elbows. The traffic eye winked from red to green and he got under way, hearing a derisive shout:

"Nigger lover!"

His hands gripped hard upon the steering wheel as he glanced at Gladys who was looking straight ahead with a serene face. Did not that insult mean anything to her?

"They spoke to *you*," he told her gently.

"I heard 'em," Gladys said, chuckling slightly, her expression unchanging.

Her reply disturbed him. Was she enjoying her role?

"What you think of stuff like that?"

"I don't let it touch me," she said proudly.

Her reaction still failed to please him.

"White folks ever bother you?"

"I wouldn't let 'em," she said defiantly.

He felt slapped. Even Tyree knuckled under to whites, and here was a slip of a defenseless girl boasting that she would not let them touch her. Was that her sly way of bragging about her white skin? Didn't she care about what other black folks suffered? Or was she pretending she never got angry? Perhaps she did not have enough imagination to grasp what it all really meant?

"I could *kill* them bastards!" he spat.

"Aw, they just crazy, mixed-up kids," she mumbled calmly.

"Crazy hell," he said. "That craziness gits folks killed!"

"They don't know what they doing." Irritation was in her voice.

"The hell they don't!" he contradicted her.

"Honey, let's don't talk *race*," Gladys begged. "It's so wonderful out . . ."

Fishbelly's sky darkened. She defended white people! Maybe she thinks she's *white!* Well, she sure *looked* white. Maybe she came often to this part of town? She could walk these streets among white people as much as she liked and nobody in the Black Belt would be the wiser. Hell, maybe she had customers among white men! He had never before considered that possibility and it fanned his rising hate of her color. He loved her because she was whitish, and yet he was now feeling that her whiteness was eluding him even though she sat there in the car beside him, even though she was willing to let him hold her in his arms tonight.

"You ever pass, Gladys?" he asked with soft suddenness. It took her so long to answer that he thought that she had not heard. "Tell me," he urged her; there was an edge in his voice now. "You ever pass?"

"Well," Gladys began, still looking ahead, her silky hair blowing behind her in the hot wind, "not for *real,* anyhow."

He hated her so much at that moment that he could have grabbed a handful of her diaphanous hair and flung her from the car. He saw her delicately tapering white fingers lift wisps of flowing hair and toss them from her eyes. He could almost feel the crown of hair on his head, hair that had been straightened, and he was ashamed of it. Bet she sure loves that damned hair of hers, he growled silently to himself.

"What you mean, 'Not for real'?" he imitated her with a jeer.

"I never pass 'cause I want to," she explained. "When I go to a department store to buy something, they treat me white and I *let* 'em. It's too much trouble to start explaining. . . . You know."

"I don't know," he said.

"Aw, Fish!"

"You don't tell 'em you white, but you don't tell you black either, hunh?" He was trying to hurt her.

"Fish, try to understand. It's just easy for me that way, that's all. If they don't *know* I'm colored, they take me for white," she spoke reluctantly.

"But do you *tell* 'em you colored?" he insisted.

Her cheeks blazed red with anger.

"What you want me to do? Carry a sign saying: I'M COL-ORED?"

"Skip it," he muttered.

"What's the matter, honey?"

"I said skip it," he snapped.

"Don't be mad at me, Fish."

"I ain't mad." Her pleading tone had mollified him a bit.

"When they know I ain't white they treat me just like they do you," she said.

"Not the *men*," he could not help but say.

"Naw," she admitted. "The men insult me on the street." She spoke without anger, her eyes pensive.

The traffic thickened and Fishbelly braked and found himself in a double lane surrounded by cars in which white people sat. He was alongside a big black Buick and saw a white family inside staring at him and Gladys.

"Look at me till your eyes rot," he muttered.

"Aw, Fish, forget 'em."

The car ahead of him advanced and he rolled forward and stopped alongside a white man in a Ford. The man's head poked inquisitively out of the window and for a split second Fishbelly could see, like an image in a half-forgotten dream, the picture of a white man's blood-streaked face pinned beneath that overturned Oldsmobile in the woods on that far-off summer day and he stared hard and unblinkingly back at the white man in the Ford while the image dissolved.

"Where you-all from?" the white man asked bluntly.

"China!" Fishbelly flung at him contemptuously and pulled swiftly ahead, leaving the man staring.

"Good for you!" Gladys yelled, laughing.

Goddamn . . . What the hell was there to laugh about? Didn't she know that the white man had been trying to find out if he had the right to interfere, to raise a mob against him? Didn't she know that black men were killed for riding in cars, side by side with women of her color? Or did she regard it all as a child's game? It was plain that he would have to educate her, tell her what the racial score was. They were cruising now on the outskirts of town, driving past wealthy white homes set amid green lawns.

"Let's git a drink at Henry's," he suggested.

"Okay," Gladys said.

Henry's was the main Black-Belt bar, but it was almost empty at that hour of the afternoon. They took a table in a corner. He sat looking at her. He was planning to take over this woman completely, but he would have to get her straightened out about many things; he would have to pry into her and find out how she really felt about black people and white people. Didn't she know how he felt? Couldn't she guess? Or did she know and didn't respect it?

"Gladys, what do you think of white folks?"

"What you mean, Fish?"

"I asked you a question—"

"Fish, they just *white*," she answered earnestly.

He realized in a flash that, though black of skin, he was really much whiter mentally than she was or ever could be, though she was whiter of skin than he. Gladys did not possess enough imagination to see herself or the life she lived in terms that white people saw black people, terms which he had experienced at their hands, terms which he *knew*. Fishbelly hotly rejected the terms in which white people weighed or saw him, for those terms made him feel agonizingly inferior; then, in his reacting against his sense of inferiority, he had to try to be like them in order to prove to himself and to them that he was not inferior. Yet, in his trying to be like them he was trapping himself; he had to admit his inferiority of situation, accept it before he could rise above it. And he was astounded that Gladys could feel or sense none of this. In a certain way she was mentally much *blacker* than he was, though she looked *white!* He stared dreamily out of the door of the bar, hearing firecrackers popping in the streets, seeing an American flag billowing lazily in the hot breeze.

"Ever had any trouble with white folks?" he asked her.

"Naw," she said. "What you worrying about, Fish?"

He gaped. Her whole life was and had been a big, nasty trouble from white folks and she was calmly denying it. She was a half-white bastard whore who had given birth to a half-white bastard girl child who was most likely destined to grow up and give birth to yet another half-white bastard girl child who would grow up to be a whore, yet she had never had any trouble from white folks. Maybe Gladys did not know what trouble was? Maybe what had happened to her appeared merely normally unfortunate? Suddenly he realized that she had already told him the truth: *she agreed with the whites!* They were right and she was wrong! An accident had anchored her on the wrong side of the racial fence and she had merely sighed and accepted it, as though someday another accident would redress the mishap and make up for all the inconvenience. In her daily life Gladys could, in a limited sense, be either white or black; and, because she could be white sometimes, she felt that it was right for the streets in the white areas to be clean, and, because the streets in the white areas were clean, the whites were, therefore right. They had money and the say-so and that was proof of their rightness.

"You think they treat us *right?*" he asked sipping his whiskey.

"Fish, stop worrying about *them,* " she said. "Look, you got a car. You got money. You wear better clothes than them poor white-trash white boys who hollered at me in front of the drugstore—"

"You think it's money and that's *all?*" he asked.

"Money's a lot," she said.

"My Papa's got money and he acts and lives like a nigger—"

"Don't talk like that about your papa," she reproved him.

"It's the truth," he insisted. "Do they *treat* us right?"

"In what *way*, Fish?" she asked with pleading eyes.

"Hell, Gladys, can't you *see?* We go to black schools and their schools are better'n ours—"

"Oh, that?" she asked softly, simply.

"Yeah, *that,*" he said scornfully, realizing that her mind was incapable of comprehending the elementary complexity of it all. "And they *kill* us too," he added bitterly.

"But who's talking about killing anybody?" she asked, offended.

"They killed Chris—"

"Oh!" She stared at him hard. "You talked about him once," she said wonderingly. "Was he kin to you or something?"

Anger rendered him speechless. She was hopeless. Yet he loved her. He wanted to be with her. Was it her racial innocence that made him love her? Was it because she was a shadowy compromise that was white and not white? Was it because she looked white and had to live in the Black Belt with him? He stared deep into the amber fluid in his glass and tried to think of life and race in the terms that Gladys felt them. If the black man that the white people killed was your father or brother, then they were bothering you, but if they killed a black stranger, then it was none of your goddamn business. . . . Yeah, poor little Gladys was just a woman and didn't know. He would take this woman and teach her.

"Gladys," he whispered.

"Yeah, baby. Don't worry—"

"I got something real serious to tell you."

"Hunh huh."

He relished the power he had over her; he could tell from the manner in which she had responded that she had no notion of what he was about to reveal.

"Sweetheart, I'm taking you out of that Grove," he told her.

The idea was so alien, unexpected, that it took time to sink home. Then her head shot up and her petulant lips parted in astonishment.

"What you mean, Fish?"

"I got a three-room flat for you over—"

"Fish!" Her eyes were round, moist circles of brown. "Really?"

"Yeah. It's on Bowman Street."

"Fish, you fooling?" she asked in a tremulous whisper.

"Baby, I mean it."

Her lips moved soundlessly, as though she were afraid to speak.

"Fish, you really want me?" she asked incredulously.

"Goddammit, I do."

Her white hands flew across the table and seized hold of him, tightly, spasmodically.

"And your folks, Fish?"

"Mama won't know. But it's okay with Papa. Anything I do is okay with 'im if I don't make no trouble."

"I won't make no trouble, Fish. I swear. I'll obey you!"

A string of firecrackers popped outside like a machine gun and Gladys flinched and leaned hard against him.

"I want you to stay home and be *true* to me," he warned.

Tears flooded her eyes; she flung herself into his arms.

"I'll do anything you say."

"I won't be able to be there all the time."

"I'll wait for you, Fish," she gasped. "I never thought you wanted me that much. . . . I didn't think this could happen to me. . . ." She stared at him through tears, smiling sadly, reluctantly. "I'll cook for you. I can sew. Git me a sewing machine, hunh?" She did not wait for an answer; she moved nervously in her chair. "Darling, I want to ask you something . . ."

"Sure."

"Can I bring my baby there?"

"Hell, it's your place and—"

"Aw, Fish!" she wailed. She clutched him. "Fish, tell me

something," she said in a rush of words. "You—" Her voice
choked off in a sob.

"What's the matter, honey?"

She closed her eyes before she spoke.

"You won't never hold what I was against me?"

He pressed her close to him.

"The past is past," he said. "From now, it's *all* past."

She opened her eyes and stared at him—eyes that were
begging redemption, salvation.

"Fish, I'm older'n you. I ain't asking to marry—"

"Papa wouldn't let me marry nohow. And I ain't ready for
that," he told her frankly but tenderly.

"Why d-didn't you t-tell me b-before?" she asked in gasps.

"I didn't know if I could work it out," he told her. "Now,
Gladys, you free to do what I ask?"

"I'm *free!* I'm yours and nobody else's; I'm yours for as long
as you want me," she swore.

"Okay. I'm sending a truck for your things in the morning."

"Yeah. Anything you say, Fish."

She threw back her head and looked off, then swabbed her
wet eyes with a balled handkerchief. He had never before
seen a woman in the throes of redemption, had never before
witnessed the light in the face of a woman whose destiny had
been changed in the twinkling of an eye. He saw lines of
tension about her mouth already leaving. Then fear showed
in her eyes.

"Fish, you wouldn't fool me about something like this?"

"Naw! Naw!"

"If you fooling me, I swear I'll just lay down and die. . . ."

"I'm keeping you. That Grove's finished."

She grabbed him again and wept. Then she asked slyly:

"Take me to the Grove for the last time. I want to dance.
Then I'm taking you home with me, for keeps!"

"Sure thing."

He paid and they left. Dusk was falling when they neared

the Grove and, as they turned into the dirt road leading to
it, they smelled the cloying scent of magnolias and heard hot
jazz filling the gloam.

"I want to dance!" Gladys yelled excitedly.

He parked the car and they ran inside and slid rhythmically onto the dance floor, swaying and dipping to the music's
beat.

"I'm dreaming," Gladys whispered.

"You a dream," he said. "A dream in the daytime."

"Nobody'll never know how happy I am tonight," she
sighed.

They danced a second time. The Grove was hot, like a
steam bath. Eyes closed, the black musicians played furiously, shaking their sweaty faces.

"Look at them cats," Gladys said. "They really sent,
hunh?"

"They gone," he said.

Outside, detonations blasted the summer night. Fishbelly
was tired.

"Say, let's git some air," he said. "I can't breathe in here."

"If you want to," she said.

He felt her vibrant body bouncing alongside his as they
went outside where a faint breeze blew. They found a grassy
spot beneath an elm tree and sat and looked at a sky burning
with huge yellow stars.

"Darling, lissen . . . If I'm moving tomorrow, I ought to tell
Fats right now. He's a mean thing and losing me might make
'im mad if I wait till the last minute, see? Fats been in jail a
lot and he's got some evil ways about 'im."

"Sure enough? Didn't know Fats was ever a jailbird."

"He's been in four or five times," Gladys said.

"No wonder he can run this outfit," Fishbelly mused.
"Okay. Tell 'im. I'll be here, waiting for you."

He rose and pulled her to her feet. She kissed him with a
new kiss, a kiss that had no reserves. Then she pulled away.

"Fish, you sweet, I can't *believe* it!"

She ran like a shadow across the darkened fields and vanished into the rear door of the Grove. Fishbelly could see golden lights gleaming through the wooden beams and the thick-hanging moss suspended from the tin roof. Thunderous jazz rocked hypnotically. He sat and lit a cigarette. He was tired, but things were going his way. He had done it; he would be with Gladys. It was not for always, but it was enough; it was what he wanted. And he would talk to Gladys, change her, make her understand what it was like to live day and night under that white shadow.

A month's drudgery had depleted him and his nerves tingled as his fatigue ebbed. He stretched out upon the grass and eddied smoke through his nostrils. Far off, a firecracker exploded. Next came a soft, swishing sound that echoed eerily. "Fourth of July," he muttered. "Somebody shooting off a rocket." Then he was staring at a strange, faint radiance in the sky above him; it was as though a full moon had burst from behind a dark bank of clouds. He looked wonderingly at the sheen while a vague disturbance moved in him. He cocked his head, hearing a confusion of dim, incomprehensible voices. He thought he heard a muffled scream, but he was not sure. He frowned, turned his head, and saw the Grove glowing white inside. The music had stopped at some moment in the immediate past, a moment that he could not remember. The wind wafted him a whiff of smoke. Yes, it was that bright light in the Grove that had cast that funny sheen upon the sky. A medley of slurred speech reached his ears. What's happening? Oh yes; they had turned on those powerful spotlights that they used when some member of the band was playing a wicked solo. But, naw! *There was no music!* He stood abruptly, peering intently at the dance hall. He took an involuntary step forward and stood still. A soft, greenish halo suddenly enveloped the moss-covered building, a halo that turned quickly blue and deepened. He was hearing piercing screams now and the bluish light became a radiant sea of orange-colored flames roiling upward toward the sky.

"Some fool nigger's done started a fire!" he spoke aloud.

He was running wildly toward the Grove before he knew it. A mountain of billowing smoke gushed up and out of the dance hall from all sides, then a sheet of red flame erupted and where the Grove had stood was now an immense column of leaping fire, filling the world, roaring whirlwind-like, casting up surging floods of sparks.

"Gawd, it's on fire!" he panted, galloping forward.

He sprinted to the Grove's back door, through which Gladys had vanished. He stopped, gaping. The door was open, but jammed with human bodies, piled one atop the other. Their faces were distorted and their mouths were open. But they were making no sounds. He felt enclosed in a nightmare. Behind the bodies were solid walls of flying flame.

"Gladys! Gladys!" he screamed.

Hellish heat hit his face. Save for crackling, licking fire, all was profoundly quiet. There had been screams, but now not one voice came from the interior of the raging dance hall. The black faces stuffed in the doorway seemed to be gasping for breath. The heat was increasing so rapidly that he had to back off. He could not react to what he saw; it was not true ... But it *was* ... The blinding glare of hurling flames gouged at his eyes.

"Gladys!" he screamed, then waited, his body shaking.

Oh Gawd, she *couldn't* be in there! He grew aware of dark forms of people milling slowly, aimlessly about and he heard a babble of distraught voices. He turned, looking; people walked as though in their sleep, dazed. He spied one of the Grove's bartenders, Clarence; he ran to him and grabbed him, feeling waving flames lashing hotly at his back.

"Clarence, you seen Gladys?" he asked in a tense whisper.

"Hunh?" Clarence grunted. "I just got out myself ... I feel dizzy. My head. Say, you got a match?"

Clarence's request rattled Fishbelly. Automatically he fumbled in his pockets, found a folder of matches, struck one, and held the flame to Clarence's cigarette and watched the man suck greedily, his black face lit by boiling lava and rolling fire.

"Thanks," Clarence mumbled, moving off unaware, it seemed, that twisting flames were leaping twenty feet from him.

Then, with a sense of shock, Fishbelly realized that the dance hall was burning and that he did not know where Gladys was. He felt snared in a net of shadows. What had happened? He wanted to perform a mental act and annul the fire and live again in a normal world. But, no . . . Again he ran to the doorway; behind the heaped-up bodies was a background of banks of glowing, white fire. Jesus . . . *Naw!*

He dashed madly, circling the blazing, smoking inferno, wondering why no sounds were coming from it, and rushed to within twenty feet of the front door. It, too, was heaped with bodies, some of which had most of their clothes torn from them. It was clear that they had been trying to get out, had grappled and trampled one another. The searing heat would not let him approach the door. He was frantic. Gladys was in there and he had to go in and get her out! But how? The dance hall had two doors and he had been to both of them and they were blocked with inert bodies. He looked about desperately. Yes; high up in the back wall was a small opening for ventilation; he recalled it now. He raced breathlessly to the rear again and stared up; the opening was white hot with seething jets of leaping fire.

He glared about at the survivors. They were whimpering, their stunned, unblinking eyes staring at the flaming building. A crying black girl was threading her way through the crowd, calling:

"Where's Bob? Oh Gawd! Bob! Didn't he git out?"

Fishbelly saw Teddy arrive, stop, stare, then yell:

"Susie's in there!"

Oh Gawd . . . Susie was Teddy's sister. Teddy tried to rush

toward the roaring building and several men caught him and held him.

"You can't go in there, you fool! You'll git—"

"I got to git Susie!" Teddy screamed, breaking loose and running toward the back door.

A huge black man stepped in front of the sprinting Teddy and clipped him on the jaw.

"Take that fool away! He'll burn in there. . . ."

Fishbelly watched a group of men drag the hysterical Teddy off, fling him to the ground, and hold him as he screamed and moaned.

A brown girl whom Fishbelly knew as Cecile came limping, her dress half torn off her.

"Cecile!" Fishbelly called to her.

The girl did not answer; she stared at him blankly, then wandered off, dragging her right leg. He followed her, grabbed her and yelled:

"You see Gladys in there?"

"I just got out . . . Oh Gawd, my leg . . ." Cecile looked at Fishbelly and blinked. "Aw, yeah . . . I saw Gladys . . ." Her voice died away.

He moaned, feeling his knees buckling. *Gladys lost?* That could not be. . . . Again he raced around the dance hall, seeing dazed figures wandering about. He began to hear acutely; it was as though until now the shock of the fire had rendered him deaf. The fire was mountainous, circling, spiraling upward in humming whiplashes of flame.

"It's on fire!"

"They all still *in* there!"

"Lawd, somebody *do* something!" an old woman called.

"Git the fire engines!" a man called.

"What happened?" Fishbelly asked the man.

"A fire broke out like *that*," the man answered, clapping his hands. "They *in* there, they *in* there . . ."

Fishbelly groaned, not wanting to believe it. He felt like screaming. Gladys gone? NAW! A hand came upon his shoulder and he turned. It was Buck, one of the doormen who had been on night duty.

"Fish, my Gawd, they all in there!" Buck wailed. *"All* of 'em!"

"You seen Gladys?" Fishbelly asked him.

"It was that damned moss," Buck keened. "It went up like lightning—"

"You seen Gladys?" Fishbelly screamed at him.

"Hunh? Naw . . . I don't know," Buck mumbled, confused.

For minutes the suddenness of the fire stunned the survivors, but more people were beginning to scream now. Fishbelly stood in a stooped, mute posture before the roaring blaze, feeling lancing waves of heat cutting into his body and forcing him farther and farther back. Entering that furnace was out of the question; one could not advance into it for six feet without being charred. Tall red flames shot up, trembling and shaking against the black sky, blotting out the stars, raining sparks far and wide.

For the second time Fishbelly felt that he was dreaming and would awaken to find the Grove as it had always been. An explosion sounded deep in the heart of the flames; some beams began falling inward and the heat became blistering, driving him farther back. At the very tiptop of the fire a tongue of flame detached itself and floated red and gleaming, a curving roll of sharp fire slicing like a pulsing scythe into the black trees.

Timber cracked and popped. The fire sang, seeming to create a wind of its own that whipped across his tightened, hot face. The night was filled with screams now. A man came running and, in the glare, his face was like a glistening black mask; the man shouted:

"Let's knock a wall down! It ain't too late! Let's git a pole!"

"What pole?" Fishbelly asked, eager but bewildered.

"Did somebody go for the fire engines?" a man asked.

"Look, I got a car. Who'll go?" Fishbelly asked.

"I'll go, Fish," Buck volunteered.

Fishbelly tossed his car keys to Buck and pointed to the jalopy.

"Go, man!"

Buck ran toward the car.

A man heaved in sight, pulling a long, heavy pole, his mouth gaping from effort, his teeth gleaming in the fire's glare.

"Let's try and knock a wall down!" he called.

Fishbelly joined several men who took hold of the pole and backing off a few feet, ran forward, jamming it ramrod-like into the outer, flimsy beams. Smoke almost blinded them. The second attempt made them choke and bend double, stagger back from blasts of heat, their eyes streaming tears. Fishbelly saw that one man's eyebrows had singed off and he noticed red sparks smoldering in another man's kinky hair. They made a last attempt with the pole, but were driven off by baleful tides of heat, stumbling, coughing. A wind current blew the total heat of the fire into their midst; they froze in their tracks, shivering, gasping, speechless. The men dropped the pole and backed creepingly off. The dance hall spluttered like a giant, glowing torch.

From directly behind Fishbelly came a terrifying scream; he turned and saw an old woman, her hands lifted, her knees bent, screaming without stopping; her eyes, glistening in the glaze of the flames, stared at the fire-ravaged building and the tears on her shriveled cheeks glittered like rubies.

"Some of her folks must be in there," Fishbelly muttered, moved.

"It's that damned moss," a man was whimpering.

"How many folks in there?" Fishbelly asked.

"A heap of 'em. Only some got out. They jammed the doors and blocked the others, trapping 'em," the man explained. "I lost my horn . . ."

He was one of the musicians and he looked with dull, bloodshot eyes at the choiring flames.

"What can we do?" Fishbelly screamed.

Out of the red dark Maybelle loomed, running toward him; she passed him as though she had not seen him. He took out after her, yelling:

"Maybelle! Where Gladys? Maybelle, stop! Where Gladys?"

He caught up with her and spun her around. She stared at him with wide, scared eyes.

"Where Gladys?"

"Hunh?" she answered, blinking.

"Gladys . . . Ain't you *seen* her?" he asked, coughing, feeling strangled by smoke.

Maybelle shook her head, her black skin gleaming like polished metal.

"Naw. I was home—"

"Gladys home?"

"I don't know," Maybelle mumbled, disorientated.

Aw Gawd maybe Gladys was home! Fishbelly circled the gutting flames to escape the sizzling heat, seeing flowery clusters of red sparks showering in the night, and found the path leading to Gladys's house. He dashed down it, looking disbelievingly back every second at a fire so ferocious that no one could get near it. He followed a curve in the path, leaving the sight of the conflagration, imagining Gladys as he wanted to see her, that is, at home in her bedroom, powdering her face. He came to her front door and rattled the knob violently. It was locked.

"Gladys! Gladys! Gladys!" he screamed and pounded his fists against the door.

There was no response. He gritted his teeth, wondering if he were wasting time. Maybe there was something back there that he could do where the flames were leaping? Then he backed off a few steps and hurled himself against the door. There was a splintering of wood, but the door held. He crashed himself a second time against it and it sagged in and collapsed flat. He entered, fumbling for the light switch.

"Gladys!" his voice echoed through the house.

A repugnant possibility shocked him. What if she had come here to turn a fast trick? As revolting as the idea was, he wished it were true. He lumbered from room to room, clicking on lights; he came to the kitchen and found it empty. Good Gawd! One moment there had been peace and hope, then fire and tragedy. Reeling, he went back through the house and stood upon the front porch and saw rising red flames turning night into day. Screams, honking auto horns, and racing motors sounded far and near. He recalled Gladys's going into the dance hall to talk to Fats. . . . *That's it!* Find Fats! He loped again to the scene of the fire. The crowd had grown vast, but it was an awed, quiet crowd.

He saw Maybelle again; this time she was calm.

"It was that moss, Fish," she said tearfully. "Them fire folks had warned 'em a heap of times—"

"Maybelle, think . . . You seen Gladys?"

"I don't know. Not tonight, Fish," she said. "I took a man to my house and left 'em dancing. I heard Fats say there must've been a hundred in there. Looks like about fifty got out. The rest was trapped. . . ."

"You seen Fats?"

"Last time I saw Fats he was in there," Maybelle told him.

"Oh Gawd! Poor Gladys," he sobbed, squeezing his eyelids shut.

"LOOK!" Maybelle screamed, grabbing him and pointing.

"What?" Fishbelly opened his eyes and followed the line of her arm.

"LOOK AT THEIR HANDS!" she screamed, still pointing.

He saw what she saw. In the upper part of the fire-filled building the moss had burned away and, extending through the wide-spaced two-by-fours, were black hands and legs.

"They *moving;* they ain't *dead,*" Maybelle whispered.

He stared; the shadows cast by the waving flames gave the illusion that the hands and legs were in motion. He edged closer. Naw . . . Those hands and legs had been thrust through the spaces between the beams by those who had tried desperately to get out. . . . Fishbelly clasped his hands before him, feeling that he was looking at Gladys's dead body.

Fire roared unabated, the throb of its heat beating upon his eardrums, drying the sweat on his face. There sounded a series of dull explosions in the lower portion of the fire and, presently, a strong, suffocating stench of alcoholic steam filled the air.

"That's them beer barrels cracking open!" a man called out.

Fishbelly felt a nervously trembling hand came upon his arm; he looked around; it was a stout black woman who was unaware that she was clutching him. He held still for a moment, then gently disengaged his arm from her hysterical grip and walked off a few feet, leaving the woman with her hand uplifted, the fingers moving imploringly in emptiness, her bulging eyes glassily reflecting the churning flames.

From the distance came the wail of fire engine sirens, but he knew that the firemen would be too late. What baffled him had been the awful silence of the people in the dance hall; in the beginning there had been a few screams, but they had died away strangely. More cars sped up, their wheels skidding in the dust of the road, their yellow lances of light stabbing the darkness.

"Gladys," Fishbelly wailed for the last time, then was gripped by shivering despair.

The full sense of the tragedy had now sunk home to the people and there was uncontrollable weeping and moaning calls toward the white-hot building. The sirens were closer. Fishbelly wanted to act, to smash something and end this nightmare.

He saw his jalopy roll up and Buck leap out.

"They coming," Buck said. "Any folks git out?"

"Naw . . . Buck, stop and think . . . *Did you see Gladys?*"

"Man, Fats told me to git some ice. I went and got a bucketful and was coming back when I seen the fire and I run like hell—"

"Did you see Gladys come *out?*"

"Fish, I didn't see her."

Though the heat of the flames singed his face, he felt like a lump of ice. He glanced down at himself and saw that his coat was ripped; the backs of his hands were skinned and blistered. Pain throbbed in his left leg.

"It's dying down a little," a man called.

The flames and the smoke were abating, but the tin roof was an incandescent lake shimmering in the night. Fire engines screamed up, their sirens blasting the air, their headlights slicing the dark. Braking wheels lifted clouds of clay dust, palling the trees. White firemen leaped from trucks and Fishbelly saw them working frantically with their hoses.

"Jesus Christ!" one exclaimed.

"It's already *gone!*" another said.

Fishbelly watched the firemen unlimber a hose and a gleaming stream of water shot up, made an arc, and hit the molten tin roof; there was a furious sizzling and hissing as the water bounced from the glowing roof; spraying hot showers of rain into the dazed crowd.

"Git the folks back!" a fireman yelled.

"Anybody in there?" a tall white fireman asked.

"A lot of folks, young folks," a black man breathed.

"Good God!" the fireman said.

Somebody grabbed Fishbelly's arm and spun him around. It was Zeke.

"Zeke!" he screamed.

"Jesus, man!" Zeke said, staring at him. "I was scared for you. You seen Beth?"

"Naw. Ain't she with *you?*"

"Naw. Oh Gawd."

"And Gladys? You seen her?"

"Naw. Was she in there?"

"Zeke, she went in five minutes 'fore it started," Fishbelly moaned. "Goddamn . . ." He recovered himself. "Tony and Sam?"

"They on their way here. We had to meet our gals here . . ."

They stared at each other, unable to speak. Zeke turned and walked off, his mouth twisting.

The water of the fire hoses pounded the hot tin roof, hissing, bubbling, sending bright columns of fog high into the night while a scalding drizzle floated down. The dirt road leading to the Grove was choked with whites and Negroes thronging forward. Then came the high-pitched wail of another siren, different from the others.

"That's the fire chief," somebody said.

A small red car skidded, halted, and a big-boned white man with white hair leaped out and stood.

"Hold it!" the fire chief shouted.

The white streams of turgid water slackened, dribbling away.

"How long has it been going?" the fire chief demanded.

"Only a few minutes, Chief. But it's lost," a fireman answered.

"Were there many in there?" the fire chief asked.

"The doors are blocked with 'em. And there're plenty inside."

"What happened?" the fire chief asked.

"That moss blazed up and nobody could get near it," a fireman explained.

"I warned those niggers about those violations," the chief muttered. He lifted his voice. "Okay! Let the water go and get these people back!"

Ten streams of water now thundered against the roof, boiling, jutting upward.

"Whoever's in there is sure gone now," the fire chief said, shaking his head. "If they weren't burned, they're smothered."

A fireman went to the chief and reported:

"Chief, it must've happened *quick*. . . . That moss burned like wildfire. All the air was cut off and the smoke did the rest.

The people in there were asphyxiated in two minutes flat."

"What a freak of a fire," the fire chief muttered, taking off his hat.

Fishbelly turned away. Minutes later he found himself wandering along a dirt road, crying: "Gladys . . . Why did I let her go in there?" He tramped doggedly back to the fire, seeing drifting clouds of steam through his tears. The police were arriving now, their sirens filling the night, drowning out the shouts and screams of the firemen and the crowd. More cars came, emptying out men and women, black and white, who rushed to the perimeter of the dance hall that was now one solid mass of baleful heat. Water dripped; steam shrouded the trees; then Fishbelly smelled a curious odor that drowned out the scent of magnolias, that overcame the stench of evaporating beer, and made even the acrid sting of the smoke unimportant.

"Jesus, I know that smell," a fireman said. "They ain't burning they're *cooking!*"

Fishbelly felt like vomiting; he could no longer stand upon his feet. He got into his jalopy and laid his face flat against the steering wheel and stared at the streams of shooting water. He caught snatches of conversation:

". . . they say most of 'em were smothered . . ."

". . . how many were in there? . . ."

". . . somebody said about fifty . . ."

"All niggers?"

". . . all niggers, nothing but niggers . . ."

". . . some Fourth of July . . ."

". . . whoever heard of covering a dance hall with *moss?*"

". . . who owns the place? . . ."

". . . some nigger doctor called Bruce or something . . ."

". . . it's dying down now; the firemen are gitting close to the front door . . ."

Fishbelly went back to the shell of a dance hall, whose interior still seethed with fire. As the heat died down, people edged closer, shielding their faces from the heat with their hands, peering, murmuring, pointing to the tangled and charred bodies cramming the doorway. Firemen were trying to dislodge the bodies while streams of water hurtled above their heads.

"Give us a hand here, will you?" a white fireman called.

Several black men rushed forward and tugged at the bodies, pulling them free and stretching them out upon the grass. Fishbelly saw a woman's arm partially dissolved, the flesh failing to adhere to the bones. He shuddered. Firemen were crowding into the front doorway now, sending streams of water before them. Fishbelly tried to enter to search for Gladys, but a white fireman pushed him back, bawling:

"Keep out, nigger! Too much smoke!"

He gave up. He saw the chief of the fire department and went and stood discreetly near him. A fireman staggered out of the front door, his face red, his eyes streaming tears, coughing.

"What's up, Bob?" the chief demanded.

"There're forty-two bodies in there," the fireman said.

"Naw!" the chief exclaimed.

"Yessir. Most of 'em are asphyxiated . . . Only a few burned. The fire raged all around 'em and above 'em, Chief. Strange thing. It was that damned moss, dry as hell. . . . It cut off all the air."

"By God, somebody's going to pay for this," the chief growled.

Crowds swarmed over the fields amid smoke and steam, looking at the smoldering ruins, walking timidly among bodies sprawled upon the grass. As the flames waned, the firemen mounted spotlights whose beams enabled them to continue working. Then Maybelle was at Fishbelly's side, calling:

"Fish! They just found Fats. He's over in the woods."

"In the woods? He dead?"

"Naw. But he's mighty bad hurt. Come on."

Hope leaped into him. Maybe Gladys was somewhere too, living. . . . He followed Maybelle into a patch of woods to the left of the Grove. A knot of people stood about a prone figure. It was Fats, breathing heavily, writhing in pain.

"Fats," Fishbelly called softly.

"Hi, Fish," Fats breathed.

"How you feeling?"

"Kind of bad."

"You seen Gladys?"

Fats shook his head. Fishbelly knelt beside him.

"Was she *in* there?" he asked Fats.

"S-she said she wanted to s-see me about something . . . Told her to w-wait . . . Heard the phone ringing and w-went to answer it . . . First thing I know the p-place's on fire . . . Fire everywhere . . . Broke a p-plank under the s-steps . . . Crawled through . . . S-started running . . . I fell . . . Too w-weak . . . Passed out . . ." Fats's whispers died away.

He had now spoken to the last person who had seen Gladys alive; there was no hope. He watched them place Fats upon a stretcher and bear him toward an ambulance, then he stumbled along, half conscious, his lackluster eyes staring vacantly; he was seeing again that dim photo of that smiling white woman that he had choked down his throat that day in the police car. Gladys had been a living white-and-black fantasy and she had gone up in smoke; he had felt that she could have redeemed everything for him and now she had vanished. Yet he was already following her in his future seekings.

Maybelle came running to him, her black face tight with anger.

"Now, this is a bitch!" she cried through her tears. "That white doctor says Fats needs a blood transfusion, and needs it quick! Now, there's a goddamn *white* hospital about half a mile from here, but they got to take Fats *ten* miles to a black hospital! That's a real bitchy thing! Goddam these white folks!"

Fishbelly was dismayed that Fats could not get prompt medical treatment, but he was too grief-stricken to respond properly. Gladys still haunted him; he walked at random among the crowds, unable to give her up. Aw, maybe she was lying suffering somewhere in the woods like Fats had lain? He re-entered the woods. Then he was still. Ahead of him was a familiar figure. He went toward it.

"Fish!" the figure called.

It was Dr. Bruce.

"Doc!" he exclaimed. "You here?"

"Sh," Dr. Bruce cautioned him.

The doctor's face was ashen, wet, and blotched. Why was he dodging here in the woods when he was needed?

"What the matter, Doc?"

"I don't want anybody to see me here," Dr. Bruce said, his arm shaking. "Fish, how many people died in that fire?"

"Somebody told the fire chief there was forty-two—"

"Naw! Good God!" Dr. Bruce exclaimed and staggered. He caught hold of a tree; his body shook.

The doctor took a bottle out of his pocket and emptied a fistful of white pellets into a trembling palm and lifted that palm toward his mouth. Fishbelly leaped instinctively forward and slapped the doctor's hand, knocking the bottle and scattering its contents to the ground.

"Don't do that, Doc!" Fishbelly cried.

"You don't understand!" Dr. Bruce wailed. "I'm *responsible* for those people, Fish!"

"Wasn't your fault." Fishbelly comforted the doctor by putting his arm about his shoulders. "Don't take it that way, Doc."

The doctor grew gradually calm.

"I d-don't kn-know," the doctor said. "Where's Fats?"

"He hurt. They took 'im to the hospital—"

"Have you seen Tyree?" the doctor asked.

"Nawsir . . . Doc, I lost my gal in that fire . . ." he wept.

"Take it easy, Fish." Fishbelly's state brought the doctor back to his professional attitude. He stopped and retrieved the bottle.

"Naw, Doc!" Fishbelly protested through his tears.

The doctor shook out two pellets and tossed the bottle away.

"Take one; it won't hurt you," the doctor said, handing Fishbelly a pellet. "I'm taking one too."

"W-what they for, Doc?"

"It'll calm you," the doctor said, inserting a pellet into his mouth and swallowing.

Hesitantly, Fishbelly swallowed a pellet.

"Fish, I got to see Tyree. Is he at his office?"

"Don't know. Mebbe Papa's there."

Dr. Bruce left, weaving unsteadily among the dark trees. Fishbelly watched him until he was lost from view.

"Gawd, poor Doc's scared to death about them folks dying in that fire," Fishbelly mumbled to himself.

He returned to the scene of the fire and met Buck.

"Aw, Fish," Buck said, clutching his arm. "They found Gladys,"

"Where?"

"She laid out on the grass—"

"Naw! Naw!"

The worst had been confirmed. That sadly smiling white face had been swallowed up in flames. Then he felt suddenly calm; it must have been the pellet that he had taken. He followed Buck, stepping over corpses, and then he was standing above her, looking down into her face. Her posture made her look as though she were sleeping; her lips were slightly parted, with just the ghost of a petulant smile on them. The only disfiguring mark was a tiny cut on the left side of her chin. She seemed about to speak, except that her brown eyes were opened and filmed. "Naw, she'll never speak again . . ."

He whimpered and turned away, stumbling toward the road in the dark. He passed Beth; she was lying on her back, her head swollen to twice its normal size. "Poor Zeke," he whispered. "Good thing he's going to the Army . . ."

He had loved Gladys and in one night he had won her and

lost her. The tension in him suddenly gave way; yes, it was that pill that Dr. Bruce had given him, for his mind was as clear as a bell. He gazed calmly over the wide litter of dead bodies and he smelled the odor of death: "cooked niggers..." He looked at the staring and murmuring white men and women, his mind now anchored in the logic of the workaday world. These bodies had to be buried and burying people was his father's profession. He saw the chief of police, the man to whom Tyree paid bribes each week. Yeah, that was the man to talk to. He approached the chief of police and confronted him.

"Chief," he addressed him softly.

"Yeah, boy. What do you want?"

"I'm Fish, sir. Tyree's son."

"Fish Tucker, hunh? Well, you look like your father. Where is he?"

"Don't know, sir."

"He'd better look into this mess," the chief of police said.

"Chief, where they taking these bodies?"

"Don't know. Our morgue's not big enough for all these niggers."

"Well, sir, there's our high-school gym—"

"By God, you're right."

"It's got running water and everything—"

"Yeah?"

"We can lay out everybody there for identification—"

"Yeeah?"

"And there's them rub-down tables that we can use for embalming. And right above 'em is a lot of pegs for clothes; we can use 'em for hanging gravity bottles. I heard somebody say there was about forty-two bodies. . . . Takes about two hours to fix up a body. That's eighty-four hours of work, if we git at it night and day. . . . In all this heat, we ought to start on 'em tonight, sir."

"That's right," the chief of police muttered, speaking through his teeth and rocking on his heels, looking at Fishbelly with unblinking eyes.

"You know Papa and if you just tell the coroner to give us the death certificates, we'll handle 'em all."

"You would, hunh?"

"Yessir," Fishbelly assured him.

The chief of police turned and yelled:

"Say, Dupree!"

"Yeah!" Dupree said.

Dupree, middle-aged, stocky, wearing eyeglasses, came forward.

"Dupree, you're the coroner and I want you to get a load of this . . . This is Fish Tucker, Tyree's son. Well, he's got it all figured out. He says we can use the gym of the nigger high school for a makeshift morgue. He says that, after the inquest, you can make out all the death certificates and send 'em to Tyree's place—"

"Now, I've heard everything," Dupree said, blinking.

"Well, Chief, *somebody's* got to bury these people," Fishbelly argued.

"Did Tyree send you to me?" the chief asked him.

"Nawsir."

"You just thought this up all by yourself?"

"Yessir. Burying folks is our business."

The chief of police chuckled and looked out over the smoking ruins of the Grove.

"Well, goddammit, I'm going to give 'em to you," the chief said grimly. "Is that all right with you, Dupree?"

"Anything you say, Chief," Dupree mumbled with a tight smile.

"Thank you, sir," Fishbelly said.

"Goddammit, you're the biggest, boldest body snatcher that ever hit this part of the country." The chief of police laughed.

"Boy, tell your papa that when he comes to the city hall we're going to give 'im a medal," the coroner said, moving away.

"You and your papa are go-getters, aren't you?" the

chief of police said. "You deal in hot meat, cold meat, and houses—"

"Don't mean no harm, Chief," Fishbelly mumbled, confused.

"That's the trouble. You don't mean any harm. All right. They're yours." The chief swept his hand over the sweep of corpses. "I hope you make a million dollars." He laughed and turned away, muttering: "Tyree's going to need it."

Fishbelly was puzzled. What did the chief of police mean? Well, anyway, he'd gotten the business. Tyree would be glad. The flames had now completely died away, leaving only lingering wisps of white smoke floating above the scorched trees. He looked up; dawn showed in the sky. A few remote and pale stars gleamed overhead. It seemed impossible that the night had fled. He ambled down the dusty road, tired, overwrought, gripped by a curious state of unfeeling. He started in surprise as he came upon his jalopy, for Tyree was sitting in it, his head lowered, his eyes hard upon him.

"Papa!" he called.

Tyree leaped from the car and ran to his son and hugged him frantically.

"Goddammit, I thought I'd lost you, son! Nobody'd *seen* you!"

"But I was there all the time, Papa."

"I asked and asked—"

"Why didn't you come and look—?"

"You alive," Tyree whispered hoarsely, ignoring Fishbelly's question. "That's all I care about. . . ."

"I lost Gladys, Papa."

He wept now; he felt that he could. Before, amidst all the people, white and black, there on the field near the Grove, he had not felt like weeping; but now here with his father, he could weep.

"Easy, son. It's going to be awright," Tyree said, patting his back.

"She was good to me, Papa."

"I know, son."

"We'd taken a flat—"

"Poor Fish," Tyree sighed.

"And she was so happy. . . ."

"Son, come on," Tyree said with a sudden change of tone. "Get in my car. Quick. Leave your jalopy; Jake'll come for it. . . . I know you all broken up, but we got work to do."

He stared at Tyree's face through his tears, knowing better than to ask questions. He ran alongside Tyree until they came to his car, got in, and a few moments later they were rolling through Black-Belt streets. A red fireball of sun hung on the rim of the east. The excitement caused by the fire had filled the streets with men and women who stood about gossiping.

"Goddamn," Tyree muttered.

"What's the matter, Papa?"

"Nothing, son."

"You can tell *me!*" he urged Tyree.

"You got enough to worry about, Fish. That poor Gladys—"

"Papa, Dr. Bruce's looking for you," Fishbelly told him. "He was hiding in the woods by the Grove. You know, Papa, he tried to kill himself . . ."

Tyree stopped the car by slamming the brake to the floor. "When?"

"A few minutes ago. He was upset about the fire. Said he had to see you."

"Mebbe he's at my office now," Tyree said.

"And, Papa," Fishbelly blurted, "the bodies, *all* of 'em, are for *us!*"

"What bodies?"

"Them folks that died in the fire, Papa. I got the chief of police to tell the coroner to give us all the death certificates. They going to use the high-school gym for a morgue—"

"How many bodies?" Tyree asked quietly.

"More'n forty, Papa. And that chief of police says he hopes you make a million dollars."

Tyree was staring dead ahead of him and sweat was oozing on his face.

"You asked 'im right *there* at the fire?"

"Sure, Papa. I got to 'im 'fore anybody else did." Fishbelly explained. "He was a little surprised, but he said yes."

"Hunh huh," Tyree grunted.

Something was wrong. Tyree did not seem pleased.

"Didn't I do right, Papa?"

"Sure. It's awright, son," Tyree said in a tone of false approbation.

The car rolled in silence. What was wrong? Didn't you go for business that was lying right under your nose? Tyree's right hand opened the glove compartment and took out his gun. Fishbelly felt goose-pimples breaking out over his skin, for he remembered the last time that he had seen Tyree handle the gun like that.

"What's happening, Papa?"

"There's trouble, Fish," Tyree said heavily.

"*Race* trouble, Papa?"

"Something like that, Fish," Tyree mumbled. "It's all mixed up."

"Any white folks after *us*, Papa?"

"There's more'n forty folks dead, son. And somebody's got to pay—"

"Papa, that's *just* what the fire chief said."

Tyree started, then stared; he lifted his right palm to his forehead and wiped away sweat. His eyes grew glassily bloodshot.

"The *fire chief* said that?"

"Yessir. But we ain't got *nothing* to do with that fire, Papa."

"Goddamn," Tyree growled, then bit his lips.

"But, Papa, w-we ain't m-mixed up in that *fire* . . .?"

"Yeah and naw, son," Tyree said in a whisper.

"How? What you mean, Papa?"

"It's a long story, son," Tyree sighed. "Just you stick by me and you'll find out everything. This is going to be awful rough—"

"But I'm tired, Papa. I want to git some sleep—"

"This ain't no time to sleep, Fish," Tyree chastised him. "You said you wanted to be a *man*. Awright, you a man now. You got to be at my side night and day from this minute on, till this business is finished. This is the hardest fight I ever had in all my life. If *I* lose, *you* lose. I'm fighting for you now, son. If they beat me, you got to take over and run things, even though you just a kid." Tyree swallowed and paused. "Mebbe you was right in quitting school, 'cause in the trouble I'm facing I can't trust nobody on this earth but my own flesh and blood, my own son."

Fishbelly felt horribly guilty; he had been thinking of his own comfort when Tyree had dire need of him.

"Sorry, Papa. I'll stay with you, by you . . . But what's wrong?"

"Stick close to me and look and lissen. You'll see what it is," Tyree said, looking compassionately at his son. "You grieving for Gladys, but you just got to forgit her, son."

Tyree held the gun in his right hand and steered the car with his left, looking around, and peering out of the rear window.

"Papa, is somebody *after* us?" he asked a second time.

"For a fact, I don't know, Fish," Tyree confessed.

"Is it the *white* folks?"

"Mebbe."

"Tell me, Papa!" Fishbelly was boiling with anxiety. "I want a gun too, Papa!"

"Naw!"

"You got a gun! I want to help, Papa!"

"If there's going to be any shooting, I'm doing it, son."

Fishbelly sighed, watching Tyree's washed-out face, a face that looked thinner, bolder, but, at the same time, more vital than he had ever seen it. He's scared . . . *But about what?* They entered the neighborhood of the undertaking parlor, but kept rolling.

"Where we going, Papa?"

"Keep quiet, Fish."

He settled back and waited. The car stopped in front of Gloria's house. Tyree reached into his pocket and pulled out a flat packet wrapped in brown paper, then peered at Gloria's dark, shut windows.

"Reckon she up yit?"

"Want me to go and see, Papa?"

"Yeah. Ring her bell. When she comes to the door, tell her I want to see her. Quick."

He got out of the car and ran across the walk and up the wooden steps and pushed his thumb against the doorbell. There was no response. He rang again, this time longer.

"Who's there?" came Gloria's voice.

"Me. Fish. Open the door, Gloria."

Gloria's white face showed against the semidark background of the hallway and fear leaped into him for a moment, then it was gone. She was in her bathrobe.

"What's the matter, Fish?"

"Papa's in the car. He wants to see you. Quick!"

"All right," Gloria said after a moment's hesitation.

He accompanied Gloria to the car, the rear door of which was held open by Tyree. She sat huddled on the edge of the back seat, her face thrust anxiously forward.

"What's happened, honey?" she asked.

"Gloria, lissen and do just what I tell you," Tyree began quietly. "I ain't got much time, see? Me and Doc's in trouble. This package's something the chief of police wants to git his hands on. . . . It's the canceled checks I done give 'im for the last five year—"

"Oh God!" Gloria said. "What happened, Tyree?"

"Don't ask no questions, honey," Tyree said. "Just hide these checks, and hide 'em good and don't let nobody see you do it. You know a place for 'em?"

Gloria stared, biting her lips.

"There's an old well in the shed; it's dry. I can put 'em down in it in a bucket. Nobody'll think of looking in there. And the well's top is all covered with firewood—"

"That's the place. That's all, honey."

"But, Tyree, what's *happened?*" Gloria begged.

"Ain't you heard? The Grove burned down last night," Tyree said.

"There's more'n forty dead," Fishbelly told her.

Gloria put her doubled fist against her teeth.

"God in heaven," she moaned. Her round, frightened eyes clung to Tyree's face. "Poor Tyree . . ."

"It's awright," Tyree mumbled. "You go and git them checks hid, *quick*. And if I don't see you for a few days, you'll know why."

Gloria turned beseechingly to Fishbelly.

"Fish, take care of your father—"

"I'm with 'im night and day," he told her.

Gloria thrust the packet into her bosom and got out of the car.

"Darling, keep in touch, won't you?"

"Sure. Git going."

She fled down the walk and vanished through the front door.

"That's done," Tyree sighed.

When Fishbelly realized that Tyree was hiding evidence of the corruption of the chief of police, apprehension filled him. He recalled now that when he had asked the chief of police for the right to bury the forty-two dead, the chief had joked brutally with him.

"Papa, did I do something wrong in gitting that business?"

"Forgit it, son," Tyree mumbled.

They rolled again, this time toward the undertaking parlor. Jim was waiting on the porch. He ran down the steps to the car.

"Tyree, the chief of police has been phoning you for an hour," Jim said.

"I know," Tyree said. He got out of the car and spoke slowly. "Lissen good, Jim. Take Fish's car keys and tell Jake to git his jalopy; it's parked out by the Grove. Then you got to handle something big. We got more'n forty bodies to fix up—"

"Wheew," Jim whistled. "The fire?"

"Yeah. Fish got the business. They giving us the death certificates. Now, Jim, we don't want the other nigger undertakers gitting jealous, see? Phone 'em in all the other towns and ask 'em to meet you at the coroner's office. Then divide up the bodies, but be on the level with 'em. This fire's making a big stink and we don't want 'em saying we hogging the business. Go easy on the dead folks' relatives. Most times the family'll let whoever's got the death certificate handle the body. But this time, Jim, if a family don't want us to handle the body, then give it up. Me and Doc's on the spot and we don't want 'em saying that niggers made money out of the Grove and then made money burying the folks that got killed in the fire . . . It's sticky, Jim. Can you handle it?"

"I'll try, Tyree," Jim mumbled.

"Tell Curley Meeks, Joe Nash, Jim Poplar, and Dick Paley to bring their emergency embalming kits. And no fuss with nobody, see? Anybody ask you anything, tell 'em to see Tyree. Now, Jim, you got to haul all them bodies to the high-school gym for identification. Git the casket companies to lend you some trucks, 'cause nobody in town's got enough hearses to handle that many dead folks. You going to need a lot of extra formaldehyde, plaster of Paris, hardening fluid. . . . Better git your orders in quick.

"Now, Jim, we going to cut funeral costs 10 per cent, 'cause this is kind of wholesale business, see? I reckon you'll have to drape black crepe on some trucks to git them folks to the graveyard. Jim, you got to do all this yourself: gitting gravity bottles, clothes, cosmetics—everything. I'm going to be tied up. There's trouble about that Grove fire. . . ."

"I see," Jim murmured. "You got it tough. Say, Dr. Bruce's waiting for you in the office."

"Yeah? Now, look, Jim . . . I ain't in to the chief of police till I done talked to Doc, see?"

"I get you, Tyree," Jim said sadly.

Fishbelly followed Tyree into the office where Dr. Bruce sat huddled and mute. The two men did not speak. Fishbelly sat and stared at them, wondering what was happening. One man was a doctor and the other an undertaker; one was his father and the other his friend; one was ignorant and cunning and the other was educated and frightened. He knew that when they talked he would learn what the fear, the whispers, and the creeping about in the dark had been for.

TYREE LOWERED THE WINDOW shade against the sun's growing glare, then switched on the desk lamp, whose sheen threw into relief the three black faces in the room. Tyree next lifted the phone's receiver from the hook, brought out a bottle of whiskey and three glasses, and placed them upon the desk. Fishbelly knew that something awful had to be discussed, that something mortally serious had to be decided, and his teeth felt on edge from suspense.

"Take what you want, Doc," Tyree mumbled, pouring himself a third of a glass.

"I need it," Dr. Bruce said. The doctor's fingers trembled as he poured a stiff drink and gulped it, then stared blankly. "We haven't got much time, Tyree."

"I know," Tyree said. "That's why I cut the phone. We ain't talking to nobody till we done settled things, hunh?"

"Tyree, the chief of police and the chief of the fire department were at my house three times this morning," Dr. Bruce began.

"Let's face it, Doc," Tyree said softly. "They going to arrest you. When forty-two folks, black or white, die all at once, folk git *scared.*"

"They want a scapegoat," Dr. Bruce said. "And I'm *it.*"

"Yeah, but take it easy, Doc, I'm with you all the way," Tyree said. "We hiring the best lawyers in this country and fighting this case all the way to the Supreme Court—"

"Hell, Tyree." Dr. Bruce spoke huskily. "Lawyers can't help me. The evidence is against me—"

"Man, money *talks!*" Tyree said thunderously.

Dr. Bruce leaped to his feet, his face twitching.

"Tyree, don't hand me that bunk! I'm *black!* They're after me! They—!"

"And I'm with you, man!" Tyree shouted his whisper. "I'm behind you."

"You going to hire lawyers while I sit in jail and rot?" Dr. Bruce asked mockingly. "Hell, no!"

"Don't git excited, Doc," Tyree said uneasily. "What you gitting at?"

"Tyree, you're my partner. We're in this Grove business fifty-fifty—"

Aw Gawd! Fishbelly had been hoping against hope that that was not true. He felt his tongue grow dry and hot.

"Sure," Tyree agreed smoothly. "But I'm your *silent* partner. We agreed on that; we said my name wasn't to have *nothing* to do with that Grove!"

"I knew it!" Dr. Bruce hissed, his face livid with fury. "As soon as trouble starts, you *run!* But, goddammit, Tyree, you *can't!* The grand jury's going to indict me for manslaughter and I won't stand trial alone for the death of forty-two people! We split the profits fifty-fifty and we're going to shoulder the responsibilities fifty-fifty! We face this together, both *you* and *me!*"

"Take it easy, Doc," Tyree begged nervously. "Let's think this over. . . ."

Stunned, Fishbelly could scarcely believe what he had heard. Tyree owned half of the Grove! He leaned back in his chair and his breath escaped him in a deep sigh. He understood now why Dr. Bruce had been hiding in those woods, why he had tried to kill himself, why the chief of police had stared at him and had said: "You're the boldest, biggest body snatcher that ever hit this part of the country." Tyree owned a part of the Grove in which forty-two black people had lost their lives and the owner's son was asking for the business of burying those who had perished! *That white man must've thought I was crazy.* Then another realization hit him: he and his family had been living off the immoral earnings of Gladys! The money he had paid her for the right to sleep with her had found its way back into his own pocket! He hung his head in shame. He was a kind of superpimp. . . . And he had condemned Gladys because she had not shared his feelings toward white people. It was only after a few moments that he could lift his head and follow the bitter argument raging between Tyree and the doctor.

"Let's git the record straight!" Tyree thundered. *"You* own that goddamn Grove, *I* don't! I only put up half the operating money—"

"Tyree, you got half of the profits!" Dr. Bruce shouted. "You're my *de facto* partner."

"What that *de facto* mean, Doc?" Tyree asked, blinking, a dangerous glint entering his eyes.

"Papa, it means you a partner in fact and in law," Fishbelly told him.

"And that's correct," Dr. Bruce argued. "The law will hold you to it."

"What good's my going to jail along with you?" Tyree tried another approach. "I can't pull strings if I'm in a cell. Doc, you upset. Calm down. You *scared—*"

"Don't insult me," Dr. Bruce's body quivered. "I'm fifty years old and I could get ten years in prison for the death of those forty-two people—"

"It won't come to that, I tell you," Tyree tried to reassure him.

"Tyree, I don't know the men in the city hall. You do. They're friends of yours. And, so help me God, you're going to stand at my side in this thing." Dr. Bruce was adamant. "I can prove that you were my partner. So admit it!"

Fishbelly was inclined toward Dr. Bruce's logic, but he felt that Tyree was right to insist upon the terms of the original agreement.

"We don't have to make up our minds now." Tyree evaded the issue.

"By God, we do! We'll decide it *now!*" Dr. Bruce screamed. "I'll be arrested any minute . . . AND I WON'T ACCEPT THIS ALONE, TYREE!"

There was silence. Tyree drained his glass and stared at the floor. Fishbelly heard the small clock on the desk ticking as loud as thunder. He looked at it; it was nearly noon. A knock came upon the door and they all started.

"Who's there?" Tyree called.

"Jim!"

Tyree rose and unlocked the door. Jim leaned to him and whispered:

"It's your wife, Tyree. She's upset. She's had no word—"

"Oh Gawd," Tyree moaned. "I clean forgot—"

"Tyree! Tyree!" Emma's hysterical voice filled the hallway. "Where Fish? Oh Lawd, my poor baby. . . . Tell me, Tyree!"

"Come in, Emma," Tyree called. He turned to Fishbelly. "Your mama worried about you."

Emma entered with a fearful, creeping movement, her tear-wet face turning from man to man, then she sank to the floor, sobbing.

"Child, I thought you was dead," she cried. "Nobody told me *nothing!*"

"Fish's awright, Emma," Tyree said soothingly. "Sorry, but I been busy's hell. . . ."

Fishbelly went to his mother and lifted her tenderly.

"I'm awright, see?" he said.

"You ain't hurt none?" Emma asked him. "Your *clothes!* They torn and burned—"

"It ain't nothing, Mama. I was just trying to help the others."

"Git hold of yourself, Emma. You can't stay here. We got serious business. Jim's taking you to the car and Jake'll drive you home."

"Right, Tyree," Jim said.

"Go along with 'im, Mama," Fishbelly said. "We'll be along when we through here . . ."

"My boy . . . I thought you was dead," Emma sobbed as Jim led her away.

Tyree shut the door, frowning.

"Goddammit, I can't think of everything," he moaned.

"Tyree, are you my partner or not?" Dr. Bruce resumed his attack.

A tremor went through Tyree's body and his eyes were wild, glassy. He took another drink and stared at his son, at Dr. Bruce, then at the floor.

"If that's the way you want it, what the hell can I do?" he consented bitterly.

"Then we fight *together,*" Dr. Bruce said, his eyes gushing tears. "That's all I wanted, Tyree. Just be loyal. . . ."

"Have it your way," Tyree mumbled in defeat.

"What's our defense going to be?" the doctor asked logically.

"There's a lot of angles, Doc," Tyree said.

"What, for instance?"

"I got evidence against that chief."

"How can we use it?"

"We can blackmail 'im into making 'im help us."

"What else?"

"We might try to find somebody to take the rap for us."

"Who?"

"Don't know . . . You still want me in that courtroom? I could be more help to you if I was free—"

"You *got* to be with me, Tyree. You just *got* to be."

A loud knock sounded upon the front door. Tyree crept to the window and peered out from behind the edge of the shade.

"It's the chief of police," he whispered.

"What're we going to do?" Dr. Bruce asked in terror.

" 'What we going to do?' " Tyree echoed the doctor's words scornfully. "We going to let 'im in. What the hell you think we can do?"

Dr. Bruce half rose, then sat, his eyes crazed with anxiety.

"Goddammit, git yourself together, Doc." Tyree snorted contemptuously. "Mebbe you ought to take a pill or something." He went out of the office.

THE CHIEF OF POLICE entered. Tyree, cringing a bit, followed. The tall, heavy-set white man stood, his eyes roving. He wore the blue uniform of his office and his left arm gleamed with gold braid for long service. His gray eyes finally settled on Dr. Bruce.

"My men are looking everywhere for you, Doc," the chief said.

"I'm right here drinking with my friend," Dr. Bruce said.

The chief looked from Dr. Bruce to Tyree, then to Fishbelly.

"Well, you got the business, Tyree," the chief said, lighting a cigarette. "By God, Fish was there grabbing at those bodies before they were cold. . . . Ha, ha!"

Embarrassed silence hung in the room and the clock's ticking sounded like the salvos of a cannon. The smile on every face in the room hid hate, fear, and anxiety. Tyree clapped Fishbelly on the back and, forcing a hollow laugh, crooned:

"Yessir, Chief. Fish's my right hand. Ain't you, son?"

"Yessir, Papa," Fishbelly replied meekly, his heart thumping.

"And your left hand too," the chief growled out of the corner of his mouth.

When the chief had entered the room Fishbelly had felt a sense of dreaminess, of mental confusion. All the bitterly turgid arguments that had raged had had meaning only in terms of this white ambassador from the white world. His coming had annulled the reality of their lives, for the black men present were not their own masters. And Fishbelly knew what was making Tyree move with stooping shoulders, with a perpetual grin on his sweaty face, with bloodshot eyes

looking always out of their corners, with knees slightly bent
—it was the presence of a white man. Tyree was masking his
motives to mislead the white man, to put him at a disadvan-
tage; he was making himself the semblance of compliance, of
a castrated shadow man who would always say yes. And Fishbelly knew that Dr. Bruce's saying that Tyree was his friend
had had a strong effect upon the chief, for it was clear in his
stony look that the chief had not expected to find the two
black men forming a common front. That big-boned white
man was hatching what tactics? "He's wondering if them two
niggers is planning something against 'im," Fishbelly whispered to himself, feeling something within him withdrawing,
dwindling in the face of this white enemy who negatively
ruled the Black Belt, who sold justice, right, liberty, who said
what could or could not be done.

"Drink, Chief?" Tyree asked.

"Don't mind if I do," the chief murmured, pouring a quarter of a glass and downing it. "Good whiskey, Tyree."

"Help yourself, Chief," Tyree forced a grin.

"Thanks, Tyree." The chief cleared his throat and, rising,
walked aimlessly about the office, then suddenly pulled off
his coat and draped it over the back of his chair. "Tyree?" he
called softly.

"Right here, Chief," Tyree sang with make-believe eagerness.

"Who am I dealing with? You *and* Doc, or *just* you?"

"Well . . ." Tyree hedged.

"We're partners, Chief," Dr. Bruce said in a steady voice.

"What does this nigger doctor know, Tyree?" the chief
asked in an ice-cold tone, hitching his thumbs into the cartridge belt girting his waist and making the gun butt jiggle.

"What you mean, Chief?" Tyree played ignorant with
wide eyes.

"This is damned dangerous business, Tyree," the chief
stated. "I know I can depend on you to keep a stiff upper lip.
. . . You've been before that grand jury three times and never

spilled a thing. But I didn't bargain on this nigger doctor, see? Okay; he's here. What does he know?"

"*Know*, Chief? You know what we know," Tyree cried naïvely.

Fishbelly had bristled when the chief had used the word "nigger"; but his tension ebbed when Tyree failed to react. Then he realized that the chief had been trying to see if the black men before him were subservient.

"Listen, Tyree, I'm giving it to you straight." The chief spoke in exasperation. "You've been paying me by check. I told you not to. But, because I know you, I was a damn fool and took them. Now, your bank sends you the canceled checks at the end of each month. Tyree, where the hell are those canceled checks? I'm asking because this goddamn fire mess has blown the lid off everything. You're going to be put on the witness stand again and that special district attorney's going to want to know how the Grove remained open in face of all the fire-violation notices that were sent out. . . . What're you going to say if they press you about that fire? I know men, Tyree. You're on the spot. But don't get any ideas in your head about swapping some canceled checks to get off about that fire . . ."

Fishbelly sat crushed. The chief's voice had been murderous, cold. He watched Tyree leap to his feet, his eyes popping with that exaggerated fear that black people knew that white people expected from them.

"Chief!" Tyree's voice was shrill. "You done known me for twenty years! You can trust me, Chief! I told you a thousand times I burn them checks!" Tyree lied with all the force of his histrionic art.

"Where do you keep your checkbooks and papers, Tyree?" the chief asked.

"Right here. In this office," Tyree said, as though suspecting nothing. "Why, Chief?"

"Open your safe and let me see what you've got," the chief ordered. "If you're not hiding anything, you'll let me look—"

"Good Gawd, Chief!" Tyree hollered in a high-pitched whisper. "You don't believe me? Well, I do declare! Sure. You can look. . . . I ain't never thought of nothing like hiding your checks, Chief. You my friend. . . . Lawd, Chief, you make me think you don't trust me no more." Tyree's voice sounded full of tears. "You can see anything I got. Fish, open the safe for the chief."

"Sure, Papa." He rose and removed the calendar screening the safe in the wall.

"Chief, have you a warrant for that kind of search?" Dr. Bruce asked, his face twitching.

The chief spun on his heel and faced the doctor.

"Goddammit, I was waiting for that!" the chief snarled. "I know an uppity nigger when I see one! What the hell do I need a warrant for? Nigger, understand one thing: Tyree's my *friend.*" He looked at Tyree. "Ain't you, Tyree?"

"Sure, Chief! You can see *anything* I got!" Tyree pretended breathlessly. He leered at Dr. Bruce with a face twisted with simulated rage. "Doc, you just keep out of this! You talk too goddamn much. This is something between *me* and the *chief!*" He turned to Fishbelly. "Got that safe open, son?"

"Almost, Papa." He trembled as he twirled the dial.

"A nigger talking about warrants," the chief sneered. His voice dropped low, menacing. "Be careful, nigger."

"It's open, Papa." Fishbelly called, stepping aside, feeling secure, knowing that Gloria had hidden the checks. He smiled grimly as he watched the chief rummaging in the safe, tossing bundles of greenbacks upon the desk.

"That's just my money." Tyree cautiously implied ownership.

"I'm not interested in your money, Tyree," the chief said. Then he stiffened, spun, shouting: "By God, *here's one!*" The chief held aloft a canceled check. "Goddamn nigger says he burns 'em! Why the hell didn't you burn *this?*"

Fishbelly blinked, feeling about to drop. What had happened?

"Where?" Tyree demanded in a wail. "Let me see that!"

"Are you lying to me, Tyree?" the chief asked.

"Lawd Gawd in heaven!" Tyree's voice was a pleading chant. "Honest, Chief, that one come in night 'fore last. . . . I ain't had time to burn it yit. 'Fore Jesus, that's the truth! Look for more of 'em, Chief! You'll see there *ain't* no more!" Tyree extended his hand. "Give me that check, Chief. I'll show you what I do with 'em!" He snatched the check and scratched a match and held the check over the flame, and, with hard, fixed eyes, watched the paper blaze up, turning it in his fingers. He dropped the remainder into an ash tray and it turned into a charred, crinkly black wisp. "There, Chief. I was going to burn that last night, so help me Gawd, if it hadn't been for that damned Grove fire." And he gazed at the white man with the eyes of a dog. "Chief, if I'd been a-trying to fool you, I would've took everything out of there. You can trust me, Chief."

The chief sighed, relaxed; his lips twisted in a wry smile.

"All right, Tyree," he said. "If you'd been holding out on me, you sure would've got rid of that." He sat heavily and took another drink. "After this, no more goddamn checks, see?"

"Just as you say, Chief," Tyree sang his agreement.

"Nigger, did I need a warrant for that?" the chief asked Dr. Bruce.

"A warrant?" Tyree went into a gale of counterfeit laughter. "You *know* you don't need no warrant with me, Chief!"

Fishbelly wondered how on earth Tyree had overlooked that check!

"Chief," Tyree called in a small, timid voice.

"Yeah, Tyree," the chief said.

Tyree rose, sat, closed his eyes and rested his head in his palms; then he straightened and stared at the white man. Fishbelly knew that gesture; Tyree was ready to counterattack. The quieter, the more nervous Tyree became, the more dangerous he was.

"Chief, you coming here looking for them checks makes

me think you know something's about to happen." Tyree's accusation was impersonal.

"Listen, Tyree, the syndicate can't touch that special district attorney, Lou Bell, that the state legislature's put in there. We got a friend or two around the grand jury, but we can't control that jury. That means that you're going to be *indicted*. And Doc too. It's that goddamned fire; it's an open-and-shut case. You'll get out on bail. When the case comes into court the syndicate'll go into action and make things as easy as it can for you."

Fishbelly felt chilled. He knew that fear had driven the chief to look into Tyree's safe, for he was afraid that Tyree might talk under pressure. Guilt for the Grove fire had trapped the black men and even the chief of police could scarcely help them. But Tyree could turn state's evidence and gain a risky immunity.

"Oh Lawd, Chief," Tyree moaned.

"What's the matter?" the chief asked.

"You know what's bothering me, Chief," Tyree whispered reprovingly. "I know too goddamn much to sit on a witness stand! How can I protect Doc, me, and *you*—"

"What're you scared of, Tyree?"

"Chief, they going to ask me how that Grove managed to run with all them fire violations against it—"

"And what're you going to tell 'em?" the chief asked crisply.

"What *can* I tell 'em?" Tyree countered the chief's question.

Fishbelly listened with clamped teeth. They were at the heart of the problem now. How could Tyree, on the witness stand, explain that the Grove remained open in spite of fire violations, and *not* implicate the chief of police? The white man was asking Tyree to protect him in his testimony before the grand jury, and he was promising to help Tyree when the case came to trial.

"I'm behind you; you'll come out all right," the chief promised.

"Chief, when I'm on that witness stand, if I talk, I'm guilty, and if I don't talk, I'm guilty. What can I *say?*"

"Keep your testimony strictly to that fire," the chief advised coldly. "You don't know *anything* else."

Three pairs of black eyes roved, weighing possibilities. Could the chief bribe the jury when the case came to trial? *Would* he? Could they trust a white man that much? Dare they hint that they had hidden evidence and would blackmail him unless he made a strong effort to help them? Or would the chief want to kill them if he suspected that? The black faces in the room were coated with sweat.

"I agree with the chief," Dr. Bruce said suddenly.

"The nigger doctor's got sense," the chief muttered.

Fishbelly knew that Dr. Bruce was hiding behind Tyree, that he was banking on the chief protecting Tyree in order to protect himself.

"I don't want to git on no witness stand," Tyree murmured with closed eyes, pretending to tremble. "That district attorney might *make* me *talk* . . ."

Fishbelly saw fright flash in the chief's eyes.

"Testify about the fire and keep your mouth shut about us," the chief insisted. "We'll help you. We always have. . . . That fire's got the whole town roused. The fire chief sent *seven* notices of fire violation to Doc—"

"I didn't see 'em!" Dr. Bruce said stoutly.

"Goddammit!" the chief exploded. "Can't you niggers understand? There's a *record* of those violations! People are wanting to know if the fire's the fault of the fire department or your fault." The chief rose and placed his palms against his chest. "Don't blame me for the fire; I didn't start it. Tomorrow the grand jury's indicting the owners of the Grove. That's certain."

Tyree's sigh was like a moan; then he threw himself tentatively upon the mercy of the white man he trusted least on earth.

"What can we do, Chief?" he asked.

The chief screwed up his eyes and pronounced judgment:

"Sell your property and prepare to defend yourselves!"

Fishbelly flinched. What the chief had said could mean anything. Tyree would be indicted and, during the course of the trial, the whites would bleed him of every penny he had ever made. But did not this scheming white man, in order to keep on collecting his weekly bribes, wish hotly to save Tyree from jail? Fishbelly recalled that Gladys had told him that Fats had been in prison four or five times. By Gawd, why could not an old jailbird like Fats be made to take the rap? Should he suggest it?

"Papa," Fishbelly called.

"Yeah, Fish," Tyree encouraged him.

"Gladys told me something about Fats. . . . Seems like he's been in jail four or five times. Let's say that Fats got them notices and didn't know what they was. . . . Fats can't read and he just threw 'em away."

"Fats can't *read?*" Tyree asked with eager indignation.

"That's right," Dr. Bruce said. "Fats wouldn't know his name if it were painted on the side of a boxcar in letters a yard high."

"There's our man," Tyree said emphatically.

"Goddamn," the chief mused, shifting in his chair. "I remember that Fats. Bad nigger . . ."

"Bad, bad, *bad,*" Tyree cried. "You can have ninety-nine colored folks, and there'll always be *one nigger!* Fats uses guns, knives, and he's been mixed up with dope, Chief." Tyree's eyes reflected a combination of aggressive balefulness and fear. "Let's git that nigger, Chief."

"Yeah, that nigger's been in all kinds of trouble," the chief said slowly.

"What about Fats, Chief?" Tyree asked with an urgent glare in his eyes.

"Could be," the chief said, pulling down a corner of his mouth.

"How much time would he git if he confessed the fire was his fault, Chief?" Tyree prodded the white man to guess.

"Maybe five years, with time off for good behavior," the chief hazarded.

"That ain't bad," Tyree judged. "Fats is used to jails."

They stared at one another, weighing this probability.

"Fats is plenty wise," the chief warned them. "You'd better make 'im a pretty good offer."

"Two thousand dollars," Dr. Bruce offered.

"Make it four thousand and Fats might bite," the chief suggested.

"Four thousand dollars? I buy that. Okay," Tyree said.

"You want me to talk to him?" Dr. Bruce asked. "I'm a doctor and I can see him—"

"Wait," the chief said. "It'd be better if I saw 'im first and softened 'im up a bit. If I start poking around into Fats's past, he'll get worried and by the time Doc gets to 'im he'll be ripe."

"Check," Dr. Bruce agreed. "Let's phone right now and see if he can receive visitors. He's in the Booker T. Washington Hospital."

"Why not?" the chief said.

"Now, we using our heads for something more'n a place to hang our hats," Tyree crooned, leaping monkeylike across the room and grabbing the phone and stealthily easing the receiver back upon the hook and pushing the phone into the white man's hand. "Here, Chief."

"Sure. I'll help you. I'll throw the book at that nigger," the chief said. He dialed and, while waiting for a response, he spoke gently to Tyree: "Tyree, I'll have to have some cash to work on this."

"Sure, Chief. How much?" Tyree's teeth showed in a false grin.

"Make it fifty for the moment," the chief said.

"Right, Chief," Tyree said, taking out his billfold and extracting a fifty-dollar note and extending it.

"Hold it," the chief said. "Hello," he spoke into the phone. "(. . .)"

"Don't move, Chief," Tyree whispered gently, tucking the bill into the white man's top shirt pocket.

"Thanks, Tyree," the chief whispered. ". . . Hello. This is Chief of Police Gerald Cantley speaking . . . Yeah. I want to know if you got a nigger there by the name of Fats . . . Hold it a second." He looked at Dr. Bruce. "What's Fats last name, Doc?"

"Brown," Dr. Bruce said with dry throat.

"Fats Brown," the chief continued into the phone. "Yeah. He was injured last night in the Grove fire. . . . Yeah. Okay." The chief turned to Tyree and Dr. Bruce. "They're checking . . ."

There seemed to be hope. Fishbelly prayed that Fats could be a stand-in for Tyree and Dr. Bruce.

"Yeah?" the chief spoke into the transmitter.

"(. . .)"

"Yeah. That's right?"

"(. . .)"

"Oh! Okay. 'By."

The chief hung up and lifted his glass and drained it.

"No dice," he said. "Fats died about an hour ago."

"Hell," Tyree muttered and sank loosely upon his chair. "We back where we started."

Fishbelly gritted his teeth, staring at Tyree's drawn, sweaty face.

"Anything else, Tyree?" the chief asked, rising and putting on his coat.

Fishbelly stifled a sob. Gawd, this couldn't happen!

"I'm afraid I'll have to send for you two tomorrow," the chief said. "The grand jury meets in the morning. If there's an indictment, I'll have to pick you up about noon." The chief pursed his lips, staring into space. "Naw . . . I don't want your people to see you're being arrested, Tyree. I'll phone you the grand-jury decision and you two come down to the city hall. You're not running away; you've got property. I'm sure you'll be out on bail before sundown."

"Chief." Tyree chanted, high-pitched, desperate.

"Yeah, Tyree," the chief replied, eying Tyree with a certain degree of pity.

"I know what to do, Chief!" Tyree cried in singsong through his nose. "But I'm *scared—!*"

"Scared of what?"

"I'm scared you won't help me."

"I'll help you, Tyree," the chief consoled him.

Tyree and the chief looked at each other. The white man's eyes were blank, free of fear, devoid of emotional commitments; the black man's eyes were evasive, filled with distrust, juggling imponderables. Fishbelly knew that Tyree was trying to decide if he should leave his case in the white man's hands. Instinct said no. Ought they not fight instead with the weapons of the canceled checks? Since they were all, white as well as black, guilty; since the Grove could not have operated in violation of the fire laws without the connivance of the police; why should only the black men alone stand trial? But what would happen if Tyree exposed the partnership he had with the police in order to lessen the pressure upon him and Dr. Bruce? If the chief of police were there in the dock with him, much of the blame could be lifted from his shoulders. But it would be almost worth his life to unmask the men in the city hall. And if he were indicted and free on bail, the chief could come to him repeatedly for money, on this pretext or that, and he would have to give. Since he could not trust the police, and since he could not fight them, could not there be a compromise? Tyree lowered his head, his lips hanging loose and open. He backed slowly to a chair and sat, staring at the floor.

"I want to say something, Chief," he whispered.

"Go ahead, Tyree."

"Now, lissen, Chief, don't go *misunderstanding* me—"

"I'll try to understand. What is it, Tyree?"

Clashing impulses were so powerful in Tyree that he rose and walked nervously to the shaded window, then back again to the chief. His voice came tense, cracked:

"Chief, you done known me for twenty years and I'm straight and solid . . ."

"Yeah," the chief said, blinking slowly, trying to anticipate Tyree.

"Chief, you know I ain't no agitator; don't you?"

"Yeah, Tyree. I know that."

"I ain't no sorehead neither. You know that?"

"You're okay, Tyree," the chief said, nodding.

"I was 'fore that grand jury three times and was loyal to you. That district attorney *begged* me to testify for the state and told me nobody could touch me if I did—"

"I know all that, Tyree."

"Now, you say they going to indict me—"

"That's right, Tyree. But these two things are *different*. Our business is *one* thing; that fire's *another*—"

"That district attorney couldn't tempt me to go against you—"

"Tyree, we're in a syndicate together; that was our *bargain!*"

"Now, you pushing me out there all alone, Chief!"

"Nigger, do you want to change your testimony before the grand jury?" the chief asked him bluntly.

"Oh Lawd Gawd, nawsir, Chief! I'm loyal to you! But, Gawd knows, I need *help* now—"

"But we're going to *help* you, Tyree!"

"I'm a nigger you can trust. . . . Tell me: You believe that, Chief?" His voice terminated somewhere in his head in a squeal.

"I trust you, Tyree."

"Now, look, Chief, you know I ain't no politician." Tyree hummed his case, staring at the white man; he swallowed, groped for words. "I'm just a nigger trying to save his skin—my life's savings for my son sitting there right 'fore your eyes. He's young and he's got his whole life 'fore 'im. Now, Chief, there ain't but one way to *really save* me. . . . But it's hard for me to say it. I ain't never said nothing like it to no white men. . . ."

"Speak, Tyree. What's on your mind?"

"I ain't never been for no social equality. You know that, don't you, Chief?"

"Yeah," the chief drawled thoughtfully. "But what—?"

"Chief, just let me talk for five minutes and *promise* you won't stop me. Will you?" Tyree begged, his voice running off into little squeaks, his face oozing sweat, his knees bent in unconscious supplication.

"All right. But what are you getting at?" the chief asked, frowning.

"You won't stop me from talking?" Tyree hedged further.

"Why are you asking me that?" The chief was wary now.

"Chief, just *promise* you won't stop me till I done finished," Tyree cried.

"Talk, Tyree. I won't stop you," the chief committed himself with uneasy compassion.

Tyree took his lungs full of air and when he spoke his voice was strained, tremulous, higher-pitched than a woman's.

"Chief, them folks don't know a thing about us," he began. "They—"

"*Who?*" the chief asked, puzzled.

"The white folks, Chief," Tyree whispered as though communicating a dreadful secret. He swallowed, blinked. "You said you was going to let me talk; you *promised*—"

"I'm not stopping you," the chief's voice was low, guarded.

"Chief, there's something in the law about a jury of your *peers*. . . ." Tyree paused, watching the white man's face for its reaction. "Now, Chief, I know that law ain't meant for us niggers and I ain't saying it is. . . ."

The chief blinked and rubbed his chin reflectively.

". . . and your folks don't know us black folks, how we live, what we feel, what we got to do to git along. . . ." Tyree's eyes weighed the chief. "Chief, only *black* folks can understand *black* folks. Chief, I don't want to be judged by your white law. Now, when time comes for our trial, if only that jury could have just six black folks on it—that jury that's trying me, see?—just *six* niggers, Chief—"

The chief rose and opened his mouth, but Tyree ran forward with uplifted hands, pleading:

"Please, Chief! Don't talk! You done *promised!* Just let me finish! If I'm wrong, then you tell me. You know I'll listen to you, Chief. . . ." Tyree's voice broke from sheer passion; he went to the desk and fortified himself with another drink. "Now, Chief, I know there ain't never been no jury in this town with no niggers on it. *I know that, Chief.* But I ain't preaching no race mixture. I'm just a scared nigger trying to save my skin. . . . There ain't a nigger in this town, nowhere in this whole county, that would sit on that jury without saving *me* and *you!* Put six niggers on that jury, and to sit on that jury who'd be fool enough to vote me guilty. Now, just think, Chief. You git my meaning?"

The chief sat and sighed.

"Goddamn," he breathed, looking off. "I never thought I'd hear you say anything like that, Tyree." He stared at the black man in amazement, then said flatly: "I know what you mean, Tyree; but, goddammit, it just *can't* be. It can *never* happen. You're talking wild, crazy—"

"It could be just for *once,*" Tyree begged in a singsong. "Just for *me,* Chief."

"Hunh," the chief grunted meditatively. "That's Judge Moon's court and he's a Ku-Kluxer. Hell, he doesn't like niggers, Tyree. He's not like me. He even hates that black gown of justice he wears in that courtroom. If I talked to 'im about your wild idea, he'd run me out of town pronto. I see what you're getting at, but it'll never work around here. So forget it, Tyree."

"It could work *once*," Tyree sobbed now. "Then I'd be free, Chief. And you won't have to worry none. . . ." His tear-drenched eyes widened knowingly. "Then that jury could go back being all white, see, Chief? All I'm asking is a favor from my good white friends, a *special* favor. This ain't no social equality. . . ."

"Tyree, don't take me for a fool!" the chief bellowed in sudden anger. "Wouldn't the niggers have to sit in the same jury box with the whites? That's social equality!"

"But, Chief, the judge could say it's a special day, like Easter or Thanksgiving—"

"Nigger, you've gone nuts." The chief spat in disgust.

"Chief, they could put a board in that jury box to separate the white folks from the niggers, like they got on the street-cars and busses," Tyree whimpered out of compromise.

"Aw, Tyree, you talk like a baby—"

"I'm burying niggers every day in *black* graves right alongside *white* graves with a wall between 'em." Tyree tried to make his idea seem normal.

Fishbelly had listened with a deepening sense of despair. He had not been able to disagree when the chief had characterized Tyree's plea as babyish, for he knew that Tyree had appealed as a child appeals to a parent. Even had Tyree won his claim, he would, in winning, have lost.

"Tyree, that's a pipe dream," the chief said. He looked at the impassive face of Dr. Bruce. "Hell, I thought that Doc would've been coming up with a damnfool notion like that, not *you*, Tyree. . . ."

Tyree sat for several seconds, mute, frozen; then he sprang tigerishly forward, sliding to the floor and grabbing hold of the chief's legs.

"I'm lost!" he cried. "I been your friend for twenty years and you done turned your back on me!"

"Let me go, Tyree," the chief said, moved, amazed.

"I been loyal to you, ain't I, Chief? You can't let me go to jail and rot—"

"What the hell can I *do*, Tyree?" the chief yelled at the black man at his feet. "You're getting dangerous to me *and* yourself!"

"Tell 'em to try a mixed jury, Chief. Just for *once*, just for *me*, for poor old *Tyree*. . . ." He lifted his sweaty face and glared at the chief. "You can't let this happen to me," he spoke with almost human dignity. Then, as though afraid, he let out a drawn-out moan of a woman with ten children telling her husband that he could *never* leave her.

"Oh, to hell with you, Tyree!" the chief thundered. "What're you doing to me?" He shook himself loose from Tyree's clinging arms, moved to the center of the room and stood glaring as though snared by invisible coils.

Fishbelly saw Tyree's red-rimmed, tear-brimming eyes watching the bayed white man's face with a coldly calculative stare.

"Goddamn!" the chief shouted and banged his fists upon the desk, rattling the whiskey bottle and glasses.

Fishbelly was transfixed. *Was that his father?* It couldn't be. Yet it was. . . . There were two Tyrees: one was a Tyree resolved unto death to save himself and yet daring not to act out his resolve; the other was a make-believe Tyree, begging, weeping—a Tyree who was a weapon in the hands of the determined Tyree. The nigger, with moans and wailing, had sunk the harpoon of his emotional claim into the white man's heart. But why was the chief so moved? Why was he reacting to this outlandishly presented claim? Frightened of the elementary emotion before him, Fishbelly swallowed and moved nervously. What kind of compassion had Tyree evoked in the chief and how deep was it? The chief was guilty along with Tyree and Dr. Bruce, guilty of accepting bribes from them. But now all the plotting and counterplotting had been forgotten. With all the strength of his being, the slave was fighting the master. Fishbelly saw that the terrible stare in the chief's eyes was so evenly divided between hate and pity that he did not know what the chief would do; the chief could just as easily have drawn his gun and shot Tyree as he could have embraced him.

"You got to do it! You got to save me, Chief!" Tyree sobbed, advancing slowly, nodding his head.

Fishbelly wanted to scream in protest. Yet he realized that Tyree had no other method of fighting, of defending himself.

"Papa," Fishbelly called, weeping for shame.

"GODDAMN YOU, TYREE!" the chief screamed, paradoxically pleading for mercy.

"Have pity on me, Chief!" Tyree begged, pressing home his advantage. "If they going to put me in jail, it's better for you to kill me, Chief! *Shoot me, Chief!*"

The chief's face flushed beet red. He lifted his clenched fists and hammered furiously upon the desk, crying out through shut teeth:

"Oh, goddamn this sonofabitching world! Goddamn everything!"

Tyree began to time his moves; he hung his head, his lowered eyes watching the emotionally wrought-up white man like a cat following the scurryings of a cornered mouse. The chief turned, not looking at anything or anybody. Fishbelly knew that Tyree was weighing whether to act further; then he sniffled and remained silent. The chief lumbered to his chair and sat heavily.

"Goddamn, Tyree," he spoke forlornly. "Maybe I can tell 'em *something.*" He straightened warningly: "But they're not going to *do* it; they'll *never* do it!"

"Please, Chief," Tyree purred. "Just for *me.* . . ."

Fishbelly saw Tyree's chest heaving and he felt that he was watching something obscene.

"Tyree, I'm going to tell Judge Moon just what you told me. I'm going to ask 'im if he can make this an exceptional case. I'll ask 'im to do it for you *personally.* . . . Because you're a goddamn good nigger."

"Thanks, Chief," Tyree sighed through his nostrils.

"Tyree, would the niggers on such a jury acquit you?" the chief asked with lifted eyebrows.

"If they didn't, I'd kill 'em," Tyree vowed through tears.

"Okay," the chief sighed. "You'll hear from me."

The chief left, with Tyree showing him out. Returning, Tyree collapsed upon a chair and whispered:

"I did all I could, Doc."

"You did," Dr. Bruce said reverently. "That was why I wanted you with me, Tyree."

"You got to know how to handle these goddamn white folks," Tyree muttered. "But it took everything out of me. I'm *beat* like I was never beat in all my life."

"Tyree, you scared me," the doctor said. "I thought you'd hidden those canceled checks."

Tyree threw a scornful look at the doctor and laughed compassionately.

"Doc, I know the white man inside out. I left that *one* check in that safe on purpose," Tyree explained. "If that chief had found no checks in that safe, he would've been dead sure I was lying. Now he thinks I just forgot that one check.... *And he feels safe.*" He hitched up his trousers with an upward-shrugging motion of his arms and elbows and spoke in a growling masculine voice: "Hell, Doc, I done saved up enough evidence against that goddamn chief to send 'im to jail for ten years!"

Minutes later they stood facing one another upon the front porch. The sun's hard glare showed their drawn, pinched faces. From the right came a truck bearing a legend: THE GOLDEN DELL CASKET SERVICE. It rumbled into the driveway and went to the rear of the building.

"Coffins," Dr. Bruce mumbled, wiping sweat from his face.

"Yeah," Tyree said.

"I hope we're not in jail this time tomorrow," the doctor sighed.

"Yeah," Tyree said absent-mindedly. "So long, Doc."

The doctor climbed into his car.

" 'By, Tyree. 'By, Fish," he called as he drove off.

"See you," Fishbelly called. "Come on, Papa. You tired. I'll drive you home in my jalopy."

"Naw, son," Tyree rejected the offer. "We going in my car. Your convertible's too goddamn open for me. I want to ride where I can have my gun on my lap."

EMMA RECEIVED THEM tearfully, exhorting them to eat; but they were too emotionally depleted to take more than a mouthful. Spurning Emma's pleas to be told what was wrong, Tyree stretched out upon the sofa in the living room and stared silently at the ceiling. Fishbelly hovered nearby, chain-smoking, brooding upon how he could help. He knew that the chief was certain that Tyree's fears of white reprisal would keep him loyal to his police partners in crime. But why should the chief be carefree and only Tyree bear the burden of fear? The line of race was drawn even among thieves. . . . Each tentative solution that Fishbelly's mind entertained was compulsively formed of whites controlling black destinies. His fantasies had often pictured him as heroically battling in the racial arena, but he had never visualized racial war having this form. His imagination had always pitted him physically against a personal enemy, but this enemy was vague, was part white, part black, was everywhere and nowhere, was within as well as without, and had allies in the shape of tradition, habit, and attitude. The acute compassion that had gripped the chief could have made him kiss Tyree as readily as kill him. Fishbelly now realized that had it not been for that fire he would never have known the real attitude of the chief. White people lived with niggers, shared with them, worked with them, but owed them no human recognition.

"Papa, tell me something," Fishbelly requested.

"What, son?"

"That chief . . . Is he kind? He ever help you?"

"Fish, white folks give us what's left over and call it kindness," Tyree said, looking at his son with a smile so bland that it was bitter.

"Papa, that chief's your friend. Now, if you was white, wouldn't he be trying to keep you out of jail?"

"Hunh," Tyree grunted. "White folks think jails was *built* for folks like us."

Guilt stirred Fishbelly's memory. He had proposed Fats as a sacrificial stand-in for Tyree. He had acted toward his people like the white acted. What had that chief thought of that?

"Then that chief looks at *us* just like he looks at *low* niggers like Fats?" Fishbelly asked.

"Fish, there ain't no *low* niggers and *high* niggers for white folks," Tyree mumbled tiredly. "We all the same to them, except when they can git something out of us."

He knew that Tyree was telling him the truth now, for he could feel the hard logic of living embedded in it. He yearned to help, and his eagerness made him toy with the notion of acting out something that he did not feel.

"Papa, can't we serve 'em in some way and git 'em to help us?"

"Sure, Fish," Tyree said, lifting his whiskey bottle. "Me and Doc's going to jail. That's serving 'em. They'll feel safe and think no more dance halls'll burn down."

Fishbelly sighed, brooding. He was tired; he dozed in the armchair, his left leg twitching.

Late that afternoon Zeke and Tony came to say good-by; they were leaving that night for Army training. The occasion was awkwardly inarticulate, for all of them had lost loved ones in the fire.

"I wish to Gawd I was going with you-all," Fishbelly told them.

"I'm glad to go," Zeke confessed. "After that fire, I don't want to stay here."

"Me neither," Tony said.

"You niggers going to forgit to write," Fishbelly accused them.

"Hell, naw, man. We going to write," Tony pledged.

"We ain't dropping our old buddies," Zeke swore.

"After you through training, where they sending you?" Fishbelly asked.

"Don't know. Mebbe Germany. Mebbe France," Zeke said.

"We'll git a chance to go to Paris, mebbe," Zeke opined.

"I done heard of that cool town." Fishbelly sighed.

"Man, they say the wine's bitter and the women's sweet in Paris," Zeke smiled.

"They say they don't bother colored folks there," Tony said.

"Damn! Ain't no place like that in this whole world," Fishbelly mumbled, laughing ruefully.

"They say in Paris white folks and black folks walk down the street *together*," Tony sang in a tone of frightened hope.

"I ain't going to believe that till I see it," Zeke said. He rubbed his fingers against the seat of his chair. "I'm touching wood."

Zeke and Tony left to walk to the railroad station, leaving Fishbelly feeling doubly abandoned. He returned to Tyree's side and found him opening another bottle.

"Not too much, Papa," he pleaded.

"I can handle it, son."

Jim phoned from the office to report progress in the high-school gym and to ask advice. Emma moved about ghostlike, frequently passing the living-room door to observe the mood of her husband and son, but not daring to ask for details. At seven o'clock she timidly begged to bring them plates of food. Tyree consented. Father and son ate sitting on the sofa, resting their plates on their knees, chewing wordlessly, swallowing mouthfuls that they could not taste. Finished, Tyree took another pull from the bottle.

"Why don't you go to bed, son?"

"I ain't sleepy. I want to stay with you."

"Good boy," Tyree said, patting his son's shoulder. "Don't worry. It'll be awright. I been through things tougher'n this."

At ten o'clock they heard a car stop, start, then enter the driveway.

"See who it is, Fish," Tyree ordered, rousing himself, taking his gun from under a pillow on the sofa and pocketing it.

Fishbelly rushed to the window and peered out.

"A big Buick, Papa," Fishbelly whispered. "White man's in it. He got a nigger chauffeur. Somebody important . . . The white man's coming to the door, Papa."

Tyree rose and put on his coat. The doorbell pealed. Emma went hurrying past in the hallway.

"Emma, let Fish git it," Tyree checked her.

Emma's eyes flashed with apprehension and she vanished into her room. Fishbelly opened the door and confronted a tall, heavy white man dressed in black.

"Is Tyree in?"

"Who calling, sir?"

"I'm Mayor Wakefield," the man said.

"Oh Lawd, it's my old friend, Mr. Mayor!" Tyree called with loud, false glee. "Come in, Mr. Mayor! Ain't seen you in a coon's age, sir!"

"Thanks, Tyree." Mayor Wakefield advanced into the living room, looking about. "Nice place you got, Tyree."

"Oh, Mr. Mayor, it ain't bad. It'll do for a poor man like me." Tyree bared his teeth in a mirthless grin. "You like a little drink, sir?"

"No, Tyree. I stopped by to have a word with you," the mayor said, sitting, keeping on his hat, and looking wonderingly at Fishbelly.

"That's my son, my side-kick and partner," Tyree crooned proudly. "Gitting old, Mr. Mayor, and I'm glad to have a boy like that to take over someday."

"I see," the mayor said. He turned sharply to Tyree. "How old are you, Tyree? You're about my age, aren't you?"

"Me, Mr. Mayor? He, he! I was forty-eight last March," he chortled.

"The older a man gets, the more sense he ought to have," the mayor observed.

"That's right, Mr. Mayor." Tyree bubbled with manufactured joy. "Older and wiser." He swallowed, waiting.

Fishbelly was on edge; the highest official of the town had called on his father, but the honor was eclipsed by anxiety.

"Tyree," the mayor began, "I been hearing some strange things about you."

"What you mean, Mr. Mayor?" Tyree asked without moving his lips, his posture suddenly abject, frozen, tense.

"Judge Moon came to me an hour ago," the mayor said. "He was upset. He said that the chief of police reported to him that you're agitating for niggers to sit on juries—"

"Nawsir!" Tyree cried, rising. "Mr. Mayor, I swear 'fore Gawd I ain't done nothing like *that!* I don't mean to dispute you, sir. But that ain't what I meant—"

"Then what in hell did you mean?" the mayor asked brutally.

"Mr. Mayor, this is a great big misunderstanding—"

"Tyree"—the mayor spoke flintily—" are you in touch with Communists?"

Tyree blinked several times to convey the impression that he was stupidly foolish; then he wet his lips with his tongue.

"Gawd, nawsir, Mr. Mayor!" Tyree breathed in meek despair. He advanced, stopped, and stared humbly into the mayor's face. "Mr. Mayor, I don't know no Commonists. Ain't got no use for 'em. If I saw one, I'd kill 'im, so help me Gawd." Tyree felt uncertain of his ground. "That is, if he wasn't *white.* . . . I ain't killing no *white* folks—"

"Now, you're talking like a good nigger," the mayor said.

"Aw, nawsir, Mr. Mayor," Tyree singsonged to reassure the white man. "I ain't messing in no politics." He began a low whining. "Mr. Mayor, I'm in trouble 'cause of that Fats nigger. He got all them niggers burned up in that Grove fire 'cause he got them notices about fire violations, but he couldn't *read*. He didn't know what them notices was and he threw 'em away 'fore Doc could see 'em. . . ."

"So?" the mayor asked coldly.

"Now, that grand jury wants to indict me and Doc for manslaughter—"

"That's *natural!* You were *careless!*" the mayor's words shot neat and clean.

"But I ain't guilty of no manslaughter!" Tyree wailed.

"You owned a part of that dance hall, didn't you?"

"Nawsir, I didn't *own* it. Doc *owned* it—"

"You put up money; you had half interest in the *profits.*"

"But I didn't have no part in *running* it," Tyree cried with tear-filled eyes.

"Didn't you and that nigger doctor give orders to that Fats nigger?" the mayor asked.

Tyree was silent.

"Answer me, Tyree!"

"Yessir," Tyree moaned.

"Then what are you beefing about?" the mayor demanded.

Like a cut shot in a movie, Tyree was transformed. He lifted his head and closed his eyes.

"That grand jury's going to find me guilty of something I ain't guilty of!" Tyree yodeled his misery in a whinnying holler of despair. "That's how this business of us niggers sitting on the jury came up when I was talking to the chief. I ain't no Commonist and I ain't asking for no social equality. Mr. Mayor, you know we niggers is satisfied. . . . And there ain't nothing on this earth I hate more'n them Commonists. I just said to the chief that if, for *once,* just ONCE, six niggers was on that *particular* jury, then I could git me some justice—"

"Nigger, you've gone crazy," the mayor said flatly. The mayor stared at Tyree, then asked with a disdainful smile: "How could you make six niggers on a jury vote for you?"

"They just wouldn't vote against me, Mr. Mayor," he whimpered.

"You want to pack our juries with niggers who'll vote for niggers?" the mayor asked.

"Niggers voting for me's *justice,*" Tyree wept. "Mr. Mayor, don't judge me like you judge your folks. I'm *black!* You know what that means here in the South. I ain't complaining, but I need help . . . Tell me what to do, *please,* sir!"

"Sell your property and prepare to defend yourself. You're in trouble, Tyree," the mayor told him. "And forget this nonsense about niggers sitting on juries; that'll never happen in this state. And tell that nigger doctor the same thing."

Tyree leaned forward and rested his head on the arm of the sofa.

"Moooooum, mooooooum," he moaned a wordless plea.

"Stop that whining and face up to what you've done," the mayor snapped at him. "The families of those dead people are going to sue you. Do you realize that?"

"They wouldn't sue if I wasn't found guilty," Tyree sobbed. "I ain't got no money—"

"You're the richest nigger in town," the mayor said snortingly. "And God only knows how you made it. How much money have you got, Tyree?"

Without replying, Tyree rocked and moaned with shut eyes. Fishbelly knew that Tyree was acting, but that acting was so real that shame wrenched him.

"Don't carry on like that!" the mayor shouted, moved.

"I done served you faithfully! No matter what you asked me to do, I did it! The Bible says: 'Even if you slay me, yet will I trust you'! Now, I need friends and my white folks turn their backs on me," Tyree keened with shut eyes.

The mayor rose and gazed silently at the sobbing black man; he glanced at the door, as though about to leave, then sat again. He shivered, then sighed.

"I'll see what I can do, Tyree," he said slowly. Then, as though to himself: "What in hell can we do with you niggers . . . ? Now, listen, Tyree. Forget this damned business about niggers on juries!"

"I ain't never said nothing like that, Mr. Mayor," Tyree rose, sweating through tears. "But you got to *save* me—"

"You'll get out on bail. Come to me and let me know what your resources are. I'll advise you how to clean up this mess," the mayor said with a smile.

"Yessir. Thank you, sir," Tyree mumbled with downcast eyes.

"I'm going now. Get your affairs straightened out."

"Thank you, sir." Tyree sighed dispiritedly. "Fish, see Mr. Mayor out. . . . Good night, Mr. Mayor."

"Good night, Tyree."

Fishbelly let the mayor out of the front door and watched him enter his car, the door of which was held open by a black chauffeur. When the car had driven off, he returned to the living room and was surprised to see Tyree putting on his hat.

"Where you going, Papa?"

"Fish," Tyree growled, his eyes blazing red, "I don't like what that goddamned white man said. I see it *all* now. *They jealous of me.* They done made up their minds to break me. We got to see Doc. These white folks think I won't fight 'em. But I will; I'll fight 'em and ride the black cat off the deep end to hell, so help me Gawd! When a man asks you how much money you got, he's planning to pick you clean, take every cent you got. And I ain't going to let that happen. I'll *die* first."

"Sh, Papa," Fishbelly warned. "Don't let Mama hear you."

"Come on," Tyree said, leading the way to the front door.

"Tyree!" Emma called distressfully. "Tell me what's happening!"

"Go to bed, Emma. See you later," Tyree said, pulling Fishbelly after him.

A moment later they were in the car. The motor roared and Tyree headed into the street, whimpering in despair:

"Gawd, I'll kill 'fore I lose all my money. . . . I'll kill, kill, *kill!*"

"What we going to do, Papa?"

"Fish, I'm gitting them canceled checks from Gloria," Tyree muttered firmly. "We got to use 'em. It's now or never. If I'm on trial, that goddamn chief of police's going to be right in that courtroom with me!"

Fishbelly sucked in his breath. Tyree was resolved to strike against the men in the city hall, hoping that such a blow would relieve him of pressure. How would that chief respond? He would most certainly react violently, for his official career and honor were at stake. Fishbelly sighed, realizing how fragile and helpless was the position of his people. The naked fact was that there was nothing left for them but flight. Tyree should stall for time, sell his property, and go away. Where? North? No. He could be extradited. . . . Then maybe go to a foreign country where people spoke another language, ate other foods, had alien habits. But such a world was beyond Fishbelly's imagination.

"Papa, you reckon you ought to do it?"

"Fish, you want to be poor and hungry?" Tyree countered. "That's what it *means.* Either I fight and win, or I do nothing and lose. And *you lose* too. If I do nothing, they'll clean me out. I'm throwing away my life to let 'em take all I ever made. Life comes to just *nothing.* I brought you into this world and I ain't going to leave you here black and naked and scared and hungry and alone. It ain't *right.* You see me crying and begging—well, that's a way of fighting. And when that way don't git me nothing, I have to do something else."

"Yessir, Papa. But don't go too far."

"A man's got to do what he's got to do," Tyree said.

They halted in front of Gloria's house.

"Fish, git that package from Gloria and put it in your pocket and come here to me," Tyree ordered. "If the chief's men come along, I'll drive off and you take the package back and tell Gloria to hide it again. Understand?"

"I got you, Papa."

"And don't let Gloria follow you out here."

"Okay, Papa."

Gloria received him in her bathrobe. But when she heard what he wanted she could scarcely move or speak.

"I want to talk to Tyree," she said.

"He ain't coming in and said for you not to come out."

"But this is *bad!*" she cried.

"Gloria, he's waiting in the car. We in a hurry."

"I must speak to him—"

"Papa ain't going to talk to you, Gloria!"

"Fish, for God's sake, don't let him do anything foolish. He's wanting those checks because he's desperate. I know Tyree. But, God in heaven, he can't fight the police and win! *They'll kill him!*"

"Look, Papa knows what he wants to do," he told her.

Gloria bit her lips and closed her eyes.

"He oughtn't do it; he oughtn't do it," she repeated.

"Papa's waiting, Gloria!" he told her tensely.

"All right," she relented despairingly. "Wait here."

She ran from the room. He stood looking at the bed that still bore the imprint of her body, studying the rouge, powder, lipstick, and perfume arranged neatly upon her dressing table. How calm and ordered was her life compared with the seething fury of Tyree's!

Gloria entered, her eyes circles of fear, hugging the package to her bosom, not wanting to surrender it. She sank upon her bed and stared blankly before her.

"I oughtn't give 'em to you," she whimpered, blinking against tears.

"Naw! Give 'em here, Gloria," he commanded.

She bent over convulsively for a long moment, then straightened and handed him the checks, sobbing.

"Papa's going to be awright," he consoled her.

"What's happening?" she asked in a tiny voice.

"I'm scared Papa's got to go to jail," he told her. "That grand jury's indicting 'im 'less he can head it off."

"Tell Tyree to do *nothing*," she whispered fiercely. "He can't *win!* He ought to *leave!*"

"But he's got to try to fight—"

"But he can't win against whites!" she sobbed. "They have the law, the guns, the juries—*everything!*"

Her intelligence, her whiteness, her flawless manner of enunciation made him endow her with the magical power and cruel cunning of the white world and he began to believe her. Maybe Tyree ought to give up and flee. . . .

"Fish, tell Tyree *not* to fight," she pleaded.

"They going to put 'im in jail and take all his money—"

"Let them *have* it!" she was emphatic.

"Aw, Gloria . . . Papa's waiting . . ."

He hurried from the house, feeling more depressed than ever. He entered the car and slid in beside Tyree.

"How come you was so long?" Tyree asked.

"She all upset, Papa. She didn't want to give 'em."

"Yeah. I thought that." Tyree sighed and started the motor. "Women can't understand these things."

Tyree drove through dark, quiet streets, handling the car with his left hand, keeping his gun in his right, now and then resting it upon his knees while shifting gears. They parked about a block from where Dr. Bruce lived. Tyree got out and looked left and right.

"Come on, Fish."

They went to the house and around to the back door.

"Don't want them goddamn white folks seeing me meeting Doc," Tyree grumbled. "They'll think we plotting." He rapped upon the windowpane. "Let me in, Doc! Quick! It's Tyree!"

A moment later Dr. Bruce opened the door.

"What's happened, Tyree?"

"I got to talk to you, Doc."

"Come in, Tyree," Dr. Bruce said. "But you've got to meet somebody first. A newspaperman's here—"

"Man, I don't want to meet no reporters," Tyree wailed. "White man or nigger?"

"One of us. . . . From up North," Dr. Bruce explained. "He's already written an article about us."

"What it say?"

"It said we violated the fire laws—"

"Goddamn! There they go trying us 'fore we git into court!" Tyree exploded.

"We've got to straighten this man out," Dr. Bruce said. "He's got his story from the city hall."

"Don't like no newspapers," Tyree grumbled, following Dr. Bruce into the receiving room.

A tall, skinny black man sat with pencil and paper in hand. He rose.

"The name's Simpson," the man said. "You're Mr. Tucker?"

"That's me. Now, what's this you putting in the papers about us? And what paper?" Tyree was aggressive.

"The Chicago *Guardian*," Simpson said. "A purely factual—"

"There ain't no facts about me that you can print without hurting me," Tyree declared. "Print the truth about me, and I'd be dead 'fore sunup."

"Tyree, the story of this fire has gone all over the country," Dr. Bruce said. "Let's face it."

"Goddamn," Tyree scowled. "How come you didn't come to us instead of sucking around them goddam white folks at City Hall? You can't prove that fire's our fault. Can we help it if that Fats nigger couldn't read—?"

"I'm not fighting you, Mr. Tucker," Simpson said. "I want the story."

Fishbelly stared at the black man from Chicago, noticing his ease, detachment, and superior manner.

"You writing fellows do a lot of harm," Tyree growled.

"Hell, I'd give you a thousand dollars to keep that story out of the papers—"

"I'm writing another one," Simpson said, laughing. "I'll sell it to you for that thousand dollars, Mr. Tucker."

"Hell," Tyree said, laughing. "I ain't in favor of no kind of writing, especially if it's about *me*. . . . But there's more to this fire mess than you can see—"

"What?" Simpson asked.

"Man, I live in a trap with these goddamn white folks and I can't tell what I know," Tyree sighed.

"Simpson, let me try to explain our position," Dr. Bruce said. "We're all black in this room, hunh? Let's talk straight."

"I appreciate that," Simpson said.

"I'm a doctor," Dr. Bruce began. "I serve our people. They have little money. I don't make enough out of my practice to live on. I treat most of my patients for almost nothing. That's why so many professional black men operate businesses on the side. Business is a side line that enables me to make both ends meet. The same's true with Tyree. . . . Understand the motive behind our operating a dance hall; it's important—"

"It's a common pattern," Simpson said. He turned to Tyree. "Mr. Tucker, there's a rumor that you're demanding that our folks be put on juries . . ."

"Now, look, Simpson," Tyree drawled. "There ain't going to be no niggers on juries down here. Not now, anyway. I just mentioned that jury business to let the white folks know that we know that they got things stacked against us. Put that in your paper, but don't say I said it. If you do, I'll sue you for lying about me."

Nervous laughter floated through the room.

"Well, that's about all," Simpson said, rising. "I'll do my best."

Dr. Bruce guided Simpson out and Tyree paced, brooding. Each event was lifting him to a higher pitch of nervousness. Fishbelly was afraid that Tyree was verging on vio-

810

lence. When Dr. Bruce returned, Tyree said:

"Doc, the mayor was by to see me tonight."

"Good God! What did he want?"

"I know what the score is now, Doc. They aim to pick us clean; they got us in a crack and they ain't going to let us go till they done squeezed us dry."

"I feared that," Dr. Bruce said heavily.

"The mayor told me to sell everything I got. And he said the same goes for you."

"What can we do, Tyree?" the doctor asked. "I'm pretty old to start all over again."

"I ain't aiming to start all over again," Tyree vowed darkly. "If they pull me down, so help me Gawd, I'll drag 'em down with me."

"How?"

Tyree tossed the batch of canceled checks upon the sofa.

"Doc, I'm going to spill *everything,*" Tyree said.

Dr. Bruce swallowed. He walked aimlessly about the room, then sat.

"You think you ought to, Tyree?" he asked quietly.

"Once they indict us, they got us licked." Tyree was logical.

"Yeah," Dr. Bruce sighed his agreement.

"The only way to stop 'em is to blow things sky-high!"

"But how? Who'll take these checks and act on them? If that chief just *thought* you were thinking of doing this, he'd kill you like—"

"That's what I want to talk to you about," Tyree told him.

Dr. Bruce lifted the packet of canceled checks, undid them and sorted through them at random; he repacked them and flung them on the sofa.

"This is a life and death matter, Tyree," he said.

"That chief's got enemies aplenty," Tyree reminded him.

"And all of 'em are scared to death of him," Dr. Bruce pointed out.

"Just tell me the name of *one* white man in this town who ain't scared," Tyree demanded.

"There's McWilliams," Dr. Bruce said. "He ran against the mayor in the last election. He's outspoken and he's a reformer. But would he act on *this?* Hell, he's a Mississippi white man too. Nine times out of ten he feels toward us like that chief does."

"Yeah, but we got to take a chance," Tyree was desperate.

"Then McWilliams is your man," Dr. Bruce said. "He's the only one with guts." The doctor shook his head. "Suppose McWilliams took these checks and made a deal with them? Where would that leave us?"

"You think there ain't no hope, Doc?"

"It's possible."

Tyree rose; his face twitched; his lips quivered.

"Then, by Gawd, I ain't going to let 'em git away with it!" he yelled. "I'll drag 'em down with me! I'll kill a white sonofabitch 'fore I let 'em break me! I swear!"

Fishbelly knew that Tyree had reached the breaking point.

"Papa," he called reprovingly.

Tyree pulled his gun and waved it wildly in the air.

"I'll kill! I ain't no coward!"

"Tyree!" the doctor shouted at him.

"I ain't going to lose like this, Doc!" Tyree raged. "For twenty years I grinned and slaved and bowed and scraped and took every insult that a man can know to git something, and now they ask me to give it all up! I won't! I'll die first!"

"Tyree, sit down! Calm yourself," Dr. Bruce urged. "Here, take this. . . ." He handed Tyree a pill and a glass of water. "You can't think straight feeling like that, man."

Tyree glared about, then swallowed the pill. He began weeping. The doctor patted his shoulder.

"That's better. Let it come out like that."

Fishbelly sat beside Tyree's racked body, hating the flowing tears, convinced that any reaction was preferable to weeping. Gloria was right: they should all clear out. . . . Oh,

Baby Jesus, how poverty-stricken was their outlook, their chances, their hopes! All of their hours were spent frenziedly within the life area mapped out by white men. Suddenly he willed himself as far away from this sodden hopelessness as possible. But the moment his mind tried to embrace the idea of something different, it went blank. He had heard of Jews wandering from nation to nation, of refugees roaming the face of the earth, but black folks remained in the same spot in peace and war, in summer and winter; they either obeyed or dodged the laws of the white man and never moved except from one set of white masters to another. They had grown used to accepting white tormentors as a part of the world, like trees, rivers, mountains—like the sun and the moon and the stars. . . . All right, since they did not know enough to run, it was better to lash out at something, no matter what.

"Let's show these damned checks to that McWilliams," Fishbelly said. "It's better'n *nothing.*"

"You right," Tyree said.

"There's nothing else we can do," the doctor said.

Fishbelly now felt afraid; they had agreed with him too quickly. He had made a random suggestion based on despair and they had leaped to embrace it. Well, why not act? Any action was better than this rot of uncertainty.

"If we going to do it, we better do it quick and give 'em to McWilliams tonight so he'll have time to think about it," he told them.

"I'm ready to see 'im now," Tyree said.

Dr. Bruce hesitated.

"You know what this means? We're carrying the fight into the camp of the enemy—"

"But there's nowhere else to fight, man," Tyree declared.

"If we can git them white folks fighting amongst themselves, mebbe some pressure'll lift off us," Fishbelly put in.

Dr. Bruce picked up the phone book and leafed through it.

"Here's his number. Want me to call him?"

"What we going to tell 'im?" Tyree asked.

"He's heard about that fire," Dr. Bruce said. "I'll tell him that we've got something on it that ought to interest him politically."

They were silent. They were playing their last card and they had to be sure that they were playing it right.

"Wonder if that McWilliams hates niggers more'n he hates crooked chiefs of police?" Fishbelly asked slowly.

"Only God knows that," Dr. Bruce said. "That's something we have to find out. You think a man's got cancer, but you never really know until you open him up. I'm all for operating."

Tyree smiled bitterly.

"Awright, Doc. Goddammit to hell. Let's operate!"

DR. BRUCE PHONED. McWilliams was in and he listened most intently to Dr. Bruce's guarded explanations. Yes, he was definitely interested and wanted to see the canceled checks. When could he visit Dr. Bruce and Tyree? Right now. He would be over in half an hour. And tell no one else. Dr. Bruce hung up.

"He's coming. He sounded interested as hell, but you never know."

"Let's git together," Tyree said determinedly. "McWilliams is white, and he ain't no friend of ours. . . . He's for good government and all that. Awright, we hand 'im this stuff and ask 'im to git it to the grand jury. Now, I'm dead sure that the chief's had to split his take with the higher-ups. So, if they indict us, they got to indict all the rest of 'em, see? *That's the deal.* The burning of the Grove, the women doing their business, all them folks being dead was not 'cause of fire violations. The law was paid to let the Grove run." His voice sank low. "It ain't going to keep us out of jail, but I want them white bastards in that court answering questions right alongside of me. If they git off, I git off. They just as guilty as me."

"It's desperate, but it's our only chance," Dr. Bruce said.

The phone rang. They looked at one another. Dr. Bruce picked up the receiver and spoke into the transmitter.

"Dr. Bruce speaking." He listened, then glanced sharply at Tyree. "I see," he murmured, his eyes roving the room. "We'll discuss it," Dr. Bruce said. "If we come, we'll be there in half an hour. If we don't, then we won't be there. Goodby." He hung up.

"Who was that?" Tyree asked.

"McWilliams. He says he can't come. He says it's better for us to come to his house—"

"I ain't going!" Tyree shouted. "He's acting like all the other goddamn white men. He done thought it over and got scared."

"He swears he's interested," Dr. Bruce said, scratching his head. "I don't get it." Baffled, he shut his eyes. "He wants those checks. Why won't he come for 'em?"

"You reckon it's a trap?" Fishbelly asked.

"Could be," Tyree said. "White men don't invite niggers to their *houses*. When visiting's done, white folks come to *us*. I ain't never been in the mayor's house, but he's been in mine."

"Well, we can drop it. Or go and take our chances," Dr. Bruce summed it up. He looked at his watch. "Thank God, it's night. That's a swanky neighborhood McWilliams lives in. Even the chief of police lives out there somewhere." He bared his teeth in a grimace. "Maybe we ought to sell our property, burn those damned checks, and get the hell out—"

"They can git us anywheres, Doc," Tyree said. "There ain't no place to run to."

The stillness was so profound that they could hear one another's breathing. Occasionally their feet moved nervously on the carpet. The sudden sound of sharp rain dashing against the shingled roof made them lift their heads. Dr.

Bruce shut the windows as lightning zipped across the sky and thunder pealed from east to west, dying rumblingly away. The phone's ringing made them start. Dr. Bruce lifted the receiver.

"Dr. Bruce speaking."

"(. . .)"

"Just a moment, Mr. McWilliams." Dr. Bruce covered the transmitter with his palm. "He wants to talk to you, Tyree."

"Give me that phone," Tyree said. He put the receiver to his ear. "Good evening, Mr. McWilliams."

"I'm waiting for you and those documents," McWilliams said.

"Well, Mr. McWilliams . . . He, he! You know we's black folks." Tyree spoke with informative humbleness. "It's best you come to see us."

"Why?"

"You want a pack of niggers tramping through your house this time of night?" Tyree asked him brutally.

"What're you afraid of?" McWilliams asked. "I'm not afraid. Come along."

Tyree's lips parted. No white man had ever spoken to him like that before.

"You reckon it's awright, Mr. McWilliams?"

"Come ahead, Tyree," McWilliams said in a flowing voice. "But let me be honest with you. I'm not fighting *for* you, Tyree. I know you by reputation. I'm fighting for justice in this town. On the basis of that, do you want to trust me?"

Tyree blinked.

"*Who* you say you fighting for, sir?"

"Justice. Justice in this town," McWilliams said.

Tyree pondered. The white man was fighting for justice, but would not fight for him. Tyree was not "legal," was outside of the law. But he was black and justice was after him, trying to send him to jail. Maybe he could sick that same justice on the police chief?

"We better go see 'im," Tyree whispered to Dr. Bruce.

"Just as you say, Tyree," Dr. Bruce sighed.

"We coming right over, Mr. McWilliams," Tyree spoke into the phone. "Good-by."

He stood and patted the gun in his pocket.

"You want to come, Fish?"

"Papa, I'm with you all the way," Fishbelly said.

"Take your car, Doc," Tyree suggested. "The police know mine."

Soon they were seated in Dr. Bruce's car, rolling through rainy night streets. Fishbelly tried to think. Were they doing right or wrong? Then he realized that there was no right or wrong in their lives. Life was a fight to keep from being killed, to keep out of jail, to avoid situations that induced too much shame. Tyree and the doctor were doing what they had to do. It was that or they fled.

"There's the house," the doctor said, pointing.

"Leave your car here. We'll walk," Tyree advised. He hesitated. "Reckon we ought to go in the back way?"

"Let's go in the front," Dr. Bruce said.

They approached the house and mounted the stone steps.

"Once we're in there, we can't back out," the doctor warned.

"We here to do what we got to do," Tyree said. "Fish, push the bell."

Fishbelly lifted his finger to jam it against the white button, and, before he could do it, the door swung open.

It was McWilliams, and Fishbelly was disturbed by the man's geniality and directness. McWilliams was in his shirt sleeves; he was tall, fortyish, spectacled.

"Come into the office," McWilliams invited them, leading the way.

Fishbelly had never before entered a white home and he was ill at ease. He followed Tyree, who trailed after Dr. Bruce. McWilliams sat behind his desk.

"Please sit down," McWilliams said.

"Thank you," Dr. Bruce said, sitting.

Fishbelly and Tyree found seats on a small sofa flanking the desk.

"Mr. McWilliams, this is my son, Fish."

McWilliams nodded toward Fishbelly, then came forward, frowning.

"I think I know what you want," McWilliams began. "But I'm not sure. I'm primarily a lawyer. Do you want to hire me to defend you or what?"

Dr. Bruce and Tyree looked at each other.

"Well, sir, I don't know," Tyree mumbled.

"If you don't know, who does?" McWilliams asked.

"Guess I just got to be honest with you, sir," Tyree said, unaware of his purring cynicism. "You heard about that Grove fire?"

"The press reported that forty-two people were asphyxiated. Seems there were some important fire violations," McWilliams said.

"Well, sir, here's the setup. Me and Doc operated the Grove," Tyree recited. "You a lawyer and I can tell you everything went on there. We made some pretty good money. The chief of police let us run—"

"Can you *prove* that, Tyree?" McWilliams shot at him.

"The proof's right here, sir," Tyree said, indicating the packet.

"Checks you gave to the chief of police?"

"Yessir."

"For what?"

"For letting us do what we wanted," Tyree said.

"And what were you doing?" McWilliams asked. "Listen, I'm not prosecuting you. You don't have to answer."

"There ain't no sense in holding back nothing now," Tyree mumbled, loath to go into details. "The only way to help ourselves is to tell the Gawd's honest truth. . . . The chief let us run, didn't bother us, see?"

"He knew what you were doing, didn't he?" McWilliams asked.

"Yessir. He knew."

"Well, what were you doing?"

"We let gals operate twenty-four hours a day there," Tyree mumbled. "Satisfying men, you know. . . . That Fats nigger handled that, collecting money from the gals. Then the chief held off the fire folks when they got rough about violations."

"And the chief's price for these services?" McWilliams asked.

"A hundred dollars a week, sir."

"Wheeeew," McWilliams whistled. "And for what else did he collect from you?" He took off his eyeglasses in a gesture of surprise.

"Well, there's a woman called Maud Williams, sir. She runs a flat, you know. She got gals there. . . . Well, I paid the chief fifty dollars a week from that—"

"What else?"

"Well, I collect ten dollars a week from four other houses for 'im. Now and then I'd kick in when a big poker or crap game got going. Stuff like that, you know."

"Give me those checks," McWilliams said.

Tyree handed over the packet and McWilliams put on his eyeglasses and examined the oblong slips of paper.

"They're made out to *him?*" McWilliams asked.

"Yessir. It was his split."

"Why was he dumb enough to accept checks?"

"Well, I been his friend for twenty years, you see. He trusted me, sir." Tyree smiled shyly.

McWilliams looked at the backs of the checks.

"He endorsed them in his own handwriting," McWilliams breathed in amazement.

"He couldn't cash 'em 'less he signed 'em," Tyree explained.

McWilliams pored over the checks, one after another.

"Five years of payments, hunh?"

"Yessir. But it's been going on for ten years, sir."

McWilliams amassed the checks and sat looking from Tyree to Dr. Bruce. His eyes finally rested upon Fishbelly.

"Is your son involved in this?"

"Nawsir. He's just sixteen. He works for me," Tyree said.

"I'm surprised that what goes on in the colored area pays off so well," McWilliams said.

"Oh, we niggers out there got money, sir." Tyree assured him.

"Why do you say 'niggers'?" McWilliams asked.

"Er . . . He, he!" Tyree stammered, laughing sheepishly. "Just a way of speaking, sir."

"These girls you were letting operate, as you call it—did any of them die in that fire?" McWilliams asked.

"Yessir. About ten of 'em?"

"What kind of girls were they?"

"Just poor gals, sir. That's all."

McWilliams rubbed his hand over his face and shook his head.

"How much money did you get from the girls?"

"What they got from the men, they split fifty-fifty with us," Tyree explained.

"And what was that for?"

"That was 'cause we managed 'em, sir. That Fats nigger did it."

"What do you mean by 'managing' them?"

"We took care of 'em, protected 'em. If they got arrested, we got 'em out of jail. The chief helped us there. . . ."

"Could these girls leave if they wanted to?"

"Oh, yessir. Sure. But they never wanted to leave us."

"Personally," McWilliams said slowly, "I detest the idea of buying and selling women, no matter what race or—"

"Well, it was us or somebody else," Tyree explained. "It's business, just like any other. You can't stop that stuff, sir. It goes on. So we just kind of organized it, sir, made it safe and regular-like, you know. . . ." Tyree felt that his ground was weak and he added quickly: "No drunk ever got rolled in the Grove, sir. And Doc took care of the gals—"

"They were *clean,*" Dr. Bruce said, not looking up.

"What do you want me to do?" McWilliams asked with a sigh.

"We want you to git these checks to that grand jury, sir. It's going to git me in trouble, but I'm awready in trouble. I lied three times to that grand jury and this is going to make me guilty of what they call perjury. But it's that or being indicted for manslaughter. . . . That chief told me to sell all I got and give 'im the money and he'd help git me off. And I just don't believe 'im, Mr. McWilliams. There ain't no reason for 'im to help me after he gits his hands on my money. Ain't natural . . ."

"You want to turn state's evidence?" McWilliams asked.

"That's right, sir," Tyree said.

"The chief of police accepted bribes from you and here is proof," McWilliams said softly. "Now, who did the bribing?"

"Me. I did," Tyree stated frankly. "You can't operate houses like the Grove and Maud Williams' place without bribes. . . ."

"It's illegal to bribe the law," McWilliams said.

Tyree blinked.

"But the *white man* is the law," Tyree pointed out.

"It's still illegal," McWilliams maintained.

"But the white man took the bribes," Tyree argued. "There ain't no law but *white* law. . . . You say it's against the law to take bribes, but the white man takes 'em."

"And now you don't want the white man to squeeze your money out of you?" McWilliams asked.

"Why should only we suffer and go to jail?" Dr. Bruce asked.

"That's a fair question," McWilliams said, nodding. "But don't you realize that you were wrong in what you did?"

"There was nothing else to do," Tyree spoke testily.

"That's no defense in a court of law," McWilliams told him.

Tyree rose and stared.

"White men make the law and they let us break it when we pay 'em," he said.

"You still broke the law," McWilliams said.

Fishbelly saw Tyree's swelling, hot bitterness reaching the boiling point. Tyree's hands trembled. What kind of a man was this McWilliams? Was he for him or against him? Why was he harping about the law? The law was the chief of police; the law could talk, could act, could accept bribes. When you wanted something, you asked a white man and he said yes or no and told you how much it would cost.

"But they *white* men!" Tyree insisted, amazed.

"That makes no difference," McWilliams maintained. "It's corrupt to *take* bribes and it's corrupt to *give* them—"

"I ain't *corrupt!*" Tyree was defiant.

"Then what are you?" McWilliams asked. "You just admitted—"

Tyree doubled his fists; he stood in the center of the room and words in wild profusion poured out of him like a torrent of water tumbling over rocks:

"Mr. McWilliams, I ain't corrupt. I'm a *nigger.* Niggers ain't corrupt. Niggers ain't got no rights but them they *buy.* You say I'm wrong to buy me some rights? How you think we niggers live? I want a wife. A car. A house to live in. The white man's got 'em. Then how come I can't have 'em? And when I git 'em the only way I can, you say I'm corrupt. Mr. McWilliams, if we niggers didn't buy justice from the white man, we'd never git any. I ain't got no rights; my papa never had any, and my papa's papa never had any; and my son sitting there ain't got none but what he can buy. Look, Mr. McWilliams, for years I done bought me rights from the white man and I done built a business. I got a home. A car. Now the same men who sold me my rights ask me to give 'em all my money. . . ." Tyree choked at the injustice of it; rage held him speechless. "They got me in a goddamn trap! Yessir, they got me!" He began to shout. "But they going to come into this trap with me! They ain't going to milk me dry! I'll die first, you hear? Mr. McWilliams, I can't vote. There ain't no black men in office in this town. We black folks is helpless and all we can do is buy a little protection. If I'm corrupt, who made me corrupt? Who took the bribes? The law, and the law's white. I live in what the white man calls Nigger Town. . . . Mr. McWilliams, I didn't make Nigger Town. White men made it. Awright. I say, 'Okay.' But, goddammit, let me *live* in Nigger Town! And don't call me corrupt when I live the only way I can live. Sure, I did wrong. But my kind of wrong is right; when you have to do wrong to live, wrong is right. . . . But I ain't never had no trouble in this town. Ask them white men in the city hall. They'll tell you Tyree's *straight.* I keep my word. When I told that goddamn chief of police I'd pay 'im a hundred and ninety dollars every Sat'day night, I *did* it. I got it out of the whores and gamblers and gave it to 'im. And he said: 'Thank you, Tyree.' Now, 'cause the fire's done made me look guilty, he wants to take all my money. I say, hell, naw! I swear 'fore Gawd he won't git it! I'll kill first. That's where I stand. I ain't mad at you, Mr. McWilliams. But you got to know straight just what this is. Ain't no use in you talking to me about law and justice. That ain't got nothing to do with me. If the law was fair, I wouldn't be in your house talking like this to you. . . . Mr. McWilliams, can't you see what I mean? This is the life I live. I live it 'cause I got to. And I don't complain. I took the white man's law and lived under it. It was *bad* law, but I made it work for me and my family, for my son there. . . . Now, just don't tell me to go and give it all up. I won't! I'll never give up what I made out of my blood!'"

Tyree finished with a dry sob and sat down. For the first time Fishbelly had heard Tyree speak out the shame and the glory that was theirs, the humiliation and the pride, the desperation and the hope. Oh, why had not Tyree said all of this to him before? Why had he to wait until this moment of danger to know how it really was with his father? He saw

McWilliams staring at Tyree with an open mouth. Dr. Bruce gaped at Tyree as though he had never seen him before.

"My God," McWilliams sighed, pulled off his eyeglasses. "I never saw it that way."

"It's the way we live every day," Tyree said.

"Do you agree with Tyree?" McWilliams asked Dr. Bruce.

"I'm a doctor, sir," Dr. Bruce said. "But I don't think I could have said it any better."

"Tyree, I don't want to hurt you. You must believe that," McWilliams said.

"Mr. McWilliams, I was hurt when I was born black with an empty gut in Mississippi," Tyree told him bitterly.

"I can do what you want," McWilliams said. "But I cannot guarantee that you won't be hurt more than you are already hurt. That's the problem. The law holds you guilty along with the others. Since you spoke, I know why you did it. But the law does not recognize that excuse. I admit that your people have been terribly provoked. There was slavery, and then there was hate on the part of the white man for the freed slave. Then your people began to *adjust* to an *unjust* situation. And that is what we are dealing with. But only a Solomon could untangle that knot. Your excuse is valid. But what can I do about it? I'll break this foul mess open. I'll chase that chief of police out of office. *But you're in danger!*"

"We awready in danger, Mr. McWilliams," Tyree mumbled.

"Let them indict *all* the guilty, not just the *black* ones," Dr. Bruce said.

"I agree," McWilliams said. "But it's a strange way to get at justice. . . ." He stared long and hard at Tyree. "I'm sorry I asked you why you called your people 'niggers.' I think I know now."

"We niggers 'cause we can't do nothing that's free," Tyree said.

"There are rumors that that city-hall mob has been trying to tamper with that grand jury," McWilliams said. "And that

police chief is a dangerous man. He'll stop at nothing,"
McWilliams said and rose.

Tyree, Fishbelly, and Dr. Bruce rose.

"Thank you for coming," McWilliams said.

They went out; it was still raining. They drove silently to
the Black Belt.

"What do you think of McWilliams, Tyree?" Dr. Bruce
asked.

"He, he! Funny kind of white man," Tyree said.

"He doesn't want to hurt us, but can he help us?" Fishbelly
said.

"That's just it." Tyree sighed.

Fishbelly and Tyree got out of the doctor's car and stood
in the rain.

"Well, we done hit back," Tyree said.

"Yes," the doctor mumbled. "But be careful."

"Right. Good night, Doc," Tyree said.

"Good night," Fishbelly called.

When they reached home, Tyree said tenderly:

"Son, let's git some sleep. I think we going to need it."

As THE NIGHT sounded with raging rain, Fishbelly entered
his room and sank limply upon his bed. So numb was he with
fatigue that he was tempted to sleep fully clad. He roused
himself, undressed, and slid beneath the covers. The excitement of striking at the police chief had temporarily washed
the terrible death of Gladys from his memory and had fogged
his realization that Tyree could, barring a miracle from
McWilliams, still be jailed, or even slain. Their disclosing the
canceled checks now compelled him to consider the possibility that he might have to face the future alone. And then the
awful futility of what they had done at McWilliams's stunned
him; they had mobilized all of their courage to deal a blow
that had not really solved anything. Their running forward
with the canceled checks had been more balm for their in-

jured vanity than a guarantee of their safety, more bitter defiance than studied wisdom.

He had constantly hankered to be on his own; yet, when faced with the awful freedom posed by the absence of Tyree, he shrank and sought means of staving it off. He wanted freedom, but with the sanction of a living, indulgent father. If Tyree were jailed, he would have to carry on with Jim's help, but he was young for that, *too* young. And if Tyree were gone, how would he face the whites? He recalled with dismay that, other than those past, bruising brushes with the police, he had no practical knowledge of whites. What would be his attitude when he met them? The mere thought made him wince. Could he imitate Tyree's tactics and make them sorry, sad—make them laugh and feel safe? *"Naw!"* he spoke aloud, then sighed in the humid darkness, hearing rainy wind lashing the windowpanes. He could not whine, grin, plead; he would die first. . . .

And he saw himself so clearly as the whites saw him that he was certain that the whites could easily detect his adoring hatred of them; they would feel it and kill him. . . . But why was he so firmly sure about the feelings of whites toward black people? He was sure, because, deep in his heart, he felt that the whites were right, but he didn't agree to belonging to that part of mankind that the whites despised! He felt rather than thought this; it came to him in flashes of intuition. On this he and Tyree agreed; the difference between them was that Tyree had automatically accepted the situation and worked willingly within it. Fishbelly also accepted the definition, but he did so consciously and therefore could never work within it. If his town had been an all-black town, he would have gone on and built up Tyree's business with no anxieties. Had his town been an all-white one (in that case, he, too, would have been white!), he could have gone on and built up Tyree's business in a normal manner. But he lived in a black-white town and he had to try to sustain Tyree's business under conditions that the whites had created but despised—and if he accepted those debased conditions and tried to fit his personality into their requirements, the whites would regard him with disdain and hatred, a disdain and hatred with which he, deep in his heart, agreed! Yet he hated himself for agreeing with them, *for he was black.*

Suddenly he half sat up in bed, leaning against his pillow, hearing the storm pounding the house, glimpsing lightning flickering blue past the edges of the shaded window. "What can I *do?*" he whispered wailingly into the dark. If he attempted to grope his way through such dense shadows, he would be killed as surely as Chris had been. Better to flee to some other spot on the earth's surface than let that overtake him. But where? He grew confused, trying to solve a problem about which he could scarcely think.

Yet, maybe, goddammit, there was an out. He would be reserved with the whites, act as sedately as they, stand aloof; then they would know that he had dignity, pride, that he was not the cringing type. But would they really believe that he had such dignity, pride? *Naw!* He honestly did not think so. Why? *He was black.*

The money he had had been made by a black buzzard of a Tyree, a crawling scavenger battening upon only the black side of human life, burying only the black dead, selling only the living black female bodies to the white or black world, buying justice, protection, comfort from those sordid dealings and calling it business. His manhood cringed as he realized once more that the money he had been spending had come partly from poor Gladys' earnings. He leaped from bed, haunted by her reluctant smile, and stood with his hot cheek resting against the wall of the room. "Creeping Jesus," he moaned. He sank back upon his bed, feeling his home and all the Black Belt about him tainted, useless, repugnant.

He shut his eyes tightly, trying to cling to a world ruled by the father he had always known, but wishing that that father could have been another and different kind of man. Then he was dreaming out his problem. . . .

... *he was sitting at the office desk making out rent receipts behind him the office door opened and he turned and saw Gladys and Gloria entering smiling sweetly and they came to him and kissed him and both of them opened their handbags and began pulling out bundles of green paper money and piling them upon the desk and he said: "But this ain't my money" and Gloria and Gladys smiled and said: "Don't be stupid; it's all yours" and he asked: "But where you git this money?" and they looked like two smiling white women and whispered: "We stole it for you from white men" and he said: "Naw" and they said: "Don't be silly; take the money and hide it" and he stuffed the bundles of money into his pockets and said: "Gawd, I'm rich!" then there was a loud knock at the door and he was terrified and whisperingly asked Gloria and Gladys: "Who's that?" and they laughingly said: "Don't be scared! It's a friend of ours" and he opened the door and the chief of police stood and said: "All right, nigger. You stole forty-two bundles of money!" and he said: "Nawsir!" and Gloria and Gladys shouted: "He's got 'em in his pockets!" and the chief said: "Empty your pockets, nigger!" and he emptied his pockets of the green bills and the chief asked: "Now, just where'd you get this money?" and he said: "I worked for it" and the chief said: "We'll see about that" and he picked up a bill and said: "This money is marked ... See? Fish, you bit the bait!" and he looked and on each bill was the smiling face of a white woman and he whirled to Gloria and Gladys and cried: "You bitches! You tricked me!" and the laughter of Gladys and Gloria echoed throughout the undertaking parlor and they said: "You're black and we're white and you'll believe anything we say!" and he turned to the chief yelling: "They're the guilty ones! Arrest them! and the chief snorted and said: "Listen to a nigger talking about justice!" and the chief pulled out a pair of handcuffs and he ducked under the chief's arm and dashed out of the office into a rear room filled with coffins and he saw his mother beckoning to him and calling whis-*

*peringly: "Fish, hide in a coffin—quick!" and he climbed
into an empty coffin and stretched out and closed his eyes
as though dead and he heard the chief running into the room
and he felt him standing over him and looking down into his
face and he fought against a desire to open his eyes to see if
the chief suspected his being alive and then he could resist
no longer and he opened his eyes and saw the chief and
Gladys and Gloria looking down at him and laughing and
the chief said: "All right, nigger. Either you're dead and
we'll bury you, or you come out of there and go to jail!"*

He awakened in the dark, swallowing as though to keep
something down, trying to blink away unwelcome images.
Free of dread, he slept again, but fitfully, grinding his teeth
in slumber.

HE OPENED HIS EYES and saw a gray, sunless morning seeping in at the edges of the window shades. He put on the light
and looked at his watch; it was ten o'clock. He bounded from
bed, flung on his robe, and ran into the living room. Tyree,
haggard-faced, was sitting on the sofa, fully dressed, fumbling with the morning's paper.

"Why didn't somebody wake me up?" Fishbelly demanded. "Say, anything new, Papa?"

"You needed sleep," Tyree said, extending the paper.
"There's something in there about McWilliams and that
grand jury. What it say?"

Fishbelly read aloud:

MCWILLIAMS CHARGES FRAUD IN HIGH PLACES
COURT CLERK ASSAULTED THIS MORNING
IN PUBLIC
GRAND JURY MEET POSTPONED

Attorney Harvey McWilliams, who ran against Mayor Wakefield
during the last city election, said this morning that vital evidence
which he had promised to submit to the grand jury had been seized
by force and violence by unknown parties.

Mr. McWilliams stated that late last night he had phoned Grand Jury Foreman Samuel Bright and had informed him that he had in his possession evidence regarding police corruption in the city. At an early hour this morning Foreman Bright dispatched Court Clerk Albert Davis to the home of McWilliams where he received a sealed envelope addressed to the grand-jury foreman.

Within a block of the McWilliams home, Albert Davis was set upon by three men who forcibly deprived him of the envelope.

"The criminal attack upon Court Clerk Davis is proof of flagrant corruption in high places," McWilliams said.

McWilliams charged that only parties who feared exposure could have engineered the deed.

Mr. Davis described his assailants as men who knew exactly what they were looking for.

"Five minutes after I left Mr. McWilliams's home, a black sedan stopped beside me and three men leaped out. Two of them held me while the third opened my brief case and extracted the envelope that McWilliams had just entrusted to me. The whole episode took place in full view of passers-by who did not realize what was happening until too late. The men got back in the car and sped off before any one could take the license number."

Mayor Wakefield said that he was stunned that any man or group of men could have the audacity to attack court personnel in such an open and criminal manner. He pledged a quick and thorough investigation.

Grand Jury Foreman Samuel Bright disclosed that the scheduled session of the grand jury that was to meet in the chambers of Augustus Moon this morning would be postponed. The grand jury had been probing into alleged connections between police officials and vice and gambling interests. . . .

"Good Gawd, Papa!" Fishbelly cried, his hands shaking.

Tyree stared stonily before him and said nothing.

"You think them checks got into the wrong hands, Papa?"

"I don't know, son," Tyree said heavily. "Something's gone wrong. . . . But it's out of our hands." Tyree stood with a hard, bleak face. "Now, now, keep calm, Fish. Finish dressing and git some coffee and come here and sit down. I got to talk to you."

"Papa, that stuff in that paper's about *us. I know it.* What can we do?"

Tyree's face was ashy but firm.

"Go do what I told you, Fish," Tyree said. "And not a word to your mama about this. All we need is for her to start blubbering."

"Okay, Papa," he said, feeling the horrible fear that Tyree was mastering. *The checks were lost!* And who could want them but the chief of police? If the chief had got hold of the checks, then Tyree was doomed. And he knew that Tyree knew it. Had they been spied upon? He dressed with shaking hands, then took the cup of coffee offered by Emma.

"How you sleep, son?" she asked him.

"Oh, awright," he mumbled.

"I'm worried. What Tyree doing, Fish?" she asked, fear and tears twisting her mouth.

"Nothing, Mama. How come you crying?"

"Son, don't let Tyree do nothing foolish," she whispered.

"What you talking about, Mama?" He wanted to scream.

"I'm scared for 'im," she whimpered, clutching his arm.

"Aw, Mama, stop!" he chided her, his nerves on edge.

"You and Tyree be careful," she sobbed. "Don't go riling them white folks. They got all the power and—"

"Mama, what you keeping on talking like that for?" He gritted his teeth.

She hugged him and he felt her hot tears on his cheeks.

"When that funeral for the folks that died in the fire, son?"

"Next Friday," he told her.

"Son, if you got any problems, take 'em to Gawd."

"Mama, ain't nothing's going to happen," he muttered. He drained his coffee cup and rose, keeping his face averted. "I got to talk to Papa." He left her abruptly.

He sat beside Tyree in the living room and looked compassionately at him.

"Papa, don't let a white face git *near* you today."

"Take it easy, Fish," Tyree said calmly. "Now, lissen . . . I told Emma I might have to go to jail for a bit. Don't tell her nothing else. Now, if anything happens, I want you to take over. Handle the office. Jim'll help you. You know what to do."

"Oh, Papa," he wailed tensely.

"And Fish, go kind of easy on your mama," Tyree advised. "She don't understand these things."

"Sure, Papa."

The phone rang and Fishbelly picked it up. Jim's voice came over the wire.

"There's a telegram here for Tyree."

"Read it, Jim, and I'll tell Papa what it says."

"Right," Jim said. "You listening?"

"Yeah."

"YOUR PRESENCE NOT NEEDED AT CITY HALL TODAY

CANTLEY"

"That all, Jim?"

"That's it."

Fishbelly hung up and turned to Tyree.

"The chief wired that you don't have to show up today, Papa."

Father and son stared at each other.

"That chief *knows,*" Tyree said softly.

"But how'd he find out, Papa?" Fishbelly asked with tortured eyes. "He don't want to arrest you now. He knows you going to talk."

"That's it, son."

"What we going to do, Papa?"

"We just got to wait, son. That's all we can do."

Again the phone pealed. It was McWilliams. Fishbelly handed the phone to Tyree.

"Tyree, do you know what's in the morning papers?" McWilliams asked.

"Yessir. I know."

"You know what it means."

"I guess that chief's got hold of them checks. That right, Mr. McWilliams?"

"Right. But we can't prove a thing."

"But how'd he know you had 'em, Mr. McWilliams?"

"Tyree, three things could've happened. There could have been a leak from around the grand jury. Cantley could have spied on you and the doctor. Or your phone was tapped. ... Now, Tyree, it seems that I've failed you. I'm not through with this case. I'll never rest till I get to the bottom of this foul mess. Tyree, I'm phoning you to warn you. You're in danger. *Be careful.*"

"Yessir. I understand."

"Don't you think you ought to have some police protection?"

"Police protection? Nawsir! I don't want no white men near me."

"I see. . . . But maybe you ought to get out of town until this is settled."

"I ain't running, Mr. McWilliams. Running says I'm guilty. And I ain't guilty."

"Well, take care, Tyree. The attack on Albert Davis was the most dastardly thing I've ever heard of. I'm going to fight this thing till I drop."

"Yessir. Good-by, sir."

"I'll see you as soon as I have something definite. Good-by."

Tyree recounted what McWilliams had said.

"They was watching us," Fishbelly mumbled despairingly.

The phone rang for the third time. It was Dr. Bruce, who, too, had received a telegram from the chief of police informing him that he need not appear at City Hall. Dr. Bruce had also talked with McWilliams over the phone.

"How come they ain't arresting us, Doc?" Tyree asked.

"If the chief's got hold of those checks, he doesn't want to see us except to kill us," Dr. Bruce said. "Tyree, for God's sake, keep out of sight until this blows over. The whites are fighting among themselves and that might give us a breathing spell. Keep your gun handy and don't leave the Black Belt."

"Right, Doc. Keep in touch, hunh? I got my gun. I ain't going nowhere but to the office.

Tyree hung up.

"Papa, that chief's plotting something. I know it," Fishbelly warned nervously.

"Son, no matter what happens," Tyree said, "we done won something. They can't git no money from me. Let's git to the office."

As they drove through sunless Black-Belt streets, Tyree reached inside his coat pocket and pulled out a long white envelope.

"Put this in your pocket, son. And hang onto it," Tyree spoke in a faraway voice. "If anything happens to me, then you read it. That lawyer Heith's got one."

"Okay, Papa."

Tyree had given him his last will and testament and he felt crushed.

"Papa, let's go away—"

"Naw. We stay here. And we got to be ready for anything."

"Naw, naw, naw, Papa." Fishbelly was growing hysterical, was beginning to weep.

Tyree stopped the car and turned to him.

"Stop that goddamn crying, Fish!" he growled.

"But, Papa, you—"

"FISH, STOP THAT CRYING!"

"Yessir," he gulped.

"It's awright to cry when it can git you something," Tyree said, driving again. "But crying now ain't no good."

Tyree, while saying a tentative good-by, was handing him the fruits of a lifetime struggle. And what could he say? Nothing. There were no words for such an act, such an occasion. But Tyree could not leave him, not yet. . . . "That can't be!" he cried inwardly. His father had draped about his shoulders an invisible cloak of authority, had made toward him a gesture of faith that went beyond the sights and sounds of the world. He was swamped by a feeling akin to religious emotion, for Tyree had performed toward him an act that linked the living with the dead. He stared out of the car window at the familiar streets that now seemed somehow strange. And his sense of awe deepened when he heard Tyree softly whistling a popular tune, as though he had unburdened himself of an awful load.

"Papa, let's *do* something," he pleaded in a whisper.

"Everything's going to be awright, son," Tyree said.

Entering the office, Tyree greeted Jim heartily.

"Hi, Jim! Everything okay at the morgue?"

"We're all set, Tyree," Jim said.

"Jim, I ain't in to nobody. Git it?"

"Right, Tyree. How're you making out with the chief?" Jim asked.

"I done straightened up and I'm flying right," Tyree sang. "You'll read about it in the papers."

Fishbelly was at Tyree's elbow all that apprehensive morning. He was amazed at how Tyree forgot his anxieties and squelched his sense of guilt for the fire victims and absorbed himself with forging a memorable event out of the mass interment. He phoned and pleaded with all the local black preachers and gained their reluctant consent to hold a collective funeral in the largest Black-Belt church, of which Reverend Amos Jutland Ragland was pastor. In defiance of suspicion pointing toward him, he organized the creation of a gigantic floral wreath "for all them poor folks who died in that terrible fire." Fishbelly scoured the white and black floral shops of the entire town for hundreds of gross of tuberoses, gladioli, lilies, carnations, peonies, dahlias, etc.

"Cover the whole goddamn front wall of the church with flowers," Tyree decreed with grim exultation. "Make it the biggest floral wreath this town ever saw. . . . To show you where my heart is, I'm donating fifty dollars out of my own pocket."

To the bereaved who called to ask timid worried questions about the origin and responsibility of the fire, Tyree did not bite his tongue as he declared, lifting a black forefinger heavenward:

"Let me tell you the Gawd's truth. Any crooked-brained sonofabitch who gives you a bum steer and tells you I had anything to do with that fire's lying! My own son, my own flesh and blood, missed going up in them flames by just five goddamn minutes. Fish could've been stretched out cold and dead and full of formaldehyde just like all the rest of 'em. You think I'd let a fire start that could burn up my own son? Don't be a fool! And don't let nobody make you believe that Doc had anything to do with it neither. That's just jealous gossip spread by them no-good white folks downtown. We told Fats to take care of things and that nigger didn't. Drinking too much, mebbe. And to show you folks that I'm on the dead level, I'm giving, without nobody asking me, 10 per cent off on every funeral. Tyree's straight and everybody knows it."

His stunned and bewildered clients accepted his explanations and, toward eleven o'clock, the office was free of weeping customers. The most stupendous funeral that Clintonville had ever seen was under way.

"Jesus," Fishbelly marveled, "when Papa's handling dead folks, there ain't a smarter nigger living."

The hours dragged calmly, *too* calmly. Other than keep track of the embalming and creating emergency viewing rooms, the day proceeded in a casual, normal manner.

"It's *too* goddamn quiet," Tyree fretted. "I don't like it."

Fishbelly watched the Black-Belt streets, but not a white face showed, not a single police car could be seen cruising.

"Papa, I want to say something," Fishbelly said.

"Yeah, son. What is it?"

"Let's go away for a few days."

"That's saying we guilty. And we ain't no more guilty than they is," Tyree said.

"We could stay three-four days in Memphis and when we

got back things'd be sort of clear," Fishbelly argued.

"Fish, I ain't running. All I got's here. And here I stay."

A few minutes before noon, Jim, wearing his white embalming jacket, came to Fishbelly and whispered:

"Fish, most of the folks are being laid out in the school gym, but Tyree told me to put Gladys in our viewing room. You want to see her?"

Fishbelly closed his eyes and was as still as stone, then he rose and followed Jim meekly back into the viewing room. Gladys lay in a plain white dress in a plain gray coffin that stood in a row of others. He stared at her pale, waxy face holding that hint of a sad smile and he recalled that she had not understood what it meant to be black, and now she was gone. His eyes clouded and he remembered Tyree's impassioned outburst last night in McWilliams's home and he wondered if he and Tyree were guilty of having killed Gladys. ... "I took the white man's law and lived under it. It was bad law, but I made it work for me and my family. ..." As always, every time he tried to think about his life, he found himself mulling over the strange reality of the white man. He returned to the office and put his hand on Tyree's shoulder.

"I want Gladys to have another box, Papa. A better one," he whimpered.

"Sure, Fish," Tyree said. "She can have what you want." He laid aside his cigar and called: "Jim!" He pushed Fishbelly gently toward a chair. "Sit down, son."

Jim appeared in the doorway.

"Put Gladys in one of the de-luxe boxes. ... Wait." Tyree rose and went to the door. "I'll show you." He led Jim out of the office.

Fishbelly leaned his head upon the desk and wept. A few moments later he felt Tyree's hand take hold of his shoulder.

"Son, life's hard, but there's some sweet things in it. Don't go letting this spoil everything, see?"

"I'll try, Papa," he mumbled with trembling lips.

When they went home for lunch, Tyree drove with his gun

on his lap, looking left and right. Emma served them with averted face. She refused to eat, pleading a headache. Back at the office, Dr. Bruce phoned and said that nothing had happened.

"I don't like this," Tyree grumbled. "It's *too* quiet."

"Papa, let's leave; let's git in the car and leave *now*—"

"Naw! Running won't help none," Tyree vetoed the idea for the third time.

A little after six o'clock Dr. Bruce was again on the phone. His voice sounded nervous and excited.

"Tyree, Maud's sick," Dr. Bruce explained. "Vera just called me. She's had some kind of an attack. I'm getting over there to see what's wrong. Just want to let you know where I am, see?"

"Okay, Doc," Tyree said. "What's the matter with Maud?"

"I don't know yet; I haven't seen her."

"Keep in touch," Tyree said. He turned to Fishbelly. "Maud's sick. Doc's gitting over there. Bet she's worried about this mess. If that grand jury cracks down, her flat'll have to close."

The hours dragged. At the final moment of daylight the sun burst through for a few moments and drenched the damp streets in gold. Jim announced that the embalming of the forty-two bodies had been completed.

"Tyree, the coroner's verdict was that they died from accidental causes, the nature of which has to be determined," Jim told him.

"That means they ain't made up their minds, hunh?" Tyree asked, staring stonily.

"That's right."

"Well, what's got to be is got to be," Tyree said. "Jim, I know you tired. You'll git a bonus for this. You been on your feet for two days and nights running—"

"I did my best for you, Tyree," Jim said modestly.

"Let's blow for home, Fish," Tyree suggested.

"Okay, Papa."

Just as they were about to leave, the phone rang and Fish-belly answered.

"Fish?" Dr. Bruce's voice hummed over the wire.

"Yeah, Doc."

"Let me talk to Tyree."

"Just a sec, Doc." Fishbelly called Tyree. "Papa, it's Doc."

As Fishbelly handed the phone to Tyree, he was vaguely aware that some cog had slipped in the turning routine of time, but he could not put his finger upon it. He listened while Tyree talked over the phone.

"Yeah, Doc."

"(. . .)"

"What?" Tyree exclaimed.

"(. . .)"

"Dead? When, man?"

"(. . .)"

"Good Lawd! About a hour ago? What was wrong?"

"(. . .)"

"Her heart, hunh?"

"(. . .)"

"Was she living when you got there?"

"(. . .)"

"Papa, what's happened?" Fishbelly asked.

"Just a minute, Doc." Tyree turned to Fishbelly. "Maud Williams is dead—dropped dead about a hour ago. It was her heart."

"Maud Williams dead?" Fishbelly exclaimed.

"You there now, Doc?" Tyree spoke into the phone.

"(. . .)"

"Yeah, I git you. Papers, hunh? You stick there till I git over. If Maud asked me to take care of her papers, there must be something in 'em she didn't want nobody to see. Git the point? What with this trouble, I better git them papers . . . Where Vera?"

"(. . .)"

There was a pause. Tyree looked distractedly about.

"Damn . . . That nigger bitch was strong's a horse. Didn't think she'd kick the bucket like that." He spoke again into the phone: "Yeah. That you, Vera?"

"(. . .)"

"Vera, honey, I'm so sorry . . . Sure. I'll be right over. Lissen, Vera, don't let nobody touch a thing belonging to Maud, see?"

"(. . .)"

"Okay. See you."

Tyree hung up and rubbed his right hand over his eyes, then walked across the office.

"You wait for one thing and something else pops up. How in hell Maud went and died like that?" He stared glumly out of the window. "That makes a problem. Vera's too young to handle the business. . . . Needs a tough woman to do a job like that." Tyree went to the door. "Jim!" he called.

"Jim, old Maud Williams died about a hour ago," Tyree announced.

"Good God!" Jim said. "What happened?"

"It was her heart, Doc says."

"Well, Tyree you have to expect things like that." Jim spoke philosophically. "We're sending for her? Dr. Bruce make out the death certificate?"

"Doc's there now. Been knowing Maud for thirty years. I better git over." Tyree put on his hat. "Fish, stick here till I git back. Won't be long."

"I want to go with you, Papa," he begged.

"Naw. It ain't far. It's in the Black Belt. Doc's there," Tyree told him. "Don't want nobody poking around Maud's things with all this Who-Shot-John going on."

"For Gawd's sake, be *careful,* Papa!"

"Sure . . . Jim, tell Jake and Guke to bring the hearse to Maud's in about half an hour, hunh?"

"Right, Tyree," Jim said in a worried tone.

Tyree lingered in the doorway, inserted a fresh cigar into his mouth and held a match flame to its end.

"I'm tired," he mumbled.

"Let me 'tend to it for you, Papa," Fishbelly begged.

"Naw, Fish. Got to do this myself," Tyree said.

"Okay, Papa."

"See you, Fish."

Dreamily, he watched Tyree drive off and he knew that his gun was on his lap as he shifted gears. You ate, slept, breathed, and lived fear. Somewhere out there in the gray void was the ever-lurking enemy who shaped your destiny, who curbed your ends, who determined your aims, and who stamped your every action with alien meanings. You existed in the bosom of the enemy, shared his ideals, spoke his tongue, fought with his weapons, and died a death usually of his choosing. Fishbelly wondered if it would always be like that. Black people paid a greater tribute to the white enemy than they did to God, whom they could sometimes forget; but the white enemy could never be forgotten. God meted out rewards and punishments only after death; you felt the white man's judgment every hour.

He slumped in a chair, sick of this season of death. Maud Williams dead? Didn't seem possible. His lips smiled dryly as he remembered the night that Tyree had taken him up on the hill and had shown him Nigger Town, and then had led him to Vera's arms; and he recalled the sly light in Maud's eyes when she had asked him if he had had a good time. . . . There were people whose personalities seemed to exempt them from death, and Maud Williams, with her cackling laughter, her brutally lewd jokes, her amorality, and her business cunning had been one of those.

He heard the evening paper hit the front porch and got it. He saw:

POLICE HEADS DENY LINK WITH VICE RACKETS

Today the city hall was in an uproar following this morning's highjacking of court clerk Albert Davis by persons unknown. Accusation and counteraccusations have come from most city government department heads.

Mayor Wakefield called publicly upon Harvey McWilliams to disclose, in the public interest, the identities of the parties that figured in the evidence which he had promised to submit to the grand jury. This evidence was presumably contained in the sealed envelope of which court clerk Albert Davis was robbed in the streets this morning.

Mr. McWilliams countercharged that he could not disclose such information without endangering the lives of his informants.

Chief of Police Gerald Cantley said that McWilliams was libeling the integrity of the police department when he inferred that any citizen went in fear of his life by co-operating with the grand jury. . . .

Fishbelly knew that that story meant that the police chief was daring McWilliams to identify Tyree directly, hinting that there would be no Tyree if it were known that Tyree had betrayed him. The white folks were fighting among themselves. . . . Tyree had been gone for more than an hour when the phone rang. Fishbelly lifted the receiver and spoke into the transmitter:

"Tyree Tucker's Funeral Home."

"Fish? That you?" came a familiar woman's voice that made the hair bristle on Fishbelly's head.

"Who this?" he asked, feeling engulfed in a dream.

"Fish, this is Maud—"

"*What?*" he asked in a shout, his skin prickling. Though he was unaware of it, he rose, gripping the phone, his eyes dancing.

"This is Maud!" the voice wailed. "You got to come *quick!*"

"*But who is this?*" he demanded slowly, his mind whirling.

"THIS IS MAUD SPEAKING!" Maud yelled at him over the wire. "Something awful's happened! Come right away!"

"B-but . . . Lissen . . . D-doc phoned . . . And Vera said you were *d-dead* . . . Is this a joke?" he asked, sensing catastrophe crawling somewhere near him.

"Fish, I can't explain everything now," Maud told him with panting breath. "But, man, come! Tyree's been shot! It was a *trap*, Fish!"

Fishbelly's eyes bulged in his head.

"W-where's Papa?" he asked stammeringly, trying to understand.

"Fish, come quick! The police done shot Tyree!"

The room reeled. His brain tied itself into a knot as he tried to think. MAUD WAS ALIVE! The afternoon flashed before his eyes: Doc had called Tyree from Maud's saying that Maud was dead; and Tyree had rushed to Maud's . . .

"W-where Papa? I want to talk to Papa—"

"Fish, for Gawd's sake, can't you *understand?*" Maud screamed. "It was a trick! Tyree's been shot! He's in my flat! Oh Lawd, it wasn't our fault . . . Tyree wants to talk to you. He don't know how long he can last, how long he can hold out—"

Fishbelly dropped the phone as the truth exploded in his tight skull. The muscles of his body jerked taut. Doc had phoned that Maud was dead and Tyree rushed over and the police had shot him! If, at that moment, he could have lifted his hand and smashed the earth upon which he stood, he would have done it. *The white folks had struck!* He doubled his fists and bellowed a harsh moan.

"Gawd, if they killed my papa, I'll kill *everybody!* I'll spread blood, goddammit! Oh, Crawling Jesus, I'll spread blood everywhere!" He snatched up the phone and yelled into it: "Hello! Hello!" But the line was dead. He hurled the phone from him. "Jim! Jim!" he screamed, running into the rear of the "shop," stumbling past coffins filled with the dead. "Jim! Jim!"

"Yes, Fish," Jim came running. "What's the matter?"

"Papa! Papa's been *shot!*"

"What?" Jim blinked.

"Maud told me—"

"*Maud?*" Jim asked, staring at Fishbelly with glistening eyes.

"She just phoned—"

"But Tyree said Maud Williams was *dead!*"

"I know ... It was a trick, Jim," he sobbed. "Aw, to hell with this goddamn world! I told Papa to *leave!* We should've been watching for this!"

"But Dr. Bruce—"

"That damned doctor baited Papa for the police and I'll kill 'im!" He ran to a wall and began to beat his fists against it. "Lawd Gawd in heaven, I'll kill every chink-chink goddamn Chinaman white man on this sonofabitching bastard earth!" In frenzied madness he seized a hammer lying upon a box and began pounding walls, coffins, tables, and chairs. "I want to kill, *kill!*"

"Fish!" Jim shouted at him. "Get hold of yourself, boy!"

"Give me a gun, Jim!"

"Stop screaming, Fish," Jim said, grabbing him.

"Turn me loose!" Fishbelly shrieked.

Jim pinned the struggling boy against a wall.

"Leave me alone!" Fishbelly yelled. "I'm going to kill that lousy, stinking, bitchy Maud!"

"Fish, I won't let you run in the streets waving a hammer," Jim told him, shaking him.

Suddenly Fishbelly wilted and began to sob.

"Try to think," Jim advised him. "What did Maud say?"

"She said they baited Papa into a trap. . . . Oh, what dumb suckers we was. . . ."

"Then, Fish, let's get to Tyree," Jim said.

"Yeah. Come with me, Jim!"

They dashed out of the shop and jumped into the jalopy and tore off toward Bowman Street. Fishbelly wept as he drove. "I'll kill that chief . . . I'll kill that doctor . . ."

"You're sure that Maud phoned you?" Jim asked.

"Hell, yes. I know her voice in a million," he whimpered.

"Where's Dr. Bruce?"

"I don't know. . . . I let Papa go off like that," he sobbed in a rage of self-accusation. "White folks got next to them niggers and made 'em trick us! I could kill 'em all!"

"Let's see what happened first," Jim advised, touching

Fishbelly to calm him. "Did Maud say Tyree was shot badly?"

"She said she didn't know how long he could last. . . ."

Breathing through open lips, Fishbelly roared through streets whose outlines were blurred by his tears. He swung the car into Bowman Street and saw a small knot of people grouped before Maud's house.

"It's true; it's true," he singsonged.

He braked to a halt and leaped from the car; Jim followed. A white policeman blocked their path.

"Where you niggers going?"

"I'm Tyree's son. He's in there. He's been hurt—"

"And who are you?" the policeman asked Jim.

"He's Papa's embalmer," Fishbelly identified Jim.

"Captain Hunt!" the policeman called.

A thin, blond, red-faced policeman came forward.

"What's up? Who're these niggers?"

"Tyree's son and a nigger who works for 'em. They want to go in," the policeman explained.

Captain Hunt quickly patted Fishbelly's and Jim's pockets to see if they were armed.

"It's better for 'em to be inside than out here," the captain muttered, waving them toward the house.

Fishbelly glanced about and saw the hearse that Tyree had ordered for Maud and he burst into tears anew. He bounded up the steps. The door opened and big, black Maud confronted him, her face wet from weeping.

"Lawd, have mercy on you, son!" she screamed and folded him in her arms.

WITH MAUD CLINGING weepingly to him, Fishbelly was scarcely inside the dim hallway when Vera, her eyes swollen from crying, ran to him.

"Fish," she pleaded, "it wasn't our fault! Don't be mad at us!"

"Where Papa?" he asked apprehensively.

"You don't know what we been through today," Maud moaned.

"I want to see Papa," he begged.

"He here," Maud said absent-mindedly, caressing him clumsily. "Fish, you got to believe us . . . 'Fore Gawd, they put guns on us and *made* us do it."

"*Who?*" he asked puzzled.

"Them *police*," Maud whispered. "They been here all day."

"You know we wouldn't hurt a hair of Tyree's head," Vera babbled through tears.

They moved awkwardly down the dark hallway and he tried to grasp their ravings.

"And don't go blaming Doc," Maud said. "They made 'im do that phoning—"

"Where Doc?" he asked, feeling hot hate.

"They took 'im," Maud whispered. "Gawd knows where..."

He understood now that Tyree had been lured, and that Dr. Bruce had not been a part of the plot. Maud paused, pointing to a spot on the wall.

"Look," she said.

"What?" he asked.

"That's where one of the bullets went," Maud said.

"Where Papa?" he wailed, frustrated.

"They shot 'im in my living room," Maud whimpered.

The hysterical women seemed incapable of answering him; he grabbed Maud's shoulders and shook her.

"I want to see Papa!" he shouted.

"He here," Maud said. "Come on."

Her matter-of-fact tone made hope leap into him, but sober sense told him that Maud was more concerned with proving her innocence than with Tyree's condition. A chill settled in his blood as he realized that she had been speaking of Tyree as though he were already dead! He pushed through the door of Maud's bedroom and halted in consternation. Tyree lay wounded in a whore house! He stepped into the dim room, blinking. The shades had been drawn and for a moment he saw nothing. Then he made out Tyree's form upon the bed. He ran forward and fell upon his knees.

"Papa!" he wept, grabbing Tyree's limp, moist hand.

Tyree did not move or answer. Maud switched on a feeble bedside lamp and Fishbelly saw Tyree's tired, sweaty face, which held a cast of green pallor.

"You hurt, Papa? This is Fish . . . Oh Gawd!"

"That you, Fish?" Tyree whispered with sticky throat.

"I'm here, Papa. How you feeling?" he asked, squeezing Tyree's hand as though to impart strength to it.

"They got me," Tyree sighed.

Maud and Vera began a violent weeping.

"Sh," he signaled them. "I want to talk to 'im. . . ." He bent toward Tyree's ear and tried to speak, but his lips would make no sound. Finally he asked: "A doctor see you yit?"

Tyree shook his head and his glazed eyes closed.

"I'll git a doctor," he said, rising with sudden determination.

"Fish, them police won't let nobody in," Maud warned him.

"But he needs a doctor!" Fishbelly railed.

"Aw, Fish, you don't understand nothing!" Maud yelled at him.

"But he's hurt! He's bleeding!" he shouted back.

"Fish, we phoned the hospital and they sent a doctor, but the police wouldn't let 'im in. They say Tyree's armed and dangerous and—"

"This is a plot to let 'im bleed to death!" he screamed. "I want to git a doctor!"

"Naw! You don't understand nothing," Vera wailed. "Them police down there'll shoot you!"

Fishbelly stared. Every move he made to help Tyree was blocked by some dire warning. And he knew that Tyree's bleeding had been arranged by the chief of police.

"BUT PAPA NEEDS A DOCTOR!" he shouted in a frenzy.

As though to shield him from danger, Maud flung herself upon him, sobbing, and he knew that Maud and Vera were taking it for granted that Tyree would die without medical aid, die in accordance with the dictates of white "law"; they were obeying that white "law," though they grieved for those whom that "law" punished. Despair unhinged his joints and he sank upon his knees at the bedside, seizing Tyree's hand.

"Son," Tyree whispered.

"Yeah, Papa."

"They got me . . . I done lost a lot of blood . . . I'm weak . . . I ain't going to git up from this bed . . . So don't make no trouble . . . It won't do no good . . ."

"Did Doc trick you, Papa?"

Tyree closed his eyes as though wordlessly telling him that the manner of his betrayal did not matter. Fishbelly twisted about and stared up into the stricken faces of the two women.

"What happened?" he asked humbly, coherently now.

"Fish, them police marched Doc in here at the point of a gun right after lunch," Maud recited. "They made 'im phone Tyree twice. . . . And they put a gun at Vera's head and told her what to say over the phone. Poor thing passed out when they let her go—"

"Aw, Fish, you don't know," Vera lamented.

The doorbell pealed. Maud looked at Fishbelly and then at Jim. Tyree roused himself, then sank back to the bed.

"Bet that's the chief," Maud murmured. "Mebbe he'll let us git a doctor now. I'll see . . ."

Maud ran out of the room. Fishbelly saw Tyree's parched lips quiver, as though about to speak; the eyelids fluttered and Tyree's head rolled limply to one side.

"What happened?" Fishbelly asked again with blinking eyes.

"They brought Doc in here crying," Vera whispered rapidly, staring, reseeing the scene. "He was sure they was going to kill 'im. They put a gun at his head and made 'im phone Tyree and say Mama was sick and then phone and say Mama was dead and that Tyree had to come and see about Mama's papers. If Doc hadn't done it, they would've shot 'im."

Aw, yes . . . He had wondered at the time about the strange tone of Dr. Bruce's voice! He rubbed his eyes; he and Tyree had expected trouble from one direction and it had come from another.

"They made me do the same," Vera recited. "I was crying and I said I couldn't say it right, but they said me crying made it sound natural. . . . Fish, I was *sick*, I tell you. I passed out and Mama put water on me. . . . Them police kept talking about some checks. . . . A little later Tyree came. They handcuffed the doctor and locked him in the kitchen and they made me go to the door. I tried to whisper to Tyree, but he didn't hear me. . . . He asked me: 'Where Maud?' and I said: 'There in the living room. . . .' I didn't say she was dead and I hoped he'd catch on; but he didn't. . . . He opened the living-room door and they shot 'im. They was waiting for 'im in there. Then they left. They waited in the street and said nobody could come into the house till the chief came." Vera finished and bent to Tyree. "Tyree, tell Fish that that's right. . . ."

Tyree's hand moved upon the bedcover and was still.

"How long ago was that?" Jim asked from the doorway.

"More'n a hour ago," Vera mumbled.

"He been bleeding all this time," Fishbelly moaned. He turned to Jim. "If that's the chief, see if he'll let us call a doctor."

"Git Doc Adams," Vera suggested. "He's close by."

"Okay," Jim said and left.

Fishbelly placed his palm upon Tyree's cold and wet forehead, then buried his face in the bedcovers.

"Son, there ain't nothing to be done," Tyree murmured.

A loud, masculine voice sounded in the hallway. Fishbelly

rose and ran to the door. Chief of Police Cantley stood grim and rigid before him.

"Well, Fish is here," the chief said.

"Please, sir. Git a doctor for Papa," Fishbelly begged him.

"Now, Fish, calm down and take it easy," the chief warned coldly. "Don't get worked up. That's what happened to Tyree. . . . He wouldn't have been shot if he hadn't lost his head and threatened to shoot my men, see? Now, cool off. That nigger Jim's gone for a doctor."

Fishbelly wished hotly to dispute the chief; instead he whispered accusingly:

"He's been bleeding for more'n a hour."

"That's his own goddamn fault," the chief charged. "He rushed my men with a gun and they let him have it. We're taking no chances with a wild nigger."

Fishbelly swallowed, knowing that that had not happened. But Tyree had warned him that nothing could be done. Fishbelly sighed, turned, and went back into the room and saw that Tyree had pulled himself up upon an elbow and was staring with red, sunken, and glazed eyes. He knew that Tyree had overheard what the chief had said.

"Son," Tyree whispered thickly. "Come here, close . . ." He fell limply back upon the pillow. "I got to talk to you. . . ."

"Papa," Fishbelly wept.

"Son, don't stir 'em up. . . . They'll kill you if they think you going to make trouble. Don't accuse 'em of what they done to me."

"Aw, Papa. Don't talk none. A doctor's coming . . ."

"*We won, son!*" Tyree whispered fiercely. "I won my fight! They didn't git my money and that chief's done for. . . . You'll see. I'll be fighting that sonofabitch from my grave! You got to go it alone. They done me in, but forgit it. We won! Look at it that way. . . ."

Tyree's panting words had frightened Fishbelly so much that he glanced over his shoulder to see if the chief was near. But only Vera, her eyes tortured and fear-struck, stood in the room. Fishbelly clung to Tyree's hand and became aware of a pool of warm blood in which he was lying. He wept afresh through clenched teeth.

"They letting you bleed on purpose," he sobbed.

"Sh," Tyree cautioned; his strength was ebbing. "I'm trying to save you, son. *Do what they say!* They ain't got no claims against you, 'less you make 'em scared. . . . You won't ever want for anything. . . . Look at that letter. . . . It's my will. Make like you believe what they say. Let this blow over. . . ."

"Yes, Papa."

"The doctor's here," Maud said, entering and leading an old brown man carrying a black bag.

"Who's that there? Old Tyree?" the doctor asked.

"Yeah," Tyree breathed.

"By Gawd, this ain't no place for you," the doctor said, dropping his bag and perching himself upon the edge of the bed. He lifted Tyree's wrist, felt for the pulse; he gazed at his watch, counting heartbeats. He laid the limp arm thoughtfully aside, then unbuttoned Tyree's shirt and peered at the bloody chest. He looked up.

"Call the hospital to come and give a blood transfusion," the doctor ordered.

"I'll phone," Jim said and left the room.

Fishbelly saw the chief looming in the doorway; he knew that the white man was waiting for Tyree to die. A living Tyree was more dangerous than ever, for he could tell how he had been shot. Oh Gawd, how cool, insolent was the man who had ambushed his father! He sighed, wondering why neither he nor Tyree had suspected a trap when Dr. Bruce had phoned. "We was just too tired to think," he told himself.

"Maud, let's git his shirt off," the doctor called.

They cut away Tyree's shirt and Fishbelly saw two gaping chest wounds from which blood seeped with each heartbeat.

"Two bullets hit the lungs," the doctor murmured, swabbing the wounds with gauze to staunch the blood flow. He covered the chest, rose, took Fishbelly gently by the arm and led him from the room.

They met Jim in the hallway.

"They're sending an ambulance," Jim said.

"Okay," Fishbelly breathed.

"Your mama know about this, son?" the doctor asked.

"Nawsir. I just got here."

"Then you better git her here . . ."

"But can't we take Papa to the hospital?" Fishbelly asked. "I don't want Mama coming *here.*"

The doctor pursed his lips and stared.

"It's a question of time, son," the doctor said.

Fishbelly lifted his hand to his mouth; he heard Tyree's death sentence. Jim came forward.

"Jim, take my car and git Mama." Fishbelly paused, uncertain, then added; "And git her quick."

"Right," Jim said and left.

Fishbelly re-entered the room behind the doctor and stood beside the bed. He could hear heavy breath coming and going in Tyree's chest now; the eyes were slightly open, but seemingly without sight.

"Fish," Tyree called weakly.

"Yeah, Papa. Right here," he replied, kneeling, bending close.

"I'm tired, son."

Tyree's head moved from left to right, then was still.

"Fish," Tyree whispered again.

"Yeah, Papa," he answered and waited.

Tyree's chest labored. His body seemed to slump. A tremor went over his lips and he gave a slight cough.

"Papa," Fishbelly called softly.

The doctor lifted Tyree's wrist and felt for the pulse. Tyree's eyes fluttered slowly and his lips parted.

"Papa!" Fishbelly called.

The doctor placed Tyree's arm upon the bed, rose, and took the eyeglasses from his nostrils.

"Papa!" Fishbelly wailed.

"He can't hear you now, son," the doctor said gently. "He's gone. . . ."

"Gawd, naw, naw!" Fishbelly screamed.

He stood and looked about wildly. The chief was just inside the doorway.

"Take it easy, Fish," the chief warned. "Control yourself!"

Maud rushed to him and held him in a tight grip.

"You poor child!" she cried.

"You folks ought to git out of here now," the doctor said, extinguishing the dim bedside lamp.

"Come on, Fish," Maud said, trying to lead him forward.

"Leave me alone!" he shouted, struggling to break loose.

"Nigger, get hold of yourself! Don't make trouble!" the chief warned sternly.

Fishbelly looked lingeringly at Tyree's still, black face and let Maud lead him from the room and into the kitchen. He was too stunned to notice much; but when he saw three white policemen standing about his grief became tinged by wariness. The chief entered.

"Sit 'im down at the table, Maud," the chief ordered.

"Yessir," Maud said.

Fishbelly sat and stared at the roomful of faces.

"Give 'im a cup of coffee," the chief ordered.

"Sure, Chief," Maud said. "Vera, heat some coffee."

"Yessum," Vera hummed, moving to obey.

"Don't want no coffee," Fishbelly muttered.

"Yeah, you do," Maud said heartily, caressing his shoulder.

"Take a cup," the chief said. "Do you good."

He stared sightlessly, feeling that speech was useless. Then, though choked with sorrow, he became aware of Vera's, Maud's, the three policemen's, and the chief's eyes regarding him, not sadly, not angrily, but just coolly, calmly. He bent forward in another fit of weeping; when he lifted his head he saw that Vera had placed the cup of coffee before him.

"Drink it," the chief said gruffly. "I want to talk to you."

Feeling almost hypnotized, he reached his trembling black fingers and lifted the cup to his wet lips and took a sip, then another. The hot fluid steadied him a bit.

"Fish," the chief lectured warningly, "I want you to listen if you ever listened in your life."

"Yessir," he answered automatically.

"What's happened has *nothing* to do with *you,*" the chief said. "Understand that and it can mean a lot to you. Your father was a good man. He was my friend. But he lost his head. And when men lose their heads, they pay for it. . . . Fish, take this the *wrong* way and you'll get fouled up for the rest of your life. Take it the *right* way and settle down and you can take up where Tyree left off. . . . Hear me?"

"Yessir," he replied by reflex, understanding nothing.

"Fish, he's talking to you like a father," Maud announced, nodding sagely. "Lissen to 'im."

"Sure," he agreed without meaning to.

"Greenhouse," the chief called.

"Here, sir," a stout policeman answered.

"Tell Fish what happened," the chief ordered.

"Sure, Chief," the policeman said, looking off. "We were here talking to this nigger woman, Maud, when the doorbell rang. That nigger gal, Vera, answered it. That nigger Tyree rushed in with a drawn gun and Gus let him have it, three times. If he hadn't, that nigger would've killed us for sure. . . . We ran out; we didn't know how badly we'd wounded him. He had a gun and we weren't taking any chances, see? And we didn't go back into the house and we didn't let anybody else go in till we knew for sure that he was harmless. That's all, Chief."

A block of ice choked Fishbelly; he wanted to rise and scream: "You lying!" But he could hear Tyree's dying admonition: *Make like you believe what they say. . . . You can't do nothing. . . .*

"Did you hear that, Fish?" the chief asked.

"Yessir," he breathed. What was the use? He sighed and pushed the coffee cup away and rested his hot head on the table, unable to stem the spasmodic heaving in his chest. He was not aware when the three policemen had left. He finally looked up and saw the chief still there.

"You'll be all right, Fish," the chief said and left with a hard smile hovering about his lips.

Maud stood over him compassionately. Vera sat on the opposite side of the table, looking at the floor, her face washed of expression.

"Fish, honey, everything's going to be awright," Maud sang with sad sweetness.

The back door opened and two brown-skinned girls whom Fishbelly knew by sight entered.

"There ain't going to be no business *today* or *tomorrow*," Maud informed them. "Tyree's dead. He was my friend and his body's in the house."

"Yeah. We know," one girl said, slowly masticating a cud of gum by moving a loose lower jaw.

"Tyree was a goddamn good man," the other girl said.

"Now, just watch that lousy, bitchy mouth of yours, you black slut!" Maud chastised the girl with violent moral fervor. *"Death's* in this house!"

"Sorry," the girl mumbled and hung her head.

"Yeah, Tyree was good and straight and you could trust 'im," Maud went on, as though somebody had disputed her. "Fish, be proud of Tyree. Don't never let nobody talk against 'im to you. You take up where he left off. You hear?"

He sighed, sensing meaning in what they were saying. It was more than compassion that they were conveying: it was business! They were declaring him their new boss, pledging allegiance, signaling their willingness to obey. He knew now the purpose of the chief's lecture; it had been telling him to step into Tyree's shoes; it had hinted that if he could blot out of his mind what had happened to Tyree, things could go on as they had before. In honor of Tyree, the renting of bodies had been banned for one night and one day, but the day after tomorrow would be a day of normal trade.

"You know, Fish," Maud said with a twisted, wistful smile, "life's got to go on. Tyree wouldn't want you just to stop like that. He'd be happy if he thought you was carrying on his—"

A soft knock sounded upon the kitchen door.

"Yeah?" Maud called, irritated at the interruption.

The door opened and Jim poked his head through.

"Excuse me," he said, "Fish, your mama's outside."

"Tell her to come in," Fishbelly said.

"Well . . . Er . . . Y-you better talk to h-her," Jim said. "You know . . ."

He followed Jim down the crowded hallway in which young black whores, the doctor, the two white-coated interns milled about. There was a drone of low-voiced conversation; the atmosphere was charged with respect for Tyree, but there was no sorrow.

Jim opened the front door and Fishbelly saw, amid a small knot of people gathered at the bottom of the steps, Emma standing beside the two workmen who handled Tyree's hearse.

"Mama." Fishbelly rushed to her and attempted to embrace her.

"Don't do that, Fish!" Emma checked him curtly, stepping back.

"What's the matter?" he asked, shocked.

"Why Tyree do this to me?" she asked in helpless despair.

"Mama," he chided her, reaching to touch her.

"Naw, Fish!" She stood with more wounded dignity than grief showing in her dry, hot eyes. That her husband had been slain in a whore house was an unforgivable affront.

"Mama, Papa's dead," he said.

"Did that Gloria whore have anything to do with this?" she asked coldly.

He was stupefied. So she knew about Gloria. . . . This was

a new Emma, an Emma who had at long last emerged when the shadow of Tyree had gone from her life. Could this defiant woman be the meek creature who had had the habit of effacing herself at the merest inflection of Tyree's strident voice. She had hidden her hate of Tyree so well that he had never suspected it! He might now come under her authority and he was not used to obeying a woman. Fishbelly grew wary; he was young, but he was also very old.

"Don't you want to see Papa 'fore they take 'im away?" he asked, feeling guilty in spite of himself.

Emma shook her head, her wide, sad eyes holding a stony stare.

"Naw. Not in there," she spoke emphatically.

The black onlookers pushed closer, trying to listen. Then Fishbelly saw the towering, pole-like form of Reverend Ragland coming forward and he noticed that Emma allowed him the privilege that she had denied him; she let him slip his arm about her shoulders.

"Gawd be with you, Sister Tucker," Reverend Ragland said.

"Lawd have mercy," Emma whimpered for the first time.

Somebody in the crowd snickered and Fishbelly knew that they were laughing because Tyree had died in a whore house; he stiffened, ready to lash out at anybody daring to belittle his father.

"Son, I'll never set foot in that foul den as long's breath's in my body," Emma declared firmly, clearly. "I married Tyree for better or worse, to stick by 'im in sickness or death; but going amongst whores was no part of the bargain."

"Papa wouldn't've thought you felt like that," he reproved her.

"Son, don't force your mama," Reverend Ragland advised him.

"I ain't *forcing* nobody," he said peevishly.

"What was Tyree doing in there?" Emma asked.

Fishbelly caught a wry smile on the face of a white policeman lurking near. He leaned to Emma and whispered fiercely:

"They trapped 'im in there, Mama. It was the *white* folks."

"What he do?" Emma asked coldly.

He checked an impulse to slap her and turned his head.

"Son, Tyree couldn't hide what he was doing from Gawd," Emma declared. "Gawd brought it all to the light of day."

"Amen," Reverend Ragland intoned.

"Mama, hush! You don't know what you saying!" He defended his father. "It wasn't Papa's fault if—"

"I know right from wrong," Emma said stoutly, disdainful of being overheard. "I'll never go amongst whores, and, if I have anything to say about it, you won't neither no more. I'll see Tyree when they bring 'im to the church."

Dr. Adams came down the steps and doffed his hat to Emma.

"I'm sorry, Mrs. Tucker," he said. "It shouldn't've been like this. . . ." He turned to Fishbelly. "They taking Tyree to the morgue for the inquest. They'll be giving 'im to you sometime tomorrow, mebbe."

The doctor moved away. Fishbelly glanced appealingly at Jim, who stood discreetly apart.

"You coming home now, Fish?" Emma asked him.

"Naw," he said sullenly, perversely, burning with unspeakable resentment. "Got to git to the office and 'tend to things for Papa."

"I'll see Sister Tucker home," Reverend Ragland offered.

"Thank you, Reverend," Jim said.

Fishbelly watched the preacher lead Emma to his car and drive off. He caught Jim staring at him and he gritted his teeth.

"Where's that hearse?" he asked indignantly; he knew where the hearse was, but felt that he had to say something.

"It's here," Jake, the driver, said. "Been here for three hours."

"Don't you go gitting sassy," Fishbelly growled. "I just asked you where it was—"

"It's here and I ain't sassy," Jake muttered defiantly.

"Stop arguing with Fish and do what you're supposed to do," Jim spoke to Jake with kind but firm authority.

Jake shuffled off and Fishbelly seethed with anger.

"Goddamn," he muttered to himself. The white world and the black world had turned suddenly hostile, menacing; Tyree had gone, leaving a vast displacement that he feared that he could never fill. He felt achingly inadequate, and he knew that his mother, Jim, Maud, Reverend Ragland, and the city police were weighing and measuring him, readying themselves for attack, each from his own angle of selfishness. He made for his car. "I'm off to the office, Jim!"

A white policeman sauntered toward him.

"Don't let 'em break you down, Fish," the policeman said.

"You go to hell," Fishbelly said under his breath and jammed the accelerator to the floor and shot down the street. Tears burned his eyes and he spoke bitterly, forlornly: "If they think they going to push me around, they crazy." His right hand felt inside his coat pocket and touched the thick, white envelope that Tyree had given him that morning. "Papa left me in charge, and, goddammit, I'm going to take charge and all hell ain't going to stop me!"

IN THE USUAL SENSE of mourning, Fishbelly could not grieve for Tyree, nor could he wholeheartedly hate the men who had slain him. His apprehension of Tyree's life had been predicated too much upon reflections of white attitudes and hence had been too objective to have been based upon love alone. He had felt toward Tyree a most profound compassion, for he knew at first hand how hopeless Tyree's life had been in comparison with the white lives above him. He could no more forget Tyree than he could forget himself, for, in a sense, Tyree was that shadow of himself cast by a white world he loved because of its power and hated because of its condemnation of him. Thus, though he could not grieve for Tyree, his living had to become a kind of grieving monument to his memory and a reluctant tribute to his slayers.

Fishbelly felt each nuanced ripple in the currents of Black-Belt life with his blood. Racial conditioning told him when to act and when to play possum. He made no effort to see Chief of Police Cantley; he knew that when the white man was ready, he would come to him. The grand jury still had not met and he could only guess that Cantley had somehow seized those ill-fated canceled checks. He often thought of McWilliams, but had heard nothing from him. And since McWilliams had failed Tyree, he thought it best not to try to see him. Diligently, he collected the police tributes and divided the loot into scrupulously equal portions: white Caesar's and his own. Maud was overjoyed.

"Fish, since Tyree's gone, I been worried about being raided," she declared. "But now you taking the money and I know I'm safe. The best way to do things is the right way. Ain't nothing better'n cash on the line."

"Don't you worry none," he told her.

"Fish?" she called him gently.

"What, Maud?"

"You ain't mad at me and Vera, is you? You know in your heart we didn't have nothing to do with what happened to Tyree, don't you?"

"Yeah. I know," he mumbled shamefacedly.

"Fish, we black. We ain't got no rights."

"I understand, Maud," he told her with a sigh.

He understood, but he did not respect her. He understood, but he did not respect himself.

"It's always the *man*, hunh?" Maud asked him, laughing dolefully.

"Yeah."

"What *man?*" Maud asked teasingly.

"The *white* man," Fishbelly mumbled, grinning ruefully.

They were silent, seeing themselves as they imagined the white world saw them, their humble hearts touched with shame.

After consulting Lawyer Heith regarding the probate of the will and other current matters, Fishbelly made his first important decision: he ordered Tyree's funeral to be held in common with that of the victims of the Grove fire, a gesture that mollified the reactions of the Black Belt toward the Tucker family. Emma learned of the funeral arrangements too late to make any effective protest. Fishbelly told her coldly:

"That's the way Papa would've wanted it."

Black-Belt gossip made Fishbelly feel that he had been right:

"Tyree didn't run off like that doctor; he was sorry for what happened. He just made a mistake and anybody can do that. . . ."

"And them goddamn white folks killed 'im; if they killed 'im, it was 'cause they was scared of 'im. . . ."

"Lawd," a fat black woman exclaimed one morning as Fishbelly collected her rent, "that Tyree was a dog! He was more'n a dog; he was a tiger! He turned these white folks upside down!"

In a Black-Belt bar a drunken Negro crooned:

"That city-hall gang's a bitch! Look what happened to Tyree, the biggest nigger around here. . . . Look what happened to Dr. Bruce. . . . Go against that city hall and you either *dead* or *missing!*"

Fats Brown, whom Fishbelly, Dr. Bruce, and Tyree had wanted to make a scapegoat, was dead and his body unclaimed in the town morgue. Race-conscious Maybelle, shocked and sobered by the loss of so many of her whoring cronies, cut short the renting of her body, joined a store-front church, and planned to become a female evangelist to warn the world of evil. Having fled and his whereabouts unknown, Dr. Bruce had been indicted in absentia by the grand jury for "criminal negligence and multiple manslaughter"; in fact, all the blame had been heaped upon him. Gloria was missing and no one, not even the police, had asked about her; Fishbelly had driven slowly past her house twice, noticing milk bottles and newspapers collecting upon her porch.

Because of the sensational highjacking of court clerk Albert Davis and the furious uproar that followed in the press, the mayor had to resign "in interests of public order." The town council had elected, upon the mayor's secret instructions, one of his personal friends to serve as his temporary successor until elections could be held. Police Chief Cantley, whom everybody suspected but against whom nothing could be proved, also resigned, declaring: "Though there is not one iota of evidence against me, I gladly relinquish my office in view of the perturbed state of the public mind. Police work is not basically my line. I'd like to run for governor." A personal friend of Cantley had been appointed in his place.

An all-white coroner's jury found that Tyree's death had been caused by his "threatening police officers with a gun." Some guessed that Tyree had been killed to keep him from "appearing before the grand jury." Others hinted that he had suddenly gone "Communist and had begun to demand social equality." Whispers said that Tyree had been caught "sleeping with the nigger mistress of the police chief and had been shot to death in a nigger whore house." Cynics said that Tyree had been holding out on police graft and that the police had "rubbed 'im out." Only among the bitter, closed-mouthed prostitutes and gamblers of the Black-Belt underworld was it known that Tyree had been ambushed; but nowhere was it known that the real motive for his slaying had been the damning canceled checks that Tyree had given to McWilliams that frantic night. Only Fishbelly knew that and his lips, on the dying advice of Tyree, were sealed in self-defense.

Fishbelly took over Tyree's car and then prompted by a vague but potent instinct, amassed a varied wardrobe: ten tweed suits, five pairs of shoes, twenty shirts, ties, socks— enough clothes, as Jim put it, "to last you five years."

"And whose money is this?" Fishbelly demanded.

"It's yours," Jim admitted.

"Awright, then. Let me alone," Fishbelly requested.

On the thundery, rainy afternoon of the mass funeral, black families came into town not only in cars, but even in buggies and wagons from the surrounding countryside. On Black-Belt streets crepe-wearing men, women, and children were conspicuous. The Grove fire and the personalities connected with it were a topic for all tongues. And the Grove, its burned-out hulk, blackened beams and rafters, its buckled tin roof glaring a rusty red in the hot sun, became a local curiosity about which people clustered and spoke in awed tones. Old folks swore that they could hear, late at night, the screams and moans of the dying; wide-eyed black children told tall tales of seeing ghosts waltzing together after sundown. So many memento hunters probed about the Grove's gutted premises that the police erected signs proclaiming: KEEP OUT.

Though the victims of the fire had been of many religious denominations, Clintonville's black pastors had agreed that Reverend Ragland would deliver the funeral oration—most of the fire victims having been working-class members of his church. For three days before the funeral Reverend Ragland secluded himself to compose his collective sermon, and, when he did deliver it with stomping feet, gasps, hymns, tears, and heart-rending gestures over the forty-two fire dead and over Tyree's body, which reposed in an ornate, bronze coffin, it was declared the most memorable peroration ever heard in Black-Belt memory.

Fishbelly, garbed in black, sat beside crepe-veiled Emma in the first row of the church, his lackluster eyes gazing alternately at Tyree's ebony profile and the whitish, shy features of Gladys, whose coffin, at Fishbelly's request, stood beside that of Tyree's.

"Who that white-looking gal in that coffin by Tyree?" Emma asked.

"Friend of mine," he said.

"What become of that Gloria hussy?" Emma asked.

"Don't know," he mumbled a sullen lie.

And Emma did not mention Tyree again during the ceremony. The gray summer afternoon was stiflingly hot and the myriad banks of floral wreaths, covering the front wall of the church as Tyree had wanted, emitted odors of such cloying sweetness that Fishbelly felt that he would suffocate. The white-robed, fifty-member choir was arranged just beneath the brass pipes of the church organ. Five thousand or more black brothers and sisters and their children jammed the edifice. They were silent, sad, nervous; now and then quiet weeping could be heard. The public stood in the rear of the church, in the aisles, on the steps, outside upon the sidewalk, and even in the middle of the street, necessitating the erection of road barriers to divert traffic. Policemen strolled casually, their white skins showing distinctly amidst the sea of black faces.

Maud, Vera, and the twenty-odd black girls who did their days' work at night in the Bowman Street flat, were present. Sam was there. Fishbelly had no chance to say more than a hurried hello to him, for he had been swamped helping Jim with a multitude of details. Gladys's mother, a bent, tan-colored woman holding a two-year-old girl in her arms, came to Fishbelly and introduced herself, pointed to Gladys, then stooped and kissed his hands as she shed hot tears. Fishbelly stared at the infant's pale, yellow face and round, fixed eyes, eyes that seemed to have never held even a hint of joy. Gladys's mother backed away, weeping.

"Who was that?" Jim asked.

"Gladys's mother and Gladys's little girl," Fishbelly said.

"Good Lord," Jim said. "What'll happen to that little tot?"

The forty-three coffins were lined, oblong box beside oblong box, from one end of a row of stained-glass windows to another, right across the entire width of the church, ranging in horseshoe shape just below and in front of the pulpit, the heads of the coffins pointing toward the pulpit and their ends facing the audience. The pulpit was as yet empty. Fishbelly knew from long observance that Reverend Ragland would enter at any moment from a small door on the left. From the ceiling's vault six huge electric fans hung, their wooden blades spinning slowly in the moist hot air.

Aggie West, church organist, walked with a too-careful manner upon the platform, seated himself at the organ keys, and rubbed his black fingers together. Suddenly Aggie wet his lips with his tongue, bent forward, touched the organ keys, and there rolled forth a deep-voweled hymn of melancholy sound in which the audience and choir joined:

> *"Sunset and evening star,*
> *And one clear call for me!*
> *And may there be no moaning of the bar*
> *When I put out to sea.*
> *But such a tide as moving seems asleep,*
> *Too full for sound and foam,*
> *When that which drew forth out the boundless deep*
> *Turns again home."*

Amid the singing and the organ's roll a few black women gave forth crying sobs.

> *"Twilight and evening bell,*
> *And after that the dark!*
> *And may there be no sadness of farewell*
> *When I embark;*
> *For though from out our bourne of time and place*
> *The flood may bear me far,*
> *I hope to see my Pilot face to face*
> *When I have crossed the bar. . . ."*

Deep-bassed "Amens!" rose and mingled with screams; several black women were escorted by ushers out of the church. Fishbelly saw Aggie dab his balled handkerchief delicately to his damp brow, close his eyes, and bend again to the organ keys:

> *"One sweetly solemn thought*
> *Comes to me o'er and o'er:*
> *I'm nearer my home today*
> *Than I have ever been before. . . ."*

Captured by liquid sorrow of dying organ peals, Fishbelly stared sightlessly, then started nervously: there was Reverend Ragland, tall, black, gaunt of face, red of eye, his expression seemingly furiously belligerent. He lifted his two long arms into the air and stretched them dramatically wide. Silence gripped the black brothers and sisters. Reverend opened his mouth and emitted a rich, carrying baritone:

"Death!"

He moved agilely to the left of the pulpit and bellowed: *"Death!"*

He glided to the right of the pulpit and leaned over the upturned faces in the coffins and screamed:

"DEATH!"

Reverend now strode briskly to the pulpit and lifted his eyes to the soaring ceiling and announced in slow, ringing tones of sad amazement.

"Death's been a-riding through this land! I say Death's been a-riding through this old world! Lawd Gawd Awmighty, Death's been a-riding through our hearts! And now you just look, *look,* LOOK—!" His long, skinny, moving finger pointed to the cold, still black faces in the curving array of coffins. "LOOK, I say, at what Death's done done! Death's been a-riding and He done left His calling cards! Death's been a-riding and He done left His fingerprints! Lawd Gawd Awmighty, I can hear old Death's rustling black robe stealing softly away!"

"Gloooory!" an old black woman screamed.

"Yes, yes, yes," a man agreed with trembling joy.

The electrified, sorrow-gripped audience leaned forward, holding its breath. Reverend turned and looked at the so-lemn-faced choir, nodded, and launched into a song in which the choir joined:

> "God moves in a mysterious way
> His wonders to perform!
> He plants His footsteps in the sea
> And rides upon the storm.
>
> "Ye fearful saints, fresh courage take!
> The clouds ye so much dread
> Are big with mercy, and shall break
> In blessings on your head."

Reverend signaled for the end of the song as cries swept the church:

"Tell it! Tell it!"

"Look down on us, Lawd!"

"Mercy, mercy, have mercy, Jesus!"

"Who dares," the reverend asked in a wild cry, "say 'No!' when that old Angel of Death calls? You can be in your grocery store ringing up a hundred-dollar sale on the cash register and Death'll call and you'll have to drop the sale and go! You can be a-riding around in your Buick and Death'll call and you have to go! You about to git out of your bed to go to your job and old Death'll call and you'll have to go! Mebbe you building a house and done called in the mason and the carpenter and then old Death calls and you have to go! 'Cause Death's asking you to come into your *last* home! Mebbe you planning on gitting married and your wonderful bride's a-waiting at the altar and you on your way and old Death calls: 'Young man, I got another bride for you! Your *last* bride!' "

"Lawd, it's true!"

"Gawd's Master!"

"Be with us, Lawd!"

"Don't matter if you white, black, rich, poor, man, woman, or child, Death can knock on your door," the reverend whispered hoarsely. Then he crooned sadistically: "You dancing to sweet music, cheek to cheek with your sweetheart on the dance floor, and Death'll call you in a low voice: 'Come and waltz with me!' "

"Susie! My poor little Susie!" Teddy's mother wailed.

A rhythmic swaying of bodies and a nodding of heads filled the church. Fishbelly sat stolid; he had heard funeral sermons all his life and he could, if pushed, have preached one himself; but this sermon was different. Tyree lay before him, forever gone, and now there was no one between him and that hostile world of whites.

"Now, don't be a fool and go blaming Death!" Reverend warmed up to his theme. "Death ain't nothing but Gawd's *special* messenger! His Pullman car is the cyclone! His airplane is the wind! His streetcar is the thunderbolt! There ain't but one thing you can say when Death taps on your door: May the Good Lawd have mercy on my soul!"

"Be with us, Lawd!"

"It's Gawd's business!"

Reverend signaled for a song and lifted his voice with that of the choir and the organ's booming peals:

"We give Thee but Thine own,
Whate'er the gift may be:
All that we have is Thine alone,
A trust, O Lord, from Thee. . . ."

Reverend waved for silence, advanced to the edge of the platform, stared down at the coffins filled with mute, black faces and spoke in quiet, matter-of-fact tones:

"Some folks in this town's talking about trying to find out who's guilty of causing these folks to die. They even talking about sending folks to jail." Looking out over the sea of black faces, he gave forth an ironic, hollow laugh: "Ha, ha! Don't them fools know that no man can kill 'less Gawd wants it done? Not a sparrow flies 'less Gawd lets it fly. Not a raindrop falls 'less Gawd says: 'Yes, rain, you can fall!' You think you so powerful that you can kill another man? You a fool! You kill and call it killing, but you only putting a name on something that Gawd's done done! When Gawd's a-working, you shut your big mouth and keep still! When Gawd calls you, it's for your own good! Oh, if we could, just for one second, see through Gawd's eyes, how foolish and ignorant we would know we is!"

Agitation swept the audience. Reverend stared down into the cold, dead, black faces while voices chanted dolefully:

"It's the truth!"

"Lawd, save us!"

"Right there 'fore my eyes is one of the men who owned the Grove dance hall!" Reverend pointed to Tyree, then to another coffin. "And there's a man who worked for 'im! Death trapped the boss and the worker!" Reverend pointed to yet another black face. "There's a man who blew a horn for the girls and boys to dance!" He turned, pointing to a batch of rather plain coffins. "There's the boys and girls who did the dancing!" Reverend walked to his pulpit and banged his fist down upon the open leaves of the Bible and demanded: "Now, who figgered all that out? Who understands the Divine Plan of Justice? On the Fourth of July, Gawd reared back and said:

" 'Death, come here!' "

"Wonderful Jesus!"

" 'Death, go down to that place called *America!*' "

"Lissen to the Lawd!"

" 'Death, find that state they call *Mississippi!*' "

"Gawd's a-talking!"

" 'Death, go to a town called *Clintonville!*' "

"Lawd, Lawd, Lawd!"

" 'Death, find me a man called *Tyree Tucker!*' "

"Gawd's King!"

" 'Death, I want you to tell Tyree Tucker that I want to see 'im!' "

"Have mercy, Jesus!"

A black woman gave a prolonged scream and began leaping about; ushers rushed to her and led her bounding body out of the church.

" 'Death, tell Tyree that I don't care *what* he's doing, he's got to come home!' "

Fishbelly felt an involuntary chill go over him. Emma clutched his arm and bent forward and sobbed. Reverend stepped back as he impersonated God; his face registered shock, surprise. Still speaking for God, he said:

" 'What you saying to me, Death? You say Tyree's busy? You say he's got some mighty important men to see? Death lissen to me. This is Gawd Awmighty talking! Now, you just go right back down to America, to Mississippi, to Clintonville, and tell that Tyree Tucker to stop being sassy! Tell 'im to drop everything this *minute!* 'Cause His Maker wants to see 'im!' "

"Just lissen to Gawd!"

Reverend walked angrily from one end of the pulpit to the other, speaking in a low, intimate, furious tone:

"Imagine telling Gawd that Tyree's busy!" He paused, stooped, pointed his right hand to the vault of the church and screamed: "When Gawd calls you, you have to answer whether you want to or *not!*"

"Amen!"

"Glory, glory, glory!"

Reverend walked back to his pulpit, took off his eyeglasses, stared down into the cold black faces and spoke to them tenderly:

"And you-all answered 'Im, didn't you? You obeyed 'Im, didn't you?" Reverend glared balefully at his audience and asked tersely: "Who out there'll dare say that these folks standing this minute 'fore Gawd's throne's sorry? What you know about Gawd's business? *Nothing!* When Gawd speaks, lift your eyes and sing:

> *When I survey that wondrous cross*
> *On which the Prince of Glory died,*
> *My richest gain I count but loss*
> *And pour contempt on all my pride. . . ."*

"Hallelujah!"

"Holy, holy, holy!"

He returned to the edge of the platform, sopped his dripping brow with a white handkerchief, and spoke scoldingly to his hearers:

"You can have your say. . . . Gawd'll let you. . . . He's patient, all-knowing. . . ." Then, thunderously: "You can talk your old big black mouth off, He don't care none! Huh! There's folks who think they tough . . . they hard . . . they done killed and cheated and lied and ain't scared of nothing. . . ." Reverend advanced to the extreme tip of the platform and looked down into the thin, black face of a young man in a plain coffin and said: "Charlie Moore, they tell me you done been in a lot of jails. They say you done faced a lot of judges in the courtrooms. . . . Well, Charlie, you in your *last* courtroom now!" His voice grew lyrically sadistic: "You now facing the Most Powerful Judge of 'em *all!* Tell me, Charlie, who's going to be your lawyer now?"

"Tell 'im, Preacher!"

Reverend bent forward and whispered hoarsely: "Lissen, Charlie, I'm going to sing you a song:

> *"There's a land that is fairer than day*
> *And by faith we can see it afar;*
> *For the Father waits over the way,*
> *To prepare us a dwelling place there.*

> *"In the sweet by and by*
> *We shall meet on that beautiful shore. . . ."*

"Gawd's done said it!"

"He's preparing a place for us!"

Reverend flicked sweat from his brow and returned to the attack:

"Who would've said a month ago that I'd be standing here saying the last words over forty-three of Gawd's children? Who dares say how many of us'll be here a year from now? Your future's in the hollow of Gawd's Hands! Now, there's men in this town who say that they run it!" Reverend's voice became scathing: "Let 'em go on thinking they run it! The men who run this town can be white as snow, but *we* know who's boss! GAWD'S THE BOSS! And He's more powerful than the president, the governor, the mayor, the chief of police . . ."

Chronology

1908	Birth of Richard Nathanael Wright, first son to Nathan and Ella, born Wilson, on September 4, on a plantation in Roxie, near Natchez, Mississippi.
1912–24	The Wrights move from Natchez to Memphis, Tennessee, then to Elaine, and finally to West Helena, Arkansas. His father having deserted the family, Richard suffers from hunger, poverty, and learns the ways of the streets. In 1915 he and his brother Leon (b. 1910) are placed in an orphanage.
1925	After his mother suffers repeated illnesses, she and the two boys return to her family in Mississippi. Richard receives his diploma from the Smith-Robinson High School in Jackson, Mississippi, on June 29. He scrapes together enough money to go to Memphis, Tennessee, and there finds a job and makes his first attempts at serious writing.
1927–32	He leaves Memphis for Chicago in December, 1927. Once in Chicago he works at a succession of odd jobs to support himself and later his family. Unable to find a job for a few months because of the Depression, he applies at the Cook County Relief Station for temporary assistance. During this time he continues to explore "great literature" and struggles with his own writing.

1933   Wright joins the Chicago John Reed Club, a literary club, and later, the Communist Party, and begins work on two novels and some short stories.

1934   In January, two of Wright's poems, "Rest for the Weary" and "A Red Love Note," are published by *Left Front*, and by April he is co-editor of the magazine. *The Anvil* prints his "Strength" and "Child of the Dead and Forgotten Gods," and in June his poem "I Have Seen Black Hands" is accepted by *New Masses*.

1935   Wright is admitted to the Illinois Federal Writers' Project in April and attends the first congress of the League of American Writers in New York as a delegate. The October 8 issue of *New Masses* publishes Wright's first piece of journalism, "Joe Louis Uncovers Dynamite."

1936   From September to November Wright works as a publicity agent for the Chicago Federal Negro Theater and helps Charles DeSheim produce Paul Green's *Hymn to the Rising Sun*, but the play is suppressed. He continues working on the novellas later included in *Uncle Tom's Children*.

1937   In June he leaves for New York City, helps launch *New Challenge*, and becomes an editor for the Harlem Bureau of the *Daily Worker*.

1938   In February Wright wins the *Story* magazine contest with "Fire and Cloud" and on Marcy 25 his volume of short stories, *Uncle Tom's Children*, is published by Harper & Brothers.

1938–39 Wright works on *Native Son*. "Fire and Cloud" receives the O'Henry Memorial Prize. In August, 1939, he marries Dhimah Meadman.

1940   In January the short story "Almos' a Man" is published in *Harper's Bazaar*. *Native Son* is published in March by Harper & Brothers, is a Book of the Month Club selection and becomes a best seller.

Wright's marriage falters, and ends in divorce. He
begins research for *Twelve Million Black Voices*.
In October Harper & Brothers publishes *Uncle
Tom's Children: Five Long Stories*.

1941   He marries Ellen Poplar on March 12. On March
25 a dramatization of *Native Son*, produced by
John Houseman and directed by Orson Welles
opens on Broadway. A daughter, Julia, is born. On
November 15 *Twelve Million Black Voices* is published by Viking Press.

1942–43 Following a lecture on growing up in America at
Fisk University, Wright starts work on his autobi-
ography. He also completes a first version of "The
Man Who Lived Underground."

1944   In August *The Atlantic Monthly* publishes
Wright's "I Tried to Be a Communist," which
marks the beginning of the Party's open hostility
toward him.

1945   A Book of the Month Club selection for February,
Black Boy, published by Harper & Brothers,
becomes an instant best seller. From June to September the Wrights vacation in Canada and then
from October to December, he tours the North
and West of the U.S. lecturing on Afro-American
literature.

1946   In May the Wrights sail to France as official guests
of the French government. In France they live in
the Latin Quarter in Paris for several months and
make friends with Gertrude Stein.

1947–48 In January, 1947, the Wrights return to the U.S.,
summer on Long Island and sail back to Paris in
August. Wright helps Leopold Senghor, Aimé Cé-
saire and Alioune Diop launch *Présence Africaine*.

1949   On January 17, 1949, a second daughter, Rachel is
born to the Wrights. In December he sponsors the
Gary Davis movement for peace and world citizenship.

1950   At the end of August Wright leaves with film director Pierre Chenal to shoot *Native Son* in Chicago and Buenos Aires. He played Bigger Thomas in the film.

1951   Back in Paris, Wright founds the French-American Fellowship.

1952   Wright spends a few months in London where he writes the final version of his novel, *The Outsider*.

1953   *The Outsider* is published in March and receives some adverse criticism. Wright spends the summer in the Gold Coast (now Ghana) gathering material for a travel diary.

1954   *Black Power: A Report of Reactions in a Land of Pathos*, is completed in May. Wright spends August and September touring Spain for another travel narrative. On September 22 *Black Power* is published.

1955   Wright spends a month in Spain, prior to a trip to Indonesia, where he is to report on the Bandoeng Conference held in mid-April.

1956   Wright is instrumental in organizing the first Congress of Negro Writers and Artists. During the fall he tours Germany and Scandinavia lecturing on Africa, the psychological problems of oppressed people, and on Afro-American literature.

1957   *Pagan Spain* is published by Harper & Brothers on February 20. In October Doubleday publishes *White Man Listen,* a collection of lectures.

1958   *The Long Dream* is published by Doubleday. Wright is refused permission to live in London by British officials.

1959   On May 27 Wright's adaptation of Louis Sapin's *Daddy Goodness* is produced by the USIS company. After visiting Africa, during the summer Wright falls ill from amoebic dysentery and is hospitalized in the American Hospital in Neuilly where he starts writing his haiku poetry.

1960   In March Wright is quite sick from recurring attacks of dysentery. In September he prepares a
series of radio talks on his writings and the racial
situation. On November 28 around 11 P.M. Wright
dies unexpectedly at the Clinique Eugene Gibez
where he was spending a week resting and expecting a check-up. He is cremated at the Père-
Lachaise Cemetery on December 5. The following Wright works were published posthumously:
Eight Men (1961), *Lawd Today* (1963), and
American Hunger (1977).

Bibliography

This chronological bibliography lists all of Wright's published nonfiction, poetry, and fiction in book form, and his most important uncollected, short nonfiction pieces. For a complete bibliography and a list of works on Wright's career see Michel Fabre, *The Unfinished Quest of Richard Wright*, New York, William Morrow, 1973, pp. 625–38.

NONFICTION

Books

12 Million Black Voices: A Folk History of the Negro in the United States. Photo direction by Edwin Rosskam. New York: Viking Press, 1941.

Black Boy: A Record of Childhood and Youth. New York: Harper & Brothers, 1945.

Black Power: A Record of Reactions in a Land of Pathos. New York: Harper & Brothers, 1954.

The Color Curtain. Cleveland and New York: World Publishing Company, 1956.

Pagan Spain. New York: Harper & Brothers, 1956.

White Man Listen. New York: Doubleday, 1957.

American Hunger. New York: Harper & Row, 1977. A continuation to *Black Boy* published posthumously.

Important short pieces, articles, reviews, letters, etc. not included in books

"Joe Louis Uncovers Dynamite." *New Masses*, 17 (Oct. 8, 1935).

"Two Million Black Voices." *New Masses*, 18 (Feb. 25, 1936).

"A Tale of Folk Courage." *Partisan Review and Anvil*, 3 (April 1936). Review of *Black Thunder* by Arna Bontemps.

"Between Laughter and Tears." *New Masses*, 25 (Oct. 5, 1937), 22–25. Review of *These Low Grounds* by Waters E. Turpin and *Their Eyes Were Watching God* by Zora Neale Hurston.

"Blueprint for Negro Writing," *New Challenge*, II (Fall, 1937), 53–65. The text published in *Amistad II* (1970) is an earlier version of this essay.

"How He Did It, and Oh!—Where Were Hitler's Pagan Gods?" *Daily Worker*, June 24, 1938, pp. 1, 8. On Joe Louis's victory over Schmeling.

"High Tide in Harlem." *New Masses*, 28 (July 5, 1938), 18–20. On Louis's victory over Schmeling.

"Lynching Bee." *New Republic*, 102 (March 11, 1940), 351. Review of *Trouble in July* by Erskine Caldwell.

"How 'Bigger' Was Born." *Saturday Review*, 22 (June 1, 1940), 4–5, 17–20.

"Inner Landscape." *New Republic*, 103 (Aug. 5, 1940), 195. Review of *The Heart Is a Lonely Hunter* by Carson McCullers.

"Forerunner and Ambassador." *New Republic*, 103 (Oct. 24, 1940), 600. Review of *The Big Sea* by Langston Hughes.

"Not My Peoples' War," *New Masses*, 39 (June 17, 1941), 8–9, 12.

"Richard Wright Describes the Birth of *Black Boy*." *New York Post*, Nov. 30, 1944, p. B6.

"Introduction," in Horace R. Cayton and St. Clair Drake, *Black Metropolis*. New York: Harcourt Brace, 1945, xvii–xxxiv.

"Richard Wright and Antonio Frasconi: an Exchange of Letters." *Twice a Year,* no. 12–13 (1945), 256–61.

"Gertrude Stein's Story Is Drenched in Hitler's Horrors." *P.M. Magazine,* March 11, 1945, p. m15. Review of *Wars I Have Seen* by Gertrude Stein.

"Alger Revisited, or My Stars! Did We Read That Stuff?" *P.M. Magazine,* Sept. 16, 1945, p. m8. Review of Horatio Alger's *Collected Novels.*

"Two Novels of the Crushing of Men, One White, One Black." *P.M. Magazine,* Nov. 25, 1945, pp. m7–m8. Review of *Focus* by Arthur Miller and *If He Hollers Let Him Go* by Chester Himes.

"American G.I.'s Fears Worry Gertrude Stein." *P.M. Magazine,* July 26, 1946, pp. m15–m16. Review of *Brewsie and Willie* by Gertrude Stein in the form of a letter to Roger Pipett.

"How Jim Crow Feels." *True Magazine,* Nov. 1946, 25–27, 154–56. On Wright's trip to Mexico and the South in the summer of 1940.

"A World View of the American Negro." *Twice A Year,* no. 14–15 (Fall 1946–Winter 1947), 346–348.

"Urban Misery in an American City: Juvenile Delinquency in Harlem." *Twice A Year,* no. 14–15 (Fall 1946–Winter 1947), 339–45.

"Two letters to Dorothy Norman," in *Art and Action.* New York, 1948, 65–73. Includes a letter dated February 28, 1948 (pp. 65–71) and a letter dated March 9, 1948 (pp. 72–73) both from Paris, on the state of things in France and Europe.

"The Shame of Chicago." *Ebony,* 7 (Dec. 1951), 24–32. On Wright's return to Chicago in 1949.

"There Is Always Another Café." *The Kiosk* (Paris) no. 10, 1953, pp. 12–14.

"Introduction," in George Lamming, *In the Castle of My Skin.* New York: McGraw-Hill, 1953, ix–xii.

"Introduction," in George Padmore, *Pan-Africanism or Communism?* London: Dobson, 1956, 11–14.

"Neurosis of Conquest." *The Nation*, 183 (Oct. 20, 1956), 330–31. Review of *Prospero and Caliban* by Octave Mannoni.

"The Voiceless Ones." *Saturday Review*, 43 (April 16, 1960), 53–54. Review of *The Disinherited* by Michel Del Castillo.

POETRY

"A Red Love Note." *Left Front*, no. 3 (Jan.–Feb. 1934), 3.

"Rest for the Weary." *Left Front*, no. 3 (Jan.–Feb. 1934), 3.

"Strength." *The Anvil*, no. 5 (March–April 1934), 20.

"Child of the Dead and Forgotten Gods." *The Anvil*, no. 5 (March–April 1934), 30.

"Everywhere Burning Waters Rise." *Left Front*, no. 4 (May–June 1934), 9.

"I Have Seen Black Hands." *New Masses*, 11 (June 26, 1934), 16.

"Rise and Live." *Midland Left*, no. 2 (Feb. 1935), 13–14.

"Obsession." *Midland Left*, no. 2 (Feb. 1935) 14.

"I Am a Red Slogan." *International Literature*, 4 (April 1935), 35.

"Ah Feels It in Mah Bones." *International Literature*, 4 (April 1935), 80.

"Red Leaves of Red Books." *New Masses*, 15 (April 30, 1935), 6.

"Between the World and Me." *Partisan Review*, 2 (July–August 1935), 18–19.

"Spread Your Sunrise." *New Masses*, 16 (July 2, 1935), 26.

"Transcontinental." *International Literature*, 5 (Jan. 1936), 52–57.

"Hearst Headline Blues." *New Masses*, 19 (May 12, 1936), 14.

"Old Habit and New Love." *New Masses*, 21 (Dec. 15, 1936), 29.

"We of the Streets." *New Masses*, 23 (April 13, 1937), 14.

"Red Clay Blues." *New Masses*, 32 (Aug. 1, 1939), 14. Written in collaboration with Langston Hughes.

"King Joe" ("Joe Louis Blues"). Lyrics for OKEH record no. 6475. Reprinted in *New York Amsterdam Star News,* Oct. 18, 1941, p. c16.

"Haiku Poems." A number of haikus have appeared in Ollie Harrington, "The Last Days of Richard Wright," *Ebony* 16 (Feb. 1961), 93–94. Reprinted (1) Arna Bontemps and Langston Hughes, *The Poetry of the Negro,* Doubleday 1964 edition; (2) Constance Webb, *Richard Wright: A Biography.* New York: Putnam, 1968, pp. 393–94; (3) Richard Wright, "Haikus." *Studies in Black Literature,* I (Summer 1970), 1; (4) "10 Haiku." *New Letters,* 38 (Winter 1971), 100–101.

FICTION

"Superstition." *Abbot's Monthly Magazine,* 2 (April 1931), 45–47, 64–66, 72–73. Signed Richard N. Wright.

"Big Boy Leaves Home," in *The New Caravan* (eds. Alfred Kreymborg et al., New York, 1936), 124–158. Included in *Uncle Tom's Children.*

"Silt." *New Masses,* 24 (August 24, 1937), 19–20. Included in *Eight Men* as "The Man Who Saw the Flood."

"Fire and Cloud." *Story Magazine,* 12 (March 1938), 9–41. Included in *Uncle Tom's Children.*

Uncle Tom's Children: Four Novellas. New York: Harper & Brothers, 1938, Included "Big Boy Leaves Home," "Down by the Riverside," "Long Black Song," and "Fire and Cloud."

"Bright and Morning Star." *New Masses,* 27 (May 10, 1938), 97–99, 116–124. Included in *Uncle Tom's Children* (1940 edition).

"Almos' a Man." *Harper's Bazaar,* 74 (Jan. 1940), 40–41. Included with slight revisions, in *Eight Men* as "The Man Who Was Almost a Man."

Native Son. New York: Harper & Brothers, 1940.

Uncle Tom's Children: Five Long Stories. New York: Harper

& Brothers, 1940. Includes "The Ethics of Living Jim Crow," the short stories printed in the 1938 edition and "Bright and Morning Star."

Native Son, the Biography of a Young American. A Play in Ten Scenes. By Paul Green and Richard Wright. New York: Harper & Brothers, 1941.

"The Man Who Lived Underground." *Cross Section* (ed. Edwin Seaver, New York, 1945), 58–102. Included in *Eight Men.*

"The Man Who Killed a Shadow." *Zero* (Paris) I (Spring 1949), 45–53. Included in *Eight Men.*

The Outsider. New York: Harper & Brothers, 1953.

Savage Holiday. New York: Avon, 1954.

"Big Black Good Man." *Esquire,* 50 (Nov. 1957), 76–80. Included in *Eight Men.*

The Long Dream. New York: Doubleday, 1958.

Eight Men. Cleveland and New York: World Publishing Company, 1961. Includes, "The Man Who Went to Chicago," "The Man Who Saw the Flood," "The Man Who Was Almost a Man," "Big Black Good Man," "Man, God Ain't Like that," "Man of All Works," "The Man Who Lived Underground," "The Man Who Killed a Shadow."

Lawd Today. New York: Walker, 1963.

"Five Episodes" in *Soon, One Morning* (ed. Herbert Hill, New York, 1963), Excerpts from "Island of Hallucinations," an unpublished novel completed in 1959.

by Richard Wright; letter by Richard Wright, "Rascoe Baiting," copyright 1940 *American Mercury; Twelve Million Black Voices* by Richard Wright, copyright 1940 by Richard Wright. Reprinted by permission of Paul R. Reynolds, Inc., 12 East 41st Street, New York, N.Y. 10017.

"I Have Seen Black Hands" originally appeared in *New Masses*, Vol. 11, June 26, 1934; "Joe Louis Uncovers Dynamite" originally appeared in *New Masses*, Vol. 17, Oct. 8, 1935; "Red Clay Blues" originally appeared in *New Masses*, Vol. 32, August 1, 1939; Review of *Wars I Have Seen* by Gertrude Stein originally appeared in *P.M. Magazine*, March 1945; "Richard Wright and Antonio Frasconi: An Exchange of Letters" originally appeared in *Twice a Year*, No.12–13, 1945; and "There's Always Another Café" originally appeared in *Kiosk*, No. 10, 1953. Reprinted by permission of Mrs. Ellen Wright.

The photographs in *Twelve Million Black Voices*—with a few exceptions—were taken by Farm Security photographers as they roamed the country during the 1940s, and are now part of the permanent Farm Security Administration picture collection held by the U.S. Library of Congress. In this reprinting of the book, three new pictures have been included which were not in the original edition. These are designated by an asterisk (*). All other pictures are by Farm Security photographers.

We wish to thank the Library of Congress for providing these pictures for this edition and credit the following photographers for their work.

Page

146	*Dorothea Lange:* Sharecropper's hands, Alabama
147	*Jack Delano:* Sharecropper, Georgia.
154 (top)	*Jack Delano:* Maid, Washington, D.C.
154 (bottom)	*Arthur Rothstein:* Steelworker, Pennsylvania.
155 (top)	*Russell Lee:* Stevedores, Houston, Texas.
155 (bottom)	*Russell Lee:* Entertainers in night club, Chicago, Ill.
156 (top)	*Roland L. Freeman.* © 1977 Roland L. Freeman: Sharecropper.
156* (bottom)	*Jack Delano:* Waiter, Washington, D.C.
160*	*Bruce Davidson.* © 1965 Magnum Photos: Sharecroppers and Sons.

161	*Dorothea Lange:* Cotton hoers going to work, Mississippi.
162	*Marion Post:* Plowing cotton, Georgia.
163	*Ben Shahn:* Cotton pickers, Arkansas.
166	*Jack Delano:* Rural Negro family on their porch, South Carolina.
168	*Russell Lee:* Cotton pickers' feet, Arkansas.
171	*Marion Post:* Cotton buyer and negro farmer discussing price, Mississippi.
172 (top)	*John Vachon:* Courtroom scene, Virginia.
172 (bottom)	Wide World Photos: Lynching, Georgia.
178 (top)	*Dorothea Lange:* Cotton fields and sharecroppers' shacks, Mississippi.
178 (bottom)	*Dorothea Lange:* Plowing cotton, Georgia.
179 (top)	*Dorothea Lange:* Hoeing cotton, Alabama.
179 (bottom)	*Ben Shahn:* Cotton pickers, Arkansas.
180 (top)	*Arthur Rothstein:* Plow in eroded cotton field, Alabama.
180 (bottom)	*Walker Evans:* Sharecropper's grave, Alabama.
182	*Russell Lee:* Tenant's house, Oklahoma.
184	*Russell Lee:* Sharecropper family, Oklahoma.
185	*Arthur Rothstein:* Sharecropper family, Alabama.
186	*Dorothea Lange:* Rural child making butter, North Carolina.
187	*Jack Delano:* Rural child asleep at home, Maryland.
188	*Russell Lee:* Tenants' children reading, Oklahoma.
189	*Arthur Rothstein:* Rural Negro school, Alabama.
190 (top)	*Jack Delano:* Rural Negroes dressed to go to church, Georgia.
190 (bottom)	*Jack Delano:* Church service, Georgia.
191	*Russell Lee:* Church service, Illinois.
192	*Jack Delano:* Church service, Georgia.
193	*Marion Post:* Negroes dancing, Mississippi.
195 (top)	*Russell Lee:* Sharecropper's son, Missouri.
195 (bottom)	*Arthur Rothstein:* Eroded land, Alabama.
196	*Marion Post:* Tractors in cotton field, Mississippi.
197 (top)	*Marion Post:* Migrant workers in cabbage field, Florida.

197 (bottom)   *Jack Delano:* Migrant potato picker, North Carolina.

198 (top)   *Jack Delano:* Migrant workers asleep, North Carolina.

198 (bottom)   *Jack Delano:* Woman migrant worker asleep, North Carolina.

201   *Arthur Rothstein:* Evicted sharecroppers, Missouri.

202   *Russell Lee:* Negro dwelling, Chicago, Ill.

203   *Russell Lee:* Church service, Illinois.

208   *Arthur Rothstein:* Negro section, Pittsburgh, Pa.

211   *Edwin Rosskam:* Entrance to apartment house, Chicago, Ill.

212   *Russell Lee:* Toilet in "kitchenette" apartment house, Chicago, Ill.

213 (top)   *Russell Lee:* Bedroom, Chicago, Ill.

213 (bottom)   *Russell Lee:* Negro family, Chicago, Ill.

214 (top)   *Russell Lee:* Interior of "kitchenette," Chicago, Ill.

214 (bottom)   *Arthur Rothstein:* Interior, Washington, D.C.

218 (top)   *Russell Lee:* Empty lot and houses, Chicago, Ill.

218 (bottom)   *Russell Lee:* Negro housing, Chicago, Ill.

222   *John Vachon:* Negro foundry workers, Maryland.

227   *Russell Lee:* Roller-skating rink, Chicago, Ill.

228   *Russell Lee:* Roller-skating rink, Chicago, Ill.

231 (top)   *Russell Lee:* Mother and son, Chicago, Ill.

231 (bottom)   *Marion Post:* Maid, Georgia.

232   *Russell Lee:* Store-front church on Easter Sunday, Chicago, Ill.

234   *Edwin Rosskam:* Boy in front of apartment house, Chicago, Ill.

235 (top)   *Edwin Rosskam:* Street scene, Chicago, Ill.

235 (bottom)   *Russell Lee:* Street scene under the elevated, Chicago, Ill.

236   *Arthur Rothstein:* Steelworker, Pennsylvania.

237*   *Wide World Photos:* Demonstration.

241   *Carl Mydans:* Back yard of alley dwelling, Washington, D.C.

Other titles of interest